Linux®
Command Line and
Shell Scripting
Bible

Linux®
Command Line and
Shell Scripting
Bible

Richard Blum

WILEY

Wiley Publishing, Inc.

Linux®Command Line and Shell Scripting Bible

Published by
Wiley Publishing, Inc.
10475 Crosspoint Boulevard
Indianapolis, IN 46256
www.wiley.com

Copyright © 2008 by Wiley Publishing, Inc., Indianapolis, Indiana

Published simultaneously in Canada

ISBN: 978-0-470-25128-7

Manufactured in the United States of America

10 9 8 7 6 5 4 3 2 1

For general information on our other products and services or to obtain technical support, please contact our Customer Care Department within the U.S. at (800) 762-2974, outside the U.S. at (317) 572-3993 or fax (317) 572-4002.

Library of Congress Cataloging-in-Publication Data is available from the publisher.

To all the people who've helped form my education. Parents, relatives, teachers, coworkers, and even anonymous posters on the Internet. Always be prepared to accept education from wherever you find it. Always continue to learn new things. "For the LORD gives wisdom, and from his mouth come knowledge and understanding." Proverbs 2:6 (NIV)

About the Author

Richard Blum has worked in the IT industry for over 19 years as both a systems and network administrator. During this time he has administered Unix, Linux, Novell, and Microsoft servers, as well as helped design and maintain a 3500-user network utilizing Cisco switches and routers. He has used Linux servers and shell scripts to perform automated network monitoring, and has written shell scripts in just about every Unix shell environment.

Rich has a bachelor of science degree in Electrical Engineering, and a master of science degree in Management, specializing in management information systems, from Purdue University. He is the author of several Linux books, including *sendmail for Linux, Running qmail, Postfix, Open Source E-mail Security, Network Performance Open Source Toolkit*, and *Professional Assembly Language Programming*. He's also a coauthor of *Professional Linux Programming* and *Linux For Dummies, 8th Edition*. When he's not being a computer nerd, Rich plays bass guitar for his church worship band and enjoys spending time with his wife, Barbara, and their two daughters, Katie Jane and Jessica.

Credits

Acquisitions Editor
Jenny Watson

Senior Development Editor
Tom Dinse

Technical Editor
John Kennedy

Production Editor
Angela Smith

Copy Editor
Foxxe Editorial Services

Editorial Manager
Mary Beth Wakefield

Production Manager
Tim Tate

Vice President and Executive Group Publisher
Richard Swadley

Vice President and Executive Publisher
Joseph B. Wikert

Project Coordinator, Cover
Lynsey Stanford

Proofreader
Word One New York

Indexer
Melanie Belkin

Contents at a Glance

Contents at a Glance

Contents

Contents

Contents

Part II Shell Scripting Basics

Chapter 8: Basic Script Building 201

Chapter 9: Using Structured Commands 229

Part III Advanced Shell Scripting

Contents

Contents

Part IV Alternative Linux Shells

Part V Advanced Topics

Acknowledgments

First, all glory and praise go to God, who through His Son makes all things possible, and gives us the gift of eternal life.

Many thanks go to the great team of people at John Wiley & Sons for their outstanding work on this project. Thanks to Jenny Watson, the acquisitions editor, for offering me the opportunity to work on this book. Also thanks to Tom Dinse, the development editor, for keeping things on track and making this book more presentable. The technical editor, John Kennedy, did an amazing job of double-checking all the work in this book, plus making suggestions to improve the content. Thanks, John, for your hard work and diligence. I would also like to thank Carole McClendon at Waterside Productions, Inc. for arranging this opportunity for me, and for helping out in my writing career.

Finally, I would like to thank my parents, Mike and Joyce Blum, for their dedication and support while raising me, and my wife, Barbara, and daughters, Katie Jane and Jessica, for their love, patience, and understanding, especially while I was writing this book.

Introduction

Welcome to *Linux Command Line and Shell Scripting Bible*. Like all books in the Bible series, you can expect to find both hands-on tutorials and real-world practical application information, as well as reference and background information that provides a context for what you are learning. This book is a fairly comprehensive resource on the Linux command line and shell commands. By the time you have completed *Linux Command Line and Shell Scripting Bible*, you will be well prepared to write your own shell scripts that can automate practically any task on your Linux system.

Who Should Read This Book

If you're a system administrator in a Linux environment, you'll benefit greatly by knowing how to write shell scripts. The book doesn't walk through setting up a Linux system, but once you have it running, you'll want to start automating some of the routine administrative tasks. That's where shell scripting comes in, and that's where this book will help you out. This book will demonstrate how to automate any administrative task using shell scripts, from monitoring system statistics and data files to generating reports for your boss.

If you're a home Linux enthusiast, you'll also benefit from *Linux Command Line and Shell Scripting Bible*. Nowadays it's easy to get lost in the graphical world of prebuilt widgets. Most desktop Linux distributions try their best to hide the Linux system from the typical user. However, there are times when you have to know what's going on under the hood. This book shows you how to access the Linux command line prompt, and what to do once you get there. Often performing simple tasks, such as file management, can be done more quickly from the command line than from a fancy graphical interface. There's a wealth of commands you can use from the command line, and this book shows you just how to use them.

How This Book Is Organized

This book is organized in a way that leads you through the basics of the Linux command line all the way to creating your own shell scripts. The book is divided into five parts, each one building on the previous parts.

Part I assumes that you either have a Linux system running or are looking into getting a Linux system. Chapter 1, "Starting with Linux Shells," describes the parts of a total Linux system and shows how the shell fits in. After learning the basics of the Linux system, this section continues with:

- Using a terminal emulation package to access the shell (Chapter 2)
- Introducing the basic shell commands (Chapter 3)
- Using more advanced shell commands to peek at system information (Chapter 4)
- Working with shell variables to manipulate data (Chapter 5)
- Understanding the Linux filesystem and security (Chapter 6)
- Knowing how to use the Linux editors to start writing shell scripts (Chapter 7)

In Part II, you'll start writing shell scripts:

- Learn how to create and run shell scripts (Chapter 8)
- Alter the program flow in a shell script (Chapter 9)
- Iterate through code sections (Chapter 10)
- Handle data from the user in your scripts (Chapter 11)
- See different methods for storing and displaying data from your script (Chapter 12)
- Control how and when your shell scripts run on the system (Chapter 13)

Part III dives into more advanced areas of shell script programming:

- Create your own functions to use in all your scripts (Chapter 14)
- See different methods for interacting with your script users (Chapter 15)
- Use advanced Linux commands to filter and parse data files (Chapter 16)
- Use regular expressions to define data (Chapter 17)
- Learn advanced methods of manipulating data in your scripts (Chapter 18)
- See how to generate reports from raw data (Chapter 19)

In Part IV, you'll get to see how to write shell scripts using some of the alternative shells available in the Linux environment:

- Write scripts for the ash or dash shells (Chapter 20)
- See how writing scripts in the tcsh shell is different (Chapter 21)
- Work with floating-point numbers in the ksh93 shell (Chapter 22)
- Use advanced network and math features in the zsh shell (Chapter 23)

The last section of the book, Part V, demonstrates how to use shell scripts in real-world environments:

- See how to use popular open source databases in your shells scripts (Chapter 24)
- Learn how to extract data from Web sites, and send data between systems (Chapter 25)
- Use e-mail to send notifications and reports to external users (Chapter 26)
- Write shell scripts to automate your daily system administration functions (Chapter 27)

Conventions and Features

There are many different organizational and typographical features throughout this book designed to help you get the most out of the information.

Throughout the book, special typography indicates code and commands. Commands and code are shown in a monospaced font. In a regular paragraph, programming code words `look like this`. Lines of code are presented like this:

```
$ cat test2
#!/bin/bash
# testing a bad command
if asdfg
then
    echo "it didn't work"
fi
echo "we're outside of the if statement"
$ ./test2
./test2: line 3: asdfg: command not found
we're outside of the if statement
$
```

Notes and Cautions

Whenever the author wants to bring something important to your attention, the information will appear in a Note or Caution.

NOTE Notes provide additional, ancillary information that is helpful, but somewhat outside of the current presentation of information.

CAUTION This information is important and is set off in a separate paragraph with a special icon. Cautions provide information about things to watch out for, whether simply inconvenient or potentially hazardous to your data or systems.

Minimum Requirements

Linux Command Line and Shell Scripting Bible looks at Linux from a generic point of view, so you'll be able to follow along in the book using any Linux system you have available. The bulk of the book references the bash shell, which is the default shell for most Linux systems.

Where to Go from Here

Once you've completed *Linux Command Line and Shell Scripting Bible*, you'll be well on your way to incorporating Linux commands in your daily Linux work. In the ever-changing world of Linux, it's always a good idea to stay in touch with new developments. Often Linux distributions will change, adding new features and removing older ones. To keep your knowledge of Linux fresh, always stay well informed. Find a good Linux forum site and monitor what's happening in the Linux world. There are many popular Linux news sites, such as Slashdot and Distrowatch, that provide up-to-the-minute information about new advances in Linux.

Part I

The Linux Command Line

Chapter 1

Starting with Linux Shells

Before you can dive into working with the Linux command line and shells, it's a good idea to first understand what Linux is, where it came from, and how it works. This chapter walks you through what Linux is, and explains where the shell and command line fit in the overall Linux picture.

What Is Linux?

If you've never worked with Linux before, you may be confused as to why there are so many different versions of it available. I'm sure that you have heard various terms such as distribution, LiveCD, and GNU when looking at Linux packages and been confused. Trying to wade through the world of Linux for the first time can be a tricky experience. This chapter will take some of the mystery out of the Linux system before we start working on commands and scripts.

For starters, there are four main parts that make up a Linux system:

- The Linux kernel
- The GNU utilities
- A graphical desktop environment
- Application software

Each of these four parts has a specific job in the Linux system. Each of the parts by itself isn't very useful. Figure 1-1 shows a basic diagram of how the parts fit together to create the overall Linux system.

3

FIGURE 1-1

The Linux system

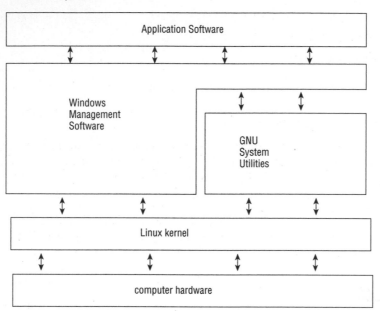

This section describes these four main parts in detail, and gives you an overview of how they work together to create a complete Linux system.

Looking into the Linux kernel

The core of the Linux system is the *kernel*. The kernel controls all of the hardware and software on the computer system, allocating hardware when necessary, and executing software when required.

If you've been following the Linux world at all, no doubt you've heard the name Linus Torvalds. Linus is the person responsible for creating the first Linux kernel software while he was a student at the University of Helsinki. He intended it to be a copy of the Unix system, at the time a popular operating system used at many universities.

After developing the Linux kernel, Linus released it to the Internet community and solicited suggestions for improving it. This simple process started a revolution in the world of computer operating systems. Soon Linus was receiving suggestions from students as well as professional programmers from around the world.

Allowing anyone to change programming code in the kernel would result in complete chaos. To simplify things, Linus acted as a central point for all improvement suggestions. It was ultimately Linus's decision whether or not to incorporate suggested code in the kernel. This same concept is still in place with the Linux kernel code, except that instead of just Linus controlling the kernel code, a team of developers has taken on the task.

The kernel is primarily responsible for four main functions:

- System memory management
- Software program management
- Hardware management
- Filesystem management

The following sections explore each of these functions in more detail.

System memory management

One of the primary functions of the operating system kernel is memory management. Not only does the kernel manage the physical memory available on the server, it can also create and manage virtual memory, or memory that does not actually exist.

It does this by using space on the hard disk, called the *swap space*. The kernel swaps the contents of virtual memory locations back and forth from the swap space to the actual physical memory. This allows the system to think there is more memory available than what physically exists (shown in Figure 1-2).

FIGURE 1-2

The Linux system memory map

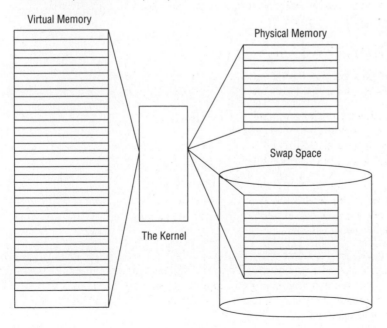

5

The memory locations are grouped into blocks called *pages*. The kernel locates each page of memory either in the physical memory or the swap space. The kernel then maintains a table of the memory pages that indicates which pages are in physical memory, and which pages are swapped out to disk.

The kernel keeps track of which memory pages are in use and automatically copies memory pages that have not been accessed for a period of time to the swap space area (called *swapping out*), even if there's other memory available. When a program wants to access a memory page that has been swapped out, the kernel must make room for it in physical memory by swapping out a different memory page, and swap in the required page from the swap space. Obviously, this process takes time, and can slow down a running process. The process of swapping out memory pages for running applications continues for as long as the Linux system is running.

You can see the current status of the virtual memory on your Linux system by viewing the special /proc/meminfo file. Here's an example of a sample /proc/meminfo entry:

```
# cat /proc/meminfo
MemTotal:        255392 kB
MemFree:           4336 kB
Buffers:           1236 kB
Cached:           48212 kB
SwapCached:        1028 kB
Active:          182932 kB
Inactive:         44388 kB
HighTotal:            0 kB
HighFree:             0 kB
LowTotal:        255392 kB
LowFree:           4336 kB
SwapTotal:       524280 kB
SwapFree:        514528 kB
Dirty:              456 kB
Writeback:            0 kB
AnonPages:       176940 kB
Mapped:           40168 kB
Slab:             16080 kB
SReclaimable:      4048 kB
SUnreclaim:       12032 kB
PageTables:        4048 kB
NFS_Unstable:         0 kB
Bounce:               0 kB
CommitLimit:     651976 kB
Committed_AS:    442296 kB
VmallocTotal:    770040 kB
VmallocUsed:       3112 kB
VmallocChunk:    766764 kB
HugePages_Total:      0
```

```
HugePages_Free:      0
HugePages_Rsvd:      0
Hugepagesize:     4096 kB

#
```

The Mem: line shows that this Linux server has 256 MB of physical memory. It also shows that about 4 MB is not currently being used (free). The output also shows that there is about 512 MB of swap space memory available on this system.

By default, each process running on the Linux system has its own private memory pages. One process cannot access memory pages being used by another process. The kernel maintains its own memory areas. For security purposes, no processes can access memory used by the kernel processes.

To facilitate data sharing, you can create shared memory pages. Multiple processes can read and write to and from a common shared memory area. The kernel maintains and administers the shared memory areas and allows individual processes access to the shared area.

The special ipcs command allows you to view the current shared memory pages on the system. Here's the output from a sample ipcs command:

```
# ipcs -m

------ Shared Memory Segments --------
key        shmid    owner    perms    bytes     nattch    status
0x00000000 0        rich     600      52228     6         dest
0x395ec51c 1        oracle   640      5787648   6

#
```

Each shared memory segment has an owner that created the segment. Each segment also has a standard Linux permissions setting that sets the availability of the segment for other users. The key value is used to allow other users to gain access to the shared memory segment.

Software program management

The Linux operating system calls a running program a *process*. A process can run in the foreground, displaying output on a display, or it can run in background, behind the scenes. The kernel controls how the Linux system manages all the processes running on the system.

The kernel creates the first process, called the *init process*, to start all other processes on the system. When the kernel starts, it loads the init process into virtual memory. As the kernel starts each additional process, it gives it a unique area in virtual memory to store the data and code that the process uses.

Some Linux implementations contain a table of processes to start automatically on bootup. On Linux systems this table is usually located in the special file /etc/inittabs.

The Linux operating system uses an init system that utilizes *run levels*. A run level can be used to direct the init process to run only certain types of processes, as defined in the /etc/inittabs file. There are five init run levels in the Linux operating system.

At run level 1, only the basic system processes are started, along with one console terminal process. This is called single user mode. Single user mode is most often used for emergency filesystem maintenance when something is broken. Obviously, in this mode only one person (usually the administrator) can log in to the system to manipulate data.

The standard init run level is 3. At this run level most application software such as network support software is started. Another popular run level in Linux is run level 5. This is the run level where the system starts the graphical X Window software, and allows you to log in using a graphical desktop window.

The Linux system can control the overall system functionality by controlling the init run level. By changing the run level from 3 to 5, the system can change from a console-based system to an advanced, graphical X Window system.

Later on (in Chapter 4) you'll see how to use the ps command to view the processes currently running on the Linux system. Here's an example of what you'll see using the ps command:

```
$ ps ax
  PID TTY       STAT    TIME COMMAND
    1 ?         S       0:03 init
    2 ?         SW      0:00 [kflushd]
    3 ?         SW      0:00 [kupdate]
    4 ?         SW      0:00 [kpiod]
    5 ?         SW      0:00 [kswapd]
  243 ?         SW      0:00 [portmap]
  295 ?         S       0:00 syslogd
  305 ?         S       0:00 klogd
  320 ?         S       0:00 /usr/sbin/atd
  335 ?         S       0:00 crond
  350 ?         S       0:00 inetd
  365 ?         SW      0:00 [lpd]
  403 ttyS0     S       0:00 gpm -t ms
  418 ?         S       0:00 httpd
  423 ?         S       0:00 httpd
  424 ?         SW      0:00 [httpd]
  425 ?         SW      0:00 [httpd]
  426 ?         SW      0:00 [httpd]
  427 ?         SW      0:00 [httpd]
  428 ?         SW      0:00 [httpd]
  429 ?         SW      0:00 [httpd]
  430 ?         SW      0:00 [httpd]
```

```
436 ?        SW      0:00 [httpd]
437 ?        SW      0:00 [httpd]
438 ?        SW      0:00 [httpd]
470 ?        S       0:02 xfs -port -1
485 ?        SW      0:00 [smbd]
495 ?        S       0:00 nmbd -D
533 ?        SW      0:00 [postmaster]
538 tty1     SW      0:00 [mingetty]
539 tty2     SW      0:00 [mingetty]
540 tty3     SW      0:00 [mingetty]
541 tty4     SW      0:00 [mingetty]
542 tty5     SW      0:00 [mingetty]
543 tty6     SW      0:00 [mingetty]
544 ?        SW      0:00 [prefdm]
549 ?        SW      0:00 [prefdm]
559 ?        S       0:02 [kwm]
585 ?        S       0:06 kikbd
594 ?        S       0:00 kwmsound
595 ?        S       0:03 kpanel
596 ?        S       0:02 kfm
597 ?        S       0:00 krootwm
598 ?        S       0:01 kbgndwm
611 ?        S       0:00 kcmlaptop -daemon
666 ?        S       0:00 /usr/libexec/postfix/master
668 ?        S       0:00 qmgr -l -t fifo -u
787 ?        S       0:00 pickup -l -t fifo
790 ?        S       0:00 telnetd: 192.168.1.2 [vt100]
791 pts/0    S       0:00 login -- rich
792 pts/0    S       0:00 -bash
805 pts/0    R       0:00 ps ax
$
```

The first column in the output shows the *process ID* (or PID) of the process. Notice that the first process is our friend the init process, and assigned PID 1 by the Linux system. All other processes that start after the init process are assigned PIDs in numerical order. No two processes can have the same PID.

The third column shows the current status of the process (S for sleeping, SW for sleeping and waiting, and R for running). The process name is shown in the last column. Processes that are in brackets are processes that have been swapped out of memory to the disk swap space due to inactivity. You can see that some of the processes have been swapped out, but most of the running processes have not.

Hardware management

Still another responsibility for the kernel is hardware management. Any device that the Linux system must communicate with needs driver code inserted inside the kernel code. The driver code allows the kernel to pass data back and forth to the device, acting as a middle man between applications and the hardware. There are two methods used for inserting device driver code in the Linux kernel:

- Drivers compiled in the kernel
- Driver modules added to the kernel

Previously, the only way to insert device driver code was to recompile the kernel. Each time you added a new device to the system, you had to recompile the kernel code. This process became even more inefficient as Linux kernels supported more hardware. Fortunately, Linux developers devised a better method to insert driver code into the running kernel.

Programmers developed the concept of kernel modules to allow you to insert driver code into a running kernel without having to recompile the kernel. Also, a kernel module could be removed from the kernel when the device was finished being used. This greatly simplified and expanded using hardware with Linux.

The Linux system identifies hardware devices as special files, called *device files*. There are three different classifications of device files:

- Character
- Block
- Network

Character device files are for devices that can only handle data one character at a time. Most types of modems and terminals are created as character files. Block files are for devices that can handle data in large blocks at a time, such as disk drives.

The network file types are used for devices that use packets to send and receive data. This includes network cards and a special loopback device that allows the Linux system to communicate with itself using common network programming protocols.

Linux creates special files, called nodes, for each device on the system. All communication with the device is performed through the device node. Each node has a unique number pair that identifies it to the Linux kernel. The number pair includes a major and a minor device number. Similar devices are grouped into the same major device number. The minor device number is used to identify a specific device within the major device group. This is an example of a few device files on a Linux server:

```
$ ls -al sda* ttyS*
brw-rw----  1 root     disk      8,   0 May  5 2006 sda
brw-rw----  1 root     disk      8,   1 May  5 2006 sda1
brw-rw----  1 root     disk      8,  10 May  5 2006 sda10
brw-rw----  1 root     disk      8,  11 May  5 2006 sda11
brw-rw----  1 root     disk      8,  12 May  5 2006 sda12
brw-rw----  1 root     disk      8,  13 May  5 2006 sda13
```

```
brw-rw----  1 root    disk     8,  14 May   5  2006 sda14
brw-rw----  1 root    disk     8,  15 May   5  2006 sda15
brw-rw----  1 root    disk     8,   2 May   5  2006 sda2
brw-rw----  1 root    disk     8,   3 May   5  2006 sda3
brw-rw----  1 root    disk     8,   4 May   5  2006 sda4
brw-rw----  1 root    disk     8,   5 May   5  2006 sda5
brw-rw----  1 root    disk     8,   6 May   5  2006 sda6
brw-rw----  1 root    disk     8,   7 May   5  2006 sda7
brw-rw----  1 root    disk     8,   8 May   5  2006 sda8
brw-rw----  1 root    disk     8,   9 May   5  2006 sda9
crw-------  1 root    tty      4,  64 Jun  29 16:09 ttyS0
crw-------  1 root    tty      4,  65 May   5  2006 ttyS1
crw-------  1 root    tty      4,  66 May   5  2006 ttyS2
crw-------  1 root    tty      4,  67 May   5  2006 ttyS3
$
```

Different Linux distributions handle devices using different device names. In this distribution, the sda device is the first SCSI hard drive, and the ttyS devices are the standard IBM PC COM ports. The listing shows all of the sda devices that were created on the sample Linux system. Not all are actually used, but they are created in case the administrator needs them. Similarly, the listing shows all of the ttyS devices created.

The fifth column is the major device node number. Notice that all of the sda devices have the same major device node, 8, while all of the ttyS devices use 4. The sixth column is the minor device node number. Each device within a major number has its own unique minor device node number.

The first column indicates the permissions for the device file. The first character of the permissions indicates the type of file. Notice that the SCSI hard drive files are all marked as block (b) device, while the COM port device files are marked as character (c) devices.

Filesystem management

Unlike some other operating systems, the Linux kernel can support different types of filesystems to read and write data to and from hard drives. Besides having over a dozen filesystems of its own, Linux can read and write to and from filesystems used by other operating systems, such as Microsoft Windows. The kernel must be compiled with support for all types of filesystems that the system will use. Table 1-1 lists the standard filesystems that a Linux system can use to read and write data.

Any hard drive that a Linux server accesses must be formatted using one of the filesystem types listed in Table 1-1.

The Linux kernel interfaces with each filesystem using the Virtual File System (VFS). This provides a standard interface for the kernel to communicate with any type of filesystem. VFS caches information in memory as each filesystem is mounted and used.

TABLE 1-1

Linux Filesystems

Filesystem	Description
ext	Linux Extended filesystem — the original Linux filesystem
ext2	Second extended filesystem, provided advanced features over ext
ext3	Third extended filesystem, supports journaling
hpfs	OS/2 high-performance filesystem
jfs	IBM's journaling file system
iso9660	ISO 9660 filesystem (CD-ROMs)
minix	MINIX filesystem
msdos	Microsoft FAT16
ncp	Netware filesystem
nfs	Network File System
ntfs	Support for Microsoft NT filesystem
proc	Access to system information
ReiserFS	Advanced Linux file system for better performance and disk recovery
smb	Samba SMB filesystem for network access
sysv	Older Unix filesystem
ufs	BSD filesystem
umsdos	Unix-like filesystem that resides on top of MSDOS
vfat	Windows 95 filesystem (FAT32)
XFS	High-performance 64-bit journaling filesystem

The GNU utilities

Besides having a kernel to control hardware devices, a computer operating system needs utilities to perform standard functions, such as controlling files and programs. While Linus created the Linux system kernel, he had no system utilities to run on it. Fortunately for him, at the same time he was working, a group of people were working together on the Internet trying to develop a standard set of computer system utilities that mimicked the popular Unix operating system.

The GNU organization (GNU stands for GNU's Not Unix) developed a complete set of Unix utilities, but had no kernel system to run them on. These utilities were developed under a software philosophy called open source software (OSS).

The concept of OSS allows programmers to develop software and then release it to the world with no licensing fees attached. Anyone can use the software, modify it, or incorporate it into his or her own system without having to pay a license fee. Uniting Linus's Linux kernel with the GNU operating system utilities created a complete, functional, free operating system.

While the bundling of the Linux kernel and GNU utilities is often just called Linux, you will see some Linux purists on the Internet refer to it as the GNU/Linux system to give credit to the GNU organization for its contributions to the cause.

The core GNU utilities

The GNU project was mainly designed for Unix system administrators to have a Unix-like environment available. This focus resulted in the project porting many common Unix system command line utilities. The core bundle of utilities supplied for Linux systems is called the *coreutils* package.

The GNU coreutils package consists of three parts:

- Utilities for handling files
- Utilities for manipulating text
- Utilities for managing processes

These three main groups of utilities each contain several utility programs that are invaluable to the Linux system administrator and programmer. This book covers each of the utilities contained in the GNU coreutils package in detail.

The shell

The GNU/Linux shell is a special interactive utility. It provides a way for users to start programs, manage files on the filesystem, and manage processes running on the Linux system. The core of the shell is the command prompt. The command prompt is the interactive part of the shell. It allows you to enter text commands, interprets the commands, then executes the commands in the kernel.

The shell contains a set of internal commands that you use to control things such as copying files, moving files, renaming files, displaying the programs currently running on the system, and stopping programs running on the system. Besides the internal commands, the shell also allows you to enter the name of a program at the command prompt. The shell passes the program name off to the kernel to start it.

There are quite a few Linux shells available to use on a Linux system. Different shells have different characteristics, some being more useful for creating scripts and some being more useful for managing processes. The default shell used in all Linux distributions is the bash shell. The bash shell was developed by the GNU project as a replacement for the standard Unix shell, called the Bourne shell (after its creator). The bash shell name is a play on this wording, referred to as the "Bourne again shell".

TABLE 1-2

Linux Shells

Shell	Description
ash	A simple, lightweight shell that runs in low-memory environments but has full compatibility with the bash shell
korn	A programming shell compatible with the Bourne shell but supporting advanced programming features like associative arrays and floating-point arithmetic
tcsh	A shell that incorporates elements from the C programming language into shell scripts
zsh	An advanced shell that incorporates features from bash, tcsh, and korn, providing advanced programming features, shared history files, and themed prompts

Besides the bash shell we will cover several other popular shells in this book. Table 1-2 lists the different shells we will examine.

Most Linux distributions include more than one shell, although usually they pick one of them to be the default. If your Linux distribution includes multiple shells, feel free to experiment with different shells and see which one fits your needs.

The Linux desktop environment

In the early days of Linux (the early 1990s) all that was available was a simple text interface to the Linux operating system. This text interface allowed administrators to start programs, control program operations, and move files around on the system.

With the popularity of Microsoft Windows, computer users expected more than the old text interface to work with. This spurred more development in the OSS community, and the Linux graphical desktops emerged.

Linux is famous for being able to do things in more than one way, and no place is this more relevant than in graphical desktops. There are a plethora of graphical desktops you can choose from in Linux. The following sections describe a few of the more popular ones.

The X Windows system

There are two basic elements that control your video environment — the video card in your PC and your monitor. To display fancy graphics on your computer, the Linux software needs to know how to talk to both of them. The X Windows software is the core element in presenting graphics.

The X Windows software is a low-level program that works directly with the video card and monitor in the PC, and controls how Linux applications can present fancy windows and graphics on your computer.

Linux isn't the only operating system that uses X Windows; there are versions written for many different operating systems. In the Linux world, there are only two software packages that can implement it.

The XFree86 software package is the older of the two, and for a long time was the only X Windows package available for Linux. As its name implies, it's a free open source version of the X Windows software.

Recently, a new package called X.org has come onto the Linux scene. It too provides an open source software implementation of the X Windows system. It is becoming increasingly popular, with many Linux distributions starting to use it instead of the older XFree86 system.

Both packages work the same way, controlling how Linux uses your video card to display content on your monitor. To do that, they have to be configured for your specific system. That is supposed to happen automatically when you install Linux.

When you first install a Linux distribution, it attempts to detect your video card and monitor and then creates an X Windows configuration file that contains the required information. During installation you may notice a time when the installation program scans your monitor for supported video modes. Sometimes this causes your monitor to go blank for a few seconds. Because there are lots of different types of video cards and monitors out there, this process can take a little while to complete.

This is where many of the customized Linux distributions can be lifesavers. Most of them take great effort to automatically detect video hardware and settings without asking you any technical questions.

Unfortunately, sometimes the installation can't autodetect what video settings to use, especially with some of the newer, more complicated video cards. Unfortunately, some Linux distributions will fail to install if they can't find your specific video card settings. Others will ask a few questions during installation to help manually gather the necessary information. Still others default to the lowest common denominator and produce a screen image that is not customized for your video environment.

To complicate matters more, many PC users have fancy video cards, such as 3-D accelerator cards, so they can play high-resolution games. In the past, this caused a lot of problems if you tried to install Linux. But lately, video card companies are helping to solve this problem by providing Linux drivers. And many of the customized Linux distributions now include drivers for specialty video cards.

The core X Windows software produces a graphical display environment, but nothing else. While this is fine for running individual applications, it is not too useful for day-to-day computer use. There is no desktop environment allowing users to manipulate files or launch programs. To do that, you need a desktop environment on top of the X Windows system software.

The KDE desktop

The K Desktop Environment (KDE) was first released in 1996 as an open source project to produce a graphical desktop similar to the Microsoft Windows environment. The KDE desktop incorporates all of the features you are probably familiar with if you are a Windows user. Figure 1-3 shows a sample KDE desktop running on Linux.

The KDE desktop allows you to place both application and file icons on the desktop area. If you single-click an application icon, the Linux system starts the application. If you single-click on a file icon, the KDE desktop attempts to determine what application to start to handle the file.

The bar at the bottom of the desktop is called the Panel. The Panel consists of four parts:

- **The K menu:** Similarly to the Windows Start menu, the K menu contains links to start installed applications.

- **Program shortcuts:** These are quick links to start applications directly from the Panel.

- **The taskbar:** The taskbar shows icons for applications currently running on the desktop.

- **Applets:** These are small applications that have an icon in the Panel that often can change depending on information from the application.

FIGURE 1-3

The KDE desktop on a SimplyMEPIS Linux system

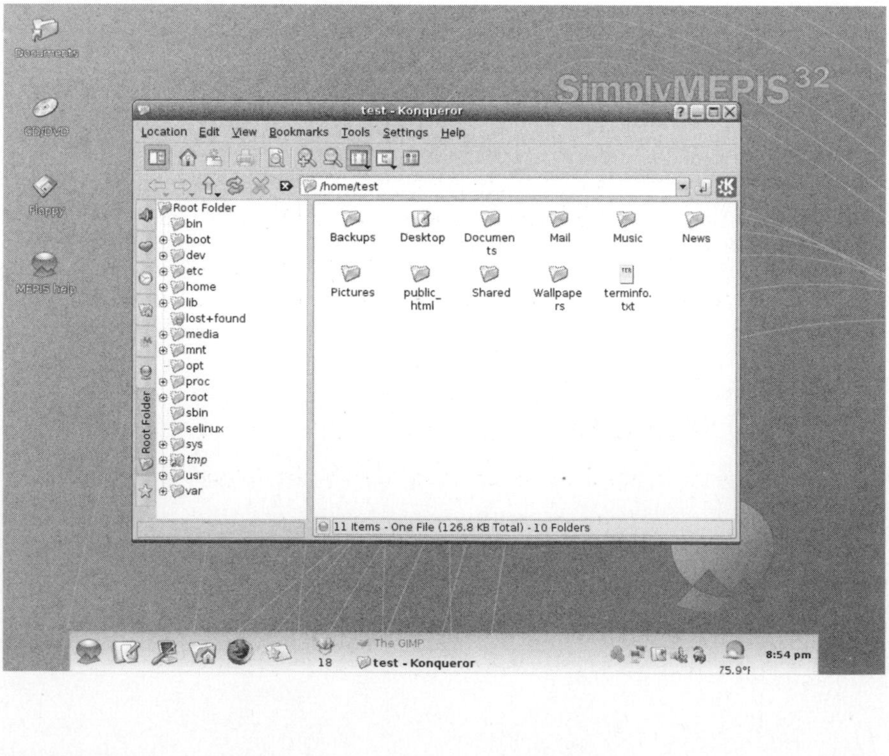

TABLE 1-3

KDE Applications

Application	Description
amaroK	Audio file player
digiKam	Digital camera software
K3b	CD-burning software
Kaffeine	Video player
Kmail	E-mail client
Koffice	Office applications suite
Konqueror	File and Web browser
Kontact	Personal information manager
Kopete	Instant messaging client

All of the Panel features are similar to what you would find in Windows. Besides the desktop features, the KDE project has produced a wide assortment of applications that run in the KDE environment. These applications are shown in Table 1-3. (You may notice the trend of using a capital K in KDE application names.)

This is only a partial list of applications produced by the KDE project. There are lots more applications that are included with the KDE desktop.

The GNOME desktop

The GNU Network Object Model Environment (GNOME) is another popular Linux desktop environment. First released in 1999, GNOME has become the default desktop environment for many Linux distributions (the most popular being Red Hat Linux).

While GNOME chose to depart from the standard Microsoft Windows look-and-feel, it incorporates many features that most Windows users are comfortable with:

■ A desktop area for icons
■ Two panel areas
■ Drag-and-drop capabilities

Figure 1-4 shows the standard GNOME desktop used in the Fedora Linux distribution.

Not to be outdone by KDE, the GNOME developers have also produced a host of graphical applications that integrate with the GNOME desktop. These are shown in Table 1-4.

As you can see, there are also quite a few applications available for the GNOME desktop. Besides all of these applications, most Linux distributions that use the GNOME desktop also incorporate the KDE libraries, allowing you to run KDE applications on your GNOME desktop.

FIGURE 1-4

A GNOME desktop on a Fedora Linux system

Other desktops

The downside to a graphical desktop environment is that they require a fair amount of system resources to operate properly. In the early days of Linux, a hallmark and selling feature of Linux was its ability to operate on older, less powerful PCs that the newer Microsoft desktop products couldn't run on. However, with the popularity of KDE and GNOME desktops, this hallmark has changed, as it takes just as much memory to run a KDE or GNOME desktop as the latest Microsoft desktop environment.

If you have an older PC, don't be discouraged. The Linux developers have banded together to take Linux back to its roots. They've created several low-memory-oriented graphical desktop applications that provide basic features that run perfectly fine on older PCs.

While these graphical desktops don't have a plethora of applications designed around them, they still run many basic graphical applications that support features such as word processing, spreadsheets, databases, drawing, and, of course, multimedia support.

TABLE 1-4

GNOME Applications

Application	Description
epiphany	Web browser
evince	Document viewer
gcalc-tool	Calculator
gedit	GNOME text editor
gnome-panel	Desktop panel for launching applications
gnome-nettool	Network diagnostics tool
gnome-terminal	Terminal emulator
nautilus	Graphical file manager
nautilus-cd-burner	CD-burning tool
sound juicer	Audio CD–ripping tool
tomboy	Note-taking software
totem	Multimedia player

TABLE 1-5

Other Linux Graphical Desktops

Desktop	Description
fluxbox	A bare-bones desktop that doesn't include a Panel, only a pop-up menu to launch applications
xfce	A desktop that's similar to the KDE desktop, but with less graphics for low-memory environments
fvwm	Supports some advanced desktop features such as virtual desktops and Panels, but runs in low-memory environments
fvwm95	Derived from fvwm, but made to look like a Windows 95 desktop

Table 1-5 shows some of the smaller Linux graphical desktop environments that can be used on lower-powered PCs and laptops.

These graphical desktop environments are not as fancy as the KDE and GNOME desktops, but they provide basic graphical functionality just fine. Figure 1-5 shows what the fluxbox desktop used in the SimplyMEPIS antiX distribution looks like.

FIGURE 1-5

The fluxbox desktop as seen in the SimplyMEPIS antiX distribution

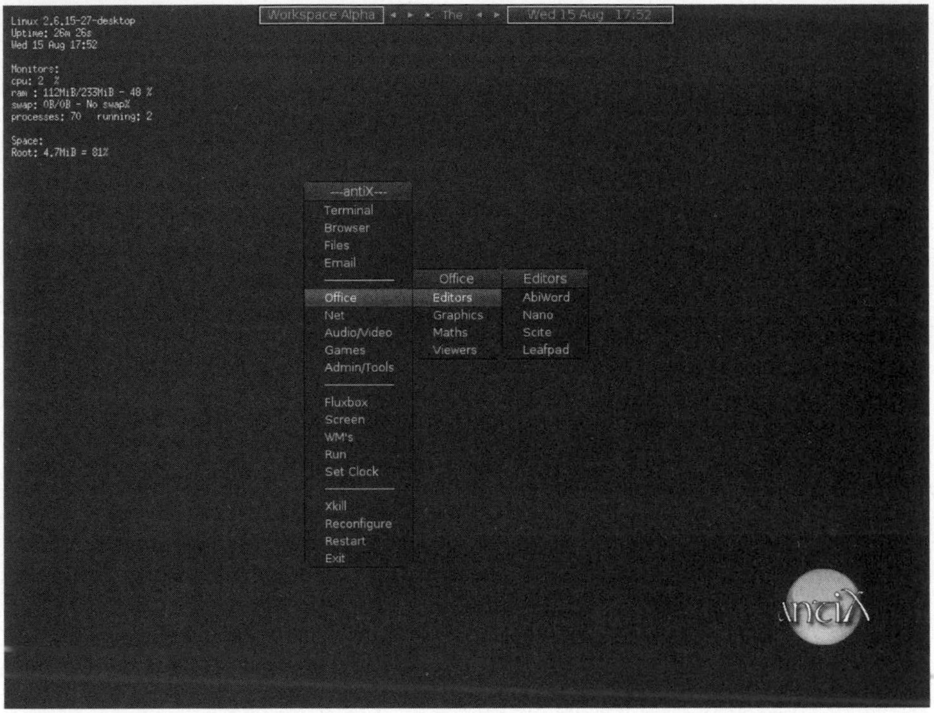

If you are using an older PC, try a Linux distribution that uses one of these desktops and see what happens. You may be pleasantly surprised.

Linux Distributions

Now that you have seen the four main components required for a complete Linux system, you may be wondering how you are going to get them all put together to make a Linux system. Fortunately, there are people who have already done that for us.

A complete Linux system package is called a *distribution*. There are lots of different Linux distributions available to meet just about any computing requirement you could have. Most distributions are customized for a specific user group, such as business users, multimedia enthusiasts, software developers, or normal home users. Each customized distribution includes the software packages required to support specialized functions, such as audio- and video-editing software for multimedia enthusiasts, or compilers and integrated development environments (IDEs) for software developers.

The different Linux distributions are often divided into three categories:

- Full core Linux distributions
- Specialized distributions
- LiveCD test distributions

The following sections describe these different types of Linux distributions, and show some examples of Linux distributions in each category.

Core Linux distributions

A core Linux distribution contains a kernel, one or more graphical desktop environments, and just about every Linux application that is available, precompiled for the kernel. It provides one-stop shopping for a complete Linux installation. Table 1-6 shows some of the more popular core Linux distributions.

In the early days of Linux, a distribution was released as a set of floppy disks. You had to download groups of files and then copy them onto disks. It would usually take 20 or more disks to make an entire distribution! Needless to say, this was a painful experience.

Nowadays, with home computers commonly having CD and DVD players built in, Linux distributions are released as either a CD set or a single DVD. This makes installing Linux much easier.

However, beginners still often run into problems when they install one of the core Linux distributions. To cover just about any situation in which someone might want to use Linux, a single distribution has to include lots of application software. They include everything from high-end Internet database servers to common games. Because of the quantity of applications available for Linux, a complete distribution often takes four or more CDs.

TABLE 1-6

Core Linux Distributions

Distribution	Description
Slackware	One of the original Linux distribution sets, popular with Linux geeks
Red Hat	A commercial business distribution used mainly for Internet servers
Fedora	A spin-off from Red Hat but designed for home use
Gentoo	A distribution designed for advanced Linux users, containing only Linux source code
Mandriva	Designed mainly for home use (previously called Mandrake)
openSuSe	Different distributions for business and home use (now owned by Novell)
Debian	Popular with Linux experts and commercial Linux products

While having lots of options available in a distribution is great for Linux geeks, it can become a nightmare for beginning Linux users. Most distributions ask a series of questions during the installation process to determine which applications to load by default, what hardware is connected to the PC, and how to configure the hardware. Beginners often find these questions confusing. As a result, they often either load way too many programs on their computer or don't load enough and later discover that their computer won't do what they want it to.

Fortunately for beginners, there's a much simpler way to install Linux.

Specialized Linux distributions

A new subgroup of Linux distributions has started to appear. These are typically based on one of the main distributions but contain only a subset of applications that would make sense for a specific area of use.

Besides providing specialized software (such as only office products for business users), customized Linux distributions also attempt to help beginning Linux users by autodetecting and autoconfiguring common hardware devices. This makes installing Linux a much more enjoyable process.

Table 1-7 shows some of the specialized Linux distributions available and what they specialize in.

That's just a small sampling of specialized Linux distributions. There are literally hundreds of specialized Linux distributions, and more are popping up all the time on the Internet. No matter what your specialty, you'll probably find a Linux distribution made for you.

Many of the specialized Linux distributions are based on the Debian Linux distribution. They use the same installation files as Debian but package only a small fraction of a full-blown Debian system.

TABLE 1-7

Specialized Linux Distributions

Distribution	Description
Linspire	A commercial Linux package configured to look like Windows
Xandros	A commercial Linux package configured for beginners
SimplyMEPIS	A free distribution for home use
Ubuntu	A free distribution for school and home use
PCLinuxOS	A free distribution for home and office use
dyne:bolic	A free distribution designed for audio and MIDI applications
Puppy Linux	A free small distribution that runs well on older PCs

TABLE 1-8

Linux LiveCD Distributions

Distribution	Description
Knoppix	A German Linux, the first Linux LiveCD developed
SimplyMEPIS	Designed for beginning home Linux users
PCLinuxOS	Full-blown Linux distribution on a LiveCD
Ubuntu	A worldwide Linux project, designed for many languages
Slax	A live Linux CD based on Slackware Linux
Puppy Linux	A full-featured Linux designed for older PCs

The Linux LiveCD

A relatively new phenomenon in the Linux world is the bootable Linux CD distribution. This lets you see what a Linux system is like without actually installing it. Most modern PCs can boot from a CD instead of the standard hard drive. To take advantage of this, some Linux distributions create a bootable CD that contains a sample Linux system (called a *Linux LiveCD*). Because of the limitations of the single CD size, the sample can't contain a complete Linux system, but you'd be surprised at all the software they can cram in there. The result is that you can boot your PC from the CD and run a Linux distribution without having to install anything on your hard drive!

This is an excellent way to test various Linux distributions without having to mess with your PC. Just pop in a CD and boot! All of the Linux software will run directly off the CD. There are lots of Linux LiveCDs that you can download from the Internet and burn onto a CD to test drive.

Table 1-8 shows some popular Linux LiveCDs that are available.

You may notice a familiarity in this table. Many specialized Linux distributions also have a Linux LiveCD version. Some Linux LiveCD distributions, such as Ubuntu, allow you to install the Linux distribution directly from the LiveCD. This enables you to boot with the CD, test drive the Linux distribution, and then if you like it, install it on your hard drive. This feature is extremely handy and user-friendly.

As with all good things, Linux LiveCDs have a few drawbacks. Since you access everything from the CD, applications run more slowly, especially if you're using older, slower computers and CD drives. Also, since you can't write to the CD, any changes you make to the Linux system will be gone the next time you reboot.

But there are advances being made in the Linux LiveCD world that help to solve some of these problems. These advances include the ability to:

- Copy Linux system files from the CD to memory
- Copy system files to a file on the hard drive

■ Store system settings on a USB memory stick

■ Store user settings on a USB memory stick

Some Linux LiveCDs, such as Puppy Linux, are designed with a minimum number of Linux system files and copy them directly into memory when the CD boots. This allows you to remove the CD from the computer as soon as Linux boots. Not only does this make your applications run much faster (since applications run faster from memory), but it also gives you a free CD tray to use for ripping audio CDs or playing video DVDs from the software included in Puppy Linux.

Other Linux LiveCDs use an alternative method that allows you to remove the CD from the tray after booting. It involves copying the core Linux files onto the Windows hard drive as a single file. After the CD boots, it looks for that file and reads the system files from it. The dyne:bolic Linux LiveCD uses this technique, which is called docking. Of course, you must copy the system file to your hard drive before you can boot from the CD.

A very popular technique for storing data from a live Linux CD session is to use a common USB memory stick (also called a flash drive and a thumb drive). Just about every Linux LiveCD can recognize a plugged-in USB memory stick (even if the stick is formatted for Windows) and read and write files to and from it. This allows you to boot a Linux LiveCD, use the Linux applications to create files, store them on your memory stick, and then access them from your Windows applications later (or from a different computer). How cool is that?

Summary

This chapter discussed where the Linux system came from and how it works. The Linux kernel is the core of the system, controlling how memory, programs, and hardware all interact with each other. The GNU utilities are also an important piece in the Linux system. The Linux shell, which is the main focus of this book, is part of the GNU core utilities. The chapter also discussed the final piece of a Linux system, the Linux desktop environment. Things have changed over the years, and Linux now supports several graphical desktop environments.

Next, the chapter talked about the various Linux distributions. A Linux distribution bundles the various parts of a Linux system into a simple package that you can easily install on your PC. The Linux distribution world consists of full-blown Linux distributions that include just about every application imaginable, as well as specialized Linux distributions that only include applications focused on a special function. The Linux LiveCD craze has created another group of Linux distributions that allow you to easily test drive Linux without even having to install it on your hard drive.

In the next chapter, we'll look at what we need to start our command line and shell scripting experience. You'll see what you need to do to get to the Linux shell utility from your fancy graphical desktop environment. These days that's not always an easy thing.

Chapter 2

Getting to the Shell

I n the old days of Linux, all that was available to work with was the shell. System administrators, programmers, and system users all sat at the Linux console terminal entering text commands, and viewing text output. These days, with our fancy graphical desktop environments, it's getting harder just to find a shell prompt on the system to work from. This chapter discusses what is required to provide a command line environment, then walks you through the terminal emulation packages you may run into in the various Linux distributions.

Terminal Emulation

Back before the days of graphical desktops, the only way to interact with a Unix system was through a text *command line interface* (CLI) provided by the shell. The CLI allowed text input only, and could only display text and rudimentary graphics output.

Because of this restriction, output devices did not have to be very fancy. Often a simple dumb terminal was all that was required to interact with the Unix system. A dumb terminal was usually nothing more than a monitor and keyboard (although later on in life they started getting fancier by utilizing a mouse) connected to the Unix system via a communication cable (usually a multi-wire serial cable). This simple combination provided an easy way to enter text data into the Unix system and view text results.

As you well know, things are significantly different in today's Linux environment. Just about every Linux distribution uses some type of graphical desktop environment. However, to access the shell you still need a text display to interact with a CLI. The problem now is getting to one. With all of the new graphical Linux desktop features, sometimes finding a way to get a CLI in a Linux distribution is not an easy task.

One way to get to a CLI is to take the Linux system out of graphical desktop mode and place it in text mode. This provides nothing more than a simple shell CLI on the monitor, just like the days before graphical desktops. This mode is called the *Linux console*, since it emulates the old days of a hard-wired console terminal, and is a direct interface to the Linux system.

The alternative to being in the Linux console is to use a *terminal emulation package* from within the graphical Linux desktop environment. A terminal emulation package simulates working on a dumb terminal, all within a graphical window on the desktop. Figure 2-1 shows an example of a terminal emulator running in a graphical Linux desktop environment.

Each terminal emulation package has the ability to emulate one or more specific types of dumb terminal. If you're going to work with the shell in Linux, unfortunately you'll need to know a little bit about terminal emulation.

Knowing the core features of the old dumb terminals will help you decide which emulation type to select when you're using a graphical terminal emulator, and use all of the available features to their full capabilities. The main features used in the dumb terminal can be broken down into two areas: the graphics capabilities and the keyboard. This section describes these features and discusses how they relate to the different types of terminal emulators.

FIGURE 2-1

A simple terminal emulator running on a Linux desktop

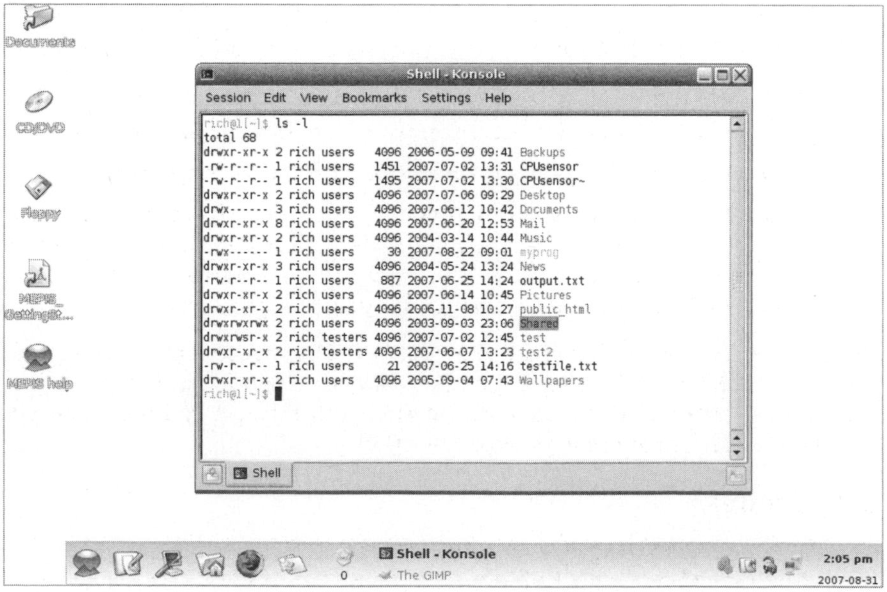

Graphics capabilities

The most important part of terminal emulation is how it displays information on the monitor. When you hear the phrase "text mode," the last thing you'd think to worry about is graphics. However, even the most rudimentary dumb terminals supported some method of screen manipulation (such as clearing the screen and displaying text at a specific location on the screen).

This section describes the graphics features that make each of the different terminal types unique, and what to look for in the terminal emulation packages.

Character sets

All terminals must display characters on the screen (otherwise, text mode would be pretty useless). The trick is in what characters to display, and what codes the Linux system needs to send to display them. A *character set* is a set of binary commands that the Linux system sends to a monitor to display characters. There are several character sets that are supported by various terminal emulation packages:

- **ASCII** The American Standard Code for Information Interchange. This character set contains the English characters stored using a 7-bit code, and consists of 128 English letters (both upper and lower case), numbers, and special symbols. This character set was adopted by the American National Standards Institute (ANSI) as US-ASCII. You will often see it referred to in terminal emulators as the ANSI character set.

- **ISO-8859-1 (commonly called Latin-1)** An extension of the ASCII character set developed by the International Organization for Standardization (ISO). It uses an 8-bit code to support the standard ASCII characters as well as special foreign language characters for most Western European languages. The Latin-1 character set is popular in multinational terminal emulation packages.

- **ISO-8859-2** ISO character set that supports Eastern European language characters.

- **ISO-8859-6** ISO character set that supports Arabic language characters.

- **ISO-8859-7** ISO character set that supports Greek language characters.

- **ISO-8859-8** ISO character set that supports Hebrew language characters.

- **ISO-10646 (commonly called Unicode)** ISO 2-byte character set that contains codes for most English and non-English languages. This single character set contains all of the codes defined in all of the ISO-8859-x series of character sets. The Unicode character set is quickly becoming popular among open source applications.

By far the most common character set in use today in English-speaking countries is the Latin-1 character set. The Unicode character set is becoming more popular, and may very well one day become the new standard in character sets. Most popular terminal emulators allow you to select which character set to use in the terminal emulation.

Control codes

Besides being able to display characters, terminals must have the ability to control special features on the monitor and keyboard, such as the cursor location on the screen. They accomplish this using a system of *control codes*. A control code is a special code not used in the character set, which signals the terminal to perform a special, nonprintable operation.

Common control code functions are the carriage return (return the cursor to the beginning of the line), line feed (put the cursor on the next horizontal row), horizontal tab (shift the cursor over a preset number of spaces), arrow keys (up, down, left, and right), and the page up/page down keys. While these codes mainly emulate features that control where the cursor is placed on the monitor, there are also several other codes, such as clearing the entire screen, and even a bell ring (emulating the old typewriter end-of-carriage bell).

Control codes were also used in controlling the communication features of dumb terminals. Dumb terminals were connected to the computer system via some type of communication channel, often a serial communication cable. Sometimes data needed to be controlled on the communication channel, so developers devised special control codes just for data communication purposes. While these codes aren't necessarily required in modern terminal emulators, most support these codes to maintain compatibility. The most common codes in this category are the XON and XOFF codes, which start and stop data transmission to the terminal, respectively.

Block mode graphics

As dumb terminals became more popular, manufacturers started experimenting with rudimentary graphics capabilities. By far the most popular type of "graphical" dumb terminal used in the Unix world was the DEC VT series of terminals. The turning point for dumb terminals came with the release of the DEC VT100 in 1978. The DEC VT100 terminal was the first terminal to support the complete ANSI character set, including block mode graphic characters.

The ANSI character set contains codes that not only allowed monitors to display text but also rudimentary graphics symbols, such as boxes, lines, and blocks. By far one of the most popular dumb terminals used in Unix operations during the 1980s was the VT102, an upgraded version of the VT100. Most terminal emulation programs emulate the operation of the VT102 display, supporting all of the ANSI codes for creating block mode graphics.

Vector graphics

The Tektronix company produced a popular series of terminals that used a display method called vector graphics. Vector graphics deviated from the DEC method of block mode graphics by making all screen images (including characters) a series of line segments (vectors). The Tektronix 4010 terminal was the most popular graphical dumb terminal produced. Many terminal emulation packages still emulate its capabilities.

The 4010 terminal displays images by drawing a series of vectors using an electron beam, much like drawing with a pencil. Since vector graphics doesn't use dots to create lines, it has the ability to draw geometric shapes using higher precision than most dot-oriented graphics terminals. This was a popular feature among mathematicians and scientists.

Terminal emulators use software to emulate the vector graphics drawing capabilities of the Tektronix 4010 terminals. This is still a popular feature for people who need precise graphical drawings, or those who still run applications that used the vector graphics routines to draw complicated charts and diagrams.

Display buffering

A key to graphics displays is the ability of the terminal to buffer data. Buffering data requires having additional internal memory within the terminal itself to store characters not currently being displayed on the monitor.

The DEC VT series of terminals utilized two types of data buffering:

- Buffering data as it scrolled off of the main display window (called a history)
- Buffering a completely separate display window (called an alternate screen)

The first type of buffering is known as a *scroll region*. The scroll region is the amount of memory the terminal has that enables it to "remember" data as it scrolls off of the screen. A standard DEC VT102 terminal contained a viewing area for 25 lines of characters. As the terminal displays a new line of characters, the previous line is scrolled upward. When the terminal reaches the bottom line of the display, the next line causes the top line to scroll off the display.

The internal memory in the VT102 terminal allowed it to save the last 64 lines that had scrolled off of the display. Users had the ability to lock the current screen display and use arrow keys to scroll backward through the previous lines that had "scrolled off" of the display. Terminal emulation packages allow you to use either a side scrollbar or a mouse scroll button to scroll through the saved data without having to lock the display. Of course, for full emulation compatibility, most terminal emulation packages also allow you to lock the display and use arrow and page up/page down to scroll through the saved data.

The second type of buffering is known as an *alternative screen*. Normally, the terminal writes data directly to the normal display area on the monitor. A method was developed to crudely implement animation by using two screen areas to store data. Control codes were used to signal the terminal to write data to the alternative screen instead of the current display screen. That data was held in memory. Another control code would signal the terminal to switch the monitor display between the normal screen data and the data contained in the alternative screen almost instantaneously. By storing successive data pages in the alternative screen area, then displaying it, you could crudely simulate moving graphics.

Terminals that emulate the VT00 series of terminals have the ability to support the alternative screen method.

Color

Even back in the black-and-white (or green) dumb terminal days, programmers were experimenting with different ways to present data. Most terminals supported special control codes to produce the following types of special text:

- Bold characters
- Underline characters

- Reverse video (black characters on white background)
- Blinking
- Combinations of all of the above features

Back in the old days, if you wanted to get someone's attention, you used bold, blinking, reverse video text. Now there's something that could hurt your eyes!

As color terminals became available, programmers added special control codes to display text in various colors and shades. The ANSI character set includes control codes for specifying specific colors for both foreground text and the background color displayed on the monitor. Most terminal emulators support the ANSI color control codes.

The keyboard

There is more to a terminal than just how the monitor operates. If you have ever worked with different types of dumb terminals, I'm sure you have seen that they often contain different keys on the keyboard. Trying to emulate specific keys on a specific dumb terminal has proven to be a difficult task for terminal emulation packages.

It was impossible for the creators of the PC keyboard to include keys for every possible type of special key found in dumb terminals. Some PC manufacturers experimented with including special keys for special functions, but eventually the PC keyboard keys became somewhat standardized.

For a terminal emulation package to completely emulate a specific type of dumb terminal, it must remap any dumb terminal keys that don't appear on the PC keyboard. This remapping feature can often become confusing, especially when different systems use different control codes for the same key.

Some common special keys you'll see in terminal emulation packages are:

- **BREAK:** Sends a stream of zeroes to the host. This is often used to interrupt the currently executing program in the shell.
- **SCROLL LOCK:** Also called no scroll, this stops the output on the display. Some terminals included memory to hold the contents of the display so the user could scroll backward through previously viewed information while the scroll lock was enabled.
- **Repeat:** When held down with another key, this caused the terminal to repeatedly send the other key's value to the host.
- **Return:** Commonly used to send a carriage return character to the host. Most often used to signify the end of a command for the host to process (now called Enter on PC keyboards).
- **Delete:** While basically a simple feature, the Delete key causes grief for terminal emulation packages. Some terminals delete the character at the current cursor location, while

others delete the preceding character. To resolve this dilemma, PC keyboards include two delete keys, Backspace and Delete.

- **Arrow keys:** Commonly used to position the cursor at a specific place; for example, when scrolling through a listing.

- **Function keys:** A combination of specialty keys that can be assigned unique values in programs similar to the PC F1 through F12 keys). The DEC VT series of terminals actually had two sets of function keys, F1 through F20, and PF1 through PF4.

Keyboard emulation is a crucial element in a terminal emulation package. Unfortunately, often applications are written requiring users to hit specific keys for specific functions. I've seen many a communications package that used the old DEC PF1 through PF4 keys, which are often a hard thing to find on a terminal emulation keyboard.

The terminfo Database

Now that you have a terminal emulation package that can emulate different types of terminals, you need a way for the Linux system to know exactly what terminal you're emulating. The Linux system needs to know what control codes to use when communicating with the terminal emulator. This is done by using an environment variable (see Chapter 5) and a special set of files collectively called the *terminfo database*.

The terminfo database is a set of files that identify the characteristics of various terminals that can be used on the Linux system. The Linux system stores the terminfo data for each terminal type as a separate file in the terminfo database directory. The location of this directory often varies from distribution to distribution. Some common locations are /usr/share/terminfo, /etc/terminfo, and /lib/terminfo.

To help with organization (often there are lots of different terminfo files), you will see that the terminfo database directory contains directories for different letters of the alphabet. The individual files for specific terminals are stored under the appropriate letter directory for their terminal name.

An individual terminfo file is a binary file that is the result of compiling a text file. This text file contains code words that define screen functions, associated with the control code required to implement the function on the terminal.

Since the terminfo database files are binary, you cannot see the codes within these files. However, you can use the infocmp command to convert the binary entries into text. An example of using this command is:

```
$ infocmp vt100
#  Reconstructed via infocmp from file: /lib/terminfo/v/vt100
vt100|vt100-am|dec vt100 (w/advanced video),
        am, msgr, xenl, xon,
```

31

```
                    cols#80, it#8, lines#24, vt#3,
                    acsc=``aaffggjjkkllmmnnooppqqrrssttuuvvwwxxyyzz{{||}}~~,
                    bel=^G, blink=\E[5m$<2>, bold=\E[1m$<2>,
                    clear=\E[H\E[J$<50>, cr=^M, csr=\E[%i%p1%d;%p2%dr,
                    cub=\E[%p1%dD, cub1=^H, cud=\E[%p1%dB, cud1=^J,
                    cuf=\E[%p1%dC, cuf1=\E[C$<2>,
                    cup=\E[%i%p1%d;%p2%dH$<5>, cuu=\E[%p1%dA,
                    cuu1=\E[A$<2>, ed=\E[J$<50>, el=\E[K$<3>, el1=\E[1K$<3>,
                    enacs=\E(B\E)0, home=\E[H, ht=^I, hts=\EH, ind=^J, ka1=\EOq,
                    ka3=\EOs, kb2=\EOr, kbs=^H, kc1=\EOp, kc3=\EOn, kcub1=\EOD,
                    kcud1=\EOB, kcuf1=\EOC, kcuu1=\EOA, kent=\EOM, kf0=\EOy,
                    kf1=\EOP, kf10=\EOx, kf2=\EOQ, kf3=\EOR, kf4=\EOS, kf5=\EOt,
                    kf6=\EOu, kf7=\EOv, kf8=\EOl, kf9=\EOw, rc=\E8,
                    rev=\E[7m$<2>, ri=\EM$<5>, rmacs=^O, rmam=\E[?7l,
                    rmkx=\E[?1l\E>, rmso=\E[m$<2>, rmul=\E[m$<2>,
                    rs2=\E>\E[?3l\E[?4l\E[?5l\E[?7h\E[?8h,
                    sc=\E7,
                    sgr0=\E[m\017$<2>, smacs=^N, smam=\E[?7h, smkx=\E[?1h\E=,
                    smso=\E[7m$<2>, smul=\E[4m$<2>, tbc=\E[3g,
          $
```

The terminfo entry defines the terminal name (in this case vt100), along with any alias names that can be associated with the terminal name. Notice that the first line shows the location of the terminfo file the values were extracted from.

Following that, the infocmp command lists the capabilities of the terminal definition, along with the control codes used to emulate the individual capabilities. Some capabilities are either enabled or disabled (such as the am, auto-right-margin, feature). If the capability appears in the list, it's enabled by the terminal definition. Other capabilities must define a specific control code sequence to perform the task (such as clearing the monitor display). Table 2-1 shows a list of some of the capabilities you see in the vt100 terminfo definition file listed.

The Linux shell uses the TERM environment variable to define which terminal emulation setting in the terminfo database to use for a specific session. When the TERM environment variable is set to vt100, the shell knows to use the control codes associated with the vt100 terminfo database entry for sending control codes to the terminal emulator. To see the TERM environment variable, you can just echo it from the CLI:

```
$ echo $TERM
xterm
$
```

This example shows that the current terminal type is set to the xterm entry in the terminfo database.

TABLE 2-1

Terminfo Capability Codes

Code	Description
am	Set right-side auto-margin
msgr	Safe to move cursor in standout mode
xenl	Newline characters ignored after 80 columns
xon	Terminal uses XON/XOFF characters for flow control
cols#80	80 columns in a line
it#8	Tab character set to eight spaces
lines#24	24 lines on a screen
vt#3	Virtual terminal number 3
bel	Control code to use to emulate the bell
blink	Control code used to produce blinking text
bold	Control code used to produce bold text
clear	Control code used to clear the screen
cr	Control code used to enter a carriage return
csr	Control code used to change scroll region
cub	Move one character to the left without erasing
cub1	Move cursor back one space
cud	Move cursor down one line
cud1	Control code to move cursor down one line
cuf	Move one character to the right without erasing
cuf1	Control code to move the cursor right one space without erasing
cup	Control code to move to row one, column two on the display
cuu	Move cursor up one line
cuu1	Control code to move cursor up one line
ed	Clear to the end of the screen
el	Clear to the end of the line
el1	Clear to the beginning of the line.

continued

TABLE 2-1	(continued)
Code	Description
enacs	Enable the alternate character set
home	Control code to move cursor to the home position — row one, column two (same as cup)
ht	Tab character
hts	Set tab in every row at current column
ind	Scroll text up
ka1	Upper-left key in keypad
ka3	Upper-right key in keypad
kb2	Center key in keypad
kbs	Backspace key
kc1	Lower-left key in keypad
kc3	Lower-right key in keypad
kcub1	The left arrow key
kcud1	Control code for down arrow key
kcuf1	The right arrow key
kcuu1	The up arrow key
kent	The Enter key
kf0	The F0 function key
kf1	The F1 function key
kf10	The F10 function key
rc	Restore cursor to last saved position
rev	Reverse video mode
ri	Scroll text down
rmacs	End alternate character set
rmam	Turn off automatic margins
rmkx	Exit keyboard transmit mode
rmso	Exit standout mode
rmul	Exit underline mode
rs2	Reset

TABLE 2-1	*(continued)*
Code	**Description**
sc	Save current cursor position
sgr	Define video attributes
sgr0	Turn off all attributes
smacs	Start alternate character set
smam	Turn on automatic margins
smkx	Start keyboard transmit mode
smso	Begin standout mode
smul	Begin underline mode
tbc	Clear all tab stops

The Linux Console

In the early days of Linux, when you booted up your system you would see a login prompt on your monitor, and that's all. As mentioned earlier, this is called the Linux console. It was the only place you could enter commands for the system.

With modern Linux systems, when the Linux system starts it automatically creates several *virtual consoles*. A virtual console is a terminal session that runs in memory on the Linux system. Instead of having six dumb terminals connected to the PC, the Linux system starts seven (or sometimes even more) virtual consoles that you can access from the single PC keyboard and monitor.

In most Linux distributions, you can access the virtual consoles using a simple keystroke combination. Usually you must hold down the Ctl+Alt key combination, then press a function key (F1 through F8) for the virtual console you want to use. Function key F1 produces virtual console 1, key F2 produces virtual console 2, and so on.

The first six virtual consoles use a full-screen text terminal emulator to display a text login screen, as shown in Figure 2-2.

After logging in with your user ID and password, you are taken to the Linux bash shell CLI. In the Linux console you do not have the ability to run any graphical programs. You can only use text programs to display on the Linux text consoles.

After logging in to a virtual console, you can keep it active and switch to another virtual console without losing your active session. You can switch between all of the virtual consoles, with multiple active sessions running.

FIGURE 2-2

The Linux console login screen

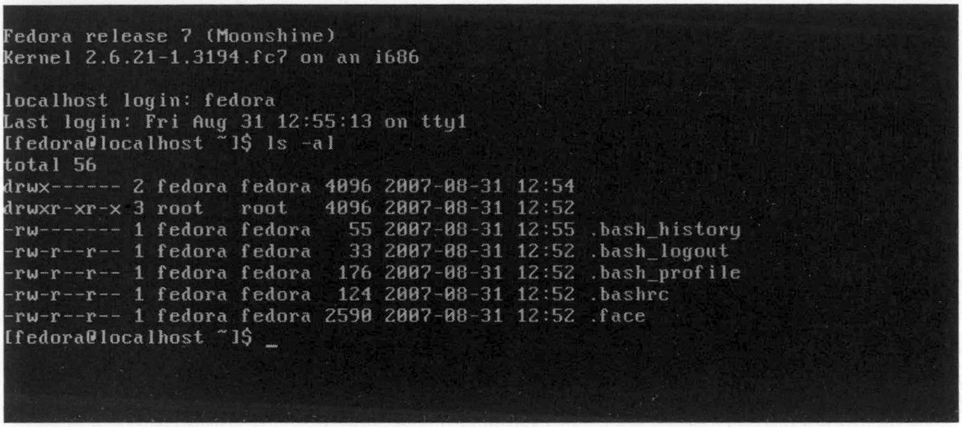

```
Fedora release 7 (Moonshine)
Kernel 2.6.21-1.3194.fc7 on an i686

localhost login: fedora
Last login: Fri Aug 31 12:55:13 on tty1
[fedora@localhost ~]$ ls -al
total 56
drwx------ 2 fedora fedora 4096 2007-08-31 12:54
drwxr-xr-x 3 root   root   4096 2007-08-31 12:52
-rw------- 1 fedora fedora   55 2007-08-31 12:55 .bash_history
-rw-r--r-- 1 fedora fedora   33 2007-08-31 12:52 .bash_logout
-rw-r--r-- 1 fedora fedora  176 2007-08-31 12:52 .bash_profile
-rw-r--r-- 1 fedora fedora  124 2007-08-31 12:52 .bashrc
-rw-r--r-- 1 fedora fedora 2590 2007-08-31 12:52 .face
[fedora@localhost ~]$ _
```

The last two virtual consoles are normally reserved for X Windows graphical desktops. Some distributions only assign one or the other, so you may have to test both Ctl+Alt+F7 and Ctl+Alt+F8 to see which one your particular distribution uses. Most distributions automatically switch to one of the graphical virtual consoles after the boot sequence completes, providing a complete graphical login and desktop experience.

Logging in to a text virtual terminal session then switching over to a graphical one can get tedious. Fortunately, there's a better way to jump between graphical and text mode on the Linux system: terminal emulation packages are a popular way to access the shell CLI from within a graphical desktop session. The following sections describe the most common software packages that provide terminal emulation in a graphical window.

The xterm Terminal

The oldest and most basic of X Windows terminal emulation packages is *xterm*. The xterm package has been around since the original days of X Windows, and is included by default in most X Window packages.

The xterm package provides both a basic VT102/220 terminal emulation CLI and a graphical Tektronix 4014 environment (similar to the 4010 environment). While xterm is a full terminal emulation package, it doesn't require many resources (such as memory) to operate. Because of this feature, the xterm package is still popular in Linux distributions designed to run on older hardware. Some graphical desktop environments, such as fluxbox, use it as the default terminal emulation package.

FIGURE 2-3

The basic xterm display

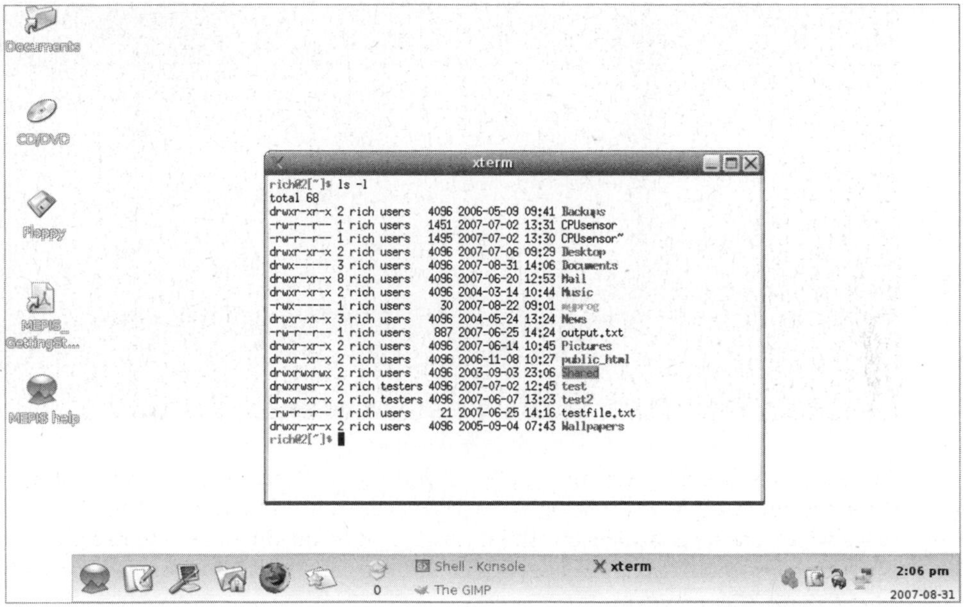

While not offering many fancy features, the xterm package does one thing extremely well, and that is emulate a VT220 terminal. The newer versions of xterm even emulate the VT series of color control codes, allowing you to use color in your scripts (discussed in Chapter 15).

Figure 2-3 shows what the basic xterm display looks like running on a graphical Linux desktop.

The xterm package allows you to set individual features using both command line parameters and a series of four simple graphical menus. The following sections discuss these features and how to change them.

Command line parameters

The list of xterm command line parameters is extensive. There are lots of features you can control to customize the terminal emulation features, such as enabling or disabling individual VT emulations.

The xterm command line parameters use the plus (+) and minus (-) signs to signify how a feature is set. A plus sign indicates that the feature should be returned to the default setting. A minus sign indicates that you are setting the feature to a non-default value. Table 2-2 lists some of the more common features that you can set using the command line parameters.

TABLE 2-2

xterm Command Line Parameters

Parameter	Description
132	By default xterm does not allow 132 characters per line mode
ah	Always highlight the text cursor
aw	Auto-line-wrap is enabled
bc	Enables text cursor blinking
bg color	Specify the color to use for the background
cm	Disables recognition of ANSI color change control codes
fb font	Specify the font to use for bold text
fg color	Specify the color to use for the foreground text
fn font	Specify the font to use for text
fw font	Specify the font to use for wide text
hc color	Specify the color to use for highlighted text
j	Use jump scrolling, scrolling multiple lines at a time
l	Enable logging screen data to a log file
lf filename	Specify the file name to use for screen logging
mb	Ring a margin bell when the cursor reaches the end of a line
ms color	Specify the color used for the text cursor
name name	Specify the name of the application that appears in the titlebar
rv	Enable reverse video by swapping the background and foreground colors
sb	Use a side scrollbar to allow scrolling of saved scroll data
t	Start xterm in Tektronix mode
tb	Specify that xterm should display a toolbar at the top

It is important to note that not all implementations of xterm support all of these command line parameters. You can determine which parameters your xterm implements by using the -help parameter when you start xterm on your system.

The xterm main menu

The main xterm menu contains configuration items that apply to both the VT102 and Tektronix windows. You can access the main menu by holding down the Ctrl key and clicking the mouse button once (the left button on a right-hand mouse, the right button on a left-hand mouse) while in an xterm session window. Figure 2-4 shows what the xterm main menu looks like.

There are four sections in the xterm main menu, as described in the following sections.

X event commands

The X event commands section contains features that allow you to manage how xterm interacts with the X Window display.

- **Toolbar:** If the xterm installation supports the toolbar, this entry enables or disables displaying the toolbar in the xterm window (the same as the `tb` command line parameter).
- **Secure Keyboard:** Restricts the keyboard keystrokes to a specific xterm window. This is useful when typing passwords to ensure they don't get hijacked by another window.
- **Allow SendEvents:** Allows X Window events generated by other X Window applications to be accepted by the xterm window.
- **Redraw Window:** Instructs X Windows to refresh the xterm window.

FIGURE 2-4

The xterm main menu

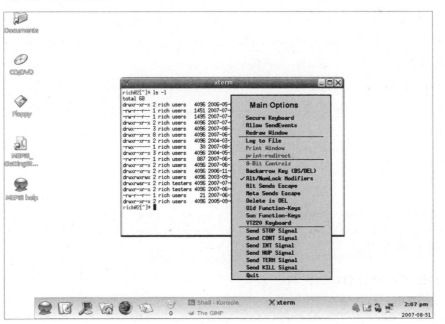

Again, all of these features may not be supported by your particular xterm implementation. If they're not supported, they'll appear grayed-out in the menu.

Output capturing

The xterm package allows you to capture data displayed in the window and either log it to a file or send it to a default printer defined in X Windows. The features that appear in this section are:

- **Log to file:** Sends all data displayed in the xterm window to a text file.
- **Print window:** Sends all data displayed in the current window to the default X Window printer.
- **Redirect to printer:** Sends all data displayed in the xterm window to the default X Window printer as well. This feature must be turned off to stop printing data.

The capturing feature can get messy if you are using graphics characters or control characters (such as colored text) in your display area. All characters sent to the display, including control characters, are stored in the log file or sent to the printer.

The xterm print feature assumes that you define a default printer in the X Window system. If you have no printer defined, the feature will appear grayed out in the menu.

Keyboard settings

The keyboard settings section contains features that allow you to customize how xterm sends keyboard characters to the host system.

- **8-bit controls:** Sends 8-bit control codes, used in VT220 terminals, rather than 7-bit ASCII control codes.
- **Backarrow key:** Toggles the back arrow key between sending a backspace character or a delete character.
- **Alt/Numlock Modifiers:** Controls whether the Alt or Numlock keys change the PC numberpad behavior.
- **Alt Sends Escape:** The Alt key sends an escape control code along with the other key pressed.
- **Meta sends Escape:** Controls whether the function keys send a two-character control code, including the escape control code.
- **Delete is DEL:** The PC Delete key sends a delete character instead of a backspace character.
- **Old Function keys:** The PC functions keys emulate the DEC VT100 function keys.
- **HP Function keys:** The PC function keys emulate the HP terminal function keys.
- **Sun Function keys:** The PC function keys emulate the Sun Workstation function keys.
- **VT220 keyboard:** The PC function keys emulate the DEC VT220 function keys.

As you can see, setting keyboard preferences often depends on the specific application and/or environment you're working in. There's also a fair amount of personal preference involved as well. Often it's just a matter of what works best for you as to which keyboard settings to make.

The VT options menu

The VT options menu sets features xterm uses in the VT102 emulation. You access the VT options menu by holding down the Control key and clicking the second mouse button. Normally the second mouse button is the middle mouse button. If you're using a two-button mouse, most Linux X Window configurations emulate the middle mouse button when you click both the left and right mouse buttons together. Figure 2-5 shows what the VT options menu looks like.

As you can see from Figure 2-5, many of the VT features that you can set from the command line parameters can also be set from the VT options menu. This produces quite a large list of available options. The VT options are divided into three sets of commands, described in the following sections.

FIGURE 2-5

The xterm VT options menu

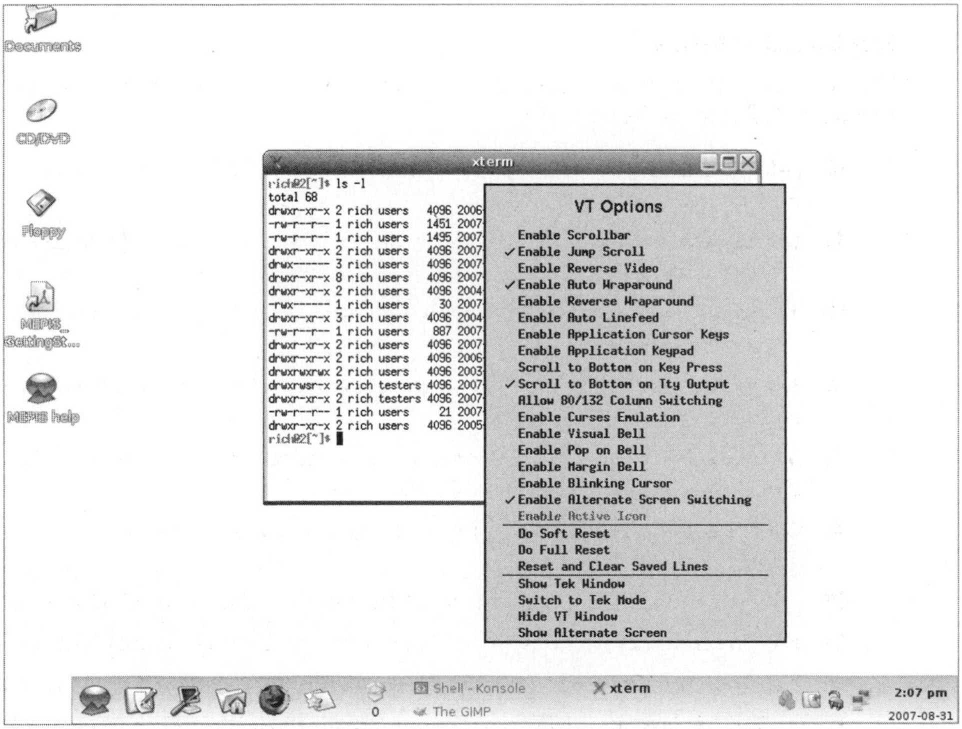

VT features

The VT features commands change the features of how xterm implements the VT102/220 emulation. They include:

- Enable Scrollbar
- Enable Jump Scrollbar
- Enable Reverse Video
- Enable Auto Wraparound
- Enable Reverse Wraparound
- Enable Auto Linefeed
- Enable Application Cursor Keys
- Enable Application Keypad
- Scroll to Bottom on Keypress
- Scroll to Bottom on TTY Output
- Allow 80/132 Column Switching
- Select to Clipboard
- Enable Visual Bell
- Enable Pop on Bell
- Enable Margin Bell
- Enable Blinking Cursor
- Enable Alternate Screen Switching
- Enable Active Icon

You can enable or disable each of these features by clicking on the feature in the menu. An enabled feature will have a checkmark next to it.

VT commands

The VT commands section sends a specific reset command to the xterm emulation window. They include:

- Do Soft Reset
- Do Full Reset
- Reset and Clear Saved Lines

The soft reset sends a control code to reset the screen area. This is convenient if a program sets the scroll region incorrectly. The full reset clears the screen, resets any set tab positions, and resets any terminal mode feature set during the session to the initial state. The Reset and Clear Saved Lines command performs a full reset, and also clears out the scroll area history file.

Current screen commands

The current screen commands section sends commands to the xterm emulator that affect which screen is the currently active screen.

- **Show Tek Window:** Display the Tektronix terminal window along with the VT100 terminal window.

- **Switch to Tek Window:** Hide the VT100 terminal window and display the Tektronix terminal window.

- **Hide VT Window:** Hide the VT100 terminal window while displaying the Tektronix terminal window.

- **Show Alternate Screen:** Display the data currently stored in the VT100 alternate screen area.

The xterm terminal emulator provides the ability to start in either VT100 terminal mode (by default) or in the Tektronix terminal mode (by using the t command line parameter). After you start in either mode, you can use this menu area to switch to the other mode during your session.

The VT fonts menu

The VT fonts menu sets the font style used in the VT100/220 emulation window. You can access this menu by holding the Control key and clicking on mouse button three (the right button on a right-handed mouse, or the left button on a left-handed mouse). Figure 2-6 shows what the VT fonts menu looks like.

FIGURE 2-6

The xterm VT fonts menu

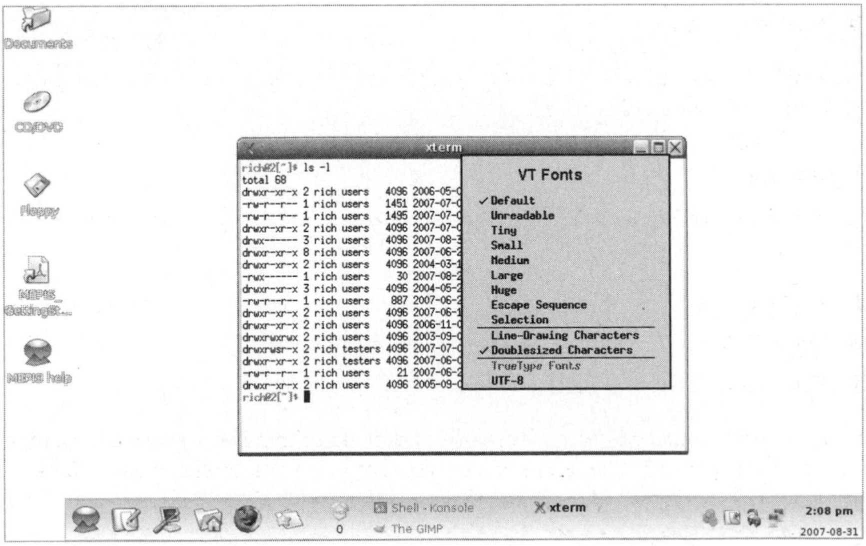

The VT fonts menu, covered in the following sections, contains three sections of selections.

Set the font

These menu options set the size of the font used in the xterm window. The available sizes are:

- Default
- Unreadable
- Tiny
- Small
- Medium
- Large
- Huge
- Escape the Sequence
- Selection

The default font is the standard-sized font used to display text in the current X Window frame. The unreadable font is pretty much what it says. It shrinks the xterm window down to a size that is not really usable. This is handy, however, when you want to minimize the window on your desktop without completely minimizing it on the system. The large and huge font options produce extremely large font sizes for visually-impaired users.

The Escape the Sequence option sets the font to the last font set by the VT100 `set font` control code. The Selection option allows you to save the current font with a special font name.

Display the font

This section of menu options defines the type of characters used to create the text. There are two options available:

- **Line Drawing Characters:** Tells the Linux system to produce ANSI graphical lines instead of using line characters from the chosen font
- **Doublesized characters:** Tells the Linux system to scale the set font to double the normal size

The line drawing characters allow you to determine which types of graphical features to use when drawing in text mode. You can use either characters provided by the selected font source or characters provided by the DEC VT100 control codes.

Specify the font

This section of the menu provides options for what type of fonts are used to create the characters:

- TrueType Fonts
- UTF-8 Fonts

The TrueType fonts are popular in graphical environments. Instead of each character taking the same amount of space in the line, characters are proportioned by their natural sizes. Thus, the letter i takes up less space on the line than the letter m. The UTF-8 font allows you to temporarily switch to use the Unicode character set for applications that don't support foreign characters.

The Konsole Terminal

The KDE Desktop Project has created its own terminal emulation package called *Konsole*. The Konsole package incorporates the basic xterm features, along with more advanced features that we now expect from a Windows application. This section describes the features of the Konsole terminal, and shows how to use them.

Command line parameters

Often a Linux distribution provides a method for starting applications directly from the graphical desktop menu system. If your distribution doesn't provide this feature, you can manually start Konsole by using the format:

```
konsole parameters
```

Just like xterm, the Konsole package uses command line parameters to set features in the new sessions. Table 2-3 shows the available Konsole command line parameters.

Sessions

When you start Konsole, you'll notice that it has a tabbed window, with one tab open to a terminal emulation session. This is the default session, and it is normally a standard bash shell CLI. You can define many different sessions for Konsole, and even have multiple sessions open at the same time.

The default configuration for Konsole includes several different types of sessions that you can access from the Konsole window:

- A standard shell session using the xterm terminal emulation
- A Linux console session using the text mode terminal emulation
- A shell session logged in as the Linux root user (you must supply the password)
- A Midnight Commander file management session (if installed in your distribution)
- A session using the Python interactive CLI for testing programs written in the Python language (if Python is installed in your distribution)
- A shell started at a saved bookmark area (discussed in "The menu bar" section later in this chapter)

TABLE 2-3

The Konsole Command Line Parameters

Parameter	Description
-e command	Execute command instead of a shell.
--keytab file	Use the specified key file to define key mappings.
--keytabs	List all of the available keytabs.
--ls	Start the Konsole session with a login screen.
--name name	Set the name that appears in the Konsole titlebar.
--noclose	Prevent the Konsole window from closing when the last session has been closed.
--noframe	Start Konsole without a frame.
--nohist	Prevent Konsole from saving scroll history in sessions.
--nomenubar	Start Konsole without the standard menubar options.
--noresize	Prevent changing the size of the Konsole window area.
--notabbar	Start Konsole without the standard tab area for sessions.
--noxft	Start Konsole without support for aliasing smaller fonts.
--profile file	Start Konsole with settings saved in the specified file.
--profiles	List all of the available Konsole profiles.
--schema name	Start Konsole using the specified schema name or file.
--schemata	List the schemes available in Konsole.
-T title	Set the Konsole window title.
--type type	Start a Konsole session using the specified type.
--types	List all of the available Konsole session types.
--vt_sz CxL	Specify the terminal columns (C) and rows (L).
--workdir dir	Specify the working directory for Konsole to store temporary files.

Konsole allows you to have multiple sessions active at the same time. Each session is contained within its own tabbed window. Konsole places a tab on each session window to allow you to easily switch between sessions. You'll notice the tabs at either the top or bottom of the window area. This is a great feature for programmers who need to edit code in one session, while testing the code in another session. It's easy to flip back and forth between different active sessions in Konsole. Figure 2-7 shows a Konsole window with three active sessions.

FIGURE 2-7

The Konsole terminal emulator with three active sessions

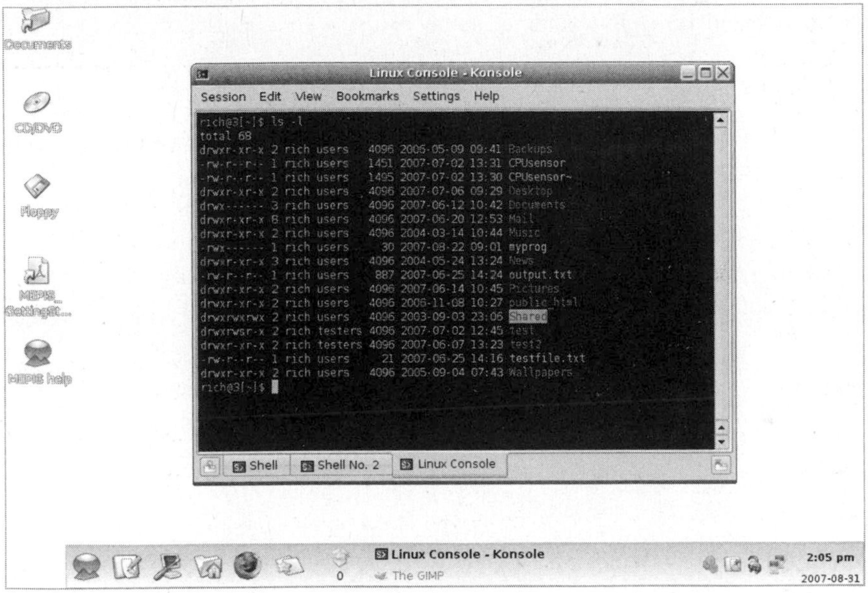

There is a new session button at the left side of the tab area. Click this button to automatically start a new session using the standard shell. Click and hold the button to see a session menu which allows you to select the type of new session to start.

Similar to the xterm terminal emulator, Konsole provides a simple menu by right-clicking in the active session area. If you right-click in the session area, a menu appears with the following options:

- **Set Selection End:** Select the session window area from the cursor to the location of the mouse pointer.
- **Copy:** Copy the selected text to the clipboard.
- **Paste:** Paste the contents of the clipboard to the selected area.
- **Send Signal:** Send a Linux control signal to the system.
- **Detach session:** Move a tabbed session to a new Konsole session window (only available if there is more than one session active).
- **Rename session:** Change the X Windows name of the session.
- **Bookmarks:** Add a session bookmark at the current session location. You can recall the bookmark later to return to the same directory in another session.
- **Close session:** Terminate the session. If it is the last session in the Konsole window, Konsole will close.

Konsole also provides another quick way to access the new session menu by holding down the Ctl key and right-clicking in the session area.

Besides the session tabs and new session button, by default Konsole uses a menu bar to provide additional functionality so that you can modify and save your Konsole sessions.

The menu bar

The default Konsole setup uses a menu bar for you to easily view and change options and features in your sessions. The menu bar consists of six items described in the following sections.

Session

The Session menu bar item provides yet another location for you to start a new session type. Besides listing the standard session types to start a new session, it also contains the following entries:

- Start a new Konsole window with a default session
- Print the screen of the current session
- Close the current session
- Quit the Konsole application

When you select one of the session types from the menu, the new session appears as a new tabbed window frame in the Konsole window.

Edit

The Edit menu bar provides options for handling text in the session:

- **Copy:** Copies selected text (that was highlighted with the mouse) to the system clipboard.
- **Paste:** Pastes text currently in the system clipboard to the current cursor location. If the text contains newline characters, they will be processed by the shell.
- **Send Signal:** Sends a Linux control signal to the system. The control signals available are:
  - **STOP:** Stops the currently running program
  - **CONT:** Continue if interrupted
  - **HUP:** Resets the currently running program
  - **INT:** Interrupts the currently running program
  - **TERM:** Terminates the current session
  - **KILL:** Kills the current session
  - **USR1:** User-defined signal 1
  - **USR2:** User-defined signal 2

- **ZModem Upload:** Uploads a file to the system using the ZModem protocol.
- **Clear terminal:** Clears all text from the current session window.
- **Reset and Clear Terminal:** Sends the control code to reset the terminal emulator, and clears the current session window.
- **Find in History:** Locates a text string in the previous lines of output text in the session.
- **Find Next:** Locates the next occurrence of the text string in the previous lines of output text in the session.
- **Find Previous:** Locates the previous occurrence of the text string in the previous lines of output text in the session.
- **Save History As:** Saves the current history as a file.
- **Clear History:** Clears the previous lines of output text in the session.
- **Clear All Histories:** Clears the previous lines of output text in all sessions.

Konsole retains a history area for each active session. The history area contains the output text for lines that scroll out of the viewing area of the terminal emulator. By default Konsole retains the last 1000 lines of output in the history area. You can scroll through the history area by using the scrollbar in the viewing area, or by pressing the Shift key and the Up Arrow key to scroll line by line, or the Page Up key to scroll page (24 lines) by page.

View

The View menu bar item contains items for controlling the individual sessions in the Konsole window. These selections include:

- **Detach Session:** Remove the current session from the Konsole window, and start a new Konsole window using the current session as the default session. This is only available when more than one active session is available.
- **Rename Session:** Change the name of the current session. The new name appears on the session tab, allowing you to identify tabs more easily.
- **Monitor for Activity:** Sets the session so that the session tab shows a special icon if new text appears in the screen area. This is allows you to switch to another session while waiting for output from an application, then notifies you when the output appears. This feature is toggled between on and off.
- **Monitor for Silence:** Sets the session so the session tab shows a special icon when no new text appears in the screen area for 10 seconds. This allows you to switch to another session while waiting for output from an application to stop, such as when compiling a large application. This feature is toggled between on and off.
- **Send Input to All Sessions:** Sends the text typed in one session to all the active sessions.
- **Move Session Left:** Moves the current session tab left in the window list.
- **Move Session Right:** Moves the current session tab right in the window list.

After the standard menu options, the View menu bar area contains a list of the current active sessions. You can switch between sessions by selecting a specific session icon.

Bookmarks

The Bookmarks menu items provide a way to manage bookmarks set in the Konsole window. A bookmark enables you to save your directory location in an active session and then easily return there in either the same session or a new session. Have you ever drilled down several directories deep to find something on the Linux system, exited, and then forgotten how you got there? Bookmarks will solve that problem. When you get to your desired directory location, just add a new bookmark. When you want to return, look at the Bookmarks for your new bookmark, and it'll automatically perform the directory change to the desired location for you. The bookmark entries include:

- **Add Bookmark:** Create a new bookmark at the current directory location.
- **Edit Bookmarks:** Edit existing bookmarks.
- **New Bookmark Folder:** Create a new storage folder for bookmarks.

There is no limit to how many bookmarks you can store in Konsole, but having lots of bookmarks can get confusing. By default they all appear at the same level in the Bookmark area. You can organize them by creating new bookmark folders and moving individual bookmarks to the new folders using the Edit Bookmarks item.

Settings

The Settings menu bar area allows you to customize the appearance of a specific session. This area includes:

- **Hide Menubar:** Remove the menu bar from the Konsole window.
- **Tab bar:** Place the window tabs at the top or bottom of the windows, or hide them altogether.
- **Scrollbar:** Place the scrollbar at the right or left side of the window, or hide it altogether.
- **Fullscreen:** Toggle between fullscreen mode (similar to the Linux console) and as a windowed application.
- **Bell:** Sets the action for the bell control code. This can set an audible tone, notify the Linux system, flash the Konsole window, or do nothing.
- **Font:** Set the character font, style, and size.
- **Encoding:** Select the character set to use in the terminal emulation.
- **Keyboard:** Select a keyboard mapping file to use for the session.
- **Schema:** Select a color schema for the background and text colors.
- **Size:** Set the number of columns and rows viewable in the session window.
- **History:** Set how much (if any) data is saved in the history scroll area.

- **Save as Default:** Save the current session configurations as the default.

- **Save Session Profile:** Save the current open sessions as a profile that you can recall later.

- **Configure Notifications:** Set actions for specific session events.

- **Configure Shortcuts:** Create keyboard shortcuts for Konsole commands.

- **Configure Konsole:** Create custom Konsole schemas and sessions.

Most of these settings you should recognize from the discussion on terminal emulators. Konsole allows you to select character sets, keyboard layouts, and colors, and even control how the bell control code is emulated within the Konsole session window.

The Configure Notifications area is pretty cool. It allows you to associate five specific events that can occur within a session with six different actions. When one of the events occurs, the defined action (or actions) are taken.

The Configure Konsole settings provides for advanced control over setting session features, including creating new color schemes. Figure 2-8 shows the main Configure Konsole dialog box.

FIGURE 2-8

The Konsole configuration dialog box

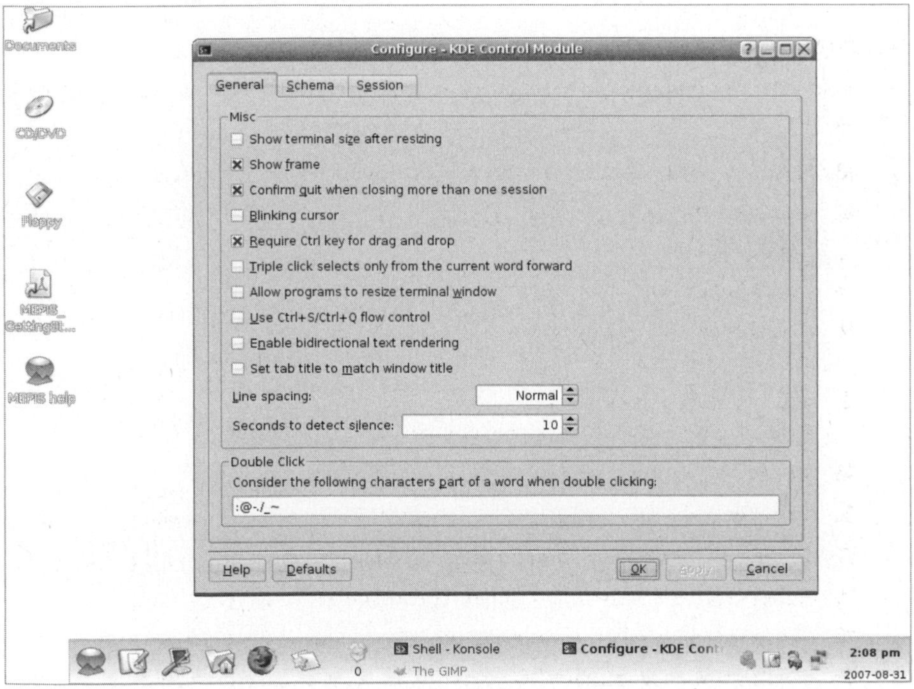

Within the configuration dialog box there are three tabbed areas:

- **General:** Allows you to set terminal emulation features such as a blinking cursor, allowing running programs to resize the terminal window using control codes, setting the line spacing, and setting the number of seconds before the session is considered inactive.

- **Schema:** Allows you to save a color schema for the session, and save it so that you can use it in later sessions.

- **Session:** Allows you to configure new and existing Konsole sessions. You can configure new sessions that start either with a standard shell or with a specific command, such as an editor.

Help

The Help menu item provides the full Konsole handbook (if KDE handbooks were installed in your Linux distribution), a "tip of the day" feature that shows interesting little-known shortcuts and tips each time you start Konsole, and the standard About Konsole dialog box.

The GNOME Terminal

As you would expect, the GNOME desktop project has its own terminal emulation program. The GNOME Terminal software package has many of the same features as Konsole and xterm. This section walks through the various parts of configuring and using GNOME Terminal.

The command line parameters

The GNOME Terminal application also provides a wealth of command line parameters that allow you to control its behavior when starting it. Table 2-4 lists the parameters available.

TABLE 2-4

The GNOME Terminal Command Line Parameters

Parameter	Description
-e command	Execute the argument inside a default terminal window.
-x	Execute the entire contents of the command line after this parameter inside a default terminal window.
--window	Open a new window with a default terminal window. You may add multiple --window parameters to start multiple windows.
--window-with-profile=	Open a new window with a specified profile. You may also add this parameter multiple times to the command line.

continued

TABLE 2-4	(continued)
Parameter	**Description**
--tab	Open a new tabbed terminal inside the last opened terminal window.
--tab-with-profile=	Open a new tabbed terminal inside the last opened terminal window using the specified profile.
--role=	Set the role for the last specified window.
--show-menubar	Enable the menu bar at the top of the terminal window.
--hide-menubar	Disable the menu bar at the top of the terminal window.
--full-screen	Display the terminal window fully maximized.
--geometry=	Specify the X Window geometry parameter.
--disable-factory	Don't register with the activation nameserver.
--use-factory	Register with the activation nameserver.
--startup-id=	Set the ID for the Linux startup notification protocol.
-t, --title=	Set the window title for the terminal window.
--working-directory=	Set the default working directory for the terminal window.
--zoom=	Set the terminal's zoom factor.
--active	Set the last specified terminal tab as the active tab.

The GNOME Terminal command line parameters allow you to set lots of features automatically as GNOME Terminal starts. However, you can also set most of these features from within the GNOME Terminal window after it starts.

Tabs

The GNOME Terminal calls each session a *tab*, as it uses tabs to keep track of multiple sessions running within the window. Figure 2-9 shows a GNOME Terminal window with three session tabs active.

You can right-click in the tab window to see the tab menu. This quick menu provides a few actions for your use in the tab session:

■ **Open Terminal:** Open a new GNOME Terminal window with a default tab session.

■ **Open Tab:** Open a new session tab in the existing GNOME Terminal window.

■ **Close Tab:** Close the current session tab.

■ **Copy:** Copy highlighted text in the current session tab to the clipboard.

■ **Paste:** Paste data in the clipboard into the current session tab at the current cursor location.

■ **Change Profile:** Change the profile for the current session tab.

■ **Edit Current Profile:** Edit the profile for the current session tab.

■ **Show Menubar:** Toggle whether the menubar is hidden or visible.

The quick menu provides easy access to commonly used actions that are available from the standard menu bar in the terminal window.

The menu bar

The main operation of GNOME Terminal happens in the menu bar. The menu bar contains all of the configuration and customization options you'll need to make your GNOME Terminal just the way you want it. The following sections describe the different items in the menu bar.

FIGURE 2-9

The GNOME Terminal with three active sessions

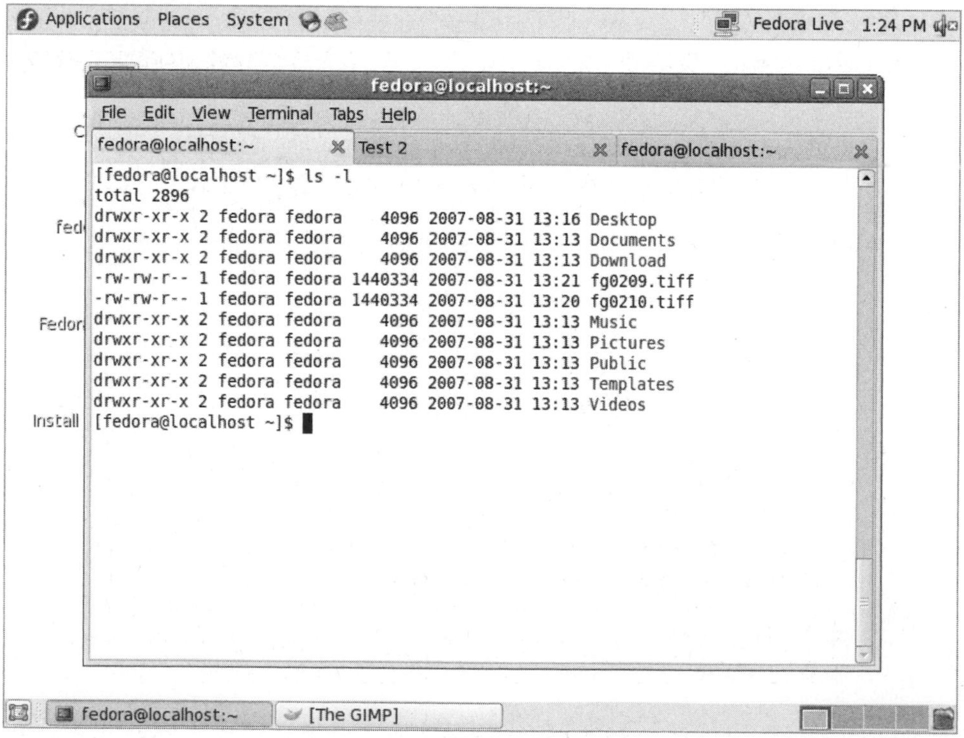

File

The File menu item contains items to create and manage the terminal tabs:

- **Open Terminal:** Start a new shell session in a new GNOME Terminal window.
- **Open Tab:** Start a new shell session on a new tab in the existing GNOME Terminal window.
- **New Profile...:** Allows you to customize the tab session and save it as a profile which you can recall for use later.
- **Close Tab:** Close the current tab in the window.
- **Close Window:** Close the current GNOME Terminal session, closing all active tabs.

Most of the items in the File menu are also available by right-clicking in the session tab area. The New Profile entry allows you to customize your session tab settings and save them for future use.

The New Profile first requests that you provide a name for the new profile, then produces the Editing Profile dialog box, shown in Figure 2-10.

FIGURE 2-10

The GNOME Terminal Editing Profile dialog box

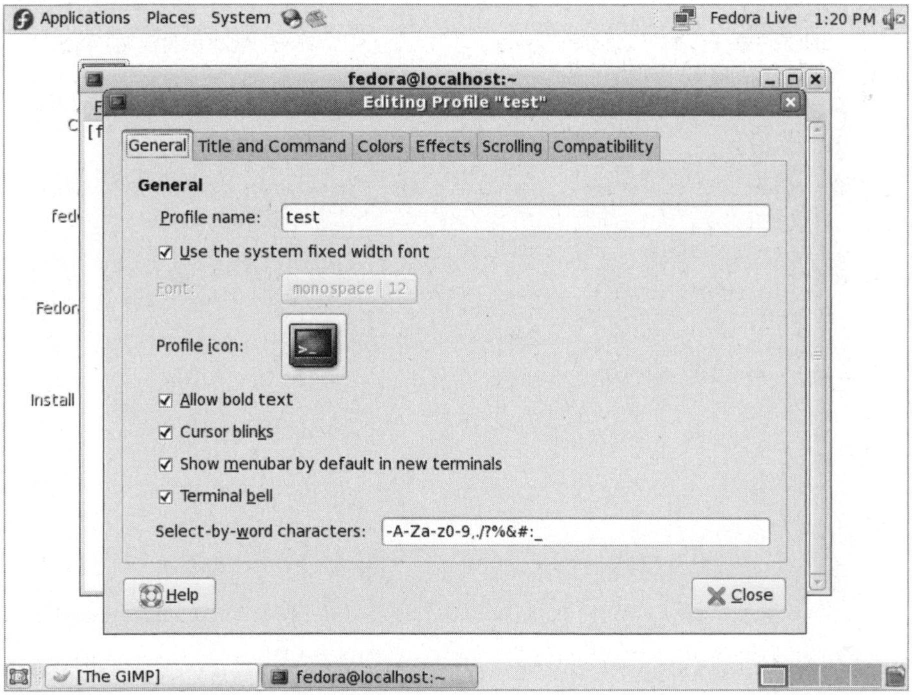

This is the area where you can set the terminal emulation features for the session. It consists of six areas:

- **General:** Provides general settings such as font, the bell, and the menubar
- **Title and Command:** Allows you to set the title for the session tab (displayed on the tab) and determine if the session starts with a special command rather than a shell
- **Colors:** Sets the foreground and background colors used in the session tab
- **Effects:** Allows you to set a background image for the session tab, or make it transparent so you can see the desktop through the session tab
- **Scrolling:** Controls whether a scroll region is created, and how large
- **Compatibility:** Allows you to set which control codes the Backspace and Delete keys send to the system.

Once you configure a profile, you can specify it when opening new session tabs.

Edit

The Edit menu item contains items for handling text within the tabs. You can use your mouse to copy and paste texts anywhere within the tab window. This allows you to easily copy text from the command line output to a clipboard and import it into an editor. You can also paste text from another GNOME application into the tab session.

- **Copy:** Copy selected text to the GNOME clipboard.
- **Paste:** Paste text from the GNOME clipboard into the tab session.
- **Profiles...:** Add, delete, or modify profiles in the GNOME Terminal.
- **Keyboard Shortcuts...:** Create key combinations to quickly access GNOME Terminal features.
- **Current Profile...:** Provides a quick way to edit the profile used for the current session tab.

The profile-editing feature is an extremely powerful tool for customizing several profiles, and then changing profiles as you change sessions.

View

The View menu item contains items for controlling how the session tab windows appear. They include:

- **Show Menubar:** Either shows or hides the menu bar
- **Full Screen:** Enlarges the GNOME Terminal window to the entire desktop
- **Zoom In:** Makes the font in the session windows larger

- **Zoom Out:** Makes the font in the session windows smaller
- **Normal Size:** Returns the session font to the default size

If you hide the menubar, you can easily get it back by right-clicking in any session tab and toggling the Show Menubar item.

Terminal

The Terminal menu item contains items for controlling the terminal emulation features of the tab session. They include:

- **Change Profile:** Allows you to switch to another configured profile in the session tab.
- **Set Title...:** Sets the title on the session tab to easily identify it.
- **Set Character Encoding:** Selects the character set used to send and display characters.
- **Reset:** Sends the reset control code to the Linux system.
- **Reset and Clear:** Sends the reset control code to the Linux system and clears any text currently showing in the tab area.

The character encoding offers a large list of available character sets to choose from. This is especially handy if you must work in a language other than English.

Tabs

The Tabs menu item provides items for controlling the location of the tabs and selecting which tab is active.

- **Previous Tab:** Make the previous tab in the list active.
- **Next Tab:** Make the next tab in the list active.
- **Move Tab to the Left:** Shuffle the current tab in front of the previous tab.
- **Move Tab to the Right:** Shuffle the current tab in front of the next tab.
- **Detach Tab:** Remove the tab and start a new GNOME Terminal window using this tab session.
- **The Tab list:** Lists the currently running session tabs in the terminal window. Select a tab to quickly jump to that session.

This section allows you to manage your tabs, which can come in handy if you have several tabs open at once.

Help

The Help menu item provides a full GNOME Terminal manual so that you can research individual items and features used in the GNOME Terminal.

Summary

To start learning Linux command line commands, you need access to a command line. In a world of graphical interfaces, this can sometimes be challenging. This chapter discussed different things you should consider when trying to get to the Linux command line from within a graphical desktop environment. First, the chapter covered terminal emulation and showed what features you should know about to ensure that the Linux system can properly communicate with your terminal emulation package, and display text and graphics properly.

After discussing terminal emulators, three different types of terminal emulators were discussed. The xterm terminal emulator package was the first available for Linux. It emulates both the VT102 and Tektronix 4014 terminals. The KDE desktop project created the Konsole terminal emulation package. It provides several fancy features, such as the ability to have multiple sessions in the same window, using both console and xterm sessions, with full control of terminal emulation parameters.

Finally, the chapter discussed the GNOME desktop project's GNOME Terminal emulation package. GNOME Terminal also allows multiple terminal sessions from within a single window, plus it provides a convenient way to set many terminal features.

In the next chapter, you'll start looking at the Linux command line commands. I'll walk you through the commands necessary to navigate around the Linux filesystem, and create, delete, and manipulate files.

Chapter 3

Basic bash Shell Commands

The default shell used in all Linux distributions is the GNU bash shell. This chapter describes the basic features available in the bash shell, and walks you through how to work with Linux files and directories using the basic commands provided by the bash shell. If you're already comfortable working with files and directories in the Linux environment, feel free to skip this chapter and continue with Chapter 4 to see more advanced commands.

Starting the Shell

The GNU bash shell is a program that provides interactive access to the Linux system. It runs as a regular program, normally started whenever a user logs in to a terminal. The shell that the system starts depends on your user ID configuration.

The /etc/passwd file contains a list of all the system user accounts, along with some basic configuration information about each user. Here's a sample entry from a /etc/passwd file:

```
rich:x:501:501:Rich Blum:/home/rich:/bin/bash
```

Each entry has seven data fields, with each field separated by a colon. The system uses the data in these fields to assign specific features for the user. These fields are:

- The username
- The user's password (or a placeholder if the password is stored in another file)

- The user's system user ID number
- The user's system group ID number
- The user's full name
- The user's default home directory
- The user's default shell program

Most of these entries will be discussed in more detail in Chapter 6. For now, just pay attention to the shell program specified.

Most Linux systems use the default bash shell when starting a command line interface (CLI) environment for the user. The bash program also uses command line parameters to modify the type of shell you can start. Table 3-1 lists the command line parameters available in bash that define what type of shell to use.

TABLE 3-1

The bash Command Line Parameters

Parameter	Description
-c string	Read commands from string and process them.
-r	Start a restricted shell, limiting the user to the default directory.
-i	Start an interactive shell, allowing input from the user.
-s	Read commands from the standard input.

By default, when the bash shell starts, it automatically processes commands in the .bashrc file in the user's home directory. Many Linux distributions use this file to also load a common file that contains commands and settings for everyone on the system. This common file is normally located in the file /etc/bashrc. This file often sets environment variables (described in Chapter 5) used in various applications.

The Shell Prompt

Once you start a terminal emulation package or log in from the Linux console, you get access to the shell CLI *prompt*. The prompt is your gateway to the shell. This is the place where you enter shell commands.

The default prompt symbol for the bash shell is the dollar sign ($). This symbol indicates that the shell is waiting for you to enter text. However, you can change the format of the prompt used by your shell. The different Linux distributions use different formats for the prompt. On my SimplyMEPIS Linux system, the bash shell prompt looks like this:

```
rich@1[~]$
```

On my Fedora Linux system, it looks like this:

```
[rich@testbox ~]$
```

You can configure the prompt to provide basic information about your environment. The first example above shows three pieces of information in the prompt:

- The username that started the shell
- The current virtual console number
- The current directory (the tilde sign is shorthand for the home directory)

The second example provides similar information, except that it uses the hostname instead of the virtual console number. There are two environment variables that control the format of the command line prompt:

- **PS1:** Controls the format of the default command line prompt
- **PS2:** Controls the format of the second-tier command line prompt

The shell uses the default PS1 prompt for initial data entry into the shell. If you enter a command that requires additional information, the shell displays the second-tier prompt specified by the PS2 environment variable.

To display the current settings for your prompts, use the echo command:

```
rich@1[~]$ echo $PS1
\u@\l[\W]\$
rich@1[~]$ echo $PS2
>
rich@1[~]$
```

The format of the prompt environment variables can look pretty odd. The shell uses special characters to signify elements within the command line prompt. Table 3-2 shows the special characters that you can use in the prompt string.

Notice that all of the special prompt characters begin with a backslash (\). This is what delineates a prompt character from normal text in the prompt. In the earlier example, the prompt contained both prompt characters and a normal character (the "at" sign, and the square brackets). You can create any combination of prompt characters in your prompt. To create a new prompt, just assign a new string to the PS1 variable:

```
[rich@testbox ~]$ PS1="[\t][\u]\$ "
[14:40:32][rich]$
```

This new shell prompt now shows the current time, along with the username. The new PS1 definition only lasts for the duration of the shell session. When you start a new shell, the default shell prompt definition is reloaded. In Chapter 5 you'll see how you can change the default shell prompt for all shell sessions.

| TABLE 3-2 | |

bash Shell Prompt Characters

Character	Description
\a	The bell character
\d	The date in the format "Day Month Date"
\e	The ASCII escape character
\h	The local hostname
\H	The fully qualified domain hostname
\j	The number of jobs currently managed by the shell
\l	The basename of the shell's terminal device name
\n	The ASCII newline character
\r	The ASCII carriage return
\s	The name of the shell
\t	The current time in 24-hour HH:MM:SS format
\T	The current time in 12-hour HH:MM:SS format
\@	The current time in 12-hour am/pm format
\u	The username of the current user
\v	The version of the bash shell
\V	The release level of the bash shell
\w	The current working directory
\W	The basename of the current working directory
\!	The bash shell history number of this command
\#	The command number of this command
\$	A dollar sign if a normal user, or a pound sign if the root user
\nnn	The character corresponding to the octal value nnn
\\	A backslash
\[	Begins a control code sequence
\]	Ends a control code sequence

The bash Manual

Most Linux distributions include an online manual for looking up information on shell commands, as well as lots of other GNU utilities included in the distribution. It is a good idea to become familiar with the manual, as it's invaluable for working with utilities, especially when trying to figure out various command line parameters.

The man command provides access to the manual pages stored on the Linux system. Entering the man command followed by a specific utility name provides the manual entry for that utility. Figure 3-1 shows an example of looking up the manual pages for the date command.

The manual page divides information about the command into separate sections, shown in Table 3-3.

You can step through the man pages by pressing the spacebar or using the arrow keys to scroll forward and backward through the man page text (assuming that your terminal emulation package supports the arrow key functions).

FIGURE 3-1

Displaying the manual pages for the Linux date command

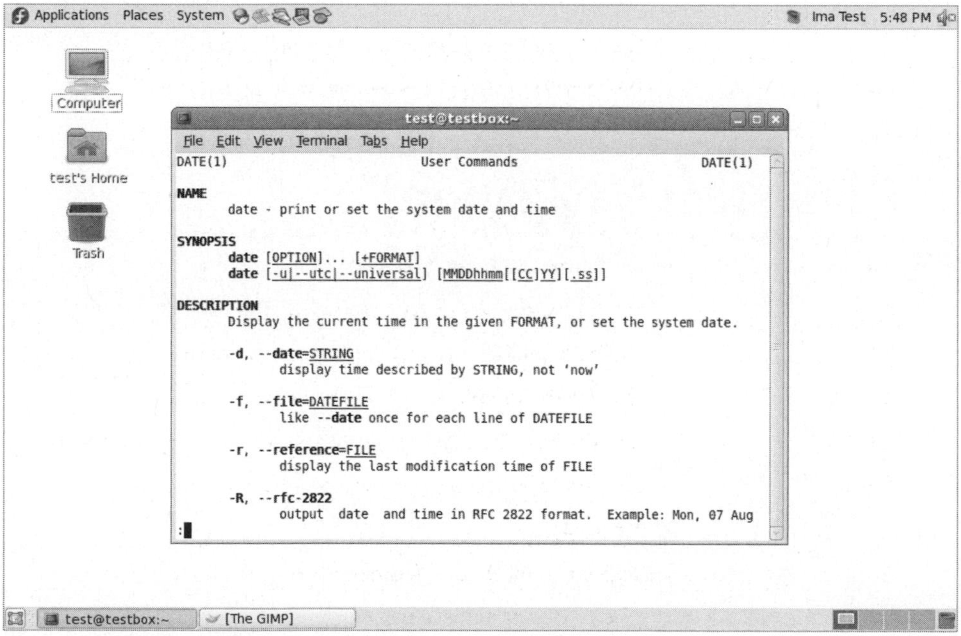

TABLE 3-3

The Linux man Page Format

Section	Description
Name	Displays the command name and a short description
Synopsis	Shows the format of the command
Description	Describes each command option
Author	Provides information on the person who developed the command
Reporting bugs	Provides information on where to report any bugs found
Copyright	Provides information on the copyright status of the command code
See Also	Refers you to any similar commands available

To see information about the bash shell, look at the man pages for it using the command:

```
$ man bash
```

This allows you to step through the entire man pages for the bash shell. This is extremely handy when building scripts, as you don't have to refer back to books or Internet sites to look up specific formats for commands. The manual is always there for you in your session.

Filesystem Navigation

As you can see from the shell prompt, when you start a shell session you are usually placed in your home directory. Most often, you will want to break out of your home directory and want to explore other areas in the Linux system. This section describes how to do that using command line commands. Before we do that though, we should take a tour of just what the Linux filesystem looks like so we know where we're going.

The Linux filesystem

If you're new to the Linux system, you may be confused by how it references files and directories, especially if you're used to the way that the Microsoft Windows operating system does that. Before exploring the Linux system, it helps to have an understanding of how it's laid out.

The first difference you'll notice is that Linux does not use drive letters in pathnames. In the Windows world, the physical drives installed on the PC determine the pathname of the file. Windows assigns a letter to each physical disk drive, and each drive contains its own directory structure for accessing files stored on it.

For example, in Windows you may be used to seeing the file paths such as:

`c:\Documents and Settings\Rich\My Documents\test.doc.`

This indicates that the file `test.doc` is located in the directory `My Documents`, which itself is located in the directory `rich`. The `rich` directory is contained under the directory `Documents and Settings`, which is located on the hard disk partition assigned the letter `C` (usually the first hard drive on the PC).

The Windows file path tells you exactly which physical disk partition contains the file named `test.doc`. If you wanted to save a file on a floppy disk, you would click the icon for the `A` drive, which automatically uses the file path `a:\test.doc`. This path indicates that the file is located at the root of the drive assigned the letter `A`, which is usually the PC's floppy disk drive.

This is not the method used by Linux. Linux stores files within a single directory structure, called a *virtual directory*. The virtual directory contains file paths from all the storage devices installed on the PC, merged into a single directory structure.

The Linux virtual directory structure contains a single base directory, called the root. Directories and files beneath the root directory are listed based on the directory path used to get to them, similar to the way Windows does it.

> **TIP** You'll notice that Linux uses a forward slash (/) instead of a backward slash (\) to denote directories in filepaths. The backslash character in Linux denotes an escape character, and causes all sorts of problems when you use it in a filepath. This may take some getting used to if you're coming from a Windows environment.

For example, the Linux file path `/home/rich/Documents/test.doc` only indicates that the file `test.doc` is in the directory `Documents`, under the directory `rich`, which is contained in the directory `home`. It doesn't provide any information as to which physical disk on the PC the file is stored on.

The tricky part about the Linux virtual directory is how it incorporates each storage device. The first hard drive installed in a Linux PC is called the *root drive*. The root drive contains the core of the virtual directory. Everything else builds from there.

On the root drive, Linux creates special directories called *mount points*. Mount points are directories in the virtual directory where you assign additional storage devices.

The virtual directory causes files and directories to appear within these mount point directories, even though they are physically stored on a different drive.

Often the system files are physically stored on the root drive, while user files are stored on a different drive, as shown in Figure 3-2.

In Figure 3-2, there are two hard drives on the PC. One hard drive is associated with the root of the virtual directory (indicated by a single forward slash). Other hard drives can be mounted anywhere in the virtual directory structure. In this example, the second hard drive is mounted at the location /home, which is where the user directories are located.

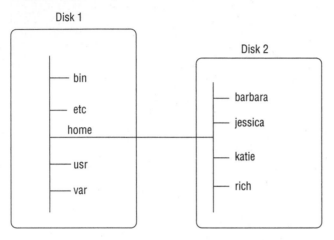

FIGURE 3-2

The Linux file structure

The Linux filesystem structure has evolved from the Unix file structure. Unfortunately, the Unix file structure has been somewhat convoluted over the years by different flavors of Unix. Nowadays it seems that no two Unix or Linux systems follow the same filesystem structure. However, there are a few common directory names that are used for common functions. Table 3-4 lists some of the more common Linux virtual directory names.

When you start a new shell prompt your session starts in your home directory, which is a unique directory assigned to your user account. When you create a user account, the system normally assigns a unique directory for the account (see Chapter 6).

In the Windows world, you're probably used to moving around the directory structure using a graphical interface. To move around the virtual directory from a CLI prompt, you'll need to learn to use the cd command.

Traversing directories

The change directory command (cd) is what you'll use to move your shell session to another directory in the Linux filesystem. The format of the cd command is pretty simplistic:

```
cd destination
```

The cd command may take a single parameter, *destination*, which specifies the directory name you want to go to. If you don't specify a destination on the cd command, it will take you to your home directory.

The destination parameter, though, can be expressed using two different methods:

■ An absolute filepath
■ A relative filepath

TABLE 3-4	

Common Linux Directory Names

Directory	Usage
/	The root of the virtual directory. Normally, no files are placed here.
/bin	The binary directory, where many GNU user-level utilities are stored.
/boot	The boot directory, where boot files are stored.
/dev	The device directory, where Linux creates device nodes.
/etc	The system configuration files directory.
/home	The home directory, where Linux creates user directories.
/lib	The library directory, where system and application library files are stored.
/media	The media directory, a common place for mount points used for removable media.
/mnt	The mount directory, another common place for mount points used for removable media.
/opt	The optional directory, often used to store optional software packages.
/root	The root home directory.
/sbin	The system binary directory, where many GNU admin-level utilities are stored.
/tmp	The temporary directory, where temporary work files can be created and destroyed.
/usr	The user-installed software directory.
/var	The variable directory, for files that change frequently, such as log files.

The following sections describe the differences between these two methods.

Absolute filepaths

You can reference a directory name within the virtual directory using an *absolute filepath*. The absolute filepath defines exactly where the directory is in the virtual directory structure, starting at the root of the virtual directory. Sort of like a full name for a directory.

Thus, to reference the apache directory, that's contained within the lib directory, which in turn is contained within the usr directory, you would use the absolute filepath:

```
/usr/lib/apache
```

With the absolute filepath there's no doubt as to exactly where you want to go. To move to a specific location in the filesystem using the absolute filepath, you just specify the full pathname in the cd command:

```
rich@1[~]$cd /etc
rich@1[etc]$
```

The prompt shows that the new directory for the shell after the cd command is now /etc. You can move to any level within the entire Linux virtual directory structure using the absolute filepath:

```
rich@1[~]$ cd /usr/lib/apache
rich@1[apache]$
```

However, if you're just working within your own home directory structure, often using absolute filepaths can get tedious. For example, if you're already in the directory /home/rich, it seems somewhat cumbersome to have to type the command:

```
cd /home/rich/Documents
```

just to get to your Documents directory. Fortunately, there's a simpler solution.

Relative filepaths

Relative filepaths allow you to specify a destination filepath relative to your current location, without having to start at the root. A relative filepath doesn't start with a forward slash, indicating the root directory.

Instead, a relative filepath starts with either a directory name (if you're traversing to a directory under your current directory), or a special character indicating a relative location to your current directory location. The two special characters used for this are:

- The dot (.) to represent the current directory
- The double dot (..) to represent the parent directory

The double dot character is extremely handy when trying to traverse a directory hierarchy. For example, if you are in the Documents directory under your home directory and need to go to your Desktop directory, also under your home directory, you can do this:

```
rich@1[Documents]$ cd ../Desktop
rich@1[Desktop]$
```

The double dot character takes you back up one level to your home directory, then the /Desktop portion then takes you back down into the Desktop directory. You can use as many double dot characters as necessary to move around. For example, if you are in your home directory (/home/rich) and want to go to the /etc directory, you could type:

```
rich@1[~]$ cd ../../etc
rich@1[etc]$
```

Of course, in a case like this, you actually have to do more typing to use the relative filepath rather than just typing the absolute filepath, /etc!

File and Directory Listing

The most basic feature of the shell is the ability to see what files are available on the system. The list command (ls) is the tool that helps do that. This section describes the ls command, and all of the options available to format the information it can provide.

Basic listing

The ls command at its most basic form displays the files and directories located in your current directory:

```
$ ls
4rich  Desktop   Download Music  Pictures store     store.zip test
backup Documents Drivers  myprog Public   store.sql Templates Videos
$
```

Notice that the ls command produces the listing in alphabetical order (in columns rather than rows). If you're using a terminal emulator that supports color, the ls command may also show different types of entries in different colors. The LS_COLORS environment variable controls this feature. Different Linux distributions set this environment variable depending on the capabilities of the terminal emulator.

If you don't have a color terminal emulator, you can use the -F parameter with the ls command to easily distinguish files from directories. Using the -F parameter produces the following output:

```
$ ls -F
4rich/      Documents/ Music/     Public/    store.zip   Videos/
backup.zip  Download/  myprog*    store/     Templates/
Desktop/    Drivers/   Pictures/  store.sql  test
$
```

The -F parameter now flags the directories with a forward slash, to help identify them in the listing. Similarly, it flags executable files (like the myprog file above) with an asterisk, to help you find the files that can be run on the system easier.

The basic ls command can be somewhat misleading. It shows the files and directories contained in the current directory, but not necessarily all of them. Linux often uses *hidden files* to store configuration information. In Linux, hidden files are files with filenames that start with a period. These files don't appear in the default ls listing (thus they are called hidden).

To display hidden files along with normal files and directories, use the -a parameter. Figure 3-3 shows an example of using the -a parameter with the ls command.

Wow, that's quite a difference. In a home directory for a user who has logged in to the system from a graphical desktop, you'll see lots of hidden configuration files. This particular example is from a user logged in to a GNOME desktop session. Also notice that there are three files that begin with `.bash`. These files are hidden files that are used by the bash shell environment. These features are covered in detail in Chapter 5.

The `-R` parameter is another command `ls` parameter to use. It shows files that are contained within directories in the current directory. If you have lots of directories, this can be quite a long listing. Here's a simple example of what the `-R` parameter produces:

```
$ ls -F -R
.:
file1 test1/  test2/

./test1:
myprog1*  myprog2*

./test2:
$
```

FIGURE 3-3

Using the -a parameter with the ls command

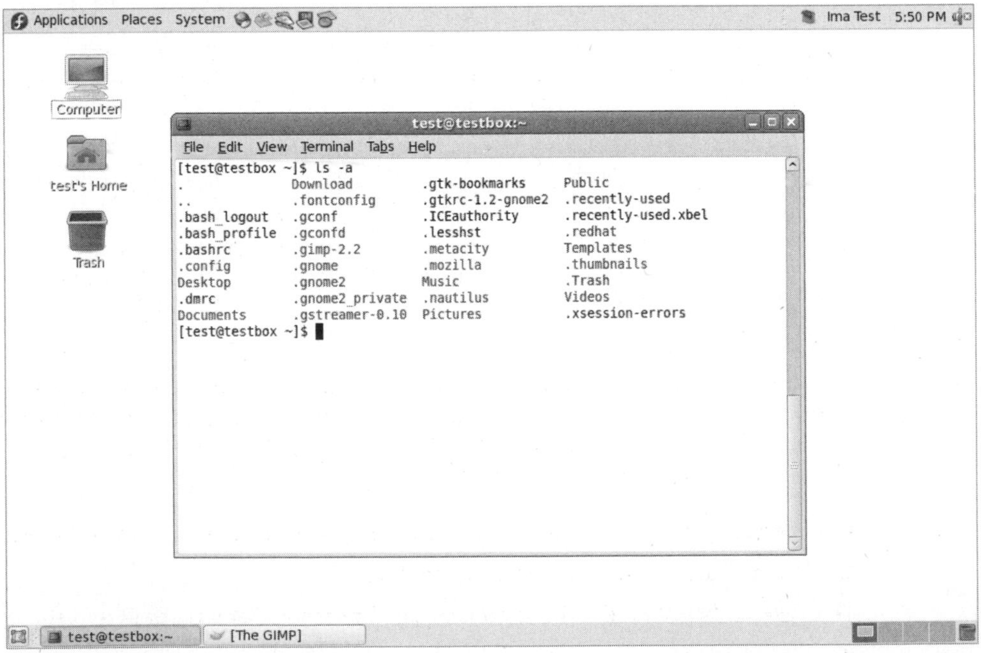

Notice that first, the -R parameter shows the contents of the current directory, which is a file (file1) and two directories (test1 and test2). Following that, it traverses each of the two directories, showing if any files are contained within each directory. The test1 directory shows two files (myprog1 and myprog2), while the test2 directory doesn't contain any files. If there had been further subdirectories within the test1 or test2 directories, the -R parameter would have continued to traverse those as well. As you can see, for large directory structures this can become quite a large output listing.

Modifying the information presented

As you can see in the basic listings, the ls command doesn't produce a whole lot of information about each file. For listing additional information, another popular parameter is -l. The -l parameter produces a long listing format, providing more information about each file in the directory:

```
$ ls -l
total 2064
drwxrwxr-x  2 rich rich     4096 2007-08-24 22:04 4rich
-rw-r--r--  1 rich rich  1766205 2007-08-24 15:34 backup.zip
drwxr-xr-x  3 rich rich     4096 2007-08-31 22:24 Desktop
drwxr-xr-x  2 rich rich     4096 2001-11-01 04:06 Documents
drwxr-xr-x  2 rich rich     4096 2001-11-01 04:06 Download
drwxrwxr-x  2 rich rich     4096 2007-07-26 18:25 Drivers
drwxr-xr-x  2 rich rich     4096 2001-11-01 04:06 Music
-rwxr--r--  1 rich rich       30 2007-08-23 21:42 myprog
drwxr-xr-x  2 rich rich     4096 2001-11-01 04:06 Pictures
drwxr-xr-x  2 rich rich     4096 2001-11-01 04:06 Public
drwxrwxr-x  5 rich rich     4096 2007-08-24 22:04 store
-rw-rw-r--  1 rich rich    98772 2007-08-24 15:30 store.sql
-rw-r--r--  1 rich rich   107507 2007-08-13 15:45 store.zip
drwxr-xr-x  2 rich rich     4096 2001-11-01 04:06 Templates
drwxr-xr-x  2 rich rich     4096 2001-11-01 04:06 Videos
[rich@testbox ~]$
```

The long listing format lists each file and directory contained in the directory on a single line. Besides the filename, it shows additional useful information. The first line in the output shows the total number of blocks contained within the directory. Following that, each line contains the following information about each file (or directory):

- The file type (such as directory (d), file (-), character device (c), or block device (b))
- The permissions for the file (see Chapter 6)
- The number of hard links to the file (see the section "Linking files" in this chapter)
- The username of the owner of the file

- The group name of the group the file belongs to
- The size of the file in bytes
- The time the file was modified last
- The file or directory name

The -l parameter is a powerful tool to have. Armed with this information you can see just about any information you need to for any file or directory on the system.

The complete parameter list

There are lots of parameters for the ls command that can come in handy as you do file management. If you use the man command for ls, you'll see several pages of available parameters for you to use to modify the output of the ls command.

The ls command uses two types of command line parameters:

- Single-letter parameters
- Full-word (long) parameters

The single-letter parameters are always preceded by a single dash. Full-word parameters are more descriptive and are preceded by a double dash. Many parameters have both a single-letter and full-word version, while some have only one type. Table 3-5 lists some of the more popular parameters that'll help you out with using the bash ls command.

You can use more than one parameter at a time if you want to. The double dash parameters must be listed separately, but the single dash parameters can be combined together into a string behind the dash. A common combination to use is the -a parameter to list all files, the -i parameter to list the *inode* for each file, the -l parameter to produce a long listing, and the -s parameter to list the block size of the files. The inode of a file or directory is a unique identification number the kernel assigns to each object in the filesystem. Combining all of these parameters creates the easy-to-remember -sail parameter:

```
$ ls -sail
total 2360
301860    8 drwx------ 36 rich rich   4096 2007-09-03 15:12 .
 65473    8 drwxr-xr-x  6 root root   4096 2007-07-29 14:20 ..
360621    8 drwxrwxr-x  2 rich rich   4096 2007-08-24 22:04 4rich
301862    8 -rw-r--r--  1 rich rich    124 2007-02-12 10:18 .bashrc
361443    8 drwxrwxr-x  4 rich rich   4096 2007-07-26 20:31 .ccache
301879    8 drwxr-xr-x  3 rich rich   4096 2007-07-26 18:25 .config
301871    8 drwxr-xr-x  3 rich rich   4096 2007-08-31 22:24 Desktop
301870    8 -rw-------  1 rich rich     26 2001-11-01 04:06 .dmrc
301872    8 drwxr-xr-x  2 rich rich   4096 2001-11-01 04:06 Download
360207    8 drwxrwxr-x  2 rich rich   4096 2007-07-26 18:25 Drivers
301882    8 drwx------  5 rich rich   4096 2007-09-02 23:40 .gconf
301883    8 drwx------  2 rich rich   4096 2007-09-02 23:43 .gconfd
360338    8 drwx------  3 rich rich   4096 2007-08-06 23:06 .gftp
```

TABLE 3-5

Some Popular ls Command Parameters

Single Letter	Full Word	Description
-a	--all	Don't ignore entries starting with a period.
-A	--almost-all	Don't list the . and .. files.
	--author	Print the author of each file.
-b	--escape	Print octal values for nonprintable characters.
	--block-size=size	Calculate the block sizes using size-byte blocks.
-B	--ignore-backups	Don't list entries with the tilde (~) symbol (used to denote backup copies).
-c		Sort by time of last modification.
-C		List entries by columns.
	--color=when	When to use colors (always, never, or auto).
-d	--directory	List directory entries instead of contents, and don't dereference symbolic links.
-F	--classify	Append file-type indicator to entries.
	--file-type	Only append file-type indicators to some filetypes (not executable files).
	--format=word	Format output as either across, commas, horizontal, long, single-column, verbose, or vertical.
-g		List full file information except for the file's owner.
	--group-directories-first	List all directories before files.
-G	--no-group	In long listing don't display group names.
-h	--human-readable	Print sizes using K for kilobytes, M for megabytes, and G for gigabytes.
	--si	Same as -h, but use powers of 1000 instead of 1024.
-i	--inode	Display the index number (inode) of each file.
-l		Display the long listing format.
-L	--dereference	Show information for the original file for a linked file.
-n	--numeric-uid-gid	Show numeric userid and groupid instead of names.

continued

73

TABLE 3-5	(continued)	
Single Letter	**Full Word**	**Description**
-o		In long listing don't display owner names.
-r	--reverse	Reverse the sorting order when displaying files and directories.
-R	--recursive	List subdirectory contents recursively.
-s	--size	Print the block size of each file.
-S	--sort=size	Sort the output by file size.
-t	--sort=time	Sort the output by file modification time.
-u		Display file last access time instead of last modification time.
-U	--sort=none	Don't sort the output listing.
-v	--sort=version	Sort the output by file version.
-x		List entries by line instead of columns.
-X	--sort=extension	Sort the output by file extension.

Besides the normal -1 parameter output information, you'll see two additional numbers added to each line. The first number in the listing is the file or directory inode number. The second number is the block size of the file. The third entry is a diagram of the type of file, along with the file's permissions. We'll dive into that in more detail in Chapter 6.

Following that, the next number is the number of hard links to the file (discussed later in the "Linking file" section), the owner of the file, the group the file belongs to, the size of the file (in bytes), a timestamp showing the last modification time by default, and finally, the actual filename.

Filtering listing output

As you've seen in the examples, by default the ls command lists all of the files in a directory. Sometimes this can be overkill, especially when you're just looking for information on a single file.

Fortunately, the ls command also provide a way for us to define a filter on the command line. It uses the filter to determine which files or directories it should display in the output.

The filter works as a simple text-matching string. Include the filter after any command line parameters you want to use:

```
$ ls -l myprog
-rwxr--r-- 1 rich rich 30 2007-08-23 21:42 myprog
$
```

When you specify the name of specific file as the filter, the ls command only shows the information for that one file. Sometimes you might not know the exact name of the file you're looking for. The ls command also recognizes standard wildcard characters and uses them to match patterns within the filter:

- A question mark to represent one character
- An asterisk to represent zero or more characters

The question mark can be used to replace exactly one character anywhere in the filter string. For example:

```
$ ls -l mypro?
-rw-rw-r-- 1 rich rich  0 2007-09-03 16:38 myprob
-rwxr--r-- 1 rich rich 30 2007-08-23 21:42 myprog
$
```

The filter mypro? matched two files in the directory. Similarly, the asterisk can be used to match zero or more characters:

```
$ ls -l myprob*
-rw-rw-r-- 1 rich rich 0 2007-09-03 16:38 myprob
-rw-rw-r-- 1 rich rich 0 2007-09-03 16:40 myproblem
$
```

The asterisk matches zero characters in the myprob file, but it matches three characters in the myproblem file.

This is a powerful feature to use when searching for files when you're not quite sure of the filenames.

File Handling

The bash shell provides lots of commands for manipulating files on the Linux filesystem. This section walks you through the basic commands you will need to work with files from the CLI for all your file-handling needs.

Creating files

Every once in a while you will run into a situation where you need to create an empty file. Sometimes applications expect a log file to be present before they can write to it. In these situations, you can use the touch command to easily create an empty file:

```
$ touch test1
$ ls -il test1
1954793 -rw-r--r--  1 rich     rich          0 Sep  1 09:35 test1
$
```

The touch command creates the new file you specify, and assigns your username as the file owner. Since I used the -il parameters for the ls command, the first entry in the listing shows the inode number assigned to the file. Every file on the Linux system has a unique inode number.

Notice that the file size is zero, since the touch command just created an empty file. The touch command can also be used to change the access and modification times on an existing file without changing the file contents:

```
$ touch test1
$ ls -l test1
-rw-r--r--    1 rich     rich          0 Sep  1 09:37 test1
$
```

The modification time of test1 is now updated from the original time. If you want to change only the access time, use the -a parameter. To change only the modification time, use the -m parameter. By default touch uses the current time. You can specify the time by using the -t parameter with a specific timestamp:

```
$ touch -t 200812251200 test1
$ ls -l test1
-rw-r--r--    1 rich     rich          0 Dec 25  2008 test1
$
```

Now the modification time for the file is set to a date significantly in the future from the current time.

Copying files

Copying files and directories from one location in the filesystem to another is a common practice for system administrators. The cp command provides this feature.

In it's most basic form, the cp command uses two parameters: the source object and the destination object:

```
cp source destination
```

When both the *source* and *destination* parameters are filenames, the cp command copies the source file to a new file with the filename specified as the destination. The new file acts like a brand new file, with an updated file creation and last modified times:

```
$ cp test1 test2
$ ls -il
total 0
1954793 -rw-r--r--    1 rich     rich          0 Dec 25  2008 test1
1954794 -rw-r--r--    1 rich     rich          0 Sep  1 09:39 test2
$
```

The new file test2 shows a different inode number, indicating that it's a completely new file. You'll also notice that the modification time for the test2 file shows the time that it was created.

If the destination file already exists, the cp command will prompt you to answer whether or not you want to overwrite it:

```
$ cp test1 test2
cp: overwrite `test2'? y
$
```

If you don't answer y, the file copy will not proceed. You can also copy a file to an existing directory:

```
$ cp test1 dir1
$ ls -il dir1
total 0
1954887 -rw-r--r--    1 rich     rich          0 Sep  6 09:42 test1
$
```

The new file is now under the dir1 directory, using the same filename as the original. These examples all used relative pathnames, but you can just as easily use the absolute pathname for both the source and destination objects.

To copy a file to the current directory you're in, you can use the dot symbol:

```
$ cp /home/rich/dir1/test1 .
cp: overwrite `./test1'?
```

As with most commands, the cp command has a few command line parameters to help you out. These are shown in Table 3-6.

Use the -p parameter to preserve the file access or modification times of the original file for the copied file.

```
$ cp -p test1 test3
$ ls -il
total 4
1954886 drwxr-xr-x    2 rich     rich       4096 Sep  1 09:42 dir1/
1954793 -rw-r--r--    1 rich     rich          0 Dec 25  2008 test1
1954794 -rw-r--r--    1 rich     rich          0 Sep  1 09:39 test2
1954888 -rw-r--r--    1 rich     rich          0 Dec 25  2008 test3
$
```

Now, even though the test3 file is a completely new file, it has the same timestamps as the original test1 file.

The -R parameter is extremely powerful. It allows you to recursively copy the contents of an entire directory in one command:

```
$ cp -R dir1 dir2
$ ls -l
total 8
```

```
drwxr-xr-x    2 rich    rich         4096 Sep  6 09:42 dir1/
drwxr-xr-x    2 rich    rich         4096 Sep  6 09:45 dir2/
-rw-r--r--    1 rich    rich            0 Dec 25  2008 test1
-rw-r--r--    1 rich    rich            0 Sep  6 09:39 test2
-rw-r--r--    1 rich    rich            0 Dec 25  2008 test3
$
```

Now dir2 is a complete copy of dir1. You can also use wildcard characters in your cp commands:

```
$ cp -f test* dir2
$ ls -al dir2
total 12
drwxr-xr-x    2 rich    rich         4096 Sep  6 10:55 ./
drwxr-xr-x    4 rich    rich         4096 Sep  6 10:46 ../
-rw-r--r--    1 rich    rich            0 Dec 25  2008 test1
-rw-r--r--    1 rich    rich            0 Sep  6 10:55 test2
-rw-r--r--    1 rich    rich            0 Dec 25  2008 test3
$
```

TABLE 3-6

The cp Command Parameters

Parameter	Description
-a	Archive files by preserving their attributes.
-b	Create a backup of each existing destination file instead of overwriting it.
-d	Preserve.
-f	Force the overwriting of existing destination files without prompting.
-i	Prompt before overwriting destination files.
-l	Create a file link instead of copying the files.
-p	Preserve file attributes if possible.
-r	Copy files recursively.
-R	Copy directories recursively.
-s	Create a symbolic link instead of copying the file.
-S	Override the backup feature.
-u	Copy the source file only if it has a newer date and time than the destination (update).
-v	Verbose mode, explaining what's happening.
-x	Restrict the copy to the current filesytem.

This command copied all of the files that started with *test* to dir2. I included the -f parameter to force the overwrite of the test1 file that was already in the directory without asking.

Linking files

You may have noticed a couple of the parameters for the cp command referred to linking files. This is a pretty cool option available in the Linux filesystems. If you need to maintain two (or more) copies of the same file on the system, instead of having separate physical copies, you can use one physical copy and multiple virtual copies, called *links*. A link is a placeholder in a directory that points to the real location of the file. There are two different types of file links in Linux:

■ A symbolic, or soft, link

■ A hard link

The hard link creates a separate file that contains information about the original file and where to locate it. When you reference the hard link file, it's just as if you're referencing the original file:

```
$ cp -l test1 test4
$ ls -il
total 16
1954886 drwxr-xr-x    2 rich      rich      4096 Sep  1 09:42 dir1/
1954889 drwxr-xr-x    2 rich      rich      4096 Sep  1 09:45 dir2/
1954793 -rw-r--r--    2 rich      rich         0 Sep  1 09:51 test1
1954794 -rw-r--r--    1 rich      rich         0 Sep  1 09:39 test2
1954888 -rw-r--r--    1 rich      rich         0 Dec 25  2008 test3
1954793 -rw-r--r--    2 rich      rich         0 Sep  1 09:51 test4
$
```

The -l parameter created a hard link for the test1 file called test4. When I performed the file listing, you can see that the inode number of both the test1 and test4 files are the same, indicating that, in reality, they are both the same file. Also notice that the link count (the third item in the listing) now shows that both files have two links.

NOTE   You can only create a hard link between files on the same physical medium. You can't create a hard link between files under separate mount points. In that case, you'll have to use a soft link.

On the other hand, the -s parameter creates a symbolic, or soft, link:

```
$ cp -s test1 test5
$ ls -il test*
total 16
1954793 -rw-r--r--    2 rich      rich         6 Sep  1 09:51 test1
1954794 -rw-r--r--    1 rich      rich         0 Sep  1 09:39 test2
1954888 -rw-r--r--    1 rich      rich         0 Dec 25  2008 test3
1954793 -rw-r--r--    2 rich      rich         6 Sep  1 09:51 test4
1954891 lrwxrwxrwx    1 rich      rich         5 Sep  1 09:56 test5 -> test1
$
```

There are a couple of things to notice in the file listing, First, you'll notice that the new `test5` file has a different inode number than the `test1` file, indicating that the Linux system treats it as a separate file. Second, the file size is different. A linked file needs to store only information about the source file, not the actual data in the file. The filename area of the listing shows the relationship between the two files.

> **TIP** Instead of using the `cp` command, if you want to link files you can also use the `ln` command. By default the `ln` command creates hard links. If you want to create a soft link, you'll still need to use the `-s` parameter.

Be careful when copying linked files. If you use the `cp` command to copy a file that's linked to another source file, all you're doing is making another copy of the source file. This can quickly get confusing. Instead of copying the linked file, you can create another link to the original file. You can have many links to the same file with no problems. However, you also don't want to create soft links to other soft-linked files. This creates a chain of links that can not only be confusing but also be easily broken, causing all sorts of problems.

Renaming files

In the Linux world, renaming files is called *moving*. The `mv` command is available to move both files and directories to another location:

```
$ mv test2 test6
$ ls -il test*
1954793 -rw-r--r--   2 rich     rich     6 Sep  1 09:51 test1
1954888 -rw-r--r--   1 rich     rich     0 Dec 25  2008 test3
1954793 -rw-r--r--   2 rich     rich     6 Sep  1 09:51 test4
1954891 lrwxrwxrwx   1 rich     rich     5 Sep  1 09:56 test5 -> test1
1954794 -rw-r--r--   1 rich     rich     0 Sep  1 09:39 test6
$
```

Notice that moving the file changed the filename but kept the same inode number and the timestamp value. Moving a file with soft links is a problem:

```
$ mv test1 test8
$ ls -il test*
total 16
1954888 -rw-r--r--   1 rich     rich     0 Dec 25  2008 test3
1954793 -rw-r--r--   2 rich     rich     6 Sep  1 09:51 test4
1954891 lrwxrwxrwx   1 rich     rich     5 Sep  1 09:56 test5 -> test1
1954794 -rw-r--r--   1 rich     rich     0 Sep  1 09:39 test6
1954793 -rw-r--r--   2 rich     rich     6 Sep  1 09:51 test8
[rich@test2 clsc]$ mv test8 test1
```

The `test4` file that uses a hard link still uses the same inode number, which is perfectly fine. However, the `test5` file now points to an invalid file, and it is no longer a valid link.

You can also use the `mv` command to move directories:

```
$ mv dir2 dir4
```

The entire contents of the directory are unchanged. The only thing that changes is the name of the directory.

Deleting files

Most likely at some point in your Linux career you'll want to be able to delete existing files. Whether it's to clean up a filesystem or to remove a software package, there's always opportunities to delete files.

In the Linux world, deleting is called *removing*. The command to remove files in the bash shell is rm. The basic form of the rm command is pretty simple:

```
$ rm -i test2
rm: remove `test2'? y
$ ls -l
total 16
drwxr-xr-x    2 rich      rich      4096 Sep  1 09:42 dir1/
drwxr-xr-x    2 rich      rich      4096 Sep  1 09:45 dir2/
-rw-r--r--    2 rich      rich         6 Sep  1 09:51 test1
-rw-r--r--    1 rich      rich         0 Dec 25  2008 test3
-rw-r--r--    2 rich      rich         6 Sep  1 09:51 test4
lrwxrwxrwx    1 rich      rich         5 Sep  1 09:56 test5 -> test1
$
```

Notice that the command prompts you to make sure that you're serious about removing the file. There's no trashcan in the bash shell. Once you remove a file it's gone forever.

Now, here's an interesting tidbit about deleting a file that has links to it:

```
$ rm test1
$ ls -l
total 12
drwxr-xr-x    2 rich      rich      4096 Sep  1 09:42 dir1/
drwxr-xr-x    2 rich      rich      4096 Sep  1 09:45 dir2/
-rw-r--r--    1 rich      rich         0 Dec 25  2008 test3
-rw-r--r--    1 rich      rich         6 Sep  1 09:51 test4
lrwxrwxrwx    1 rich      rich         5 Sep  1 09:56 test5 -> test1
$ cat test4
hello
$ cat test5
cat: test5: No such file or directory
$
```

I removed the test1 file, which had both a hard link with the test4 file and a soft link with the test5 file. Noticed what happened. Both of the linked files still appear, even though the test1 file is now gone (although on my color terminal the test5 filename now appears in red). When I look at the contents of the test4 file that was a hard link, it still shows the contents of the file. When I look at the contents of the test5 file that was a soft link, bash indicates that it doesn't exist any more.

Remember that the hard link file uses the same inode number as the original file. The hard link file maintains that inode number until you remove the last linked file, preserving the data! All the soft link file knows is that the underlying file is now gone, so it has nothing to point to. This is an important feature to remember when working with linked files.

One other feature of the `rm` command, if you're removing lots of files and don't want to be bothered with the prompt, is to use the `-f` parameter to force the removal. Just be careful!

> **TIP** As with copying files, you can use wildcard characters with the `rm` command. Again, use caution when doing this, as anything your remove, even by accident, is gone forever!

Directory Handling

In Linux there are a few commands that work for both files and directories (such as the `cp` command), and some that only work for directories. To create a new directory, you'll need to use a specific command, which I'll discuss in this section. Removing directories can get interesting, so we'll look at that as well in this section.

Creating directories

There's not much to creating a new directory in Linux, just use the `mkdir` command:

```
$ mkdir dir3
$ ls -il
total 16
1954886 drwxr-xr-x    2 rich      rich      4096 Sep  1 09:42 dir1/
1954889 drwxr-xr-x    2 rich      rich      4096 Sep  1 10:55 dir2/
1954893 drwxr-xr-x    2 rich      rich      4096 Sep  1 11:01 dir3/
1954888 -rw-r--r--    1 rich      rich         0 Dec 25  2008 test3
1954793 -rw-r--r--    1 rich      rich         6 Sep  1 09:51 test4
$
```

The system creates a new directory and assigns it a new inode number.

Deleting directories

Removing directories can be tricky, but there's a reason for that. There are lots of opportunity for bad things to happen when you start deleting directories. The bash shell tries to protect us from accidental catastrophes as much as possible. The basic command for removing a directory is `rmdir`:

```
$ rmdir dir3
$ rmdir dir1
rmdir: dir1: Directory not empty
$
```

By default, the rmdir command only works for removing empty directories. Since there is a file in the dir1 directory, the rmdir command refuses to remove it. You can remove nonempty directories using the --ignore-fail-on-non-empty parameter.

Our friend the rm command can also help us out some when handling directories.

If you try using it with not parameters, as with files, you'll be somewhat disappointed:

```
$ rm dir1
rm: dir1: is a directory
$
```

However, if you really want to remove a directory, you can use the -r parameter to recursively remove the files in the directory, then the directory itself:

```
$ rm -r dir2
rm: descend into directory `dir2'? y
rm: remove `dir2/test1'? y
rm: remove `dir2/test3'? y
rm: remove `dir2/test4'? y
rm: remove directory `dir2'? y
$
```

While this works, it's somewhat awkward. Notice that you still must verify every file that gets removed. For a directory with lots of files and subdirectories, this can become tedious.

The ultimate solution for throwing caution to the wind and removing an entire directory, contents and all, is the rm command with both the -r and -f parameters:

```
$ rm -rf dir2
$
```

That's it. No warnings, no fanfare, just another shell prompt. This, of course, is an extremely dangerous tool to have, especially if you're logged in as the root user account. Use it sparingly, and only after triple checking to make sure that you're doing exactly what you want to do.

NOTE   You may have noticed in the last example that I combined two command line parameters using one dash. This is a feature in the bash shell that allows us to combine command line parameters to help cut down on typing.

Viewing File Contents

So far we've covered everything there is to know about files, except for how to peek inside of them. There are several commands available for taking a look inside files without having to pull out an editor (see Chapter 7). This section demonstrates a few of the commands you have available to help you examine files.

Viewing file statistics

You've already seen that the `ls` command can be used to provide lots of useful information about files. However, there's still more information that you can't see in the `ls` command (or at least not all at once).

The `stat` command provides a complete rundown of the status of a file on the filesystem:

```
$ stat test10
  File: "test10"
  Size: 6              Blocks: 8          Regular File
Device: 306h/774d      Inode: 1954891     Links: 2
Access: (0644/-rw-r--r--)  Uid: (  501/ rich) Gid: ( 501/ rich)
Access: Sat Sep  1 12:10:25 2007
Modify: Sat Sep  1 12:11:17 2007
Change: Sat Sep  1 12:16:42 2007

$
```

The results from the `stat` command show just about everything you'd want to know about the file being examined, even down the major and minor device numbers of the device where the file is being stored.

Viewing the file type

Despite all of the information the `stat` command produces, there's still one piece of information missing — the file type. Before you go charging off trying to list out a 1000-byte file, it's usually a good idea to get a handle on what type of file it is. If you try listing a binary file, you'll get lots of gibberish on your monitor, and possibly even lock up your terminal emulator.

The `file` command is a handy little utility to have around. It has the ability to peek inside of a file and determine just what kind of file it is:

```
$ file test1
test1: ASCII text
$ file myscript
myscript: Bourne shell script text executable
$ file myprog
myprog: ELF 32-bit LSB executable, Intel 80386, version 1 (SYSV),
dynamically linked (uses shared libs), not stripped
$
```

The `file` command classifies files into three categories:

- **Text files:** Files that contain printable characters
- **Executable files:** Files that you can run on the system
- **Data files:** Files that contain nonprintable binary characters, but that you can't run on the system

The first example shows a text file. The `file` command determined not only that the file contains text but also the character code format of the text. The second example shows a text script file. While the file is text, since it's a script file you can execute (run) it on the system. The final example is a binary executable program. The `file` command determines the platform that the program was compiled for and what types of libraries it requires. This is an especially handy feature if you have a binary executable program from an unknown source.

Viewing the whole file

If you have a large text file on your hands, you may want to be able to see what's inside of it. There are three different commands in Linux that can help you out here.

The cat command

The `cat` command is a handy tool for displaying all of the data inside a text file:

```
$ cat test1
hello

This is a test file.


That we'll use to        test the cat command.
$
```

Nothing too exciting, just the contents of the text file. There are a few parameters you can use with the `cat` command, though, that can help you out.

The `-n` parameter numbers all of the lines for us:

```
$ cat -n test1
     1  hello
     2
     3  This is a test file.
     4
     5
     6  That we'll use to        test the cat command.
$
```

That feature will come in handy when you're examining scripts. If you just want to number the lines that have text in them, the `-b` parameter is for you:

```
$ cat -b test1
     1  hello

     2  This is a test file.


     3  That we'll use to        test the cat command.
$
```

Fancy! If you need to compress multiple blank lines into a single blank line, use the -s parameter:

```
$ cat -s test1
hello

This is a test file.

That we'll use to        test the cat command.
$
```

Finally, if you don't want tab characters to appear, use the -T parameter:

```
$ cat -T test1
hello

This is a test file.


That we'll use to^Itest the cat command.
$
```

The -T parameter replaces any tabs in the text with the ^I character combination.

FIGURE 3-4

Using the more command to display a text file

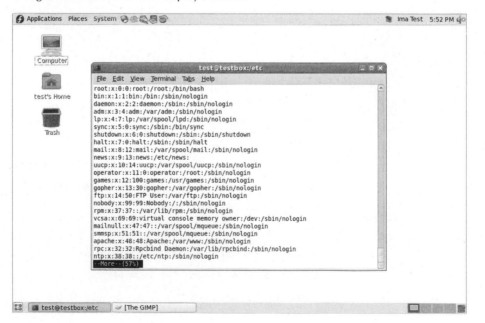

For large files, the `cat` command can be somewhat annoying. The text in the file will just quickly scroll off of the monitor without stopping. Fortunately, there's a simple way to solve this problem.

The more command

The main drawback of the `cat` command is that you can't control what's happening once you start it. To solve that problem, developers created the `more` command. The `more` command displays a text file, but stops after it displays each page of data. A sample `more` screen is shown in Figure 3-4.

Notice that at the bottom of the screen in Figure 3-4 the `more` command displays a tag showing that you're still in the `more` application and how far along in the text file you are. This is the prompt for the `more` command. At this point you can enter one of several options, shown in Table 3-7.

TABLE 3-7

The more Command Options

Option	Description
H	Display a help menu.
spacebar	Display the next screen of text from the file.
z	Display the next screen of text from the file.
ENTER	Display one more line of text from the file.
d	Display a half-screen (11 lines) of text from the file.
q	Exit the program.
s	Skip forward one line of text.
f	Skip forward one screen of text.
b	Skip backward one screen of text.
/expression	Search for the text *expression* in the file.
n	Search for the next occurrence of the last specified expression.
'	Go to the first occurrence of the specified expression.
!cmd	Execute a shell command.
v	Start up the vi editor at the current line.
CTRL-L	Redraw the screen at the current location in the file.
=	Display the current line number in the file.
.	Repeat the previous command.

Viewing a file using the less command

The `more` command allows some rudimentary movement through the text file. For more advanced features, try the `less` command.

The less command

Although from its name it sounds like it shouldn't be as advanced as the `more` command, the `less` command is actually a play on words and is an advanced version of the `more` command (the `less` command uses the phrase "less is more"). It provides several very handy features for scrolling both forward and backward through a text file, as well as some pretty advanced searching capabilities.

The `less` command also has the feature of being able to display the contents of a file before it finishes reading the entire file. This is a serious drawback for both the `cat` and `more` commands when using extremely large files.

The `less` command operates much the same as the `more` command, displaying one screen of text from a file at a time. Figure 3-5 shows the `less` command in action.

Notice that the `less` command provides additional information in its prompt, showing the total number of lines in the file, and the range of lines currently displayed. The `less` command supports the same command set as the `more` command, plus lots more options. To see all of the options available, look at the `man` pages for the `less` command. One set of features is that the less command recognizes the up and down arrow keys, as well as the page up and page down keys (assuming that you're using a properly defined terminal). This gives you full control when viewing a file.

Viewing parts of a file

Often the data you want to view is located either right at the top or buried at the bottom of a text file. If the information is at the top of a large file, you still need to wait for the cat or more commands to load the entire file before you can view it. If the information is located at the bottom of a file (such as a log file), you need to wade through thousands of lines of text just to get to the last few entries. Fortunately, Linux has specialized commands to solve both of these problems.

The tail command

The tail command displays the last group of lines in a file. By default, it'll show the last 10 lines in the file, but you can change that with command line parameters, shown in Table 3-8.

The -f parameter is a pretty cool feature of the tail command. It allows you to peek inside a file as it's being used by other processes. The tail command stays active and continues to display new lines as they appear in the text file. This is a great way to monitor the system log file in real-time mode.

The head command

While not as exotic as the tail command, the head command does what you'd expect, it displays the first group of lines at the start of a file. By default, it'll display the first 10 lines of text. Similar to the tail command, it supports the -c, and -n parameters so that you can alter what's displayed.

TABLE 3-8

The tail Command Line Parameters

Parameter	Description
-c bytes	Display the last bytes number of bytes in the file.
-n lines	Display the last lines number of lines in the file.
-f	Keeps the tail program active and continues to display new lines as they're added to the file.
--pid=PID	Along with -f, follows a file until the process with ID PID terminates.
-s sec	Along with -f, sleeps for sec seconds between iterations.
-v	Always displays output headers giving the filename.
-q	Never displays output headers giving the filename.

Usually the beginning of a file doesn't change, so the head command doesn't support the -f parameter feature. The head command is a handy way to just peek at the beginning of a file if you're not sure what's inside, without having to go through the hassle of displaying the entire file.

Summary

This chapter covered the basics for working with the Linux filesystem from a shell prompt. It started out by discussing the bash shell and showed you how to interact with the shell. The command line interface (CLI) uses a prompt string to indicate when it's ready for you to enter commands. You can customize the prompt string to display useful information about your system, your logon ID, and even dates and times.

The bash shell provides a wealth of utilities you can use to create and manipulate files. Before you start playing with files, it's a good idea to understand how Linux stores them. This chapter discussed the basics of the Linux virtual directory and showed how Linux references store media devices. After describing the Linux filesystem, the chapter walked you through using the cd command to move around the virtual directory.

After showing you how to get to a directory, the chapter demonstrated how to use the ls command to list the files and subdirectories. There are lots of parameters that customize the output of the ls command. You can obtain information on files and directories just by using the ls command.

The touch command is useful for creating empty files and for changing the access or modification times on an existing file. The chapter also discussed using the cp command to copy existing files from one location to another. It walked you through the process of linking files instead of copying them, providing an easy way to have the same file in two locations without making a separate copy. The cp command does this, as does the ln command.

Next, you learned how to rename files (called *moving*) in Linux using the mv command, and saw how to delete files (called *removing*) using the rm command. It also showed how to perform the same tasks with directories, using the mkdir and rmdir commands.

Finally, the chapter closed with a discussion on viewing the contents of files. The cat, more, and less commands provide easy methods for viewing the entire contents of a file, while the tail and head commands are great for peeking inside a file to just see a small portion of it.

The next chapter continues the discussion on bash shell commands. We'll take a look at more advanced administrator commands that'll come in handy as you administer your Linux system.

Chapter 4

More bash Shell Commands

hapter 3 covered the basics of rummaging through the Linux filesystem and working with the files and directories. File and directory management is a major feature of the Linux shell; however, there are some more things we should look at before we start our script programming. This chapter digs into the Linux system management commands, showing you how to peek inside your Linux system using command line commands. After that, it shows you a few handy commands that you can use to work with data files on the system.

Monitoring Programs

One of the toughest jobs of being a Linux system administrator is keeping track of what's running on the system — especially now, when graphical desktops take a handful of programs just to produce a single desktop. There are always a lot of programs running on the system.

Fortunately, there are a few command line tools that can help make life easier for you. This section covers a few of the basic tools you'll need to know how to use to manage programs on your Linux system.

Peeking at the processes

When a program runs on the system, it's referred to as a *process*. To examine these processes, you'll need to become familiar with the ps command, the Swiss Army knife of utilities. It can produce lots of information about all the programs running on your system.

Unfortunately, with this robustness comes complexity — in the form of numerous parameters — making the ps command probably one of the most difficult commands to master. Most system administrators find a subset of these parameters that provide the information they want, and then stick with using only those.

That said, however, the basic ps command doesn't really provide all that much information:

```
$ ps
  PID TTY          TIME CMD
 3081 pts/0    00:00:00 bash
 3209 pts/0    00:00:00 ps
$
```

Not too exciting. By default the ps command shows only the processes that belong to the current user and that are running on the current terminal. In this case, I only had my bash shell running (remember, the shell is just another program running on the system) and, of course, the ps command itself.

The basic output shows the process ID (PID) of the programs, the terminal (TTY) that they are running from, and the CPU time the process has used.

> **NOTE**   The tricky feature of the ps command (and the part that makes it so complicated) is that at one time there were two versions of it. Each version had its own set of command line parameters controlling what information it displayed, and how. Recently, Linux developers have combined the two ps command formats into a single ps program (and of course added their own touches).

The GNU ps command that's used in Linux systems supports three different types of command line parameters:

- Unix-style parameters, which are preceded by a dash
- BSD-style parameters, which are not preceded by a dash
- GNU long parameters, which are preceded by a double dash

The following sections examine the three different parameter types and show examples of how they work.

Unix-style parameters

The Unix-style parameters originated with the original ps command that ran on the AT&T Unix systems invented by Bell Labs. These parameters are shown in Table 4-1.

TABLE 4-1

The ps Command Unix Parameters

Parameter	Description
-A	Show all processes.
-N	Show the opposite of the specified parameters.

continued

TABLE 4-1	(continued)
Parameter	Description
-a	Show all processes except session headers and processes without a terminal.
-d	Show all processes except session headers.
-e	Show all processes.
-C *cmslist*	Show processes contained in the list *cmdlist*.
-G *grplist*	Show processes with a group ID listed in *grplist*.
-U *userlist*	Show processes owned by a userid listed in *userlist*.
-g *grplist*	Show processes by session or by groupid contained in *grplist*.
-p *pidlist*	Show processes with PIDs in the list *pidlist*.
-s *sesslist*	Show processes with session ID in the list *sesslist*.
-t *ttylist*	Show processes with terminal ID in the list *ttylist*.
-u *userlist*	Show processes by effective userid in the list *userlist*.
-F	Use extra full output.
-O *format*	Display specific columns in the list *format*, along with the default columns.
-M	Display security information about the process.
-c	Show additional scheduler information about the process.
-f	Display a full format listing.
-j	Show job information.
-l	Display a long listing.
-o *format*	Display only specific columns listed in *format*.
-y	Don't show process flags.
-Z	Display the security context information.
-H	Display processes in a hierarchical format (showing parent processes).
-n *namelist*	Define the values to display in the WCHAN column.
-w	Use wide output format, for unlimited width displays
-L	Show process threads
-V	Display the version of ps

That's a lot of parameters, and remember, there are still more! The key to using the ps command is not to memorize all of the available parameters, only those you find most useful. Most Linux system administrators have their own sets of commonly used parameters that they remember for extracting pertinent information. For example, if you need to see everything running on the system, use the -ef parameter combination (the ps command lets you combine parameters together like this):

```
$ ps -ef
UID          PID   PPID  C STIME TTY          TIME CMD
root           1      0  0 11:29 ?        00:00:01 init [5]
root           2      0  0 11:29 ?        00:00:00 [kthreadd]
root           3      2  0 11:29 ?        00:00:00 [migration/0]
root           4      2  0 11:29 ?        00:00:00 [ksoftirqd/0]
root           5      2  0 11:29 ?        00:00:00 [watchdog/0]
root           6      2  0 11:29 ?        00:00:00 [events/0]
root           7      2  0 11:29 ?        00:00:00 [khelper]
root          47      2  0 11:29 ?        00:00:00 [kblockd/0]
root          48      2  0 11:29 ?        00:00:00 [kacpid]
68          2349      1  0 11:30 ?        00:00:00 hald
root        2489      1  0 11:30 tty1     00:00:00 /sbin/mingetty tty1
root        2490      1  0 11:30 tty2     00:00:00 /sbin/mingetty tty2
root        2491      1  0 11:30 tty3     00:00:00 /sbin/mingetty tty3
root        2492      1  0 11:30 tty4     00:00:00 /sbin/mingetty tty4
root        2493      1  0 11:30 tty5     00:00:00 /sbin/mingetty tty5
root        2494      1  0 11:30 tty6     00:00:00 /sbin/mingetty tty6
root        2956      1  0 11:42 ?        00:00:00 /usr/sbin/httpd
apache      2958   2956  0 11:42 ?        00:00:00 /usr/sbin/httpd
apache      2959   2956  0 11:42 ?        00:00:00 /usr/sbin/httpd
root        2995      1  0 11:43 ?        00:00:00 auditd
root        2997   2995  0 11:43 ?        00:00:00 /sbin/audispd
root        3078   1981  0 12:00 ?        00:00:00 sshd: rich [priv]
rich        3080   3078  0 12:00 ?        00:00:00 sshd: rich@pts/0
rich        3081   3080  0 12:00 pts/0    00:00:00 -bash
rich        4445   3081  3 13:48 pts/0    00:00:00 ps -ef
$
```

I've cut out quite a few lines from the output to save space, but as you can see, there are lots of processes running on a Linux system. This example uses two parameters, the -e parameter, which shows all of the processes running on the system, and the -f parameter, which expands the output to show a few useful columns of information:

- UID: The user responsible for launching the process
- PID: The process ID of the process
- PPID: The PID of the parent process (if a process is started by another process)
- C: Processor utilization over the lifetime of the process
- STIME: The system time when the process started
- TTY: The terminal device from which the process was launched

- TIME: The cumulative CPU time required to run the process

- CMD: The name of the program that was started

This produces a reasonable amount of information, which is what many system administrators would like to see. For even more information, you can use the -l parameter, which produces the long format output:

```
$ ps -l
F S  UID PID  PPID C PRI NI ADDR SZ WCHAN TTY     TIME   CMD
0 S  500 3081 3080 0 80  0  -  1173 wait pts/0  00:00:00 bash
0 R  500 4463 3081 1 80  0  -  1116 -    pts/0  00:00:00 ps
$
```

Notice the extra columns that appear when you use the -l parameter:

- F: System flags assigned to the process by the kernel

- S: The state of the process (O = running on processor; S = sleeping; R = runnable, waiting to run; Z = zombie, process terminated but parent not available; T = process stopped)

- PRI: The priority of the process (higher numbers mean lower priority)

- NI: The nice value, which is used for determining priorities

- ADDR: The memory address of the process

- SZ: Approximate amount of swap space required if the process was swapped out

- WCHAN: Address of the kernel function where the process is sleeping

Before moving on, there's one more extremely handy parameter to remember, -H. The -H parameter organizes the processes in a hierarchical format, showing which processes started which other processes. Here's an extraction from an -efH-formatted listing:

```
$ ps -efH
UID    PID    PPID  C STIME TTY    TIME      CMD
root   3078   1981  0 12:00 ?      00:00:00  sshd: rich [priv]
rich   3080   3078  0 12:00 ?      00:00:00   sshd: rich@pts/0
rich   3081   3080  0 12:00 pts/0  00:00:00    -bash
rich   4803   3081  1 14:31 pts/0  00:00:00     ps -efH
```

Notice the shifting in the CMD column output. This shows the hierarchy of the processes that are running. First, the sshd process started by the root user (this is the Secure Shell (SSH) server session, which listens for remote SSH connections). Next, when I connected from a remote terminal to the system, the main SSH process spawned a terminal process (pts/0), which in turn spawned a bash shell.

From there, I executed the ps command, which appears as a child process from the bash process. On a multi-user system, this is a very useful tool when trying to troubleshoot runaway processes, or when trying to track down which userid or terminal they belong to.

BSD-style parameters

Now that you've seen the Unix parameters, let's take a look at the BSD-style parameters. The Berkeley Software Distribution (BSD) was a version of Unix developed at (of course) the University of California, Berkeley. It had many subtle differences from the AT&T Unix system, thus sparking many Unix wars over the years. The BSD version of the ps command parameters are shown in Table 4-2.

TABLE 4-2

The ps Command BSD Parameters

Parameter	Description
T	Show all processes associated with this terminal.
a	Show all processes associated with any terminal.
g	Show all processes including session headers.
r	Show only running processes.
x	Show all processes, even those without a terminal device assigned.
U *userlist*	Show processes owned by a userid listed in *userlist*.
p *pidlist*	Show processes with a PID listed in *pidlist*.
t *ttylist*	Show processes associated with a terminal listed in *ttylist*.
O *format*	List specific columns in *format* to display along with the standard columns.
X	Display data in the register format.
Z	Include security information in the output.
j	Show job information.
l	Use the long format.
o *format*	Display only columns specified in *format*.
s	Use the signal format.
u	Use the user-oriented format.
v	Use the virtual memory format.
N *namelist*	Define the values to use in the WCHAN column.
O *order*	Define the order in which to display the information columns.
S	Sum numerical information, such as CPU and memory usage, for child processes into the parent process.

continued

TABLE 4-2	(continued)
Parameter	**Description**
c	Display the true command name (the name of the program used to start the process).
e	Display any environment variables used by the command.
f	Display processes in a hierarchical format, showing which processes started which processes.
h	Don't display the header information.
k *sort*	Define the column(s) to use for sorting the output.
n	Use numeric values for user and group IDs, along with WCHAN information.
w	Produce wide output for wider terminals.
H	Display threads as if they were processes.
m	Display threads after their processes.
L	List all format specifiers.
V	Display the version of ps.

As you can see, there's a lot of overlap between the Unix and BSD types of parameters. Most of the information you can get from one you can also get from the other. Most of the time which one you use depends on which format you're more comfortable with (for example, if you were used to a BSD environment before using Linux).

When you use the BSD-style parameters, the ps command automatically changes the output to simulate the BSD format. Here's an example using the l parameter:

```
$ ps l
F  UID  PID PPID PRI  NI  VSZ  RSS WCHAN  STAT TTY      TIME COMMAND
0  500 3081 3080  20   0 4692 1432 wait   Ss   pts/0    0:00 -bash
0  500 5104 3081  20   0 4468  844 -      R+   pts/0    0:00 ps l
$
```

Notice that while many of the output columns are the same as when we used the Unix-style parameters, there are a couple of different ones:

- VSZ: The size in kilobytes of the process in memory
- RSS: The physical memory that a process has used that isn't swapped out
- STAT: A two-character state code representing the current process state

Many system administrators like the BSD-style l parameter because it produces a more detailed state code for processes (the STAT column). The two-character code more precisely defines exactly what's happening with the process than the single-character Unix-style output.

The first character uses the same values as the Unix-style S output column, showing when a process is sleeping, running, or waiting. The second character further defines the process's status:

- <: The process is running at high priority.
- N: The process is running at low priority.
- L: The process has pages locked in memory.
- s: The process is a session leader.
- l: The process is multi-threaded.
- +: The process is running in the foreground.

From the simple example shown above, you can see that the bash command is sleeping, but it is a session leader (it's the main process in my session), while the ps command was running in the foreground on the system.

The GNU long parameters

Finally, the GNU developers put their own touches on the new, improved ps command by adding a few more options to the parameter mix. Some of the GNU long parameters copy existing Unix- or BSD-style parameters, while others provide new features. Table 4-3 lists the GNU long parameters available.

You can combine GNU long parameters with either Unix- or BSD-style parameters to really customize your display. One cool feature of GNU long parameters that I really like is the --forest parameter. It displays the hierarchical process information, but using ASCII characters to draw cute charts:

```
 1981 ?         00:00:00 sshd
 3078 ?         00:00:00  \_ sshd
 3080 ?         00:00:00      \_ sshd
 3081 pts/0     00:00:00          \_ bash
16676 pts/0     00:00:00              \_ ps
```

This format makes tracing child and parent processes a snap!

Real-time process monitoring

The ps command is great for gleaning information about processes running on the system, but it has one drawback. The ps command can only display information for a specific point in time. If you're trying to find trends about processes that are frequently swapped in and out of memory, it's hard to do that with the ps command.

Instead, the top command can solve this problem. The top command displays process information similarly to the ps command, but it does it in real-time mode. Figure 4-1 is a snapshot of the top command in action.

TABLE 4-3

The ps Command GNU Parameters

Parameter	Description
`--deselect`	Show all processes except those listed in the command line.
`--Group grplist`	Show processes whose group ID is listed in *grplist*.
`--User userlist`	Show processes whose user ID is listed in *userlist*.
`--group grplist`	Show processes whose effective group ID is listed in *grplist*.
`--pid pidlist`	Show processes whose process ID is listed in *pidlist*.
`--ppid pidlist`	Show processes whose parent process ID is listed in *pidlist*.
`--sid sidlist`	Show processes whose session ID is listed in *sidlist*.
`--tty ttylist`	Show processes whose terminal device ID is listed in *ttylist*.
`--user userlist`	Show processes whose effective user ID is listed in *userlist*.
`--format format`	Display only columns specified in the *format*.
`--context`	Display additional security information.
`--cols n`	Set screen width to *n* columns.
`--columns n`	Set screen width to *n* columns.
`--cumulative`	Include stopped child process information.
`--forest`	Display processes in a hierarchical listing showing parent processes.
`--headers`	Repeat column headers on each page of output.
`--no-headers`	Don't display column headers.
`--lines n`	Set the screen height to *n* lines.
`--rows n`	Set the screen height to *n* rows.
`--sort order`	Define the column(s) to use for sorting the output.
`--width n`	Set the screen width to *n* columns.
`--help`	Display the help information.
`--info`	Display debugging information.
`--version`	Display the version of the ps program.

FIGURE 4-1

The output of the top command while it is running

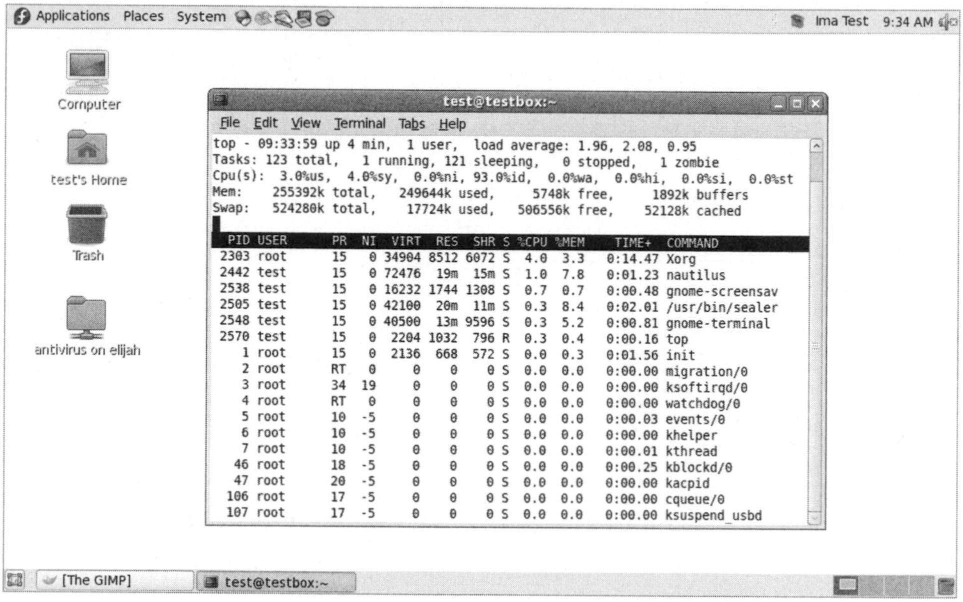

The first section of the output shows general system information. The first line shows the current time, how long the system has been up, the number of users logged in, and the load average on the system.

The load average appears as three numbers, the 1-minute, 5-minute, and 15-minute load averages. The higher the values, the more load the system is experiencing. It's not uncommon for the 1-minute load value to be high for short bursts of activity. If the 15-minute load value is high, your system may be in trouble.

NOTE The trick in Linux system administration is defining what exactly a high load average value is. This value depends on what's normally running on your system and the hardware configuration. What's high for one system might be normal for another. Usually, if your load averages start getting over 2, things are getting busy on your system.

The second line shows general process information (called *tasks* in top): how many processes are running, sleeping, stopped, and zombie (have finished but their parent process hasn't responded).

The next line shows general CPU information. The top display breaks down the CPU utilization into several categories depending on the owner of the process (user versus system processes) and the state of the processes (running, idle, or waiting).

Following that, there are two lines that detail the status of the system memory. The first line shows the status of the physical memory in the system, how much total memory there is, how much is currently being used, and how much is free. The second memory line shows the status of the swap memory area in the system (if any is installed), with the same information.

Finally, the next section shows a detailed list of the currently running processes, with some information columns that should look familiar from the ps command output:

- PID: The process ID of the process
- USER: The user name of the owner of the process
- PR: The priority of the process
- NI: The nice value of the process
- VIRT: The total amount of virtual memory used by the process
- RES: The amount of physical memory the process is using
- SHR: The amount of memory the process is sharing with other processes
- S: The process status (D = interruptible sleep, R = running, S = sleeping, T = traced or stopped, or Z = zombie)
- %CPU: The share of CPU time that the process is using
- %MEM: The share of available physical memory the process is using
- TIME+: The total CPU time the process has used since starting
- COMMAND: The command line name of the process (program started)

By default, when you start top it sorts the processes based on the %CPU value. You can change the sort order by using one of several interactive commands while top is running. Each interactive command is a single character you can press while top is running and changes the behavior of the program. These commands are shown in Table 4-4.

You have lots of control over the output of the top command. Using this tool, you can often find offending processes that have taken over your system. Of course, once you find one, the next job is to stop it, which brings us to the next topic.

Stopping processes

A crucial part of being a system administrator is knowing when and how to stop a process. Sometimes a process gets hung up and just needs a gentle nudge to either get going again or stop. Other times, a process runs away with the CPU and refuses to give it up. In both cases, you need a command that will allow you to control a process. Linux follows the Unix method of interprocess communication.

In Linux, processes communicate between each other using *signals*. A process signal is a predefined message that processes recognize and may choose to ignore or act on. The developers program how a process handles signals. Most well-written applications have the ability to receive and act on the standard Unix process signals. These signals are shown in Table 4-5.

There are two commands available in Linux that allow us to send process signals to running processes.

TABLE 4-4

The top Interactive Commands

Command	Description
1	Toggle the single CPU and Symmetric Multiprocessor (SMP) state.
b	Toggle the bolding of important numbers in the tables.
I	Toggle Irix/Solaris mode.
z	Configure color for the table.
l	Toggle the displaying of the load average information line.
t	Toggle the displaying of the CPU information line.
m	Toggle the displaying of the MEM and SWAP information lines.
f	Add or remove different information columns.
o	Change the display order of information columns.
F or O	Select a field on which to sort the processes (%CPU by default).
< or >	Move the sort field one column left (<) or right (>).
r	Toggle the normal or reverse sort order.
h	Toggle the showing of threads.
c	Toggle the showing of the command name or the full command line (including parameters) of processes.
i	Toggle the showing of idle processes.
S	Toggle the showing of the cumulative CPU time or relative CPU time.
x	Toggle highlighting of the sort field.
y	Toggle highlighting of running tasks.
z	Toggle color and mono mode.
b	Toggle bold mode for x and y modes.
u	Show processes for a specific user.
n or #	Set the number of processes to display.
k	Kill a specific process (only if process owner or if root user).
r	Change the priority (renice) of a specific process (only if process owner or if root user).
d or s	Change the update interval (default three seconds).
W	Write current settings to a configuration file.
q	Exit the top command.

TABLE 4-5

Linux Process Signals

Signal	Name	Description
1	HUP	Hang up.
2	INT	Interrupt.
3	QUIT	Stop running.
9	KILL	Unconditionally terminate.
11	SEGV	Segment violation.
15	TERM	Terminate if possible.
17	STOP	Stop unconditionally, but don't terminate.
18	TSTP	Stop or pause, but continue to run in background.
19	CONT	Resume execution after STOP or TSTP.

The kill command

The kill command allows you to send signals to processes based on their process ID (PID). By default the kill command sends a TERM signal to all the PIDs listed on the command line. Unfortunately, you can only use the process PID instead of its command name, making the kill command difficult to use sometimes.

To send a process signal, you must either be the owner of the process or be logged in as the root user.

```
$ kill 3940
-bash: kill: (3940) - Operation not permitted
$
```

The TERM signal tells the process to kindly stop running. Unfortunately, if you have a runaway process, most likely it'll ignore the request. When you need to get forceful, the -s parameter allows you to specify other signals (either using their name or signal number).

The generally accepted procedure is to first try the TERM signal. If the process ignores that, try the INT or HUP signals. If the program recognizes these signals, it'll try to gracefully stop doing what it was doing before shutting down. The most forceful signal is the KILL signal. When a process receives this signal, it immediately stops running. This can lead to corrupt files.

As you can see from the following example, there's no output associated with the kill command.

```
# kill -s HUP 3940
#
```

To see if the command was effective, you'll have to perform another ps or top command to see if the offending process stopped.

The killall command

The `killall` command is a powerful way to stop processes by using their names rather than the PID numbers. The `killall` command allows you to use wildcard characters as well, making it a very useful tool when you've got a system that's gone awry.

> **CAUTION** Be extremely careful using the `killall` command when logged in as the root user. It's easy to get carried away with wildcard characters and accidentally stop important system processes. This could lead to a damaged filesystem.

Monitoring Disk Space

Another important task of the system administrator is to keep track of the disk usage on the system. Whether you're running a simple Linux desktop or a large Linux server, you'll need to know how much space you have for your applications.

There are a few command line commands you can use to help you manage the media environment on your Linux system. This section describes the core commands you'll likely run into during your system administration duties.

Mounting media

As discussed in Chapter 3, the Linux filesystem combines all media disks into a single virtual directory. Before you can use a new media disk on your system, you need to place it in the virtual directory. This task is called *mounting*.

In today's graphical desktop world, most Linux distributions have the ability to automatically mount specific types of *removable media*. A removable media device is a medium that (obviously) can be easily removed from the PC, such as CD-ROMs, floppy disks, and, recently, USB memory sticks.

If you're not using a distribution that automatically mounts and unmounts removable media, you'll have to do it yourself. This section describes the Linux command line commands to help you manage your removable media devices.

The mount command

Oddly enough, the command used to mount media is called `mount`. By default, the `mount` command displays a list of media devices currently mounted on the system:

```
$ mount
/dev/mapper/VolGroup00-LogVol00 on / type ext3 (rw)
proc on /proc type proc (rw)
sysfs on /sys type sysfs (rw)
devpts on /dev/pts type devpts (rw,gid=5,mode=620)
/dev/sda1 on /boot type ext3 (rw)
```

```
tmpfs on /dev/shm type tmpfs (rw)
none on /proc/sys/fs/binfmt_misc type binfmt_misc (rw)
sunrpc on /var/lib/nfs/rpc_pipefs type rpc_pipefs (rw)
/dev/sdb1 on /media/disk type vfat
(rw,nosuid,nodev,uhelper=hal,shortname=lower,uid=503)
$
```

There are four pieces of information the `mount` command provides:

- The device location of the media
- The mount point in the virtual directory where the media is mounted
- The filesystem type
- The access status of the mounted media

The last entry in the example above is a USB memory stick that the GNOME desktop automatically mounted at the `/media/disk` mount point. The `vfat` filesystem type shows that it was formatted on a Microsoft Windows PC.

To manually mount a media device in the virtual directory, you'll need to be logged in as the root user. The basic command for manually mounting a media device is:

```
mount -t type device directory
```

The `type` parameter defines the filesystem type the disk was formatted under. There are lots and lots of different filesystem types that Linux recognizes. If you share removable media devices with your Windows PCs, the types you're most likely to run into are:

- `vfat`: Windows long filesystem.
- `ntfs`: Windows advanced filesystem used in Windows NT, XP, and Vista.
- `iso9660`: The standard CD-ROM filesystem.

Most USB memory sticks and floppies are formatted using the `vfat` filesystem. If you need to mount a data CD, you'll have to use the `iso9660` filesystem type.

The next two parameters define the location of the device file for the media device and the location in the virtual directory for the mount point. For example, to manually mount the USB memory stick at device `/dev/sdb1` at location `/media/disk`, you'd use the command:

```
mount -t vfat /dev/sdb1 /media/disk
```

Once a media device is mounted in the virtual directory, the root user will have full access to the device, but access by other users will be restricted. You can control who has access to the device using directory permissions (discussed in Chapter 6).

In case you need to use some of the more exotic features of the `mount` command, the available parameters are shown in Table 4-6.

TABLE 4-6

The mount Command Parameters

Parameter	Description
-a	Mount all filesystems specified in the /etc/fstab file.
-f	Causes the mount command to simulate mounting a device, but not actually mount it.
-F	When used with the -a parameter, mounts all filesystems at the same time.
-v	Verbose mode, explains all the steps required to mount the device.
-I	Don't use any filesystem helper files under /sbin/mount.filesystem.
-l	Add the filesystem labels automatically for ext2, ext3, or XFS filesystems.
-n	Mount the device without registering it in the /etc/mstab mounted device file.
-p num	For encrypted mounting, read the passphrase from the file descriptor num.
-s	Ignore mount options not supported by the filesystem.
-r	Mount the device as read-only.
-w	Mount the device as read-write (the default).
-L label	Mount the device with the specified label.
-U uuid	Mount the device with the specified uuid.
-O	When used with the -a parameter, limits the set of filesystems applied.
-o	Add specific options to the filesytem.

The -o option allows you to mount the filesystem with a comma-separated list of additional options. The popular options to use are:

- ro: Mount as read-only.
- rw: Mount as read-write.
- user: Allow an ordinary user to mount the filesystem.
- check=none: Mount the filesystem without performing an integrity check.
- loop: Mount a file.

A popular thing in Linux these days is to distribute a CD as a .iso file. The .iso file is a complete image of the CD in a single file. Most CD-burning software packages can create a new CD based on the .iso file. A feature of the mount command is that you can mount a .iso file directly to your Linux virtual directory without having to burn it onto a CD. This is accomplished using the -o parameter with the loop option:

```
$ mkdir mnt
$ su
Password:
# mount -t iso9660 -o loop MEPIS-KDE4-LIVE-DVD_32.iso mnt
# ls -l mnt
total 16
-r--r--r-- 1 root root  702 2007-08-03 08:49 about
dr-xr-xr-x 3 root root 2048 2007-07-29 14:30 boot
-r--r--r-- 1 root root 2048 2007-08-09 22:36 boot.catalog
-r--r--r-- 1 root root  894 2004-01-23 13:22 cdrom.ico
-r--r--r-- 1 root root 5229 2006-07-07 18:07 MCWL
dr-xr-xr-x 2 root root 2048 2007-08-09 22:32 mepis
dr-xr-xr-x 2 root root 2048 2007-04-03 16:44 OSX
-r--r--r-- 1 root root  107 2007-08-09 22:36 version
# cd mnt/boot
# ls -l
total 4399
dr-xr-xr-x 2 root root    2048 2007-06-29 09:00 grub
-r--r--r-- 1 root root 2392512 2007-07-29 12:53 initrd.gz
-r--r--r-- 1 root root   94760 2007-06-14 14:56 memtest
-r--r--r-- 1 root root 2014704 2007-07-29 14:26 vmlinuz
#
```

The mount command mounted the .iso CD image file just as if it were a real CD and allowed us to maneuver around within its filesystem.

The umount command

To remove a removable media device, you should never just remove it from the system. Instead, you should always *unmount* it first.

> **TIP** Linux doesn't allow you to eject a mounted CD. If you ever have trouble removing a CD from the drive, most likely it means the CD is still mounted in the virtual directory. Unmount it first, then try to eject it.

The command used to unmount devices is umount (yes, there's no "n" in the command, which gets confusing sometimes). The format for the umount command is pretty simple:

```
umount [directory | device ]
```

The umount command gives you the choice of defining the media device by either its device location or its mounted directory name. If there are any open files contained on the device, the system won't let you unmount it.

```
[root@testbox boot]# umount /home/rich/mnt
umount: /home/rich/mnt: device is busy
```

```
umount: /home/rich/mnt: device is busy
[root@testbox boot]# cd /home/rich
[root@testbox rich]# umount /home/rich/mnt
[root@testbox rich]# ls -l mnt
total 0
[root@testbox rich]#
```

In this example, even though I was not using a file from the mounted .iso image file, I was still in a directory within the filesystem structure, so the umount command wouldn't let me unmount the image file. Once I moved out of the image file filesystem, I was able to successfully unmount the image file.

Using the df command

Sometimes you need to see how much disk space is available on an individual device. The df command allows us to easily see what's happening on all of the mounted disks:

```
$ df
Filesystem           1K-blocks      Used Available Use% Mounted on
/dev/sda2             18251068   7703964   9605024  45% /
/dev/sda1               101086     18680     77187  20% /boot
tmpfs                   119536         0    119536   0% /dev/shm
/dev/sdb1               127462    113892     13570  90% /media/disk
$
```

The df command shows each mounted filesystem that contains data. As you can see from the mount command earlier, some mounted devices are used for internal system purposes. The command displays:

- The device location of the device
- How many 1024-byte blocks of data it can hold
- How many 1024-byte blocks are used
- How many 1024-byte blocks are available
- The amount of used space as a percentage
- The mount point where the device is mounted

There are a few different command line parameters available with the df command, most of which you'll never use. One popular parameter is -h, which shows the disk space in human-readable form, usually as an M for megabytes or a G for gigabytes:

```
$ df -h
Filesystem      Size  Used Avail Use% Mounted on
/dev/sdb2        18G  7.4G  9.2G  45% /
/dev/sda1        99M   19M   76M  20% /boot
tmpfs           117M     0  117M   0% /dev/shm
/dev/sdb1       125M  112M   14M  90% /media/disk
$
```

Now instead of having to decode those ugly block numbers, all of the disk sizes are shown using "normal" sizes. The df command is invaluable in troubleshooting disk space problems on the system.

NOTE Remember, the Linux system always has processes running in the background that handle files. The values from the df command reflect what the Linux system thinks are the current values at that point in time. It's possible that you have a process running that has created or deleted a file, but has not released the file yet. This value is not included in the free space calculation.

Using the du command

With the df command, knowing that a disk is running out of space is easy. The next problem for the system administrator is to know what to do when that happens.

Another useful command to help us out is the du command. The du command shows the disk usage for a specific directory (by default, the current directory). This is a quick way to determine if you have any obvious disk hogs on the system.

By default, the du command displays all of the files, directories, and subdirectories under the current directory, and it shows how many disk blocks each file or directory takes. For a standard-sized directory, this can be quite a listing. Here's a partial listing of using the du command:

```
$ du
484      ./.gstreamer-0.10
8        ./Templates
8        ./Download
8        ./.ccache/7/0
24       ./.ccache/7
368      ./.ccache/a/d
384      ./.ccache/a
424      ./.ccache
8        ./Public
8        ./.gphpedit/plugins
32       ./.gphpedit
72       ./.gconfd
128      ./.nautilus/metafiles
384      ./.nautilus
72       ./.bittorrent/data/metainfo
20       ./.bittorrent/data/resume
144      ./.bittorrent/data
152      ./.bittorrent
8        ./Videos
8        ./Music
16       ./.config/gtk-2.0
40       ./.config
8        ./Documents
```

The number at the right of each line is the number of disk blocks that each file or directory takes. Notice that the listing starts at the bottom of a directory and works its way up through the files and subdirectories contained within the directory.

The du command by itself can be somewhat useless. It's nice to be able to see how much disk space each individual file and directory takes up, but it can be meaningless when you have to wade through pages and pages of information before you find what you're looking for.

There are a few command line parameters that you can use with the du command to make things a little more legible:

- -c: Produce a grand total of all the files listed.
- -h: Print sizes in human-readable form, using K for kilobyte, M for megabyte, and G for gigabyte.
- -s: Summarize each argument.

The next step for the system administrator is to use some file-handling commands for manipulating large amounts of data. That's exactly what the next section covers.

Working with Data Files

When you have a large amount of data, it's often difficult to handle the information and make it useful. As you saw with the du command in the previous section, it's easy to get data overload when working with system commands.

The Linux system provides several command line tools to help us manage large amounts of data. This section covers the basic commands that every system administrator — as well as any everyday Linux user — should know how to use to make their lives easier.

Sorting data

One popular function that comes in handy when working with large amounts of data is the sort command. The sort command does what it says — it sorts data.

By default, the sort command sorts the data lines in a text file using standard sorting rules for the language you specify as the default for the session.

```
$ cat file1
one
two
three
four
five
$ sort file1
five
```

```
four
one
three
two
$
```

Pretty simple. However, things aren't always as easy as they appear. Take a look at this example:

```
$ cat file2
1
2
100
45
3
10
145
75
$ sort file2
1
10
100
145
2
3
45
75
$
```

If you were expecting the numbers to sort in numerical order, you were disappointed. By default, the sort command interprets numbers as characters and performs a standard character sort, producing output that might not be what you want. To solve this problem, use the -n parameter, which tells the sort command to recognize numbers as numbers instead of characters, and to sort them based on their numerical values:

```
$ sort -n file2
1
2
3
10
45
75
100
145
$
```

Now, that's much better! Another common parameter that's used is -M, the month sort. Linux log files usually contain a timestamp at the beginning of the line to indicate when the event occurred:

```
Sep 13 07:10:09 testbox smartd[2718]: Device: /dev/sda, opened
```

If you sort a file that uses timestamp dates using the default sort, you'll get something like this:

```
$ sort file3
Apr
Aug
Dec
Feb
Jan
Jul
Jun
Mar
May
Nov
Oct
Sep
$
```

Not exactly what you wanted. If you use the -M parameter, the sort command recognizes the three-character month nomenclature, and sorts appropriately:

```
$ sort -M file3
Jan
Feb
Mar
Apr
May
Jun
Jul
Aug
Sep
Oct
Nov
Dec
$
```

There are several other handy sort parameters to use, shown in Table 4-7.

The -k and -t parameters are handy when sorting data that uses fields, such as the /etc/passwd file. Use the -t parameter to specify the field separator character, and the -k parameter to specify which field to sort on. For example, to sort the password file based on numerical userid, just do this:

```
$ sort -t ':' -k 3 -n /etc/passwd
root:x:0:0:root:/root:/bin/bash
bin:x:1:1:bin:/bin:/sbin/nologin
daemon:x:2:2:daemon:/sbin:/sbin/nologin
adm:x:3:4:adm:/var/adm:/sbin/nologin
lp:x:4:7:lp:/var/spool/lpd:/sbin/nologin
sync:x:5:0:sync:/sbin:/bin/sync
```

```
shutdown:x:6:0:shutdown:/sbin:/sbin/shutdown
halt:x:7:0:halt:/sbin:/sbin/halt
mail:x:8:12:mail:/var/spool/mail:/sbin/nologin
news:x:9:13:news:/etc/news:
uucp:x:10:14:uucp:/var/spool/uucp:/sbin/nologin
operator:x:11:0:operator:/root:/sbin/nologin
games:x:12:100:games:/usr/games:/sbin/nologin
gopher:x:13:30:gopher:/var/gopher:/sbin/nologin
ftp:x:14:50:FTP User:/var/ftp:/sbin/nologin
```

Now the data is perfectly sorted based on the third field, which is the numerical userid value.

The -n parameter is great for sorting numerical outputs, such as the output of the du command:

```
$ du -sh * | sort -nr
1008k    mrtg-2.9.29.tar.gz
972k     bldg1
888k     fbs2.pdf
760k     Printtest
680k     rsync-2.6.6.tar.gz
660k     code
516k     fig1001.tiff
496k     test
496k     php-common-4.0.4pl1-6mdk.i586.rpm
448k     MesaGLUT-6.5.1.tar.gz
400k     plp
```

Notice that the -r option also sorts the values in descending order, so you can easily see what files are taking up the most space in your directory.

TABLE 4-7

The sort Command Parameters

Single Dash	Double Dash	Description
-b	--ignore-leading-blanks	Ignore leading blanks when sorting.
-C	--check=quiet	Don't sort, but don't report if data is out of sort order.
-c	--check	Don't sort, but check if the input data is already sorted. Report if not sorted.
-d	--dictionary-order	Consider only blanks and alphanumeric characters; don't consider special characters.
-f	--ignore-case	By default, sort orders capitalized letters first. This parameter ignores case.
-g	--general-numeric-sort	Use general numerical value to sort.

continued

TABLE 4-7	*(continued)*	
Single Dash	**Double Dash**	**Description**
-i	--ignore-nonprinting	Ignore nonprintable characters in the sort.
-k	--key=POS1[,POS2]	Sort based on position POS1, and end at POS2 if specified.
-M	--month-sort	Sort by month order using three-character month names.
-m	--merge	Merge two already sorted data files.
-n	--numeric-sort	Sort by string numerical value.
-o	-output=file	Write results to file specified.
-R	--random-sort	Sort by a random hash of keys.
	--random-source=FILE	Specify the file for random bytes used by the -R parameter.
-r	--reverse	Reverse the sort order (descending instead of ascending.
-S	--buffer-size=SIZE	Specify the amount of memory to use.
-s	--stable	Disable last-resort comparison.
-T	--temporary-direction=DIR	Specify a location to store temporary working files.
-t	--field-separator=SEP	Specify the character used to distinguish key positions.
-u	--unique	With the -c parameter, check for strict ordering; without the -c parameter, output only the first occurrence of two similar lines.
-z	--zero-terminated	End all lines with a NULL character instead of a newline.

Searching for data

Often in a large file you have to look for a specific line of data buried somewhere in the middle of the file. Instead of manually scrolling through the entire file, you can let the grep command search for you. The command line format for the grep command is:

```
grep [options] pattern [file]
```

The grep command searches either the input or the file you specify for lines that contain characters that match the specified pattern. The output from grep is the lines that contain the matching pattern.

Here are two simple examples of using the grep command with the file1 file used in the Sorting data section:

```
$ grep three file1
three
$ grep t file1
two
three
$
```

The first example searches the file `file1` for text matching the pattern `three`. The `grep` command produces the line that contains the matching pattern. The next example searches the file `file1` for the text matching the pattern *t*. In this case, there were two lines that matched the specified pattern, and both are displayed.

Because of the popularity of the `grep` command, it has undergone lots of development changes over its lifetime. There are lots of features that have been added to the `grep` command. If you look over the `man` pages for the `grep` command, you'll see how versatile it really is.

If you want to reverse the search (output lines that don't match the pattern) use the `-v` parameter:

```
$ grep -v t file1
one
four
five
$
```

If you need to find the line numbers where the matching patterns are found, use the `-n` parameter:

```
$ grep -n t file1
2:two
3:three
$
```

If you just need to see a count of how many lines contain the matching pattern, use the `-c` parameter:

```
$ grep -c t file1
2
$
```

If you need to specify more than one matching pattern, use the `-e` parameter to specify each individual pattern:

```
$ grep -e t -e f file1
two
three
four
five
$
```

This example outputs lines that contain either the string `t` or the string `f`.

By default, the grep command uses basic Unix-style regular expressions to match patterns. A Unix-style regular expression uses special characters to define how to look for matching patterns.

CROSS-REF For a more detailed explanation of regular expressions, see Chapter 17.

Here's a simple example of using a regular expression in a grep search:

```
$ grep [tf] file1
two
three
four
five
$
```

The square brackets in the regular expression indicate that grep should look for matches that contain either a t or an f character. Without the regular expression, grep would search for text that would match the string tf.

The egrep command is an offshoot of grep, which allows you to specify POSIX extended regular expressions, which contain more characters for specifying the matching pattern (again, see Chapter 17 for more details). The fgrep command is another version that allows you to specify matching patterns as a list of fixed-string values, separated by newline characters. This allows you to place a list of strings in a file, then use that list in the fgrep command to search for the strings in a larger file.

Compressing data

If you've done any work in the Microsoft Windows world, no doubt you've used zip files. It became such a popular feature that Microsoft eventually incorporated it into the Windows XP operating system. The zip utility allows you to easily compress large files (both text and executable) into smaller files that take up less space.

Linux contains several file compression utilities. While this may sound great, it often leads to confusion and chaos when trying to download files. Table 4-8 lists the file compression utilities available for Linux.

The compress file compression utility is not often found on Linux systems. If you download a file with a .Z extension, you can usually install the compress package (called ncompress in many Linux distributions) and then uncompress the file with the uncompress command.

The bzip2 utility

The bzip2 utility is a relatively new compression package that is gaining popularity, especially when compressing large binary files. The utilities in the bzip2 package are:

- bzip2 for compressing files
- bzcat for displaying the contents of compressed text files
- bunzip2 for uncompressing compressed .bz2 files
- bzip2recover for attempting to recover damaged compressed files

TABLE 4-8

Linux File Compression Utilities

Utility	File extension	Description
bzip2	.bz2	Uses the Burrows-Wheeler block sorting text compression algorithm and Huffman coding
compress	.Z	Original Unix file compression utility; starting to fade away into obscurity
gzip	.gz	The GNU Project's compression utility; uses Lempel-Ziv coding
zip	.zip	The Unix version of the PKZIP program for Windows

By default, the bzip2 command attempts to compress the original file, and replaces it with the compressed file, using the same filename with a .bz2 extension:

```
$ ls -l myprog
-rwxrwxr-x 1 rich rich 4882 2007-09-13 11:29 myprog
$ bzip2 myprog
$ ls -l my*
-rwxrwxr-x 1 rich rich 2378 2007-09-13 11:29 myprog.bz2
$
```

The original size of the myprog program was 4882 bytes, and after the bzip2 compression it is now 2378 bytes. Also, notice that the bzip2 command automatically renamed the original file with the .bz2 extension, indicating what compression technique we used to compress it.

To uncompress the file, just use the bunzip2 command:

```
$ bunzip2 myprog.bz2
$ ls -l myprog
-rwxrwxr-x 1 rich rich 4882 2007-09-13 11:29 myprog
$
```

As you can see, the uncompressed file is back to the original file size. Once you compress a text file, you can't use the standard cat, more, or less commands to view the data. Instead, you need to use the bzcat command:

```
$ bzcat test.bz2
This is a test text file.
The quick brown fox jumps over the lazy dog.
This is the end of the test text file.
$
```

The bzcat command displays the text inside the compressed file, without uncompressing the actual file.

The gzip utility

By far the most popular file compression utility in Linux is the gzip utility. The gzip package is a creation of the GNU Project, in their attempt to create a free version of the original Unix compress utility. This package includes the files:

- gzip for compressing files
- gzcat for displaying the contents of compressed text files
- gunzip for uncompressing files

These utilities work the same way as the bzip2 utilities:

```
$ gzip myprog
$ ls -l my*
-rwxrwxr-x 1 rich rich 2197 2007-09-13 11:29 myprog.gz
$
```

The gzip command compresses the file you specify on the command line. You can also specify more than one filename or even use wildcard characters to compress multiple files at once:

```
$ gzip my*
$ ls -l my*
-rwxr--r--    1 rich     rich          103 Sep  6 13:43 myprog.c.gz
-rwxr-xr-x    1 rich     rich         5178 Sep  6 13:43 myprog.gz
-rwxr--r--    1 rich     rich           59 Sep  6 13:46 myscript.gz
-rwxr--r--    1 rich     rich           60 Sep  6 13:44 myscript~.gz
$
```

The gzip command compresses every file in the directory that matches the wildcard pattern.

The zip utility

The zip utility is compatible with the popular PKZIP package created by Phil Katz for MS-DOS and Windows. There are four utilities in the Linux zip package:

- zip creates a compressed file containing listed files and directories.
- zipcloak creates an encrypted compress file containing listed files and directories.
- zipnote extracts the comments from a zip file.
- zipsplit splits a zip file into smaller files of a set size (used for copying large zip files to floppy disks).
- unzip extracts files and directories from a compressed zip file.

To see all of the options available for the zip utility, just enter it by itself on the command line:

```
$ zip
Copyright (C) 1990-2005 Info-ZIP
Type 'zip "-L"' for software license.
Zip 2.31 (March 8th 2005). Usage:
```

```
zip [-options] [-b path] [-t mmddyyyy] [-n suffixes] [zipfile list]
[-xi list]
    The default action is to add or replace zipfile entries from list,
which can include the special name - to compress standard input.
  If zipfile and list are omitted, zip compresses stdin to stdout.
-f freshen: only changed files  -u update: only changed or new files
-d delete entries in zipfile    -m move into zipfile (delete files)
-r recurse into directories     -j junk directory names
-0 store only                   -l convert LF to CR LF
-1 compress faster              -9 compress better
-q quiet operation              -v verbose operation
-c add one-line comments        -z add zipfile comment
-@ read names from stdin        -o make file as old as latest entry
-x exclude the following names  -i include only the following names
-F fix zipfile (-FF try harder) -D do not add directory entries
-A adjust self-extracting exe   -J junk zipfile prefix (unzipsfx)
-T test zipfile integrity       -X eXclude eXtra file attributes
-y store symbolic links as the link instead of the referenced file
-R PKZIP recursion (see manual)
-e encrypt                      -n don't compress these suffixes
$
```

The power of the zip utility is its ability to compress entire directories of files into a single compressed file. This makes it ideal for archiving entire directory structures:

```
$ zip -r testzip test
  adding: test/ (stored 0%)
  adding: test/test1/ (stored 0%)
  adding: test/test1/myprog2 (stored 0%)
  adding: test/test1/myprog1 (stored 0%)
  adding: test/myprog.c (deflated 39%)
  adding: test/file3 (deflated 2%)
  adding: test/file4 (stored 0%)
  adding: test/test2/ (stored 0%)
  adding: test/file1.gz (stored 0%)
  adding: test/file2 (deflated 4%)
  adding: test/myprog.gz (stored 0%)
$
```

This example creates the zip file named testzip.zip, and recurses through the directory test, adding each file and directory found to the zip file. Notice from the output that not all of the files stored in the zip file could be compressed. The zip utility automatically determines the best compression type to use for each individual file.

CAUTION When you use the recursion feature in the zip command, files are stored in the same directory structure in the zip file. Files contained in subdirectories are stored in the zip file within the same subdirectories. You must be careful when extracting the files, the unzip command will rebuild the entire directory structure in the new location. Sometimes this gets confusing when you have lots of subdirectories and files.

Archiving data

While the `zip` command works great for compressing and archiving data into a single file, it's not the standard utility used in the Unix and Linux worlds. By far the most popular archiving tool used in Unix and Linux is the `tar` command.

The `tar` command was originally used to write files to a tape device for archiving. However, it can also write the output to a file, which has become a popular way to archive data in Linux.

The format of the `tar` command is:

```
tar function [options] object1 object2 ...
```

The `function` parameter defines what the `tar` command should do, as shown in Table 4-9.

Each function uses *options* to define a specific behavior for the `tar` archive file. Table 4-10 lists the common options that you can use with the `tar` command.

These options are usually combined to create the following scenarios:

```
tar -cvf test.tar test/ test2/
```

TABLE 4-9

The tar Command Functions

Function	Long name	Description
-A	--concatenate	Append an existing tar archive file to another existing tar archive file.
-c	--create	Create a new tar archive file.
-d	--diff	Check the differences between a tar archive file and the filesystem.
	--delete	Delete from an existing tar archive file.
-r	--append	Append files to the end of an existing tar archive file.
-t	--list	List the contents of an existing tar archive file.
-u	--update	Append files to an existing tar archive file that are newer than a file with the same name in the existing archive.
-x	--extract	Extract files from an existing archive file.

TABLE 4-10

The tar Command Options

Option	Description
-C dir	Change to the specified directory.
-f file	Output results to file (or device) *file*.
-j	Redirect output to the bzip2 command for compression.
-p	Preserve all file permissions.
-v	List files as they are processed.
-z	Redirect the output to the gzip command for compression.

This creates an archive file called test.tar containing the contents of both the test directory and the test2 directory.

    tar -tf test.tar

This lists (but doesn't extract) the contents of the tar file: test.tar.

    tar -xvf test.tar

This extracts the contents of the tar file test.tar. If the tar file was created from a directory structure, the entire directory structure is recreated starting at the current directory.

As you can see, using the tar command is a simple way to create archive files of entire directory structures. This is a common method for distributing source code files for open source applications in the Linux world.

> **TIP** If you download open source software, often you'll see filenames that end in .tgz. These are gzipped tar files, and can be extracted using the command tar -zxvf filename.tgz.

Summary

This chapter discussed some of the more advanced bash commands used by Linux system administrators and programmers. The ps and top commands are vital in determining the status of the system, allowing you to see what applications are running and how many resources they are consuming.

In this day of removable media, another popular topic for system administrators is mounting storage devices. The `mount` command allows you to mount a physical storage device into the Linux virtual directory structure. To remove the device, use the `umount` command.

Finally, the chapter discussed various utilities used for handling data. The `sort` utility easily sorts large data files to help you organize data, and the `grep` utility allows you to quickly scan through large data files looking for specific information. There are a few different file compression utilities available in Linux, including `bzip2`, `gzip`, and `zip`. Each one allows you to compress large files to help save space on your filesystem. The Linux `tar` utility is a popular way to archive directory structures into a single file that can easily be ported to another system.

The next chapter discusses Linux environment variables. Environment variables allow you to access information about the system from your scripts, as well as provide a convenient way to store data within your scripts.

Chapter 5

Using Linux Environment Variables

IN THIS CHAPTER

Using environment variables

Setting your own environment variables

Advanced variable techniques

Using aliases

Linux environment variables help define your Linux shell experience. However, they can be a confusing topic for new Linux users. Many programs and scripts use environment variables to obtain system information and store temporary data and configuration information. There are lots of places where environment variables are set on the Linux system, and it's important to know where these places are. This chapter walks you through the world of Linux environment variables, showing where they are, how to use them, and even how to create your own. The chapter finishes off with a related topic, defining and using aliases in your shell session.

What Are Environment Variables?

The bash shell uses a feature called *environment variables* to store information about the shell session and the working environment (thus the name environment variables). This feature also allows you to store data in memory that can be easily accessed by any program or script running from the shell. This is a handy way to store persistent data that identifies features of the user account, system, shell, or anything else you need to store.

There are two types of environment variables in the bash shell:

- Global variables
- Local variables

This section describes each type of environment variables, and shows how to see and use them.

> **NOTE**   Even though the bash shell uses specific environment variables that are consistent, different Linux distributions often add their own environment variables. The environment variable examples you see in this chapter may differ slightly from what's available in your specific distribution. If you run into an environment variable not covered here, check the documentation for your Linux distribution.

Global environment variables

Global environment variables are visible from the shell session, and any child processes that the shell spawns. Local variables are only available in the shell that creates them. This makes global environment variables useful in applications that spawn child processes that require information from the parent process.

The Linux system sets several global environment variables when you start your bash session (for more details about what variables are started at that time, see the "Locating System Environment Variables" section later in this chapter). The system environment variables always use all capital letters to differentiate them from normal user environment variables.

To view the global environment variables, use the `printenv` command:

```
$ printenv
HOSTNAME=testbox.localdomain
TERM=xterm
SHELL=/bin/bash
HISTSIZE=1000
SSH_CLIENT=192.168.1.2 1358 22
OLDPWD=/home/rich/test/test1
SSH_TTY=/dev/pts/0
USER=rich
LS_COLORS=no=00:fi=00:di=00;34:ln=00;36:pi=40;33:so=00;35:
bd=40;33;01:cd=40;33;01:or=01;05;37;41:mi=01;05;37;41:ex=00;32:
*.cmd=00;32:*.exe=00;32:*.com=00;32:*.btm=00;32:*.bat=00;32:
*.sh=00;32:*.csh=00;32:*.tar=00;31:*.tgz=00;31:*.arj=00;31:
*.taz=00;31:*.lzh=00;31:*.zip=00;31:*.z=00;31:*.Z=00;31:
*.gz=00;31:*.bz2=00;31:*.bz=00;31:*.tz=00;31:*.rpm=00;31:
*.cpio=00;31:*.jpg=00;35:*.gif=00;35:*.bmp=00;35:*.xbm=00;35:
*.xpm=00;35:*.png=00;35:*.tif=00;35:
MAIL=/var/spool/mail/rich
PATH=/usr/kerberos/bin:/usr/lib/ccache:/usr/local/bin:/bin:/usr/bin:
/home/rich/bin
INPUTRC=/etc/inputrc
PWD=/home/rich
LANG=en_US.UTF-8
SSH_ASKPASS=/usr/libexec/openssh/gnome-ssh-askpass
SHLVL=1
HOME=/home/rich
LOGNAME=rich
CVS_RSH=ssh
```

```
SSH_CONNECTION=192.168.1.2 1358 192.168.1.4 22
LESSOPEN=|/usr/bin/lesspipe.sh %s
G_BROKEN_FILENAMES=1
_=/usr/bin/printenv
$
```

As you can see, there are lots of global environment variables that get set for the bash shell. Most of them are set by the system during the login process.

To display the value of an individual environment variable, use the `echo` command. When referencing an environment variable, you must place a dollar sign before the environment variable name:

```
$ echo $HOME
/home/rich
$
```

As I mentioned, global environment variables are also available to child processes running under the current shell session:

```
$ bash
$ echo $HOME
/home/rich
$
```

In this example, after starting a new shell using the `bash` command, I displayed the current value of the HOME environment variable, which the system sets when I log into the main shell. Sure enough, the value is also available from the child shell process.

Local environment variables

Local environment variables, as their name implies, can be seen only in the local process in which they are defined. Don't get confused though about local environment variables, they are just as important as global environment variables. In fact, the Linux system also defines standard local environment variables for you by default.

Trying to see the list of local environment variables is a little tricky. Unfortunately there isn't a command that displays only local environment variables. The `set` command displays all of the environment variables set for a specific process. However, this also includes the global environment variables.

Here's the output from a sample `set` command:

```
$ set
BASH=/bin/bash
BASH_ARGC=()
BASH_ARGV=()
BASH_LINENO=()
BASH_SOURCE=()
```

```
BASH_VERSINFO=([0]="3" [1]="2" [2]="9" [3]="1" [4]="release"
[5]="i686-redhat-linux-gnu")
BASH_VERSION='3.2.9(1)-release'
COLORS=/etc/DIR_COLORS.xterm
COLUMNS=80
CVS_RSH=ssh
DIRSTACK=()
EUID=500
GROUPS=()
G_BROKEN_FILENAMES=1
HISTFILE=/home/rich/.bash_history
HISTFILESIZE=1000
HISTSIZE=1000
HOME=/home/rich
HOSTNAME=testbox.localdomain
HOSTTYPE=i686
IFS=$' \t\n'
INPUTRC=/etc/inputrc
LANG=en_US.UTF-8
LESSOPEN='|/usr/bin/lesspipe.sh %s'
LINES=24
LOGNAME=rich
LS_COLORS='no=00:fi=00:di=00;34:ln=00;36:pi=40;33:so=00;35:bd=40;33;
01:cd=40;33;01:or=01;05;37;41:mi=01;05;37;41:ex=00;32:*.cmd=00;32:
*.exe=00;32:*.com=00;32:*.btm=00;32:*.bat=00;32:*.sh=00;32:
*.csh=00;32:*.tar=00;31:*.tgz=00;31:*.arj=00;31:*.taz=00;31:
*.lzh=00;31:*.zip=00;31:*.z=00;31:*.Z=00;31:*.gz=00;31:*.bz2=00;31:
*.bz=00;31:*.tz=00;31:*.rpm=00;31:*.cpio=00;31:*.jpg=00;35:
*.gif=00;35:*.bmp=00;35:*.xbm=00;35:*.xpm=00;35:*.png=00;35:
*.tif=00;35:'
MACHTYPE=i686-redhat-linux-gnu
MAIL=/var/spool/mail/rich
MAILCHECK=60
OPTERR=1
OPTIND=1
OSTYPE=linux-gnu
PATH=/usr/kerberos/bin:/usr/lib/ccache:/usr/local/bin:/bin:/usr/bin:
/home/rich/bin
PIPESTATUS=([0]="0")
PPID=3702
PROMPT_COMMAND='echo -ne
"\033]0;${USER}@${HOSTNAME%%.*}:${PWD/#$HOME/~}"; echo -ne "\007"'
PS1='[\u@\h \W]\$ '
PS2='> '
PS4='+ '
PWD=/home/rich
SHELL=/bin/bash
SHELLOPTS=braceexpand:emacs:hashall:histexpand:history:
```

```
interactive-comments:monitor
SHLVL=2
SSH_ASKPASS=/usr/libexec/openssh/gnome-ssh-askpass
SSH_CLIENT='192.168.1.2 1358 22'
SSH_CONNECTION='192.168.1.2 1358 192.168.1.4 22'
SSH_TTY=/dev/pts/0
TERM=xterm
UID=500
USER=rich
_=-H
consoletype=pty
$
```

You'll notice that all of the global environment variables seen from the `printenv` command appear in the output from the `set` command. However, there are quite a few additional environment variables that now appear. These are the local environment variables.

Setting Environment Variables

You can set your own environment variables directly from the bash shell. This section shows how to create your own environment variables and reference them from your interactive shell or shell script program.

Setting local environment variables

Once you start a bash shell (or spawn a shell script), you're allowed to create local variables that are visible within your shell process. You can assign either a numeric or a string value to an environment variable by assigning the variable to a value using the equal sign:

```
$ test=testing
$ echo $test
testing
$
```

That was simple! Now any time you need to reference the value of the test environment variable, just reference it by the name $test.

If you need to assign a string value that contains spaces, you'll need to use a single quotation mark to delineate the beginning and the end of the string:

```
$ test=testing a long string
-bash: a: command not found
$ test='testing a long string'
$ echo $test
testing a long string
$
```

Without the single quotation marks, the bash shell assumes that the next character is another command to process. Notice that for the local environment variable I defined, I used lower-case letters, while the system environment variables we've seen so far have all used upper-case letters.

This is a standard convention in the bash shell. If you create new environment variables, it is recommended (but not required) that you use lower-case letters. This helps distinguish your personal environment variables from the scores of system environment variables.

CAUTION   It's extremely important that there are no spaces between the environment variable name, the equal sign, and the value. If you put any spaces in the assignment, the bash shell interprets the value as a separate command:

```
$ test2 = test
-bash: test2: command not found
$
```

Once you set a local environment variable, it's available for use anywhere within your shell process. However, if you spawn another shell, it's not available in the child shell:

```
$ bash
$ echo $test

$ exit
exit
$ echo $test
testing a long string
$
```

In this example I started a child shell. As you can see, the test environment variable is not available in the child shell (it contains a blank value). After I exited the child shell and returned to the original shell, the local environment variable was still available.

Similarly, if you set a local environment variable in a child process, once you leave the child process the local environment variable is no longer available:

```
$ bash
$ test=testing
$ echo $test
testing
$ exit
exit
$ echo $test

$
```

The test environment variable set in the child shell doesn't exist when I go back to the parent shell.

Setting global environment variables

Global environment variables are visible from any child processes created by the process that sets the global environment variable. The method used to create a global environment variable is to create a local environment variable, then export it to the global environment.

This is done by using the `export` command:

```
$ echo $test
testing a long string
$ export test
$ bash
$ echo $test
testing a long string
$
```

After exporting the local environment variable `test`, I started a new shell process and viewed the value of the `test` environment variable. This time, the environment variable kept its value, as the `export` command made it global.

CAUTION **Notice that when exporting a local environment variable, you don't use the dollar sign to reference the variable's name.**

Removing Environment Variables

Of course, if you can create a new environment variable, it makes sense that you can also remove an existing environment variable. This is done by using the `unset` command:

```
$ echo $test
testing
$ unset test
$ echo $test

$
```

When referencing the environment variable in the `unset` command, remember not to use the dollar sign.

When dealing with global environment variables, things get a little tricky. If you're in a child process and unset a global environment variable, it only applies to the child process. The global environment variable is still available in the parent process:

```
$ test=testing
$ export test
$ bash
$ echo $test
testing
$ unset test
```

```
$ echo $test

$ exit
exit
$ echo $test
testing
$
```

In this example I set a local environment variable called `test`, then exported it to make it a global environment variable. I then started a child shell process and checked to make sure that the global environment variable `test` was still available. Next, while still in the child shell, I used the `unset` command to remove the global environment variable `test`, then exited the child shell. Now back in the original parent shell, I checked the `test` environment variable value, and it is still valid.

Default Shell Environment Variables

There are specific environment variables that the bash shell uses by default to define the system environment. You can always count on these variables being set on your Linux system. Since the bash shell is a derivative of the original Unix Bourne shell, it also includes environment variables originally defined in that shell.

Table 5-1 shows the environment variables the bash shell provides that are compatible with the original Unix Bourne shell.

By far the most important environment variable in this list is the `PATH` environment variable. When you enter a command in the shell command line interface (CLI), the shell must search the system to find the program. The `PATH` environment variable defines the directories it searches looking for commands. On my Linux system, the `PATH` environment variable looks like this:

```
$ echo $PATH
/usr/kerberos/bin:/usr/lib/ccache:/usr/local/bin:/bin:/usr/bin:
/home/rich/bin
$
```

This shows that there are six directories where the shell looks for commands. Each directory in the `PATH` is separated by a colon. There's nothing at the end of the `PATH` variable indicating the end of the directory listing. You can add additional directories to the `PATH` simply by adding another colon, and adding the new directory. The `PATH` also shows the order in which it looks for commands.

Besides the default Bourne environment variables, the bash shell also provides a few variables of its own, shown in Table 5-2.

TABLE 5-1

The bash Shell Bourne Variables

Variable	Description
CDPATH	A colon-separated list of directories used as a search path for the cd command.
HOME	The current user's home directory.
IFS	A list of characters that separate fields used by the shell to split text strings.
MAIL	The filename for the current user's mailbox. The bash shell checks this file for new mail.
MAILPATH	A colon-separated list of multiple filenames for the current user's mailbox. The bash shell checks each file in this list for new mail.
OPTARG	The value of the last option argument processed by the getopts command.
OPTIND	The index value of the last option argument processed by the getopts command.
PATH	A colon-separated list of directories where the shell looks for commands.
PS1	The primary shell command line interface prompt string.
PS2	The secondary shell command line interface prompt string.

TABLE 5-2

The bash Shell Environment Variables

Variable	Description
BASH	The full pathname to execute the current instance of the bash shell.
BASH_ENV	When set, each bash script attempts to execute a startup file defined by this variable before running.
BASH_VERSION	The version number of the current instance of the bash shell.
BASH_VERSINFO	A variable array that contains the individual major and minor version numbers of the current instance of the bash shell.
COLUMNS	Contains the terminal width of the terminal used for the current instance of the bash shell.
COMP_CWORD	An index into the variable COMP_WORDS, which contains the current cursor position.
COMP_LINE	The current command line.

continued

TABLE 5-2	*(continued)*
Variable	**Description**
COMP_POINT	The index of the current cursor position relative to the beginning of the current command.
COMP_WORDS	A variable array that contains the individual words on the current command line.
COMPREPLY	A variable array that contains the possible completion codes generated by a shell function.
DIRSTACK	A variable array that contains the current contents of the directory stack.
EUID	The numeric effective user ID of the current user.
FCEDIT	The default editor used by the fc command.
FIGNORE	A colon-separated list of suffixes to ignore when performing filename completion.
FUNCNAME	The name of the currently executing shell function.
GLOBIGNORE	A colon-separated list of patterns defining the set of filenames to be ignored by filename expansion.
GROUPS	A variable array containing the list of groups of which the current user is a member.
histchars	Up to three characters which control history expansion.
HISTCMD	The history number of the current command.
HISTCONTROL	Controls what commands are entered in the shell history list.
HISTFILE	The name of the file to save the shell history list (.bash_history by default).
HISTFILESIZE	The maximum number of lines to save in the history file.
HISTIGNORE	A colon-separated list of patterns used to decide which commands are ignored for the history file.
HISTSIZE	The maximum number of commands stored in the history file.
HOSTFILE	Contains the name of the file that should be read when the shell needs to complete a hostname.
HOSTNAME	The name of the current host.
HOSTTYPE	A string describing the machine the bash shell is running on.
IGNOREEOF	The number of consecutive EOF characters the shell must receive before exiting. If this value doesn't exist, the default is one.

TABLE 5-2	(continued)
Variable	**Description**
INPUTRC	The name of the Readline initialization file (the default is .inputrc).
LANG	The locale category for the shell.
LC_ALL	Overrides the LANG variable, defining a locale category.
LC_COLLATE	Sets the collation order used when sorting string values.
LC_CTYPE	Determines the interpretation of characters used in filename expansion and pattern matching.
LC_MESSAGES	Determines the locale setting used when interpreting double-quoted strings preceded by a dollar sign.
LC_NUMERIC	Determines the locale setting used when formatting numbers.
LINENO	The line number in a script currently executing.
LINES	Defines the number of lines available on the terminal.
MACHTYPE	A string defining the system type in *cpu-company-system* format
MAILCHECK	How often (in seconds) the shell should check for new mail (default is 60).
OLDPWD	The previous working directory used in the shell.
OPTERR	If set to 1, the bash shell displays errors generated by the getopts command.
OSTYPE	A string defining the operating system the shell is running on.
PIPESTATUS	A variable array containing a list of exit status values from the processes in the foreground process.
POSIXLY_CORRECT	If set, bash starts in POSIX mode.
PPID	The process ID (PID) of the bash shell's parent process.
PROMPT_COMMAND	If set, the command to execute before displaying the primary prompt.
PS3	The prompt to use for the select command.
PS4	The prompt displayed before the command line is echoed if the bash -x parameter is used.
PWD	The current working directory.
RANDOM	Returns a random number between 0 and 32767. Assigning a value to this variable seeds the random number generator.
REPLY	The default variable for the read command.

continued

TABLE 5-2	(continued)
Variable	**Description**
SECONDS	The number of seconds since the shell was started. Assigning a value resets the timer to the value.
SHELLOPTS	A colon-separated list of enabled bash shell options.
SHLVL	Indicates the shell level, incremented by one each time a new bash shell is started.
TIMEFORMAT	A format specifying how the shell displays time values.
TMOUT	The value of how long (in seconds) the select and read commands should wait for input. The default of zero indicates to wait indefinitely.
UID	The numeric real user id of the current user.

You may notice that not all of the default environment variables are shown when I used the set command. The reason for this is that although these are the default environment variables, not all of them are required to contain a value.

Setting the PATH Environment Variable

The PATH environment variable seems to cause the most problem on Linux systems. It defines where the shell looks for commands you enter on the command line. If it can't find the command, it produces an error message:

```
$ myprog
-bash: myprog: command not found
$
```

The problem is that often applications place their executable programs in directories that aren't in the PATH environment variable. The trick is ensuring that your PATH environment variable includes all of the directories where your applications reside.

You can add new search directories to the existing PATH environment variable without having to rebuild it from scratch. The individual directories listed in the PATH are separated by a colon. All you need to do is reference the original PATH value, and add any new directories to the string. This looks something like this:

```
$ echo $PATH
/usr/kerberos/bin:/usr/lib/ccache:/usr/local/bin:/bin:/usr/bin:/home
/rich/bin
$ PATH=$PATH:/home/rich/test
```

```
$ echo $PATH
/usr/kerberos/bin:/usr/lib/ccache:/usr/local/bin:/bin:/usr/bin:/home
/rich/bin:/home/rich/test
$ myprog
The factorial of 5 is 120.
$
```

By adding the directory to the PATH environment variable, you can now execute your program from anywhere in the virtual directory structure:

```
[rich@testbox ~]$ cd /etc
[rich@testbox etc]$ myprog
The factorial of 5 is 120
[rich@testbox etc]$
```

A common trick for programmers is to include the single dot symbol in their PATH environment variable. The single dot symbol represents the current directory (see Chapter 3):

```
[rich@testbox ~]$ PATH=$PATH:.
[rich@testbox ~]$ cd test2
[rich@testbox test2]$ myprog2
The factorial of 6 is 720
[rich@testbox test2]$
```

In the next section you'll see how you can make changes to environment variables permanent on your system, so you can always execute your programs.

Locating System Environment Variables

The Linux system uses environment variables to identify itself in programs and scripts. This provides a convenient way to obtain system information for your programs. The trick is in how these environment variables are set.

When you start a bash shell by logging in to the Linux system, by default bash checks several files for commands. These files are called *startup files*. The startup files bash processes depend on the method you use to start the bash shell. There are three ways of starting a bash shell:

- As a default login shell at login time
- As an interactive shell that is not the login shell
- As a non-interactive shell to run a script

The following sections describe the startup files the bash shell executes in each of these startup methods.

Login shell

When you log in to the Linux system, the bash shell starts as a login shell. The login shell looks for four different startup files to process commands from. The order in which the bash shell processes the files is:

- `/etc/profile`
- `$HOME/.bash_profile`
- `$HOME/.bash_login`
- `$HOME/.profile`

The `/etc/profile` file is the main default startup file for the bash shell on the system. Every user on the system executes this startup file when they log in. The other three startup files are specific for each user and can be customized for each user's requirements. Let's take a closer look at these files.

The /etc/profile file

The `/etc/profile` file is the main default startup file for the bash shell. Whenever you log in to the Linux system, bash executes the commands in the `/etc/profile` startup file. Different Linux distributions place different commands in this file. On my Linux system, it looks like this:

```
$ cat /etc/profile
# /etc/profile

# System wide environment and startup programs, for login setup
# Functions and aliases go in /etc/bashrc

pathmunge () {
        if ! echo $PATH | /bin/egrep -q "(^|:)$1($|:)" ; then
           if [ "$2" = "after" ] ; then
              PATH=$PATH:$1
           else
              PATH=$1:$PATH
           fi
        fi
}

# ksh workaround
if [ -z "$EUID" -a -x /usr/bin/id ]; then
        EUID=`id -u`
        UID=`id -ru`
fi

# Path manipulation
```

```
if [ "$EUID" = "0" ]; then
        pathmunge /sbin
        pathmunge /usr/sbin
        pathmunge /usr/local/sbin
fi

# No core files by default
ulimit -S -c 0 > /dev/null 2>&1

if [ -x /usr/bin/id ]; then
        USER="`id -un`"
        LOGNAME=$USER
        MAIL="/var/spool/mail/$USER"
fi

HOSTNAME=`/bin/hostname`
HISTSIZE=1000

if [ -z "$INPUTRC" -a ! -f "$HOME/.inputrc" ]; then
    INPUTRC=/etc/inputrc
fi

export PATH USER LOGNAME MAIL HOSTNAME HISTSIZE INPUTRC

for i in /etc/profile.d/*.sh ; do
    if [ -r "$i" ]; then
        . $i
    fi
done

unset i
unset pathmunge
$
```

Most of the commands and scripts you see in this file are covered in more detail later on in Chapter 8. The important thing to notice now is the environment variables that are set in this startup file. Notice the export line near the bottom of the file:

```
export PATH USER LOGNAME MAIL HOSTNAME HISTSIZE INPUTRC
```

This ensures that these environment variables are available to all child processes spawned from the login shell.

There's also another tricky feature that the profile file uses. There's a for statement that iterates through any files located in the /etc/profile.d directory. (for statements are discussed in detail in Chapter 10.) This provides a place for the Linux system to place application-specific startup files that will be executed by the shell when you log in. On my Linux system, I have the following files in the `profile.d` directory:

```
$ ls -l /etc/profile.d
total 168
-rw-r--r-- 1 root root   88 2007-03-15 10:08 ccache.csh
-rw-r--r-- 1 root root   87 2007-03-15 10:08 ccache.sh
-rw-r--r-- 1 root root  764 2007-02-26 08:04 colorls.csh
-rw-r--r-- 1 root root  713 2007-02-26 08:04 colorls.sh
-rw-r--r-- 1 root root   80 2007-07-11 09:00 cvs.csh
-rw-r--r-- 1 root root   78 2007-07-11 09:00 cvs.sh
-rw-r--r-- 1 root root  192 2004-09-09 01:17 glib2.csh
-rw-r--r-- 1 root root  192 2005-12-12 00:58 glib2.sh
-rw-r--r-- 1 root root   58 2007-03-20 05:17 gnome-ssh-askpass.csh
-rw-r--r-- 1 root root   70 2007-03-20 05:17 gnome-ssh-askpass.sh
-rw-r--r-- 1 root root  218 2004-09-09 03:12 krb5-devel.csh
-rw-r--r-- 1 root root  229 2006-01-19 13:05 krb5-devel.sh
-rw-r--r-- 1 root root  218 2004-09-09 03:12 krb5-workstation.csh
-rw-r--r-- 1 root root  229 2006-01-19 13:05 krb5-workstation.sh
-rwxr-xr-x 1 root root 3006 2007-06-25 12:57 lang.csh
-rwxr-xr-x 1 root root 3329 2007-06-25 12:57 lang.sh
-rw-r--r-- 1 root root  122 2007-02-07 07:55 less.csh
-rw-r--r-- 1 root root  108 2007-02-07 07:55 less.sh
-rw-r--r-- 1 root root   74 2007-06-27 05:11 vim.csh
-rw-r--r-- 1 root root  248 2007-06-27 05:11 vim.sh
-rwxr-xr-x 1 root root  170 2007-01-22 05:48 which-2.sh
$
```

You'll notice that these are mostly related to specific applications on the system. Most applications create two startup files, one for the bash shell (using the `.sh` extension) and one for the csh (using the `.csh` extension). We'll be talking about the differences between these two shells later on in Chapter 21.

The `lang.csh` and `lang.sh` files attempt to determine the default language character set used on the system, and set the LANG environment variable appropriately.

The $HOME startup files

The remaining three startup files are all used for the same function — to provide a user-specific startup file for defining user-specific environment variables. Most Linux distributions use only one of these three startup files:

- `$HOME/.bash_profile`
- `$HOME/.bash_login`
- `$HOME/.profile`

Notice that all three files start with a dot, making them hidden files (they don't appear in a normal `ls` command listing). Since they are in the user's HOME directory, each user can edit the files and add his or her own environment variables that are active for every bash shell session they start.

My Linux system contains the following `.bash_profile` file:

```
$ cat .bash_profile
# .bash_profile

# Get the aliases and functions
if [ -f ~/.bashrc ]; then
        . ~/.bashrc
fi

# User specific environment and startup programs

PATH=$PATH:$HOME/bin

export PATH
$
```

The `.bash_profile` startup file first checks to see if there's another startup file present in the HOME directory, called `.bashrc` (which we'll talk about next in the "Interactive Shell" section). If it's there, the startup file executes the commands in it. Next, the startup file adds a directory to the PATH environment variable, providing a common location to place executable files in your HOME directory.

Interactive shell

If you start a bash shell without logging into a system (such as if you just type `bash` at a CLI prompt), you start what's called an *interactive shell*. The interactive shell doesn't act like the login shell, but it still provides a CLI prompt for you to enter commands.

If bash is started as an interactive shell, it doesn't process the `/etc/profile` file. Instead, it checks for the `.bashrc` file in the user's HOME directory.

On my Linux distribution, this file looks like this:

```
[rich@testbox ~]$ cat .bashrc
# .bashrc

# Source global definitions
if [ -f /etc/bashrc ]; then
        . /etc/bashrc
fi

# User specific aliases and functions
[rich@testbox ~]$
```

The `.bashrc` file does two things. First, it checks for a common bashrc file in the `/etc` directory. Second, it provides a place for the user to enter personal aliases (discussed later in the Using Command Aliases section) and private script functions (described in Chapter 14).

The common `/etc/bashrc` startup file is run by everyone on the system who starts an interactive shell session. On my Linux distribution it looks like this:

```
$ cat /etc/bashrc
# /etc/bashrc

# System wide functions and aliases
# Environment stuff goes in /etc/profile

# By default, we want this to get set.
# Even for non-interactive, non-login shells.
if [ $UID -gt 99 ] && [ "`id -gn`" = "`id -un`" ]; then
        umask 002
else
        umask 022
fi

# are we an interactive shell?
if [ "$PS1" ]; then
    case $TERM in
        xterm*)
                if [ -e /etc/sysconfig/bash-prompt-xterm ]; then
                        PROMPT_COMMAND=/etc/sysconfig/bash-prompt-
xterm
                else
                PROMPT_COMMAND='echo -ne
"\033]0;${USER}@${HOSTNAME%%.*}:${PWD/#$HOME/~}"; echo -ne "\007"'
                fi
                ;;
        screen)
                if [ -e /etc/sysconfig/bash-prompt-screen ]; then
                        PROMPT_COMMAND=/etc/sysconfig/bash-prompt-
screen
                else
                PROMPT_COMMAND='echo -ne
"\033_${USER}@${HOSTNAME%%.*}:${PWD/#$HOME/~}"; echo -ne "\033\\"'
                fi
                ;;
        *)
                [ -e /etc/sysconfig/bash-prompt-default ] &&
PROMPT_COMMAND=/etc/sysconfig/bash-prompt-default
            ;;
    esac
    # Turn on checkwinsize
    shopt -s checkwinsize
```

```
          [ "$PS1" = "\\s-\\v\\\$ " ] && PS1="[\u@\h \W]\\$ "
fi

if ! shopt -q login_shell ; then # We're not a login shell
       # Need to redefine pathmunge, it get's undefined at the end
of /etc/profile
    pathmunge () {
              if ! echo $PATH | /bin/egrep -q "(^|:)$1($|:)" ; then
                     if [ "$2" = "after" ] ; then
                            PATH=$PATH:$1
                     else
                            PATH=$1:$PATH
                     fi
              fi
       }

       for i in /etc/profile.d/*.sh; do
              if [ -r "$i" ]; then
                     . $i
       fi
       done
       unset i
       unset pathmunge
fi
# vim:ts=4:sw=4
$
```

The default file sets a few environment variables, but notice that it doesn't use the export command to make them global. Remember, the interactive shell startup file runs each time a new interactive shell starts; thus, any child shell will automatically execute the interactive shell startup file.

You'll also notice that the /etc/bashrc file also executes the application-specific startup files located in the /etc/profile.d directory.

Non-interactive shell

Finally, the last type of shell is a non-interactive shell. This is the shell that the system starts to execute a shell script. This is different in that there isn't a CLI prompt to worry about. However, there may still be specific startup commands you want to run each time you start a script on your system.

To accommodate that situation, the bash shell provides the BASH_ENV environment variable. When the shell starts a non-interactive shell process, it checks this environment variable for the name of a startup file to execute. If one is present, the shell executes the commands in the file. On my Linux distribution, this environment value is not set by default.

Variable Arrays

A really cool feature of environment variables is that they can be used as *arrays*. An array is a variable that can hold multiple values. Values can be referenced either individually or as a whole for the entire array.

To set multiple values for an environment variable, just list them in parentheses, with each value separated by a space:

```
$ mytest=(one two three four five)
$
```

Not much excitement there. If you try to display the array as a normal environment variable, you'll be disappointed:

```
$ echo $mytest
one
$
```

Only the first value in the array appears. To reference an individual array element, you must use a numerical index value, which represents its place in the array. The numeric value is enclosed in square brackets:

```
$ echo ${mytest[2]}
three
$
```

> **CAUTION** Environment variable arrays start with an index value of zero. This often gets confusing.

To display an entire array variable, you use the asterisk wildcard character as the index value:

```
$ echo ${mytest[*]}
one two three four five
$
```

You can also change the value of an individual index position:

```
$ mytest[2]=seven
$ echo ${mytest[*]}
one two seven four five
$
```

You can even use the unset command to remove an individual value within the array, but be careful, as this gets tricky. Watch this example:

```
$ unset mytest[2]
$ echo ${mytest[*]}
```

```
one two four five
$
$ echo ${mytest[2]}

$ echo ${mytest[3]}
four
$
```

This example uses the unset command to remove the value at index value 2. When you display the array, it appears that the other index values just dropped down one. However, if you specifically display the data at index value 2, you'll see that that location is empty.

Finally, you can remove the entire array just by using the array name in the unset command:

```
$ unset mytest
$ echo ${mytest[*]}

$
```

Sometimes variable arrays just complicate matters, so they're often not used in shell script programming. They're not very portable to other shell environments, which is a downside if you do lots of shell programming for different shells. There are a couple of bash system environment variables that use arrays (such as BASH_VERSINFO), but overall you probably won't run into them very often.

Using Command Aliases

While not environment variables per se, shell command aliases behave in much the same manner. A *command alias* allows you to create an alias name for common commands (along with their parameters) to help keep your typing to a minimum.

Most likely your Linux distribution has already set some common command aliases for you. To see a list of the active aliases, use the alias command with the -p parameter:

```
$ alias -p
alias l.='ls -d .* --color=tty'
alias ll='ls -l --color=tty'
alias ls='ls --color=tty'
alias vi='vim'
alias which='alias | /usr/bin/which --tty-only --read-
alias--show-dot --show-tilde'
$
```

Notice that on my Linux distribution, they use an alias to override the standard ls command. It automatically provides the --color parameter, indicating that the terminal supports color mode listings.

You can create your own aliases by using the `alias` command:

```
[rich@testbox ~]$ alias li='ls -il'
[rich@testbox ~]$ li
total 989292
 360621 drwxrwxr-x  2 rich rich         4096 2007-08-24 22:04 4rich
 301871 drwxr-xr-x  4 rich rich     4096 2007-09-18 08:38 Desktop
 301875 drwxr-xr-x  2 rich rich         4096 2001-11-01 01:10 Documents
 301872 drwxr-xr-x  2 rich rich         4096 2001-11-01 04:06 Download
 360207 drwxrwxr-x  2 rich rich         4096 2007-07-26 18:25 Drivers
 327362 drwxrwxr-x  2 rich rich     4096 2007-09-18 08:38 mnt
 301876 drwxr-xr-x  2 rich rich         4096 2001-11-01 04:06 Music
 301942 -rw-rw-r--  1 rich rich            0 2007-09-03 16:38 myprob
 301963 -rw-rw-r--  1 rich rich            0 2007-09-03 16:40 myproblem
 301974 -rwxr--r--  1 rich rich           30 2007-08-23 21:42 myprog
 301877 drwxr-xr-x  2 rich rich         4096 2001-11-01 04:06 Pictures
 301874 drwxr-xr-x  2 rich rich         4096 2001-11-01 04:06 Public
 360262 drwxrwxr-x  5 rich rich         4096 2007-08-24 22:04 store
```

Once you define an alias value, you can use it at any time in your shell, including in shell scripts.

Command aliases act like local environment variables. They're only valid for the shell process in which they're defined:

```
$ alias li='ls -il'
$ bash
$ li
bash: li: command not found
$
```

Of course, now you know a way to solve that problem. The bash shell always reads the `$HOME/.bashrc` startup file when starting a new interactive shell. This is a great place to put command alias statements (as was pointed out in the `.bashrc` file comments).

Summary

This chapter examined the world of Linux environment variables. Global environment variables can be accessed from any child process spawned by the process they're defined in. Local environment variables can only be accessed from the process in which they're defined.

The Linux system uses both global and local environment variables to store information about the system environment. You can access this information from the shell command line interface, as well as within shell scripts. The bash shell uses the system environment variables defined in the original Unix Bourne shell, as well as lots of new environment variables. The PATH environment variable defines the search pattern the bash shell takes to find an executable command. You can modify the PATH environment variable to add your own directories, or even the current directory symbol, to make running your programs easier.

You can also create your own global and local environment variables for your own use. Once you create an environment variable, it's accessible for the entire duration of your shell session.

There are several startup files that the bash shell executes when it starts up. These startup files can contain environment variable definitions to set standard environment variables for each bash session. When you log in to the Linux system, the bash shell accesses the /etc/profile startup file, and also three local startup files for each user, $HOME/.bash_profile, $HOME/.bash_login, and $HOME/.profile. Users can customize these files to include environment variables and startup scripts for their own use.

The bash shell also provides for environment variable arrays. These environment variables can contain multiple values in a single variable. You can access the values either individually by referencing an index value or as a whole by referencing the entire environment variable array name.

Finally, the chapter discussed the use of command aliases. While not environment variables, command aliases behave similar to environment variables. They allow you to define an alias name for a command, along with its parameters. Instead of having to type in a long command and parameters, you can just assign it to a simple alias and use the alias at any time in your shell session.

The next chapter dives into the world of Linux file permissions. This is possibly the most difficult topic for novice Linux users. However, to write good shell scripts, you need to understand how file permissions work and be able to use them in your Linux system.

Chapter 6

Understanding Linux File Permissions

N
o system is complete without some form of security. There must be a mechanism available to protect files from unauthorized viewing or modification. The Linux system follows the Unix method of file permissions, allowing individual users and groups access to files based on a set of security settings for each file and directory. This chapter discusses how to use the Linux file security system to protect data when necessary and share data when desired.

Linux Security

The core of the Linux security system is the *user account*. Each individual who accesses a Linux system should have a unique user account assigned. The permissions users have to objects on the system depend on the user account they log in with.

User permissions are tracked using a *user ID* (often called a UID), which is assigned to an account when it's created. The UID is a numerical value, unique for each user. However, you don't log in to a Linux system using your UID. Instead, you use a *login name*. The login name is an alphanumeric text string of eight characters or fewer that the user uses to log in to the system (along with an associated password).

The Linux system uses special files and utilities to track and manage user accounts on the system. Before we can discuss file permissions, we need to discuss how Linux handles user accounts. This section describes the files and utilities required for user accounts so that you can understand how to use them when working with file permissions.

The /etc/passwd file

The Linux system uses a special file to match the login name to a corresponding UID value. This file is the /etc/passwd file. The /etc/passwd file contains several pieces of information about the user. Here's what the /etc/passwd file looks like on my Linux system:

```
$ cat /etc/passwd
root:x:0:0:root:/root:/bin/bash
bin:x:1:1:bin:/bin:/sbin/nologin
daemon:x:2:2:daemon:/sbin:/sbin/nologin
adm:x:3:4:adm:/var/adm:/sbin/nologin
lp:x:4:7:lp:/var/spool/lpd:/sbin/nologin
sync:x:5:0:sync:/sbin:/bin/sync
shutdown:x:6:0:shutdown:/sbin:/sbin/shutdown
halt:x:7:0:halt:/sbin:/sbin/halt
mail:x:8:12:mail:/var/spool/mail:/sbin/nologin
news:x:9:13:news:/etc/news:
uucp:x:10:14:uucp:/var/spool/uucp:/sbin/nologin
operator:x:11:0:operator:/root:/sbin/nologin
games:x:12:100:games:/usr/games:/sbin/nologin
gopher:x:13:30:gopher:/var/gopher:/sbin/nologin
ftp:x:14:50:FTP User:/var/ftp:/sbin/nologin
nobody:x:99:99:Nobody:/:/sbin/nologin
rpm:x:37:37::/var/lib/rpm:/sbin/nologin
vcsa:x:69:69:virtual console memory owner:/dev:/sbin/nologin
mailnull:x:47:47::/var/spool/mqueue:/sbin/nologin
smmsp:x:51:51::/var/spool/mqueue:/sbin/nologin
apache:x:48:48:Apache:/var/www:/sbin/nologin
rpc:x:32:32:Rpcbind Daemon:/var/lib/rpcbind:/sbin/nologin
ntp:x:38:38::/etc/ntp:/sbin/nologin
nscd:x:28:28:NSCD Daemon:/:/sbin/nologin
tcpdump:x:72:72::/:/sbin/nologin
dbus:x:81:81:System message bus:/:/sbin/nologin
avahi:x:70:70:Avahi daemon:/:/sbin/nologin
hsqldb:x:96:96::/var/lib/hsqldb:/sbin/nologin
sshd:x:74:74:Privilege-separated SSH:/var/empty/sshd:/sbin/nologin
rpcuser:x:29:29:RPC Service User:/var/lib/nfs:/sbin/nologin
nfsnobody:x:65534:65534:Anonymous NFS User:/var/lib/nfs:/sbin/nologin
haldaemon:x:68:68:HAL daemon:/:/sbin/nologin
xfs:x:43:43:X Font Server:/etc/X11/fs:/sbin/nologin
gdm:x:42:42::/var/gdm:/sbin/nologin
rich:x:500:500:Rich Blum:/home/rich:/bin/bash
mama:x:501:501:Mama:/home/mama:/bin/bash
katie:x:502:502:katie:/home/katie:/bin/bash
jessica:x:503:503:Jessica:/home/jessica:/bin/bash
mysql:x:27:27:MySQL Server:/var/lib/mysql:/bin/bash
$
```

The `root` user account is the administrator for the Linux system and is always assigned UID 0. As you can see, the Linux system creates lots of user accounts for various functions that aren't actual users. These are called *system accounts*. A system account is a special account that services running on the system use to gain access to resources on the system. All services that run in background mode need to be logged in to the Linux system under a system user account.

Before security became a big issue, these services often just logged in using the `root` user account. Unfortunately, if an unauthorized person broke into one of these services, he instantly gained access to the system as the `root` user. To prevent this, now just about every service that runs in background on a Linux server has its own user account to log in with. This way, if a troublemaker does compromise a service, he still can't necessarily get access to the whole system.

Linux reserves UIDs below 500 for system accounts. Some services even require specific UIDs to work properly. When you create accounts for normal users, most Linux systems assign the first available UID starting at 500 (although this is not necessarily true for all Linux distributions).

You probably noticed that the `/etc/passwd` file contains lots more than just the login name and UID for the user. The fields of the `/etc/passwd` file contain the following information:

- The login username
- The password for the user
- The numerical UID of the user account
- The numerical group ID (GID) of the user account
- A text description of the user account (called the comment field)
- The location of the `HOME` directory for the user
- The default shell for the user

The password field in the `/etc/passwd` file is set to an `x`. This doesn't mean that all of the user accounts have the same password. In the old days of Linux, the `/etc/passed` file contained an encrypted version of the user's password. However, since lots of programs need to access the `/etc/passwd` file for user information, this became somewhat of a security problem. With the advent of software that could easily decrypt encrypted passwords, the bad guys had a field day trying to break user passwords stored in the `/etc/passwd` file. Linux developers needed to rethink that policy.

Now, most Linux systems hold user passwords in a separate file (called the *shadow* file, located at `/etc/shadow`). Only special programs (such as the login program) are allowed access to this file.

As you can see, the `/etc/passwd` file is a standard text file. You can use any text editor to manually perform user management functions (such as adding, modifying, or removing user accounts) directly in the `/etc/passwd` file. However, this is an extremely dangerous practice. If the `/etc/passwd` file becomes corrupt, the system won't be able to read it, and it will prevent anyone (even the root user) from logging in. Instead, it's safer to use the standard Linux user management utilities to perform all user management functions.

The /etc/shadow file

The /etc/shadow file provides more control over how the Linux system manages passwords. Only the root user has access to the /etc/shadow file, making it more secure than the /etc/passwd file.

The /etc/shadow file contains one record for each user account on the system. A record looks like this:

```
rich:$1$.FfcKOns$f1UgiyHQ25wrB/hykCnO20:11627:0:99999:7:::
```

There are nine fields in each /etc/shadow file record:

- The login name corresponding to the login name in the /etc/passwd file
- The encrypted password
- The number of days since January 1, 1970 that the password was last changed
- The minimum number of days before the password can be changed
- The number of days before the password must be changed
- The number of days before password expiration that the user is warned to change the password
- The number of days after a password expires before the account will be disabled
- The date (stored as the number of days since January 1, 1970) since the user account was disabled
- A field reserved for future use

Using the shadow password system, the Linux system has much finer control over user passwords. It can control how often a user must change his or her password, and when to disable the account if the password hasn't been changed.

Adding a new user

The primary tool used to add new users to your Linux system is useradd. This command provides an easy way to create a new user account and set up the user's HOME directory structure all at once. The useradd command uses a combination of system default values and command line parameters to define a user account. To see the system default values used on your Linux distribution, enter the useradd command with the -D parameter:

```
# /usr/sbin/useradd -D
GROUP=100
HOME=/home
INACTIVE=-1
EXPIRE=
SHELL=/bin/bash
SKEL=/etc/skel
CREATE_MAIL_SPOOL=yes
#
```

Some Linux distributions place the Linux user and group utilities in the /usr/sbin directory, which may not be in your PATH environment variable. If that's the case in your Linux distribution, either add the directory to your PATH or use the absolute filepath to run it.

The -D parameter shows what defaults the useradd command uses if you don't specify them in the command line when creating a new user account. This example shows the following default values:

- The new user will be added to a common group with group ID 100.
- The new user will have a HOME account created in the directory /home/loginname.
- The account will not be disabled when the password expires.
- The new account will not be set to expire at a set date.
- The new account will use the bash shell as the default shell.
- The system will copy the contents of the /etc/skel directory to the user's HOME directory.
- The system will create a file in the mail directory for the user account to receive mail.

The next-to-the-last value is interesting. The useradd command allows an administrator to create a default HOME directory configuration, then uses that as a template to create the new user's HOME directory. This allows you to place default files for the system in every new user's HOME directory automatically. On my Linux system, the /etc/skel directory has the following files:

```
# ls -al /etc/skel
total 48
drwxr-xr-x   2 root root  4096 2001-11-01 00:23 .
drwxr-xr-x 107 root root 12288 2007-09-20 16:53 ..
-rw-r--r--   1 root root    33 2007-02-12 10:18 .bash_logout
-rw-r--r--   1 root root   176 2007-02-12 10:18 .bash_profile
-rw-r--r--   1 root root   124 2007-02-12 10:18 .bashrc
#
```

You should recognize these file from Chapter 5. These are the standard startup files for the bash shell environment. The system automatically copies these default files into every user's HOME directory you create.

You can test this by creating a new user account using the default system parameters and then looking at the HOME directory for the new user:

```
# /usr/sbin/useradd test
# ls -al /home/test
total 40
drwx------ 2 test test 4096 2007-09-20 18:23 .
drwxr-xr-x 7 root root 4096 2007-09-20 18:23 ..
-rw-r--r-- 1 test test   33 2007-09-20 18:23 .bash_logout
-rw-r--r-- 1 test test  176 2007-09-20 18:23 .bash_profile
-rw-r--r-- 1 test test  124 2007-09-20 18:23 .bashrc
#
```

As expected, the useradd command created the new HOME directory, using the files in the /etc/skel directory.

If you want to override a default value when creating a new user, you can do that with command line parameters. These are shown in Table 6-1.

As you can see, you can override all of the system default values when creating a new user account just by using command line parameters. However, if you find yourself having to override a value all the time, it's easier to just change the system default value.

You can change the system default new user values by using the -D parameter, along with a parameter representing the value you need to change. These parameters are shown in Table 6-2.

TABLE 6-1

The useradd Command Line Parameters

Parameter	Description
-c *comment*	Add text to the new user's comment field.
-d *home_dir*	Specify a different name for the home directory other than the login name.
-e *expire_date*	Specify a date, in YYYY-MM-DD format, when the account will expire.
-f *inactive_days*	Specify the number of days after a password expires when the account will be disabled. A value of 0 disables the account as soon as the password expires; a value of -1 disables this feature.
-g *initial_group*	Specify the group name or GID of the user's login group.
-G *group...*	Specify one or more supplementary groups the user belongs to.
-k	Copy the /etc/skel directory contents into the user's HOME directory (must use -m as well).
-m	Create the user's HOME directory.
-M	Don't create a user's HOME directory (used if the default setting is to create one).
-n	Create a new group using the same name as the user's login name.
-r	Create a system account
-p *passwd*	Specify a default password for the user account.
-s *shell*	Specify the default login shell.
-u *uid*	Specify a unique UID for the account.

TABLE 6-2

The useradd Change Default Values Parameters

Parameter	Description
-b *default_home*	Change the location of where users' HOME directories are created.
-e *expiration_date*	Change the expiration date on new accounts.
-f *inactive*	Change the number of days after a password has expired before the account is disabled.
-g *group*	Change the default group name or GID used.
-s *shell*	Change the default login shell.

Changing the default values is a snap:

```
# useradd -D -s /bin/tsch
# useradd -D
GROUP=100
HOME=/home
INACTIVE=-1
EXPIRE=
SHELL=/bin/tsch
SKEL=/etc/skel
CREATE_MAIL_SPOOL=yes
#
```

Now, the useradd command will use the tsch shell as the default login shell for all new user accounts you create.

Removing a user

If you want to remove a user from the system, the userdel command is what you need. By default, the userdel command only removes the user information from the /etc/passwd file. It doesn't remove any files the account owns on the system.

If you use the -r parameter, userdel will remove the user's HOME directory, along with the user's mail directory. However, there may still be other files owned by the deleted user account on the system. This can be a problem in some environments.

Here's an example of using the userdel command to remove an existing user account:

```
# /usr/sbin/userdel -r test
# ls -al /home/test
ls: cannot access /home/test: No such file or directory
#
```

After using the -r parameter, the user's old /home/test directory no longer exists.

> **CAUTION** Be careful when using the -r parameter in an environment with lots of users. You never know if a user had important files stored in his or her HOME directory that are used by someone else or another program. Always check before removing a user's HOME directory!

Modifying a user

Linux provides a few different utilities for modifying the information for existing user accounts. Table 6-3 shows these utilities.

TABLE 6-3

User Account Modification Utilities

Command	Description
usermod	Edits user account fields, as well as specifying primary and secondary group membership
passwd	Changes the password for an existing user
chpasswd	Reads a file of login name and password pairs, and updates the passwords
chage	Changes the password's expiration date
chfn	Changes the user account's comment information
chsh	Changes the user account's default shell

Each of these utilities provides a specific function for changing information about user accounts. The following sections describe each of these utilities.

usermod

The usermod command is the most robust of the user account modification utilities. It provides options for changing most of the fields in the /etc/passwd file. To do that you just need to use the command line parameter that corresponds to the value you want to change. The parameters are mostly the same as the useradd parameters (such as -c to change the comment field, -e to change the expiration date, and -g to change the default login group). However, there are a couple of additional parameters that might come in handy:

- -l to change the login name of the user account
- -L to lock the account so the user can't log in
- -p to change the password for the account
- -U to unlock the account so that the user can log in

The -L parameter is especially handy. Use this to lock an account so that a user can't log in without having to remove the account and the user's data. To return the account to normal, just use the -U parameter.

passwd and chpasswd

A quick way to change just the password for a user is the passwd command:

```
# passwd test
Changing password for user test.
New UNIX password:
Retype new UNIX password:
passwd: all authentication tokens updated successfully.
#
```

If you just use the passwd command by itself, it'll change your own password. Any user in the system can change their own password, but only the root user can change someone else's password.

The -e option is a handy way to force a user to change the password on the next log in. This allows you to set the user's password to a simple value, then force them to change it to something harder that they can remember.

If you ever need to do a mass password change for lots of users on the system, the chpasswd command can be a lifesaver. The chpasswd command reads a list of login name and password pairs (separated by a colon) from the standard input, and automatically encrypts the password and sets it for the user account.

chsh, chfn, and chage

The chsh, chfn, and chage utilities are specialized for specific functions. The chsh command allows you to quickly change the default login shell for a user. You must use the full pathname for the shell, and not just the shell name:

```
# chsh -s /bin/csh test
Changing shell for test.
Shell changed.
#
```

The chfn command provides a standard method for storing information in the comments field in the /etc/passwd file. Instead of just inserting random text, such as names, nicknames, or even just leaving the comment field blank, the chfn command uses specific information used in the Unix finger command to store information in the comment field. The finger command allows you to easily find information about people on your Linux system:

```
# finger rich
Login: rich                          Name: Rich Blum
Directory: /home/rich                Shell: /bin/bash
```

```
On since Thu Sep 20 18:03 (EDT) on pts/0 from 192.168.1.2
No mail.
No Plan.
#
```

> **NOTE**   Because of security concerns, many Linux system administrators disable the `finger`
> command on their systems.

If you use the `chfn` command with no parameters, it queries you for the appropriate values to
enter in to the comment field:

```
# chfn test
Changing finger information for test.
Name []: Ima Test
Office []: Director of Technology
Office Phone []: (123)555-1234
Home Phone []: (123)555-9876

Finger information changed.
# finger test
Login: test                            Name: Ima Test
Directory: /home/test                  Shell: /bin/csh
Office: Director of Technology         Office Phone: (123)555-1234
Home Phone: (123)555-9876
Never logged in.
No mail.
No Plan.
#
```

If you now look at the entry in the /etc/passwd file, it looks like this:

```
# grep test /etc/passwd
test:x:504:504:Ima Test,Director of Technology,(123)555-
1234,(123)555-9876:/home/test:/bin/csh
#
```

All of the `finger` information is neatly stored away in the /etc/passwd file entry.

Finally, the `chage` command helps us manage the password aging process for user accounts.
There are several parameters to set individual values, shown in Table 6-4.

The `chage` date values can be expressed using one of two methods:

- A date in YYYY-MM-DD format
- A numerical value representing the number of days since January 1, 1970

One neat feature of the `chage` command is that it allows you to set an expiration date for an
account. Using this feature, you can create temporary user accounts that automatically expire
on a set date, without your having to remember to delete them! Expired accounts are similar to
locked accounts. The account still exists, but the user can't log in with it.

TABLE 6-4	

The chage Command Parameters

Parameter	Description
-d	Set the number of days since the password was last changed.
-E	Set the date the password will expire.
-I	Set the number of days of inactivity after the password expires to lock the account.
-m	Set the minimum number of days between password changes.
-W	Set the number of days before the password expires that a warning message appears.

Using Linux Groups

User accounts are great for controlling security for individual users, but they aren't so good at allowing groups of users to share resources. To accomplish this, the Linux system uses another security concept, called *groups*.

Group permissions allow multiple users to share a common set of permissions for an object on the system, such as a file, directory, or device (more on that later in the "Decoding File Permissions" section).

Linux distributions differ somewhat on how they handle default group memberships. Some Linux distributions create just one group which contains all of the user accounts as members. You need to be careful if your Linux distribution does this, as your files may be readable by all other users on the system. Other distributions create a separate user account for each user, to provide a little more security.

Each group has a unique GID, which, like UIDs, is a unique numerical value on the system. Along with the GID, each group has a unique group name. There are a few group utilities you can use to create and manage your own groups on the Linux system. This section discusses how group information is stored, and how to use the group utilities to create new groups and modify existing groups.

The /etc/group file

Just like user accounts, group information is stored in a file on the system. The /etc/group file contains information about each group used on the system. Here are a few examples from the /etc/group file on my Linux system:

```
root:x:0:root
bin:x:1:root,bin,daemon
```

```
daemon:x:2:root,bin,daemon
sys:x:3:root,bin,adm
adm:x:4:root,adm,daemon
rich:x:500:
mama:x:501:
katie:x:502:
jessica:x:503:
mysql:x:27:
test:x:504:
```

Similarly to UIDs, GIDs are assigned using a special format. Groups used for system accounts are assigned GIDs below 500, and user groups are assigned GIDs starting at 500. The /etc/group file uses four fields:

- The group name
- The group password
- The GID
- The list of user accounts that belong to the group

The group password allows a non-group member to temporarily become a member of the group by using the password. This feature is not used all that commonly, but it does exist.

You should never add users to groups by editing the /etc/group file. Instead, use the usermod command (discussed earlier in the "Linux Security" section) to add a user account to a group. Before you can add users to different groups, you must create the groups.

NOTE   The list of user accounts is somewhat misleading. You'll notice that there are several groups in the list that don't have any users listed. This isn't because they don't have any members. When a user account uses a group as the default group in the /etc/passwd file, the user account doesn't appear in the /etc/group file as a member. This has caused confusion for more than one system administrator over the years!

Creating new groups

The groupadd command allows you to create new groups on your system:

```
# /usr/sbin/groupadd shared
# tail /etc/group
haldaemon:x:68:
xfs:x:43:
gdm:x:42:
rich:x:500:
mama:x:501:
katie:x:502:
jessica:x:503:
mysql:x:27:
```

```
test:x:504:
shared:x:505:
#
```

When you create a new group, there are no users assigned to it by default. The groupadd command doesn't provide an option for adding user accounts to the group. Instead, to add new users, use the usermod command:

```
# /usr/sbin/usermod -G shared rich
# /usr/sbin/usermod -G shared test
# tail /etc/group
haldaemon:x:68:
xfs:x:43:
gdm:x:42:
rich:x:500:
mama:x:501:
katie:x:502:
jessica:x:503:
mysql:x:27:
test:x:504:
shared:x:505:rich, test
#
```

The shared group now has two members, test and rich. The -G parameter in usermod appends the new group to the list of groups for the user account.

CAUTION Be careful when assigning groups for user accounts. If you use the -g parameter, the group name you specify replaces the default group for the user account. The -G parameter adds the group to the list of groups the user belongs to, keeping the default group intact.

Modifying groups

As you can see from the /etc/group file, there isn't too much information about a group for you to modify. The groupmod command allows you to change the GID (using the -g parameter) or the group name (using the -n parameter) of an existing group:

```
# /usr/sbin/groupmod -n sharing shared
# tail /etc/group
haldaemon:x:68:
xfs:x:43:
gdm:x:42:
rich:x:500:
mama:x:501:
katie:x:502:
jessica:x:503:
mysql:x:27:
test:x:504:
sharing:x:505:test,rich
#
```

When changing the name of a group, the GID and group members remain the same, only the group name changes. Since all security permissions are based on the GID, you can change the name of a group as often as you wish without adversely affecting file security.

Decoding File Permissions

Now that you know about users and groups, it's time to decode the cryptic file permissions you've seen when using the ls command. This section describes how to decipher the permissions and where they come from.

Using file permission symbols

If you remember from Chapter 3, the ls command allows us to see the file permissions for files, directories, and devices on the Linux system:

```
$ ls -l
total 68
-rw-rw-r-- 1 rich rich   50 2007-09-13 07:49 file1.gz
-rw-rw-r-- 1 rich rich   23 2007-09-13 07:50 file2
-rw-rw-r-- 1 rich rich   48 2007-09-13 07:56 file3
-rw-rw-r-- 1 rich rich   34 2007-09-13 08:59 file4
-rwxrwxr-x 1 rich rich 4882 2007-09-18 13:58 myprog
-rw-rw-r-- 1 rich rich  237 2007-09-18 13:58 myprog.c
drwxrwxr-x 2 rich rich 4096 2007-09-03 15:12 test1
drwxrwxr-x 2 rich rich 4096 2007-09-03 15:12 test2
$
```

The first field in the output listing is a code that describes the permissions for the files and directories. The first character in the field defines the type of the object:

- ■ - for files
- ■ d for directories
- ■ l for links
- ■ c for character devices
- ■ b for block devices
- ■ n for network devices

After that, there are three sets of three characters. Each set of three characters defines an access permission triplet:

- ■ r for read permission for the object
- ■ w for write permission for the object
- ■ x for execute permission for the object

If a permission is denied, a dash appears in the location. The three sets relate the three levels of security for the object:

- The owner of the object
- The group that owns the object
- Everyone else on the system

This is broken down in Figure 6-1.

FIGURE 6-1

The Linux file permissions

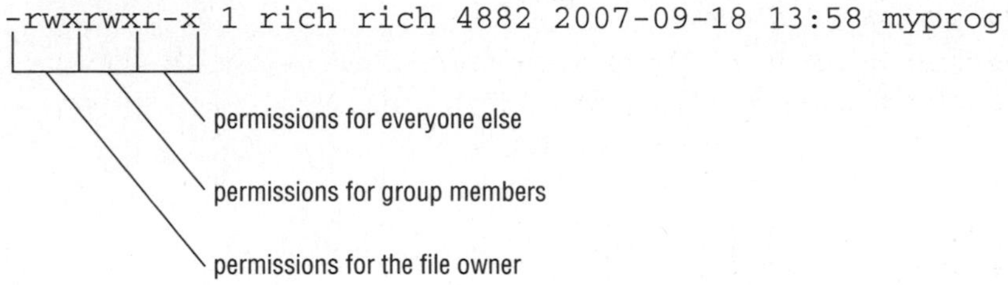

```
-rwxrwxr-x 1 rich rich 4882 2007-09-18 13:58 myprog
```
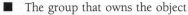

permissions for everyone else

permissions for group members

permissions for the file owner

The easiest way to discuss this is to take an example and decode the file permissions one by one:

```
-rwxrwxr-x 1 rich rich 4882 2007-09-18 13:58 myprog
```

The file myprog has the following sets of permissions:

- rwx for the file owner (set to the login name rich)
- rwx for the file group owner (set to the group name rich)
- r-x for everyone else on the system

These permissions indicate that the user login name rich can read, write, and execute the file (considered full permissions). Likewise, members in the group rich can also read, write, and execute the file. However, anyone else not in the rich group can only read and execute the file; the w is replaced with a dash, indicating that write permissions are not assigned to this security level.

Default file permissions

You may be wondering about where these file permissions come from. The answer, is *umask*. The umask command sets the default permissions for any file or directory you create:

```
$ touch newfile
$ ls -al newfile
-rw-r--r--    1 rich      rich             0 Sep 20 19:16 newfile
$
```

The touch command created the file using the default permissions assigned to my user account. The umask command shows and sets the default permissions:

```
$ umask
0022
$
```

Unfortunately, the umask command setting isn't overtly clear, and trying to understand exactly how it works makes things even muddier. The first digit represents a special security feature called the *sticky bit*. We'll talk more about that later on in this chapter in the "Sharing Files" section.

The next three digits represent the octal values of the umask for a file or directory. To understand how umask works, you first need to understand octal mode security settings.

Octal mode security settings take the three rwx permission values and convert them into a 3-bit binary value, represented by a single octal value. In the binary representation, each position is a binary bit. Thus, if the read permission is the only permission set, the value becomes r--, relating to a binary value of 100, indicating the octal value of 4. Table 6-5 shows the possible combinations you'll run into.

Octal mode takes the octal permissions and lists three of them in order for the three security levels (user, group, and everyone). Thus, the octal mode value 664 represents read and write permissions for the user and group, but read-only permission for everyone else.

Now that you know about octal mode permissions, the umask value becomes even more confusing. The octal mode shown for the default umask on my Linux system is 0022, but the file I created had an octal mode permission of 644. How did that happen?

TABLE 6-5

Linux File Permission Codes

Permissions	Binary	Octal	Description
---	000	0	No permissions
--x	001	1	Execute-only permission
-w-	010	2	Write-only permission
-wx	011	3	Write and execute permissions
r--	100	4	Read-only permission
r-x	101	5	Read and execute permissions
rw-	110	6	Read and write permissions
rwx	111	7	Read, write, and execute permissions

The umask value is just that, a mask. It masks out the permissions you don't want to give to the security level. Now we have to dive into some octal arithmetic to figure out the rest of the story.

The umask value is subtracted from the full permission set for an object. The full permission for a file is mode 666 (read/write permission for all), but for a directory it's 777 (read/write/execute permission for all).

Thus, in the example, the file starts out with permissions 666, and the umask of 022 is applied, leaving a file permission of 644.

The umask value is normally set in the /etc/profile startup file (see Chapter 5). You can specify a different default umask setting using the umask command:

```
$ umask 026
$ touch newfile2
$ ls -l newfile2
-rw-r----- 1 rich     rich              0 Sep 20 19:46 newfile2
$
```

By setting the umask value to 026, the default file permissions become 640, so the new file now is restricted to read-only for the group members, and everyone else on the system has no permissions to the file.

The umask value also applies to making new directories:

```
$ mkdir newdir
$ ls -l
drwxr-x--x 2 rich     rich           4096 Sep 20 20:11 newdir/
```

Since the default permissions for a directory are 777, the resulting permissions from the umask are different from those of a new file. The 026 umask value is subtracted from 777, leaving the 751 directory permission setting.

Changing Security Settings

If you've already created a file or directory, and need to change the security settings on it, there are a few different utilities available in Linux. This section shows how to change the existing permissions, the default owner, and the default group settings for a file or directory.

Changing permissions

The chmod command allows you to change the security settings for files and directories. The format of the chmod command is:

```
chmod options mode file
```

The `mode` parameter allows you to set the security settings using either octal or symbolic mode. The octal mode settings are pretty straightforward; just use the standard three-digit octal code you want the file to have:

```
$ chmod 760 newfile
$ ls -l newfile
-rwxrw----    1 rich      rich             0 Sep 20 19:16 newfile*
$
```

The octal file permissions are automatically applied to the file indicated. The symbolic mode permissions are not so easy to implement.

Instead of using the normal string of three sets of three characters, the `chmod` command takes a different approach. The format for specifying a permission in symbolic mode is:

```
[ugoa...][[+-=][rwxXstugo...]
```

Makes perfectly good sense, doesn't it? The first group of characters defines to whom the new permissions apply:

- u for the user
- g for the group
- o for others (everyone else)
- a for all of the above

Next, a symbol is used to indicate whether you want to add the permission to the existing permissions (+), subtract the permission from the existing permission (−), or set the permissions to the value (=).

Finally, the third symbol is the permission used for the setting. You may notice that there are more than the normal `rwx` values here. The additional settings are:

- X to assign execute permissions only if the object is a directory or if it already had execute permissions
- s to set the UID or GID on execution
- t to save program text
- u to set the permissions to the owner's permissions
- g to set the permissions to the group's permissions
- o to set the permissions to the other's permissions

Using these permissions looks like this:

```
$ chmod o+r newfile
$ ls -l newfile
-rwxrw-r--    1 rich      rich             0 Sep 20 19:16 newfile*
$
```

The o+r entry adds the read permission to whatever permissions the everyone security level already had.

```
$ chmod u-x newfile
$ ls -l newfile
-rw-rw-r--   1 rich      rich              0 Sep 20 19:16 newfile
$
```

The u-x entry removes the execute permission that the user already had. Note that the settings for the ls command indicate if a file has execution permissions by adding an asterisk to the filename.

The *options* parameters provide a few additional features to augment the behavior of the chmod command. The -R parameter performs the file and directory changes recursively. You can use wildcard characters for the filename specified, changing the permissions on multiple files with just one command.

Changing ownership

Sometimes you need to change the owner of a file, such as when someone leaves an organization or a developer creates an application that needs to be owned by a system account when it's in production. Linux provides two commands for doing that. The chown command to makes it easy to change the owner of a file, and the chgrp command allows you to change the default group of a file.

The format of the chown command is:

```
chown options owner[.group] file
```

You can specify either the login name or the numeric UID for the new owner of the file:

```
# chown dan newfile
# ls -l newfile
-rw-rw-r--   1 dan      rich              0 Sep 20 19:16 newfile*
#
```

Simple. The chown command also allows you to change both the user and group of a file:

```
# chown dan.dan newfile
# ls -l newfile
-rw-rw-r--   1 dan      dan               0 Sep 20 19:16 newfile*
#
```

If you really want to get tricky, you can just change the default group for a file:

```
# chown .rich newfile
# ls -l newfile
-rw-rw-r--   1 dan      rich              0 Sep 20 19:16 newfile*
#
```

Finally, if your Linux system uses individual group names that match user login names, you can change both with just one entry:

```
# chown test. newfile
# ls -l newfile
-rw-rw-r--    1 test    test          0 Sep 20 19:16 newfile*
#
```

The chown command uses a few different option parameters. The -R parameter allows you to make changes recursively through subdirectories and files, using a wildcard character. The -h parameter also changes the ownership of any files that are symbolically linked to the file.

NOTE Only the root user can change the owner of a file. Any user can change the default group of a file, but the user must be a member of the groups the file is changed from and to.

The chgrp command provides an easy way to change just the default group for a file or directory:

```
$ chgrp shared newfile
$ ls -l newfile
-rw-rw-r--    1 rich    shared        0 Sep 20 19:16 newfile*
$
```

Now any member in the shared group can write to the file. This is one way to share files on a Linux system. However, sharing files among a group of people on the system can get tricky. The next section discusses how to do this.

Sharing Files

As you've probably already figured out, creating groups is the way to share access to files on the Linux system. However, for a complete file-sharing environment, things are more complicated.

As you've already seen in the "Decoding File Permissions" section, when you create a new file, Linux assigns the file permissions of the new file using your default UID and GID. To allow others access to the file, you need to either change the security permissions for the everyone security group or assign the file a different default group that contains other users.

This can be a pain in a large environment if you want to create and share documents among several people. Fortunately, there's a simple solution for how to solve this problem.

There are three additional bits of information that Linux stores for each file and directory:

- **The set user id (SUID):** When a file is executed by a user, the program runs under the permissions of the file owner.
- **The set group id (SGID):** For a file, the program runs under the permissions of the file group. For a directory, new files created in the directory use the directory group as the default group.
- **The sticky bit:** The file remains (sticks) in memory after the process ends.

The SGID bit is important for sharing files. By enabling the SGID bit, you can force all new files created in a shared directory to be owned by the directory's group and now the individual user's group.

The SGID is set using the chmod command. It's added to the beginning of the standard three-digit octal value (making a four-digit octal value), or you can use the symbol s in symbolic mode.

If you're using octal mode, you'll need to know the arrangement of the bits, shown in Table 6-6.

TABLE 6-6

The chmod SUID, SGID, and Sticky Bit Octal Values

Binary	Octal	Description
000	0	All bits are cleared.
001	1	The sticky bit is set.
010	2	The SGID bit is set.
011	3	The SGID and sticky bits are set.
100	4	The SUID bit is set.
101	5	The SUID and sticky bits are set.
110	6	The SUID and SGID bits are set.
111	7	All bits are set.

So, to create a shared directory that always sets the directory group for all new files, all you need to do is set the SGID bit for the directory:

```
$ mkdir testdir
$ ls -l
drwxrwxr-x    2 rich      rich        4096 Sep 20 23:12 testdir/
$ chgrp shared testdir
$ chmod g+s testdir
$ ls -l
drwxrwsr-x    2 rich      shared      4096 Sep 20 23:12 testdir/
$ umask 002
$ cd testdir
$ touch testfile
$ ls -l
total 0
-rw-rw-r--    1 rich      shared         0 Sep 20 23:13 testfile
$
```

The first step is to create a directory that you want to share using the mkdir command. Next, the chgrp command is used to change the default group for the directory to a group that contains the members who need to share files. Finally, the SGID bit is set for the directory, to ensure that any files created in the directory use the shared group name as the default group.

For this environment to work properly, all of the group members need to have their umask values set to make files writable by group members. This is why I changed my umask to 002.

After all that's done, I can go to the shared directory and create a new file. As expected, the new file uses the default group of the directory, not my user account's default group. Now any user in the shared group can access this file.

Summary

This chapter discussed the command line commands you need to know to manage the Linux security on your system. Linux uses a system of user IDs and group IDs to protect access to files, directories, and devices. Linux stores information about user accounts in the /etc/passwd file, and information about groups in the /etc/group file. Each user is assigned a unique numeric user ID, along with a text login name to identify the user in the system. Groups are also assigned unique numerical group IDs, and text group names. A group can contain one or more users to allowed shared access to system resources.

There are several commands available for managing user accounts and groups. The useradd command allows you to create new user accounts, and the groupadd command allows you to create new group accounts. To modify an existing user account, use the usermod command. Similarly, the groupmod command is used to modify group account information.

Linux uses a complicated system of bits to determine access permissions for files and directories. Each file contains three security levels of protection: the file's owner, a default group that has access to the file, and a level for everyone else on the system. Each security level is defined by three access bits: read, write, and execute. The combination of three bits is often referred to by the symbols rwx, for read, write, and execute. If a permission is denied, it's symbol is replaced with a dash (such as r-- for read-only permission).

The symbolic permissions are often referred to as octal values, with the 3 bits combined into one octal value, and three octal values representing the three security levels. The umask command is used to set the default security settings for files and directories created on the system. The system administrator normally sets a default umask value in the /etc/profile file, but you can use the umask command to change your umask value at any time.

The chmod command is used to change security settings for files and directories. Only the file's owner can change permissions for a file or directory. However, the root user can change the security settings for any file or directory on the system. The chown and chgrp commands can be used to change the default owner and group of the file.

Finally, the chapter closed out with a discussion on how to use the set GID bit to create a shared directory. The SGID bit forces any new files or directories created in a directory to use the default group name of the parent directory, not that of the user who created them. This provides an easy way to share files between users on the system.

Now that you know about Linux file security, you're almost ready to start creating some programs. However, before you start coding there's one more element we need to discuss: editors. If you plan on writing shell scripts, you'll need an environment in which to create your masterpieces. The next chapter discusses the text editors available for you to use in different Linux environments.

Chapter 7

Working with Editors

Before you can start your shell scripting career, you'll need to know how to use at least one text editor in Linux. The more you know about how to use these fancy features such as searching, cutting, and pasting, the quicker you'll be able to develop your shell scripts. This chapter discusses the main text editors you'll see in the Linux world.

The vim Editor

If you're working in command line mode, you may want to become familiar with at least one text editor that operates in the Linux console. The vi editor is the original editor used on Unix systems. It uses the console graphics mode to emulate a text-editing window, allowing you to visually see the lines of your file, move around within the file, and insert, edit, and replace text.

While it may quite possibly be the most complicated editor in the world (at least in the opinion of those who hate it), it provides many features that have made it a staple for Unix administrators for decades.

When the GNU Project ported the vi editor to the open source world, they chose to make some improvements to it. Since it no longer resembled the original vi editor found in the Unix world, they also renamed it, to vi improved, or vim.

Almost all Linux distributions create an alias name (see Chapter 5) vi to point to vim:

```
$ alias vi
alias vi='vim'
$
```

This section walks you through the basics of using the vim editor to edit your text shell script files.

The basics of vim

The vim editor works with data in a memory buffer. To start the vim editor, just type the vim command (or vi if there's an alias) and the name of the file you want to edit:

```
$ vim myprog.c
```

If you start vim without a filename, or if the file doesn't exist, vim opens a new buffer area for editing. If you specify an existing file on the command line, vim will read the entire contents of the file into a buffer area, where it is ready for editing, as shown in Figure 7-1.

The vim editor detects the terminal type for the session (see Chapter 2) and uses a full-screen mode to use the entire console window for the editor area.

FIGURE 7-1

The vim main window

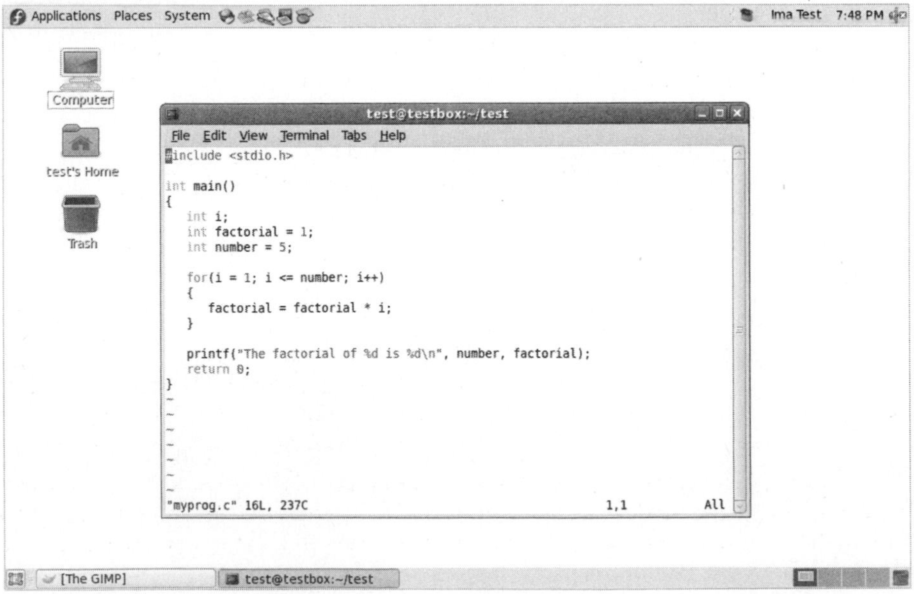

The initial vim edit window shows the contents of the file (if there are any) along with a message line at the bottom of the window. If the file contents don't take up the entire screen, vim places a tilde on lines that are not part of the file (as shown in Figure 7-1).

The message line at the bottom indicates information about the edited file, depending on the status of the file, and the default settings in your vim installation. If the file is new, the message [New File] appears.

The vim editor has two modes of operation:

- Normal mode
- Insert mode

When you first open a file (or start a new file) for editing, the vim editor enters *normal* mode. In normal mode, the vim editor interprets keystrokes as commands (more on those later).

In *insert* mode, vim inserts every key you type at the current cursor location in the buffer. To enter insert mode, press the i key. To get out of insert mode and go back into normal mode, press the Escape key on the keyboard.

In normal mode, you can move the cursor around the text area by using the arrow keys (as long as your terminal type is detected properly by vim). If you happen to be on a flaky terminal connection that doesn't have the arrow keys defined, hope is not lost. The vim commands include commands for moving the cursor:

- h to move left one character.
- j to move down one line (the next line in the text).
- k to move up one line (the previous line in the text).
- l to move right one character

Moving around within large text files line by line can get tedious. Fortunately, vim provides a few commands to help speed things along:

- PageDown (or Ctl-f) to move forward one screen of data
- PageUp (or Ctl-b) to move backward one screen of data
- G to move to the last line in the buffer
- *num* G to move to the line number *num* in the buffer.
- gg to move to the first line in the buffer

The vim editor has a special feature within normal mode called *command line mode*. The command line mode provides an interactive command line where you can enter additional commands to control the actions in vim. To get to command line mode, press the colon key in normal mode. The cursor moves to the message line, and a colon appears, waiting for you to enter a command.

Within the command line mode are several commands for saving the buffer to the file, and exiting vim:

- q to quit if no changes have been made to the buffer data
- q! to quit and discard any changes made to the buffer data
- w *filename* to save the file under a different filename
- wq to save the buffer data to the file and quit

After seeing just a few basic vim commands you might understand why some people absolutely hate the vim editor. To be able to use vim to its fullest, you must know plenty of obscure commands. However, once you get a few of the basic vim commands down, you can quickly edit files directly from the command line, no matter what type of environment you're in.

Editing data

While in insert mode, you can insert data into the buffer; however, sometimes you need to add or remove data after you've already entered it into the buffer. While in normal mode, the vim editor provides several commands for editing the data in the buffer. Table 7-1 lists some common editing commands for vim.

Some of the editing commands also allow you to use a numeric modifier to indicate how many times to perform the command. For example, the command 2x deletes two characters, starting from the current cursor position, and the command 5dd deletes five lines, starting at the line from the current cursor position.

CAUTION Be careful when trying to use the PC keyboard Backspace or Delete keys while in the vim editor. The vim editor usually recognizes the Delete key as the functionality of the x command, deleting the character at the current cursor location. Usually, the vim editor doesn't recognize the Backspace key.

Copy and paste

A standard feature of modern editors is the ability to cut or copy data, then paste it elsewhere in the document. The vim editor provides a way to do this.

Cutting and pasting is relatively easy. You've already seen the commands in Table 7-1 that can remove data from the buffer. However, when vim removes data, it actually keeps it stored in a separate register. You can retrieve that data by using the p command.

For example, you can use the dd command to delete a line of text, then move the cursor to the location in the buffer where you want to place it, then use the p command. The p command inserts the text after the line at the current cursor position. You can do this with any command that removes text.

Copying text is a little bit trickier. The copy command in vim is y (for yank). You can use the same second character with y as with the d command (yw to yank a word, y$ to yank to the end of a line). After you yank the text, move the cursor to the location where you want to place the text, and use the p command. The yanked text now appears at that location.

TABLE 7-1

vim Editing Commands

Command	Description
x	Delete the character at the current cursor position.
dd	Delete the line at the current cursor position.
dw	Delete the word at the current cursor position.
d$	Delete to the end of the line from the current cursor position.
J	Delete the line break at the end of the line at the current cursor position.
a	Append data after the current cursor position.
A	Append data to the end of the line at the current cursor position.
r *char*	Replace a single character at the current cursor position with *char*.
R *text*	Overwrite the data at the current cursor position with *text*, until you press Escape.

Yanking is tricky in that you can't see what happened, since you're not affecting the text that you yank. You never know for sure what you yanked until you paste it somewhere. But there's another feature in vim that helps us out with yanking.

The *visual mode* highlights text as you move the cursor. You use visual mode to select text to yank for pasting. To enter visual mode, move the cursor to the location where you want to start yanking, and press v. You'll notice that the text at the cursor position is now highlighted. Next, move the cursor to cover the text you want to yank (you can even move down lines to yank more than one line of text). As you move the cursor, vim highlights the text in the yank area. After you've covered the text you want to copy, press the y key to activate the yank command. Now that you've got the text in the register, just move the cursor to where you want to paste, and use the p command.

Search and substitute

You can easily search for data in the buffer using the vim search command. To enter a search string, press the forward slash (/) key. The cursor goes to the message line, and vim displays a forward slash. Enter the text you want to find, and press the Enter key. The vim editor responds with one of three actions:

- If the word appears after the current cursor location, it jumps to the first location where the text appears.

- If the word doesn't appear after the current cursor location, it wraps around the end of the file to the first location in the file where the text appears (and indicates this with a message).

- It produces an error message stating that the text was not found in the file.

To continue searching for the same word, press the forward slash character, then press the Enter key, or you can use the n key, for *next*.

The substitute command allows you to quickly replace (substitute) one word for another in the text. To get to the substitute command you must be in command line mode. The format for the substitute command is:

   `:s/old/new/`

The vim editor jumps to the first occurrence of the text `old` and replaces it with the text `new`. There are a few modifications you can make to the substitute command to substitute more than one occurrence of the text:

- `:s/old/new/g` to replace all occurrences of `old` in a line
- `:#,#s/old/new/g` to replace all occurrences of `old` between two line numbers
- `:%s/old/new/g` to replace all occurrences of `old` in the entire file
- `:%s/old/new/gc` to replace all occurrences of `old` in the entire file, but prompt for each occurrence

As you can see, for a command line text editor, vim contains quite a few advanced features. Since every Linux distribution includes it, it's a good idea to at least know the basics of the vim editor so that you can always edit scripts, no matter where you are or what you have available.

The emacs Editor

The emacs editor is an extremely popular editor that appeared before even Unix was around. Developers liked it so much they ported it to the Unix environment, and now it's been ported to the Linux environment. The emacs editor started out life as a console editor, much like vi, but has made the migration to the graphical world.

The emacs editor still provides the original console mode editor, but now it also has the ability to use a graphical X Windows window to allow editing text in a graphical environment. Normally, when you start the emacs editor from a command line, it'll determine if you have an available X Window session and start in graphical mode. If you don't, it'll start in console mode.

This section describes both the console mode and graphical mode emacs editors so that you'll know how to use either one if you want (or need) to.

Using emacs on the console

The console mode version of emacs is another editor that uses lots of key commands to perform editing functions. The emacs editor uses key combinations involving the Control key (the Ctrl key on the PC keyboard) and the Meta key. In most PC terminal emulator packages, the Meta key is mapped to the PC's Alt key. The official emacs documents abbreviate the Ctrl key as `C-` and the Meta key as `M-`, Thus, if you enter a Ctrl-x key combination, the document shows `C-x`. I'll do the same here so as not to confuse you.

FIGURE 7-2

Editing a file using the emacs editor in console mode

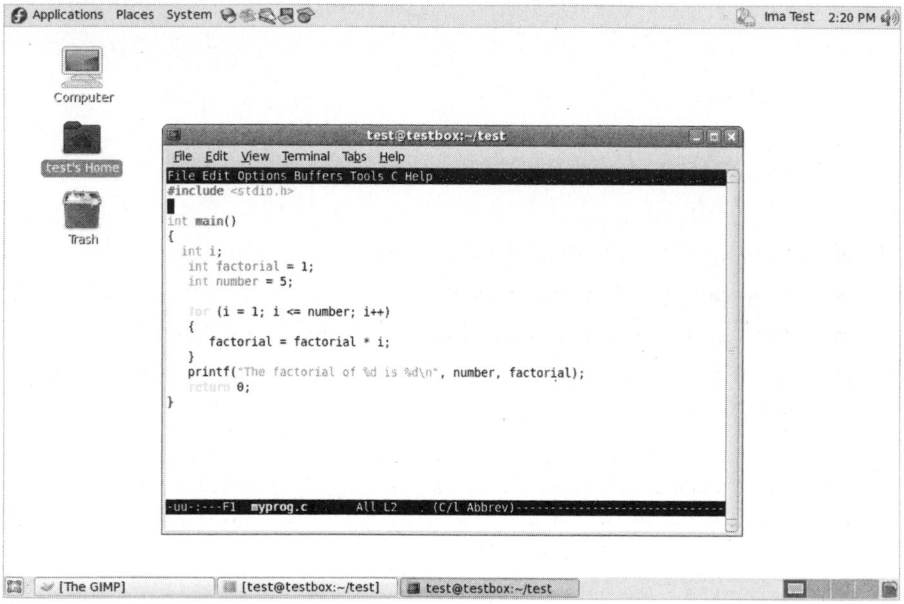

The basics of emacs

To edit a file using emacs, from the command line, enter:

```
$ emacs myprog.c
```

The emacs console mode window appears with a short introduction and help screen. Don't be alarmed; as soon as you press a key, emacs loads the file into the active buffer and displays the text, as shown in Figure 7-2.

You'll notice that the top of the console mode window shows a typical menubar. Unfortunately, you won't be able to use the menubar in console mode, only in graphical mode.

Unlike the vim editor, where you have to move in to and out of insert mode to switch between entering commands and inserting text, the emacs editor only has one mode. If you type a printable character, emacs inserts it at the current cursor position. If you type a command, emacs executes the command.

To move the cursor around the buffer area, you can use the arrow keys and the PageUp and PageDown keys, assuming that emacs detected your terminal emulator correctly. If not, there are commands for moving the cursor around:

- C-p to move up one line (the previous line in the text).
- C-b to move left (back) one character.

- `C-f` to move right (forward) one character.
- `C-n` to move down one line (the next line in the text).

There are also commands for making longer jumps with the cursor within the text:

- `M-f` moves right (forward) to the next word.
- `M-b` moves left (backward) to the previous word.
- `C-a` moves to the beginning of the current line.
- `C-e` moves to the end of the current line.
- `M-a` moves to the beginning of the current sentence.
- `M-e` moves to the end of the current sentence.
- `M-v` moves back one screen of data.
- `C-v` moves forward one screen of data.
- `M-<` to move the first line of the text.
- `M->` to move to the last line of the text.

There are several commands you should know for saving the editor buffer back into the file, and exiting emacs:

- `C-x C-s` to save the current buffer contents to the file.
- `C-z` to exit emacs but keep it running in your session so that you can come back to it.
- `C-x C-c` to exit emacs and stop the program.

You'll notice that two of these features require two key commands. The `C-x` command is called the *extend command*. This provides yet another whole set of commands to work with.

Editing data

The emacs editor is pretty robust about inserting and deleting text in the buffer. To insert text, just move the cursor to the location where you want to insert the text and start typing. To delete text, emacs uses the Backspace key to delete the character before the current cursor position and the Delete key to delete the character at the current cursor location.

The emacs editor also has commands for killing text. The difference between deleting text and killing text is that when you kill text, emacs places it in a temporary area where you can retrieve it (see the "Copying and pasting" section). Deleted text is gone forever.

There are a few commands for killing text in the buffer:

- `M-Backspace` to kill the word before the current cursor position.
- `M-d` to kill the word after the current cursor position.
- `C-k` to kill from the current cursor position to the end of the line.
- `M-k` to kill from the current cursor position to the end of the sentence.

The emacs editor also includes a fancy way of mass-killing text. Just move the cursor to the start of the area you want to kill, and press either the C-@ or C-Spacebar keys. Then move the cursor to the end of the area you want to kill and press the C-w command keys. All of the text between the two locations is killed.

If you happen to make a mistake when killing text, the C-u command will undo the kill command, and return the data the state it was in before you killed it.

Copying and pasting

You've seen how to cut data from the emacs buffer area; now it's time to see how to paste it somewhere else. Unfortunately, if you use the vim editor, this process may confuse you when you use the emacs editor.

In an unfortunate coincidence, pasting data in emacs is called *yanking*. In the vim editor, copying is called yanking, which is what makes this a difficult thing to remember if you happen to use both editors.

After you kill data using one of the kill commands, move the cursor to the location where you want to paste the data, and use the C-y command. This yanks the text out of the temporary area and pastes it at the current cursor position. The C-y command yanks the text from the last kill command. If you've performed multiple kill commands, you can cycle through them using the M-y command.

To copy text, just yank it back into the same location you killed it from, then move to the new location and use the C-y command again. You can yank text back as many times as you desire.

Searching and replacing

Searching for text in the emacs editor is done by using the C-s and C-r commands. The C-s command performs a forward search in the buffer area from the current cursor position to the end of the buffer, whereas the C-r command performs a backward search in the buffer area from the current cursor position to the start of the buffer.

When you enter either the C-s or C-r command, a prompt appears in the bottom line, querying you for the text to search. There are two types of searches that emacs can perform.

In an *incremental* search, the emacs editor performs the text search in real-time mode as you type the word. When you type the first letter, it highlights all of the occurrences of that letter in the buffer. When you type the second letter, it highlights all of the occurrences of the two letter combination in the text, and so on until you complete the text you're searching for.

In a *non-incremental* search, press the Enter key after the C-s or C-r commands. This locks the search query into the bottom line area and allows you to type the search text in full before searching.

To replace an existing text string with a new text string, you have to use the M-x command. This command requires a text command, along with parameters.

The text command is `replace-string`. After typing the command, press the Enter key, and emacs will query you for the existing text string. After entering that, press the Enter key again, and emacs will query you for the new replacement text string.

Using buffers in emacs

The emacs editor allows you to edit multiple files at the same time by having multiple buffer areas. You can load files into a buffer and switch between buffers while editing.

To load a new file into a buffer while you're in emacs, use the `C-x C-f` key combination. This is the emacs *find a file* mode. It takes you to the bottom line in the window and allows you to enter the name of the file you want to start to edit. If you don't know the name or location of the file, just press the Enter key. This brings up a file browser in the edit window, as shown in Figure 7-3.

From here, you can browse to the file you want to edit. To traverse up a directory level, go to the double dot entry, and press the Enter key. To traverse down a directory, go to the directory entry and press the Enter key. When you've found the file you want to edit, just press the Enter key, and emacs will load it into a new buffer area.

FIGURE 7-3

The emacs find a file mode browser

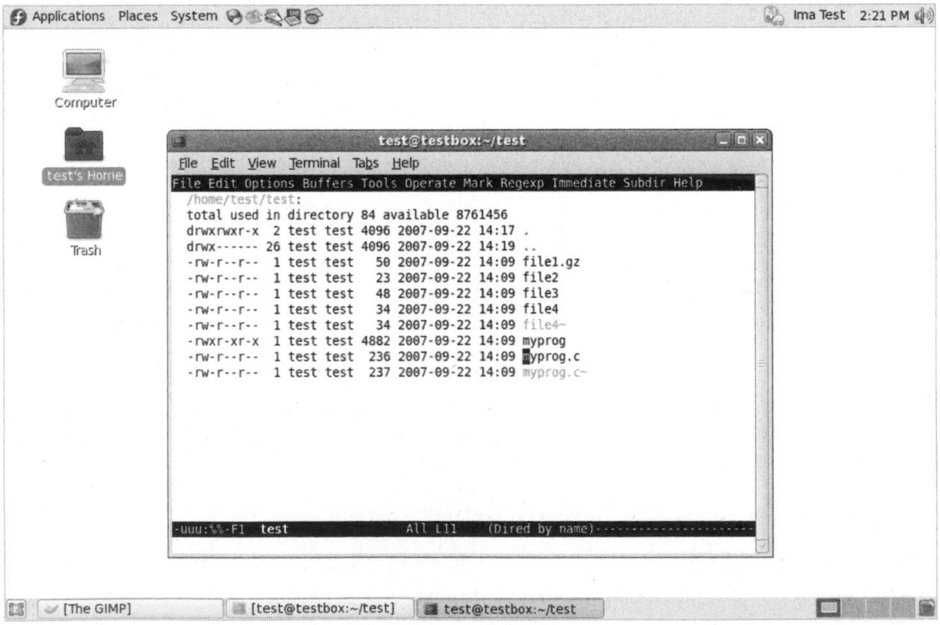

You can list the active buffer areas by pressing the C-x C-b extended command combination. The emacs editor splits the editor window and displays a list of buffers in the bottom window. There are always two buffers that emacs provides besides your main editing buffer:

- A scratch area called *scratch*
- A message area called *Messages*

The scratch area allows you to enter LISP programming commands, as well as enter notes to yourself. The message area shows messages generated by emacs while operating. If any errors occur while using emacs, they will appear in the message area.

There are two ways to switch to a different buffer area in the window:

- C-x o to switch to the buffer listing window. Use the arrow keys to move to the buffer area you want, and press the Enter key.
- C-x b to type in the name of the buffer area you want to switch to.

When you select the option to switch to the buffer listing window, emacs will open the buffer area in the new window area. The emacs editor allows you to have multiple windows open in a single session. The following section discusses how to manage multiple windows in emacs.

Using windows in console mode emacs

The console mode emacs editor was developed many years before the idea of graphical windows appeared. However, it was advanced for its time, in that it could support multiple editing windows within the main emacs window.

You can split the emacs editing window into multiple windows by using one of two commands:

- C-x 2 splits the window horizontally into two windows.
- C-x 3 splits the window vertically into two windows.

To move from one window to another, use the C-x o command. You'll notice that when you create a new window, emacs uses the buffer area from the original window in the new window. Once you move into the new window, you can use the C-x C-f command to load a new file, or one of the commands to switch to a different buffer area in the new window.

To close a window, move to it and use the C-x 0 (that's a zero) command. If you want to close all of the windows except the one you're in, use the C-x 1 (that's a numerical one) command.

Using emacs in X Windows

If you use emacs from an X Windows environment (such as the KDE or GNOME desktops), it'll start in graphical mode, as shown in Figure 7-4.

FIGURE 7-4

The emacs graphical window

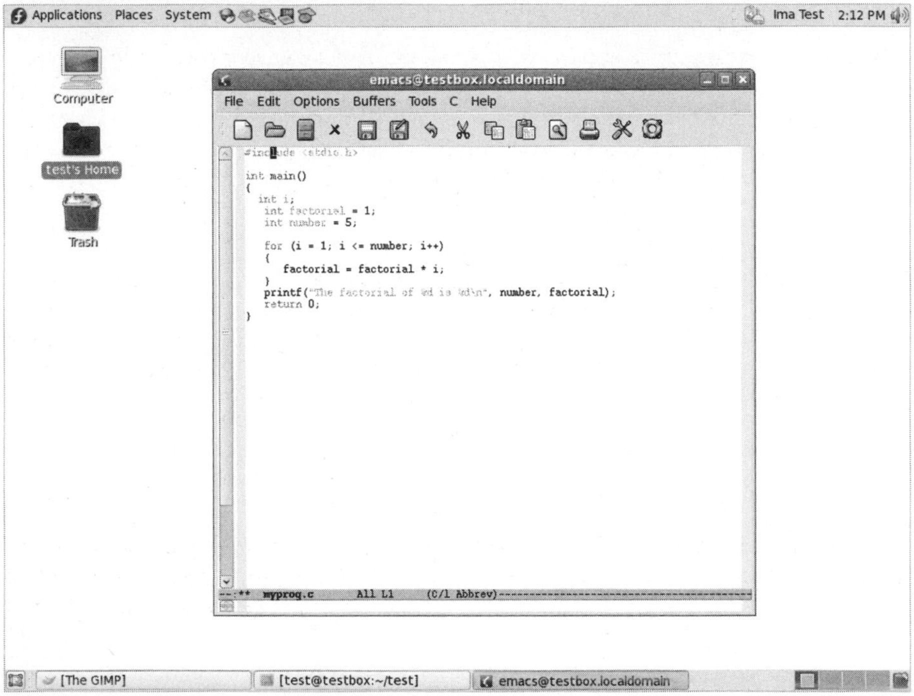

If you've already used emacs in console mode, you should be fairly familiar with the X Windows mode. All of the key commands are available as menubar items. The emacs menubar contains the following items:

- **File** allows you to open files in the window, create new windows, close windows, save buffers, and print buffers.

- **Edit** allows you to cut and copy selected text to the clipboard, paste clipboard data to the current cursor position, search for text, and replace text.

- **Options** provides settings for many more emacs features, such as highlighting, word wrap, cursor type, and setting fonts.

- **Buffers** lists the current buffers available and allows you to easily switch between buffer areas.

- **Tools** provides access to the advanced features in emacs, such as the command line interface access, spell checking, comparing text between files (called diff), sending an e-mail message, calendar, and the calculator.

- **Help** provides the emacs manual online for access to help on specific emacs functions.

Besides the normal graphical emacs menubar items, there is often a separate item specific to the file type in the editor buffer. In Figure 7-4, I opened a C program, so emacs provided a C menu item, allowing advanced settings for highlighting C syntax, and compiling, running, and debugging the code from a command prompt.

The graphical emacs window is an example of an older console application making the migration to the graphical world. Now that many Linux distributions provide graphical desktops (even on servers that don't need them), graphical editors are becoming more commonplace. Both of the popular Linux desktop environments (KDE and GNOME) have also provided graphical text editors specifically for their environments, which are covered in the rest of this chapter.

The KDE Family of Editors

If you're using a Linux distribution that uses the KDE desktop (see Chapter 1), there are a couple of options for you when it comes to text editors. The KDE project officially supports two different text editors:

- **KWrite**: A single-screen text-editing package
- **Kate:** Full-featured multi-window text editing package

Both of these editors are graphical text editors that contain many advanced features. The Kate editor provides more advanced features, plus extra niceties not often found in standard text editors. This section describes each of the editors and shows some of the features that you can use to help with your shell script editing.

The KWrite editor

The basic editor for the KDE environment is KWrite. It provides simple word-processing-style text editing, along with support for code syntax highlighting and editing. The default KWrite editing window is shown in Figure 7-5.

You can't tell from Figure 7-5, but the KWrite editor recognizes several types of programming languages and uses color coding to distinguish constants, functions, and comments. Also, notice that the for loop has an icon that links the opening and closing braces. This is called a *folding marker*. By clicking the icon, you can collapse the function into a single line. This is a great feature when working through large applications.

The KWrite editing window provides full cut and paste capabilities, using the mouse and the arrow keys. Just as in a word processor, you can highlight and cut (or copy) text anywhere in the buffer area and paste it at any other place.

To edit a file using KWrite, you can either select KWrite from the KDE menu system on your desktop (some Linux distributions even create a Panel icon for it) or start it from the command line prompt:

```
$ kwrite factorial.sh
```

183

FIGURE 7-5

The default KWrite window editing a shell script program

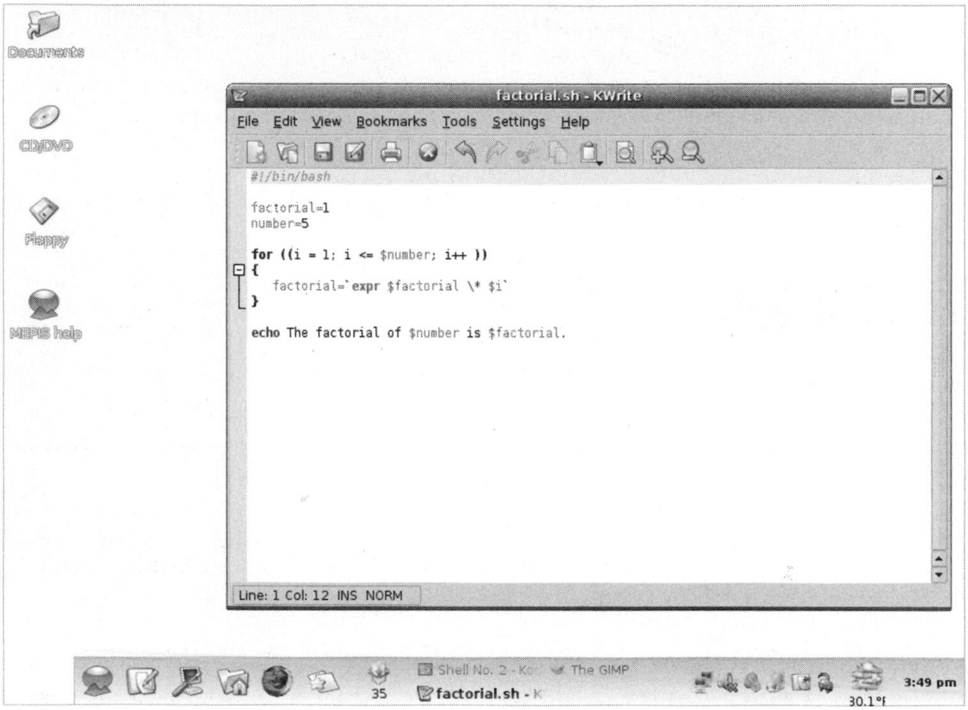

The kwrite command has several command line parameters you can use to customize how it starts:

- --stdin causes KWrite to read data from the standard input device instead of a file.
- --encoding specifies a character encoding type to use for the file.
- --line specifies a line number in the file to start at in the editor window.
- --column specifies a column number in the file to start at in the editor window.

The KWrite editor provides both a menubar and a toolbar at the top of the edit window, allowing you to select features and change configuration settings of the KWrite editor.

The menubar contains the following items:

- **File** to load, save, print, and export text from files.
- **Edit** to manipulate text in the buffer area.
- **View** to manage how the text appears in the editor window.

- **Bookmarks** for handling pointers to return to specific locations in the text.
- **Tools** contains specialized features to manipulate the text.
- **Settings** for configuring the way the editor handles text.
- **Help** for getting information about the editor and commands.

The Edit menubar item provides commands for all of your text editing needs. Instead of having to remember cryptic key commands (which by the way, KWrite also supports), you can just select items in the Edit menubar, as shown in Table 7-2.

The Find Text dialog box, shown in Figure 7-6, is a powerful tool for searching for text in the buffer area.

TABLE 7-2

The KWrite Edit Menu Items

Item	Description
Undo	Reverse the last action or operation.
Redo	Reverse the last undo action.
Cut	Deletes the selected text and places it in the clipboard.
Copy	Copies the selected text to the clipboard.
Copy as HTML	Copies the selected text to the clipboard as HTML code.
Paste	Inserts the current contents of the clipboard at the current cursor position.
Select All	Selects all text in the editor.
Deselect	Deselects any text that is currently selected.
Block Selection Mode	When enabled, allows you to select text between columns instead of whole lines.
Overwrite Mode	Toggles insert mode to overwrite mode, replacing text with new typed text instead of just inserting the new text.
Find	Produces the Find Text dialog box, which allows you to customize a text search.
Find Next	Repeats the last find operation forward in the buffer area.
Find Previous	Repeats the last find operation backwards in the buffer area.
Replace	Produces the Replace With dialog box, which allows you to customize a text search and replace.
Go to Line	Produces the Goto dialog box, which allows you to enter a line number. The cursor moves to the specified line.

FIGURE 7-6

The KWrite Find Text dialog box

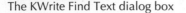

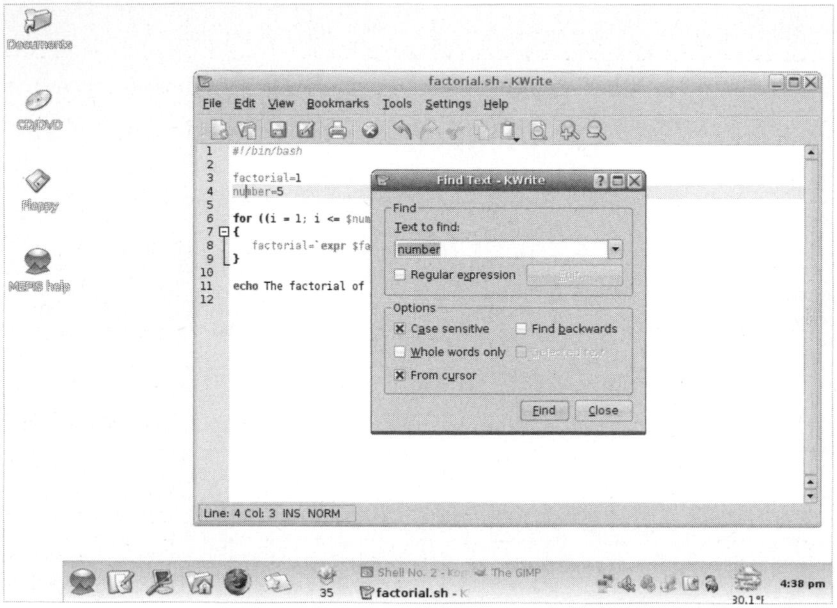

The Find Text dialog box uses the word at the current cursor location as the default text value to search for. It also provides for you to use a regular expression (discussed in Chapter 17) for the search. There are a few checkboxes you can use to customize the search as well, indicating, for example, whether or not to perform a case-sensitive search, or to look only for whole words instead of finding the text within words.

The Tools menubar item provides several handy features for working with the text in the buffer area. Table 7-3 describes the tools available in KWrite.

There are lots of tools for a simple text editor!

The Settings menu includes the Configure Editor dialog box, shown in Figure 7-7.

The Configuration dialog box uses icons on the left side for you to select the feature in KWrite to configure. When you select an icon, the right side of the dialog box shows the configuration settings for the feature.

The Appearance feature allows you to set several features controlling how the text appears in the text editor window. You can enable word wrap, line numbers (great for programmers), and the folder markers from here. With the Fonts & Colors feature, you can customize the complete color scheme for the editor, determining what colors to make each category of text in the program code.

TABLE 7-3

The KWrite Tools

Tool	Description
Read Only Mode	Locks the text so no changes can be made while in the editor.
Filetype	Selects the filetype scheme used in the text.
Highlighting	Highlights text based on content, such as program code or a configuration file.
Indentation	Automatically indents lines based on a selection..
Encoding	Sets the character set encoding used by the text.
Spelling	Starts the spellcheck program at the start of the text.
Spelling (from cursor)	Starts the spellcheck program from the current cursor position.
Spellcheck Selection	Starts the spellcheck program only on the selected section of text.
Indent	Increases the paragraph indentation by one.
Unindent	Decreases the paragraph indentation by one.
Clean Indentation	Returns all paragraph indentation to the original settings.
Align	Forces the current line or the selected lines to return to the default indentation settings.
Comment	Adds a comment symbol to the current line based on the detected file type.
Uncomment	Removes a comment symbol from the current line based on the detected file type.
Uppercase	Sets the selected text, or the character at the current cursor position to upper case.
Lowercase	Sets the selected text, or the character at the current cursor position to lower case.
Capitalize	Uppercases the first letter of the selected text or the word at the current cursor position.
Join Lines	Combines the selected lines, or the line at the current cursor position and the next line into one line.
Word Wrap Document	Enable word wrapping in the text. If a line extends past the editor window edge, the line continues on the next line.

FIGURE 7-7

The KWrite Configure Editor dialog box

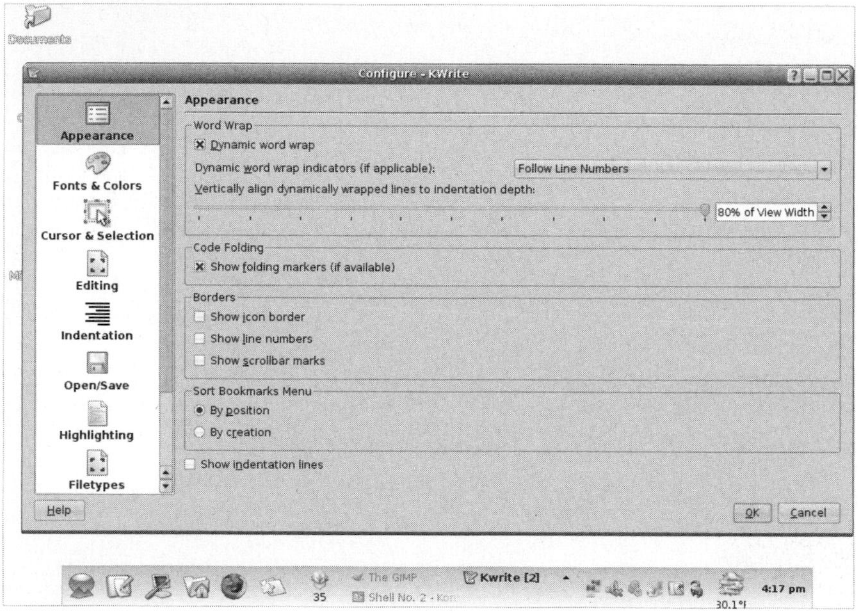

FIGURE 7-8

The Kate session dialog box

The Kate editor

The Kate editor is the flagship editor for the KDE Project. It uses the same text editor as the KWrite application (so most of those features are the same), but it incorporates lots of other features into a single package.

The first thing you'll notice when you start the Kate editor, is that the editor doesn't start! Instead, you get a dialog box, as shown in Figure 7-8.

The Kate editor handles files in sessions. You can have multiple files open in a session, and you can have multiple sessions saved. When you start Kate, it provides you with the choice of which session to return to. When you close your Kate session, it remembers the documents you had open, and displays them the next time you start Kate.

After selecting a session, you'll see the main Kate editor window, shown in Figure 7-9.

The left side frame shows the documents currently open in the session. You can switch between documents just by clicking the document name. To edit a new file, click the Filesystem Browser tab on the left side. The left frame is now a full graphical filesystem browser, allowing you to graphically browse to locate your files.

FIGURE 7-9

The main Kate editing window

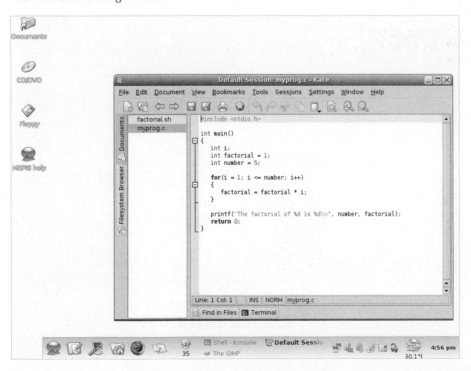

FIGURE 7-10

The Kate built-in terminal window

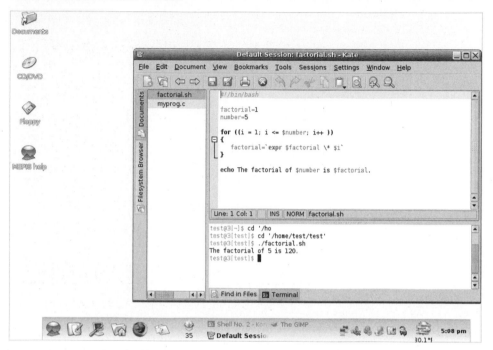

One of my favorite features of the Kate editor is the built-in terminal window, shown in Figure 7-10.

The terminal tab at the bottom of the text editor window starts the built-in terminal emulator in Kate (using the KDE Konsole terminal emulator). This feature horizontally splits the current editing window, creating a new window with Konsole running in it. You can now enter command line commands, start programs, or check on system settings without having to leave the editor! To close the terminal window, just type **exit** at the command prompt.

As you can tell from the terminal feature, Kate also supports multiple windows. The Window menubar item provides options to:

- Create a new Kate window using the current session
- Split the current window vertically to create a new window
- Split the current window horizontally to create a new window
- Close the current window

To set the configuration settings in Kate, select the Configure Kate item under the Settings menubar item. The Configuration dialog box, shown in Figure 7-11, appears.

FIGURE 7-11

The Kate configuration settings dialog box

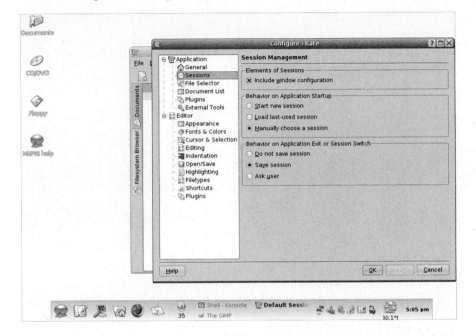

You'll notice that the Editor settings area is exactly the same as for KWrite. This is because the two editors share the same text editor engine. The Application settings area allows you to configure settings for the Kate items, such as controlling sessions (shown in Figure 7-11), the documents list, and the filesystem browser. Kate also supports external plugin applications, which can be activated here.

The GNOME Editor

If you're working on a Linux system using the GNOME desktop environment, there's a graphical text editor that you can use as well. The gedit text editor is a basic text editor, with a few advanced features thrown in just for fun. This section walks you through the features of gedit and demonstrates how to use it for your shell script programming.

Starting gedit

Most GNOME desktop environments include gedit in the Accessories Panel menu item. If you can't find gedit there, you can start it from the command line prompt:

```
$ gedit factorial.sh myprog.c
```

191

FIGURE 7-12

The gedit main editor window

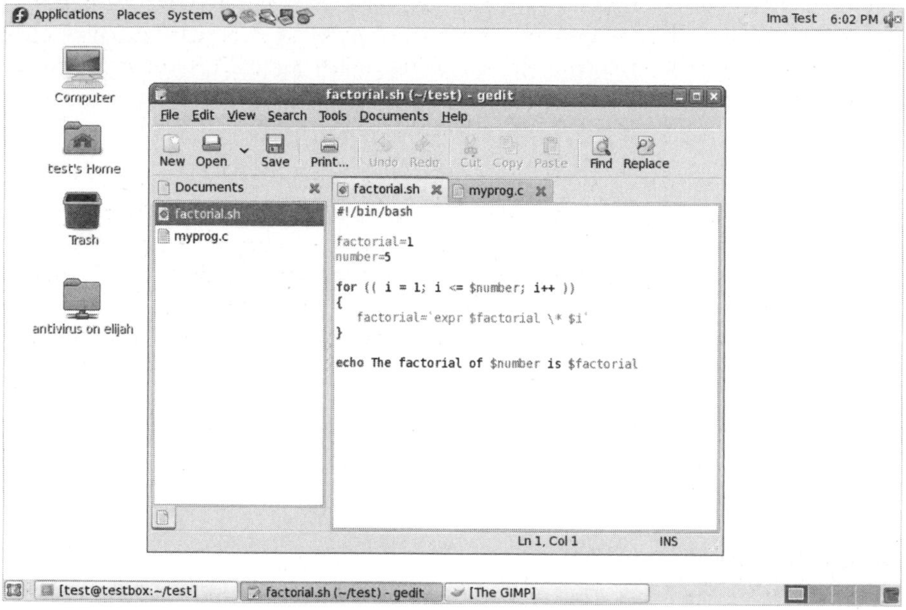

When you start gedit with multiple files, it loads all of the files into separate buffers and displays each one as a tabbed window within the main editor window, as shown in Figure 7-12.

The left frame in the gedit main editor window shows the documents you're currently editing. The right side shows the tabbed windows that contain the buffer text. If you hover your mouse pointer over each tab, a dialog box appears, showing the full pathname of the file, the MIME type, and the character set encoding it uses.

Basic gedit features

Besides the editor windows, gedit uses both a menubar and toolbar that allow you to set features and configure settings. The toolbar provides quick access to menubar items. The menubar items available are:

- **File** for handling new files, saving existing files, and printing files.
- **Edit** to manipulate text in the active buffer area and set the editor preferences.
- **View** to set the editor features to display in the window and to set the text highlighting mode.
- **Search** to find and replace text in the active editor buffer area.
- **Tools** to access plugin tools installed in gedit.

- **Documents** to manage files open in the buffer areas.
- **Help** to access the full gedit manual.

There shouldn't be anything too surprising here. The File menu provides the option Open Location, which allows you to open a file from the network using the standard Uniform Resource Identifier (URI) format popular in the World Wide Web world. This format identifies the protocol used to access the file (such as HTTP or FTP), the server where the file is located, and the complete path on the server to access the file.

The Edit menu contains the standard cut, copy, and paste functions, along with a neat feature that allows you to easily enter the date and time in the text in several different formats. The Search menu provides a standard find function, which produces a dialog box where you can enter the text to find, along with the capability to select how the find should work (matching case, matching the whole word, and the search direction). It also provides an incremental search feature, which works in real-time mode, finding text as you type characters of the word.

Setting preferences

The Edit menu contains a Preferences item, which produces the gedit Preferences dialog box, shown in Figure 7-13.

FIGURE 7-13

The gedit Preferences dialog box

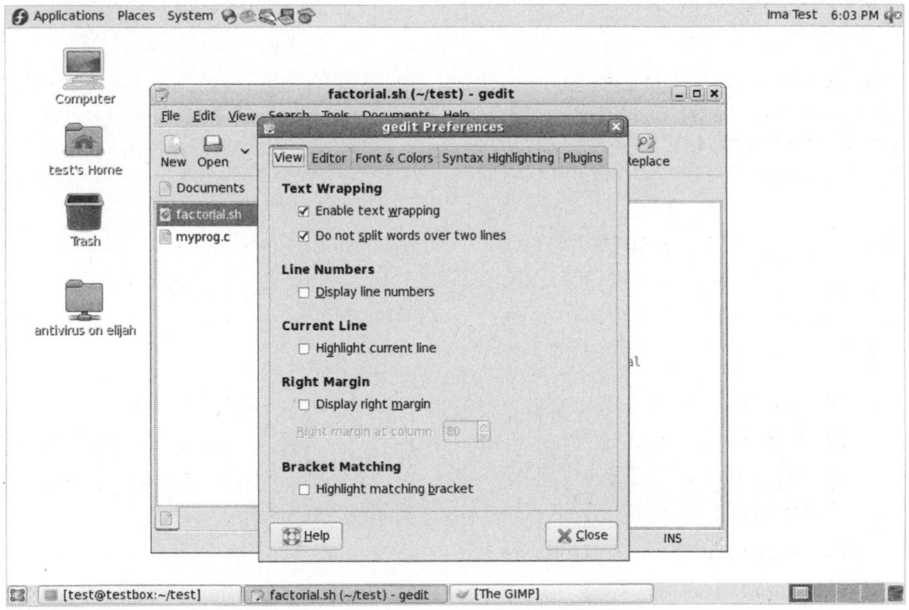

This is where you can customize the operation of the gedit editor. The Preferences dialog box contains five tabbed areas for setting the features and behavior of the editor.

View

The View tab provides options for how gedit displays the text in the editor window:

- **Text Wrapping** determines how to handle long lines of text in the editor. The Enabling text wrapping option wraps long lines to the next line of the editor. The Do Not Split Words Over Two Lines option prevents the auto-inserting of hyphens into long words, to prevent them being split between two lines.

- **Line Numbers** displays line numbers in the left margin in the editor window.

- **Current Line** highlights the line where the cursor is currently positioned, enabling you to easily find the cursor position.

- **Right Margin** enables the right margin and allows you to set how many columns should be in the editor window. The default value is 80 columns.

- **Bracket Matching**, when enabled, highlights bracket pairs in programming code, allowing you to easily match brackets in if-then statements, for and while loops, and other coding elements that use brackets.

The line-numbering and bracket-matching features provide an environment for programmers to troubleshoot code that's not often found in text editors.

Editor

The Editor tab provides options for how the gedit editor handles tabs and indentation, along with how files are saved:

- **Tab Stops** sets the number of spaces skipped when you press the Tab key. The default value is eight. This feature also includes a checkbox that, when checked, inserts spaces instead of a tab skip.

- **Automatic Indentation**, when enabled, causes gedit to automatically indent lines in the text for paragraphs and code elements (such as if-then statements and loops).

- **File Saving** provides two features for saving files: whether or not to create a backup copy of the file when opened in the edit window, and whether or not to automatically save the file at a preselected interval.

The auto-save feature is a great way to ensure that your changes are saved on a regular basis to prevent catastrophes from crashes or power outages.

Font & Colors

The Font & Colors tab allows you to configure (not surprisingly) two items:

- **Font** allows you to select the default font of Monospace 10, or to select a customized font and font size from a dialog box.
- **Colors** allows you to select the default color scheme used for text, background, selected text, and selection colors, or choose a custom color for each category.

The default colors for gedit match the standard GNOME desktop theme selected for the desktop. These colors will change to match the scheme you select for the desktop.

Syntax Highlighting

The Syntax Highlighting tab provides options to configure how gedit highlights elements in programming code. The gedit editor has the capability to detect the programming language contained in a text file and to automatically set the appropriate syntax highlighting for the text.

You can also customize the syntax-highlighting feature by selecting colors for various elements of a programming code file. The elements change depending on the programming code type you select. For shell scripts, select the sh highlighting mode. This mode contains color schemes for the following code elements:

- Text within a backtick string
- Built-in shell commands
- Common commands
- Shell functions
- Line comments
- Multiline string (two versions)
- Shell operator
- Shell punctuator
- Shell redirection
- Self
- Two types of strings
- Two types of variables

This provides an amazing amount of control when selecting your shell-script-editing environment. You can customize your own work area, down to the colors you prefer for the code highlighting.

FIGURE 7-14

The gedit Plugins Preferences tab

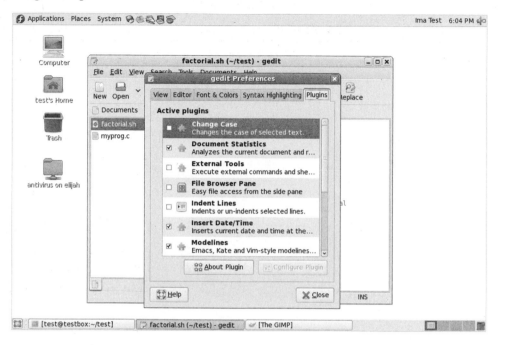

Plugins

The Plugins tab provides control over the plugins used in gedit. Plugins are separate programs that can interface with gedit to provide additional functionality. The Plugins tab is shown in Figure 7-14.

There are several plugins available for gedit, but not all of them are installed by default. Table 7-4 describes the plugins that are currently available in gedit.

Plugins that are enabled show a checkmark in the checkbox next to their name. Some plugins, such as the External Tools plugin, also provide additional configuration features after you select them. It allows you to set a shortcut key to start the terminal, where gedit displays output, and the command to use to start the shell session.

Unfortunately, not all plugins are installed in the same place in the gedit menubar. Some plugins appear in the Tools menubar item (such as the Spell Checker and External Tools plugins), while others appear in the Edit menubar item (such as the Change Case and Insert Date/Time plugins).

TABLE 7-4

The gedit Plugins

Plugin	Description
Change Case	Changes the case of selected text.
Document Statistics	Reports the number of words, lines, characters, and non-space characters.
External Tools	Provides a shell environment in the editor to execute commands and scripts.
File Browser Pane	Provides a simple file browser to make selecting files for editing easier.
Indent Lines	Provides advanced line indentation and un-indentation.
Insert Date/Time	Inserts the current date and time in several formats at the current cursor position.
Modelines	Provides emacs-style message lines at the bottom of the editor window.
Python Console	Provides an interactive console at the bottom of the editor window for entering commands using the Python programming language.
Snippets	Allows you to store often-used pieces of text for easy retrieval anywhere in the text.
Sort	Quickly sorts the entire file or selected text.
Spell Checker	Provides dictionary spellchecking for the text file.
Tag List	Provides a list of commonly used strings you can easily enter into your text.
User name	Inserts the current user's login name at the current cursor position.

Summary

When it comes to creating shell scripts, you'll need some type of text editor. There are several popular text editors available for the Linux environment. The most popular editor in the Unix world, vi, has been ported to the Linux world as the vim editor. The vim editor provides simple text editing from the console, using a rudimentary full-screen graphical mode. The vim editor provides many advanced editor features, such as text searching and replacement.

Another popular Unix editor, emacs, has also made its way to the Linux world. The Linux version of emacs has both console and an X Windows graphical mode, making it the bridge between the old world and the new. The emacs editor provides multiple buffer areas, allowing you to edit multiple files simultaneously.

The KDE Project created two editors for use in the KDE desktop. The KWrite editor is a simple editor that provides the basic text-editing features, along with a few advanced features such as syntax highlighting for programming code, line numbering, and code folding. The Kate editor provides more advanced features for programmers. One great feature in Kate is a built-in terminal window. You can open a command line interface session directly in the Kate editor without having to open a separate terminal emulator window. The Kate editor also allows you to open multiple files, providing different windows for each opened file.

The GNOME Project also provides a simple text editor for programmers. The gedit editor is a basic text editor that provides some advanced features such as code syntax highlighting and line numbering, but it was designed to be a bare-bones editor. To spruce up the gedit editor, developers created plugins, which expand the features available in gedit. Current plugins include a spellchecker, a terminal emulator, and a file browser.

This wraps up the background chapters on working with the command line in Linux. The next part of the book dives into the shell-scripting world. The next chapter starts you off by showing you how to create a shell script file and how to run it on your Linux system. It'll also show you the basics of shell scripts, allowing you to create simple programs by stringing multiple commands together into a script you can run.

Part II

Shell Scripting Basics

## Chapter 8

Basic Script Building

Now that we've covered the basics of the Linux system and the command line, it's time to start coding. This chapter discusses the basics of writing shell scripts. You'll need to know these basic concepts before you can start writing your own shell script masterpieces.

Using Multiple Commands

So far you've seen how to use the command line interface (CLI) prompt of the shell to enter commands and view the command results. The key to shell scripts is the ability to enter multiple commands, and process the results from each command, even possibly passing the results of one command to another. The shell allows you to chain commands together into a single step.

If you want to run two commands together, you can enter them on the same prompt line, separated with a semicolon:

```
$ date ; who
Mon Sep 24 19:44:35 EST 2007
rich    :0      2007-09-24 18:23 (console)
rich    pts/1   2007-09-24 18:24
rich    pts/0   2007-09-24 18:42
barbara pts/2   2007-09-24 19:30
katie   pts/3   2007-09-24 19:39
$
```

Congratulations, you just wrote a shell script! This simple script uses just two bash shell commands. The date command runs first, displaying the current date and time, followed by the output of the who command, showing who is currently logged on to the system. Using this technique, you can string together as many commands as you wish, up to the maximum command line character count of 255 characters.

While using this technique is fine for small scripts, it has a major drawback in that you have to enter the entire command at the command prompt every time you want to run it. Instead of having to manually enter the commands onto a command line, you can combine the commands into a simple text file. When you need to run the commands, just simply run the text file.

Creating a Script File

To place shell commands in a text file, first you'll need to use a text editor (see Chapter 7) to create a file, then enter the commands into the file.

When creating a shell script file, you must specify the shell you are using in the first line of the file. The format for this is:

```
#!/bin/bash
```

In a normal shell script line, the pound sign (#) is used as a comment line. A comment line in a shell script isn't processed by the shell. However, the first line of a shell script file is a special case, and the pound sign followed by the exclamation point tells the shell what shell to run the script under (yes, you can be using a bash shell and run your script using another shell).

After indicating the shell, commands are entered onto each line of the file, followed by a carriage return. As mentioned, comments can be added by using the pound sign. An example looks like this:

```
#!/bin/bash
# This script displays the date and who's logged on
date
who
```

And that's all there is to it. You can use the semicolon and put both commands on the same line if you want to, but in a shell script, you can list commands on separate lines. The shell will process commands in the order in which they appear in the file.

Also notice that I added another line that starts with the pound symbol and adds a comment. Lines that start with the pound symbol (other than the first #! line) aren't interpreted by the shell. This is a great way to leave comments for yourself about what's happening in the script, so when you come back to it two years later you can easily remember what you did.

Save this script in a file called test1, and you are almost ready. I say "almost" because there are still a couple of things to do before you can run your new shell script file.

If you try running the file now, you'll be somewhat disappointed to see this:

```
$ test1
bash: test1: command not found
$
```

The first hurdle to jump is getting the bash shell to find your script file. If you remember from Chapter 5, the shell uses an environment variable called PATH to find commands. Looking at the PATH environment variable explains my problem:

```
$ echo $PATH
/usr/local/bin:/bin:/usr/bin:/usr/X11R6/bin:/usr/X11R6/bin
$
```

The PATH environment variable is set to look for commands only in a handful of directories. To get the shell to find my test1 script, I need to do one of two things:

- Add the directory where my shell script file is located to the PATH environment variable.
- Use an absolute or relative filepath to reference my shell script file in the prompt.

> **TIP** Some Linux distributions add the $HOME/bin directory to the PATH environment variable. This creates a place in every user's HOME directory to place files where the shell can find them to execute.

For this example, I'll use the second method to tell the shell exactly where my script file is located. Remember, to reference a file in the current directory, you can use the single dot operator in the shell:

```
$ ./test1
bash: ./test1: Permission denied
$
```

Now the shell found the shell script file just fine, but there's another problem. The shell indicated that I don't have permission to execute the file. A quick look at the file permissions should show what's going on here:

```
$ ls -l test1
-rw-r--r--    1 rich     rich              73 Sep 24 19:56 test1
$
```

When I created the new test1 file, my umask value determined the default permission settings for the new file. Since my umask is set to 022 (see Chapter 6), the system created the file with only read/write permissions for myself.

The next step is to give myself permission to execute the file, using the chmod command (see Chapter 6):

```
$ chmod u+x test1
$ ./test1
Mon Sep 24 19:58:35 EST 2007
rich     :0          2007-09-24 18:23 (console)
rich     pts/1       2007-09-24 18:24
rich     pts/0       2007-09-24 18:42
barbara  pts/2       2007-09-24 19:30
katie    pts/3       2007-09-24 19:39
$
```

Success! Now all of the pieces are in the right places to execute the new shell script file.

Displaying Messages

Most shell commands produce their own output, which is displayed on the console monitor where the script is running. Many times though you will want to add your own text messages to help the script user know what is happening within the script. This is done using the echo command. The echo command can display a simple text string if you add the string following the command:

```
$ echo This is a test
This is a test
$
```

Notice that by default you don't need to use quotes to delineate the string you're displaying. However, sometimes this can get tricky if you are using quotes within your string:

```
$ echo Let's see if this'll work
Lets see if thisll work
$
```

The echo command uses either double or single quotes to delineate text strings. If you use them within your string, you need to use one type of quote within the text, and the other type to delineate the string:

```
$ echo "This is a test to see if you're paying attention"
This is a test to see if you're paying attention
$ echo 'Rich says "scripting is easy".'
Rich says "scripting is easy".
$
```

Now all of the quotation marks appear properly in the output.

You can add echo statements anywhere in your shell scripts where you need to display additional information:

```
$ cat test1
#!/bin/bash
# This script displays the date and who's logged on
echo  The time and date are:
date
echo "Let's see who's logged into the system:"
who
$
```

When you run this script, it produces the output:

```
$ chmod u+x test1
$ ./test1
The time and date are:
Mon Sep 24 20:09:35 EST 2007
Let's see who's logged into the system:
rich    :0      2007-09-24 18:23 (console)
rich    pts/1   2007-09-24 18:24
rich    pts/0   2007-09-24 18:42
barbara pts/2   2007-09-24 19:30
katie   pts/3   2007-09-24 19:39
$
```

That's nice, but what if you want to echo a text string on the same line as a command output? You can use the -n parameter for the echo statement to do that. Just change the first echo statement line to:

```
echo -n "The time and date are: "
```

You'll need to use quotes around the string to ensure that there's a space at the end of the echoed string. The command output begins exactly where the string output stops. The output will now look like:

```
$ ./test1
The time and date are: Mon Sep 24 20:11:35 EST 2007
Let's see who's logged into the system:
rich    :0      2007-09-24 18:23 (console)
rich    pts/1   2007-09-24 18:24
rich    pts/0   2007-09-24 18:42
barbara pts/2   2007-09-24 19:30
katie   pts/3   2007-09-24 19:39
$
```

Perfect! The echo command is a crucial piece of shell scripts that interact with users. You'll find yourself using it in many situations, especially when you want to display the values of script variables. Let's look at that next.

Using Variables

Just running individual commands from the shell script is useful, but this has its limitations. Often you'll want to incorporate other data in your shell commands to process information. You can do this by using *variables*. Variables allow you to temporarily store information within the shell script for use with other commands in the script. This section shows how to use variables in your shell scripts.

Environment variables

You've already seen one type of Linux variable in action. Chapter 5 described the environment variables available in the Linux system. You can access these values from your shell scripts as well.

The shell maintains environment variables that track specific system information, such as the name of the system, the name of the user logged in to the system, the user's system ID (called UID), the default home directory of the user, and the search path used by the shell to find programs. You can display a complete list of active environment variables available by using the set command:

```
$ set
BACKSPACE=Delete
BASH=/bin/bash
EUID=1000
HISTFILE=/home/rich/.bash_history
HISTFILESIZE=1000
HISTSIZE=1000
HOME=/home/rich
HOSTNAME=testing
HOSTTYPE=i586
LANG=en
LANGUAGE=en_US:en
LINES=24
LOGNAME=rich
...
```

You can tap into these environment variables from within your scripts by using the environment variable's name preceded by a dollar sign. This is demonstrated in the following script:

```
$ cat test2
#!/bin/bash
# display user information from the system.
echo "User info for userid: $USER"
echo UID: $UID
echo HOME: $HOME
$
```

The $USER, $UID, and $HOME environment variables are used to display the pertinent information about the logged-in user. The output should look something like this:

```
$chmod u+x test2
$ ./test2
User info for userid:  rich
UID: 501
HOME: /home/rich
$
```

Notice that the environment variables in the echo commands are replaced by their current values when the script is run. Also notice that we were able to place the $USER system variable within the double quotation marks in the first string, and the shell script was still able to figure out what we meant. There is a drawback to using this method though. Look at what happens in this example:

```
$ echo "The cost of the item is $15"
The cost of the item is 5
```

That is obviously not what I intended. Whenever the script sees a dollar sign within quotes, it assumes you're referencing a variable. In this example the script attempted to display the variable $1 (which was not defined), then the number 5. To display an actual dollar sign, you must precede it with a backslash character:

```
$ echo "The cost of the item is \$15"
The cost of the item is $15
```

That's better. The backslash allowed the shell script to interpret the dollar sign as an actual dollar sign, and not a variable. The next section shows how to create your own variables in your scripts.

> **NOTE** You may also see variables referenced using the format ${variable}. The extra braces around the variable name are often used to help identify the variable name from the dollar sign.

User variables

Besides the environment variables, a shell script allows you to set and use your own variables within the script. Setting variables allows you to temporarily store data and use it throughout the script, making the shell script more like a real computer program.

User variables can be any text string of up to 20 letters, digits, or an underscore character. User variables are case sensitive, so the variable Var1 is different from the variable var1. This little rule often gets novice script programmers in trouble.

Values are assigned to user variables using an equal sign. No spaces can appear between the variable, the equal sign, and the value (another trouble spot for novices). Here are a few examples of assigning values to user variables:

```
var1=10
var2=-57
var3=testing
var4="still more testing"
```

The shell script automatically determines the data type used for the variable value. Variables defined within the shell script maintain their values throughout the life of the shell script but are deleted when the shell script completes.

Just like system variables, user variables can be referenced using the dollar sign:

```
$ cat test3
#!/bin/bash
# testing variables
days=10
guest="Katie"
echo "$guest checked in $days days ago"
days=5
guest="Jessica"
echo "$guest checked in $days days ago"
$
```

Running the script produces the output:

```
$ chmod u+x test3
$ ./test3
Katie checked in 10 days ago
Jessica checked in 5 days ago
$
```

Each time the variable is referenced, it produces the value currently assigned to it. It's important to remember that when referencing a variable value you use the dollar sign, but when referencing the variable to assign a value to it, you do not use the dollar sign. Here's an example of what I mean:

```
$ cat test4
#!/bin/bash
# assigning a variable value to another variable

value1=10
value2=$value1
echo The resulting value is $value2
$
```

When you use the value of the `value1` variable in the assignment statement, you must still use the dollar sign. This code produces the output:

```
$ chmod u+x test4
$ ./test4
The resulting value is 10
$
```

If you forget the dollar sign, and make the `value2` assignment line look like:

```
value2=value1
```

you get the following output:

```
$ ./test4
The resulting value is value1
$
```

Without the dollar sign the shell interprets the variable name as a normal text string, which is most likely not what you wanted.

The backtick

One of the most useful features of shell scripts is the lowly back quote character, usually called the backtick (`) in the Linux world. Be careful, this is not the normal single quotation mark character you are used to using for strings. Since it is not used very often outside of shell scripts, you may not even know where to find it on your keyboard. You should become familiar with it, because it's a crucial component of many shell scripts (hint: on a U.S. keyboard, it is usually on the same key as the tilde symbol ($\sim$)).

The backtick allows you to assign the output of a shell command to a variable. While this doesn't seem like much, it is a major building block in script programming.

You must surround the entire command line command with backtick characters:

```
testing=`date`
```

The shell runs the command within the backticks, and assigns the output to the variable `testing`. Here's an example of creating a variable using the output from a normal shell command:

```
$ cat test5
#!/bin/bash
# using the backtick character
testing=`date`
echo "The date and time are: " $testing
$
```

The variable `testing` receives the output from the `date` command, and it is used in the `echo` statement to display it. Running the shell script produces the following output:

```
$ chmod u+x test5
$ ./test5
The date and time are:  Mon Sep 24 20:23:25 EDT 2007
$
```

That's not all that exciting in this example (you could just as easily just put the command in the `echo` statement), but once you capture the command output in a variable, you can do anything with it.

Here's a popular example of how the backtick is used to capture the current date and use it to create a unique filename in a script:

```
#!/bin/bash
# copy the /usr/bin directory listing to a log file
today=`date +%y%m%d`
ls /usr/bin -al > log.$today
```

The `today` variable is assigned the output of a formatted `date` command. This is a common technique used to extract date information for log filenames. The `+%y%m%d` format instructs the `date` command to display the date as a two-digit year, month, and day:

```
$ date +%y%m%d
070922
$
```

The script assigns the value to a variable, which is then used as part of a filename. The file itself contains the redirected output (discussed later in the "Redirecting Output" section) of a directory listing. After running the script, you should see a new file in your directory:

```
-rw-r--r--    1 rich     rich            769 Sep 22 10:15 log.070922
```

The log file appears in the directory using the value of the `$today` variable as part of the filename. The contents of the log file are the directory listing from the `/usr/bin` directory. If the script is run the next day, the log filename will be `log.070923`, thus creating a new file for the new day.

Redirecting Input and Output

There are times when you'd like to save the output from a command instead of just having it displayed on the monitor. The bash shell provides a few different operators that allow you to *redirect* the output of a command to an alternative location (such as a file). Redirection can be used for input as well as output, redirecting a file to a command for input. This section describes what you need to use redirection in your shell scripts.

Output redirection

The most basic type of redirection is sending output from a command to a file. The bash shell uses the greater-than symbol for this:

```
command > outputfile
```

Anything that would appear on the monitor from the command instead is stored in the output file specified:

```
$ date > test6
$ ls -l test6
-rw-r--r--    1 rich     rich              29 Sep 24 17:56 test6
$ cat test6
Tue Sep 24 17:56:58 EDT 2007
$
```

The redirect operator created the file test6 (using the default umask settings) and redirected the output from the date command to the test6 file. If the output file already exists, the redirect operator overwrites the existing file with the new file data:

```
$ who > test6
$ cat test6
rich     pts/0    Sep 24 17:55
$
```

Now the contents of the test6 file contain the output from the who command.

Sometimes, instead of overwriting the file's contents, you may need to append output from a command to an existing file, for example if you're creating a log file to document an action on the system. In this situation, you can use the double greater-than symbol (>>) to append data:

```
$ date >> test6
$ cat test6
rich     pts/0    Sep 24 17:55
Tue Sep 24 18:02:14 EDT 2007
$
```

The test6 file still contains the original data from the who command processed earlier, plus now it contains the new output from the date command.

Input redirection

Input redirection is the opposite of output redirection. Instead of taking the output of a command and redirecting it to a file, input redirection takes the content of a file and redirects it to a command.

The input redirection symbol is the less-than symbol (<):

```
command < inputfile
```

The easy way to remember this is that the command is always listed first in the command line, and the redirection symbol "points" to the way the data is flowing. The less-than symbol indicates that the data is flowing from the input file to the command.

Here's an example of using input redirection with the wc command:

```
$ wc < test6
      2      11      60
$
```

The wc command provides a count of text in the data. By default it produces three values:

- The number of lines in the text
- The number of words in the text
- The number of bytes in the text

By redirecting a text file to the wc command, you can get a quick count of the lines, words, and bytes in the file. The example shows that there are 2 lines, 11 words, and 60 bytes in the test6 file.

There's another method of input redirection, called *inline input redirection*. This method allows you to specify the data for input redirection on the command line instead of in a file. This may seem somewhat odd at first, but there are a few applications for this process (such as those shown in the "Performing Math" section later).

The inline input redirection symbol is the double less-than symbol (<<). Besides this symbol, you must specify a text marker that delineates the beginning and end of the data used for input. You can use any string value for the text marker, but it must be the same at the beginning of the data and the end of the data:

```
command << marker
data
marker
```

When using inline input redirection on the command line, the shell will prompt for data using the secondary prompt, defined in the PS2 environment variable (see Chapter 5). Here's how this looks when you use it:

```
$ wc << EOF
> test string 1
> test string 2
> test string 3
> EOF
      3       9      42
$
```

The secondary prompt continues to prompt for more data until you enter the text marker. The wc command performs the line, word, and byte counts of the data supplied by the inline input redirection.

Pipes

There are times when you need to send the output of one command to the input of another command. This is possible using redirection, but somewhat clunky:

```
$ rpm -qa > rpm.list
$ sort < rpm.list
a2ps-4.13b-65.fc7
acl-2.2.39-3.1.fc7
alacarte-0.11.3-3.fc7
alsa-lib-1.0.14-3.fc7
alsa-utils-1.0.14-1.fc7
anacron-2.3-47.fc7
apr-1.2.8-6
apr-util-1.2.8-7
aspell-0.60.5-3.fc7
aspell-en-6.0-7.fc7
at-3.1.10-13.fc7
atk-1.18.0-1.fc7
at-spi-1.18.1-1.fc7
...
```

The rpm command manages the software packages installed on systems using the Red Hat Package Management system (RPM), such as my Fedora system as shown. When used with the -qa parameters, it produces a list of the existing packages installed, but not necessarily in any specific order. If you're looking for a specific package, or group of packages, it can be difficult to find it using the output of the rpm command.

Using the standard output redirection, I was able to redirect the output from the rpm command to a file, called rpm.list. After the command finished, the rpm.list file contained a list of all the installed software packages on my system. Next, I used input redirection to send the contents of the rpm.list file to the sort command to sort the package names alphabetically.

That was useful, but again, a somewhat clunky way of producing the information. Instead of redirecting the output of a command to a file, you can redirect the output to another command. This process is called piping. The pipe symbol is the bar operator (|):

```
command1 | command2
```

Piping provides a way to link commands to provide more detailed output. Don't think of piping as running two commands back to back though. The Linux system actually runs both commands at the same time, linking them together internally in the system. As the first command produces output, it's sent immediately to the second command. No intermediate files or buffer areas are used to transfer the data.

Now, using piping you can easily pipe the output of the `rpm` command directly to the `sort` command to produce your results:

```
$ rpm -qa | sort
a2ps-4.13b-65.fc7
acl-2.2.39-3.1.fc7
alacarte-0.11.3-3.fc7
alsa-lib-1.0.14-3.fc7
alsa-utils-1.0.14-1.fc7
anacron-2.3-47.fc7
apr-1.2.8-6
apr-util-1.2.8-7
aspell-0.60.5-3.fc7
aspell-en-6.0-7.fc7
at-3.1.10-13.fc7
atk-1.18.0-1.fc7
at-spi-1.18.1-1.fc7
...
```

Unless you're a (very) quick reader, you probably couldn't keep up with the output generated by this command. Since the piping feature operates in real time, as soon as the `rpm` command produces data, the `sort` command gets busy sorting it. By the time the `rpm` command finishes outputting data, the `sort` command already has the data sorted and starts displaying it on the monitor.

There's no limit to the number of pipes you can use in a command (up to the 255 character limit on the line length). You can continue piping the output of commands to other commands to refine your operation.

In this case, since the output of the `sort` command zooms by so quickly, we can use one of the text paging commands (such as `less` or `more`) to force the output to stop at every screen of data:

```
$ rpm -qa | sort | more
```

This command sequence runs the `rpm` command, pipes the output to the `sort` command, then pipes that output to the `more` command to display the data, stopping after every screen of information. This now lets you pause and read what's on the display before continuing, as shown in Figure 8-1.

To get even fancier, you can use redirection along with piping, to save your output to a file:

```
$ rpm -qa | sort > rpm.list
$more rpm.list
ammonite-1.0.0-1mdk
anacron-2.3-7mdk
```

```
apache-1.3.19-3mdk
apache-common-1.3.19-3mdk
apache-conf-1.3.19-3mdk
apache-mod_perl-1.3.19_1.25-3mdk
apache-modules-1.3.19-3mdk
apache-suexec-1.3.19-3mdk
arts-2.1.1-7mdk
ash-0.2-24mdk
aspell-0.32.5-4mdk
aspell-en-0.32.5-4mdk
at-3.1.7-21mdk
...
```

As expected, the data in the rpm.list file is now sorted!

By far one of the most popular uses of piping is piping the results of commands that produce long output to the more command. This is especially common with the ls command, as shown in Figure 8-2.

The ls -l command produces a long listing of all the files in the directory. For directories with lots of files, this can be quite a listing. By piping the output to the more command, you force the output to stop at the end of every screen of data.

FIGURE 8-1

Using piping to send data to the more command

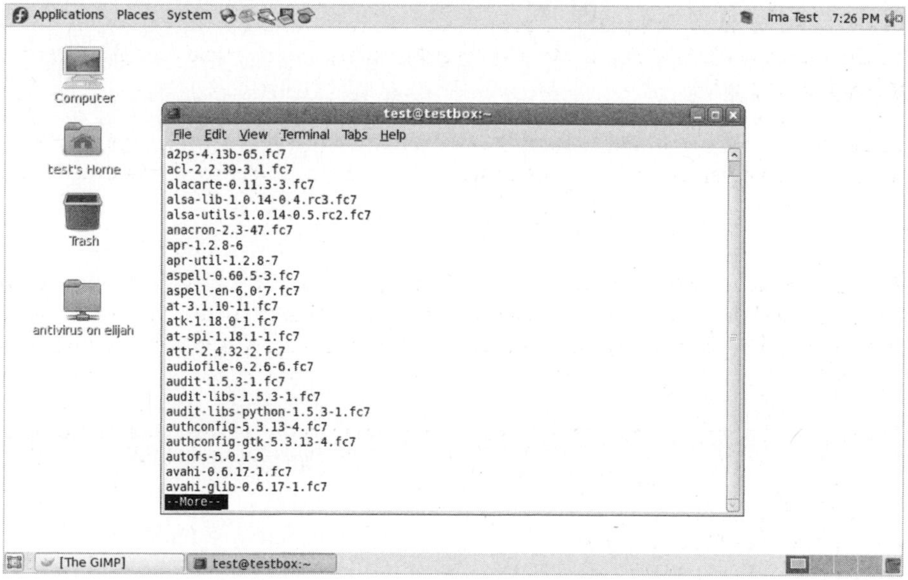

FIGURE 8-2

Using the more command with the ls command

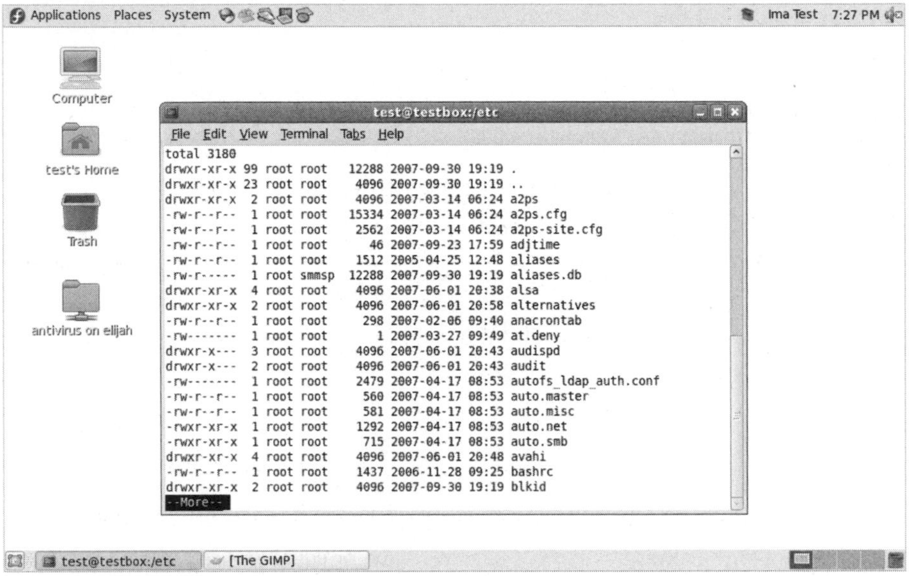

Performing Math

Another feature crucial to any programming language is the ability to manipulate numbers. Unfortunately, for shell scripts this process is a bit awkward. There a two different ways to perform mathematical operations in your shell scripts.

The expr command

Originally, the Bourne shell provided a special command that was used for processing mathematical equations. The expr command allowed the processing of equations from the command line, but it is extremely clunky:

```
$ expr 1 + 5
6
```

The expr command recognizes a few different mathematical and string operators, shown in Table 8-1.

While the standard operators work fine in the expr command, the problem comes in actually using them from a script or the command line. Many of the expr command operators have other meanings in the shell (such as the asterisk). Using them in the `expr` command produces odd results:

```
$ expr 5 * 2
expr: syntax error
$
```

TABLE 8-1

The expr Command Operators

Operator	Description
ARG1 | ARG2	Return ARG1 if neither argument is null or zero; otherwise, return ARG2.
ARG1 & ARG2	Return ARG1 if neither argument is null or zero; otherwise, return 0.
ARG1 < ARG2	Return 1 if ARG1 is less than ARG2; otherwise, return 0.
ARG1 <= ARG2	Return 1 if ARG1 is less than or equal to ARG2; otherwise, return 0.
ARG1 = ARG2	Return 1 if ARG1 is equal to ARG2; otherwise, return 0.
ARG1 != ARG2	Return 1 if ARG1 is not equal to ARG2; otherwise, return 0.
ARG1 >= ARG2	Return 1 if ARG1 is greater than or equal to ARG2; otherwise, return 0.
ARG1 > ARG2	Return 1 if ARG1 is greater than ARG2; otherwise, return 0.
ARG1 + ARG2	Return the arithmetic sum of ARG1 and ARG2.
ARG1 - ARG2	Return the arithmetic difference of ARG1 and ARG2.
ARG1 * ARG2	Return the arithmetic product of ARG1 and ARG2.
ARG1 / ARG2	Return the arithmetic quotient of ARG1 divided by ARG2.
ARG1 % ARG2	Return the arithmetic remainder of ARG1 divided by ARG2.
STRING : REGEXP	Return the pattern match if REGEXP matches a pattern in STRING.
match STRING REGEXP	Return the pattern match if REGEXP matches a pattern in STRING.
substr STRING POS LENGTH	Return the substring LENGTH characters in length, starting at position POS (starting at 1).
index STRING CHARS	Return position in STRING where CHARS is found; otherwise, return 0.
length STRING	Return the numeric length of the string STRING.
+ TOKEN	Interpret TOKEN as a string, even if it's a keyword.
(EXPRESSION)	Return the value of EXPRESSION.

To solve this problem, you need to use the shell escape character (the backslash) to identify any characters that may be misinterpreted by the shell before being passed to the `expr` command:

```
$ expr 5 \* 2
10
$
```

Now that's really starting to get ugly! Using the `expr` command in a shell script is equally cumbersome:

```
#!/bin/bash
# An example of using the expr command
var1=10
var2=20
var3=`expr $var2 / $var1`
echo The result is $var3
```

To assign the result of a mathematical equation to a variable, you have to use the backtick character to extract the output from the `expr` command:

```
$ ./test6
The result is 2
$
```

Fortunately, the bash shell has an improvement for processing mathematical operators.

Using brackets

The bash shell includes the `expr` command to stay compatible with the Bourne shell; however, it also provides a much easier way of performing mathematical equations. In bash, when assigning a mathematical value to a variable, you can enclose the mathematical equation using a dollar sign and square brackets (`$[ operation ]`):

```
$ var1=$[1 + 5]
$ echo $var1
6
$ var2 = $[$var1 * 2]
$ echo $var2
12
$
```

Using brackets makes shell math much easier than with the `expr` command. This same technique also works in shell scripts:

```
$ cat test7
#!/bin/bash
var1=100
```

```
var2=50
var3=45
var4=$[$var1 * ($var2 - $var3)]
echo The final result is $var4
$
```

Running this script produces the output:

```
$ chmod u+x test7
$ ./test7
The final result is 500
$
```

Also notice that when using the square brackets method for calculating equations you don't need to worry about the multiplication symbol, or any other characters, being misinterpreted by the shell. The shell knows that it's not a wildcard character, since it is within the square brackets.

There's one major limitation to performing math in the bash shell script. Take a look at this example:

```
$ cat test8
#!/bin/bash
var1=100
var2=45
var3=$[$var1 / $var2]
echo The final result is $var3
$
```

Now run it and see what happens:

```
$ chmod u+x test8
$ ./test8
The final result is 2
$
```

The bash shell mathematical operators only support integer arithmetic. This is a huge limitation if you're trying to do any sort of real-world mathematical calculations.

NOTE   The z shell (zsh) provides full floating-point arithmetic operations. If you require floating-point calculations in your shell scripts, you might consider checking out the z shell (discussed in Chapter 23).

A floating-point solution

There have been several solutions for overcoming the bash integer limitation. The most popular solution uses the built-in bash calculator (called bc).

The basics of bc

The bash calculator is actually a programming language that allows you to enter floating-point expressions at a command line, then interprets the expressions, calculates them, and returns the result. The bash calculator recognizes:

- Numbers (both integer and floating point)
- Variables (both simple variables and arrays)
- Comments (lines starting with a pound sign or the C language /* */ pair)
- Expressions
- Programming statements (such as if-then statements)
- Functions

You can access the bash calculator from the shell prompt using the bc command:

```
$ bc
bc 1.06
Copyright 1991-1994, 1997, 1998, 2000 Free Software Foundation, Inc.
This is free software with ABSOLUTELY NO WARRANTY.
For details type `warranty'.
12 * 5.4
64.8
3.156 * (3 + 5)
25.248
quit
$
```

The example starts out by entering the expression 12 * 5.4. The bash calculator returns the answer. Each subsequent expression entered into the calculator is evaluated, and the result is displayed. To exit the bash calculator, you must enter quit.

The floating-point arithmetic is controlled by a built-in variable called scale. You must set this value to the desired number of decimal places you want in your answers, or you won't get what you were looking for:

```
$ bc -q
3.44 / 5
0
scale=4
3.44 / 5
.6880
quit
$
```

The default value for the scale variable is zero. Before the scale value is set, the bash calculator provides the answer to zero decimal places. After you set the scale variable value to four, the bash calculator displays the answer to four decimal places. The -q command line parameter suppresses the lengthy welcome banner from the bash calculator.

Besides normal numbers, the bash calculator also understands variables:

```
$ bc -q
var1=10
var1 * 4
40
var2 = var1 / 5
print var2
2
quit
$
```

Once a variable value is defined, you can use the variable throughout the bash calculator session. The `print` statement allows you to print variables and numbers.

Using bc in scripts

Now you may be wondering how the bash calculator is going to help us with floating-point arithmetic in your shell scripts. Do you remember our friend the backtick character? Yes, you can use the backtick to run a `bc` command, and assign the output to a variable! The basic format to use is:

```
variable=`echo "options; expression" | bc`
```

The first portion, `options`, allows us to set variables. If you need to set more than one variable, separate them using the semicolon. The `expression` parameter defines the mathematical expression to evaluate using `bc`. While this looks pretty odd, trust me, it works like a champ. Here's a quick example of doing this in a script:

```
$ cat test9
#!/bin/bash
var1=`echo " scale=4; 3.44 / 5" | bc`
echo The answer is $var1
$
```

This example sets the `scale` variable to four decimal places, then specifies a specific calculation for the expression. Running this script produces the following output:

```
$ chmod u+x test9
$ ./test9
The answer is .6880
$
```

Now that's fancy! You aren't limited to just using numbers for the expression value. You can also use variables defined in the shell script:

```
$ cat test10
#!/bin/bash
var1=100
```

```
var2=45
var3=`echo "scale=4; $var1 / $var2" | bc`
echo The answer for this is $var3
$
```

The script defines two variables, which are used within the expression sent to the bc command. Remember to use the dollar sign to signify the value for the variables, and not the variables themselves. The output of this script is:

```
$ ./test10
The answer for this is 2.2222
$
```

And of course, once a value is assigned to a variable, that variable can be used in yet another calculation:

```
$ cat test11
#!/bin/bash
var1=20
var2=3.14159
var3=`echo "scale=4; $var1 * $var1" | bc`
var4=`echo "scale=4; $var3 * $var2" | bc`
echo The final result is $var4
$
```

This method works fine for short calculations, but sometimes you need to get more involved with your numbers. If you have more than just a couple of calculations, it gets confusing trying to list multiple expressions on the same command line.

There's a simple solution to this problem. The bc command recognizes input redirection, allowing you to redirect a file to the bc command for processing. However, this can just as easily get confusing, as you'd need to store your expressions in a file.

Instead of using a file for redirection, you can use the inline input redirection method, which allows you to redirect data directly from the command line. In the shell script, you can assign the output to a variable. This looks like this:

```
variable=`bc << EOF
options
statements
expressions
EOF
`
```

The EOF text string indicates the beginning and end of the inline redirection data. Remember that the backtick characters are still needed to assign the output of the bc command to the variable.

Now you can place all of the individual bash calculator elements on separate lines in the script file. Here's an example of using this technique in a script:

```
$ cat test12
#!/bin/bash
```

```
var1=10.46
var2=43.67
var3=33.2
var4=71

var5=`bc << EOF
scale = 4
a1 = ( $var1 * $var2)
b1 = ($var3 * $var4)
a1 + b1
EOF
`

echo The final answer for this mess is $var5
$
```

Using this you can place each option and expression on a separate line in your script, making things cleaner and easier to read and follow. The EOF string indicates the start and end of the data to redirect to the bc command. Of course, you need to use the backtick characters to indicate the command to assign to the variable.

You'll also notice in this example that you can assign variables within the bash calculator. It's important to remember that any variables created within the bash calculator are only valid within the bash calculator and can't be used in the shell script.

Exiting the Script

So far, in our sample scripts we terminated things pretty abruptly. When we were done with our last command, we just ended the script. There's a more elegant way of completing things available to us.

Every command that runs in the shell uses an *exit status* to indicate to the shell that it's done processing. The exit status is an integer value between 0 and 255 that's passed by the command to the shell when the command finishes running. You can capture this value and use it in your scripts.

Checking the exit status

Linux provides the $? special variable that holds the exit status value from the last command that executed. You must view or use the $? variable immediately after the command you want to check. It changes values to the exit status of the last command executed by the shell:

```
$ date
Sat Sep 29 10:01:30 EDT 2007
$ echo $?
0
$
```

By convention, the exit status of a command that successfully completes is zero. If a command completes with an error, then a positive integer value is placed in the exit status:

```
$ asdfg
-bash: asdfg: command not found
$ echo $?
127
$
```

The invalid command returns an exit status of 127. There's not much of a standard convention to Linux error exit status codes. However, there are a few guidelines you can use, as shown in Table 8-2.

An exit status value of 126 indicates that the user didn't have the proper permissions set to execute the command:

```
$ ./myprog.c
-bash: ./myprog.c: Permission denied
$ echo $?
126
$
```

Another common error you'll encounter occurs if you supply an invalid parameter to a command:

```
$ date %t
date: invalid date `%t'
$ echo $?
1
$
```

TABLE 8-2

Linux Exit Status Codes

Code	Description
0	Successful completion of the command
1	General unknown error
2	Misuse of shell command
126	The command can't execute
127	Command not found
128	Invalid exit argument
128+x	Fatal error with Linux signal x
130	Command terminated with Ctl-C
255	Exit status out of range

This generates the general exit status code of one, indicating an unknown error occurred in the command.

The exit command

By default, your shell script will exit with the exit status of the last command in your script:

```
$ ./test6
The result is 2
$ echo $?
0
$
```

You can change that to return your own exit status code. The exit command allows you to specify an exit status when your script ends:

```
$ cat test13
#!/bin/bash
# testing the exit status
var1=10
var2=30
var3=$[ $var1 + var2 ]
echo The answer is $var3
exit 5
$
```

When you check the exit status of the script, you'll get the value used as the parameter of the exit command:

```
$ chmod u+x test13
$ ./test13
The answer is 40
$ echo $?
5
$
```

You can also use variables in the exit command parameter:

```
$ cat test14
#!/bin/bash
# testing the exit status
var1=10
var2=30
var3=$[ $var1 + var2 ]
exit $var3
$
```

When you run this command, it produces the following exit status:

```
$ chmod u+x test14
$ ./test14
```

```
$ echo $?
40
$
```

You should be careful with this feature though, as the exit status codes can only go up to 255. Watch what happens in this example:

```
$ cat test14b
#!/bin/bash
# testing the exit status
var1=10
var2=30
var3=$[ $var1 * var2 ]
echo The value is $var3
exit $var3
$
```

Now when you run it, you get:

```
$ ./test14b
The value is 300
$ echo $?
44
$
```

The exit status code is reduced to fit in the 0 to 255 range. The shell does this by using modulo arithmetic. The *modulo* of a value is the remainder after a division. The resulting number is the remainder of the specified number divided by 256. In the case of 300 (the result value), the remainder is 44, which is what appears as the exit status code.

In Chapter 9, you'll see how you can use the if-then statement to check the error status returned by a command to see if the command was successful or not.

Summary

The bash shell script allows you to string commands together into a script. The most basic way of creating a script is to separate multiple commands on the command line using a semicolon. The shell executes each command in order, displaying the output of each command on the monitor.

You can also create a shell script file, placing multiple commands in the file for the shell to execute in order. The shell script file must define the shell used to run the script. This is done in the first line of the script file, using the #! symbol, followed by the full path of the shell.

Within the shell script you can reference environment variable values by using a dollar sign in front of the variable. You can also define your own variables for use within the script, and assign values and even the output of a command by using the backtick character. The variable value can be used within the script by placing a dollar sign in front of the variable name.

The bash shell allows you to redirect both the input and output of a command from the standard behavior. You can redirect the output of any command from the monitor display to a file by using the greater-than symbol, followed by the name of the file to capture the output. You can append output data to an existing file by using two greater-than symbols. The less-than symbol is used to redirect input to a command. You can redirect input from a file to a command.

The Linux pipe command (the bar symbol) allows you to redirect the output of a command directly to the input of another command. The Linux system runs both commands at the same time, sending the output of the first command to the input of the second command without using any redirect files.

The bash shell provides a couple of ways for you to perform mathematical operations in your shell scripts. The `expr` command is a simple way to perform integer math. In the bash shell you can also perform basic math calculations by enclosing equations in square brackets, preceded by a dollar sign. To perform floating-point arithmetic, you need to utilize the `bc` calculator command, redirecting input from inline data and storing the output in a user variable.

Finally, the chapter discussed how to use the exit status in your shell script. Every command that runs in the shell produces an exit status. The exit status is an integer value between 0 and 255 that indicates if the command completed successfully, and if not, what the reason may have been. An exit status of 0 indicates that the command completed successfully. You can use the `exit` command in your shell script to declare a specific exit status upon the completion of your script.

So far in your shell scripts, things have proceeded in an orderly fashion from one command to the next. In the next chapter, you'll see how you can use some logic flow control to alter which commands are executed within the script.

Using Structured Commands

I n the shell scripts presented in Chapter 8, the shell processed each individual command in the shell script in the order it appeared. This works out fine for sequential operations, where you want all of the commands to process in the proper order. However, this isn't how all programs operate.

Many programs require some sort of logic flow control between the commands in the script. This means that the shell executes certain commands given one set of circumstances, but it has the ability to execute other commands given a different set of circumstances. There is a whole class of commands that allows the script to skip over or loop through commands based on conditions of variable values, or the result of other commands. These commands are generally referred to as *structured commands*.

The structured commands allow you to alter the flow of operation of the program, executing some commands under some conditions, while skipping others under other conditions. There are quite a few structured commands available in the bash shell, so we'll look at them individually. In this chapter, we'll look at the if-then statement.

Working with the if-then Statement

The most basic type of structured command is the if-then statement. The if-then statement has the following format:

```
if command
then
    commands
fi
```

229

If you're use to using if-then statements in other programming languages, this format may be somewhat confusing. In other programming languages, the object after the if statement is an equation that is evaluated for a TRUE or FALSE value. That's not how the bash shell if statement works.

The bash shell if statement runs the command defined on the if line. If the exit status of the command (see Chapter 8) is zero (the command completed successfully), the commands listed under the then section are executed. If the exit status of the command is anything else, the then commands aren't executed, and the bash shell moves on to the next command in the script.

Here's a simple example to demonstrate this concept:

```
$ cat test1
#!/bin/bash
# testing the if statement
if date
then
    echo "it worked"
fi
```

This script uses the date command on the if line. If the command completes successfully, the echo statement should display the text string. When you run this script from the command line, you'll get the following results:

```
$ ./test1
Sat Sep 29 14:09:24 EDT 2007
it worked
$
```

The shell executed the date command listed on the if line. Since the exit status was zero, it also executed the echo statement listed in the then section.

Here's another example:

```
$ cat test2
#!/bin/bash
# testing a bad command
if asdfg
then
    echo "it didn't work"
fi
echo "we're outside of the if statement"
$ ./test2
./test2: line 3: asdfg: command not found
we're outside of the if statement
$
```

In this example, I deliberately use a command I know won't work in the if statement line. Since this is a bad command, it'll produce an exit status that's non-zero, and the bash shell skips the echo statement in the then section. Also notice that the error message generated from running the command in the if statement still appears in the output of the script. There'll be times when you won't want this to happen. Chapter 12 discusses how this can be avoided.

You're not limited to just one command in the then section. You can list commands just as in the rest of the shell script. The bash shell treats the commands as a block, executing all of them if the command in the if statement line returns a zero exit status or skipping all of them if the command returns a non-zero exit status:

```
$ cat test3
#!/bin/bash
# testing multiple commands in the then section
testuser=rich
if grep $testuser /etc/passwd
then
    echo The bash files for user $testuser are:
    ls -a /home/$testuser/.b*
fi
```

The if statement line uses the grep comment to search the /etc/passwd file to see if a specific username is currently used on the system. If there's a user with that logon name, the script displays some text, then lists the bash files in the user's HOME directory:

```
$ ./test3
rich:x:500:500:Rich Blum:/home/rich:/bin/bash
The files for user rich are:
/home/rich/.bash_history   /home/rich/.bash_profile
/home/rich/.bash_logout    /home/rich/.bashrc
$
```

However, if you set the testuser variable to a user that doesn't exist on the system, nothing happens:

```
$ ./test3
$
```

That's not all too exciting. It would be nice if we could display a little message saying that the username wasn't found on the system. Well, we can, using another feature of the if-then statement.

> **NOTE** You might see an alternative form of the if-then statement used in some scripts:
>
> ```
> if command; then
>     commands
> fi
> ```
>
> By putting a semicolon at the end of the command to evaluate, you can include the then statement on the same line, which looks more like how if-then statements are handled in some other programming languages.

The if-then-else Statement

In the `if-then` statement, you only have one option of whether or not a command is successful. If the command returns a non-zero exit status code, the bash shell just moves on to the next command in the script. In this situation, it would be nice to be able to execute an alternate set of commands. That's exactly what the `if-then-else` statement is for.

The `if-then-else` statement provides another group of commands in the statement:

```
if command
then
    commands
else
    commands
fi
```

If the command in the `if` statement line returns with an exit status code of zero, the commands listed in the `then` section are executed, just as in a normal `if-then` statement. If the command in the `if` statement line returns a non-zero exit status code, the bash shell executes the commands in the `else` section.

Now you can modify the test script to look like this:

```
$ cat test4
#!/bin/bash
# testing the else section
testuser=badtest
if grep $testuser /etc/passwd
then
    echo The files for user $testuser are:
    ls -a /home/$testuser/.b*
else
    echo "The user name $testuser doesn't exist on this system"
fi
$ ./test4
The user name badtest doesn't exist on this system
$
```

That's more user-friendly. Just like the `then` section, the `else` section can contain multiple commands. The `fi` statement delineates the end of the `else` section.

Nesting ifs

Sometimes you must check for several situations in your script code. Instead of having to write separate `if-then` statements, you can use an alternative version of the else section, called `elif`.

The `elif` continues an `else` section with another `if-then` statement:

```
if command1
then
    commands
elif command2
then
    more commands
fi
```

The elif statement line provides another command to evaluate, similarly to the original if statement line. If the exit status code from the elif command is zero, bash executes the commands in the second then statement section.

You can continue to string elif statements together, creating one huge if-then-elif conglomeration:

```
if command1
then
    command set 1
elif command2
then
    command set 2
elif command3
then
    command set 3
elif command4
then
    command set 4
fi
```

Each block of commands is executed depending on which command returns the zero exit status code. Remember, the bash shell will execute the if statements in order, and only the first one that returns a zero exit status will result in the then section being executed. Later on in "The case Command" section you'll see how to use the case command instead of having to nest lots of if-then statements.

The test Command

So far all you've seen in the if statement line are normal shell commands. You might be wondering if the bash if-then statement has the ability to evaluate any condition other than the exit status code of a command.

The answer is no, it can't. However, there's a neat utility available in the bash shell that helps us evaluate other things, using the if-then statement.

The test command provides a way to test different conditions in an if-then statement. If the condition listed in the test command evaluates to true, the test command exits with a zero exit status code, making the if-then statement behave in much the same way that if-then statements work in other programming languages. If the condition is `false`, the `test` command exits with a one, which causes the `if-then` statement to fail.

The format of the `test` command is pretty simple:

```
test condition
```

The *condition* is a series of parameters and values that the `test` command evaluates. When used in an `if-then` statement, the `test` command looks like this:

```
if test condition
then
    commands
fi
```

The bash shell provides an alternative way of declaring the `test` command in an `if-then` statement:

```
if [ condition ]
then
    commands
fi
```

The square brackets define the condition that's used in the `test` command. Be careful; you must have a space after the first bracket, and a space before the last bracket or you'll get an error message.

There are three classes of conditions the `test` command can evaluate:

- Numeric comparisons
- String comparisons
- File comparisons

The next sections describe how to use each of these classes of tests in your `if-then` statements.

Numeric comparisons

The most common method for using the test command is to perform a comparison of two numeric values. Table 9-1 shows the list of condition parameters used for testing two values.

The numeric test conditions can be used to evaluate both numbers and variables. Here's an example of doing that:

```
$ cat test5
#!/bin/bash
# using numeric test comparisons
val1=10
```

```
val2=11

if [ $val1 -gt 5 ]
then
    echo "The test value $val1 is greater than 5"
fi

if [ $val1 -eq $val2 ]
then
    echo "The values are equal"
else
    echo "The values are different"
fi
```

TABLE 9-1

The test Numeric Comparisons

Comparison	Description
n1 -eq *n2*	Check if *n1* is equal to *n2*.
n1 -ge *n2*	Check if *n1* is greater than or equal to *n2*.
n1 -gt *n2*	Check if *n1* is greater than *n2*.
n1 -le *n2*	Check if *n1* is less than or equal to *n2*.
n1 -lt *n2*	Check if *n1* is less than *n2*.
n1 -ne *n2*	Check if *n1* is not equal to *n2*.

The first test condition:

```
if [ $val1 -gt 5 ]
```

tests if the value of the variable val1 is greater than 5. The second test condition:

```
if [ $val1 -eq $val2 ]
```

tests if the value of the variable val1 is equal to the value of the variable val2. Run the script and watch the results:

```
$ ./test5
The test value 10 is greater than 5
The values are different
$
```

Both of the numeric test conditions evaluated as expected.

There is a limitation to the `test` numeric conditions though. Try this script:

```
$ cat test6
#!/bin/bash
# testing floating point numbers
val1=` echo "scale=4; 10 / 3 " | bc`
echo "The test value is $val1"
if [ $val1 -gt 3 ]
then
    echo "The result is larger than 3"
fi
$ ./test6
The test value is 3.3333
./test6: line 5: [: 3.3333: integer expression expected
$
```

This example uses the bash calculator to produce a floating-point value, stored in the `val1` variable. Next, it uses the `test` command to evaluate the value. Something obviously went wrong here.

In Chapter 8, you learned how to trick the bash shell into handling floating-point values; there's still a problem in this script. The `test` command wasn't able to handle the floating-point value that was stored in the `val1` variable.

Remember, the only numbers the bash shell can handle are integers. When we utilize the bash calculator, we just fool the shell into storing a floating-point value in a variable as a string value. This works perfectly fine if all you need to do is display the result, using an `echo` statement, but this doesn't work in numeric-oriented functions, such as our numeric test condition. The bottom line is that you're not able to use integer values in the `test` command.

String comparisons

The `test` command also allows you to perform comparisons on string values. Performing comparisons on strings can get tricky, as you'll see. Table 9-2 shows the comparison functions you can use to evaluate two string values.

The following sections describe the different string comparisons available.

String equality

The equal and not equal conditions are fairly self-explanatory with strings. It's pretty easy to know when two string values are the same or not:

```
$cat test7
#!/bin/bash
```

```
# testing string equality
testuser=rich

if [ $USER = $testuser ]
then
    echo "Welcome $testuser"
fi
$ ./test7
Welcome rich
$
```

Similarly, using the not equals string comparison:

TABLE 9-2

The test Command String Comparisons

Comparison	Description
str1 = *str2*	Check if *str1* is the same as string *str2*.
str1 != *str2*	Check if *str1* is not the same as *str2*.
str1 < *str2*	Check if *str1* is less than *str2*.
str1 > *str2*	Check if *str1* is greater than *str2*.
-n *str1*	Check if *str1* has a length greater than zero.
-z *str1*	Check if *str1* has a length of zero.

```
$ cat test8
#!/bin/bash
# testing string equality
testuser=baduser

if [ $USER != $testuser ]
then
    echo "This isn't $testuser"
else
    echo "Welcome $testuser"
fi
$ ./test8
This isn't baduser
$
```

The test comparison takes all punctuation and capitalization into account when comparing strings for equality.

String order

Trying to determine if one string is less than or greater than another is where things start getting tricky. There are two problems that often plague shell programmers when trying to use the greater-than or less-than features of the test command:

- The greater-than and less-than symbols must be escaped, or the shell will use them as redirection symbols, with the string values as filenames.

- The greater-than and less-than order is not the same as that used with the sort command.

The first item can result in a huge problem that often goes undetected when programming your scripts. Here's a typical example of what sometimes happens to novice shell script programmers:

```
$ cat badtest
#!/bin/bash
# mis-using string comparisons

val1=baseball
val2=hockey

if [ $val1 > $val2 ]
then
    echo "$val1 is greater than $val2"
else
    echo "$val1 is less than $val2"
fi
$ ./badtest
baseball is greater than hockey
$ ls -l hockey
-rw-r--r--    1 rich      rich                  0 Sep 30 19:08 hockey
$
```

By just using the greater-than symbol itself in the script, no errors are generated, but the results are wrong. The script interpreted the greater-than symbol as an output redirection, so it created a file called hockey. Since the redirection completed successfully, the test command returns a zero exit status code, which the if statement evaluates as though things completed successfully!

To fix this problem, you need to properly escape the greater-than symbol:

```
$ cat test9
#!/bin/bash
# mis-using string comparisons

val1=baseball
val2=hockey

if [ $val1 \> $val2 ]
```

```
then
   echo "$val1 is greater than $val2"
else
   echo "$val1 is less than $val2"
fi
$ ./test9
baseball is less than hockey
$
```

Now that answer is more along the lines of what you would expect from the string comparison.

The second issue is a little more subtle, and you may not even run across it unless you're working with upper-case and lower-case letters. The way the sort command handles upper-case letters is opposite of the way the test command considers them. Let's test this feature in a script:

```
$ cat test9b
#!/bin/bash
# testing string sort order
val1=Testing
val2=testing

if [ $val1 \> $val2 ]
then
   echo "$val1 is greater than $val2"
else
   echo "$val1 is less than $val2"
fi
$ ./test9b
Testing is less than testing
$ sort testfile
testing
Testing
$
```

Capitalized letters appear less than lower-case letters in the test command. However, when you put the same strings in a file and use the sort command, the lower-case letters appear first. This is due to the ordering technique each command uses. The test command uses standard ASCII ordering, using each character's ASCII numeric value to determine the sort order. The sort command uses the sorting order defined for the system locale language settings. For the English language, the locale settings specify that lower-case letters appear before upper-case letters in sort order.

CAUTION   Notice that the test command uses the standard mathematical comparison symbols for string comparisons, and text codes for numerical comparisons. This is a subtle feature that many programmers manage to get reversed. If you use the mathematical comparison symbols for numeric values, the shell interprets them as string values and may not produce the correct results.

String size

The -n and -z comparisons are handy when trying to evaluate if a variable contains data or not:

```
$ cat test10
#!/bin/bash
# testing string length
val1=testing
val2=''

if [ -n $val1 ]
then
    echo "The string '$val1' is not empty"
else
    echo "The string '$val1' is empty"
fi

if [ -z $val2 ]
then
    echo "The string '$val2' is empty"
else
    echo "The string '$val2' is not empty"
fi

if [ -z $val3 ]
then
    echo "The string '$val3' is empty"
else
    echo "The string '$val3' is not empty"
fi
$ ./test10
The string 'testing' is not empty
The string '' is empty
The string '' is empty
$
```

This example creates two string variables. The val1 variable contains a string, and the val2 variable is created as an empty string. The following comparisons are made:

```
if [ -n $val1 ]
```

determines if the val1 variable is non-zero in length, which it is, so the then section is processed:

```
if [ -z $var2 ]
```

determines if the val2 variable is zero in length, which it is, so the then section is processed:

```
if [ -z $val3 ]
```

determines if the val3 variable is zero in length. This variable was never defined in the shell script, so it indicates that the string length is still zero, even though it wasn't defined.

TABLE 9-3

The test Command File Comparisons

Comparison	Description
-d *file*	Check if *file* exists and is a directory.
-e *file*	Checks if *file* exists.
-f *file*	Checks if *file* exists and is a file.
-r *file*	Checks if *file* exists and is readable.
-s *file*	Checks if *file* exists and is not empty.
-w *file*	Checks if *file* exists and is writable.
-x *file*	Checks if *file* exists and is executable.
-O file	Checks if *file* exists and is owned by the current user.
-G *file*	Checks if *file* exists and the default group is the same as the current user.
file1 -nt *file2*	Checks if *file1* is newer than *file2*.
file1 -ot *file2*	Checks if *file1* is older than *file2*.

CAUTION   Empty and uninitialized variables can have catastrophic effects on your shell script tests. If you're not sure of the contents of a variable, it's always best to test if the variable contains a value using -n or -z before using it in a numeric or string comparison.

File comparisons

The last category of test comparisons is quite possibly the most powerful and most used comparisons in shell scripting. The test command allows you to test the status of files and directories on the Linux filesystem. Table 9-3 list these comparisons.

These conditions give you the ability to check files in your filesystem within your shell scripts, and they are often used in scripts that access files. Since they're used so much, let's look at each of these individually.

Checking directories

The -d test checks if a specified filename exists as a directory on the system. This is usually a good thing to do if you're trying to write a file to a directory, or before you try to change to a directory location:

```
$ cat test11
#!/bin/bash
# look before you leap
if [ -d $HOME ]
```

```
then
    echo "Your HOME directory exists"
    cd $HOME
    ls -a
else
    echo "There's a problem with your HOME directory"
fi
$ ./test11
Your HOME directory exists
.                  Drivers         .ICEauthority      .recently
..                 .emacs.d        joomla             .redhat
4rich              .evolution      .lesshst           rpm.list
backup.zip         .fontconfig     .metacity          .spamassassin
.bash_history      .gconf          mnt                store
.bash_logout       .gconfd         .mozilla           store.sql
.bash_profile      .gftp           Music              store.zip
.bashrc            .gimp-2.2       myprob             Templates
.bittorrent        .gnome          myproblem          test
.ccache            .gnome2         myprog             test1
.config            .gnome2_private .mysql_history     .thumbnails
Desktop            .gphpedit       .nautilus          .Trash
.dmrc              .gstreamer-0.10 .openoffice.org2.0 Videos
Documents          .gtk-bookmarks  Pictures           .viminfo
Download           .gtkrc-1.2-gnome2 Public
$
```

The sample code uses the -d test condition to see if the HOME directory exists for the user. If it does, it proceeds to use the cd command to change to the HOME directory and performs a directory listing.

Checking if an object exists

The -e comparison allows you to check if a file or directory object exists before you attempt to use it in your script:

```
$ cat test12
#!/bin/bash
# checking if a directory exists
if [ -e $HOME ]
then
    echo "OK on the directory, now let's check the file"
    # checking if a file exists
    if [ -e $HOME/testing ]
    then
        # the file exists, append data to it
        echo "Appending date to existing file"
        date >> $HOME/testing
    else
        # the file doesn't exist, create a new file
```

```
            echo "Creating new file"
            date > $HOME/testing
        fi
else
    echo "Sorry, you don't have a HOME directory"
fi
$ ./test12
OK on the directory, now let's check the file
Creating new file
$ ./test12
OK on the directory, now let's check the file
Appending date to existing file
$
```

The first check uses the -e comparison to determine if the user has a HOME directory. If so, the next -e comparison checks to determine if the testing file exists in the HOME directory. If the file doesn't exist, the shell script uses the single greater-than redirect symbol, creating a new file with the output from the date command. The second time you run the shell script, it uses the double greater-than symbol, so it just appends the date output to the existing file.

Checking for a file

The -e comparison works for both files and directories. To be sure that the object specified is a file, you must use the -f comparison:

```
$ cat test13
#!/bin/bash
# check if a file
if [ -e $HOME ]
then
    echo "The object exists, is it a file?"
    if [ -f $HOME ]
    then
        echo "Yes, it's a file!"
    else
        echo "No, it's not a file!"
        if [ -f $HOME/.bash_history ]
        then
            echo "But this is a file!"
        fi
    fi
else
    echo "Sorry, the object doesn't exist"
fi
$ ./test13
The object exists, is it a file?
No, it's not a file!
But this is a file!
$
```

This little script does a whole lot of checking! First, it uses the -e comparison to test if $HOME exists. If it does, it uses -f to test if it's a file. If it isn't a file (which of course it isn't), we use the -f comparison to test if it's a file, which it is.

Can you read it?

Before trying to read data from a file, it's usually a good idea to test if you can read from the file first. This is done using the -r comparison:

```
$ cat test14
#!/bin/bash
# testing if you can read a file
pwfile=/etc/shadow

# first, test if the file exists, and is a file
if [ -f $pwfile ]
then
    # now test if you can read it
    if [ -r $pwfile ]
    then
        tail $pwfile
    else
        echo "Sorry, I'm unable to read the $pwfile file"
    fi
else
    echo "Sorry, the file $file doesn't exist"
fi
$ ./test14
Sorry, I'm unable to read the /etc/shadow file
$
```

The /etc/shadow file contains the encrypted passwords for system users, so it's not readable by normal users on the system. The -r comparison determined that I didn't have read access to the file, so the test command failed, and the bash shell executed the else section of the if-then statement.

Checking for empty files

You should use -s comparison to check if a file is empty, especially if you're trying to remove a file. Be careful, because when the -s comparison succeeds, it indicates that a file has data in it:

```
$ cat test15
#!/bin/bash
# testing if a file is empty
file=t15test
touch $file

if [ -s $file ]
then
```

```
        echo "The $file file exists and has data in it"
    else
        echo "The $file exists and is empty"
    fi

    date > $file
    if [ -s $file ]
    then
        echo "The $file file has data in it"
    else
        echo "The $file is still empty"
    fi
    $./test15
    The t15test exists and is empty
    The t15test file has data in it
    $
```

The touch command creates the file, but doesn't put any data in it. After we use the date command and redirect the output to the file, the -s comparison indicates that there's data in the file.

Checking if you can write to a file

The -w comparison determines if you have permission to write to a file:

```
$ cat test16
#!/bin/bash
# checking if a file is writeable

logfile=$HOME/t16test
touch $logfile
chmod u-w $logfile
now=`date +%Y%m%d-%H%M`

if [ -w $logfile ]
then
    echo "The program ran at: $now" > $logfile
    echo "The fist attempt succeeded"
else
    echo "The first attempt failed"
fi

chmod u+w $logfile
if [ -w $logfile ]
then
    echo "The program ran at: $now" > $logfile
    echo "The second attempt succeeded"
else
    echo "The second attempt failed"
```

```
fi
$ ./test16
The first attempt failed
The second attempt succeeded
$ cat $HOME/t16test
The program ran at: 20070930-1602
$
```

This is a pretty busy shell script! First, it defines a log file in your HOME directory, stores the filename of it in the variable logfile, creates the file, and then removes the write permission for the user, using the chmod command. Next, it creates the variable now and stores a timestamp, using the date command. After all of that, it checks if you have write permission to the new log file (which you just took away). Since you don't have write permission, you should see the failed message appear.

After that, the script uses the chmod command again to grant the write permission back for the user, and tries to write to the file again. This time the write is successful.

Checking if you can run a file

The -x comparison is a handy way to determine if you have execute permission for a specific file. While this may not be needed for most commands, if you run a lot of scripts from your shell scripts, it could come in handy:

```
$ cat test17
#!/bin/bash
# testing file execution
if [ -x test16 ]
then
    echo "You can run the script:"
    ./test16
else
    echo "Sorry, you are unable to execute the script"
fi
$ ./test17
You can run the script:
The first attempt failed
The second attempt succeeded
$ chmod u-x test16
$ ./test17
Sorry, you are unable to execute the script
$
```

This example shell script uses the -x comparison to test if you have permission to execute the test16 script. If so, it runs the script (notice that even in a shell script, you must have the proper path to execute a script that's not located in your PATH). After successfully running the test16 script the first time, change the permissions on it, and try again. This time the -x comparison fails, as you don't have execute permission for the test16 script.

Checking ownership

The -O comparison allows you to easily test if you're the owner of a file:

```
$ cat test18
#!/bin/bash
# check file ownsership

if [ -O /etc/passwd ]
then
    echo "You're the owner of the /etc/passwd file"
else
    echo "Sorry, you're not the owner of the /etc/passwd file"
fi
$ ./test18
Sorry, you're not the owner of the /etc/passwd file
$ su
Password:
# ./test18
You're the owner of the /etc/passwd file
#
```

The script uses the -O comparison to test if the user running the script is the owner of the /etc/passwd file. The first time the script is run under a normal user account, so the test fails. The second time, I used the su command to become the root user, and the test succeeded.

The -G comparison checks the default group of a file, and it succeeds if it matches the group of the default group for the user. This can be somewhat confusing, because the -G comparison only checks the default groups, and not all the groups the user belongs to. Here's an example of this:

```
$ cat test19
#!/bin/bash
# check file group test

if [ -G $HOME/testing ]
then
    echo "You're in the same group as the file"
else
    echo "The file is not owned by your group"
fi
$ ls -l $HOME/testing
-rw-rw-r-- 1 rich rich 58 2007-09-30 15:51 /home/rich/testing
$ ./test19
You're in the same group as the file
$ chgrp sharing $HOME/testing
$ ./test19
The file is not owned by your group
$
```

The first time the script is run, the $HOME/testing file is in the rich group, and the -G comparison succeeds. Next, I changed the group to the sharing group, which I'm also a member of. However, the -G comparison failed, since it only compares the default groups, not any additional groups I belong to.

Checking file date

The last set of comparisons deal with comparing the creation times of two files. This comes in handy when writing scripts to install software. Sometimes you don't want to install a file that is older than a file already installed on the system.

The -nt comparison determines if a file is newer than another file. If a file is newer, it'll have a more recent file creation time. The -ot comparison determines if a file is older than another file. If the file is older, it'll have an older file creation time:

```
$ cat test20
#!/bin/bash
# testing file dates

if [ ./test19 -nt ./test18 ]
then
    echo "The test19 file is newer than test18"
else
    echo "The test18 file is newer than test19"
fi

if [ ./test17 -ot ./test19 ]
then
   echo "The test17 file is older than the test19 file"
fi
$ ./test20
The test19 file is newer than test18
The test17 file is older than the test19 file
$ ls -l test17 test18 test19
-rwxrw-r-- 1 rich rich 167 2007-09-30 16:31 test17
-rwxrw-r-- 1 rich rich 185 2007-09-30 17:46 test18
-rwxrw-r-- 1 rich rich 167 2007-09-30 17:50 test19
$
```

The filepaths used in the comparisons are relative to the directory from where you run the script. This can cause problems if the files you're checking can be moved around. Another problem is that neither of these comparisons check if the file exists first. Try this test:

```
$ cat test21
#!/bin/bash
# testing file dates

if [ ./badfile1 -nt ./badfile2 ]
```

```
then
    echo "The badfile1 file is newer than badfile2"
else
    echo "The badfile2 file is newer than badfile1"
fi
$ ./test21
The badfile2 file is newer than badfile1
$
```

This little example demonstrates that if the files don't exist, the -nt comparison just returns a failed condition. It's imperative that you ensure the files exist before trying to use them in the -nt or -ot comparison.

Compound Condition Testing

The if-then statement allows you to use Boolean logic to combine tests. There are two Boolean operators you can use:

- [*condition1*] && [*condition2*]
- [*condition1*] || [*condition2*]

The first Boolean operation uses the AND Boolean operator to combine two conditions. Both conditions must be met for the then section to execute.

The second Boolean operation uses the OR Boolean operator to combine two conditions. If either condition evaluates to a true condition, the then section is executed.

```
$ cat test22
#!/bin/bash
# testing compound comparisons

if [ -d $HOME ] && [ -w $HOME/testing ]
then
    echo "The file exists and you can write to it"
else
    echo "I can't write to the file"
fi
$ ./test22
I can't write to the file
$ touch $HOME/testing
$ ./test22
The file exists and you can write to it
$
```

Using the AND Boolean operator, both of the comparisons must be met. The first comparison checks to see if the HOME directory exists for the user. The second comparison checks to see if there's a file called testing in the user's HOME directory, and if the user has write permissions for the file. If either of these comparisons fails, the if statement fails and the shell executes the else section. If both of the comparisons succeed, the if statement succeeds and the shell executes the then section.

Advanced if-then Features

There are two relatively recent additions to the bash shell that provide advanced features that you can use in if-then statements:

- Double parentheses for mathematical expressions
- Double square brackets for advanced string handling functions

The following sections describe each of these features in more detail.

Using double parentheses

The *double parentheses* command allows you to incorporate advanced mathematical formulas in your comparisons. The test command only allows for simple arithmetic operations in the comparison. The double parentheses command provides more mathematical symbols that programmers from other languages are used to using. The format of the double parentheses command is:

```
(( expression ))
```

The *expression* term can be any mathematical assignment or comparison expression. Besides the standard mathematical operators that the test command uses, Table 9-4 shows the list of additional operators available for use in the double parentheses command.

You can use the double parentheses command in an if statement, as well as a normal command in the script for assigning values:

```
$ cat test23
#!/bin/bash
# using double parenthesis

val1=10

if (( $val1 ** 2 > 90 ))
then
    (( val2 = $val1 ** 2 ))
    echo "The square of $val1 is $val2"
fi
$ ./test23
The square of 10 is 100
$
```

TABLE 9-4

The Double Parentheses Command Symbols

Symbol	Description
val++	post-increment
val--	post-decrement
++val	pre-increment
--val	pre-decrement
!	logical negation
~	bitwise negation
**	exponentiation
<<	left bitwise shift
>>	right bitwise shift
&	bitwise Boolean AND
|	bitwise Boolean OR
&&	logical AND
||	logical OR

Notice that you don't need to escape the greater-than symbol in the expression within the double parentheses. This is yet another advanced feature provided by the double parentheses command.

Using double brackets

The *double bracket* command provides advanced features for string comparisons. The double bracket command format is:

```
[[ expression ]]
```

The double bracketed *expression* uses the standard string comparison used in the test command. However, it provides an additional feature that the test command doesn't, *pattern matching*.

In pattern matching, you can define a regular expression (discussed in detail in Chapter 17) that's matched against the string value:

```
$ cat test24
#!/bin/bash
# using pattern matching
```

```
if [[ $USER == r* ]]
then
    echo "Hello $USER"
else
    echo "Sorry, I don't know you"
fi
$ ./test24
Hello rich
$
```

The double bracket command matches the $USER environment variable to see if it starts with the letter r. If so, the comparison succeeds, and the shell executes the then section commands.

The case Command

Often you'll find yourself trying to evaluate the value of a variable, looking for a specific value within a set of possible values. In this scenario, you end up having to write a lengthy if-then-else statement, like this:

```
$ cat test25
#!/bin/bash
# looking for a possible value

if [ $USER = "rich" ]
then
    echo "Welcome $USER"
    echo "Please enjoy your visit"
elif [ $USER = barbara ]
then
    echo "Welcome $USER"
    echo "Please enjoy your visit"
elif [ $USER = testing ]
then
    echo "Special testing account"
elif [ $USER = jessica ]
then
    echo "Don't forget to logout when you're done"
else
    echo "Sorry, you're not allowed here"
fi
$ ./test25
Welcome rich
Please enjoy your visit
$
```

The elif statements continue the if-then checking, looking for a specific value for the single comparison variable.

252

Instead of having to write all of the elif statements to continue checking the same variable value, you can use the case command. The case command checks multiple values of a single variable in a list-oriented format:

```
case variable in
pattern1 | pattern2) commands1;;
pattern3) commands2;;
*) default commands;;
esac
```

The case command compares the variable specified against the different patterns. If the variable matches the pattern, the shell executes the commands specified for the pattern. You can list more than one pattern on a line, using the bar operator to separate each pattern. The asterisk symbol is the catch-all for values that don't match any of the listed patterns. Here's an example of converting the if-then-else program to using the case command:

```
$ cat test26
#!/bin/bash
# using the case command

case $USER in
rich | barbara)
    echo "Welcome, $USER"
    echo "Please enjoy your visit";;
testing)
    echo "Special testing account";;
jessica)
    echo "Don't forget to log off when you're done";;
*)
    echo "Sorry, you're not allowed here";;
esac
$ ./test26
Welcome, rich
Please enjoy your visit
$
```

The case command provides a much cleaner way of specifying the various options for each possible variable value.

Summary

Structured commands allow you to alter the normal flow of execution on the shell script. The most basic structured command is the if-then statement. This statement allows you to evaluate a command, and perform other commands based on the outcome of the command you evaluated.

You can expand the if-then statement to include a set of commands the bash shell executes if the specified command fails as well. The if-then-else statement allows you to execute commands only if the command being evaluated returns a non-zero exit status code.

You can also link if-then-else statements together, using the elif statement. The elif is equivalent to using an else if statement, providing for additional checking if the original command that was evaluated failed.

In most scripts, instead of evaluating a command, you'll want to evaluate a condition, such as a numeric value, the contents of a string, or the status of a file or directory. The test command provides an easy way for you to evaluate all of these conditions. If the condition evaluates to a true condition, the test command produces a zero exit status code for the if-then statement. If the condition evaluates to a false condition, the test command produces a non-zero exit status code for the if-then statement.

The square bracket is a special bash command that is a synonym for the test command. You can enclose a test condition in square brackets in the if-then statement to test for numeric, string, and file conditions.

The double parentheses command allows you to perform advanced mathematical evaluations using additional operators, and the double square bracket command allows you to perform advanced string pattern-matching evaluations.

Finally, the chapter discussed the case command, which is a shorthand way of performing multiple if-then-else commands, checking the value of a single variable against a list of values.

The next chapter continues the discussion of structured commands by examining the shell looping commands. The for and while commands allow you to create loops that iterate through commands for a given period of time.

Chapter 10

More Structured Commands

In the previous chapter, you saw how to manipulate the flow of a shell script program by checking the output of commands, and the values of variables. In this chapter, we'll continue to look at structured commands that control the flow of your shell scripts. You'll see how you can perform repeating processes, commands that can loop through a set of commands until an indicated condition has been met. This chapter discusses and demonstrates the for, while, and until bash shell looping commands.

The for Command

Iterating through a series of commands is a common programming practice. Often you need to repeat a set of commands until a specific condition has been met, such as processing all of the files in a directory, all of the users on a system, or all of the lines in a text file.

The bash shell provides the for command to allow you to create a loop that iterates through a series of values. Each iteration performs a defined set of commands using one of the values in the series. The basic format of the bash shell for command is:

```
for var in list
do
    commands
done
```

You supply the series of values used in the iterations in the list parameter. There are several different ways that you can specify the values in the list.

IN THIS CHAPTER

Looping with the for statement

Iterating with the until statement

Using while statement

Combining loops

Redirecting loop output

In each iteration, the variable `var` contains the current value in the list. The first iteration uses the first item in the list, the second iteration the second item, and so on until all of the items in the list have been used.

The `commands` entered between the `do` and `done` statements can be one or more standard bash shell commands. Within the commands the `$var` variable contains the current list item value for the iteration.

> **NOTE** If you prefer, you can include the `do` statement on the same line as the `for` statement, but you must separate it from the list items using a semicolon: `for var in list; do`.

I mentioned that there are several different ways to specify the values in the list. The following sections show the various ways to do that.

Reading values in a list

The most basic use of the `for` command is to iterate through a list of values defined within the `for` command itself:

```
$ cat test1
#!/bin/bash
# basic for command

for test in Alabama Alaska Arizona Arkansas California Colorado
do
    echo The next state is $test
done
$ ./test1
The next state is Alabama
The next state is Alaska
The next state is Arizona
The next state is Arkansas
The next state is California
The next state is Colorado
$
```

Each time the `for` command iterates through the list of values provided, it assigns the `test` variable the next value in the list. The `$test` variable can be used just like any other script variable within the `for` command statements. After the last iteration, the `$test` variable remains valid throughout the remainder of the shell script. It retains the last iteration value (unless you change its value):

```
$ cat test1b
#!/bin/bash
# testing the for variable after the looping

for test in Alabama Alaska Arizona Arkansas California Colorado
do
    echo "The next state is $test"
done
```

```
          echo "The last state we visited was $test"
          test=Connecticut
          echo "Wait, now we're visiting $test"
          $ ./test1b
          The next state is Alabama
          The next state is Alaska
          The next state is Arizona
          The next state is Arkansas
          The next state is California
          The next state is Colorado
          The last state we visited was Colorado
          Wait, now we're visiting Connecticut
          $
```

The $test variable retained its value, and also allowed us to change the value and use it outside of the for command loop, as any other variable would.

Reading complex values in a list

Things aren't always as easy as they seem with the for loop. There are times when you run into data that causes problems. Here's a classic example of what can cause shell script programmers problems:

```
          $ cat badtest1
          #!/bin/bash
          # another example of how not to use the for command

          for test in I don't know if this'll work
          do
               echo "word:$test"
          done
          $ ./badtest1
          word:I
          word:dont know if thisll
          word:work
          $
```

Ouch, that hurts. The shell saw the single quotation marks within the list values and attempted to use them to define a single data value, and it really messed things up in the process.

There are two ways to solve this problem:

■ Use the escape character (the backslash) to escape the single quotation mark.

■ Use double quotation marks to define the values that use single quotation marks.

Neither solution is all that fantastic, but each one does help solve the problem:

```
          $ cat test2
          #!/bin/bash
          # another example of how not to use the for command
```

```
for test in I don\'t know if "this'll" work
do
    echo "word:$test"
done
$ ./test2
word:I
word:don't
word:know
word:if
word:this'll
word:work
$
```

In the first problem value, I added the backslash character to escape the single quotation mark in the don't value. In the second problem value, I enclosed the this'll value in double quotation marks. Both methods worked fine to distinguish the value.

Yet another problem you may run into is multi-word values. Remember, the for loop assumes that each value is separated with a space. If you have data values that contain spaces, you'll run into yet another problem:

```
$ cat badtest2
#!/bin/bash
# another example of how not to use the for command

for test in Nevada New Hampshire New Mexico New York North Carolina
do
    echo "Now going to $test"
done
$ ./badtest1
Now going to Nevada
Now going to New
Now going to Hampshire
Now going to New
Now going to Mexico
Now going to New
Now going to York
Now going to North
Now going to Carolina
$
```

Oops, that's not exactly what we wanted. The for command separates each value in the list with a space. If there are spaces in the individual data values, you must accommodate them using double quotation marks:

```
$ cat test3
#!/bin/bash
# an example of how to properly define values
```

```
for test in Nevada "New Hampshire" "New Mexico" "New York"
do
    echo "Now going to $test"
done
$ ./test3
Now going to Nevada
Now going to New Hampshire
Now going to New Mexico
Now going to New York
$
```

Now the `for` command can properly distinguish between the different values. Also, notice that when you use double quotation marks around a value, the shell doesn't include the quotation marks as part of the value.

Reading a list from a variable

Often what happens in a shell script is that you accumulate a list of values stored in a variable and then need to iterate through the list. You can do this using the `for` command as well:

```
$ cat test4
#!/bin/bash
# using a variable to hold the list

list="Alabama Alaska Arizona Arkansas Colorado"
list=$list" Connecticut"

for state in $list
do
    echo "Have you ever visited $state?"
done
$ ./test4
Have you ever visited Alabama?
Have you ever visited Alaska?
Have you ever visited Arizona?
Have you ever visited Arkansas?
Have you ever visited Colorado?
Have you ever visited Connecticut?
$
```

The `$list` variable contains the standard text list of values to use for the iterations. Notice that the code also uses another assignment statement to add (or concatenate) an item to the existing list contained in the `$list` variable. This is a common method for adding text to the end of an existing text string stored in a variable.

Reading values from a command

Yet another way to generate values for use in the list is to use the output of a command. You use the backtick characters to execute any command that produces output, then use the output of the command in the for command:

```
$ cat test5
#!/bin/bash
# reading values from a file

file="states"

for state in `cat $file`
do
    echo "Visit beautiful $state"
done
$ cat states
Alabama
Alaska
Arizona
Arkansas
Colorado
Connecticut
Delaware
Florida
Georgia
$ ./test5
Visit beautiful Alabama
Visit beautiful Alaska
Visit beautiful Arizona
Visit beautiful Arkansas
Visit beautiful Colorado
Visit beautiful Connecticut
Visit beautiful Delaware
Visit beautiful Florida
Visit beautiful Georgia
$
```

This example uses the cat command to display the contents of the file states. You'll notice that the states file includes each state on a separate line, not separated by spaces. The for command still iterates through the output of the cat command one line at a time, assuming that each state is on a separate line. However, this doesn't solve the problem of having spaces in data. If you list a state with a space in it, the for command will still take each word as a separate value. There's a reason for this, which we'll look at in the next section.

> **NOTE** The test5 code example assigned the filename to the variable using just the filename without a path. This requires that the file be in the same directory as the script. If this isn't the case, you'll need to use a full pathname (either absolute or relative) to reference the file location.

Changing the field separator

The cause of this problem is the special environment variable IFS, called the *internal field separator*. The IFS environment variable defines a list of characters the bash shell uses as field separators. By default, the bash shell considers the following characters as field separators:

- A space
- A tab
- A newline

If the bash shell sees any of these characters in the data, it'll assume that you're starting a new data field in the list. When working with data that can contain spaces (such as filenames), this can be annoying, as you saw in the previous script example.

To solve this problem, you can temporarily change the IFS environment variable values in your shell script to restrict the characters the bash shell recognizes as field separators. However, there is somewhat of an odd way of doing this. For example, if you want to change the IFS value to only recognize the newline character, you need to do this:

```
IFS=$'\n'
```

Adding this statement to your script tells the bash shell to ignore spaces and tabs in data values. Applying this to the previous script yields the following:

```
$ cat test5b
#!/bin/bash
# reading values from a file

file="states"

IFS=$'\n'
for state in `cat $file`
do
    echo "Visit beautiful $state"
done
$ ./test5b
Visit beautiful Alabama
Visit beautiful Alaska
Visit beautiful Arizona
Visit beautiful Arkansas
Visit beautiful Colorado
Visit beautiful Connecticut
Visit beautiful Delaware
Visit beautiful Florida
Visit beautiful Georgia
Visit beautiful New York
Visit beautiful New Hampshire
Visit beautiful North Carolina
$
```

Now the shell script is able to use values in the list that contain spaces.

CAUTION When working on long scripts, it's possible to change the IFS value in one place, then forget about it and assume the default value elsewhere in the script. A safe practice to get into is to save the original IFS value before changing it, then restore it when you're done.

This technique can be coded like this:

```
IFS.OLD=$IFS
IFS=$'\n'
<use the new IFS value in code>
IFS=$IFS.OLD
```

This ensures that the IFS value is returned to the default value for future operations within the script.

There are other excellent applications of the IFS environment variable. Say that you want to iterate through values in a file that are separated by a colon (such as in the /etc/passwd file). All you need to do is set the IFS value to a colon:

```
IFS=:
```

If you want to specify more than one IFS character, just string them together on the assignment line:

```
IFS=$'\n':;"
```

This assignment uses the newline, colon, semicolon, and double quotation mark characters as field separators. There's no limit to how you can parse your data using the IFS characters.

Reading a directory using wildcards

Finally, you can use the for command to automatically iterate through a directory of files. To do this, you must use a wildcard character in the file or pathname. This forces the shell to use *file globbing*. File globbing is the process of producing file or path names that match a specified wildcard character.

This feature is great for processing files in a directory, when you don't know all of the filenames:

```
$ cat test6
#!/bin/bash
# iterate through all the files in a directory

for file in /home/rich/test/*
do

    if [ -d "$file" ]
    then
        echo "$file is a directory"
    elif [ -f "$file" ]
    then
```

```
        echo "$file is a file"
    fi
done
$ ./test6
/home/rich/test/dir1 is a directory
/home/rich/test/myprog.c is a file
/home/rich/test/myprog is a file
/home/rich/test/myscript is a file
/home/rich/test/newdir is a directory
/home/rich/test/newfile is a file
/home/rich/test/newfile2 is a file
/home/rich/test/testdir is a directory
/home/rich/test/testing is a file
/home/rich/test/testprog is a file
/home/rich/test/testprog.c is a file
$
```

The for command iterates through the results of the /home/rich/test/* listing. The code tests each entry using the test command (using the square bracket method) to see if it's a directory (using the -d parameter) or a file (using the -f parameter). (See Chapter 9, "Using Structured Commands".)

Notice in this example I did something different in the if statement tests:

```
if [ -d "$file" ]
```

In Linux it's perfectly legal to have directory and filenames that contain spaces. To accommodate that, you should enclose the $file variable in double quotation marks. If you don't, you'll get an error if you run into a directory or filename that contains spaces:

```
./test6: line 6: [: too many arguments
./test6: line 9: [: too many arguments
```

The bash shell interprets the additional words as arguments within the test command, causing an error.

You can also combine both the directory search method and the list method in the same for statement, by listing a series of directory wildcards in the for command:

```
$ cat test7
#!/bin/bash
# iterating through multiple directories

for file in /home/rich/.b* /home/rich/badtest
do
    if [ -d "$file" ]
    then
        echo "$file is a directory"
    elif [ -f "$file" ]
    then
```

```
        echo "$file is a file"
    else
      echo "$file doesn't exist"
    fi
done
$ ./test7
/home/rich/.backup.timestamp is a file
/home/rich/.bash_history is a file
/home/rich/.bash_logout is a file
/home/rich/.bash_profile is a file
/home/rich/.bashrc is a file
/home/rich/badtest doesn't exist
$
```

The `for` statement first uses file globbing to iterate through the list of files that result from the wildcard character, then it iterates through the next file in the list. You can combine any number of wildcard entries in the list to iterate through.

> **CAUTION** Notice that you can enter anything in the list data — even if the file or directory doesn't exist, the `for` statement attempts to process whatever you place in the list. This can be a problem when working with files and directories. You have no way of knowing if you're trying to iterate through a nonexistent directory: It's always a good idea to test each file or directory before trying to process it.

The C-Style for Command

If you've done any programming using the C programming language, you're probably surprised by the way the bash shell uses the `for` command. In the C language, a `for` loop normally defines a variable, which it then alters automatically during each iteration. Normally, programmers use this variable as a counter, and either increment or decrement the counter by one in each iteration. The bash `for` command can also provide this functionality. This section shows how you can use a C-style `for` command in a bash shell script.

The C language for command

The C language `for` command has a specific method for specifying a variable, a condition that must remain true for the iterations to continue, and a method for altering the variable for each iteration. When the specified condition becomes false, the `for` loop stops. The condition equation is defined using standard mathematical symbols. For example, take the C language code:

```
for (i = 0; i < 10; i++)
{
    printf("The next number is %d\n", i);
}
```

This code produces a simple iteration loop, where the variable i is used as a counter. The first section assigns a default value to the variable. The middle section defines the condition under which the loop will iterate. When the defined condition becomes false, the for loop stops iterations. The last section defines the iteration process. After each iteration, the expression defined in the last section is executed. In this example, the i variable is incremented by one after each iteration.

The bash shell also supports a version of the for loop that looks similar to the C-style for loop, although it does have some subtle differences, including a couple of things that'll confuse shell script programmers. Here's the basic format of the C-style bash for loop:

```
for (( variable assignment ; condition ; iteration process ))
```

The format of the C-style for loop can be confusing for bash shell script programmers, as it uses C-style variable references instead of the shell-style variable references. Here's what a C-style for command looks like:

```
for (( a = 1; a < 10; a++ ))
```

Notice that there are a couple of things that don't follow the standard bash shell for method:

■ The assignment of the variable value can contain spaces.

■ The variable in the condition isn't preceded with a dollar sign.

■ The equation for the iteration process doesn't use the expr command format.

The shell developers created this format to more closely resemble the C-style for command. While this is great for C programmers, it can throw even expert shell programmers into a tizzy. Be careful when using the C-style for loop in your scripts.

Here's an example of using the C-style for command in a bash shell program:

```
$ cat test8
#!/bin/bash
# testing the C-style for loop

for (( i=1; i <= 10; i++ ))
do
    echo "The next number is $i"
done
$ ./test8
The next number is 1
The next number is 2
The next number is 3
The next number is 4
The next number is 5
The next number is 6
The next number is 7
The next number is 8
```

```
The next number is 9
The next number is 10
$
```

The for loop iterates through the commands using the variable defined in the for loop (the letter i in this example). In each iteration, the $i variable contains the value assigned in the for loop. After each iteration, the loop iteration process is applied to the variable, which in this example, increments the variable by one.

Using multiple variables

The C-style for command also allows you to use multiple variables for the iteration. The loop handles each variable separately, allowing you to define a different iteration process for each variable. While you can have multiple variables, you can only define one condition in the for loop:

```
$ cat test9
#!/bin/bash
# multiple variables

for (( a=1, b=10; a <= 10; a++, b-- ))
do
    echo "$a - $b"
done
$ ./test9
1 - 10
2 - 9
3 - 8
4 - 7
5 - 6
6 - 5
7 - 4
8 - 3
9 - 2
10 - 1
$
```

The a and b variables are each initialized with different values, and different iteration processes are defined. While the loop increases the a variable, it decreases the b variable for each iteration.

The while Command

The while command is somewhat of a cross between the if-then statement and the for loop. The while command allows you to define a command to test, then loop through a set of commands for as long as the defined test command returns a zero exit status. It tests the test command at the start of each iteration. When the test command returns a non-zero exit status, the while command stops executing the set of commands.

266

Basic while format

The format of the `while` command is:

```
while test command
do
 other commands
done
```

The `test command` defined in the `while` command is the exact same format as in `if-then` statements (see Chapter 9). Just as in the `if-then` statement, you can use any normal bash shell command, or you can use the `test` command to test for conditions, such as variable values.

The key to the `while` command is that the exit status of the test command specified must change, based on the commands run during the loop. If the exit status never changes, the `while` loop will get stuck in an infinite loop.

The most common situation uses the `test` command brackets to check a value of a shell variable that's used in the loop commands:

```
$ cat test10
#!/bin/bash
# while command test

var1=10
while [ $var1 -gt 0 ]
do
    echo $var1
    var1=$[ $var1 - 1 ]
done
$ ./test10
10
9
8
7
6
5
4
3
2
1
$
```

The `while` command defines the test condition to check for each iteration:

```
while [ $var1 -gt 0 ]
```

As long as the test condition is true, the `while` command continues to loop through the commands defined. Within the commands, the variable used in the test condition must be modified, or else you'll have an infinite loop. In this example, we use shell arithmetic to decrease the variable value by one:

```
var1=$[ $var1 - 1 ]
```

The while loop stops when the test condition is no longer true.

Using multiple test commands

In somewhat of an odd situation, the while command allows you to define multiple test commands on the while statement line. Only the exit status of the last test command is used to determine when the loop stops. This can cause some interesting results if you're not careful. Here's an example of what I mean:

```
$ cat test11
#!/bin/bash
# testing a multicommand while loop

var1=10

while echo $var1
      [ $var1 -ge 0 ]
do
   echo "This is inside the loop"
   var1=$[ $var1 - 1 ]
done
$ ./test11
10
This is inside the loop
9
This is inside the loop
8
This is inside the loop
7
This is inside the loop
6
This is inside the loop
5
This is inside the loop
4
This is inside the loop
3
This is inside the loop
2
This is inside the loop
1
This is inside the loop
0
```

```
This is inside the loop
-1
$
```

Pay close attention to what happened in this example. There were two test commands defined in the `while` statement:

```
while echo $var1
      [ $var1 -ge 0 ]
```

The first test command simply displays the current value of the `var1` variable. The second command uses the `test` command to determine the value of the `var1` variable. Inside the loop, an `echo` statement displays a simple message, indicating that the loop was processed. Notice when you run the example, how the output ends:

```
This is inside the loop
-1
$
```

The `while` loop executed the `echo` statement for when the `var1` variable was equal to zero, then decreased the `var1` variable value. Next, the test commands were executed for the next iteration. The `echo` test command was executed, displaying the value of the `var1` variable, which is now less than zero. It's not until the shell executes the `test` test command that the `while` loop terminates.

This demonstrates that in a multi-command `while` statement, all of the test commands are executed in each iteration, including the last iteration when the last test command fails. Be careful of this.

The until Command

The `until` command works exactly the opposite way from the `while` command. The `until` command requires that you to specify a test command that normally produces a non-zero exit status. As long as the exit status of the test command is non-zero, the bash shell executes the commands listed in the loop. Once the test command returns a zero exit status, the loop stops.

As you would expect, the format of the `until` command is:

```
until test commands
do
    other commands
done
```

Similar to the `while` command, you can have more than one *test command* in the `until` command statement. Only the exit status of the last command determines if the bash shell executes the *other commands* defined.

Here's an example of using the `until` command:

```
$ cat test12
#!/bin/bash
# using the until command

var1=100

until [ $var1 -eq 0 ]
do
   echo $var1
   var1=$[ $var1 - 25 ]
done
$ ./test12
100
75
50
25
$
```

This example tests the `var1` variable to determine when the `until` loop should stop. As soon as the value of the variable is equal to zero, the `until` command stops the loop. The same caution as for the `while` command applies when you use multiple test commands with the `until` command:

```
$ cat test13
#!/bin/bash
# using the until command

var1=100

until echo $var1
      [ $var1 -eq 0 ]
do
   echo Inside the loop: $var1
   var1=$[ $var1 - 25 ]
done
$ ./test13
100
Inside the loop: 100
75
Inside the loop: 75
50
Inside the loop: 50
25
Inside the loop: 25
0
$
```

The shell executes the test commands specified and stops only when the last command is true.

Nesting Loops

A loop statement can use any other type of command within the loop, including other loop commands. This is called a *nested loop*. Care should be taken when using nested loops, as you're performing an iteration within an iteration, which multiplies the number of times commands are being run. Not paying close attention to this can cause problems in your scripts.

Here's a simple example of nesting a `for` loop inside another `for` loop:

```
$ cat test14
#!/bin/bash
# nesting for loops

for (( a = 1; a <= 3; a++ ))
do
   echo "Starting loop $a:"
   for (( b = 1; b <= 3; b++ ))
   do
      echo "   Inside loop: $b"
   done
done
$ ./test14
Starting loop 1:
   Inside loop: 1
   Inside loop: 2
   Inside loop: 3
Starting loop 2:
   Inside loop: 1
   Inside loop: 2
   Inside loop: 3
Starting loop 3:
   Inside loop: 1
   Inside loop: 2
   Inside loop: 3
$
```

The nested loop (also called the inner loop) iterates through its values for each iteration of the outer loop. Notice that there's no difference between the `do` and `done` commands for the two loops. The bash shell knows when the first `done` command is executed that it refers to the inner loop and not the outer loop.

The same applies when you mix loop commands, such as placing a `for` loop inside a `while` loop:

```
$ cat test15
#!/bin/bash
# placing a for loop inside a while loop

var1=5
```

```
    while [ $var1 -ge 0 ]
    do
       echo "Outer loop: $var1"
       for (( var2 = 1; $var2 < 3; var2++ ))
       do
          var3=$[ $var1 * $var2 ]
          echo " Inner loop: $var1 * $var2 = $var3"
       done
       var1=$[ $var1 - 1 ]
    done
$ ./test15
Outer loop: 5
   Inner loop: 5 * 1 = 5
   Inner loop: 5 * 2 = 10
Outer loop: 4
   Inner loop: 4 * 1 = 4
   Inner loop: 4 * 2 = 8
Outer loop: 3
   Inner loop: 3 * 1 = 3
   Inner loop: 3 * 2 = 6
Outer loop: 2
   Inner loop: 2 * 1 = 2
   Inner loop: 2 * 2 = 4
Outer loop: 1
   Inner loop: 1 * 1 = 1
   Inner loop: 1 * 2 = 2
Outer loop: 0
   Inner loop: 0 * 1 = 0
   Inner loop: 0 * 2 = 0
$
```

Again, the shell was able to distinguish between the do and done commands of the inner for loop from the same commands in the outer while loop.

If you really want to test your brain, you can even combine until and while loops:

```
$ cat test16
#!/bin/bash
# using until and while loops

var1=3

until [ $var1 -eq 0 ]
do
   echo "Outer loop: $var1"
   var2=1
   while [ $var2 -lt 5 ]
   do
      var3=`echo "scale=4; $var1 / $var2" | bc`
```

```
            echo "    Inner loop: $var1 / $var2 = $var3"
            var2=$[ $var2 + 1 ]
        done
    var1=$[ $var1 - 1 ]
done
$ ./test16
Outer loop: 3
    Inner loop: 3 / 1 = 3.0000
    Inner loop: 3 / 2 = 1.5000
    Inner loop: 3 / 3 = 1.0000
    Inner loop: 3 / 4 = .7500
Outer loop: 2
    Inner loop: 2 / 1 = 2.0000
    Inner loop: 2 / 2 = 1.0000
    Inner loop: 2 / 3 = .6666
    Inner loop: 2 / 4 = .5000
Outer loop: 1
    Inner loop: 1 / 1 = 1.0000
    Inner loop: 1 / 2 = .5000
    Inner loop: 1 / 3 = .3333
    Inner loop: 1 / 4 = .2500
$
```

The outer until loop starts with a value of three and continues until the value equals zero. The inner while loop starts with a value of 1 and continues as long as the value is less than five. Each loop must change the value used in the test condition, or the loop will get stuck infinitely.

Looping on File Data

Often, you must iterate through items stored inside a file. This requires combining two of the techniques covered:

- Using nested loops
- Changing the IFS environment variable

By changing the IFS environment variable, you can force the for command to handle each line in the file as a separate item for processing, even if the data contains spaces. Once you've extracted an individual line in the file, you may have to loop again to extract data contained within it.

The classic example of this is processing data in the /etc/passwd file. This requires that you iterate through the /etc/passwd file line by line, then change the IFS variable value to a colon so that you can separate out the individual components in each line.

Here's an example of doing that:

```
#!/bin/bash
# changing the IFS value
```

273

```
IFS.OLD=$IFS
IFS=$'\n'
for entry in `cat /etc/passwd`
do
    echo "Values in $entry -"
    IFS=:
    for value in $entry
    do
        echo "    $value"
    done
done
$
```

This script uses two different IFS values to parse the data. The first IFS value parses the individual lines in the /etc/passwd file. The inner for loop next changes the IFS value to the colon, which allows you to parse the individual values within the /etc/passwd lines.

When you run this script, you'll get output something like this:

```
Values in rich:x:501:501:Rich Blum:/home/rich:/bin/bash -
    rich
    x
    501
    501
    Rich Blum
    /home/rich
    /bin/bash
Values in katie:x:502:502:Katie Blum:/home/katie:/bin/bash -
    katie
    x
    506
    509
    Katie Blum
    /home/katie
    /bin/bash
```

The inner loop parses each individual value in the /etc/passwd entry. This is also a great way to process comma-separated data, a common way to import spreadsheet data.

Controlling the Loop

You might be tempted to think that once you start a loop, you're stuck until the loop finishes all of its iterations. This is not true. There are a couple of commands that help us control what happens inside of a loop:

- The break command
- The continue command

Each command has a different use in how to control the operation of a loop. The following sections describe how you can use these commands to control the operation of your loops.

The break command

The break command is a simple way to escape out of a loop in progress. You can use the break command to exit out of any type of loop, including while and until loops.

There are several situations in which you can use the break command. This section shows each of these methods.

Breaking out of a single loop

When the shell executes a break command, it attempts to break out of the loop that's currently processing:

```
$ cat test17
#!/bin/bash
# breaking out of a for loop

for var1 in 1 2 3 4 5 6 7 8 9 10
do
    if [ $var1 -eq 5 ]
    then
        break
    fi
    echo "Iteration number: $var1"
done
echo "The for loop is completed"
$ ./test17
Iteration number: 1
Iteration number: 2
Iteration number: 3
Iteration number: 4
The for loop is completed
$
```

The for loop should normally have iterated through all of the values specified in the list. However, when the if-then condition was satisfied, the shell executed the break command, which stopped the for loop.

This technique also works for while and until loops:

```
$ cat test18
#!/bin/bash
# breaking out of a while loop

var1=1

while [ $var1 -lt 10 ]
do
```

```
        if [ $var1 -eq 5 ]
        then
            break
        fi
        echo "Iteration: $var1"
        var1=$[ $var1 + 1 ]
done
echo "The while loop is completed"
$ ./test18
Iteration: 1
Iteration: 2
Iteration: 3
Iteration: 4
The while loop is completed
$
```

The while loop terminated when the if-then condition was met, executing the break command.

Breaking out of an inner loop

When you're working with multiple loops, the break command automatically terminates the innermost loop you're in:

```
$ cat test19
#!/bin/bash
# breaking out of an inner loop

for (( a = 1; a < 4; a++ ))
do
    echo "Outer loop: $a"
    for (( b = 1; b < 100; b++ ))
    do
        if [ $b -eq 5 ]
        then
            break
        fi
        echo "   Inner loop: $b"
    done
done
$ ./test19
Outer loop: 1
   Inner loop: 1
   Inner loop: 2
   Inner loop: 3
   Inner loop: 4
Outer loop: 2
   Inner loop: 1
   Inner loop: 2
```

```
        Inner loop: 3
        Inner loop: 4
Outer loop: 3
        Inner loop: 1
        Inner loop: 2
        Inner loop: 3
        Inner loop: 4
$
```

The for statement in the inner loop specifies to iterate until the b variable is equal to 100. However, the if-then statement in the inner loop specifies that when the b variable value is equal to five, the break command is executed. Notice that even though the inner loop is terminated with the break command, the outer loop continues working as specified.

Breaking out of an outer loop

There may be times when you're in an inner loop but need to stop the outer loop. The break command includes a single command line parameter value:

```
break n
```

where n indicates the level of the loop to break out of. By default, n is one, indicating to break out of the current loop. If you set n to a value of two, the break command will stop the next level of the outer loop:

```
$ cat test20
#!/bin/bash
# breaking out of an outer loop

for (( a = 1; a < 4; a++ ))
do
    echo "Outer loop: $a"
    for (( b = 1; b < 100; b++ ))
    do
        if [ $b -gt 4 ]
        then
            break 2
        fi
        echo "   Inner loop: $b"
    done
done
$ ./test20
Outer loop: 1
    Inner loop: 1
    Inner loop: 2
    Inner loop: 3
    Inner loop: 4
$
```

Now when the shell executes the break command, the outer loop stops.

The continue command

The continue command is a way to prematurely stop processing commands inside of a loop but not terminate the loop completely. This allows you to set conditions within a loop where the shell won't execute commands. Here's a simple example of using the continue command in a for loop:

```
$ cat test21
#!/bin/bash
# using the continue command

for (( var1 = 1; var1 < 15; var1++ ))
do
    if [ $var1 -gt 5 ] && [ $var1 -lt 10 ]
    then
        continue
    fi
    echo "Iteration number: $var1"
done
$ ./test21
Iteration number: 1
Iteration number: 2
Iteration number: 3
Iteration number: 4
Iteration number: 5
Iteration number: 10
Iteration number: 11
Iteration number: 12
Iteration number: 13
Iteration number: 14
$
```

When the conditions of the if-then statement are met (the value is greater than five and less than 10), the shell executes the continue command, which skips the rest of the commands in the loop, but keeps the loop going. When the if-then condition is no longer met, things return back to normal.

You can use the continue command in while and until loops, but be extremely careful with what you're doing. Remember, when the shell executes the continue command, it skips the remaining commands. If you're incrementing your test condition variable in one of those conditions, bad things will happen:

```
$ cat badtest3
#!/bin/bash
# improperly using the continue command in a while loop

var1=0
```

```
        while echo "while iteration: $var1"
            [ $var1 -lt 15 ]
        do
            if [ $var1 -gt 5 ] && [ $var1 -lt 10 ]
            then
                continue
            fi
            echo "    Inside iteration number: $var1"
            var1=$[ $var1 + 1 ]
        done
$ ./badtest3 | more
while iteration: 0
    Inside iteration number: 0
while iteration: 1
    Inside iteration number: 1
while iteration: 2
    Inside iteration number: 2
while iteration: 3
    Inside iteration number: 3
while iteration: 4
    Inside iteration number: 4
while iteration: 5
    Inside iteration number: 5
while iteration: 6
while iteration: 6
while iteration: 6
while iteration: 6
while iteration: 6
while iteration: 6
while iteration: 6
while iteration: 6
while iteration: 6
while iteration: 6
while iteration: 6
$
```

You'll want to make sure you redirect the output of this script to the more command so you can stop things. Everything seems to be going just fine, until the if-then condition is met, and the shell executes the continue command. When the shell executes the continue command, it skips the remaining commands in the while loop. Unfortunately, that's where I incremented the counter variable that I tested in the while test command. That meant that the variable wasn't incremented, as you can see from the continually displaying output.

Just as with the break command, the continue command allows you to specify what level of loop to continue with a command line parameter:

```
continue n
```

where *n* defines the loop level to continue. Here's an example of continuing an outer for loop:

```
$ cat test22
#!/bin/bash
# continuing an outer loop

for (( a = 1; a <= 5; a++ ))
do
    echo "Iteration $a:"
    for (( b = 1; b < 3; b++ ))
    do
        if [ $a -gt 2 ] && [ $a -lt 4 ]
        then
            continue 2
        fi
        var3=$[ $a * $b ]
        echo "   The result of $a * $b is $var3"
    done
done
$ ./test22
Iteration 1:
    The result of 1 * 1 is 1
    The result of 1 * 2 is 2
Iteration 2:
    The result of 2 * 1 is 2
    The result of 2 * 2 is 4
Iteration 3:
Iteration 4:
    The result of 4 * 1 is 4
    The result of 4 * 2 is 8
Iteration 5:
    The result of 5 * 1 is 5
    The result of 5 * 2 is 10
$
```

The if-then statement:

```
if [ $a -gt 2 ] && [ $a -lt 4 ]
    then
        continue 2
    fi
```

uses the continue command to stop processing the commands inside the loop, but continue the outer loop. Notice in the script output that the iteration for the value 3 doesn't process any inner loop statements, as the continue command stopped the processing, but continues with the outer loop processing.

Processing the Output of a Loop

Finally, you can either pipe or redirect the output of a loop within your shell script. You do this by adding the processing command to the end of the `done` command:

```
for file in /home/rich/*
do
   if [ -d "$file" ]
   then
      echo "$file is a directory"
   elif
      echo "$file is a file"
   fi
done > output.txt
```

Instead of displaying the results on the monitor, the shell redirects the results of the `for` command to the file `output.txt`.

Here's an example of redirecting the output of a `for` command to a file:

```
$ cat test23
#!/bin/bash
# redirecting the for output to a file

for (( a = 1; a < 10; a++ ))
do
   echo "The number is $a"
done > test23.txt
echo "The command is finished."
$ ./test23
The command is finished.
$ cat test23.txt
The number is 1
The number is 2
The number is 3
The number is 4
The number is 5
The number is 6
The number is 7
The number is 8
The number is 9
$
```

The shell creates the file `test23.txt`, and redirects the output of the `for` command only to the file. The shell displays the `echo` statement after the `for` command just as normal.

This same technique also works for piping the output of a loop to another command:

```
$ cat test24
#!/bin/bash
# piping a loop to another command

for state in "North Dakota" Connecticut Illinois Alabama Tennessee
do
    echo "$state is the next place to go"
done | sort
echo "This completes our travels"
$ ./test24
Alabama is the next place to go
Connecticut is the next place to go
Illinois is the next place to go
North Dakota is the next place to go
Tennessee is the next place to go
This completes our travels
$
```

The state values aren't listed in any particular order in the `for` command list. The output of the `for` command is piped to the `sort` command, which will change the order of the `for` command output. Running the script indeed shows that the output was properly sorted within the script.

Summary

Looping is an integral part of programming. The bash shell provides three different looping commands that we can use in our scripts. The `for` command allows us to iterate through a list of values, either supplied within the command line, contained in a variable, or obtained by using file globbing to extract file and directory names from a wildcard character.

The `while` command provides a method to loop based on the condition of a command, using either ordinary commands or the test command, which allows us to test conditions of variables. As long as the command (or condition) produces a zero exit status, the `while` loop will continue to iterate through the specified set of commands.

The `until` command also provides a method to iterate through commands, but it bases its iterations on a command (or condition) producing a non-zero exit status. This feature allows us to set a condition that must be met before the iteration stops.

You can combine loops in shell scripts, producing multiple layers of loops. The bash shell provides the `continue` and `break` commands, which allow us to alter the flow of the normal loop process based on different values within the loop.

The bash shell also allows us to use standard command redirection and piping to alter the output of a loop. You can use redirection to redirect the output of a loop to a file, or piping to redirect the output of a loop to another command. This provides a wealth of features with which you can control your shell script execution.

The next chapter discusses how to interact with your shell script user. Often shell scripts aren't completely self-contained. They require some sort of external data that must be supplied at the time you run them. The next chapter shows different methods with which you can provide real-time data to your shell scripts for processing.

## Chapter 11

Handling User Input

So far you've seen how to write scripts that interact with data, variables, and files on the Linux system. Sometimes, you need to write a script that has to interact with the person running the script. The bash shell provides a few different methods for retrieving data from people, including command line parameters (data values added after the command), command line options (single-letter values that modify the behavior of the command), and reading input directly from the keyboard. This chapter discusses how to incorporate these different methods into your bash shell scripts to obtain data from the person running your script.

Command Line Parameters

The most basic method of passing data to your shell script is by using *command line parameters*. Command line parameters allow you to add data values to the command line when you execute the script:

```
$ ./addem 10 30
```

This example passes two command line parameters (10 and 30) to the script addem. The script handles the command line parameters using special variables. The following sections describe how to use command line parameters in your bash shell scripts.

Reading parameters

The bash shell assigns special variables, called *positional parameters*, to all of the parameters entered in a command line. This even includes the name of the program the shell executes. The positional parameter variables are standard numbers, with $0 being the name of the program, $1 being the first parameter, $2 being the second parameter, and so on, up to $9 for the ninth parameter.

Here's a simple example of using one command line parameter in a shell script:

```
$ cat test1
#!/bin/bash
# using one command line parameter

factorial=1
for (( number = 1; number <= $1 ; number++ ))
do
    factorial=$[ $factorial * $number ]
done
echo The factorial of $1 is $factorial
$ ./test1 5
The factorial of 5 is 120
$
```

You can use the $1 variable just like any other variable in the shell script. The shell script automatically assigns the value from the command line parameter to the variable, you don't need to do anything with it.

If you need to enter more command line parameters, each parameter must be separated by a space on the command line:

```
$ cat test2
#!/bin/bash
# testing two command line parameters

total=$[ $1 * $2 ]
echo The first paramerer is $1.
echo The second parameter is $2.
echo The total value is $total.
$ ./test2 2 5
The first paramerer is 2.
The second parameter is 5.
The total value is 10.
$
```

The shell assigns each parameter to the appropriate variable.

In this example, the command line parameters used were both numerical values. You can also use text strings in the command line:

```
$ cat test3
#!/bin/bash
# testing string parameters
```

```
echo Hello $1, glad to meet you.
$ ./test3 Rich
Hello Rich, glad to meet you.
$
```

The shell passes the string value entered into the command line to the script. However, you'll have a problem if you try to do this with a text string that contains spaces:

```
$ ./test3 Rich Blum
Hello Rich, glad to meet you.
$
```

Remember, each of the parameters is separated by a space, so the shell interpreted the space as just separating the two values. To include a space as a parameter value, you must use quotation marks (either single or double quotation marks):

```
$ ./test3 'Rich Blum'
Hello Rich Blum, glad to meet you.
$ ./test3 "Rich Blum"
Hello Rich Blum, glad to meet you.
$
```

Notice that the quotation marks aren't part of the data, they just delineate the beginning and end of the data.

If your script needs more than nine command line parameters, you can continue, but the variable names change slightly. After the ninth variable, you must use braces around the variable number, such as ${10}. Here's an example of doing that:

```
$ cat test4
#!/bin/bash
# handling lots of parameters

total=$[ ${10} * ${11} ]
echo The tenth parameter is ${10}
echo The eleventh parameter is ${11}
echo The total is $total
$ ./test4 1 2 3 4 5 6 7 8 9 10 11 12
The tenth parameter is 10
The eleventh parameter is 11
The total is 110
$
```

This technique allows you to add as many command line parameters to your scripts as you could possibly need.

Reading the program name

You can use the $0 parameter to determine the name of the program that the shell started from the command line. This can come in handy if you're writing a utility that can have multiple functions. However, there's a small problem that you'll have to deal with. Look what happens in this simple example:

```
$ cat test5
#!/bin/bash
# testing the $0 parameter

echo The command entered is: $0
$ ./test5
The command entered is: ./test5
$ /home/rich/test5
The command entered is: /home/rich/test5
$
```

The actual string passed in the $0 variable is the entire path used for the program, not just the program name.

If you want to write a script that performs different functions based on the name of the script run from the command line, you'll have to do a little work. You need to be able to strip off whatever path is used to run the script from the command line.

Fortunately, there's a handy little command available for us that does just that. The basename command returns just the program name without the path. Let's modify the example script and see how this works:

```
$ cat test5b
#!/bin/bash
# using basename with  the $0 parameter

name=`basename $0`
echo The command entered is: $name
$ ./test5b
The command entered is: test5b
$ /home/rich/test5b
The command entered is: test5b
$
```

Now that's much better. You can now use this technique to write scripts that perform different functions based on the script name used. Here's a simple example to demonstrate this:

```
$ cat test6
#!/bin/bash
# testing a multi-function script

name=`basename $0`
```

```
if [ $name = "addem" ]
then
    total=$[ $1 + $2 ]
elif [ $name = "multem" ]
then
    total=$[ $1 * $2 ]
fi
echo The calculated value is $total
$ chmod u+x test6
$ cp test6 addem
$ ln -s test6 multem
$ ls -l
-rwxr--r--    1 rich     rich     211 Oct 15 18:00 addem*
lrwxrwxrwx    1 rich     rich       5 Oct 15 18:01 multem -> test6*
-rwxr--r--    1 rich     rich     211 Oct 15 18:00 test6*
$ ./addem 2 5
The calculated value is 7
$ ./multem 2 5
The calculated value is 10
$
```

The example creates two separate filenames from the test6 code, one by just copying the file and the other by using a link to create the new file. In both cases, the script determines the basename of the script and performs the appropriate function based on that value.

Testing parameters

You need to be careful when using command line parameters in your shell scripts. If the script runs without the parameters, bad things can happen:

```
$ ./addem 2
./addem: line 8: 2 +  : syntax error: operand expected (error
 token is " ")
The calculated value is
$
```

When the script assumes there's data in a parameter variable, and there isn't, most likely you'll get an error message from your script. This is not a good way to write scripts. It's always a good idea to check your parameters to make sure there's really data there before using them:

```
$ cat test7
#!/bin/bash
# testing parameters before use

if [ -n "$1" ]
then
    echo Hello $1, glad to meet you.
else
    echo "Sorry, you didn't identify yourself."
fi
```

289

```
$ ./test7 Rich
Hello Rich, glad to meet you.
$ ./test7
Sorry, you didn't identify yourself.
$
```

In this example, I used the `-n` parameter in the `test` command to check if there was data in the command line parameter. In the next section you'll see there's yet another way to check for command line parameters.

Special Parameter Variables

There are a few special variables available in the bash shell that track command line parameters. This section describes what they are, and how to use them.

Counting parameters

As you saw in the last section, it's often a good idea to verify command line parameters before using them in your script. For scripts that use multiple command line parameters, this can get tedious.

Instead of testing each parameter, you can just count how many parameters were entered on the command line. The bash shell provides a special variable for this purpose.

The special `$#` variable contains the number of command line parameters included when the script was run. You can use this special variable anywhere in the script, just as a normal variable:

```
$ cat test8
#!/bin/bash
# getting the number of parameters

echo There were $# parameters supplied.
$ ./test8
There were 0 parameters supplied.
$ ./test8 1 2 3 4 5
There were 5 parameters supplied.
$ ./test8 1 2 3 4 5 6 7 8 9 10
There were 10 parameters supplied.
$ ./test8 "Rich Blum"
There were 1 parameters supplied.
$
```

Now you have the ability to test the number of parameters present before trying to use them:

```
$ cat test9
#!/bin/bash
# testing parameters

if [ $# -ne 2 ]
then
    echo Usage: test9 a b
else
    total=$[ $1 + $2 ]
    echo The total is $total
fi
$ ./test9
Usage: test9 a b
$ ./test9 10
Usage: test9 a b
$ ./test9 10 15
The total is 25
$ ./test9 10 15 20
Usage: test9 a b
$
```

The if-then statement uses the test command to perform a numeric test of the number of parameters supplied on the command line. If the correct number of parameters isn't present, you can print an error message that shows the correct usage of the script.

This variable also provides a cool way of grabbing the last parameter on the command line, without having to know how many parameters were used. However, you need to use a little trick to get there.

If you think this through, you might think that since the $# variable contains the value of the number of parameters, then using the variable ${$#} would represent the last command line parameter variable. Try that out and see what happens:

```
$ cat badtest1
#!/bin/bash
# testing grabbing last parameter

echo The last parameter was ${$#}
$ ./badtest1 10
The last parameter was 15354
$
```

291

Wow, what happened here? Obviously, something wrong happened. It turns out that you can't use the dollar sign within the braces. Instead, you must replace the dollar sign with an exclamation mark. Odd, but it works:

```
$ cat test10
#!/bin/bash
# grabbing the last parameter

params=$#
echo The last parameter is $params
echo The last paramerer is ${!#}
$ ./test10 1 2 3 4 5
The last parameter is 5
The last paramerer is 5
$ ./test10
The last parameter is 0
The last parameter is ./test10
$
```

Perfect. This test also assigned the $# variable value to the variable params, then used that variable within the special command line parameter variable format as well. Both versions worked. It's also important to notice that, when there weren't any parameters on the command line, the $# value was zero, which is what appears in the params variable, but the ${!#} variable returns the script name used on the command line.

Grabbing all the data

There are situations where you'll want to just grab all of the parameters provided on the command line and iterate through all of them. Instead of having to mess with using the $# variable to determine how many parameters are on the command line, then having to loop through all of them, you can use a couple of other special variables.

The $* and $@ variables provide one-stop shopping for all of your parameters. Both of these variables include all of the command line parameters within a single variable.

The $* variable takes all of the parameters supplied on the command line as a single word. The word contains each of the values as they appear on the command line. Basically, instead of treating the parameters as multiple objects, the $* variable treats them all as one parameter.

The $@ variable on the other hand, takes all of the parameters supplied on the command line as separate words in the same string. It allows you to iterate through the value, separating out each parameter supplied. This is most often accomplished using the for command.

It can easily get confusing as to how these two variables operate. If you take them both at face value, you won't even see the difference:

```
$ cat test11
#!/bin/bash
# testing $* and $@
```

```
echo "Using the \$* method: $*"
echo "Using the \$@ method: $@"
$ ./test11 rich barbara katie jessica
Using the $* method: rich barbara katie jessica
Using the $@ method: rich barbara katie jessica
$
```

Notice that on the surface, both variables produce the same output, showing all of the command line parameters provided at once.

Now, here's another example that'll demonstrate where the difference comes into play:

```
$ cat test12
#!/bin/bash
# testing $* and $@

count=1
for param in "$*"
do
    echo "\$* Parameter #$count = $param"
    count=$[ $count + 1 ]
done

count=1
for param in "$@"
do
    echo "\$@ Parameter #$count = $param"
    count=$[ $count + 1 ]
done
$ ./test12 rich barbara katie jessica
$* Parameter #1 = rich barbara katie jessica
$@ Parameter #1 = rich
$@ Parameter #2 = barbara
$@ Parameter #3 = katie
$@ Parameter #4 = jessica
$
```

Now we're getting somewhere. By using the for command to iterate through the special variables, you can see how they each treat the command line parameters differently. The $* variable treated all of the parameters as a single word, while the $@ variable treated each parameter separately. This is a great way to iterate through command line parameters.

Being Shifty

Another tool you have in your bash shell toolbelt is the shift command. The bash shell provides the shift command to help us manipulate command line parameters. The shift command does what it says, it shifts the command line parameters in their relative positions.

When you use the shift command, it "downgrades" each parameter variable one position by default. Thus, the value for variable $3 is moved to $2, the value for variable $2 is moved to $1, and the value for variable $1 is discarded (note that the value for variable $0, the program name, remains unchanged).

This is another great way to iterate through command line parameters, especially if you don't know how many parameters are available. You can just operate on the first parameter, shift the parameters over, then operate on the first parameter again.

Here's a short demonstration of how this works:

```
$ cat test13
#!/bin/bash
# demonstrating the shift command

count=1
while [ -n "$1" ]
do
    echo "Parameter #$count = $1"
    count=$[ $count + 1 ]
    shift
done
$ ./test13 rich barbara katie jessica
Parameter #1 = rich
Parameter #2 = barbara
Parameter #3 = katie
Parameter #4 = jessica
$
```

The script performs a while loop, testing the length of the first parameter's value. When the first parameter's length is zero, the loop ends.

After testing the first parameter, the shift command is used to shift all of the parameters one position.

Alternatively, you can perform a multiple location shift by providing a parameter to the shift command. Just provide the number of places you want to shift:

```
$ cat test14
#!/bin/bash
# demonstrating a multi-position shift

echo "The original parameters: $*"
shift 2
echo "Here's the new first parameter: $1"
$ ./test14 1 2 3 4 5
The original parameters: 1 2 3 4 5
Here's the new first parameter: 3
$
```

By using values in the shift command, you can easily skip over parameters you don't need.

> **CAUTION** Be careful when working with the `shift` command. When a parameter is shifted out, its value is lost and can't be recovered.

Working With Options

If you've been following along in the book, you've seen several bash commands that provide both parameters and options. *Options* are single letters preceded by a dash that alter the behavior of a command. This section shows three different methods for working with options in your shell scripts.

Finding your options

On the surface, there's nothing all that special about command line options. They appear on the command line immediately after the script name, just the same as command line parameters. In fact, if you want, you can process command line options the same way that you process command line parameters.

Processing simple options

In the `test13` script earlier, you saw how to use the `shift` command to walk your way down the command line parameters provided with the script program. You can use this same technique to process command line options.

As you extract each individual parameter, use the `case` statement to determine when a parameter is formatted as an option:

```
$ cat test15
#!/bin/bash
# extracting command line options as parameters

while [ -n "$1" ]
do
   case "$1" in
   -a) echo "Found the -a option" ;;
   -b) echo "Found the -b option";;
   -c) echo "Found the -c option" ;;
   *) echo "$1 is not an option";;
   esac
   shift
done
$ ./test15 -a -b -c -d
Found the -a option
Found the -b option
Found the -c option
-d is not an option
$
```

The case statement checks each parameter for valid options. When one is found, the appropriate commands are run in the case statement.

This method works, no matter what order the options are presented on the command line:

```
$ ./test15 -d -c -a
-d is not an option
Found the -c option
Found the -a option
$
```

The case statement processes each option as it finds it in the command line parameters. If any other parameters are included on the command line, you can include commands in the catch-all part of the case statement to process them.

Separating options from parameters

Often you'll run into situations where you'll want to use both options and parameters for a shell script. The standard way to do this in Linux is to separate the two with a special character code that tells the script when the options are done and when the normal parameters start.

For Linux, this special character is the double dash (--). The shell uses the double dash to indicate the end of the option list. After seeing the double dash, your script can safely process the remaining command line parameters as parameters and not options.

To check for the double dash, all you need to do is add another entry in the case statement:

```
$ cat test16
#!/bin/bash
# extracting options and parameters

while [ -n "$1" ]
do
   case "$1" in
   -a) echo "Found the -a option" ;;
   -b) echo "Found the -b option";;
   -c) echo "Found the -c option" ;;
   --) shift
       break ;;
   *) echo "$1 is not an option";;
   esac
   shift
done

count=1
for param in $@
do
   echo "Parameter #$count: $param"
   count=$[ $count + 1 ]
done
$
```

This script uses the break command to break out of the while loop when it encounters the double dash. Because we're breaking out prematurely, we need to ensure that we stick in another shift command to get the double dash out of the parameter variables.

For the first test, try running the script using a normal set of options and parameters:

```
$ ./test16 -c -a -b test1 test2 test3
Found the -c option
Found the -a option
Found the -b option
test1 is not an option
test2 is not an option
test3 is not an option
$
```

The results show that the script assumed that all the command line parameters were options when it processed them. Next, try the same thing, only this time using the double dash to separate the options from the parameters on the command line:

```
$ ./test16 -c -a -b -- test1 test2 test3
Found the -c option
Found the -a option
Found the -b option
Parameter #1: test1
Parameter #2: test2
Parameter #3: test3
$
```

When the script reaches the double dash, it stops processing options and assumes that any remaining parameters are command line parameters.

Processing options with values

Some options require an additional parameter value. In these situations, the command line looks something like this:

```
$ ./testing -a test1 -b -c -d test2
```

Your script must be able to detect when your command line option requires an additional parameter and be able to process it appropriately. Here's an example of how to do that:

```
$ cat test17
#!/bin/bash
# extracting command line options and values

while [ -n "$1" ]
do
   case "$1" in
   -a) echo "Found the -a option";;
```

297

```
        -b) param="$2"
            echo "Found the -b option, with parameter value $param"
            shift 2;;
        -c) echo "Found the -c option";;
        --) shift
            break;;
        *) echo "$1 is not an option";;
        esac
        shift
done

count=1
for param in "$@"
do
    echo "Parameter #$count: $param"
    count=$[ $count + 1 ]
done
$ ./test17 -a -b test1 -d
Found the -a option
Found the -b option, with parameter value test1
-d is not an option
$
```

In this example, the case statement defines three options that it processes. The -b option also requires an additional parameter value. Since the parameter being processed is $1, you know that the additional parameter value is located in $2 (since all of the parameters are shifted after they are processed). Just extract the parameter value from the $2 variable. Of course, since we used two parameter spots for this option, you also need to set the shift command to shift two positions.

Just as with the basic feature, this process works no matter what order you place the options in (just remember to include the appropriate option parameter with the each option):

```
$ ./test17 -b test1 -a -d
Found the -b option, with parameter value test1
Found the -a option
-d is not an option
$
```

Now you have the basic ability to process command line options in your shell scripts, but there are limitations. For example, this won't work if you try to combine multiple options in one parameter:

```
$ ./test17 -ac
-ac is not an option
$
```

It is a common practice in Linux to combine options, and if your script is going to be user-friendly, you'll want to offer this feature for your users as well. Fortunately, there's another method for processing options that can help us.

Using the getopt command

The getopt command is a great tool to have handy when processing command line options and parameters. It reorganizes the command line parameters to make parsing them in your script easier.

The command format

The getopt command can take a list of command line options and parameters, in any form, and automatically turn them into the proper format. It uses the command format:

```
getopt options optstring parameters
```

The *optstring* is the key to the process. It defines the valid option letters used in the command line. It also defines which option letters require a parameter value.

First, list each command line option letter you're going to use in your script in the optstring. Then, place a colon after each option letter that requires a parameter value. The getopt command parses the supplied parameters based on the optstring you define.

Here's a simple example of how getopt works:

```
$ getopt ab:cd -a -b test1 -cd test2 test3
 -a -b test1 -c -d -- test2 test3
$
```

The optstring defines four valid option letters, a, b, c, and d. It also defines that the option letter b requires a parameter value. When the getopt command runs, it examines the provided parameter list, and parses it based on the supplied optstring. Notice that it automatically separated the -cd options into two separate options and inserted the double dash to separate the additional parameters on the line.

If you specify an option not in the optstring, by default the getopt command produces an error message:

```
$ getopt ab:cd -a -b test1 -cde test2 test3
getopt: invalid option -- e
 -a -b test1 -c -d -- test2 test3
$
```

If you prefer to just ignore the error messages, use the -q option with the command:

```
$ getopt -q ab:cd -a -b test1 -cde test2 test3
 -a -b 'test1' -c -d -- 'test2' 'test3'
$
```

Note that the getopt command options must be listed before the optstring. Now you should be ready to use this command in your scripts to process command line options.

Using getopt in your scripts

You can use the getopt command in your scripts to format any command line options or parameters entered for your script. It's a little tricky, though, to use.

The trick is to replace the existing command line options and parameters with the formatted version produced by the getopt command. The way to do that is to use the set command.

You saw the set command back in Chapter 5. The set command works with the different variables in the shell. Chapter 5 showed how to use the set command to display all of the system environment variables.

One of the options of the set command is the double dash, which instructs it to replace the command line parameter variables with the values on the set command's command line.

The trick then is to feed the original script command line parameters to the getopt command, then feed the output of the getopt command to the set command to replace the original command line parameters with the nicely formatted ones from getopt. This looks something like this:

```
set -- `getopts -q ab:cd "$@"`
```

Now the values of the original command line parameter variables are replaced with the output from the getopt command, which formats the command line parameters for us.

Using this technique, we can now write scripts that handle our command line parameters for us:

```
$ cat test18
#!/bin/bash
# extracting command line options and values with getopt

set -- `getopt -q ab:c "$@"`
while [ -n "$1" ]
do
   case "$1" in
   -a) echo "Found the -a option" ;;
   -b) param="$2"
       echo "Found the -b option, with parameter value $param"
       shift ;;
   -c) echo "Found the -c option" ;;
   --) shift
       break;;
   *) echo "$1 is not an option";;
   esac
```

```
    shift
done

count=1
for param in "$@"
do
    echo "Parameter #$count: $param"
    count=$[ $count + 1 ]
done
$
```

You'll notice this is basically the same script as in test17. The only thing that changed is the addition of the getopt command to help format our command line parameters.

Now when you run the script with complex options, things work much better:

```
$ ./test18 -ac
Found the -a option
Found the -c option
$
```

And of course, all of the original features work just fine as well:

```
$ ./test18 -a -b test1 -cd test2 test3 test4
Found the -a option
Found the -b option, with parameter value 'test1'
Found the -c option
Parameter #1: 'test2'
Parameter #2: 'test3'
Parameter #3: 'test4'
$
```

Now things are looking pretty fancy. However, there's still one small bug that lurks in the getopt command. Check out this example:

```
$ ./test18 -a -b test1 -cd "test2 test3" test4
Found the -a option
Found the -b option, with parameter value 'test1'
Found the -c option
Parameter #1: 'test2
Parameter #2: test3'
Parameter #3: 'test4'
$
```

The getopt command isn't good at dealing with parameter values with spaces. It interpreted the space as the parameter separator, instead of following the double quotation marks and combining the two values into one parameter. Fortunately for us, there's yet another solution that solves this problem.

The more advanced getopts

The getopts command (notice that it's plural) is built into the bash shell. It looks a lot like its getopt cousin, but has some expanded features.

Unlike getopt, which produces one output for all of the processed options and parameters found in the command line, the getopts command works on the existing shell parameter variables sequentially.

It processes the parameters it detects in the command line one at a time each time it's called. When it runs out of parameters, it exits with an exit status greater than zero. This makes it great for using in loops to parse all of the parameters on the command line.

The format of the getopts command is:

```
getopts optstring variable
```

The optstring value is similar to the one used in the getopt command. List valid option letters in the optstring, along with a colon if the option letter requires a parameter value. To suppress error messages, start the optstring with a colon. The getopts command places the current parameter in the variable defined in the command line.

There are two environment variables that the getopts command uses. The OPTARG environment variable contains the value to be used if an option requires a parameter value. The OPTIND environment variable contains the value of the current location within the parameter list where getopts left off. This allows you to continue processing other command line parameters after finishing the options.

Let's take a look at a simple example that uses the getopts command:

```
$ cat test19
#!/bin/bash
# simple demonstration of the getopts command

while getopts :ab:c opt
do
   case "$opt" in
   a) echo "Found the -a option" ;;
   b) echo "Found the -b option, with value $OPTARG";;
   c) echo "Found the -c option" ;;
   *) echo "Unknown option: $opt";;
   esac
done
$ ./test19 -ab test1 -c
Found the -a option
```

```
Found the -b option, with value test1
Found the -c option
$
```

The `while` statement defines the `getopts` command, specifying what command line options to look for, along with the variable name to store them in for each iteration.

You'll notice something different about the `case` statement in this example. When the `getopts` command parses the command line options, it also strips off the leading dash, so you don't need them in the case definitions.

There are several nice features in the `getopts` command. For starters, you can now include spaces in your parameter values:

```
$ ./test19 -b "test1 test2" -a
Found the -b option, with value test1 test2
Found the -a option
$
```

Another nice feature is that you can run the option letter and the parameter value together without a space:

```
$ ./test19 -abtest1
Found the -a option
Found the -b option, with value test1
$
```

The getopts command correctly parsed the `test1` value from the `-b` option. Yet another nice feature of the `getopts` command is that it bundles any undefined option that it finds in the command line into a single output, the question mark:

```
$ ./test19 -d
Unknown option: ?
$ ./test19 -acde
Found the -a option
Found the -c option
Unknown option: ?
Unknown option: ?
$
```

Any option letter not defined in the optstring value is sent to your code as a question mark.

The `getopts` command knows when to stop processing options, and leave the parameters for you to process. As `getopts` processes each option, it increments the `OPTIND` environment variable by one. When you've reached the end of the `getopts` processing, you can just use the `OPTIND` value with the `shift` command to move to the parameters:

```
$ cat test20
#!/bin/bash
# processing options and parameters with getopts

while getopts :ab:cd opt
do
   case "$opt" in
   a) echo "Found the -a option" ;;
   b) echo "Found the -b option, with value $OPTARG";;
   c) echo "Found the -c option";;
   d) echo "Found the -d option";;
   *) echo "Unknown option: $opt";;
   esac
done
shift $[ $OPTIND - 1 ]

count=1
for param in "$@"
do
   echo "Parameter $count: $param"
   count=$[ $count + 1 ]
done
$ ./test20 -a -b test1 -d test2 test3 test4
Found the -a option
Found the -b option, with value test1
Found the -d option
Parameter 1: test2
Parameter 2: test3
Parameter 3: test4
$
```

Now you have a full-featured command line option and parameter processing utility you can use in all of your shell scripts.

Standardizing Options

When you create your shell script, obviously you're in control of what happens. It's completely up to you as to which letter options you select to use, and how you select to use them.

However, there are a few letter options that have achieved somewhat of a standard meaning in the Linux world. If you leverage these options in your shell script, it'll make your scripts more user-friendly.

TABLE 11-1

Common Linux Command Line Options

Option	Description
-a	Show all objects
-c	Produce a count
-d	Specify a directory
-e	Expand an object
-f	Specify a file to read data from
-h	Display a help message for the command
-i	Ignore text case
-l	Produce a long format version of the output
-n	Use a non-interactive (batch) mode
-o	Specify an output file to redirect all output to
-q	Run in quiet mode
-r	Process directories and files recursively
-s	Run in silent mode
-v	Produce verbose output
-x	Exclude and object
-y	Answer yes to all questions

Table 11-1 shows some of the common meanings for command line options used in Linux.

You'll probably recognize most of these option meanings just from working with the various bash commands throughout the book. Using the same meaning for your options helps users interact with your script without having to worry about manuals.

Getting User Input

While providing command line options and parameters is a great way to get data from your script users, sometimes your script needs to be more interactive. There are times when you need to ask a question while the script is running and wait for a response from the person running your script. The bash shell provides the read command just for this purpose.

Basic reading

The read command accepts input from the standard input (the keyboard), or from another file descriptor (see Chapter 12). After receiving the input, the read command places the data into a standard variable. Here's the read command at its simplest:

```
$ cat test21
#!/bin/bash
# testing the read command

echo -n "Enter your name: "
read name
echo "Hello $name, welcome to my program."
$ ./test21
Enter your name: Rich Blum
Hello Rich Blum, welcome to my program.
$
```

That's pretty simple. Notice that the echo command that produced the prompt uses the -n option. This suppresses the newline character at the end of the string, allowing the script user to enter data immediately after the string, instead of on the next line. This gives your scripts a more form-like appearance.

In fact, the read command includes the -p option, which allows you to specify a prompt directly in the read command line:

```
$ cat test22
#!/bin/bash
# testing the read -p option

read -p "Please enter your age:" age
days=$[ $age * 365 ]
echo "That makes you over $days days old!"
$ ./test22
Please enter your age:10
That makes you over 3650 days old!
$
```

You'll notice in the first example that when I typed my name, the read command assigned both my first name and last name to the same variable. The read command will assign all data entered at the prompt to a single variable, or you can specify multiple variables. Each data value entered is assigned to the next variable in the list. If the list of variables runs out before the data does, the remaining data is assigned to the last variable:

```
$ cat test23
#!/bin/bash
# entering multiple variables

read -p "Enter your name: " first last
```

```
echo "Checking data for $last, $first..."
$ ./test23
Enter your name: Rich Blum
Checking data for Blum, Rich...
$
```

You can also specify no variables on the read command line. If you do that, the read command places any data it receives in the special environment variable REPLY:

```
$ cat test24
#!/bin/bash
# testing the REPLY environment variable

read -p "Enter a number: "
factorial=1
for (( count=1; count <= $REPLY; count++ ))
do
    factorial=$[ $factorial * $count ]
done
echo "The factorial of $REPLY is $factorial"
$ ./test24
Enter a number: 5
The factorial of 5 is 120
$
```

The REPLY environment variable will contain all of the data entered in the input, and it can be used in the shell script as any other variable.

Timing out

There's a danger when using the read command. It's quite possible that your script will get stuck waiting for the script user to enter data. If the script must go on regardless of if there was any data entered, you can use the -t option specify a timer. The -t option specifies the number of seconds for the read command to wait for input. When the timer expires, the read command returns a non-zero exit status:

```
$ cat test25
#!/bin/bash
# timing the data entry

if read -t 5 -p "Please enter your name: " name
then
    echo "Hello $name, welcome to my script"
else
    echo
    echo "Sorry, too slow!"
fi
$ ./test25
```

```
Please enter your name: Rich
Hello Rich, welcome to my script
$ ./test25
Please enter your name:
Sorry, too slow!
$
```

Since the read command exits with a non-zero exit status if the timer expires, it's easy to use the standard structured statements, such as an if-then statement or a while loop to track what happened. In this example, when the timer expires, the if statement fails, and the shell executes the commands in the else section.

Instead of timing the input, you can also set the read command to count the input characters. When a preset number of characters has been entered, it automatically exits, assigning the entered data to the variable:

```
$ cat test26
#!/bin/bash
# getting just one character of input

read -n1 -p "Do you want to continue [Y/N]? " answer
case $answer in
Y | y) echo
       echo "fine, continue on...";;
N | n) echo
       echo OK, goodbye
       exit;;
esac
echo "This is the end of the script"
$ ./test26
Do you want to continue [Y/N]? Y
fine, continue on...
This is the end of the script
$ ./test26
Do you want to continue [Y/N]? n
OK, goodbye
$
```

This example uses the -n option with the value of one, instructing the read command to accept only a single character before exiting. As soon as you press the single character to answer, the read command accepts the input and passes it to the variable. There's no need to press the Enter key.

Silent reading

There are times when you need input from the script user, but you don't want that input to display on the monitor. The classic example of this is when entering passwords, but there are plenty of other types of data that you will need to hide.

The -s option prevents the data entered in the read command from being displayed on the monitor (actually, the data is displayed, but the read command sets the text color to the same as the background color). Here's an example of using the -s option in a script:

```
$ cat test27
#!/bin/bash
# hiding input data from the monitor

read -s -p "Enter your password: " pass
echo
echo "Is your password really $pass?"
$ ./test27
Enter your password:
Is your password really T3st1ng?
$
```

The data typed at the input prompt doesn't appear on the monitor but is assigned to the variable just fine for use in the script.

Reading from a file

Finally, you can also use the read command to read data stored in a file on the Linux system. Each call to the read command reads a single line of text from the file. When there are no more lines left in the file, the read command will exit with a non-zero exit status.

The tricky part of this is getting the data from the file to the read command. The most common method for doing this is to pipe the result of the cat command of the file directly to a while command that contains the read command. Here's an example of how to do this:

```
$ cat test28
#!/bin/bash
# reading data from a file

count=1
cat test | while read line
do
    echo "Line $count: $line"
    count=$[ $count + 1]
done
echo "Finished processing the file"
$ cat test
The quick brown dog jumps over the lazy fox.
This is a test, this is only a test.
O Romeo, Romeo! wherefore art thou Romeo?
$ ./test28
Line 1: The quick brown dog jumps over the lazy fox.
Line 2: This is a test, this is only a test.
```

```
Line 3: O Romeo, Romeo! wherefore art thou Romeo?
Finished processing the file
$
```

The `while` command loop continues processing lines of the file with the `read` command, until the `read` command exits with a non-zero exit status.

Summary

This chapter showed three different methods for retrieving data from the script user. Command line parameters allow users to enter data directly on the command line when they run the script. The script uses positional parameters to retrieve the command line parameters and assign them to variables.

The `shift` command allows you to manipulate the command line parameters by rotating them within the positional parameters. This command allows you to easily iterate through the parameters without knowing how many parameters are available.

There are three special variables that you can use when working with command line parameters. The shell sets the $# variable to the number of parameters entered on the command line. The $* variable contains all of the parameters as a single string, and the $@ variable contains all of the parameters as separate words. These variables come in handy when trying to process long parameter lists.

Besides parameters, your script users can also use command line options to pass information to your script. Command line options are single letters preceded by a dash. Different options can be assigned to alter the behavior of your script. The bash shell provides three ways to handle command line options.

The first way is to handle them just like command line parameters. You can iterate through the options using the positional parameter variables, processing each option as it appears on the command line.

Another way to handle command line options is with the `getopt` command. This command converts command line options and parameters into a standard format that you can process in your script. The `getopt` command allows you to specify which letters it recognizes as options and which options require an additional parameter value. The `getopt` command processes the standard command line parameters and outputs the options and parameters in the proper order.

The bash shell also includes the `getopts` command (note that it's plural). The `getopts` command provides more advanced processing of the command line parameters. It allows for multi-value parameters, along with identifying options not defined by the script.

The final method to allow data from your script users is the `read` command. The `read` command allows your scripts to interactively query users for information and wait. The `read` command places any data entered by the script user into one or more variables, which you can use within the script.

There are several options available for the read command that allow you to customize the data input into your script, such as using hidden data entry, applying timed data entry, and requesting a specific number of input characters.

In the next chapter, we'll dig deeper into how bash shell scripts output data. So far, you've seen how to display data on the monitor and redirect it to a file. Next we'll explore a few other options that you have available not only to direct data to specific locations but also to direct specific types of data to specific locations. This'll help make your shell scripts look professional!

Chapter 12

Presenting Data

S o far the scripts shown in this book display information either by echoing data to the monitor or by redirecting data to a file. Chapter 8 demonstrated how to redirect the output of a command to a file. This chapter expands on that topic by showing you how you can redirect the output of your script to different locations on your Linux system.

Understanding Input and Output

So far, you've seen two methods for displaying the output from your scripts:

- Display output on the monitor screen
- Redirect output to a file

Both methods produced an all-or-nothing approach to data output. There are times though when it would be nice to display some data on the monitor and other data in a file. For these instances, it comes in handy to know how Linux handles input and output so that you can get your script output to the right place.

The following sections describe how to use the standard Linux input and output system to your advantage, to help direct script output to specific locations.

313

Standard file descriptors

The Linux system handles every object as a file. This includes the input and output process. Linux identifies each file object using a *file descriptor*. The file descriptor is a non-negative integer, which uniquely identifies open files in a session. Each process is allowed to have up to nine open file descriptors at a time. The bash shell reserves the first three file descriptors (0, 1, and 2) for special purposes. These are shown in Table 12-1.

These three special file descriptors handle the input and output from your script. The shell uses them to direct the default input and output in the shell to the appropriate location (which by default is usually your monitor). The following sections describe each of these standard file descriptors in more detail.

STDIN

The STDIN file descriptor references the standard input to the shell. For a terminal interface, the standard input is the keyboard. The shell receives input from the keyboard on the STDIN file descriptor, and processes each character as you type it.

When you use the input redirect symbol (<), Linux replaces the standard input file descriptor with the file referenced by the redirection. It reads the file and retrieves data just as if it were typed on the keyboard.

Many bash commands accept input from STDIN, especially if no files are specified on the command line. Here's an example of using the cat command with data entered from STDIN:

```
$ cat
this is a test
this is a test
this is a second test.
this is a second test.
```

When you enter the cat command on the command line by itself, it accepts input from STDIN. As you enter each line, the cat command echoes the line to the display.

TABLE 12-1

Linux Standard File Descriptors

File Descriptor	Abbreviation	Description
0	STDIN	Standard input
1	STDOUT	Standard output
2	STDERR	Standard error

However, you can also use the STDIN redirect symbol to force the cat command to accept input from another file other than STDIN:

```
$ cat < testfile
This is the first line.
This is the second line.
This is the third line.
$
```

Now the cat command uses the lines that are contained in the testfile file as the input. You can use this technique to input data to any shell command that accepts data from STDIN.

STDOUT

The STDOUT file descriptor references the standard output for the shell. On a terminal interface, the standard output is the terminal monitor. All output from the shell (including programs and scripts you run in the shell) is directed to the standard output, which is the monitor.

Most bash commands direct their output to the STDOUT file descriptor by default. As shown in Chapter 8, you can change that using output redirection:

```
$ ls -l > test2
$ cat test2
total 20
-rw-rw-r-- 1 rich rich 53 2007-10-26 11:30 test
-rw-rw-r-- 1 rich rich  0 2007-10-26 11:32 test2
-rw-rw-r-- 1 rich rich 73 2007-10-26 11:23 testfile
$
```

With the output redirection symbol, all of the output that normally would have gone to the monitor is instead redirected to the designated redirection file by the shell.

You can also append data to a file. You do this using the >> symbol:

```
$ who >> test2
$ cat test2
total 20
-rw-rw-r-- 1 rich rich 53 2007-10-26 11:30 test
-rw-rw-r-- 1 rich rich  0 2007-10-26 11:32 test2
-rw-rw-r-- 1 rich rich 73 2007-10-26 11:23 testfile
rich     pts/0        2007-10-27 15:34 (192.168.1.2)
$
```

The output generated by the who command is appended to the data already in the test2 file.

However, if you use the standard output redirection for your scripts, you can run into a problem. Here's an example of what can happen in your script:

```
$ ls -al badfile > test3
ls: cannot access badfile: No such file or directory
```

```
$ cat test3
$
```

When a command produces an error message, the shell doesn't redirect the error message to the output redirection file. The shell created the output redirection file, but the error message appeared on the monitor screen.

The shell handles error messages separately from the normal output. If you're creating a shell script that runs in background mode, often you must rely on the output messages being sent to a log file. Using this technique, if any error messages occur, they won't appear in the log file. You'll need to do something different.

STDERR

The shell handles error messages using the special STDERR file descriptor. The STDERR file descriptor references the standard error output for the shell. This is the location where the shell sends error messages generated by the shell or programs and scripts running in the shell.

By default, the STDERR file descriptor points to the same place as the STDOUT file descriptor (even though they are assigned different file descriptor values). This means that, by default, all error messages go to the monitor display.

However, as you saw in the example, when you redirect STDOUT this doesn't automatically redirect STDERR. When working with scripts, you'll often want to change that behavior, especially if you're interested in logging error messages to a log file.

Redirecting errors

You've already seen how to redirect the STDOUT data by using the redirection symbol. Redirecting the STDERR data isn't much different, you just need to define the STDERR file descriptor when you use the redirection symbol. There are a couple of ways to do this.

Redirecting just errors

As you saw in Table 12-1, the STDERR file descriptor is set to the value 2. You can select to redirect only error messages by placing this file descriptor value immediately before the redirection symbol. The value must appear immediately before the redirection symbol or it won't work:

```
$ ls -al badfile 2> test4
$ cat test4
ls: cannot access badfile: No such file or directory
$
```

Now when you run the command, the error message doesn't appear on the monitor. Instead, the output file contains any error messages that are generated by the command. Using this method, the shell only redirects the error messages, not the normal data. Here's another example of mixing STDOUT and STDERR messages in the same output:

```
$ ls -al test badtest test2 2> test5
-rw-rw-r-- 1 rich rich 158 2007-10-26 11:32 test2
$ cat test5
ls: cannot access test: No such file or directory
ls: cannot access badtest: No such file or directory
$
```

The normal STDOUT output from the ls command still goes to the default STDOUT file descriptor, which is the monitor. Since the command redirects file descriptor 2 output (STDERR) to an output file, the shell sends any error messages generated directly to the specified redirection file.

Redirecting errors and data

If you want to redirect both errors and the normal output, you'll need to use two redirection symbols. You need to precede each with the appropriate file descriptor for the data you want to redirect, then have them point to the appropriate output file for holding the data:

```
$ ls -al test test2 test3 badtest 2> test6 1> test7
$ cat test6
ls: cannot access test: No such file or directory
ls: cannot access badtest: No such file or directory
$ cat test7
-rw-rw-r-- 1 rich rich 158 2007-10-26 11:32 test2
-rw-rw-r-- 1 rich rich   0 2007-10-26 11:33 test3
$
```

The shell redirects the normal output of the ls command that would have gone to STDOUT to the test7 file using the 1> symbol. Any error messages that would have gone to STDERR were redirected to the test6 file using the 2> symbol.

You can use this technique to separate normal script output from any error messages that occur in the script. This allows you to easily identify errors without having to wade through thousands of lines of normal output data.

Alternatively, if you want, you can redirect both STDERR and STDOUT output to the same output file. The bash shell provides a special redirection symbol just for this purpose, the &> symbol:

```
$ ls -al test test2 test3 badtest &> test7
$ cat test7
ls: cannot access test: No such file or directory
ls: cannot access badtest: No such file or directory
-rw-rw-r-- 1 rich rich 158 2007-10-26 11:32 test2
-rw-rw-r-- 1 rich rich   0 2007-10-26 11:33 test3
$
```

Using the &> symbol, all of the output generated by the command is sent to the same location, both data and errors. You'll notice that one of the error messages is out of order from what you'd expect. The error message for the badtest file (the last file to be listed) appears second in the output file. The bash shell automatically gives error messages a higher priority than the standard output. This allows you to view the error messages together, rather than scattered throughout the output file.

Redirecting Output in Scripts

You can use the STDOUT and STDERR file descriptors in your scripts to produce output in multiple locations simply by redirecting the appropriate file descriptors. There are two methods for redirecting output in the script:

- Temporarily redirecting each line
- Permanently redirecting all commands in the script

The following sections describe how each of these methods works.

Temporary redirections

If you want to purposely generate error messages in your script, you can redirect an individual output line to STDERR. All you need to do is use the output redirection symbol to redirect the output to the STDERR file descriptor. When you redirect to a file descriptor, you must precede the file descriptor number with an ampersand sign (&):

```
echo "This is an error message" >&2
```

This line displays the text wherever the STDERR file descriptor for the script is pointing, instead of the normal STDOUT. Here's an example of a script that uses this feature:

```
$ cat test8
#!/bin/bash
# testing STDERR messages

echo "This is an error" >&2
echo "This is normal output"
$
```

If you run the script as normal, you won't notice any difference:

```
$ ./test8
This is an error
This is normal output
$
```

Remember, by default Linux directs the STDERR output to STDOUT. However, if you redirect STDERR when running the script, any text directed to STDERR in the script will be redirected:

```
$ ./test8 2> test9
This is normal output
```

```
$ cat test9
This is an error
$
```

Perfect! The text that's displayed using STDOUT appears on the monitor, while the echo statement text sent to STDERR is redirected to the output file.

This method is great for generating error messages in your scripts. If someone uses your scripts, they can easily redirect the error messages using the STDERR file descriptor, as shown.

Permanent redirections

If you have lots of data that you're redirecting in your script, it can get tedious having to redirect every echo statement. Instead, you can tell the shell to redirect a specific file descriptor for the duration of the script by using the exec command:

```
$ cat test10
#!/bin/bash
# redirecting all output to a file
exec 1>testout

echo "This is a test of redirecting all output"
echo "from a script to another file."
echo "without having to redirect every individual line"
$ ./test10
$ cat testout
This is a test of redirecting all output
from a script to another file.
without having to redirect every individual line
$
```

The exec command starts a new shell, and redirects the STDOUT file descriptor to a file. All output in the script that goes to STDOUT is instead redirected to the file.

You can also redirect the STDOUT in the middle of a script:

```
$ cat test11
#!/bin/bash
# redirecting output to different locations

exec 2>testerror

echo "This is the start of the script"
echo "now reidirecting all output to another location"

exec 1>testout

echo "This output should go to the testout file"
echo "but this should go to the testerror file" >&2
$ ./test11
```

319

```
This is the start of the script
now reidirecting all output to another location
$ cat testout
This output should go to the testout file
$ cat testerror
but this should go to the testerror file
$
```

The script uses the `exec` command to redirect any output going to STDERR to the file `testerror`. Next, the script uses the `echo` statement to display a few lines to STDOUT. After that, the `exec` command is used again to redirect STDOUT to the `testout` file. Notice that even when STDOUT is redirected, you can still specify the output from an `echo` statement to go to STDERR, which in this case is still redirected to the `testerror` file.

This feature can come in handy when you want to redirect the output of just parts of a script to an alternative location, such as an error log. There's just one problem you'll run into when using this.

Once you redirect STDOUT or STDERR, you can't easily redirect them back to their original location. If you need to switch back and forth with your redirection, there's a trick you'll need to learn. The "Creating Your Own Redirection" section later in this chapter discusses what this trick is and how to use it in your shell scripts.

Redirecting Input in Scripts

You can use the same technique used to redirect STDOUT and STDERR in your scripts to redirect STDIN from the keyboard. The `exec` command allows you to redirect STDIN to a file on the Linux system:

```
exec 0< testfile
```

This command informs the shell that it should retrieve input from the file `testfile` instead of STDIN. This redirection applies anytime the script requests input. Here's an example of this in action:

```
$ cat test12
#!/bin/bash
# redirecting file input

exec 0< testfile
count=1

while read line
do
    echo "Line #$count: $line"
    count=$[ $count + 1 ]
done
```

```
$ ./test12
Line #1: This is the first line.
Line #2: This is the second line.
Line #3: This is the third line.
$
```

Chapter 11 showed how to use the `read` command to read data entered from the keyboard by a user. By redirecting STDIN to a file, when the `read` command attempts to read from STDIN, it retrieves data from the file instead of the keyboard.

This is an excellent technique to read data in files for processing in your scripts. A common task for Linux system administrators is to read data from log files for processing. This is the easiest way to accomplish that task.

Creating Your Own Redirection

When you redirect input and output in your script, you're not limited to the three default file descriptors. I mentioned that you could have up to nine open file descriptors in the shell. The other six file descriptors are numbered from three through eight and are available for you to use as either input or output redirection. You can assign any of these file descriptors to a file, then use them in your scripts as well. This section shows how to use the other file descriptors in your scripts.

Creating output file descriptors

You assign a file descriptor for output by using the `exec` command. Just as with the standard file descriptors, once you assign an alternative file descriptor to a file location, that redirection stays permanent until you reassign it. Here's a simple example of using an alternative file descriptor in a script:

```
$ cat test13
#!/bin/bash
# using an alternative file descriptor

exec 3>test13out

echo "This should display on the monitor"
echo "and this should be stored in the file" >&3
echo "Then this should be back on the monitor"
$ ./test13
This should display on the monitor
Then this should be back on the monitor
$ cat test13out
and this should be stored in the file
$
```

321

The script uses the exec command to redirect file descriptor 3 to an alternative file location. When the script executes the echo statements, they display on STDOUT as you would expect. However, the echo statements that you redirect to file descriptor 3 go to the alternative file. This allows you to keep normal output for the monitor, and redirect special information to files, such as log files.

Redirecting file descriptors

Now comes the trick to help you bring back a redirected file descriptor. You can assign an alternative file descriptor to a standard file descriptor, and vice versa. This means that you can redirect the original location of STDOUT to an alternative file descriptor, then redirect that file descriptor back to STDOUT. This might sound somewhat complicated, but in practice it's fairly straightforward. Hopefully, this simple example will clear things up for you:

```
$ cat test14
#!/bin/bash
# storing STDOUT, then coming back to it

exec 3>&1
exec 1>test14out

echo "This should store in the output file"
echo "along with this line."

exec 1>&3

echo "Now things should be back to normal"
$ ./test14
Now things should be back to normal
$ cat test14out
This should store in the output file
along with this line.
$
```

This example is a little crazy, so let's walk through it piece by piece. First, the script redirects file descriptor 3 to the current location of file descriptor 1, which is STDOUT. This means that any output sent to file descriptor 3 will go to the monitor.

The second exec command redirects STDOUT to a file. The shell will now redirect any output sent to STDOUT directly to the output file. However, file descriptor 3 still points to the original location of STDOUT, which is the monitor. If you send output data to file descriptor 3 at this point, it'll still go to the monitor, even though STDOUT is redirected.

After sending some output to STDOUT, which points to a file, the script then redirects STDOUT to the current location of file descriptor 3, which is still set to the monitor. This means that now STDOUT is pointing to its original location, the monitor.

While this method can get confusing, it's a common way to temporarily redirect output in script files then set the output back to the normal settings.

Creating input file descriptors

You can redirect input file descriptors exactly the same way as output file descriptors. Save the STDIN file descriptor location to another file descriptor before redirecting it to a file, then when you're done reading the file you can restore STDIN to its original location:

```
$ cat test15
#!/bin/bash
# redirecting input file descriptors

exec 6<&0

exec 0< testfile

count=1
while read line
do
    echo "Line #$count: $line"
    count=$[ $count + 1 ]
done
exec 0<&6
read -p "Are you done now? " answer
case $answer in
Y|y) echo "Goodbye";;
N|n) echo "Sorry, this is the end.";;
esac
$ ./test15
Line #1: This is the first line.
Line #2: This is the second line.
Line #3: This is the third line.
Are you done now? y
Goodbye
$
```

In this example, file descriptor 6 is used to hold the location for STDIN. The script then redirects STDIN to a file. All of the input for the read command comes from the redirected STDIN, which is now the input file.

When all of the lines have been read, the script returns STDIN to its original location by redirecting it to file descriptor 6. The script tests to make sure that STDIN is back to normal by using another read command, which this time waits for input from the keyboard.

Creating a read/write file descriptor

As odd as it may seem, you can also open a single file descriptor for both input and output. You can then use the same file descriptor to both read data from a file and write data to the same file.

You need to be especially careful with this method though. As you read and write data to and from a file, the shell maintains an internal pointer, indicating where it is in the file. Any reading or writing occurs where the file pointer last left off. This can produce some interesting results if you're not careful. Take a look at this example:

```
$ cat test16
#!/bin/bash
# testing input/output file descriptor

exec 3<> testfile
read line <&3
echo "Read: $line"
echo "This is a test line" >&3
$ cat testfile
This is the first line.
This is the second line.
This is the third line.
$ ./test16
Read: This is the first line.
$ cat testfile
This is the first line.
This is a test line
ine.
This is the third line.
$
```

This example uses the exec command to assign file descriptor 3 for both input and output sent to and from the file testfile. Next, it uses the read command to read the first line in the file, using the assigned file descriptor, then it displays the read line of data in STDOUT. After that, it uses the echo statement to write a line of data to the file opened with the same file descriptor.

When you run the script, at first things look just fine. The output shows that the script read the first line in the testfile file. However, if you display the contents of the testfile file after running the script, you'll see that the data written to the file overwrote the existing data.

When the script writes data to the file, it starts where the file pointer is located. The read command reads the first line of data, so it left the file pointer pointing to the first character in the second line of data. When the echo statement outputs data to the file, it places the data at the current location of the file pointer, overwriting whatever data was there.

Closing file descriptors

If you create new input or output file descriptors, the shell automatically closes them when the script exits. There are situations though when you need to manually close a file descriptor before the end of the script.

To close a file descriptor, redirect it to the special symbol &-. This is how this looks in the script:

```
exec 3>&-
```

This statement closes file descriptor 3, preventing it from being used any more in the script. Here's an example of what happens when you try to use a closed file descriptor:

```
$ cat badtest
#!/bin/bash
# testing closing file descriptors

exec 3> test17file

echo "This is a test line of data" >&3

exec 3>&-

echo "This won't work" >&3
$ ./badtest
./badtest: 3: Bad file descriptor
$
```

Once you close the file descriptor, you can't write any data to it in your script or the shell produces an error message.

There's yet another thing to be careful of when closing file descriptors. If you open the same output file later on in your script, the shell replaces the existing file with a new file. This means that if you output any data, it'll overwrite the existing file. Here's an example of this problem:

```
$ cat test17
#!/bin/bash
# testing closing file descriptors

exec 3> test17file
echo "This is a test line of data" >&3
exec 3>&-

cat test17file

exec 3> test17file
echo "This'll be bad" >&3
$ ./test17
This is a test line of data
$ cat test17file
This'll be bad
$
```

After sending a data string to the test17file and closing the file descriptor, the script uses the cat command to display the contents of the file. So far, so good. Next, the script reopens the output file and sends another data string to it. When you display the contents of the output file, all you'll see is the second data string. The shell overwrote the original output file.

Listing Open File Descriptors

With only nine file descriptors available to you, you'd think that it wouldn't be too hard keeping things straight. Sometimes, though, it's easy to get lost when trying to keep track of which file descriptor is redirected where. To help you keep your sanity, the bash shell provides the lsof command.

The lsof command lists all of the open file descriptors on the entire Linux system. This is somewhat of a controversial feature, as it can provide information about the Linux system to non-system-administrators. Because of this, many Linux systems hide this command so that users don't accidentally stumble across it.

On my Fedora Linux system, the lsof command is located in the /usr/sbin directory. To run it with a normal user account, I have to reference it by its full pathname:

```
$ /usr/sbin/lsof
```

This produces an amazing amount of output. It displays information about every file currently open on the Linux system. This includes all of the processes running on background, as well as any user accounts logged in to the system.

There are plenty of command line parameters and options available to help filter out the lsof output. The most commonly used are -p, which allows you to specify a process ID (PID), and -d, which allows you to specify the file descriptor numbers to display.

To easily determine the current PID of the process, you can use the special environment variable $$, which the shell sets to the current PID. The -a option is used to AND the results of the other two options, to produce the following:

```
$ /usr/sbin/lsof -a -p $$ -d 0,1,2
COMMAND  PID USER    FD   TYPE DEVICE SIZE NODE NAME
bash    3344 rich     0u   CHR  136,0       2 /dev/pts/0
bash    3344 rich     1u   CHR  136,0       2 /dev/pts/0
bash    3344 rich     2u   CHR  136,0       2 /dev/pts/0
$
```

This shows the default file descriptors (0, 1, and 2) for the current process (the bash shell). The default output of lsof contains several columns of information, described in Table 12-2.

The file type associated with STDIN, STDOUT, and STDERR is character mode. Since the STDIN, STDOUT, and STDERR file descriptors all point to the terminal, the name of the output file is the device name of the terminal. All three standard files are available for both reading and writing (although it does seem odd to be able to write to STDIN and read from STDOUT).

TABLE 12-2

Default lsof Output

Column	Description
COMMAND	The first nine characters of the name of the command in the process
PID	The process ID of the process
USER	The login name of the user who owns the process
FD	The file descriptor number and access type (r - read, w - write, u - read/write)
TYPE	The type of file (CHR - character, BLK - block, DIR - directory, REG - regular file)
DEVICE	The device numbers (major and minor) of the device
SIZE	If available, the size of the file
NODE	The node number of the local file
NAME	The name of the file

Now, let's take a look at the results of the lsof command from inside a script that's opened a couple of alternative file descriptors:

```
$ cat test18
#!/bin/bash
# testing lsof with file descriptors

exec 3> test18file1
exec 6> test18file2
exec 7< testfile

/usr/sbin/lsof -a -p $$ -d0,1,2,3,6,7
$ ./test18
COMMAND  PID USER   FD   TYPE DEVICE SIZE    NODE NAME
test18  3594 rich    0u   CHR  136,0            2 /dev/pts/0
test18  3594 rich    1u   CHR  136,0            2 /dev/pts/0
est18   3594 rich    2u   CHR  136,0            2 /dev/pts/0
18      3594 rich    3w   REG  253,0      0 360712 /home/rich/test18file1
18      3594 rich    6w   REG  253,0      0 360715 /home/rich/test18file2
18      3594 rich    7r   REG  253,0     73 360717 /home/rich/testfile
$
```

The script creates three alternative file descriptors, two for output (3 and 6) and one for input (7). When the script runs the lsof command, you can see the new file descriptors in the output. I truncated the first part of the output so that you could see the results of the file name. The filename shows the complete pathname for the files used in the file descriptors. It shows each of the files as type REG, which indicates that they are regular files on the filesystem.

Suppressing Command Output

There are times when you don't want to display any output from your script. This often occurs if you're running a script as a background process (see Chapter 13). If any error messages occur from the script while it's running in background, the shell e-mails them to the owner of the process. This can get tedious, especially if you run scripts that generate minor nuisance errors.

To solve that problem, you can redirect STDERR to a special file called the *null file*. The null file is pretty much what it says it is, a file that contains nothing. Any data that the shell outputs to the null file is not saved, thus lost.

The standard location for the null file on Linux systems is /dev/null. Any data you redirect to that location is thrown away and doesn't appear:

```
$ ls -al > /dev/null
$ cat /dev/null
$
```

This is a common way to suppress any error messages without actually saving them:

```
$ ls -al badfile test16 2> /dev/null
-rwxr--r--   1 rich     rich             135 Oct 29 19:57 test16*
$
```

You can also use the /dev/null file for input redirection as an input file. Since the /dev/null file contains nothing, it is often used by programmers to quickly remove data from an existing file without having to remove the file and recreate it:

```
$ cat testfile
This is the first line.
This is the second line.
This is the third line.
$ cat /dev/null > testfile
$ cat testfile
$
```

The file testfile still exists on the system, but now it is empty. This is a common method used to clear out log files that must remain in place for applications to operate.

Using Temporary Files

The Linux system contains a special directory location reserved for temporary files. Linux uses the /tmp directory for files that don't need to be kept indefinitely. Most Linux distributions configure the system to automatically remove any files in the /tmp directory at bootup.

Any user account on the system has privileges to read and write files in the /tmp directory. This feature provides an easy way for you to create temporary files that you don't necessarily have to worry about cleaning up.

There's even a specific command to use for creating a temporary file. The mktemp command allows you to easily create a unique temporary file in the /tmp folder. The shell creates the file but doesn't use your default umask value (see Chapter 6). Instead, it only assigns read and write permissions to the file's owner and makes you the owner of the file. Once you create the file, you have full access to read and write to and from it from your script, but no one else will be able to access it (other than the root user of course).

Creating a local temporary file

By default, mktemp creates a file in the local directory. To create a temporary file in a local directory with the mktemp command, all you need to do is specify a filename template. The template consists of any text filename, plus six X's appended to the end of the filename:

```
$ mktemp testing.XXXXXX
$ ls -al testing*
-rw-------   1 rich      rich        0 Oct 29 21:30 testing.UfIi13
$
```

The mktemp command replaces the six X's with a six-character code to ensure the filename is unique in the directory. You can create multiple temporary files and be assured that each one is unique:

```
$ mktemp testing.XXXXXX
testing.1DRLuV
$ mktemp testing.XXXXXX
testing.1VBtkW
$ mktemp testing.XXXXXX
testing.PgqNKG
$ ls -l testing*
-rw-------   1 rich      rich        0 Oct 29 21:57 testing.1DRLuV
-rw-------   1 rich      rich        0 Oct 29 21:57 testing.PgqNKG
-rw-------   1 rich      rich        0 Oct 29 21:30 testing.UfIi13
-rw-------   1 rich      rich        0 Oct 29 21:57 testing.1VBtkW
$
```

As you can see, the output of the mktemp command is the name of the file that it creates. When you use the mktemp command in a script, you'll want to save that filename in a variable, so you can refer to it later on in the script:

```
$ cat test19
#!/bin/bash
# creating and using a temp file

tempfile=`mktemp test19.XXXXXX`
```

```
       exec 3>$tempfile

       echo "This script writes to temp file $tempfile"

       echo "This is the first line" >&3
       echo "This is the second line." >&3
       echo "This is the last line." >&3
       exec 3>&-

       echo "Done creating temp file. The contents are:"
       cat $tempfile
       rm -f $tempfile 2> /dev/null
       $ ./test19
       This script writes to temp file test19.vCHoya
       Done creating temp file. The contents are:
       This is the first line
       This is the second line.
       This is the last line.
       $ ls -al test19*
       -rwxr--r--    1 rich      rich            356 Oct 29 22:03 test19*
       $
```

The script uses the `mktemp` command to create a temporary file and assigns the file name to the `$tempfile` variable. It then uses the temporary file as the output redirection file for file descriptor 3. After displaying the temporary file name on STDOUT, it writes a few lines to the temporary file, then it closes the file descriptor. Finally, it displays the contents of the temporary file and then uses the `rm` command to remove it.

Creating a temporary file in /tmp

The `-t` option forces `mktemp` to create the file in the temporary directory of the system. When you use this feature, the `mktemp` command returns the full pathname used to create the temporary file, not just the filename:

```
       $ mktemp -t test.XXXXXX
       /tmp/test.xG3374
       $ ls -al /tmp/test*
       -rw------- 1 rich rich 0 2007-10-29 18:41 /tmp/test.xG3374
       $
```

Since the `mktemp` command returns the full pathname, you can then reference the temporary file from any directory on the Linux system, no matter where it places the temporary directory:

```
       $ cat test20
       #!/bin/bash
       # creating a temp file in /tmp

       tempfile=`mktemp -t tmp.XXXXXX`
```

```
echo "This is a test file." > $tempfile
echo "This is the second line of the test." >> $tempfile

echo "The temp file is located at: $tempfile"
cat $tempfile
rm -f $tempfile
$ ./test20
The temp file is located at: /tmp/tmp.Ma3390
This is a test file.
This is the second line of the test.
$
```

When `mktemp` creates the temporary file, it returns the full pathname to the environment variable. You can then use that value in any command to reference the temporary file.

Creating a temporary directory

The `-d` option tells the `mktemp` command to create a temporary directory instead of a file. You can then use that directory for whatever purposes you need, such as creating additional temporary files:

```
$ cat test21
#!/bin/bash
# using a temporary directory

tempdir=`mktemp -d dir.XXXXXX`
cd $tempdir
tempfile1=`mktemp temp.XXXXXX`
tempfile2=`mktemp temp.XXXXXX`
exec 7> $tempfile1
exec 8> $tempfile2

echo "Sending data to directory $tempdir"
echo "This is a test line of data for $tempfile1" >&7
echo "This is a test line of data for $tempfile2" >&8
$ ./test21
Sending data to directory dir.ouT8S8
$ ls -al
total 72
drwxr-xr-x    3 rich     rich         4096 Oct 29 22:20 ./
drwxr-xr-x    9 rich     rich         4096 Oct 29 09:44 ../
drwx------    2 rich     rich         4096 Oct 29 22:20 dir.ouT8S8/
-rwxr--r--    1 rich     rich          338 Oct 29 22:20 test21*
$ cd dir.ouT8S8
[dir.ouT8S8]$ ls -al
total 16
drwx------    2 rich     rich         4096 Oct 29 22:20 ./
drwxr-xr-x    3 rich     rich         4096 Oct 29 22:20 ../
```

```
-rw-------    1 rich    rich          44 Oct 29 22:20 temp.N5F306
-rw-------    1 rich    rich          44 Oct 29 22:20 temp.SQslb7
[dir.ouT8S8]$ cat temp.N5F306
This is a test line of data for temp.N5F306
[dir.ouT8S8]$ cat temp.SQslb7
This is a test line of data for temp.SQslb7
[dir.ouT8S8]$
```

The script creates a directory in the current directory, then it uses the `cd` command to change to that directory before creating two temporary files. The two temporary files are then assigned to file descriptors and used to store output from the script.

Logging Messages

Sometimes it's beneficial to send output both to the monitor and to a file for logging. Instead of having to redirect output twice, you can use the special `tee` command.

The `tee` command is like a T-connector for pipes. It sends data from STDIN to two destinations at the same time. One destination is STDOUT. The other destination is a filename specified on the `tee` command line:

```
tee filename
```

Since `tee` redirects data from STDIN, you can use it with the pipe command to redirect output from any command:

```
$ date | tee testfile
Mon Oct 29 18:56:21 EDT 2007
$ cat testfile
Mon Oct 29 18:56:21 EDT 2007
$
```

The output appears in STDOUT, and it is written to the file specified. Be careful: by default, the `tee` command overwrites the output file on each use:

```
$ who | tee testfile
rich      pts/0          2007-10-29 18:41 (192.168.1.2)
$ cat testfile
rich      pts/0          2007-10-29 18:41 (192.168.1.2)
$
```

If you want to append data to the file, you must use the `-a` option:

```
$ date | tee -a testfile
Mon Oct 29 18:58:05 EDT 2007
$ cat testfile
rich      pts/0          2007-10-29 18:41 (192.168.1.2)
```

```
Mon Oct 29 18:58:05 EDT 2007
$
```

Using this technique, you can both save data in files and display the data on the monitor for your users:

```
$ cat test22
#!/bin/bash
# using the tee command for logging

tempfile=test22file

echo "This is the start of the test" | tee $tempfile
echo "This is the second line of the test" | tee -a $tempfile
echo "This is the end of the test" | tee -a $tempfile
$ ./test22
This is the start of the test
This is the second line of the test
This is the end of the test
$ cat test22file
This is the start of the test
This is the second line of the test
This is the end of the test
$
```

Now you can save a permanent copy of your output at the same time that you're displaying it to your users.

Summary

Understanding how the bash shell handles input and output can come in handy when creating your scripts. You can manipulate both how the script receives data and how it displays data, to customize your script for any environment. You can redirect the input of a script from the standard input (STDIN) to any file on the system. You can also redirect the output of the script from the standard output (STDOUT) to any file on the system.

Besides the STDOUT, you can redirect any error messages your script generates, by redirecting the STDERR output. This is accomplished by redirecting the file descriptor associated with the STDERR output, which is file descriptor 2. You can redirect STDERR output to the same file as the STDOUT output or to a completely separate file. This enables you to separate normal script messages from any error messages generated by the script.

The bash shell allows you to create your own file descriptors for use in your scripts. You can create file descriptors 3 through 9 and assign them to any output file you desire. Once you create a file descriptor, you can redirect the output of any command to it, using the standard redirection symbols.

The bash shell also allows you to redirect input to a file descriptor, providing an easy way to read data contained in a file into your script. You can use the `lsof` command to display the active file descriptors in your shell.

Linux systems provide a special file, called `/dev/null`, to allow you to redirect output that you don't want. The Linux system discards anything redirected to the `/dev/null` file. You can also use this file to produce an empty file by redirecting the contents of the `/dev/null` file to the file.

The `mktemp` command is a handy feature of the bash shell that allows you to easily create temporary files and directories. All you need to do is specify a template for the `mktemp` command, and it creates a unique file each time you call it, based on the file template format. You can also create temporary files and directories in the `/tmp` directory on the Linux system, which is a special location that isn't preserved between system boots.

The `tee` command is a handy way to send output both to the standard output and to a log file. This enables you to display messages from your script on the monitor and store them in a log file at the same time.

In Chapter 13, you'll see how to control and run your scripts. Linux provides several different methods for running scripts other than directly from the command line interface prompt. You'll see how to schedule your scripts to run at a specific time, as well as learn how to pause them while they're running.

Chapter 13

Script Control

As you start building more advanced scripts, you'll probably start to wonder how to run and control them on your Linux system. So far in this book, the only way we've run scripts is directly from the command line interface in real-time mode. This isn't the only way to run scripts in Linux. There are quite a few other options available for running your shell scripts on Linux systems. This chapter examines different ways you can use to get your scripts started. Also, sometimes you might run into the problem of a script that gets stuck in a loop and you need to figure out how to get it to stop without having to turn off your Linux system. This chapter examines the different ways you can control how and when your shell script runs on your system.

Handling Signals

Linux uses signals to communicate with processes running on the system. Chapter 4 described the different Linux signals and how the Linux system uses these signals to stop, start, and kill processes. You can also use these signals to control the operation of your shell scripts by programming your shell script to perform commands when it receives specific signals from the Linux system.

Linux signals revisited

There are over 30 Linux signals that can be generated by the system and applications. Table 13-1 lists the most common Linux system signals that you'll run across in your Linux programming.

335

TABLE 13-1		

Linux Signals

Signal	Value	Description
1	SIGHUP	Hang up the process.
2	SIGINT	Interrupt the process.
3	SIGQUIT	Stop the process.
9	SIGKILL	Unconditionally terminate the process.
15	SIGTERM	Terminate the process if possible.
17	SIGSTOP	Unconditionally stop, but don't terminate the process.
18	SIGTSTP	Stop or pause the process, but don't terminate.
19	SIGCONT	Continue a stopped process.

By default, the bash shell ignores any SIGQUIT (3) and SIGTERM (15) signals that it receives (this is so that an interactive shell can't be accidentally terminated). However, the bash shell processes any SIGHUP (1) and SIGINT (2) signals it receives.

If the bash shell receives a SIGHUP signal, it exits. Before it exits though, it passes the SIGHUP signal to any processes started by the shell (such as your shell script). With a SIGINT signal, the shell is just interrupted. The Linux kernel stops giving the shell processing time on the CPU. When this happens, the shell passes the SIGINT signal to any processes started by the shell to notify them of the situation.

The shell passes these signals to your shell script program for processing. The default behavior of shell scripts, however, is to ignore the signals, which may have an adverse effect on the operation of your script. To avoid this situation, you can program your script to recognize signals, and perform commands to prepare the script for the consequences of the signal.

Generating signals

The bash shell allows you to generate two basic Linux signals using key combinations on the keyboard. This feature comes in handy if you need to stop or pause runaway programs.

Interrupting a process

The Ctrl-C key combination generates a SIGINT signal, and sends it to any processes currently running in the shell. You can test this by running a command that normally takes a long time to finish, and pressing the Ctrl-C key combination:

```
$ sleep 100

$
```

The Ctrl-C key combination doesn't produce any output on the monitor, it just stops the current process running in the shell. The `sleep` command pauses operation for the specified number of seconds. Normally, the command prompt wouldn't return until the timer has expired. By pressing the Ctrl-C key combination before the timer expires, you can cause the `sleep` command to terminate prematurely.

Pausing a process

Instead of terminating a process, you can pause it in the middle of whatever it's doing. Sometimes this can be a dangerous thing (for example, if a script has a file lock open on a crucial system file), but often it allows you to peek inside what a script is doing without actually terminating the process.

The Ctrl-Z key combination generates a `SIGTSTP` signal, stopping any processes running in the shell. Stopping a process is different than terminating the process, as stopping the process leaves the program still in memory, and able to continue running from where it left off. In the "Job Control" section later on you'll learn how to restart a process that's been stopped.

When you use the Ctrl-Z key combination, the shell informs you that the process has been stopped:

```
$ sleep 100

[1]+  Stopped                 sleep 100
$
```

The number in the square brackets is the *job number* assigned by the shell. The shell refers to each process running in the shell as a *job*, and assigns each job a unique job number. It assigns the first process started job number 1, the second job number 2, and so on.

If you have a stopped job assigned to your shell session, bash will warn you if you try to exit the shell:

```
$ exit
logout
There are stopped jobs.
$
```

You can view the stopped job by using our friend the `ps` command:

```
$ ps au
USER PID    %CPU %MEM  VSZ  RSS TTY   STAT  START   TIME COMMAND
rich 20560  0.0  1.2   2688 1624 pts/0 S     05:15   0:00 -bash
rich 20605  0.2  0.4   1564  552 pts/0 T     05:22   0:00 sleep 100
rich 20606  0.0  0.5   2584  740 pts/0 R     05:22   0:00 ps au
$
```

The `ps` command shows the status of the stopped job as T, which indicates the command is either being traced or is stopped.

337

If you really want to exit the shell with the stopped job still active, just type the `exit` command again. The shell will exit, terminating the stopped job. Alternately, now that you know the PID of the stopped job, you can use the `kill` command to send a `SIGKILL` signal to terminate it:

```
$ kill -9 20605
$
[1]+  Killed                  sleep 100
$
```

When you kill the job, initially you won't get any response. However, the next time you do something that produces a shell prompt, you'll see a message indicating that the job was killed. Each time the shell produces a prompt, it also displays the status of any jobs that have changed states in the shell. After you kill a job, the next time you force the shell to produce a prompt, it displays a message showing that the job was killed while running.

Trapping signals

Instead of allowing your script to ignore signals, you can trap them when they appear and perform other commands. The `trap` command allows you to specify which Linux signals your shell script can watch for and intercept from the shell. If the script receives a signal listed in the `trap` command, it prevents it from being processed by the shell, and instead handles it locally.

The format of the trap command is:

```
trap commands signals
```

That's simple enough. On the `trap` command line, you just list the commands you want the shell to execute, along with a space-separated list of signals you want to trap. You can specify the signals either by their numeric value or by their Linux signal name.

Here's a simple example of using the `trap` command to ignore `SIGINT` and `SIGTERM` signals:

```
$ cat test1
#!/bin/bash
# testing output in a background job

trap "echo Haha" SIGINT SIGTERM
echo "This is a test program"
count=1
while [ $count -le 10 ]
do
    echo "Loop #$count"
    sleep 10
    count=$[ $count + 1 ]
done
echo "This is the end of the test program"
$
```

The `trap` command used in this example displays a simple text message each time it detects either the `SIGINT` or `SIGTERM` signal. Trapping these signals makes this script impervious to the user attempting to stop the program by using the bash shell keyboard `Ctrl-C` command:

```
$ ./test1
This is a test program
Loop #1
Haha
Loop #2
Loop #3
Haha
Loop #4
Loop #5
Loop #6
Loop #7
Haha
Loop #8
Loop #9
Loop #10
This is the end of the test program
$
```

Each time the Ctrl-C key combination was used, the script executed the `echo` statement specified in the `trap` command instead of ignoring the signal and allowing the shell to stop the script.

Trapping a script exit

Besides trapping signals in your shell script, you can trap them when the shell script exits. This is a convenient way to perform commands just as the shell finishes its job.

To trap the shell script exiting, just add the `EXIT` signal to the `trap` command:

```
$ cat test2
#!/bin/bash
# trapping the script exit

trap "echo byebye" EXIT

count=1
while [ $count -le 5 ]
do
    echo "Loop #$count"
    sleep 3
    count=$[ $count + 1 ]
done
$ ./test2
Loop #1
Loop #2
```

```
Loop #3
Loop #4
Loop #5
byebye
$
```

When the script gets to the normal exit point, the trap is triggered, and the shell executes the command you specify on the trap command line. The EXIT trap also works if you prematurely exit the script:

```
$ ./test2
Loop #1
Loop #2
byebye

$
```

When the Ctrl-C key combination is used to send a SIGINT signal, the script exits (since that signal isn't listed in the trap list), but before the script exits, the shell executes the trap command.

Removing a trap

You can remove a set trap by using a dash as the command and a list of the signals you want to return to normal behavior:

```
$ cat test3
#!/bin/bash
# removing a set trap

trap "echo byebye" EXIT

count=1
while [ $count -le 5 ]
do
    echo "Loop #$count"
    sleep 3
    count=$[ $count + 1 ]
done
trap - EXIT
echo "I just removed the trap"
$ ./test3
Loop #1
Loop #2
Loop #3
Loop #4
Loop #5
```

```
I just removed the trap
$
```

Once the signal trap is removed, the script ignores the signals. However, if a signal is received before the trap is removed, the script processes it per the `trap` command:

```
$ ./test3
Loop #1
Loop #2
byebye

$
```

In this example a `Ctrl-C` key combination was used to terminate the script prematurely. Since the script was terminated before the trap was removed, the script executed the command specified in the trap.

Running Scripts in Background Mode

There are times when running a shell script directly from the command line interface is inconvenient. Some scripts can take a long time to process, and you may not want to tie up the command line interface waiting. While the script is running, you can't do anything else in your terminal session. Fortunately, there's a simple solution to that problem.

When you use the `ps` command, you see a whole bunch of different processes running on the Linux system. Obviously, all of these processes aren't running on your terminal monitor. This is called running processes in the *background*. In background mode, a process runs without being associated with a STDIN, STDOUT, and STDERR on a terminal session (see Chapter 12).

You can exploit this feature with your shell scripts as well, allowing them to run behind the scenes and not lock up your terminal session. The following sections describe how to run your scripts in background mode on your Linux system.

Running in the background

Running a shell script in background mode is a fairly easy thing to do. To run a shell script in background mode from the command line interface, just place an ampersand symbol after the command:

```
$ ./test1 &
[1] 19555
$ This is test program
Loop #1
Loop #2

$ ls -l
```

```
total 8
-rwxr--r--     1 rich     rich          219 Nov  2 11:27 test1*
$ Loop #3
```

When you place the ampersand symbol after a command it separates the command from the bash shell and runs it as a separate background process on the system. The first thing that displays is the line:

```
[1] 19555
```

The number in the square brackets is the job number assigned to the background process by the shell. The next number is the PID the Linux system assigns to the process. Every process running on the Linux system must have a unique PID.

As soon as the system displays these items, a new command line interface prompt appears. You are returned back to the shell, and the command you executed runs safely in background mode.

At this point, you can enter new commands at the prompt (as shown in the example). However, while the background process is still running, it still uses your terminal monitor for STDOUT and STDERR messages. You'll notice from the example that the output from the test1 script appears in the output intermixed with any other commands that are run from the shell.

When the background process finishes, it displays a message on the terminal:

```
[1]+  Done                    ./test1
```

This shows the job number and the status of the job (Done), along with the command used to start the job.

Running multiple background jobs

You can start any number of background jobs at the same time from the command line prompt:

```
$ ./test1 &
[1] 19582
$ This is test program
Loop #1
$ ./test1 &
[2] 19597
$ This is test program
Loop #1
$ ./test1 &
[3] 19612
$ This is test program
Loop #1
Loop #2
Loop #2
Loop #2
```

Each time you start a new job, the Linux system assigns it a new job number and PID. You can see that all of the scripts are running using the ps command:

```
$ ps au
USER       PID %CPU %MEM   VSZ  RSS TTY       STAT START   TIME
COMMAND
rich 19498 0.0 1.2 2688 1628 pts/0 S 11:38 0:00 -bash
rich 19582 0.0 0.9 2276 1180 pts/0 S 11:55 0:00 /bin/bash ./test1
rich 9597  0.1 0.9 2276 1180 pts/0 S 11:55 0:00 /bin/bash ./test1
rich 19612 0.1 0.9 2276 1180 pts/0 S 11:55 0:00 /bin/bash ./test1
rich 19639 0.0 0.4 1564 552  pts/0 S 11:56 0:00 sleep 10
rich 19640 0.0 0.4 1564 552  pts/0 S 11:56 0:00 sleep 10
rich 19641 0.0 0.4 1564 552  pts/0 S 11:56 0:00 sleep 10
rich 19642 0.0 0.5 2588 744  pts/0 R 11:56 0:00 ps au
```

Each of the background processes you start appears in the ps command output listing of running processes. If all of the processes display output in your terminal session, things can get pretty messy pretty quickly. Fortunately, there's a simple way to solve that problem. which we'll discuss in the next section.

Exiting the terminal

You must be careful when using background processes from a terminal session. Notice in the output from the ps command that each of the background processes is tied to the terminal session (pts/0) terminal. If the terminal session exits, the background process also exits.

Some terminal emulators warn you if you have any running background processes associated with the terminal, while others don't. If you want your script to continue running in background mode after you've logged off the console, there's something else you need to do. The next section discusses that process.

Running Scripts without a Console

There will be times when you want to start a shell script from a terminal session, then let the script run in background mode until it finishes, even if you exit the terminal session. You can do this by using the nohup command.

The nohup command runs another command blocking any SIGHUP signals that are sent to the process. This prevents the process from exiting when you exit your terminal session.

The format used for the nohup command is:

```
$ nohup ./test1 &
[1] 19831
$ nohup: appending output to `nohup.out'
$
```

Just as with a normal background process, the shell assigns the command a job number, and the Linux system assigns a PID number. The difference is that when you use the nohup command, the script ignores any SIGHUP signals sent by the terminal session if you close the session.

Because the nohup command disassociates the process from the terminal, the process loses the STDOUT and STDERR output links. To accommodate any output generated by the command, the nohup command automatically redirects STDOUT and STDERR messages to a file, called nohup.out.

The nohup.out file contains all of the output that would normally be sent to the terminal monitor. After the process finishes running, you can view the nohup.out file for the output results:

```
$ cat nohup.out
This is a test program
Loop #1
Loop #2
Loop #3
Loop #4
Loop #5
Loop #6
Loop #7
Loop #8
Loop #9
Loop #10
This is the end of the test program
$
```

The output appears in the nohup.out file just as if the process ran on the command line!

CAUTION If you run another command using nohup, the output is appended to the existing nohup.out file. Be careful when running multiple commands from the same directory, as all of the output will be sent to the same nohup.out file, which can get confusing.

Job Control

Earlier in this chapter, you saw how to use the Ctrl-Z key combination to stop a job running in the shell. After you stop a job, the Linux system lets you either kill or restart it. You can kill the process by using the kill command. Restarting a stopped process requires sending it a SIGCONT signal.

The function of starting, stopping, killing, and resuming jobs is called *job control*. With job control, you have full control over how processes run in your shell environment.

This section describes the commands to use to view and control jobs running in your shell.

Viewing jobs

The key command for job control is the `jobs` command. The `jobs` command allows you to view the current jobs being handled by the shell:

```
$ cat test4
#!/bin/bash
# testing job control

echo "This is a test program $$"
count=1
while [ $count -le 10 ]
do
    echo "Loop #$count"
    sleep 10
    count=$[ $count + 1 ]
done
echo "This is the end of the test program"
$ ./test4
This is a test program 29011
Loop #1

[1]+  Stopped                  ./test4
$ ./test4 > test4out &
[2] 28861
$
$ jobs
[1]+  Stopped                  ./test4
[2]-  Running                  ./test4 >test4out &
$
```

The script uses the $$ variable to display the PID that the Linux system assigns to the script, then it goes into a loop, sleeping for 10 seconds at a time for each iteration. In the example, I start the first script from the command line interface, then stop it using the Ctrl-Z key combination. Next, I start another job as a background process, using the ampersand symbol. To make life a little easier, I redirected the output of that script to a file so that it wouldn't appear on the monitor.

After the two jobs were started, I used the `jobs` command to view the jobs assigned to the shell. The `jobs` command shows both the stopped and the running jobs, along with their job numbers and the commands used in the jobs.

The `jobs` command uses a few different command line parameters, shown in Table 13-2.

You probably noticed the plus and minus signs in the output. The job with the plus sign is considered the default job. It would be the job referenced by any job control commands if a job number wasn't specified in the command line. The job with the minus sign is the job that would become the default job when the current default job finishes processing. There will only be one job with the plus sign and one job with the minus sign at any time, no matter how many jobs are running in the shell.

```
TABLE 13-2
```

The jobs Command Parameters

Parameter	Description
-l	List the PID of the process along with the job number.
-n	List only jobs that have changed their status since the last notification from the shell.
-p	List only the PIDs of the jobs.
-r	List only the running jobs.
-s	List only stopped jobs.

Here's an example showing how the next job in line takes over the default status, when the default job is removed:

```
$ ./test4
This is a test program 29075
Loop #1

[1]+  Stopped                 ./test4
$ ./test4
This is a test program 29090
Loop #1

[2]+  Stopped                 ./test4
$ ./test4
This is a test program 29105
Loop #1

[3]+  Stopped                 ./test4
$ jobs -l
[1]  29075 Stopped                 ./test4
[2]- 29090 Stopped                 ./test4
[3]+ 29105 Stopped                 ./test4
$ kill -9 29105
$ jobs -l
[1]- 29075 Stopped                 ./test4
[2]+ 29090 Stopped                 ./test4
$
```

In this example, I started, then stopped, three separate processes. The jobs command listing shows the three processes and their status. Note that the default process (the one listed with the plus sign) is the last process started.

I then used the `kill` command to send a `SIGHUP` signal to the default process. In the next jobs listing, the job that previously had the minus sign is now the default job.

Restarting stopped jobs

Under bash job control, you can restart any stopped job as either a background process or a foreground process. A foreground process takes over control of the terminal you're working on, so be careful about using that feature.

To restart a job in background mode, use the `bg` command, along with the job number:

```
$ bg 2
[2]+ ./test4 &
Loop #2
$ Loop #3
Loop #4

$ jobs
[1]+  Stopped                 ./test4
[2]-  Running                 ./test4 &
$ Loop #6
Loop #7
Loop #8
Loop #9
Loop #10
This is the end of the test program

[2]-  Done                    ./test4
$
```

Since I restarted the job in background mode, the command line interface prompt appears, allowing me to continue with other commands. The output from the `jobs` command now shows that the job is indeed running (as you can tell from the output now appearing on the monitor).

To restart a job in foreground mode, use the `fg` command, along with the job number:

```
$ jobs
[1]+  Stopped                 ./test4
$ fg 1
./test4
Loop #2
Loop #3
```

Since the job is running in foreground mode, I don't get a new command line interface prompt until the jobs finishes.

Being Nice

In a multitasking operating system (which Linux is), the kernel is responsible for assigning CPU time for each process running on the system. Only one process at a time can actually be running in the CPU, so the kernel assigns CPU time to each process in turn.

By default, all processes started from the shell have the same *scheduling priority* on the Linux system. The scheduling priority is the amount of CPU time the kernel assigns to the process relative to the other processes.

The scheduling priority is an integer value, from −20 (the highest priority) to +20 (the lowest priority). By default, the bash shell starts all processes with a priority of 0.

This means that a simple script that only requires a little bit of processing time gets the same CPU time slices as a complex mathematical algorithm that can take hours to run.

Sometimes you want to change the priority of a specific command, either lowering its priority so that it doesn't take as much processing power from the CPU or giving it a higher priority so that it gets more processing time. You can do this by using the nice command.

The nice command

The nice command allows you to set the scheduling priority of a command as you start it. To make a command run with less priority, just use the `-n` command line option for nice to specify a new priority level:

```
$ nice -n 10 ./test4 > test4out &
[1] 29476
$ ps al
  F   UID   PID  PPID PRI  NI WCHAN  STAT TTY        TIME COMMAND
100   501 29459 29458  12   0 wait4  S    pts/0      0:00 -bash
000   501 29476 29459  15  10 wait4  SN   pts/0      0:00 /bin/bash .
000   501 29490 29476  15  10 nanosl SN   pts/0      0:00 sleep 10
000   501 29491 29459  14   0 -      R    pts/0      0:00 ps al
$
```

The nice command causes the script to run at a lower priority. However, if you try to increase the priority of one of your commands, you might be in for a surprise:

```
$ nice -n -10 ./test4 > test4out &
[1] 29501
$ nice: cannot set priority: Permission denied

[1]+  Exit 1                  nice -n -10 ./test4 >test4out
$
```

The nice command prevents normal system users from increasing the priority of their commands. This is a safety feature to prevent a user from starting all of his or her commands as high priority.

The renice command

Sometimes you'd like to change the priority of a command that's already running on the system. That's what the renice command is for. It allows you to specify the PID of a running process to change the priority of:

```
$ ./test4 > test4out &
[1] 29504
$ ps al
  F   UID   PID  PPID PRI  NI WCHAN  STAT TTY        TIME COMMAND
100   501 29459 29458  12   0 wait4  S    pts/0      0:00 -bash
000   501 29504 29459   9   0 wait4  S    pts/0      0:00 /bin/bash .
000   501 29518 29504   9   0 nanosl S    pts/0      0:00 sleep 10
000   501 29519 29459  14   0 -      R    pts/0      0:00 ps al
$ renice 10 -p 29504
29504: old priority 0, new priority 10
$ ps al
  F   UID   PID  PPID PRI  NI WCHAN  STAT TTY        TIME COMMAND
100   501 29459 29458  16   0 wait4  S    pts/0      0:00 -bash
000   501 29504 29459  14  10 wait4  SN   pts/0      0:00 /bin/bash .
000   501 29535 29504   9   0 nanosl S    pts/0      0:00 sleep 10
000   501 29537 29459  14   0 -      R    pts/0      0:00 ps al
$
```

The renice command automatically updates the scheduling priority of the running process. Just as with the nice command, the renice command has some limitations:

- You can only renice processes that you own.
- You can only renice your processes to a lower priority.
- The root user can renice any process to any priority.

If you want to fully control running processes, you must be logged in as the root account.

Running Like Clockwork

I'm sure that, as you start working with scripts, there'll be a situation in which you'll want to run a script at a preset time, usually at a time when you're not there. The Linux system provides three ways of running a script at a preselected time:

- The at command
- The batch command
- The cron table

Each method uses a different technique for scheduling when and how often to run scripts. The following sections describe each of these methods.

Scheduling a job using the at command

The `at` command allows you to specify a time when the Linux system will run a script. The `at` command submits a job to a queue with directions on when the shell should run the job. Another command, `atd`, runs in the background and checks the job queue for jobs to run. Most Linux distributions start this automatically at boot time.

The `atd` command checks a special directory on the system (usually `/var/spool/at`) for jobs submitted using the `at` command. By default the `atd` command checks this directory every 60 seconds. When a job is present, the `atd` command checks the time the job is set to be run. If the time matches the current time, the `atd` command runs the job.

The following sections describe how to use the `at` command to submit jobs to run and how to manage jobs.

The at command format

The basic `at` command format is pretty simple:

```
at [-f filename] time
```

By default, the `at` command submits input from `STDIN` to the queue. You can specify a filename used to read commands (your script file) using the `-f` parameter.

The `time` parameter specifies when you want the Linux system to run the job. You can get pretty creative with how you specify the time. The `at` command recognizes lots of different time formats:

- A standard hour and minute, such as 10:15
- An AM/PM indicator, such as 10:15PM
- A specific named time, such as now, noon, midnight, or teatime (4PM)

If you specify a time that's already past, the `at` command runs the job at that time on the next day.

Besides specifying the time to run the job, you can also include a specific date, using a few different date formats:

- A standard date format, such as MMDDYY, MM/DD/YY, or DD.MM.YY
- A text date, such as Jul 4 or Dec 25, with or without the year
- You can also specify a time increment:
  - Now + 25 minutes
  - 10:15PM tomorrow
  - 10:15 + 7 days

When you use the `at` command, the job is submitted into a *job queue*. The job queue holds the jobs submitted by the `at` command for processing. There are 26 different job queues available for different priority levels. Job queues are referenced using lower-case letters, `a` through `z`.

By default all `at` jobs are submitted to job queue `a`, the highest-priority queue. If you want to run a job at a lower priority, you can specify the letter using the `-q` parameter.

Retrieving job output

When the job runs on the Linux system, there's no monitor associated with the job. Instead, the Linux system uses the e-mail address of the user who submitted the job as `STDOUT` and `STDERR`. Any output destined to `STDOUT` or `STDERR` is mailed to the user via the mail system.

Here's a simple example of using the `at` command to schedule a job to run:

```
$ cat test5
#!/bin/bash
# testing the at command

time=`date +%T`
echo "This script ran at $time"
echo "This is the end of the script" >&2
$ date
Sat Nov  3 12:06:04 EST 2007
$ at -f test5 12:07
warning: commands will be executed using /bin/sh
job 6 at 2007-11-03 12:07
$ mail
Mail version 8.1.1 6/6/93.  Type ? for help.
"/var/spool/mail/rich": 1 message 1 new
>N  1 rich@testbox Sat Nov 3 12:07  14/474   "Output from your job "
&
Message 1:
From rich  Sat Nov  3 12:07:00 2007
Delivered-To: rich@testbox
Subject: Output from your job         6
Date: Sat,  3 Nov 2007 12:07:00 -0500 (EST)
From: rich@testbox (Rich)
To: undisclosed-recipients:;

This script ran at 12:07:00
This is the end of the script

&
```

The `at` command produces a warning message, indicating what shell the system uses to run the script (the default shell assigned to `/bin/sh`, which for Linux is the bash shell), along with the job number assigned to the job and the time the job is scheduled to run.

When the job completes, nothing appears on the monitor, but the system generates an e-mail message. The e-mail message shows the output generated by the script. If the script doesn't produce any output, it won't generate an e-mail message, by default. You can change that by using the -m option in the at command. This generates an e-mail message, indicating the job completed, even if the script doesn't generate any output.

Listing pending jobs

The atq command allows you to view what jobs are pending on the system:

```
$ at -f test5 10:15
warning: commands will be executed using /bin/sh
job 7 at 2007-11-04 10:15
$ at -f test5 4PM
warning: commands will be executed using /bin/sh
job 8 at 2007-11-03 16:00
$ at -f test5 1PM tomorrow
warning: commands will be executed using /bin/sh
job 9 at 2007-11-04 13:00
$ atq
7       2007-11-04 10:15 a
8       2007-11-03 16:00 a
9       2007-11-04 13:00 a
$
```

The job listing shows the job number, the date and time the system will run the job, and the job queue the job is stored in.

Removing jobs

Once you know the information about what jobs are pending in the job queues, you can use the atrm command to remove a pending job:

```
$ atrm 8
$ atq
7       2007-11-04 10:15 a
9       2007-11-04 13:00 a
$
```

Just specify the job number you want to remove. You can only remove jobs that you submit for execution. You can't remove jobs submitted by others.

Using the batch command

The batch command is a little different from the at command. Instead of scheduling a script to run at a preset time, you use the batch command to schedule a script to run when the system is at a lower usage level.

If the Linux system is experiencing high load levels, the `batch` command will defer running a submitted job until things quiet down. This is a great feature for servers that may experience different load levels at various times of the day and night. You can schedule a script to run during the quiet time without having to know exactly when that is.

The `batch` command checks the current load average of the Linux system. If the load average is below 0.8, it runs any jobs waiting in the job queue.

The command format for the `batch` command is:

```
batch [-f filename] [time]
```

Similarly to the `at` command, by default the `batch` command reads commands from `STDIN`. You can use the `-f` parameter to specify a file to read commands from. You can also optionally specify the earliest time that the `batch` command should try running the job.

Scheduling regular scripts

Using the `at` command to schedule a script to run at a preset time is great, but what if you need that script to run at the same time every day or once a week or once a month? Instead of having to continually submit `at` jobs, you can use another feature of the Linux system.

The Linux system uses the `cron` program to allow you to schedule jobs that need to run on a regular basis. The `cron` program runs in the background and checks special tables, called *cron tables*, for jobs that are scheduled to run.

The cron table

The cron table uses a special format for allowing you to specify when a job should be run. The format for the cron table is:

```
min hour dayofmonth month dayofweek command
```

The cron table allows you to specify entries as specific values, ranges of values (such as 1-5) or as a wildcard character (the asterisk). For example, if you want to run a command at 10:15 on every day, you would use the cron table entry of:

```
15 10 * * * command
```

The wildcard character used in the *dayofmonth*, *month*, and *dayofweek* fields indicates that `cron` will execute the command every day of every month at 10:15. To specify a command to run at 4:15PM every Monday, you would use:

```
15 16 * * 1 command
```

You can specify the *dayofweek* entry as either a three-character text value (mon, tue, wed, thu, fri, sat, sun) or as a numeric value, with 0 being Sunday and 6 being Saturday.

Here's another example: to execute a command at 12 noon on the first day of every month, you'd use the format:

```
00 12 1 * * command
```

The *dayofmonth* entry specifies a date value (1–31) for the month.

> **NOTE** The astute reader might be wondering just how you'd be able to set a command to execute on the last day of every month, since you can't set the *dayofmonth* value to cover every month. This problem has plagued Linux and Unix programmers, and has spawned quite a few different solutions. A common method is to add an if-then statement that uses the date command to check if tomorrow's date is 01:
>
> ```
> 00 12 * * * if [ `date +%d -d tomorrow` = 01 ] ; then ; command
> ```
>
> This will check every day at 12 noon to see if it's the last day of the month, and if so, it will run the command.

The command list must specify the full pathname of the command or shell script to run. You can add any command line parameters or redirection symbols you like, as a regular command line:

```
15 10 * * * /home/rich/test4 > test4out
```

The cron program runs the script using the user account that submitted the job. Thus, you must have the proper permissions to access the command and output files specified in the command listing.

Building the cron table

Each system user can have their own cron table (including the root user) for running scheduled jobs. Linux provides the crontab command for handling the cron table. To list an existing cron table, use the -l parameter:

```
$ crontab -l
no crontab for rich
$
```

By default, each user's cron table file doesn't exist. To add entries to your cron table, use the -e parameter. When you do that, the crontab command automatically starts the vi editor (see Chapter 7) with the existing cron table (or an empty file if it doesn't yet exist).

The anacron program

The only problem with the cron program is that it assumes that your Linux system is operational 24 hours a day, 7 days a week. Unless you're running Linux in a server environment, this may not necessarily be true.

If the Linux system is turned off at the time a job is scheduled to run by cron, the job won't run. The cron program doesn't retroactively run missed jobs when the system is turned back on. To resolve this issue, many Linux distributions also include the anacron program.

The anacron program uses timestamps to determine if a scheduled job has been run at the proper interval. If it determines that a job has missed a scheduled running, it automatically runs the job as soon as possible. This means that if your Linux system is turned off for a few days, when it starts back up any jobs scheduled to run during the time it was off are automatically run.

This is a feature that's often used for scripts that perform routine log maintenance. If the system is always off when the script should run, the log files would never get trimmed and could grow to undesirable sizes. With anacron, you're guaranteed that the log files will be trimmed at least each time the system is started.

The anacron program has its own table (usually located at /etc/anacrontab) to specify jobs. On almost all Linux distributions, this table is only accessible by the root user. The format of the anacron table is slightly different from that of the cron table:

```
period delay identifier command
```

The period entry defines how often the job should be run, specified in days. The delay entry specifies how many minutes after the anacron program determines that a command should be run it should actually run it. This allows you to set different delay values for different commands so that you don't have them all running as soon as you turn on the Linux system.

The identifier entry is a unique non-blank character string to uniquely identify the job in log messages and error e-mails.

Start At the Beginning

The last method of starting shell scripts is to have your script run automatically either as soon as the Linux system boots or whenever a user starts a new bash shell session. Starting scripts at boot time is usually reserved for special scripts that perform system functions, such as configuring a network interface or starting a server process. However, if you're a Linux system administrator, it's possible that you'll need to perform a function every time the Linux system boots, such as resetting a custom log file or starting a custom application.

The ability to run a script every time a user starts a new bash shell (even just when a specific user starts a bash shell) also can come in handy. There are times when you want to set shell features for a shell session or just ensure that a specific file has been set.

This section describes how to configure your Linux system to run your scripts either at boot time or each time a new bash shell starts.

Starting your scripts at boot

Before you can get your shell script to start at boot time, you'll need to know a little bit about how the Linux boot process works. There's a specific order that Linux uses to start scripts at boot time, and knowing that process can help you in getting your script to perform the way you want it.

TABLE 13-3

The Linux Run Levels

Run level	Description
0	Halt
1	Single-user mode
2	Multi-user mode, usually without networking support
3	Full multi-user mode, with networking
4	Unused
5	Multi-user mode, with networking and a graphical X Window session
6	Reboot

The boot process

After you turn on your Linux system, the Linux kernel loads into memory and runs. The first thing it does is run the init program. Since the init program (usually located at /sbin/init) is always the first thing to run, the kernel always assigns it PID 1. The init process is then responsible for starting all other processes on the Linux system.

As part of the boot process, the init program reads the /etc/inittab file. The inittab file lists scripts that the init program starts at different *run levels*. A Linux run level defines the operating state of the Linux system. Different run levels start different programs and scripts. Table 13-3 lists the Linux run levels.

Each run level defines what scripts the init program starts or stops. The normal run level for a graphical Linux system is run level 5. Most Linux distributions start all of the server software at run level 3, which allows multiple users to log in to the system.

The Linux system determines what programs to start at what run level by the rc script. The rc script determines the current system run level and runs the appropriate scripts for that run level.

The Linux system starts applications using *startup scripts*. A startup script is a shell script that starts an application, providing the necessary environment variables for it to run.

This is the part of the Linux boot process where things start to get a little fuzzy, mainly because different Linux distributions place startup scripts in slightly different locations. Some distributions place startup scripts in the /etc/rc.d directory, with a different directory for each run level. Others use the /etc/init.d directory, and still others use the /etc/init.d/rc.d directory.

Usually a quick glance in your /etc directory structure can easily determine what format your distribution uses.

Defining your scripts

It's best not to mess with the individual startup script files in your Linux distribution. Often distributions provide tools to automatically build these scripts as you add server applications, and manually changing these scripts can cause problems.

Instead, most Linux distributions provide a local startup file specifically to allow the system administrator to enter scripts to run at boot time. Of course, the name and location of this file are different in different Linux distributions. Table 13-4 identifies the location of the startup file in three popular Linux distributions.

Inside the local startup file, you can either specify specific commands and statements, or enter any scripts you want started at boot time. Remember, if you use a script, you'll need to specify the full pathname for the script so that the system can find it at boot time.

CAUTION   Different Linux distributions also execute the local startup script at different points in the boot process. Sometimes the script is run before things such as network support have been started. Consult your specific Linux distribution documentation to determine when the local startup script is run in your distribution.

Starting with a new shell

Each user's home directory contains two files that the bash shell uses to automatically start scripts and set environment variables:

- The .bash_profile file
- The .bashrc file

TABLE 13-4

The Linux Local Startup File Locations

Distribution	File location
Debian	/etc/init.d/rc.local
Fedora	/etc/rc.d/rc.local
openSuse	/etc/init.d/boot.local

The bash shell runs the .bash_profile file when a new shell is run as a result of a new login. Place any scripts that you want run at login time in this file.

The bash shell runs the .bashrc file any time a new shell is started, including when a new login occurs. You can test this by adding a simple echo statement to the .bashrc file in your home directory, then starting a new shell:

```
$ bash
This is a new shell!!
$
```

If you want to run a script for every user on the system, most Linux distributions provide the /etc/bashrc file (note that there's no period in front of the bashrc filename). The bash shell executes the statements in this file every time any user on the system starts a new bash shell.

Summary

The Linux system allows you to control your shell scripts by using signals. The bash shell accepts signals, and passes them on to any process running under the shell process. Linux signals allow you to easily kill a runaway process or temporarily pause a long-running process.

You can use the trap statement in your scripts to catch signals and perform commands. This feature provides a simple way to control whether a user can interrupt your script while it's running.

By default, when you run a script in a terminal session shell, the interactive shell is suspended until the script completes. You can cause a script or command to run in background mode by adding an ampersand sign (&) after the command name. When you run a script or command in background mode, the interactive shell returns, allowing you to continue entering more commands. Any background processes run using this method are still tied to the terminal session. If you exit the terminal session, the background processes also exit.

To prevent this from happening, use the nohup command. This command intercepts any signals intended for the command that would stop it, for example, when you exit the terminal session. This allows scripts to continue running in background mode even if you exit the terminal session.

When you move a process to background mode, you can still control what happens to it. The jobs command allows you to view processes started from the shell session. Once you know the job ID of a background process, you can use the kill command to send Linux signals to the process, or use the fg command to bring the process back to the foreground in the shell session. You can suspend a running foreground process by using the Ctrl-Z key combination, then place it back in background mode using the bg command.

The nice and renice commands allow you to change the priority level of a process. By giving a process a lower priority, you allow the CPU to allocate less time to it. This comes in handy when running long processes that can take lots of CPU time.

Besides controlling processes while they're running, you can also determine when a process starts on the system. Instead of running a script directly from the command line interface prompt, you can schedule the process to run at an alternative time. There are several different ways to accomplish this. The `at` and `batch` commands allow you to run a script once at a preset time. The `cron` program provides an interface that can run scripts at a regularly scheduled interval.

Finally, the Linux system provides script files for you to use for scheduling your scripts to run either at system boot time or whenever a user starts a new bash shell. The `rc.local` (or `boot.local` for openSuse) file allows you to list scripts that start each time the system boots. This allows system administrators to run special scripts for system maintenance at boot time. Similarly, the `.bash_profile` and `.bashrc` files are located in every user's home directory to provide a location to place scripts and commands that run with a new shell. The `.bash_profile` file runs scripts each time a user logs in to the system, and the `.bashrc` file runs scripts on each new shell instance.

In the next chapter, we'll look at how to write script functions. Script functions allow you to write code blocks once, then use them in multiple locations throughout your script.

Part III

Advanced Shell Scripting

Chapter 14

Creating Functions

Often while writing shell scripts you'll find yourself using the same code in multiple locations. If it's just a small code snippet, it's usually not that big of a deal. However, if you're rewriting large chunks of code multiple times in your shell script, that can get tiring. The bash shell provides a way to help you out by supporting user-defined functions. You can encapsulate your shell script code into a function, which you can then use as many times as you want anywhere in your script. This chapter walks you through the process of creating your own shell script functions, and demonstrates how to use them in other shell script applications.

IN THIS CHAPTER

Creating a function

Using parameters

Sharing functions

Basic Script Functions

As you start writing more complex shell scripts, you'll find yourself reusing parts of code that perform specific tasks. Sometimes it's something simple, such as displaying a text message and retrieving an answer from the script users. Other times it's a complicated calculation that's used multiple times in your script as part of a larger process.

In each of these situations, it can get tiresome writing the same blocks of code over and over again in your script. It would be nice to just write the block of code once, then be able to refer to that block of code anywhere in your script without having to rewrite it.

The bash shell provides a feature allowing you to do just that. *Functions* are blocks of script code that you assign a name to, then reuse anywhere in your code. Anytime you need to use that block of code in your script, all you need to do is use the function name you assigned it (referred to as *calling* the function). This section describes how to create and use functions in your shell scripts.

Creating a function

There are two formats you can use to create functions in bash shell scripts. The first format uses the keyword `function`, along with the function name you assign to the block of code:

```
function name {
    commands
}
```

The *name* attribute defines a unique name assigned to the function. Each function you define in your script must be assigned a unique name.

The *commands* are one or more bash shell commands that make up your function. When you call the function, the bash shell executes each of the commands in the order they appear in the function, just as in a normal script.

The second format for defining a function in a bash shell script more closely follows how functions are defined in other programming languages:

```
name() {
commands
}
```

The empty parentheses after the function name indicate that you're defining a function. The same naming rules apply in this format as in the original shell script function format.

Using functions

To use a function in your script, specify the function name on a line, just as you would any other shell command:

```
$ cat test1
#!/bin/bash
# using a function in a script

function func1 {
    echo "This is an example of a function"
}

count=1
while [ $count -le 5 ]
do
    func1
    count=$[ $count + 1 ]
done
```

```
echo "This is the end of the loop"
func1
echo "Now this is the end of the script"
$ ./test1
This is an example of a function
This is an example of a function
This is an example of a function
This is an example of a function
This is an example of a function
This is the end of the loop
This is an example of a function
Now this is the end of the script
$
```

Each time you reference the func1 function name, the bash shell returns to the func1 function definition and executes any commands you defined there.

The function definition doesn't have to be the first thing in your shell script, but be careful. If you attempt to use a function before it's defined, you'll get an error message:

```
$ cat test2
#!/bin/bash
# using a function located in the middle of a script

count=1
echo "This line comes before the function definition"

function func1 {
    echo "This is an example of a function"
}

while [ $count -le 5 ]
do
    func1
    count=$[ $count + 1 ]
done
echo "This is the end of the loop"
func2
echo "Now this is the end of the script"

function func2 {
    echo "This is an example of a function"
}
$ ./test2
This line comes before the function definition
This is an example of a function
This is an example of a function
This is an example of a function
This is an example of a function
```

```
This is an example of a function
This is the end of the loop
./test2: func2: command not found
Now this is the end of the script
$
```

The first function, func1, was defined after a couple of statements in the script, which is perfectly fine. When the func1 function was used in the script, the shell knew where to find it.

However, the script attempted to use the func2 function before it was defined. Since the func2 function wasn't defined, when the script reached the place where I used it, it produced an error message.

You also need to be careful about your function names. Remember, each function name must be unique, or you'll have a problem. If you redefine a function, the new definition will override the original function definition, without producing any error messages:

```
$ cat test3
#!/bin/bash
# testing using a duplicate function name

function func1 {
echo "This is the first definition of the function name"
}

func1

function func1 {
    echo "This is a repeat of the same function name"
}

func1
echo "This is the end of the script"
$ ./test3
This is the first definition of the function name
This is a repeat of the same function name
This is the end of the script
$
```

The original definition of the func1 function works fine, but after the second definition of the func1 function, any subsequent uses of the function use the second definition.

Returning a Value

The bash shell treats functions like mini-scripts, complete with an exit status (see Chapter 8). There are three different ways you can generate an exit status for your functions.

The default exit status

By default, the exit status of a function is the exit status returned by the last command in the function. After the function executes, you use the standard $? variable to determine the exit status of the function:

```
$ cat test4
#!/bin/bash
# testing the exit status of a function

func1() {
    echo "trying to display a non-existent file"
    ls -l badfile
}

echo "testing the function:"
func1
echo "The exit status is: $?"
$ ./test4
testing the function:
trying to display a non-existent file
ls: badfile: No such file or directory
The exit status is: 1
$
```

The exit status of the function is 1 since the last command in the function failed. However, you have no way of knowing if any of the other commands in the function completed successfully or not. Take a look at this example:

```
$ cat test4b
#!/bin/bash
# testing the exit status of a function

func1() {
    ls -l badfile
    echo "This was a test of a bad command"
}

echo "testing the function:"
func1
echo "The exit status is: $?"
$ ./test4b
testing the function:
ls: badfile: No such file or directory
This was a test of a bad command
The exit status is: 0
$
```

This time, since the function ended with an `echo` statement that completed successfully, the exit status of the function is 0, even though one of the commands in the function failed. Using the default exit status of a function can be a dangerous practice. Fortunately, there are a couple of other solutions for us.

Using the return command

The bash shell uses the `return` command to exit a function with a specific exit status. The `return` command allows you to specify a single integer value to define the function exit status, providing an easy way for you to programmatically set the exit status of your function:

```
$ cat test5
#!/bin/bash
# using the return command in a function

function dbl {
    read -p "Enter a value: " value
    echo "doubling the value"
    return $[ $value * 2 ]
}

dbl
echo "The new value is $?"
$
```

The `dbl` function doubles the value contained in the `$value` variable provided by the user input. It then returns the result using the `return` command, which the script displays using the `$?` variable.

You must be careful though when using this technique to return a value from a function. There are two things that can cause problems:

■ Remember to retrieve the return value as soon as the function completes.

■ Remember that an exit status can only be in the range of 0 to 255.

If you execute any other commands before retrieving the value of the function using the `$?` variable, the return value from the function will be lost (remember, the `$?` variable returns the exit status of the last executed command).

The second problem defines a limitation for using this return value technique. Since an exit status must be less than 256, the result of your function must produce an integer value less than 256. Any values over that returns an error value:

```
$ ./test5
Enter a value: 200
doubling the value
The new value is 1
$
```

You can't use this return value technique if you need to return either larger integer values or a string value. Instead, you'll need to use another method, demonstrated in the next section.

Using function output

Just as you can capture the output of a command to a shell variable, you can also capture the output of a function to a shell variable. You can use this technique to retrieve any type of output from a function to assign to a variable:

```
result=`dbl`
```

This command assigns the output of the dbl function to the $result shell variable. Here's an example of using this method in a script:

```
$ cat test5b
#!/bin/bash
# using the echo to return a value

function dbl {
    read -p "Enter a value: " value
    echo $[ $value * 2 ]
}

result=`dbl`
echo "The new value is $result"
$ ./test5b
Enter a value: 200
The new value is 400
$ ./test5b
Enter a value: 1000
The new value is 2000
$
```

The new function now uses an echo statement to display the result of the calculation. The script just captures the output of the dbl function instead of looking at the exit status for the answer.

There's a subtle trick that this example demonstrates. You'll notice that the dbl function really outputs two messages. The read command outputs a short message querying the user for the value. The bash shell script is smart enough to not consider this as part of the STDOUT output and ignores it. If you had used an echo statement to produce this message, it would have been captured by the shell variable as well as the output value.

> **NOTE** Using this technique you can also return floating point and string values, making this an extremely versatile method for returning values from functions.

Using Variables in Functions

You might have noticed in the test5 example in the previous section that I used a variable called $value within the function to hold the value that it processed. When you use variables in your functions, you need to be somewhat careful about how you define and handle them. This is a common cause of problems in shell scripts. This section goes over a few techniques for handling variables both inside and outside your shell script functions.

Passing parameters to a function

As was mentioned earlier in the "Returning a Value" section, the bash shell treats functions just like mini-scripts. This means that you can pass parameters to a function just like a regular script (see Chapter 11).

Functions can use the standard parameter environment variables to represent any parameters passed to the function on the command line. For example, the name of the function is defined in the $0 variable, and any parameters on the function command line are defined using the variables $1, $2, and so on. You can also use the special variable $# to determine the number of parameters passed to the function.

When specifying the function in your script, you must provide the parameters on the same command line as the function, like this:

```
func1 $value1 10
```

The function can then retrieve the parameter values using the parameter environment variables. Here's an example of using this method to pass values to a function:

```
$ cat test6
#!/bin/bash
# passing parameters to a function

function addem {
   if [ $# -eq 0 ] || [ $# -gt 2 ]
   then
      echo -1
   elif [ $# -eq 1 ]
   then
      echo $[ $1 + $1 ]
   else
      echo $[ $1 + $2 ]
   fi
}

echo -n "Adding 10 and 15: "
value=`addem 10 15`
echo $value
echo -n "Let's try adding just one number: "
value=`addem 10`
echo $value
echo -n "Now trying adding no numbers: "
value=`addem`
echo $value
```

```
echo -n "Finally, try adding three numbers: "
value=`addem 10 15 20`
echo $value
$ ./test6
Adding 10 and 15: 25
Let's try adding just one number: 20
Now trying adding no numbers: -1
Finally, try adding three numbers: -1
$
```

The addem function in the text6 script first checks the number of parameters passed to it by the script. If there aren't any parameters, or if there are more than two parameters, it returns a value of -1. If there's just one parameter, it adds it to itself for the result. If there are two parameters, it adds them together for the result.

Since the function uses the special parameter environment variables for its own parameter values, it can't directly access the script parameter values from the command line of the script. This example will fail:

```
$ cat badtest1
#!/bin/bash
# trying to access script parameters inside a function

function badfunc1 {
    echo $[ $1 * $2 ]
}

if [ $# -eq 2 ]
then
    value=`badfunc1`
    echo "The result is $value"
else
    echo "Usage: badtest1 a b"
fi
$ ./badtest1
Usage: badtest1 a b
$ ./badtest1 10 15
./badtest1: *  : syntax error: operand expected (error token is "*
")
The result is
$
```

Even though the function uses the $1 and $2 variables, they aren't the same $1 and $2 variables available in the main part of the script. Instead, if you want to use those values in your function, you'll have to manually pass them when you call the function:

```
$ cat test7
#!/bin/bash
# trying to access script parameters inside a function
```

```
function func7 {
    echo $[ $1 * $2 ]
}

if [ $# -eq 2 ]
then
    value=`func7 $1 $2`
    echo "The result is $value"
else
    echo "Usage: badtest1 a b"
fi
$ ./test7
Usage: badtest1 a b
$ ./test7 10 15
The result is 150
$
```

By passing the $1 and $2 variables to the function, they become available for the function to use, just like any other parameter.

Handling variables in a function

One thing that causes problems for shell script programmers is the *scope* of a variable. The scope is where the variable is visible. Variables defined in functions can have a different scope than regular variables. That is, they can be hidden from the rest of the script.

Functions use two types of variables:

- Global
- Local

The following sections describe how to use both types of variables in your functions.

Global variables

Global variables are variables that are valid anywhere within the shell script. If you define a global variable in the main section of a script, you can retrieve its value inside a function. Likewise, if you define a global variable inside a function, you can retrieve its value in the main section of the script.

By default, any variables you define in the script are global variables. Variables defined outside of a function can be accessed within the function just fine:

```
$ cat test8
#!/bin/bash
# using a global variable to pass a value
```

```
function dbl {
    value=$[ $value * 2 ]
}

read -p "Enter a value: " value
dbl
echo "The new value is: $value"
$ ./test8
Enter a value: 450
The new value is: 900
$
```

The $value variable is defined outside of the function, and assigned a value outside of the function. When the dbl function is called, the variable and its value are still valid inside the function. When the variable is assigned a new value inside the function, that new value is still valid when the script references the variable.

This can be a dangerous practice though, especially if you intend to use your functions in different shell scripts. It requires that you know exactly what variables are used in the function, including any variables used to calculate values not returned to the script. Here's an example of how things can go bad:

```
$ cat badtest2
#!/bin/bash
# demonstrating a bad use of variables

function func1 {
    temp=$[ $value + 5 ]
    result=$[ $temp * 2 ]
}

temp=4
value=6

func1
echo "The result is $result"
if [ $temp -gt $value ]
then
    echo "temp is larger"
else
    echo "temp is smaller"
fi
$ ./badtest2
The result is 22
temp is larger
$
```

Because the $temp variable was used in the function, its value is compromised in the script, producing a result that you may not have intended. There's an easy way to solve this problem in your functions, shown in the next section.

Local variables

Instead of using global variables in functions, any variables that the function uses internally can be declared as local variables. To do that, just use the `local` keyword in front of the variable declaration:

```
local temp
```

You can also use the `local` keyword in an assignment statement while assigning a value to the variable:

```
local temp=$[ $value + 5 ]
```

The `local` keyword ensures that the variable is limited to only within the function. If a variable with the same name appears outside the function in the script, the shell keeps the two variable values separate. Now you can easily keep your function variables separate from your script variables, and share only the ones you want to share:

```
$ cat test9
#!/bin/bash
# demonstrating the local keyword

function func1 {
    local temp=$[ $value + 5 ]
    result=$[ $temp * 2 ]
}

temp=4
value=6

func1
echo "The result is $result"
if [ $temp -gt $value ]
then
    echo "temp is larger"
else
    echo "temp is smaller"
fi
$ ./test9
The result is 22
temp is smaller
$
```

Now when you use the `$temp` variable within the `func1` function it doesn't affect the value assigned to the `$temp` variable in the main script.

Array Variables and Functions

Chapter 5 discussed an advanced way of allowing a single variable to hold multiple values by using arrays. Using array variable values with functions is a little tricky, and there are some special considerations. This section describes a technique that allows you to do that.

Passing arrays to functions

The art of passing an array variable to a script function can be confusing. If you try to pass the array variable as a single parameter, it won't work:

```
$ cat badtest3
#!/bin/bash
# trying to pass an array variable

function testit {
    echo "The parameters are: $@"
    thisarray=$1
    echo "The received array is ${thisarray[*]}"
}

myarray=(1 2 3 4 5)
echo "The original array is: ${myarray[*]}"
testit $myarray
$ ./badtest3
The original array is: 1 2 3 4 5
The parameters are: 1
./badtest3: thisarray[*]: bad array subscript
The received array is
$
```

If you try using the array variable as a function parameter, the function only picks up the first value of the array variable.

To solve this problem, you must disassemble the array variable into its individual values, then use the values as function parameters. Inside the function, you can reassemble all of the parameters into a new array variable. Here's an example of doing this:

```
$ cat test10
#!/bin/bash
# array variable to function test

function testit {
    local newarray
```

```
    newarray=(`echo "$@"`)
    echo "The new array value is: ${newarray[*]}"
}

myarray=(1 2 3 4 5)
echo "The original array is ${myarray[*]}"
testit ${myarray[*]}
$ ./test10
The original array is 1 2 3 4 5
The new array value is: 1 2 3 4 5
$
```

The script uses the $myarray variable to hold all of the individual array values to place them all on the command line for the function. The function then rebuilds the array variable from the command line parameters. Once inside the function, the array can be used just like any other array:

```
$ cat test11
#!/bin/bash
# adding values in an array

function addarray {
    local sum=0
    local newarray
    newarray=(`echo "$@"`)
    for value in ${newarray[*]}
    do
        sum=$[ $sum + $value ]
    done
    echo $sum
}

myarray=(1 2 3 4 5)
echo "The original array is: ${myarray[*]}"
arg1=`echo ${myarray[*]}`
result=`addarray $arg1`
echo "The result is $result"
$ ./test11
The original array is: 1 2 3 4 5
The result is 15
$
```

The addarray function iterates through the array values, adding them together. You can put any number of values in the myarray array variable, and the addarray function will add them.

Returning arrays from functions

Passing an array variable from a function back to the shell script uses a similar technique. The function uses an echo statement to output the individual array values in the proper order, then the script must reassemble them into a new array variable:

```
$ cat test12
#!/bin/bash
# returning an array value

function arraydblr {
    local origarray
    local newarray
    local elements
    local i
    origarray=(`echo "$@"`)
    newarray=(`echo "$@"`)
    elements=$[ $# - 1 ]
    for (( i = 0; i <= $elements; i++ ))
    {
        newarray[$i]=$[ ${origarray[$i]} * 2 ]
    }
    echo ${newarray[*]}
}

myarray=(1 2 3 4 5)
echo "The original array is: ${myarray[*]}"
arg1=`echo ${myarray[*]}`
result=(`arraydblr $arg1`)
echo "The new array is: ${result[*]}"
$ ./test12
The original array is: 1 2 3 4 5
The new array is: 2 4 6 8 10
```

The script passes the array value, using the $arg1 variable to the arraydblr function. The arraydblr function reassembles the array into a new array variable, and it makes a copy for the output array variable. It then iterates through the individual array variable values, doubles each value, and places it into the copy of the array variable in the function.

The arraydblr function then uses the echo statement to output the individual values of the array variable values. The script uses the output of the arraydblr function to reassemble a new array variable with the values.

Function Recursion

One feature that local function variables provides is *self-containment*. A self-contained function doesn't use any resources outside of the function, other than whatever variables the script passes to it in the command line.

This feature enables the function to be called *recursively*. Calling a function recursively is when the function calls itself to reach an answer. Usually, a recursive function has a base value that it eventually iterates down to. Many advanced mathematical algorithms use recursion to reduce a complex equation down one level repeatedly, until they get to the level defined by the base value.

The classic example of a recursive algorithm is calculating factorials. A factorial of a number is the value of the preceding numbers multiplied with the number. Thus, to find the factorial of 5, you'd perform the equation:

```
5! = 1 * 2 * 3 * 4 * 5 = 120
```

Using recursion, the equation is reduced down to the format:

```
x! = x * (x-1)!
```

or in English, the factorial of x is equal to x times the factorial of x-1. This can be expressed in a simple recursive script:

```
function factorial {
    if [ $1 -eq 1 ]
    then
        echo 1
    else
        local temp=$[ $1 - 1 ]
        local result=`factorial $temp`
        echo $[ $result * $1 ]
    fi
}
```

The factorial function uses itself to calculate the value for the factorial:

```
$ cat test13
#!/bin/bash
# using recursion

function factorial {
    if [ $1 -eq 1 ]
    then
        echo 1
    else
        local temp=$[ $1 - 1 ]
        local result=`factorial $temp`
        echo $[ $result * $1 ]
    fi
}

read -p "Enter value: " value
result=`factorial $value`
echo "The factorial of $value is: $result"
```

```
$ ./test13
Enter value: 5
The factorial of 5 is: 120
$
```

Using the factorial function is easy.

Creating a Library

It's easy to see how functions can help save typing in a single script, but how about if you just happen to use the same single code block between scripts? It would seem to not help if you have to define the same function in each script, only to use it one time in each script.

There's a solution for that problem! The bash shell allows you to create a *library file* for your functions, then reference that single library file in as many scripts as you need to.

The first step in the process is to create a common library file that contains the functions you need in your scripts. Here's a simple library file called myfuncs that defines three simple functions:

```
$ cat myfuncs
# my script functions

function addem {
   echo $[ $1 + $2 ]
}

function multem {
   echo $[ $1 * $2 ]
}

function divem {
   if [ $2 -ne 0 ]
   then
      echo $[ $1 / $2 ]
   else
      echo -1
   fi
}
$
```

The next step is to include the myfuncs library file in your script files that want to use any of the functions. This is where things get tricky.

The problem is with the scope of shell functions. Just as with environment variables, shell functions are only valid for the shell session in which you define them. If you run the myfuncs shell script from your shell command line interface prompt, the shell creates a new shell, and runs the script in that new shell. This will define the three functions for that shell, but when you try to run another script that uses those functions, they won't be available.

This applies to scripts as well. If you try to just run the library file as a regular script file, the functions won't appear in your script:

```
$ cat badtest4
#!/bin/bash
# using a library file the wrong way
./myfuncs

result=`addem 10 15`
echo "The result is $result"
$ ./badtest4
./badtest3: addem: command not found
The result is
$
```

The key to using function libraries is the source command. The source command executes commands within the current shell context instead of creating a new shell to execute them. You use the source command to run the library file script inside of your shell script. This makes the functions available to the script.

The source command has a shortcut alias, called the *dot operator*. To source the myfuncs library file in a shell script, all you need to do is add the following line:

```
. ./myfuncs
```

This example assumes that the myfuncs library file is located in the same directory as the shell script. If not, you'll need to use the appropriate path to access the file. Here's an example of creating a script that uses the myfuncs library file:

```
$ cat test14
#!/bin/bash
# using functions defined in a library file
. ./myfuncs

value1=10
value2=5
result1=`addem $value1 $value2`
result2=`multem $value1 $value2`
result3=`divem $value1 $value2`
echo "The result of adding them is: $result1"
echo "The result of multiplying them is: $result2"
echo "The result of dividing them is: $result3"
$ ./test14
The result of adding them is: 15
```

```
The result of multiplying them is: 50
The result of dividing them is: 2
$
```

The script successfully uses the functions defined in the myfuncs library file.

Using Functions on the Command Line

You can use script functions to create some pretty complex operations. Sometimes it would be nice to be able to use these functions directly on the command line interface prompt.

Just as you can use a script function as a command in a shell script, you can also use a script function as a command in the command line interface. This is a nice feature, since once you define the function in the shell, you can use it from any directory on the system; you don't have to worry about a script being in your PATH environment variable. The trick is to get the shell to recognize the function. There are a couple of ways to do that.

Creating functions on the command line

Since the shell interprets commands as you type them, you can define a function directly on the command line. There are two ways to do that.

The first method defines the function all on one line:

```
$ function divem { echo $[ $1 / $2 ];  }
$ divem 100 5
20
$
```

When you define the function on the command line, you must remember to include a semicolon at the end of each command, so the shell knows where to separate commands:

```
$ function doubleit { read -p "Enter value: " value; echo $[
 $ value * 2 ]; }
$ doubleit
Enter value: 20
40
$
```

The other method is to use multiple lines to define the function. When you do that, the bash shell uses the secondary prompt to prompt you for more commands. Using this method, you don't need to place a semicolon at the end of each command; just press the ENTER key:

```
$ function multem {
> echo $[ $1 * $2 ]
> }
```

```
$ multem 2 5
10
$
```

When you use the brace at the end of the function, the shell knows that you're done defining the function.

CAUTION Be extremely careful when creating functions on the command line. If you use a function with the same name as a built-in command or another command, the function will override the original command.

Defining functions in the .bashrc file

The obvious downside to defining shell functions directly on the command line is that when you exit the shell, your function disappears. For complex functions, this can become somewhat of a problem.

A much simpler method is to define the function in a place where it'll be reloaded by the shell each time you start a new shell.

The best place to do that is the .bashrc file. The bash shell looks for this file in your home directory each time it starts, whether interactively or as the result of starting a new shell from within an existing shell.

Directly defining functions

You can define the functions directly in the .bashrc file in your home directory. Most Linux distributions already define some things in the .bashrc file, so be careful not to remove those items. Just add your functions to the bottom of the existing file. Here's an example of doing that:

```
$ cat .bashrc
# .bashrc

# Source global definitions
if [ -r /etc/bashrc ]; then
        . /etc/bashrc
fi

function addem {
   echo $[ $1 + $2 ]
}
$
```

The function won't take effect until the next time you start a new bash shell. After you do that, you can use the function anywhere on the system.

Sourcing function files

Just as in a shell script, you can use the source command (or its alias the dot operator) to add functions from an existing library file to your .bashrc script:

```
$ cat .bashrc
# .bashrc

# Source global definitions
if [ -r /etc/bashrc ]; then
        . /etc/bashrc
fi

. /home/rich/libraries/myfuncs
$
```

Make sure that you include the proper pathname to reference the library file for the bash shell to find. The next time you start a shell, all of the functions in your library are available at the command line interface:

```
$ addem 10 5
15
$ multem 10 5
50
$ divem 10 5
2
$
```

Even better, the shell also passes any defined functions to child shell processes, so your functions are automatically available for any shell scripts you run from your shell session. You can test this by writing a script that uses the functions without defining or sourcing them:

```
$ cat test15
#!/bin/bash
# using a function defined in the .bashrc file

value1=10
value2=5
result1=`addem $value1 $value2`
result2=`multem $value1 $value2`
result3=`divem $value1 $value2`
echo "The result of adding them is: $result1"
echo "The result of multiplying them is: $result2"
echo "The result of dividing them is: $result3"
$ ./test15
The result of adding them is: 15
The result of multiplying them is: 50
The result of dividing them is: 2
$
```

Even without sourcing the library file, the functions worked perfectly in the shell script.

Summary

Shell script functions allow you to place script code that's repeated throughout the script in a single place. Instead of having to rewrite blocks of code, you can create a function containing the code block, then just reference the function name in your script. The bash shell jumps to the function code block whenever it sees the function name used in the script.

You can even create script functions that return values. This allows you to create functions that interact with the script, returning both numeric and character data. Script functions can return numeric data by using the exit status of the last command in the function, or using the `return` command. The `return` command allows you to programmatically set the exit status of your function to a specific value based on the results of the function.

Functions can also return values using the standard `echo` statement. You can capture the output data using the backtick character as you would any other shell command. This enables you to return any type of data from a function, including strings and floating-point numbers.

You can use shell variables within your functions, assigning values to variables and retrieving values from existing variables. This allows you to pass any type of data both into and out of a script function from the main script program. Functions also allow you to define local variables, which are accessible only from within the function code block. Local variables allow you to create self-contained functions, which don't interfere with any variables or processes used in the main shell script.

Functions can also call other functions, including themselves. When a function calls itself, that's called recursion. A recursive function often has a base value that is the terminal value of the function. The function continues to call itself with a decreasing parameter value until the base value is reached.

If you use lots of functions in your shell scripts, you can create library files of script functions. The library files can be included in any shell script file by using the `source` command, or its alias, the dot operator. This is called sourcing the library file. The shell doesn't run the library file but makes the functions available within the shell that runs the script. You can use this same technique to create functions that you can use on the normal shell command line. You can either define functions directly on the command line or you can add them to your `.bashrc` file so that they are available for each new shell session you start. This is a handy way to create utilities that can be used no matter what your PATH environment variable is set to.

The next chapter discusses the topic of using text graphics in your scripts. In this day of modern graphical interfaces, sometimes a plain text interface just doesn't cut it. The bash shell provides some easy ways for you to incorporate simple graphics features in your scripts to help spice things up.

Adding Color to Scripts

Over the years, shell scripts have acquired a reputation for being dull and boring. This doesn't have to be the case, though, if you plan on running your scripts in a graphical environment. There are plenty of other ways to interact with your script user other than using the read and echo statements. This chapter dives into a few different methods you can use to help add life to your interactive scripts so that they don't look so old-fashioned.

IN THIS CHAPTER

Creating text menus

Making scripts colorful

Text windows widgets

Using X Windows graphics

Creating Text Menus

The most common way to create an interactive shell script is to utilize a menu. Offering your customers a choice of various options helps guide them through exactly what the script can and can't do.

Menu scripts usually clear the display area, then show a list of options available. The customer can select an option by pressing an associated letter or number assigned to each option. Figure 15-1 shows the layout of a sample menu.

The core of a shell script menu is the case command (see Chapter 9). The case command performs specific commands, depending on what character your customer selects from the menu.

The following sections walk you through the steps you should follow to create a menu-based shell script.

FIGURE 15-1

Displaying a menu from a shell script

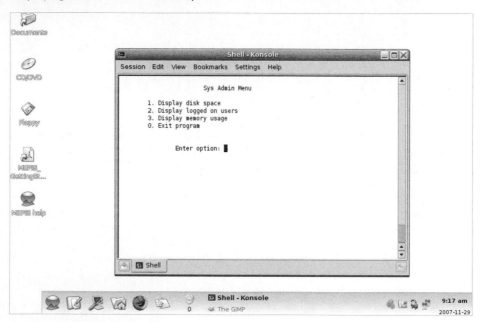

Create the menu layout

The first step in creating a menu is, obviously, to determine what elements you want to appear in the menu and lay them out the way that you want them to appear.

Before creating the menu, it's usually a good idea to clear the monitor display. This enables you to display your menu in a clean environment without distracting text.

The clear command uses the terminfo data of your terminal session (see Chapter 2) to clear any text that appears on the monitor. After the clear command, you can use the echo command to display your menu elements.

By default, the echo command can only display printable text characters. When creating menu items, it's often helpful to use nonprintable items, such as the tab and newline characters. To include these characters in your echo command, you must use the -e option. Thus, the command:

```
echo -e "1.\tDisplay disk space"
```

results in the output line:

```
1.         Display disk space
```

This greatly helps in formatting the layout of the menu items. With just a few echo commands, you can create a reasonable looking menu:

```
clear
echo
echo -e "\t\t\tSys Admin Menu\n"
echo -e "\t1. Display disk space"
echo -e "\t2. Display logged on users"
echo -e "\t3. Display memory usage"
echo -e "\t0. Exit menu\n\n"
echo -en "\t\tEnter option: "
```

The -en option on the last line displays the line without adding the newline character at the end. This gives the menu a more professional look, as the cursor will stay at the end of the line waiting for the customer's input.

The last part of creating the menu is to retrieve the input from the customer. This is done using the read command (see Chapter 11). Since we only expect single-character input, the nice thing to do is to use the -n option in the read command to only retrieve one character. This allows the customer to enter a number without having to press the Enter key:

```
read -n 1 option
```

Next, you'll need to create your menu functions.

Create the menu functions

Shell script menu options are easier to create as a group of separate functions. This enables you to create a simple, concise case command that is easy to follow.

To do that, you need to create separate shell functions for each of your menu options. The first step in creating a menu shell script is to determine what functions you want your script to perform and lay them out as separate functions in your code.

It's common practice to create *stub functions* for functions that aren't implemented yet. A stub function is a function that doesn't contain any commands yet, or possibly just an echo statement indicating what should be there eventually:

```
function diskspace {
   clear
   echo "This is where the diskspace commands will go"
}
```

This enables your menu to operate smoothly while you work on the individual functions. You don't have to code all of the functions for your menu to work. You'll notice that the function starts out with the clear command. This enables you to start the function on a clean monitor screen, without the menu showing.

One thing that helps out in the shell script menu is to create the menu layout itself as a function:

```
function menu {
   clear
   echo
   echo -e "\t\t\tSys Admin Menu\n"
   echo -e "\t1. Display disk space"
   echo -e "\t2. Display logged on users"
   echo -e "\t3. Display memory usage"
   echo -e "\t0. Exit program\n\n"
   echo -en "\t\tEnter option: "
   read -n 1 option
}
```

This enables you to easily redisplay the menu at any time just by calling the `menu` function.

Add the menu logic

Now that you have your menu layout and your functions, all you need to do is create the programming logic to put the two together. As mentioned, this requires the `case` command.

The `case` command should call the appropriate function according to the character selection expected from the menu. It's always a good idea to use the default `case` command character (the asterisk) to catch any incorrect menu entries.

Using the `case` command in a typical menu would look something like this:

```
menu
case $option in
0)
   break ;;
1)
   diskspace ;;
2)
   whoseon ;;
3)
   memusage ;;
*)
   clear
   echo "Sorry, wrong selection";;
esac
```

This code first uses the menu function to clear the monitor screen and display the menu. The `read` command in the `menu` function pauses until the customer hits a character on the keyboard. Once that's been done, the `case` command takes over. The `case` command calls the appropriate function based on the returned character. After the function completes, the `case` command exits.

388

Putting it all together

Now that you've seen all of the parts that make up a shell script menu, let's put them together and see how they all interoperate. Here's an example of a full menu script:

```
$ cat menu1
#!/bin/bash
# simple script menu

function diskspace {
    clear
    df -k
}

function whoseon {
    clear
    who
}

function memusage {
    clear
    cat /proc/meminfo
}

function menu {
    clear
    echo
    echo -e "\t\t\tSys Admin Menu\n"
    echo -e "\t1. Display disk space"
    echo -e "\t2. Display logged on users"
    echo -e "\t3. Display memory usage"
    echo -e "\t0. Exit program\n\n"
    echo -en "\t\tEnter option: "
    read -n 1 option
}

while [ 1 ]
do
    menu
    case $option in
    0)
        break ;;
    1)
        diskspace ;;
    2)
        whoseon ;;
    3)
        memusage ;;
    *)
```

```
                clear
                echo "Sorry, wrong selection";;
        esac
        echo -en "\n\n\t\t\tHit any key to continue"
        read -n 1 line
done
clear
$
```

This menu creates three functions to retrieve administrative information about the Linux system using common commands. I used a `while` loop to continually loop through the menu until the customer selects option 0, which uses the `break` command to break out of the `while` loop.

You can use this same template to create any shell script menu interface. It provides a simple way to interact with your customers.

Using the select command

You may have noticed that half the problem of creating a text menu is just creating the menu layout and retrieving the answer that you enter. The `bash` shell provides a handy little utility for you that does all of this work automatically.

The `select` command allows you to create a menu from a single command line, then retrieve the entered answer and automatically process it. The format of the `select` command is:

```
select variable in list
do
     commands
done
```

The *list* parameter is a space-separated list of text items that build the menu. The `select` command displays each item in the list as a numbered option and then displays a special prompt, defined by the PS3 environment variable, for the selection.

Here's a simple example of the select command in action:

```
$ cat smenu1
#!/bin/bash
# using select in the menu

function diskspace {
   clear
   df -k
}

function whoson {
   clear
   who
```

```
}

function memusage {
   clear
   cat /proc/meminfo
}

PS3="Enter option: "
select option in "Display disk space" "Display logged on users"
"Display memory usage" "Exit program"
do
   case $option in
   "Exit program")
         break ;;
   "Display disk space")
         diskspace ;;
   "Display logged on users")
         whoseon ;;
   "Display memory usage")
         memusage ;;
   *)
         clear
         echo "Sorry, wrong selection";;
   esac
done
clear
$
```

When you run the program, it automatically produces the following menu:

```
$ ./smenu1
1) Display disk space    3) Display memory usage
2) Display logged on users  4) Exit program
Enter option:
```

When you use the `select` command, remember that the result value stored in the variable is the entire text string and not the number associated with the menu item. The text string values are what you need to compare in your `case` statements.

Adding Color

Back in the old days of Unix, script programmers were limited to monochrome terminals, so interactive shell scripts didn't have to worry about using colors. These days, with all of the fancy terminal emulation packages around, adding colors and special effects to your interactive scripts has almost become a necessity. This section discusses and demonstrates how to add special text features to your script output.

391

The ANSI escape codes

Most all terminal emulation software recognizes the ANSI escape codes for formatting display output. The ANSI escape codes begin with a *control sequence indicator* (CSI), which tells the terminal that the data represents an escape code, followed by data indicating the operation to perform on the display.

There are ANSI escape codes for positioning the cursor at a specific location on the display, erasing parts of the display, and what we're interested in here, controlling the display format. To control the display format, you must use the Select Graphic Rendition (SGR) escape codes. The format of an SGR escape code is:

```
CSIn[;k]m
```

The m in the code indicates the SGR escape code. The n and k parameters define which display control is used. You can specify just one parameter or two at the same time, separating them using the semicolon. There are three classes of display control parameters:

- Effect control codes
- Foreground color control codes
- Background color control codes

Table 15-1 shows the effect control codes available.

Thus, to set the display to use italic font, you send the code:

```
CSI3m
```

TABLE 15-1

The ANSI SGR Effect Control Codes

Code	Description
0	Reset to normal mode.
1	Set to bold intensity.
2	Set to faint intensity.
3	Use italic font.
4	Use single underline.
5	Use slow blink.
6	Use fast blink.
7	Reverse foreground/background colors.
8	Set foreground color to background color (invisible text).

If you want to set the display to use italic font and blink, you send the code:

    CSI3;5m

The foreground and background color control codes use a two-digit code. Foreground colors use a two-digit value starting with a 3, while background colors use a two-digit value starting with a 4. The second digit in each denotes the specific color. Table 15-2 shows the color control codes available.

Thus, to specify a white foreground color, you send the code:

    CSI37m

which specifies the 3 to represent the foreground color and a 7 to specify the white color. To send a white background color, you'd use the code:

    CSI47m

You can combine up to two attributes in each control code. Thus, to set the background color to black, and the foreground color to red, you'd send the code:

    CSI31;40m

Next, it's time to look at how to send the actual codes to the terminal.

Displaying ANSI escape codes

Now that you know the ANSI escape codes, you're probably wondering how you can use them in your shell scripts. You can send the ANSI escape codes to the terminal session by using the echo command, just like normal text. The only tricky part is creating the CSI character.

TABLE 15-2

The ANSI Color Control Codes

Code	Description
0	Black
1	Red
2	Green
3	Yellow
4	Blue
5	Magenta
6	Cyan
7	White

The CSI character is normally a two-character sequence. This sequence is the ESC ASCII value, followed by the left square bracket character. Creating the ESC ASCII value in a script can be a challenge.

Obviously you can't just hit the Esc key on your keyboard, since most text editors interpret that to mean something else. Fortunately, there's a common key sequence that most editors recognize to allow you to insert the ESC ASCII value in your script. That's the Ctrl-v key combination, followed by the Esc key. When you enter this key combination, the characters ^[appear.

> **NOTE** You'll often see the ^[characters in scripts that use ANSI escape codes. When you see that character combination, remember that it's generated using the Ctrl-v ESC key combination.

So, a complete ANSI escape control code looks like this:

```
^[[0m
```

This specifies effect control code 0, which resets the display to the default settings.

You can test using ANSI escape control codes from your command line interface prompt:

```
$ echo ^[[41mThis is a test
This is a test
$
```

Of course, you can't tell from the book example, but this statement sets the background color to red on the terminal screen. The text appears in the default foreground color and with red as the background color. If you do this in your terminal emulator, you'll notice that after the shell prints the text from the echo command, the new prompt still uses the color control code. This is an important thing to remember.

> **CAUTION** ANSI color control codes remain active until another ANSI color control code changes the output.

To solve this problem, it's usually a good idea to use the reset control code (0) to reset the terminal display to normal:

```
$ echo ^[[41mThis is a test^[[0m
This is a test
$
```

After this test, the new shell prompt reverts to its original color scheme.

The same applies to effect control codes:

```
$ echo ^[[1mThis is a test^[[0m
This is a test
$
```

The text displayed by the echo command should appear in bold font in your terminal emulator, then the command line interface prompt should return to normal.

Some terminal emulators don't support the effect control codes. For example, my PuTTY terminal emulator software doesn't blink text marked with the blink escape control code. Instead, it just presents blinking text with a gray background.

If you need to set both the background and foreground colors, the ANSI escape control code allows you to specify two codes in one escape sequence:

```
$ echo "^[[33;44mThis is a test^[[0m"
This is a test
$
```

This command sets the foreground color to yellow, and the background color to blue using just one escape control code sequence.

When setting two escape control codes in an echo command, it's important to use double quotation marks around the code string. Without them, the echo command doesn't interpret the escape codes properly and produces an error message.

Using colors in scripts

You can now add ANSI escape control codes into your shell scripts to control the color format of your script output. This is especially handy when using menus, as you can control the color to direct the customer's attention to a specific part of the menu.

You must be careful though when creating scripts that use ANSI escape control codes. Remember, whenever the terminal emulator sees the code, it processes it. This is especially dangerous when using the cat command to list a script that contains ANSI escape control codes. The cat command will echo the codes to the display, which are then interpreted by the terminal emulator, changing the display. This can be annoying in large scripts that change lots of display features.

Here's a modified version of the menu script that uses color control codes to liven things up a bit:

```
$ cat menu2
#!/bin/bash
# menu using colors

function diskspace {
   clear
   df -k
}

function whoseon {
   clear
```

```
        who
    }

    function memusage {
        clear
        cat /proc/meminfo
    }

    function menu {
        clear
        echo
        echo -e "\t\t\tSys Admin Menu\n"
        echo -e "\t1. Display disk space"
        echo -e "\t2. Display logged on users"
        echo -e "\t3. Display memory usage"
        echo -e "^[[1m\t0. Exit program\n\n^[[0m^[[44;33m"
        echo -en "\t\tEnter option: "
        read -n 1 option
    }

    echo "^[[44;33m"
    while [ 1 ]
    do
        menu
        case $option in
        0)
            break ;;
        1)
            diskspace ;;
        2)
            whoseon ;;
        3)
            memusage ;;
        *)
         clear
         echo -e "^[[5m\t\t\tSorry, wrong selection^[[0m^[[44;33m";;
        esac
        echo -en "\n\n\t\t\tHit any key to continue"
        read -n 1 line
    done
    echo "^[[0m"
    clear
    $
```

The menu appears in yellow text on a blue background. Note that it's important to set your foreground and background colors before using the `clear` command; otherwise, the `clear` command will paint the terminal emulation screen with the default colors, making the menu items not blend in with the rest of the background.

When you use the bold (1) or blink (5) control codes in your script to highlight important text, you must change the foreground and background colors back, as there are no unbold or unblink control codes. Unfortunately, the reset control code just sets the display back to the default, not to whatever setting you were previously using.

Doing Windows

Using text menus and colors is a step in the right direction, but there's still a lot missing in our interactive scripts, especially if we try to compare them to the graphical Windows world. Fortunately for us, there are some very resourceful people out in the open source world that have helped us out.

The *dialog* package is a nifty little tool originally created by Savio Lam, and currently maintained by Thomas E. Dickey. This package recreates standard Windows dialog boxes in a text environment using ANSI escape control codes. You can easily incorporate these dialog boxes in your shell scripts to interact with your script users. This section describes the dialog package and demonstrates how to use it in shell scripts.

The dialog package

The `dialog` command uses command line parameters to determine what type of Windows *widget* to produce. A widget is the dialog package term for a type of Windows element. The dialog package currently supports the types of widgets shown in Table 15-3.

As you can see from Table 15-3, there are lots of different widgets to choose from. This can give your scripts a more professional look with very little effort.

To specify a specific widget on the command line, you need to use the double dash format:

```
dialog --widget parameters
```

Where `widget` is the widget name as seen in Table 15-3, and the `parameters` define the size of the widget window and any text required for the widget.

Each dialog widget provides output in two forms:

- Using STDERR
- Using the exit code status

The exit code status of the `dialog` command determines the button selected by the user. If an OK or Yes button is selected, the `dialog` command returns a zero exit status. If a Cancel or No button is selected, the `dialog` command returns a one exit status. You can use the standard `$?` variable to determine which button was selected in the dialog widget.

TABLE 15-3

The dialog Widgets

Widget	Description
calendar	Provides a calendar to select a date from
checklist	Displays multiple entries where each entry can be turned on or off
form	Allows you to build a form with labels and text fields to be filled out
fselect	Provides a file selection window to browse for a file
gauge	Displays a meter showing a percentage of completion
infobox	Displays a message without waiting for a response
inputbox	Displays a single text form box for text entry
inputmenu	Provides an editable menu
menu	Displays a list of selections to choose from
msgbox	Displays a message and requires the user to select an OK button
pause	Displays a meter showing the status of a specified pause period
passwordbox	Displays a single textbox that hides entered text
passwordform	Displays a form with labels and hidden text fields
radiolist	Provides a group of menu items where only one item can be selected
tailbox	Displays text from a file in a scroll window using the tail command
tailboxbg	Same as tailbox, but operates in background mode
textbox	Displays the contents of a file in a scroll window
timebox	Provides a window to select an hour, minute, and second
yesno	Provides a simple message with Yes and No buttons

If a widget returns any data, such as a menu selection, the dialog command sends the data to STDERR. You can use the standard bash shell technique of redirecting the STDERR output to another file or file descriptor:

```
dialog --inputbox "Enter your age:" 10 20 2>age.txt
```

This command redirects the text entered in the textbox to the age.txt file.

The following sections take a look at some examples of the more common dialog widgets you'll use in your shell scripts.

The msgbox widget

The msgbox widget is the most common type of dialog box. It displays a simple message in a window and waits for the user to click on an OK button before disappearing. The format required to use a msgbox widget is:

```
dialog --msgbox text height width
```

The text parameter is any string you want to place in the window. The dialog command will automatically wrap the text to fit the size of the window you create, using the height and width parameters. If you want to place a title at the top of the window, you can also use the --title parameter, along with the text of the title. Here's an example of using the msgbox widget:

```
$ dialog --title Testing --msgbox "This is a test" 10 20
```

After entering this command the message box will appear on the screen of the terminal emulator session you're using. Figure 15-2 shows what this looks like.

If your terminal emulator supports the mouse, you can click on the OK button. You can also use keyboard commands to simulate a click, just press the Enter key.

FIGURE 15-2

Using the msgbox widget in the dialog command

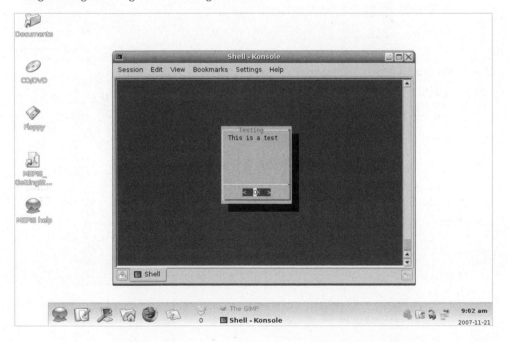

The yesno widget

The yesno widget takes the msgbox widget one step further, allowing the user to answer a yes/no question displayed in the window. It produces two buttons at the bottom of the window, one for Yes, and another for No. The user can switch between buttons by using the mouse, the tab key or the keyboard arrow keys. To select the button the user can either press the space bar or the Enter key.

Here's an example of using the yesno widget:

```
$ dialog --title "Please answer" --yesno "Is this thing on?" 10 20
$ echo $?
1
$
```

This produces the widget shown in Figure 15-3.

The exit status of the dialog command is set depending on which button the user selects. If the No button is selected, the exit status is one.

FIGURE 15-3

Using the yesno widget in the dialog command

The inputbox widget

The inputbox widget provides a simple textbox area for the user to enter a text string. The dialog command sends the value of the text string to STDERR. You must redirect that to retrieve the answer. Figure 15-4 demonstrates what the inputbox widget looks like.

As you can see in Figure 15-4, the inputbox provides two buttons, OK and Cancel. If the Cancel button is selected, the exit status of the command is one; otherwise, the exit status will be zero:

```
$ dialog --inputbox "Enter your age:" 10 20 2>age.txt
$ echo $?
0
$ cat age.txt
12$
```

You'll notice when you use the cat command to display the contents of the text file that there's no newline character after the value. This enables you to easily redirect the file contents to a variable in a shell script to extract the string entered by the user.

FIGURE 15-4

The inputbox widget

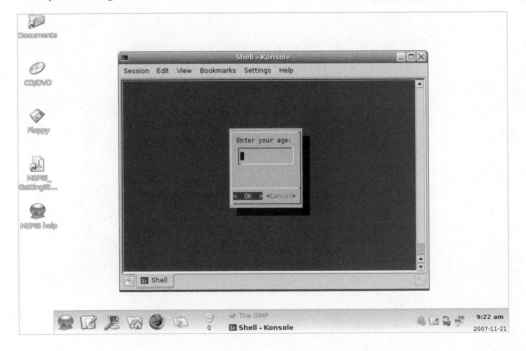

The textbox widget

The textbox widget is a great way to display lots of information in a window. It produces a scrollable window containing the text from a file specified in the parameters:

```
$ dialog --textbox /etc/passwd 15 45
```

The contents of the /etc/passwd file are shown within the scrollable text window, as shown in Figure 15-5.

You can use the arrow keys to scroll left and right, as well as up and down in the text file. The bottom line in the window shows the percent location within the file that you're viewing. The textbox only contains a single Exit button that should be selected to exit the widget.

The menu widget

The menu widget allows you to create a window version of the text menu we created earlier in this chapter. All you need to do is provide a selection tag and the text for each item:

```
$ dialog --menu "Sys Admin Menu" 20 30 10 1 "Display disk space"
2 "Display users" 3 "Display memory usage" 4 "Exit" 2> text.txt
```

FIGURE 15-5

The textbox widget

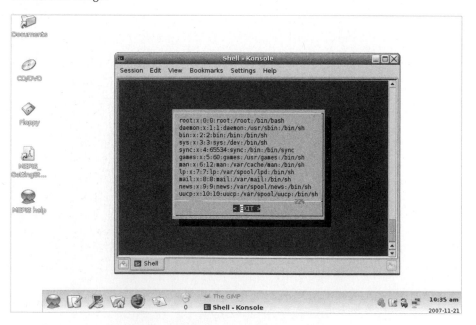

The first parameter defines a title for the menu. The next two parameters define the height and width of the menu window, while the third parameter defines the number of menu items that appear in the window at one time. If there are more menu items, you can scroll through them using the arrow keys.

Following those parameters, you must add menu item pairs. The first element is the tag used to select the menu item. Each tag should be unique for each menu item and can be selected by hitting the appropriate key on the keyboard. The second element is the text used in the menu. Figure 15-6 demonstrates the menu produced by the example command.

If a user selects a menu item by pressing the appropriate key for the tag, that menu item is highlighted but not selected. A selection isn't made until the OK button is selected, by using either the mouse or the Enter key. The dialog command sends the selected menu item text to STDERR, which you can redirect as needed.

The fselect widget

There are several fancy built-in widgets provided by the dialog command. The fselect widget is extremely handy when working with filenames. Instead of forcing the user to type in a filename, you can use the fselect widget to browse to the file location and select the file, as shown in Figure 15-7.

FIGURE 15-6

The menu widget with menu items

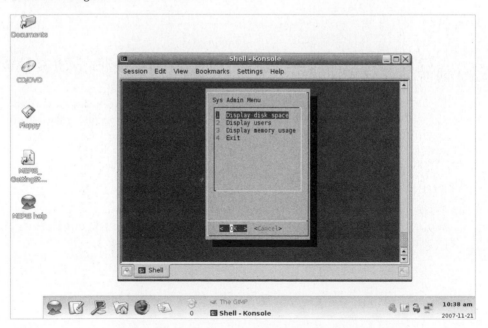

FIGURE 15-7

The fselect widget

The `fselect` widget format looks like:

```
$ dialog --title "Select a file" --fselect $HOME/ 10 50 2>file.txt
```

The first parameter after `fselect` is the starting location used in the window. The `fselect` widget window consists of a directory listing on the left side, a file listing on the right side, showing all of the files in the selected directory, and a simple textbox that contains the currently selected file or directory. You can manually type a filename in the textbox, or use the directory and file listings to select one.

The dialog options

Besides the standard widgets, you can customize lots of different options in the `dialog` command. You've already seen the `--title` parameter in action. This allows you to set a title for the widget that appears at the top of the window.

There are lots of other options available that allow you to completely customize both the appearance and the behavior of your windows. Table 15-4 shows the options available for the `dialog` command.

TABLE 15-4

The dialog Command Options

Option	Description
--add-widget	Proceed to the next dialog unless Esc or the Cancel button has been pressed.
--aspect *ratio*	Specify the width/height aspect ratio of the window.
--backtitle *title*	Specify a title to display on the background, at the top of the screen.
--begin *x y*	Specify the starting location of the top-left corner of the window.
--cancel-label *label*	Specify an alternative label for the Cancel button.
--clear	Clear the display using the default dialog background color.
--colors	Allows you to embed ANSI color codes in dialog text.
--cr-wrap	Allow newline characters in dialog text and force a line wrap.
--create-rc *file*	Dump a sample configuration file to the specified file.
--defaultno	Make the default of a yes/no dialog No.
--default-item *string*	Set the default item in a checklist, form, or menu dialog.
--exit-label *label*	Specify an alternative label for the Exit button.
--extra-button	Display an extra button between the OK and Cancel buttons.
--extra-label *label*	Specify an alternative label for the Extra button.
--help	Display the dialog command help message.
--help-button	Display a Help button after the OK and Cancel buttons.
--help-label *label*	Specify an alternative label for the Help button.
--help-status	Write the checklist, radiolist, or form information after the help information in the Help button was selected.
--ignore	Ignore options that dialog does not recognize.
--input-fd *fd*	Specify an alternative file descriptor, other than STDIN.
--insecure	Changes the password widget to display asterisks when typing.
--item-help	Adds a help column at the bottom of the screen for each tag in a checklist, radiolist, or menu for the tag item.
--keep-window	Don't clear old widgets from the screen.
--max-input *size*	Specify a maximum string size for the input. The default is 2048.

continued

TABLE 15-4   *(continued)*

Option	Description
`--nocancel`	Suppress the Cancel button.
`--no-collapse`	Don't convert tabs to spaces in dialog text.
`--no-kill`	Place the tailboxbg dialog in background and disable SIGHUP for the process.
`--no-label` *label*	Specify an alternative label for the No button.
`--no-shadow`	Don't display shadows for dialog windows.
`--ok-label` *label*	Specify an alternative label for the OK button.
`--output-fd` *fd*	Specify an alternative output file descriptor other than STDERR.
`--print-maxsize`	Print the maximum size of dialog windows allowed to the output.
`--print-size`	Print the size of each dialog window to the output.
`--print-version`	Print the dialog version to output.
`--separate-output`	Output the result of a `checklist` widget one line at a time with no quoting.
`--separator` *string*	Specify a string that separates the output for each widget.
`--separate-widget` *string*	Specify a string that separates the output for each widget.
`--shadow`	Draw a shadow to the right and bottom of each window.
`--single-quoted`	Use single quoting if needed for the checklist output.
`--sleep` *sec*	Delay for the specified number of seconds after processing the dialog window.
`--stderr`	Send output to STDERR (this is the default behavior).
`--stdout`	Send output to STDOUT.
`--tab-correct`	Convert tabs to spaces.
`--tab-len` *n*	Specify the number of spaces a tab character uses (the default is 8).
`--timeout` *sec*	Specify the number of seconds before exiting with an error code if no user input.
`--title` *title*	Specify the title of the dialog window.
`--trim`	Remove leading spaces and newline characters from dialog text.
`--visit-items`	Modify the tab stops in the dialog window to include the list of items.
`--yes-label` *label*	Specify an alternative label for the Yes button.

The --backtitle option is a handy way to create a common title for your menu through the script. If you specify it for each dialog window, it'll persist throughout your application, creating a professional look to your script.

As you can tell from Table 15-4, you can overwrite any of the button labels in your dialog window. This feature allows you to create just about any window situation you need.

Using the dialog command in a script

Using the dialog command in your scripts is a snap. There are just two things you must remember:

- Check the exit status of the dialog command if there's a Cancel or No button available.
- Redirect STDERR to retrieve the output value.

If you follow these two rules, you'll have a professional-looking interactive script in no time. Here's an example using dialog widgets to reproduce the system admin menu we created earlier in the chapter:

```
$ cat menu3
#!/bin/bash
# using dialog to create a menu

temp=`mktemp -t test.XXXXXX`
temp2=`mktemp -t test2.XXXXXX`

function diskspace {
   df -k > $temp
   dialog --textbox $temp 20 60
}

function whoseon {
   who > $temp
   dialog --textbox $temp 20 50
}

function memusage {
   cat /proc/meminfo > $temp
   dialog --textbox $temp 20 50
}

while [ 1 ]
do
dialog --menu "Sys Admin Menu" 20 30 10 1 "Display disk space" 2
"Display users" 3 "Display memory usage" 0 "Exit" 2> $temp2
if [ $? -eq 1 ]
then
    break
fi
```

```
selection=`cat $temp2`

case $selection in
1)
   diskspace ;;
2)
   whoseon ;;
3)
   memusage ;;
0)
   break ;;
*)
   dialog --msgbox "Sorry, invalid selection" 10 30
esac
done
rm -f $temp 2> /dev/null
rm -f $temp2 2> /dev/null
$
```

The script uses the `while` loop with a constant true value to create an endless loop displaying the menu dialog. This means that, after every function, the script returns to displaying the menu. Figure 15-8 shows what the dialog menu looks like.

FIGURE 15-8

The script menu using the dialog command

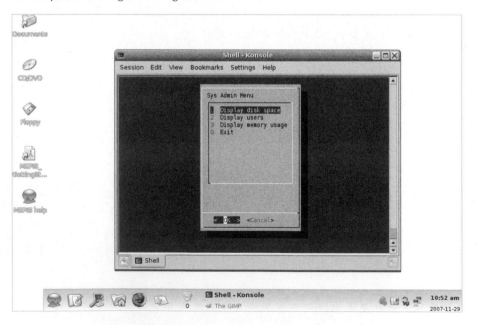

The menu dialog includes a Cancel button, so the script checks the exit status of the dialog command in case the user presses the Cancel button to exit. Since it's in a while loop, exiting is as easy as using the break command to jump out of the while loop.

The script uses the mktemp command to create two temporary files for holding data for the dialog commands. The first one, $temp, is used to hold the output of the df command so that it can be displayed in the textbox dialog. The second temporary file, $temp2, is used to hold the selection value from the main menu dialog.

Getting Graphic

If you're looking for even more graphics for your interactive scripts, you can go one step further. Both the KDE and GNOME desktop environments (see Chapter 1) have expanded on the dialog command idea and include commands that produce X Windows graphical widgets for their respective environments.

This section describes the kdialog and zenity packages, which provide graphical window widgets for the KDE and GNOME desktops, respectively.

The KDE environment

The KDE graphical environment includes the kdialog package by default. The kdialog package uses the kdialog command to generate standard windows, similar to the dialog-style widgets, within your KDE desktop. This allows you to produce Windows-quality user interfaces directly from your shell scripts!

kdialog widgets

Just like the dialog command, the kdialog command uses command line options to specify what type of window widget to use. The format of the kdialog command is:

```
kdialog display-options window-options arguments
```

The window-options options allow you to specify what type of window widget to use. The available options are shown in Table 15-5.

As you can see from Table 15-5, all of the standard window dialog box types are represented. However, when you use a kdialog window widget, it appears as a separate window in the KDE desktop, not inside the terminal emulator session!

The checklist and radiolist widgets allow you to define individual items in the lists, and whether they are selected by default:

```
$ kdialog --checklist "Items I need" 1 "Toothbrush" on 2 "Toothpaste"
off 3 "Hair brush" on 4 "Deodorant" off 5 "Slippers" off
```

TABLE 15-5

kdialog Window Options

Option	Description
`--checklist title [tag item status]`	A checklist menu, with status specifying if the item is checked or not.
`--error text`	Error message box.
`--inputbox text [init]`	Input textbox. You can specify the default value using the *init* value.
`--menu title [tag item]`	Menu selection box title and a list of items identified by a tag.
`--msgbox text`	Simple message box with specified text.
`--password text`	Password input textbox that hides user input.
`--radiolist title [tag item status]`	A radiolist menu, with status specifying if the item is selected or not.
`--separate-output`	Returns items on separate lines for checklist and radiolist menus.
`--sorry text`	Sorry message box.
`--textbox file [width] [height]`	Textbox displaying the contents of *file*, alternatively specified by width and height.
`--title title`	Specifies a title for the TitleBar area of the dialog window.
`--warningyesno text`	Warning message box with Yes and No buttons.
`--warningcontinuecancel text`	Warning message box with Continue and Cancel buttons.
`--warningyesnocancel text`	Warning message box with Yes, No, and Cancel buttons.
`--yesno text`	Question box with Yes and No buttons.
`--yesnocancel text`	Question box with Yes, No, and Cancel buttons.

The resulting checklist window is shown in Figure 15-9.

To select or deselect an item in the checklist, just click on it. If you select the OK button, the kdialog will send the tag values to STDOUT:

```
$ kdialog --checklist "Items I need" 1 "Toothbrush" on 2 "Toothpaste"
 off 3 "Hair brush" on 4 "Deodorant" off 5 "Slippers" off
"1" "3" "5"
$
```

FIGURE 15-9

A kdialog checklist dialog window

When you hit the Enter key, the kdialog box appears with the selections. When you click the OK or Cancel buttons, the kdialog command returns each tag as a string value to STDOUT (these are the "1", "3", and "5" values you see in the example). Your script must be able to parse the resulting values and match them with the original values.

Using kdialog

You can use the kdialog window widgets in your shell scripts similarly to how you use the dialog widgets. The big difference is that the kdialog window widgets output values using STDOUT instead of STDERR.

Here's a script that converts the sys admin menu created earlier into a KDE application:

```
$ cat menu4
#!/bin/bash
# using kdialog to create a menu

temp=`mktemp -t temp.XXXXXX`
temp2=`mktemp -t temp2.XXXXXX`

function diskspace {
   df -k > $temp
   kdialog --textbox $temp 1000 10
}
```

```
function whoseon {
    who > $temp
    kdialog --textbox $temp 500 10
}

function memusage {
    cat /proc/meminfo > $temp
    kdialog --textbox $temp 300 500
}

while [ 1 ]
do
kdialog --menu "Sys Admin Menu" "1" "Display disk space" "2" "Display
users" "3" "Display memory usage" "0" "Exit" > $temp2
if [ $? -eq 1 ]
then
    break
fi

selection=`cat $temp2`

case $selection in
1)
    diskspace ;;
2)
    whoseon ;;
3)
    memusage ;;
0)
    break ;;
*)
    kdialog --msgbox "Sorry, invalid selection"
esac
done
$
```

There isn't much difference from using the kdialog command and the dialog command. The resulting menu is shown in Figure 15-10.

Now things are looking like a real application! There's no limit to what you can do with your interactive scripts now.

The GNOME environment

The GNOME graphical environment supports two popular packages that can generate standard windows:

- gdialog
- zenity

FIGURE 15-10

The sys admin menu script using kdialog

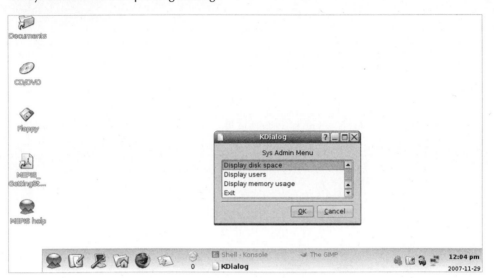

By far `zenity` is the most commonly available package found in most GNOME desktop Linux distributions (such as Ubuntu and Fedora). This section describes the features of `zenity` and demonstrates how to use it in your shell scripts.

zenity widgets

Just as you would expect, `zenity` allows you to create different windows widgets by using command line options. Table 15-6 shows the different widgets that `zenity` can produce.

The `zenity` program works somewhat different than the `kdialog` and `dialog` programs. Many of the widget types are defined using additional options on the command line, instead of including them as arguments to an option.

The `zenity` program does offer some pretty cool basic dialog windows. The calendar option produces a full month calendar, as shown in Figure 15-11

When you select a date from the calendar, zenity returns the value to `STDOUT`, just like `kdialog`:

```
$ zenity --calendar
11/25/2008
$
```

Another pretty cool window in `zenity` is the file selection option, shown in Figure 15-12.

TABLE 15-6

The zenity Windows Widgets

Option	Description
--calendar	Display a full month calendar.
--entry	Display a text entry dialog window.
--error	Display an error message dialog window.
--file-selection	Display a full pathname and filename dialog window.
--info	Display an informational dialog window.
--list	Display a checklist or radiolist dialog window.
--notification	Display a notification icon.
--progress	Display a progress bar dialog window.
--question	Display a yes/no question dialog window.
--scale	Display a scale dialog window.
--text-info	Display a textbox containing text.
--warning	Display a warning dialog window.

FIGURE 15-11

The zenity calendar dialog window

FIGURE 15-12

The zenity file selection dialog window

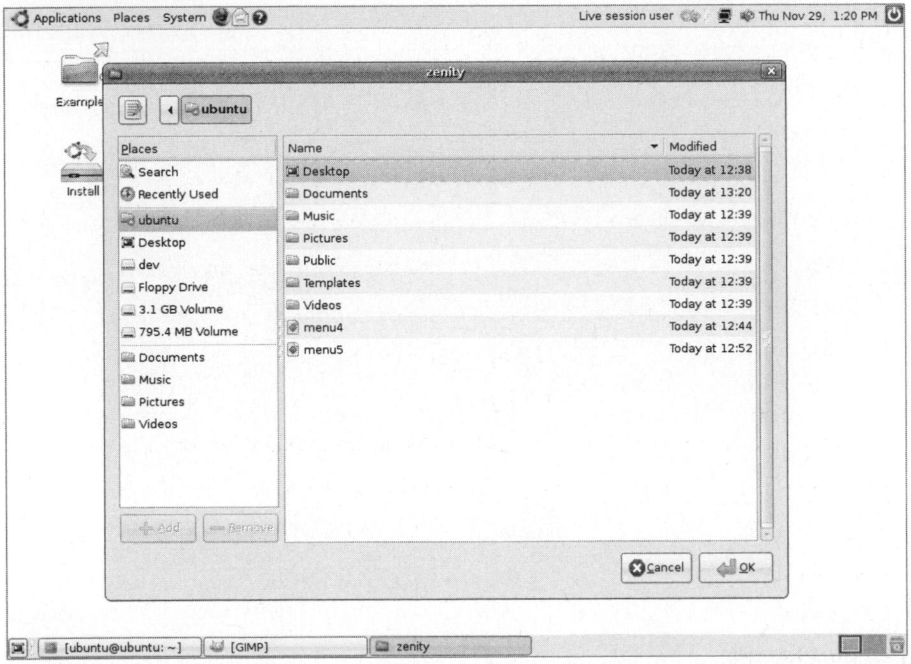

You can use the dialog window to browse to any directory location on the system (as long as you have the privileges to view the directory) and select a file. When you select a file, zenity returns the full file and pathname:

```
$ zenity --file-selection
/home/ubuntu/menu5
$
```

That's about as professional looking as you can get in the shell script world!

Using zenity in scripts

As you would expect, zenity performs well in shell scripts. Unfortunately zenity chose not to follow the option convention used in dialog and kdialog, so converting any existing interactive scripts to zenity may prove challenging.

In converting the sys admin menu from kdialog to zenity, I found that I had to do quite a bit of manipulation of the widget definitions:

```
$cat menu5
#!/bin/bash
```

```
# using zenity to create a menu

temp=`mktemp -t temp.XXXXXX`
temp2=`mktemp -t temp2.XXXXXX`

function diskspace {
   df -k > $temp
   zenity --text-info --title "Disk space" --filename=$temp
--width 750 --height 10
}

function whoseon {
   who > $temp
   zenity --text-info --title "Logged in users" --filename=$temp
--width 500 --height 10
}

function memusage {
   cat /proc/meminfo > $temp
   zenity --text-info --title "Memory usage" --filename=$temp
--width 300 --height 500
}

while [ 1 ]
do
zenity --list --radiolist --title "Sys Admin Menu" --column "Select"
--column "Menu Item" FALSE "Display disk space" FALSE "Display users"
FALSE "Display memory usage" FALSE "Exit" > $temp2
if [ $? -eq 1 ]
then
   break
fi

selection=`cat $temp2`
case $selection in
"Display disk space")
   diskspace ;;
"Display users")
   whoseon ;;
"Display memory usage")
   memusage ;;
Exit)
   break ;;
*)
   zenity --info "Sorry, invalid selection"
esac
done
$
```

FIGURE 15-13

The sys admin menu using zenity

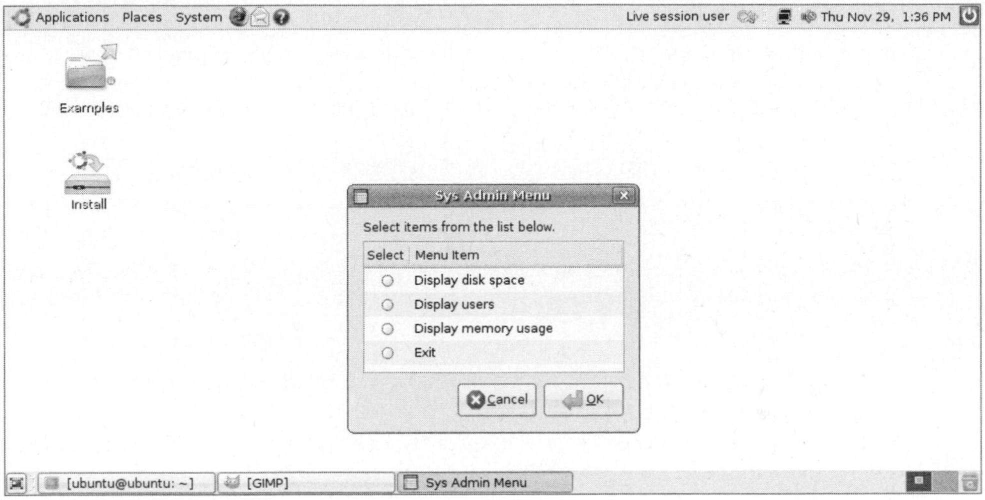

Since `zenity` doesn't support the menu dialog window, I used a radiolist type window for the main menu, as seen in Figure 15-13.

The radiolist uses two columns, each with a column heading. The first column is the radio buttons to select. The second column is the item text. The radiolist also doesn't use tags for the items. When you select an item, the full text of the item is returned to `STDOUT`. This makes life a little more interesting for the `case` command. You must use the full text from the items in the case options. If there are any spaces in the text, you need to use quotation marks around the text.

Using the `zenity` package, you can add a Windows feel to your interactive shell scripts in the GNOME desktop.

Summary

Interactive shell scripts have a reputation for being dull and boring. You can change that by using a few different techniques and tools available on most Linux systems. First, you can create menu systems for your interactive scripts by using the `case` command and shell script functions.

The `case` command allows you to paint a menu, using the standard `echo` command, and read a response from the user, using the `read` command. The `case` command then selects the appropriate shell script function based on the value entered.

You can liven up text mode menus by using the ANSI escape control codes to set colors and control features in your menu text, such as blinking and bold text. Often just changing the colors of a menu helps make the script experience more enjoyable.

The dialog program provides several prebuilt text widgets for creating Windows-like objects on a text-based terminal emulator. You can create dialog boxes for displaying text, entering text, and choosing files and dates by using the `dialog` program. This helps bring even more life to your shell script.

If you're running your shell scripts in a graphical X Windows environment, you can utilize even more tools in your interactive scripts. For the KDE desktop, there's the `kdialog` program. This program provides simple commands to create windows widgets for all of the basic windows functions. For the GNOME desktop, there are the `gdialog` and `zenity` programs. Each of these programs provides window widgets that blend into the GNOME desktop just like a real Windows application.

The next chapter dives into the subject of editing and manipulating text data files. Often the biggest use of shell scripts revolves around parsing and displaying data in text files such as log and error files. The Linux environment includes two very useful tools, `sed` and `gawk`, for working with text data in your shell scripts. The next chapter introduces you to these tools, and shows the basics of how to use them.

Chapter 16

Introducing sed and gawk

B y far, one of the most common functions that people use shell scripts for is working with text files. Between examining log files, reading configuration files, and handling data elements, shell scripts can help automate the mundane tasks of manipulating any type of data contained in text files. However, trying to manipulate the contents of text files using just shell script commands can be somewhat awkward. If you perform any type of data manipulation in your shell scripts, you'll want to become familiar with the sed and gawk tools available in Linux. These tools can greatly simplify any data-handling tasks you need to perform.

IN THIS CHAPTER

Working with text files

Discovering sed

Exploring gawk

Text Manipulation

Chapter 7 showed how to edit text files using different editor programs available in the Linux environment. These editors allow you to easily manipulate text contained in a text file, using simple commands or mouse clicks.

There are times though when you'll find yourself wanting to manipulate text in a text file on the fly, without having to pull out a full-fledged interactive text editor. In these situations, it would be useful to have a simple command line editor that could easily format, insert, modify, or delete text elements automatically.

The Linux system provides two common tools for doing just that. This section describes the two most popular command line editors used in the Linux world, sed and gawk.

The sed editor

The sed editor is called a *stream editor*, as opposed to a normal interactive text editor. In an interactive text editor, such as vim, you interactively use keyboard commands to insert, delete, or replace text in the data. A stream editor edits a stream of data based on a set of rules you supply ahead of time, before the editor processes the data.

The sed editor can manipulate data in a data stream based on commands you either enter into the command line or store in a command text file. It reads one line of data at a time from the input, matches that data with the supplied editor commands, changes data in the stream as specified in the commands, then outputs the new data to STDOUT. After the stream editor matches all of the commands against a line of data, it reads the next line of data and repeats the process. After the stream editor processes all of the lines of data in the stream, it terminates.

Since the commands are applied sequentially line by line, the sed editor only has to make one pass through the data stream to make the edits. This makes the sed editor much faster than an interactive editor, allowing you to quickly make changes to data in a file on the fly.

The format for using the sed command is:

```
sed options script file
```

The options parameters allow you to customize the behavior of the sed command, and include the options shown in Table 16-1.

The script parameter specifies a single command to apply against the stream data. If more than one command is required, you must use either the -e option to specify them in the command line or the -f option to specify them in a separate file. There are lots of commands available for manipulating data. We'll examine some of the basic commands used by the sed editor later in this chapter, then look at some of the more advanced commands in Chapter 18.

TABLE 16-1

The sed Command Options

Option	Description
-e script	Add commands specified in the script to the commands run while processing the input.
-f file	Add the commands specified in the file to the commands run while processing the input.
-n	Don't produce output for each command, but wait for the print command.

Defining an editor command in the command line

By default, the sed editor applies the specified commands to the STDIN input stream. This allows you to pipe data directly to the sed editor for processing. Here's a quick example demonstrating how to do this:

```
$ echo "This is a test" | sed 's/test/big test/'
This is a big test
$
```

This example uses the s command in the sed editor. The s command substitutes a second text string for the first text string pattern specified between the forward slashes. In this example, I substituted the words *big test* for the word *test*.

When you run this example, it should display the results almost instantaneously. That's the power of using the sed editor, you can make multiple edits to data in about the same time it takes for some of the interactive editors just to start up.

Of course, this simple test just edited one line of data. You should get the same speedy results when editing complete files of data:

```
$ cat data1
The quick brown fox jumps over the lazy dog.
The quick brown fox jumps over the lazy dog.
The quick brown fox jumps over the lazy dog.
The quick brown fox jumps over the lazy dog.
$ sed 's/dog/cat/' data1
The quick brown fox jumps over the lazy cat.
The quick brown fox jumps over the lazy cat.
The quick brown fox jumps over the lazy cat.
The quick brown fox jumps over the lazy cat.
$
```

The sed command executes and returns the data almost instantaneously. As it processes each line of data, the results are displayed. You'll start seeing results before the sed editor completes processing the entire file.

It's important to note that the sed editor doesn't modify the data in the text file itself. It only sends the modified text to STDOUT. If you look at the text file, it still contains the original data:

```
$ cat data1
The quick brown fox jumps over the lazy dog.
The quick brown fox jumps over the lazy dog.
The quick brown fox jumps over the lazy dog.
The quick brown fox jumps over the lazy dog.
$
```

Using multiple editor commands in the command line

To execute more than one command from the sed command line, just use the -e option:

```
$ sed -e 's/brown/green/; s/dog/cat/' data1
The quick green fox jumps over the lazy cat.
The quick green fox jumps over the lazy cat.
The quick green fox jumps over the lazy cat.
The quick green fox jumps over the lazy cat.
$
```

Both commands are applied to each line of data in the file. The commands must be separated with a semicolon, and there shouldn't be any spaces between the end of the command and the semicolon.

Instead of using a semicolon to separate the commands, you can use the secondary prompt in the bash shell. Just enter the first single quotation mark to open the script, and bash will continue to prompt you for more commands until you enter the closing quotation mark:

```
$ sed -e '
> s/brown/green/
> s/fox/elephant/
> s/dog/cat/' data1
The quick green elephant jumps over the lazy cat.
The quick green elephant jumps over the lazy cat.
The quick green elephant jumps over the lazy cat.
The quick green elephant jumps over the lazy cat.
$
```

You must remember to finish the command on the same line that the closing single quotation mark appears, for once the bash shell detects the closing quotation mark, it'll process the command. Once it starts, the sed command applies each command you specified to each line of data in the text file.

Reading editor commands from a file

Finally, if you have lots of sed commands you want to process, it's often easier to just store them in a separate file and use the -f option to specify the file in the sed command:

```
$ cat script1
s/brown/green/
s/fox/elephant/
s/dog/cat/
$ sed -f script1 data1
The quick green elephant jumps over the lazy cat.
The quick green elephant jumps over the lazy cat.
The quick green elephant jumps over the lazy cat.
The quick green elephant jumps over the lazy cat.
$
```

In this case, you don't put a semicolon after each command. The sed editor knows that each line contains a separate command. Just as with entering commands on the command line, the sed editor reads the commands from the specified file and applies them to each line in the data file.

We'll be looking at some other sed editor commands that'll come in handy for manipulating data in the "The sed Editor Basics" section. Before that, let's take a quick look at the other Linux data editor.

The gawk program

While the sed editor is a handy tool for modifying text files on the fly, it has its limitations. Often you need a more advanced tool for manipulating data in a file, one that provides a more programming-like environment allowing you to modify and reorganize data in a file. This is where gawk comes in.

The gawk program is the GNU version of the original awk program in Unix. The awk program takes stream editing one step further than the sed editor by providing a programming language instead of just editor commands. Within the programming language you can:

- Define variables to store data.
- Use arithmetic and string operators to operate on data.
- Use structured programming concepts, such as if-then statements and loops, to add logic to your data processing.
- Generate formatted reports by extracting data elements within the data file and repositioning them in another order or format.

The gawk program's report-generating abilities are often used for extracting data elements from large bulky text files and formatting them into a readable report. The perfect example of this is formatting log files. Trying to pore through lines of errors in a log file can be difficult. The gawk program allows you to filter just the data elements you want to view from the log file, then format them in a manner that makes reading the important data easier.

The gawk command format

The basic format of the gawk program is:

```
gawk options program file
```

Table 16-2 shows the options available with the gawk program.

The command line options provide an easy way to customize features in the gawk program. We'll be looking more closely at these as we explore using gawk.

The power of gawk is in the program script. You can write scripts to read the data within a line of text, then manipulate and display the data to create any type of output report.

TABLE 16-2

The gawk Options

Option	Description
-F *fs*	Specify a file separator for delineating data fields in a line.
-f *file*	Specify a filename to read the program from.
-v *var=value*	Define a variable and default value used in the gawk program.
-mf *N*	Specify the maximum number of fields to process in the data file.
-mr *N*	Specify the maximum record size in the data file.
-W *keyword*	Specify the compatibility mode or warning level for gawk.

Reading the program script from the command line

A gawk program script is defined by opening and closing braces. You must place script commands between the two braces. Since the gawk command line assumes that the script is a single text string, you must also enclose your script in single quotation marks. Here's an example of a simple gawk program script specified on the command line:

```
$ gawk '{print "Hello John!"}'
```

The program script defines a single command, the print command. The print command does what it says; it prints text to STDOUT. If you try running this command, you'll be somewhat disappointed, as nothing will happen right away. Since no filename was defined in the command line, the gawk program retrieves data from STDIN. When you run the program, it just waits for text to come in via STDIN.

If you type a line of text and press the Enter key, gawk will run the text through the program script:

```
$ gawk '{print "Hello World!"}'
This is a test
Hello John!
hello
Hello John!
This is another test
Hello John!

$
```

Just like the sed editor, the gawk program executes the program script on each line of text available in the data stream. Since the program script is set to display a fixed text string, no matter what text you enter in the data stream, you'll get the same text output.

To terminate the gawk program, you must signal that the data stream has ended. The bash shell provides a key combination to generate an End-of-File (EOF) character. The Ctrl-D key combination generates an EOF character in bash. Using that key combination terminates the gawk program and returns you to a command line interface prompt.

Using data field variables

As I mentioned, one of the primary features of gawk is its ability to manipulate data in the text file. It does this by automatically assigning a variable to each data element in a line. By default, gawk assigns the following variables to each data field it detects in the line of text:

- $0 represents the entire line of text.
- $1 represents the first data field in the line of text.
- $2 represents the second data field in the line of text.
- $n represents the nth data field in the line of text.

Each data field is determined in a text line by a *field separation character*. When gawk reads a line of text, it delineates each data field using the defined field separation character. The default field separation character in gawk is any whitespace character (such as the tab or space characters).

To demonstrate this, here's an example gawk program that reads a text file and displays only the first data field value:

```
$ cat data3
One line of test text.
Two lines of test text.
Three lines of test text.
$ gawk '{print $1}' data3
One
Two
Three
$
```

This program uses the $1 field variable to display only the first data field for each line of text.

If you're reading a file that uses a different field separation character, you can specify it by using the -F option:

```
$ gawk -F: '{print $1}' /etc/passwd
root
bin
daemon
adm
lp
sync
shutdown
halt
...
```

425

This short program displays the first data field in the password file on the system. Because the /etc/passwd file uses a colon to separate the data fields, if you want to separate out each data element you must specify it as the field separation character in the gawk options.

Using multiple commands in the program script

A programming language wouldn't be very useful if you could only execute one command. The gawk programming language allows you to combine commands into a normal program. To use multiple commands in the program script specified on the command line, just place a semicolon between each command:

```
$ echo "My name is Rich" | gawk '{$4="Dave"; print $0}'
My name is Dave
$
```

The first command assigns a value to the $4 field variable. The second command then prints the entire data field. Notice from the output that the gawk program replaced the fourth data field in the original text with the new value.

You can also use the secondary prompt to enter your program script commands one line at a time:

```
$ gawk '{
> $4="testing"
> print $0 }'
This is not a good test.
This is not testing good test.
$
```

After you open the single quotation mark, the bash shell provides the secondary prompt to prompt you for more data. You can add your commands one at a time on each line until you enter the closing single quotation mark. To exit the program, just press the Ctrl-D key combination to signal the end of the data.

Reading the program from a file

Just as with the sed editor, the gawk editor allows you to store your programs in a file and refer to them in the command line:

```
$ cat script2
{ print $5 "'s userid is " $1 }
$ gawk -F: -f script2 /etc/passwd
root's userid is root
bin's userid is bin
PostgreSQL Server's userid is postgres
FTP User's userid is ftp
GDM User's userid is gdm
HTDIG User's userid is htdig
```

```
Dhcpd User's userid is dhcpd
Bind User's userid is named
NSCD Daemon's userid is nscd
X Font Server's userid is xfs
MySQL server's userid is mysql
Rich's userid is rich
test account's userid is testing
postfix's userid is postfix
$
```

The `script2` program script uses the `print` command again to print the comment data field (field variable $5) of the /etc/passwd file, a short text message, then the `userid` data field (field variable $1).

You can specify multiple commands in the program file. To do so, just place each command on a separate line. There's no need to use semicolons:

```
$ cat script3
{
text="'s userid is "
print $5 text $1
}
$ awk -F: -f script3 /etc/passwd | more
root's userid is root
bin's userid is bin
PostgreSQL Server's userid is postgres
FTP User's userid is ftp
GDM User's userid is gdm
HTDIG User's userid is htdig
Dhcpd User's userid is dhcpd
Bind User's userid is named
NSCD Daemon's userid is nscd
X Font Server's userid is xfs
MySQL server's userid is mysql
Rich's userid is rich
test account's userid is testing
postfix's userid is postfix
$
```

The `script3` program script defines a variable to hold a text string used in the `print` command. You'll notice that gawk programs don't use a dollar sign when referencing a variable's value, as the shell script does.

Running scripts before processing data

The gawk program also allows you to specify when the program script is run. By default, gawk reads a line of text from the input, then executes the program script on the data in the line of text. Sometimes you may need to run a script before processing data, such as to create a header section for a report. To do that you use the BEGIN keyword. This forces gawk to execute the program script specified after the BEGIN keyword before reading the data:

```
$ gawk 'BEGIN {print "Hello World!"}'
Hello World!
$
```

This time the print command displays the text before reading any data. However, after it displays the text, it quickly exits, without waiting for any data.

The reason for that is the BEGIN keyword only applies the specified script before it processes any data. If you want to process data with a normal program script, you must define the program using another script section:

```
$ gawk 'BEGIN {print "Hello World!"} {print $0}'
Hello World!
This is a test
This is a test
This is another test
This is another test
This is the last test
This is the last test

$
```

Now after gawk executes the BEGIN script, it uses the second script to process any data that appears. To exit the program, just press the Ctrl-D key combination to signal the end of the data.

Be careful when doing this, notice that both of the scripts are still considered one text string on the gawk command line. You need to place your single quotation marks accordingly.

Running scripts after processing data

Similarly to the BEGIN keyword, the END keyword allows you to specify a program script that gawk executes after reading the data:

```
$ gawk 'BEGIN {print "Hello World!"} {print $0} END {print
    "byebye"}'
Hello World!
This is a test
This is a test
This is another test.
This is another test.
byebye
$
```

This time, after you press the Ctrl-D key combination to signal the end of the data, the gawk program executes the commands in the END script. This is a great technique to use to add footer data to reports after all the normal data has been processed.

You can put all of these elements together into a nice little program script file to create a full report from a simple data file:

```
$ cat script4
BEGIN {
print "The latest list of users and shells"
print " Userid      Shell"
print "--------     -------"
FS=":"
}

{
print $1 "        " $7
}

END {
print "This concludes the listing"
}
$
```

This script uses the BEGIN script to create a header section for the report. It also defines a special variable called FS. This is yet another way to define the field separation character. This way you don't have to count on whomever uses your script to define the field separation character in the command line options.

Here's a somewhat truncated output from running this gawk program script:

```
$ gawk -f script4 /etc/passwd
The latest list of users and shells
 Userid      Shell
--------     -------
root      /bin/bash
sync      /bin/sync
shutdown      /sbin/shutdown
halt      /sbin/halt
mysql     /bin/bash
rich      /bin/bash
test2     /bin/csh
test      /bin/bash
This concludes the listing
$
```

As expected, the BEGIN script created the header text, the program script processed the information from the specified data file (the /etc/passwd file), and the END script produced the footer text.

This gives you a small taste of the power available when you use simple gawk scripts. Chapter 19 describes some more basic programming principles available for your gawk scripts, along with some even more advanced programming concepts you can use in your gawk program scripts to create professional looking reports from even the most cryptic data files.

The sed Editor Basics

The key to successfully using the sed editor is knowing its myriad commands and formats, which are available to help you customize your text editing. This section describes some of the basic commands and features you can incorporate into your script to start using the sed editor.

More substitution options

You've already seen how to use the s command to substitute new text for the text in a line. However, there are a few other options available for the substitute command that can help make your life easier.

Substitution flags

There's a caveat to how the substitute command replaces matching patterns in the text string. Watch what happens in this example:

```
$ cat data4
This is a test of the test script.
This is the second test of the test script.
$ sed 's/test/trial/' data4
This is a trial of the test script.
This is the second trial of the test script.
$
```

The substitute command works fine in replacing text in multiple lines, but by default it only replaces the first occurrence in each line. To get the substitute command to work on different occurrences of the text, you must use a *substitution flag*. The substitution flag is set after the substitution command strings:

```
s/pattern/replacement/flags
```

There are four types of substitution flags available:

- A number, indicating the pattern occurrence for which new text should be substituted.
- g — Indicates that new text should be substituted for all occurrences of the existing text.
- p — Indicates that the contents of the original line should be printed.
- w *file* — Write the results of the substitution to a file.

In the first type of substitution, you can specify which occurrence of the matching pattern the sed editor should substitute new text for:

```
$ sed 's/test/trial/2' data4
This is a test of the trial script.
This is the second test of the trial script.
$
```

As a result of specifying a 2 as the substitution flag, the sed editor only replaces the pattern in the second occurrence in each line. The g substitution flag enables you to replace every occurrence of the pattern in the text:

```
$ sed 's/test/trial/g' data4
This is a trial of the trial script.
This is the second trial of the trial script.
$
```

The p substitution flag prints a line that contains a matching pattern in the substitute command. This is most often used in conjunction with the -n sed option:

```
$ cat data5
This is a test line.
This is a different line.
$ sed -n 's/test/trial/p' data5
This is a trial line.
$
```

The -n option suppresses output from the sed editor. However, the p substitution flag outputs any line that's been modified. Using the two in combination produces output only for lines that have been modified by the substitute command.

The w substitution flag produces the same output but stores the output in the specified file:

```
$ sed 's/test/trial/w test' data5
This is a trial line.
This is a different line.
$ cat test
This is a trial line.
$
```

The normal output of the sed editor appears in STDOUT, but only the lines that include the matching pattern are stored in the specified output file.

Replacement characters

There are times when you run across characters in text strings that aren't easy to use in the substitution pattern. One popular example in the Linux world is the forward slash.

Substituting pathnames in a file can get awkward. For example, if you wanted to substitute the Cshell for the bash shell in the /etc/passwd file, you'd have to do this:

```
$ sed 's/\/bin\/bash/\/bin\/csh/' /etc/passwd
```

Since the forward slash is used as the string delimiter, you must use a backslash to escape it if it appears in the pattern text. This often leads to confusion and mistakes.

To solve this problem, the sed editor allows you to select a different character for the string delimiter in the substitute command:

```
$ sed 's!/bin/bash!/bin/csh!' /etc/passwd
```

In this example the exclamation point is used for the string delimiter, making the pathnames much easier to read and understand.

Using addresses

By default, the commands you use in the sed editor apply to all lines of the text data. If you only want to apply a command to a specific line, or a group of lines, you must use *line addressing*.

There are two forms of line addressing in the sed editor:

- A numeric range of lines
- A text pattern that filters out a line

Both forms use the same format for specifying the address:

```
[address]command
```

You can also group more than one command together for a specific address:

```
address {
    command1
    command2
    command3
}
```

The sed editor applies each of the commands you specify only to lines that match the address specified.

This section demonstrates using both of these addressing techniques in your sed editor scripts.

Numeric line addressing

When using numeric line addressing, you reference lines using their line position in the text stream. The sed editor assigns the first line in the text stream as line number one and continues sequentially for each new line.

The address you specify in the command can be a single line number or a range of lines specified by a starting line number, a comma, and an ending line number. Here's an example of specifying a line number to which the sed command will be applied:

```
$ sed '2s/dog/cat/' data1
The quick brown fox jumps over the lazy dog
The quick brown fox jumps over the lazy cat
The quick brown fox jumps over the lazy dog
The quick brown fox jumps over the lazy dog
$
```

The sed editor modified the text only in line two per the address specified. Here's another example, this time using a range of line addresses:

```
$ sed '2,3s/dog/cat/' data1
The quick brown fox jumps over the lazy dog
The quick brown fox jumps over the lazy cat
The quick brown fox jumps over the lazy cat
The quick brown fox jumps over the lazy dog
$
```

If you want to apply a command to a group of lines starting at some point within the text, but continuing to the end of the text, you can use the special address, the dollar sign:

```
$ sed '2,$s/dog/cat/' data1
The quick brown fox jumps over the lazy dog
The quick brown fox jumps over the lazy cat
The quick brown fox jumps over the lazy cat
The quick brown fox jumps over the lazy cat
$
```

Since you may not know how many lines of data are in the text, the dollar sign often comes in handy.

Using text pattern filters

The other method of restricting which lines a command applies to is a bit more complicated. The sed editor allows you to specify a text pattern that it uses to filter lines for the command. The format for this is:

```
/pattern/command
```

You must encapsulate the *pattern* you specify in forward slashes. The sed editor applies the command only to lines that contain the text pattern that you specify.

For example, if you want to change the default shell for only the user rich, you'd use the sed command:

```
$ sed '/rich/s/bash/csh/' /etc/passwd
rich:x:500:500:Rich Blum:/home/rich:/bin/csh
barbara:x:501:501:Barbara:/home/barbara:/bin/bash
katie:x:502:502:Katie:/home/katie:/bin/bash
jessica:x:503:503:Jessica:/home/jessica:/bin/bash
test:x:504:504:Ima test:/home/test:/bin/bash
$
```

The command was only applied to the line with the matching text pattern. While using a fixed text pattern may be useful for filtering specific values, as in the userid example, it's somewhat limited in what you can do with it. The sed editor uses a feature called *regular expressions* in text patterns to allow you to create patterns that get pretty involved.

Regular expressions allow you to create advanced text pattern–matching formulas to match all sorts of data. These formulas combine a series of wildcard characters, special characters, and fixed text characters to produce a concise pattern that can match just about any text situation. Regular expressions are one of the scarier parts of shell script programming, and Chapter 17 covers them in great detail.

Grouping commands

If you need to perform more than one command on an individual line, group the commands together using braces. The sed editor will process each command listed on the address line(s):

```
$ sed '2{
> s/fox/elephant/
> s/dog/cat/
> }' data1
The quick brown fox jumps over the lazy dog.
The quick brown elephant jumps over the lazy cat.
The quick brown fox jumps over the lazy dog.
The quick brown fox jumps over the lazy dog.
$
```

Both commands are processed against the address. And of course, you can also specify an address range before the grouped commands:

```
$ sed '3,${
> s/brown/green/
> s/lazy/active/
> }' data1
The quick brown fox jumps over the lazy dog.
The quick brown fox jumps over the lazy dog.
The quick green fox jumps over the active dog.
The quick green fox jumps over the active dog.
$
```

The sed editor applies all of the commands to all of the lines in the address range.

Deleting lines

The text substitution command isn't the only command available in the sed editor. If you need to delete specific lines of text in a text stream, there's the delete command.

The delete command, d, pretty much does what it says. It'll delete any text lines that match the addressing scheme supplied. Be careful with the delete command, because if you forget to include an addressing scheme, all of the lines will be deleted from the stream:

```
$ cat data1
The quick brown fox jumps over the lazy dog
```

```
The quick brown fox jumps over the lazy dog
The quick brown fox jumps over the lazy dog
The quick brown fox jumps over the lazy dog
$ sed 'd' data1
$
```

The delete command is obviously most useful when used in conjunction with a specified address. This allows you to delete specific lines of text from the data stream, either by line number:

```
$ sed '3d' data6
This is line number 1.
This is line number 2.
This is line number 4.
$
```

or by a specific range of lines:

```
$ sed '2,3d' data6
This is line number 1.
This is line number 4.
$
```

or by using the special end of file character:

```
$ sed '3,$d' data6
This is line number 1.
This is line number 2.
$
```

The pattern-matching feature of the sed editor also applies to the delete command:

```
$ sed '/number 1/d' data6
This is line number 2.
This is line number 3.
This is line number 4.
$
```

The sed editor removes the line containing text that matches the pattern you specify.

> **NOTE** Remember that the sed editor doesn't touch the original file. Any lines you delete are only gone from the output of the sed editor. The original file still contains the "deleted" lines.

You can also delete a range of lines using two text patterns, but be careful if you do this. The first pattern you specify "turns on" the line deletion, and the second pattern "turns off" the line deletion. The sed editor deletes any lines between the two specified lines (including the specified lines):

```
$ sed '/1/,/3/d' data6
This is line number 4.
$
```

I mentioned that you need to be careful with this, as the delete feature will "turn on" whenever the sed editor detects the start pattern in the data stream. This may produce an unexpected result:

```
$ cat data7
This is line number 1.
This is line number 2.
This is line number 3.
This is line number 4.
This is line number 1 again.
This is text you want to keep.
This is the last line in the file.
$ sed '/1/,/3/d' data7
This is line number 4.
$
```

The second occurrence of a line with the number 1 in it triggered the delete command again, deleting the rest of the lines in the data stream, as the stop pattern wasn't recognized. Of course, the other obvious problem occurs if you specify a pattern that never appears in the text:

```
$ sed '/1/,/5/d' data7
$
```

Since the delete features "turned on" at the first pattern match, but never found the end pattern match, the entire data stream was deleted.

Inserting and appending text

As you would expect, like any other editor, the sed editor allows you to insert and append text lines to the data stream. The difference between the two actions can be confusing:

- The insert command (i) adds a new line before the specified line
- The append command (a) adds a new line after the specified line

A confusing thing about these two commands is their formats. You can't use these commands on a single command line. You must specify the line to insert or append on a separate line by itself. The format for doing this is:

```
sed '[address]command\
new line'
```

The text in *new line* appears in the sed editor output in the place you specify. Remember, when you use the insert command, the text appears before the data stream text:

```
$ echo "testing" | sed 'i\
> This is a test'
This is a test
testing
$
```

And when you use the append command, the text appears after the data stream text:

```
$ echo "testing" | sed 'a\
> This is a test'
testing
This is a test
$
```

When you use the sed editor from the command line interface prompt, you'll get the secondary prompt to enter the new line data. You must complete the sed editor command on this line, for once you enter the ending single quotation mark the bash shell will process the command.

This works great for adding text before or after the text in the data stream, but what about adding text inside the data stream?

To insert or append data inside the data stream lines, you must use addressing to tell the sed editor where you want the data to appear. You can only specify a single line address when using these commands. You can match either a numeric line number or a text pattern, but you can't use a range of addresses (that makes sense, as you can only insert or append before or after a single line, not a range).

Here's an example of inserting a new line before line 3 in the data stream:

```
$ sed '3i\
> This is an inserted line.' data6
This is line number 1.
This is line number 2.
This is an inserted line.
This is line number 3.
This is line number 4.
$
```

Here's an example of appending a new line after line 3 in the data stream:

```
$ sed '3a\
>This is an inserted line.' data6
This is line number 1.
This is line number 2.
This is line number 3.
This is an inserted line.
This is line number 4.
$
```

This uses the same process as the insert command; it just places the new text line after the specified line number. If you have a multiline data stream, and you want to append a new line of text to the end of a data stream, just use our new friend the dollar sign, which represents the last line of data:

```
$ sed '$a\
> This is a new line of text.' data6
```

```
This is line number 1.
This is line number 2.
This is line number 3.
This is line number 4.
This is a new line of text.
$
```

The same idea applies if you want to add a new line at the beginning of the data stream. Just insert a new line before line number one.

To insert or append more than one line of text, you must use a backslash on each line of new text until you reach the last text line where you want to insert or append text:

```
$ sed '1i\
> This is one line of new text.\
> This is another line of new text.' data6
This is one line of new text.
This is another line of new text.
This is line number 1.
This is line number 2.
This is line number 3.
This is line number 4.
$
```

Both of the specified lines are added to the data stream.

Changing lines

The change command allows you to change the contents of an entire line of text in the data stream. It works the same way as the insert and append commands, in that you must specify the new line separately from the rest of the sed command:

```
$ sed '3c\
> This is a changed line of text.' data6
This is line number 1.
This is line number 2.
This is a changed line of text.
This is line number 4.
$
```

In this example the sed editor changes the text in line number 3. You can also use a text pattern for the address:

```
$ sed '/number 3/c\
> This is a changed line of text.' data6
This is line number 1.
This is line number 2.
This is a changed line of text.
This is line number 4.
$
```

The text pattern change command will change any line of text in the data stream that it matches.

```
$ sed '/number 1/c\
> This is a changed line of text.' data7
This is a changed line of text.
This is line number 2.
This is line number 3.
This is line number 4.
This is a changed line of text.
This is yet another line.
This is the last line in the file.
$
```

You can use an address range in the change command, but the results may not be what you expect:

```
$ sed '2,3c\
> This is a new line of text.' data6
This is line number 1.
This is a new line of text.
This is line number 4.
$
```

Instead of changing both lines with the text, the sed editor uses the single line of text to replace both lines.

The transform command

The transform command (y) is the only sed editor command that operates on a single character. The transform command uses the format:

```
[address]y/inchars/outchars/
```

The transform command performs a one-to-one mapping of the *inchars* and the *outchars* values. The first character in *inchars* is converted to the first character in *outchars*. The second character in *inchars* is converted to the second character in *outchars*. This mapping continues throughout the length of the specified characters. If the *inchars* and *outchars* are not the same length, the sed editor will produce an error message.

A simple example of using the transform command is:

```
$ sed 'y/123/789/' data7
This is line number 7.
This is line number 8.
This is line number 9.
This is line number 4.
This is line number 7 again.
This is yet another line.
This is the last line in the file.
$
```

As you can see from the output, each instance of the characters specified in the *inchars* pattern has been replaced by the character in the same position in the *outchars* pattern.

The transform command is a global command, that is, it performs the transformation on any character found in the text line automatically, without regard to the occurrence:

```
$ echo "This 1 is a test of 1 try." | sed 'y/123/456/'
This 4 is a test of 4 try.
$
```

The sed editor transformed both instances of the matching character 1 in the text line. You can't limit the transformation to a specific occurrence of the character.

Printing revisited

The "More Substitution Options" section showed how to use the p flag with the substitution command to display lines that the sed editor changed. There are three commands that also can be used to print information from the data stream:

- The lowercase p command to print a text line
- The equal sign (=) command to print line numbers
- The l (lowercase L) command to list a line

The following sections look at each of these three printing commands in the sed editor.

Printing lines

Similarly to the p flag in the substitution command, the p command prints a line in the sed editor output. On its own, there's not much excitement:

```
$ echo "this is a test" | sed 'p'
this is a test
this is a test
$
```

All it does is print the data text that you already know is there. The most common use for the print command is printing lines that contain matching text from a text pattern:

```
$ sed -n '/number 3/p' data6
This is line number 3.
$
```

By using the -n option on the command line, you can suppress all of the other lines and only print the line that contains the matching text pattern.

You can also use this as a quick way to print a subset of lines in a data stream:

```
$ sed -n '2,3p' data6
This is line number 2.
```

```
This is line number 3.
$
```

Another use for the print command is when you need to see a line before it gets altered, such as with the substitution or change command. You can create a script that displays the line before it's changed:

```
$ sed -n '/3/{
p
s/line/test/p
}' data6
This is line number 3.
This is test number 3.
$
```

This sed editor command searches for lines that contain the number 3, then executes two commands. First, the script uses the p command to print the original version of the line, then it uses the s command to substitute text, along with the p flag to print the resulting text. The output shows both the original line text and the new line text.

Printing line numbers

The equal sign command prints the current line number for the line within the data stream. Line numbers are determined by using the newline character in the data stream. Each time a newline character appears in the data stream, the sed editor assumes that it terminates a line of text.

The basic use of the equal sign command isn't too exciting:

```
$ sed '=' data1
1
The quick brown fox jumps over the lazy dog.
2
The quick brown fox jumps over the lazy dog.
3
The quick brown fox jumps over the lazy dog.
4
The quick brown fox jumps over the lazy dog.
$
```

The sed editor prints the line number before the actual line of text. The equal sign command comes in handy if you're searching for a specific text pattern in the data stream:

```
$ sed -n '/number 4/{
=
p
}' data6
4
This is line number 4.
$
```

By using the -n option you can have the sed editor display only both the line number and text for the line that contains the matching text pattern.

Listing lines

The list command (1) allows you to print both the text and nonprintable ASCII characters in a data stream. Any nonprintable characters are shown using either their octal values, preceded by a backslash, or the standard C-style nomenclature for common nonprintable characters, such as \t for tab characters:

```
$ cat data8
This     line     contains           tabs.
$ sed -n 'l' data8
This\tline\tcontains\ttabs.$
$
```

The tab character locations are shown with the \t nomenclature. The dollar sign at the end of the line indicates the newline character. If you have a data stream that contains an escape character, the list command displays it using the octal code:

```
$ cat data9
This line contains an escape character
$ sed -n 'l' data9
This line contains an escape character \033[44m$
$
```

The data9 text file contains an escape control code (see Chapter 15) to change the display color. When you use the cat command to display the text file, you don't see the escape control code; it just changes the color of the display.

However, using the list command you can display the escape control code used. The \033 is the octal value of the ASCII code for the escape key.

Using files with sed

The substitution command contains flags that allow you to work with files. There are also regular sed editor commands that let you do that without having to substitute text.

Writing to a file

The w command is used to write lines to a file. The format for the w command is:

```
[address]w filename
```

The filename can be specified as either a relative or absolute pathname, but in either case the person running the sed editor must have write permissions for the file. The address can be any type of addressing method used in sed, such as a single line number, a text pattern, or a range of line numbers or text patterns.

Here's an example that prints only the first two lines of a data stream to a text file:

```
$ sed '1,2w test' data6
This is line number 1.
This is line number 2.
This is line number 3.
This is line number 4.
$ cat test
This is line number 1.
This is line number 2.
$
```

Of course, if you don't want the lines to display on STDOUT, you can use the -n option for the sed command.

This is a great tool to use if you need to create a data file from a master file on the basis of common text values, such as those in a mailing list:

```
$ cat data10
Blum, Katie       Chicago, IL
Mullen, Riley    West Lafayette, IN
Snell, Haley     Ft. Wayne, IN
Woenker, Matthew        Springfield, IL
Wisecarver, Emma        Grant Park, IL
$ sed -n '/IN/w INcustomers' data10
$ cat INcustomers
Mullen, Riley    West Lafayette, IN
Snell, Haley     Ft. Wayne, IN
$
```

The sed editor writes to a destination file only the data lines that contain the text pattern.

Reading data from a file

You've already seen how to insert data into and append text to a data stream from the sed command line. The read command (r) allows you to insert data contained in a separate file.

The format of the read command is:

```
[address]r filename
```

The filename parameter specifies either an absolute or relative pathname for the file that contains the data. You can't use a range of addresses for the read command. You can only specify a single line number or text pattern address. The sed editor inserts the text from the file after the address.

```
$ cat data11
This is an added line.
This is the second added line.
$ sed '3r data11' data6
```

```
This is line number 1.
This is line number 2.
This is line number 3.
This is an added line.
This is the second added line.
This is line number 4.
$
```

The sed editor inserts into the data stream all of the text lines in the data file. The same technique works when using a text pattern address:

```
$ sed '/number 2/r data11' data6
This is line number 1.
This is line number 2.
This is an added line.
This is the second added line.
This is line number 3.
This is line number 4.
$
```

If you want to add text to the end of a data stream, just use the dollar sign address symbol:

```
$ sed '$r data11' data6
This is line number 1.
This is line number 2.
This is line number 3.
This is line number 4.
This is an added line.
This is the second added line.
$
```

A cool application of the read command is to use it in conjunction with a delete command to replace a placeholder in a file with data from another file. For example, suppose that you had a form letter stored in a text file that looked like this:

```
$ cat letter
Would the following people:
LIST
please report to the office.
$
```

The form letter uses the generic placeholder LIST in place of a list of people. To insert the list of people after the placeholder, all you need to do is use the read command. However, this still leaves the placeholder text in the output. To remove that, just use the delete command. The result looks like this:

```
$ sed '/LIST/{
> r data10
> d
```

```
> }' letter
Would the following people:
Blum, Rich      Chicago, IL
Mullen, Riley   West Lafayette, IN
Snell, Haley    Ft. Wayne, IN
Woenker, Matthew        Springfield, IL
Wisecarver, Emma        Grant Park, IL
please report to the office.
$
```

Now the placeholder text is replaced with the list of names from the data file.

Summary

While shell scripts can do a lot of work on their own, it's often difficult to manipulate data with just a shell script. Linux provides two handy utilities to help out with handling text data. The sed editor is a stream editor that quickly processes data "on the fly" as it reads it. You must provide the sed editor with a list of editing commands, which it applies to the data.

The gawk program is a utility from the GNU organization that mimics and expands on the functionality of the Unix awk program. The awk program contains a built-in programming language that you can use to write scripts to handle and process data. You can use the gawk program to extract data elements from large data files and output them in just about any format you desire. This makes processing large log files a snap, as well as creating custom reports from data files.

A crucial piece of both the sed and gawk programs is knowing how to use regular expressions. Regular expressions are key to creating customized filters for extracting and manipulating data in text files. The next chapter dives into the often misunderstood world of regular expressions, showing how to build regular expressions for manipulating all types of data.

Chapter 17

Regular Expressions

The key to successfully working with the sed editor and the gawk program in your shell script is being comfortable using regular expressions. This is not always an easy thing to do, as trying to filter specific data from a large batch of data can (and often does) get complicated. This chapter describes how to create regular expressions in both the sed editor and the gawk program that can filter out just the data you need.

What Are Regular Expressions?

The first step to understanding regular expressions is defining just exactly what they are. This section explains just what a regular expression is and describes how Linux uses regular expressions.

A definition

A regular expression is a pattern template you define that a Linux utility uses to filter text. A Linux utility (such as the sed editor or the gawk program) matches the regular expression pattern against data as that data flows into the utility. If the data matches the pattern, it's accepted for processing. If the data doesn't match the pattern, it's rejected. This is illustrated in Figure 17-1.

The regular expression pattern makes use of wildcard characters to represent one or more characters in the data stream. There are plenty of instances in Linux where you can specify a wildcard character to represent data that you don't know about. You've already seen an example of using wildcard characters with the Linux ls command for listing files and directories (see Chapter 3).

FIGURE 17-1

Matching data against a regular expression pattern

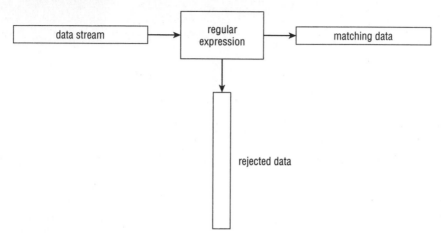

The asterisk wildcard character allows you to list only files that match a certain criteria. For example:

```
$ ls -al da*
-rw-r--r--    1 rich     rich          45 Nov 26 12:42 data
-rw-r--r--    1 rich     rich          25 Dec  4 12:40 data.tst
-rw-r--r--    1 rich     rich         180 Nov 26 12:42 data1
-rw-r--r--    1 rich     rich          45 Nov 26 12:44 data2
-rw-r--r--    1 rich     rich          73 Nov 27 12:31 data3
-rw-r--r--    1 rich     rich          79 Nov 28 14:01 data4
-rw-r--r--    1 rich     rich         187 Dec  4 09:45 datatest
$
```

The da* parameter instructs the ls command to list only the files whose name starts with da. There can be any number of characters after the da in the filename (including none). The ls command reads the information regarding all of the files in the directory but only displays the ones that match the wildcard character.

Regular expression wildcard patterns work in a similar way. The regular expression pattern contains text and/or special characters that define a template for the sed editor and the gawk program to follow when matching data. There are different special characters you can use in a regular expression to define a specific pattern for filtering data.

Types of regular expressions

The biggest problem with using regular expressions is that there isn't just one set of them. Several different applications use different types of regular expressions in the Linux environment.

These include such diverse applications as programming languages (Java, Perl, and Python), Linux utilities (such as the sed editor, the gawk program, and the grep utility), and mainstream applications (such as the MySQL and PostgreSQL database servers).

A regular expression is implemented using a *regular expression engine*. A regular expression engine is the underlying software that interprets regular expression patterns and uses those patterns to match text.

In the Linux world, there are two popular regular expression engines:

- The POSIX Basic Regular Expression (BRE) engine
- The POSIX Extended Regular Expression (ERE) engine

Most Linux utilities at a minimum conform to the POSIX BRE engine specifications, recognizing all of the pattern symbols it defines. Unfortunately, some utilities (such as the sed editor) only conform to a subset of the BRE engine specifications. This is due to speed constraints, as the sed editor attempts to process text in the data stream as quickly as possible.

The POSIX ERE engine is often found in programming languages that rely on regular expressions for text filtering. It provides advanced pattern symbols as well as special symbols for common patterns, such as matching digits, words, and alphanumeric characters. The gawk program uses the ERE engine to process its regular expression patterns.

Since there are so many different ways to implement regular expressions, it's hard to present a single, concise description of all the possible regular expressions. The following sections show the most commonly found regular expressions and demonstrate how to use them in the sed editor and gawk program.

Defining BRE Patterns

The most basic BRE pattern is matching text characters in a data stream. This section demonstrates how you can define text in the regular expression pattern and what to expect from the results.

Plain text

Chapter 16 demonstrated how to use standard text strings in the sed editor and the gawk program to filter data. Here's an example to refresh your memory:

```
$ echo "This is a test" | sed -n '/test/p'
This is a test
$ echo "This is a test" | sed -n '/trial/p'
$
$ echo "This is a test" | gawk '/test/{print $0}'
This is a test
$ echo "This is a test" | gawk '/trial/{print $0}'
$
```

The first pattern defines a single word `test`. The sed editor and gawk program scripts each use their own version of the print command to print any lines that match the regular expression pattern. Since the `echo` statement contains the word `test` in the text string, the data stream text matches the defined regular expression pattern, and the sed editor displays the line.

The second pattern again defines just a single word, this time the word `trial`. Since the `echo` statement text string doesn't contain that word, the regular expression pattern doesn't match, so neither the sed editor nor the gawk program print the line.

You probably already noticed that the regular expression doesn't care where in the data stream the pattern occurs. It also doesn't matter how many times the pattern occurs. Once the regular expression can match the pattern anywhere in the text string, it passes the string along to the Linux utility that's using it.

The key is matching the regular expression pattern to the data stream text. It's important to remember that regular expressions are extremely picky about matching patterns. The first rule to remember is that regular expression patterns are case sensitive. This means they'll only match patterns with the proper case of characters:

```
$ echo "This is a test" | sed -n '/this/p'
$
$ echo "This is a test" | sed -n '/This/p'
This is a test
$
```

The first attempt failed to match since the word `this` doesn't appear in all lower case in the text string., while the second attempt, which uses the upper-case letter in the pattern, worked just fine.

You don't have to limit yourself to whole words in the regular expression. If the defined text appears anywhere in the data stream, the regular expression will match:

```
$ echo "The books are expensive" | sed -n '/book/p'
The books are expensive
$
```

Even though the text in the data stream is `books`, the data in the stream contains the regular expression `book`, so the regular expression pattern matches the data. Of course, if you try the opposite, the regular expression will fail:

```
$ echo "The book is expensive" | sed -n '/books/p'
$
```

The complete regular expression text didn't appear in the data stream, so the match failed and the sed editor didn't display the text.

You also don't have to limit yourself to single text words in the regular expression. You can include spaces and numbers in your text string as well:

```
$ echo "This is line number 1" | sed -n '/ber 1/p'
This is line number 1
$
```

Spaces are treated just like any other character in the regular expression:

```
$ echo "This is line number1" | sed -n '/ber 1/p'
$
```

If you define a space in the regular expression, it must appear in the data stream. You can even create a regular expression pattern that matches multiple contiguous spaces:

```
$ cat data1
This is a normal line of text.
This is  a line with too many spaces.
$ sed -n '/  /p' data1
This is  a line with too many spaces.
$
```

The line with two spaces between words matches the regular expression pattern. This is a great way to catch spacing problems in text files!

Special characters

As you use text strings in your regular expression patterns, there's something you need to be aware of. There are a few exceptions when defining text characters in a regular expression. Regular expression patterns assign a special meaning to a few characters. If you try to use these characters in your text pattern, you won't get the results you were expecting.

The special characters recognized by regular expressions are:

```
.*[]^${}\+?|()
```

As the chapter progresses, you'll find out just what these special characters do in a regular expression. For now though, just remember that you can't use these characters by themselves in your text pattern.

If you want to use one of the special characters as a text character, you need to *escape* it. When you escape the special characters, you add a special character in front of it to indicate to the regular expression engine that is should interpret the next character as a normal text character. The special character that does this is the backslash character (\).

For example, if you want to search for a dollar sign in your text, just precede it with a backslash character:

```
$ cat data2
The cost is $4.00
$ sed -n '/\$/p' data2
The cost is $4.00
$
```

Since the backslash is a special character, if you need to use it in a regular expression pattern you'll need to escape it as well, producing a double backslash:

```
$ echo "\ is a special character" | sed -n '/\\/p'
\ is a special character
$
```

Finally, although the forward slash isn't a regular expression special character, if you use it in your regular expression pattern in the sed editor or the gawk program, you'll get an error:

```
$ echo "3 / 2" | sed -n '///p'
sed: -e expression #1, char 2: No previous regular expression
$
```

To use a forward slash you'll need to escape that as well:

```
$ echo "3 / 2" | sed -n '/\//p'
3 / 2
$
```

Now the sed editor can properly interpret the regular expression pattern, and all is well.

Anchor characters

As shown in the "Plain Text " section, by default, when you specify a regular expression pattern, if the pattern appears anywhere in the data stream, it will match. There are two special characters you can use to anchor a pattern to either the beginning or the end of lines in the data stream.

Starting at the beginning

The caret character (^) defines a pattern that starts at the beginning of a line of text in the data stream. If the pattern is located any place other than the start of the line of text, the regular expression pattern fails.

To use the caret character, you must place it before the pattern specified in the regular expression:

```
$ echo "The book store" | sed -n '/^book/p'
$
$ echo "Books are great" | sed -n '/^Book/p'
Books are great
$
```

The caret anchor character checks for the pattern at the beginning of each new line of data, as determined by the newline character:

```
$ cat data3
This is a test line.
this is another test line.
A line that tests this feature.
Yet more testing of this
$ sed -n '/^this/p' data3
this is another test line.
$
```

As long as the pattern appears at the start of a new line, the caret anchor will catch it.

If you position the caret character in any place other than at the beginning of the pattern, it'll act like a normal character and not as a special character:

```
$ echo "This ^ is a test" | sed -n '/s ^/p'
This ^ is a test
$
```

Since the caret character is listed last in the regular expression pattern, the sed editor uses it as a normal character to match text.

NOTE If you need to specify a regular expression pattern using only the caret character, you don't need to escape it with a backslash. However, if you specify the caret character first, followed by additional text in the pattern, you'll need to use the escape character before the caret character.

Looking for the ending

The opposite of looking for a pattern at the start of a line is looking for it at the end of a line. The dollar sign ($) special character defines the end anchor. Add this special character after a text pattern to indicate that the line of data must end with the text pattern:

```
$ echo "This is a good book" | sed -n '/book$/p'
This is a good book
$ echo "This book is good" | sed -n '/book$/p'
$
```

The problem with an ending text pattern is that you must be careful of what you're looking for:

```
$ echo "There are a lot of good books" | sed -n '/book$/p'
$
```

Making the book word plural at the end of the line means that it no longer matches the regular expression pattern, even though book is in the data stream. The text pattern must be the last thing on the line for the pattern to match.

Combining anchors

There are a couple of common situations where you can combine both the start and end anchor on the same line. In the first situation, suppose that you want to look for a line of data containing only a specific text pattern:

```
$ cat data4
this is a test of using both anchors
I said this is a test
this is a test
I'm sure this is a test.
$ sed -n '/^this is a test$/p' data4
this is a test
$
```

The sed editor ignores the lines that include other text besides the specified text.

The second situation may seem a little odd at first, but is extremely useful. By combining both anchors together in a pattern with no text, you can filter blank lines from the data stream. Look at this example:

```
$ cat data5
This is one test line.

This is another test line.
$ sed '/^$/d' data5
This is one test line.
This is another test line.
$
```

The regular expression pattern defined looks for lines that have nothing between the start and end of the line. Since blank lines contain no text between the two newline characters, they match the regular expression pattern. The sed editor uses the delete command to delete lines that match the regular expression pattern, thus removing all blank lines from the text. This is an effective way to remove blank lines from documents.

The dot character

The dot special character is used to match any single character except a newline character. The dot character must match a character though; if there's no character in the place of the dot, then the pattern will fail.

Let's take a look at a few examples of using the dot character in a regular expression pattern:

```
$ cat data6
This is a test of a line.
The cat is sleeping.
That is a very nice hat.
This test is at line four.
```

```
at ten o'clock we'll go home.
$ sed -n '/.at/p' data6
The cat is sleeping.
That is a very nice hat.
This test is at line four.
$
```

You should be able to figure out why the first line failed and why the second and third lines passed. The fourth line is a little tricky. Notice that we matched the at, but there's no character in front of it to match the dot character. Ah, but there is! In regular expressions, spaces count as characters, so the space in front of the at matches the pattern. The fifth line proves this, by putting the at in the front of the line, which fails to match the pattern.

Character classes

The dot special character is great for matching a character position against any character, but what if you want to limit what characters to match? This is called a *character class* in regular expressions.

You can define a class of characters that would match a position in a text pattern. If one of the characters from the character class is in the data stream, it matches the pattern.

To define a character class, you use square brackets. The brackets should contain any character that you want to include in the class. You then use the entire class within a pattern just like any other wildcard character. This takes a little getting used to at first, but once you catch on it can generate some pretty amazing results.

Here's an example of creating a character class:

```
$ sed -n '/[ch]at/p' data6
The cat is sleeping.
That is a very nice hat.
$
```

Using the same data file as in the dot special character example, we came up with a different result. This time we managed to filter out the line that just contained the word at. The only words that match this pattern are cat and hat. Also notice that the line that started with at didn't match as well. There must be a character in the character class that matches the appropriate position.

Character classes come in handy if you're not sure which case a character is in:

```
$ echo "Yes" | sed -n '/[Yy]es/p'
Yes
$ echo "yes" | sed -n '/[Yy]es/p'
yes
$
```

You can use more than one character class in a single expression:

```
$ echo "Yes" | sed -n '/[Yy][Ee][Ss]/p'
Yes
$ echo "yEs" | sed -n '/[Yy][Ee][Ss]/p'
yEs
$ echo "yeS" | sed -n '/[Yy][Ee][Ss]/p'
yeS
$
```

The regular expression used three character classes to cover both lower and upper cases for all three character positions.

Character classes don't have to contain just letters; you can use numbers in them as well:

```
$ cat data7
This line doesn't contain a number.
This line has 1 number on it.
This line a number 2 on it.
This line has a number 4 on it.
$ sed -n '/[0123]/p' data7
This line has 1 number on it.
This line a number 2 on it.
$
```

The regular expression pattern matches any lines that contain the numbers 0, 1, 2, or 3. Any other numbers are ignored, as are lines without numbers in them.

You can combine character classes to check for properly formatted numbers, such as phone numbers and zip codes. However, when you're trying to match a specific format, you must be careful. Here's an example of a zip code match gone wrong:

```
$ cat data8
60633
46201
223001
4353
22203
$ sed -n '
>/[0123456789][0123456789][0123456789][0123456789][0123456789]/p
>' data8
60633
46201
223001
22203
$
```

This might not have produced the result you were thinking of. It did a fine job of filtering out the number that was too short to be a zip code, as the last character class didn't have a character to match against. However, it still passed the six-digit number, even though we only defined five character classes.

Remember, the regular expression pattern can be found anywhere in the text of the data stream. There can always be additional characters besides the matching pattern characters. If you want to ensure that you only match against five numbers, you need to delineate them somehow, either with spaces, or as in this example, by showing that they're at the start and end of the line:

```
$ sed -n '
> /^[0123456789][0123456789][0123456789][0123456789][0123456789]$/p
> ' data8
60633
46201
22203
$
```

Now that's much better! Later on we'll look at how to simplify this even further.

One extremely popular use for character classes is parsing words that might be misspelled, such as data entered from a user form. You can easily create regular expressions that can accept common misspellings in data:

```
$ cat data9
I need to have some maintenence done on my car.
I'll pay that in a seperate invoice.
After I pay for the maintenance my car will be as good as new.
$ sed -n '
/maint[ea]n[ae]nce/p
/sep[ea]r[ea]te/p
' data9
I need to have some maintenence done on my car.
I'll pay that in a seperate invoice.
After I pay for the maintenance my car will be as good as new.
$
```

The two sed print commands in this example utilize regular expression character classes to help catch the misspelled words maintenance and separate in the text. The same regular expression pattern also matches the properly spelled occurrence of maintenance.

Negating character classes

In regular expression patterns, you can also reverse the effect of a character class. Instead of looking for a character contained in the class, you can look for any character that's not in the class. To do that, just place a caret character at the beginning of the character class range:

```
$ sed -n '/[^ch]at/p' data6
This test is at line two.
$
```

By negating the character class, the regular expression pattern matches any character that's neither a c nor an h, along with the text pattern. Since the space character fits this category, it passed the pattern match. However, even with the negation, the character class must still match a character, so the line with the at in the start of the line still doesn't match the pattern.

Using ranges

You may have noticed when I showed the zip code example earlier it was somewhat awkward having to list all of the possible digits in each character class. Fortunately, you can use a shortcut to prevent having to do that.

You can use a range of characters within a character class by using the dash symbol. Just specify the first character in the range, a dash, then the last character in the range. The regular expression includes any character that's within the specified character range, according to the character set used by the Linux system (see Chapter 2).

Now you can simplify the zip code example by specifying a range of digits:

```
$ sed -n '/^[0-9][0-9][0-9][0-9][0-9]$/p' data8
60633
46201
45902
$
```

That saved a lot of typing! Each character class will match any digit from 0 to 9. The pattern will fail if a letter is present anywhere in the data:

```
$ echo "a8392" | sed -n '/^[0-9][0-9][0-9][0-9][0-9]$/p'
$
$ echo "1839a" | sed -n '/^[0-9][0-9][0-9][0-9][0-9]$/p'
$
$ echo "18a92" | sed -n '/^[0-9][0-9][0-9][0-9][0-9]$/p'
$
```

The same technique also works with letters:

```
$ sed -n '/[c-h]at/p' data6
The cat is sleeping.
That is a very nice hat.
$
```

The new pattern [c-h]at matches words where the first letter is between the letter c and the letter h. In this case, the line with only the word at failed to match the pattern.

You can also specify multiple, noncontinuous ranges in a single character class:

```
$ sed -n '/[a-ch-m]at/p' data6
The cat is sleeping.
That is a very nice hat.
$
```

The character class allows the ranges a through c, and h through m to appear before the at text. This range would reject any letters between d and g:

```
$ echo "I'm getting too fat." | sed -n '/[a-ch-m]at/p'
$
```

This pattern rejected the fat text, as it wasn't in the specified range.

Special character classes

Besides defining your own character classes, the BRE contains special character classes you can use to match against specific types of characters. Table 17-1 describes the BRE special characters you can use.

You use the special character classes just as you would a normal character class in your regular expression patterns:

```
$ echo "abc" | sed -n '/[[:digit:]]/p'
$
$ echo "abc" | sed -n '/[[:alpha:]]/p'
abc
$ echo "abc123" | sed -n '/[[:digit:]]/p'
abc123
$ echo "This is, a test" | sed -n '/[[:punct:]]/p'
This is, a test
$ echo "This is a test" | sed -n '/[[:punct:]]/p'
$
```

TABLE 17-1

BRE Special Character Classes

Class	Description
[[:alpha:]]	Match any alphabetical character, either upper or lower case.
[[:alnum:]]	Match any alphanumeric character 0–9, A–Z, or a–z.
[[:blank:]]	Match a space or Tab character.
[[:digit:]]	Match a numerical digit from 0 through 9.
[[:lower:]]	Match any lower-case alphabetical character a–z.
[[:print:]]	Match any printable character.
[[:punct:]]	Match a punctuation character.
[[:space:]]	Match any whitespace character: space, Tab, NL, FF, VT, CR.
[[:upper:]]	Match any upper-case alphabetical character A–Z.

Using the special character classes is an easy way to define ranges. Instead of having to use a range [0-9], you can just use [[:digit:]].

The asterisk

Placing an asterisk after a character signifies that the character must appear zero or more times in the text to match the pattern:

```
$ echo "ik" | sed -n '/ie*k/p'
ik
$ echo "iek" | sed -n '/ie*k/p'
iek
$ echo "ieek" | sed -n '/ie*k/p'
ieek
$ echo "ieeek" | sed -n '/ie*k/p'
ieeek
$ echo "ieeeek" | sed -n '/ie*k/p'
ieeeek
$
```

This pattern symbol is commonly used for handling words that have a common misspelling or variations in language spellings. For example, if you need to write a script that may be used in either American or British English, you could write:

```
$ echo "I'm getting a color TV" | sed -n '/colou*r/p'
I'm getting a color TV
$ echo "I'm getting a colour TV" | sed -n '/colou*r/p'
I'm getting a colour TV
$
```

The u* in the pattern indicates that the letter u may or may not appear in the text to match the pattern. Similarly, if you know of a word that is commonly misspelled, you can accommodate it by using the asterisk:

```
$ echo "I ate a potatoe with my lunch." | sed -n '/potatoe*/p'
I ate a potatoe with my lunch.
$ echo "I ate a potato with my lunch." | sed -n '/potatoe*/p'
I ate a potato with my lunch.
$
```

Placing an asterisk next to the possible extra letter allows you to accept the misspelled word.

Another handy feature is combining the dot special character with the asterisk special character. This combination provides a pattern to match any number of any characters. It's often used between two text strings that may or may not appear next to each other in the data stream:

```
$ echo "this is a regular pattern expression" | sed -n '
> /regular.*expression/p'
this is a regular pattern expression
$
```

Using this pattern, you can easily search for multiple words that may appear anywhere in a line of text in the data stream.

The asterisk can also be applied to a character class. This allows you to specify a group or range of characters that can appear more than once in the text:

```
$ echo "bt" | sed -n '/b[ae]*t/p'
bt
$ echo "bat" | sed -n '/b[ae]*t/p'
bat
$ echo "bet" | sed -n '/b[ae]*t/p'
bet
$ echo "btt" | sed -n '/b[ae]*t/p'
$
$ echo "baat" | sed -n '/b[ae]*t/p'
baat
$ echo "baaeeet" | sed -n '/b[ae]*t/p'
baaeeet
$ echo "baeeaeeat" | sed -n '/b[ae]*t/p'
baeeaeeat
$ echo "baabeeet" | sed -n '/b[ae]*t/p'
$
```

As long as the a and e characters appear in any combination between the b and t characters (including not appearing at all), the pattern matches. If any other character outside of the defined character class appears, the pattern match fails.

Extended Regular Expressions

The POSIX ERE patterns include a few additional symbols that are used by some Linux applications and utilities. The gawk program recognizes the ERE patterns, but the sed editor doesn't.

CAUTION It's important to remember that there is a difference between the regular expression engines in the sed editor and the gawk program. The gawk program can use most of the extended regular expression pattern symbols, and it can provide some additional filtering capabilities that the sed editor doesn't have. However, because of this, it is often slower in processing data streams.

This section describes the more commonly found ERE pattern symbols that you can use in your gawk program scripts.

The question mark

The question mark is similar to the asterisk, but with a slight twist. The question mark indicates that the preceding character can appear zero or one time, but that's all. It doesn't match repeating occurrences of the character:

```
$ echo "bt" | gawk '/be?t/{print $0}'
bt
$ echo "bet" | gawk '/be?t/{print $0}'
bet
```

```
$ echo "beet" | gawk '/be?t/{print $0}'
$
$ echo "beeet" | gawk '/be?t/{print $0}'
$
```

If the e character doesn't appear in the text, or as long as it appears only once in the text, the pattern matches.

Just as with the asterisk, you can use the question mark symbol along with a character class:

```
$ echo "bt" | gawk '/b[ae]?t/{print $0}'
bt
$ echo "bat" | gawk '/b[ae]?t/{print $0}'
bat
$ echo "bot" | gawk '/b[ae]?t/{print $0}'
$
$ echo "bet" | gawk '/b[ae]?t/{print $0}'
bet
$ echo "baet" | gawk '/b[ae]?t/{print $0}'
$
$ echo "beat" | gawk '/b[ae]?t/{print $0}'
$
$ echo "beet" | gawk '/b[ae]?t/{print $0}'
$
```

If zero or one character from the character class appears, the pattern match passes. However, if either both characters appear, or if one of the characters appears twice, the pattern match fails.

The plus sign

The plus sign is another pattern symbol that's similar to the asterisk, but with a different twist than the question mark. The plus sign indicates that the preceding character can appear one or more times, but must be present at least once. The pattern doesn't match if the character is not present:

```
$ echo "beeet" | gawk '/be+t/{print $0}'
beeet
$ echo "beet" | gawk '/be+t/{print $0}'
beet
$ echo "bet" | gawk '/be+t/{print $0}'
bet
$ echo "bt" | gawk '/be+t/{print $0}'
$
```

If the e character is not present, the pattern match fails. The plus sign also works with character classes, the same way as the asterisk and question mark do:

```
$ echo "bt" | gawk '/b[ae]+t/{print $0}'
$
```

```
$ echo "bat" | gawk '/b[ae]+t/{print $0}'
bat
$ echo "bet" | gawk '/b[ae]+t/{print $0}'
bet
$ echo "beat" | gawk '/b[ae]+t/{print $0}'
beat
$ echo "beet" | gawk '/b[ae]+t/{print $0}'
beet
$ echo "beeat" | gawk '/b[ae]+t/{print $0}'
beeat
$
```

This time if either character defined in the character class appears, the text matches the specified pattern.

Using braces

Curly braces are available in ERE to allow you to specify a limit on a repeatable regular expression. This is often referred to as an *interval*. You can express the interval in two formats:

■ *m*: The regular expression appears exactly *m* times.

■ *m*, *n*: The regular expression appears at least *m* times, but no more than *n* times.

This feature allows you to fine-tune exactly how many times you allow a character (or character class) to appear in a pattern.

CAUTION   By default, the gawk program doesn't recognize regular expression intervals. You must specify the --re-interval command line option for the gawk program to recognize regular expression intervals.

Here's an example of using a simple interval of one value:

```
$ echo "bt" | gawk --re-interval '/be{1}t/{print $0}'
$
$ echo "bet" | gawk --re-interval '/be{1}t/{print $0}'
bet
$ echo "beet" | gawk --re-interval '/be{1}t/{print $0}'
$
```

By specifying an interval of one, you restrict the number of times the character can be present for the string to match the pattern. If the character appears more times, the pattern match fails.

There are lots of times when specifying the lower and upper limit comes in handy:

```
$ echo "bt" | gawk --re-interval '/be{1,2}t/{print $0}'
$
$ echo "bet" | gawk --re-interval '/be{1,2}t/{print $0}'
bet
```

```
$ echo "beet" | gawk --re-interval '/be{1,2}t/{print $0}'
beet
$ echo "beeet" | gawk --re-interval '/be{1,2}t/{print $0}'
$
```

In this example, the e character can appear once or twice for the pattern match to pass; otherwise, the pattern match fails.

The interval pattern match also applies to character classes:

```
$ echo "bt" | gawk --re-interval '/b[ae]{1,2}t/{print $0}'
$
$ echo "bat" | gawk --re-interval '/b[ae]{1,2}t/{print $0}'
bat
$ echo "bet" | gawk --re-interval '/b[ae]{1,2}t/{print $0}'
bet
$ echo "beat" | gawk --re-interval '/b[ae]{1,2}t/{print $0}'
beat
$ echo "beet" | gawk --re-interval '/b[ae]{1,2}t/{print $0}'
beet
$ echo "beeat" | gawk --re-interval '/b[ae]{1,2}t/{print $0}'
$
$ echo "baeet" | gawk --re-interval '/b[ae]{1,2}t/{print $0}'
$
$ echo "baeaet" | gawk --re-interval '/b[ae]{1,2}t/{print $0}'
$
```

This regular expression pattern will match if there are exactly one or two a's or e's in the text pattern, but it will fail if there are any more in any combination.

The pipe symbol

The pipe symbol allows to you to specify two or more patterns that the regular expression engine uses in a logical OR formula when examining the data stream. If any of the patterns match the data stream text, the text passes. If none of the patterns match, the data stream text fails.

The format for using the pipe symbol is:

```
expr1|expr2|...
```

Here's an example of this:

```
$ echo "The cat is asleep" | gawk '/cat|dog/{print $0}'
The cat is asleep
$ echo "The dog is asleep" | gawk '/cat|dog/{print $0}'
The dog is asleep
$ echo "The sheep is asleep" | gawk '/cat|dog/{print $0}'
$
```

This example looks for the regular expression cat or dog in the data stream. You can't place any spaces within the regular expressions and the pipe symbol, or they'll be added to the regular expression pattern.

The regular expressions on either side of the pipe symbol can use any regular expression pattern, including character classes, to define the text:

```
$ echo "He has a hat." | gawk '/[ch]at|dog/{print $0}'
He has a hat.
$
```

This example would match cat, hat, or dog in the data stream text.

Grouping expressions

Regular expression patterns can also be grouped by using parentheses. When you group a regular expression pattern, the group is treated like a standard character. You can apply a special character to the group just as you would to a regular character. For example:

```
$ echo "Sat" | gawk '/Sat(urday)?/{print $0}'
Sat
$ echo "Saturday" | gawk '/Sat(urday)?/{print $0}'
Saturday
$
```

The grouping of the day ending along with the question mark allows the pattern to match either the full day name or the abbreviated name.

It's common to use grouping along with the pipe symbol to create groups of possible pattern matches:

```
$ echo "cat" | gawk '/(c|b)a(b|t)/{print $0}'
cat
$ echo "cab" | gawk '/(c|b)a(b|t)/{print $0}'
cab
$ echo "bat" | gawk '/(c|b)a(b|t)/{print $0}'
bat
$ echo "bab" | gawk '/(c|b)a(b|t)/{print $0}'
bab
$ echo "tab" | gawk '/(c|b)a(b|t)/{print $0}'
$
$ echo "tac" | gawk '/(c|b)a(b|t)/{print $0}'
$
```

The pattern (c|b)a(b|t) matches any combination of the letters in the first group along with any combination of the letters in the second group.

Regular Expressions in Action

Now that you've seen the rules and a few simple demonstrations of using regular expression patterns, it's time to put that knowledge into action. The following sections demonstrate some common regular expression examples within shell scripts.

Counting directory files

To start things out, let's look at a shell script that counts the executable files that are present in the directories defined in your PATH environment variable. To do that, you'll need to parse out the PATH variable into separate directory names. Chapter 5 showed how to display the PATH environment variable:

```
$ echo $PATH
/usr/local/bin:/bin:/usr/bin:/usr/X11R6/bin:/usr/games:/usr/java/
j2sdk1.4.1_01/bin
$
```

Your PATH environment variable will differ, depending on where the applications are located on your Linux system. The key is to recognize that each directory in the PATH is separated by a colon. To get a listing of directories that you can use in a script, you'll have to replace each colon with a space. You now recognize that the sed editor can do just that using a simple regular expression:

```
$ echo $PATH | sed 's/:/ /g'
/usr/local/bin /bin /usr/bin /usr/X11R6/bin /usr/games /usr/java/
j2sdk1.4.1_01/bin
$
```

Once you've got the directories separated out, you can use them in a standard for statement (see Chapter 10) to iterate through each directory:

```
mypath=`echo $PATH | sed 's/:/ /g'`
for directory in $mypath
do
...
done
```

Once you have each directory, you can use the ls command to list each file in each directory, and use another for statement to iterate through each file, incrementing a counter for each file.

The final version of the script looks like this:

```
$ cat countfiles
#!/bin/bash
# count number of files in your PATH
```

```
mypath=`echo $PATH | sed 's/:/ /g'`
count=0
for directory in $mypath
do
   check=`ls $directory`
   for item in $check
   do
         count=$[ $count + 1 ]
   done
   echo "$directory - $count"
   count=0
done
$ ./countfiles
/usr/local/bin - 79
/bin - 86
/usr/bin - 1502
/usr/X11R6/bin - 175
/usr/games - 2
/usr/java/j2sdk1.4.1_01/bin - 27
$
```

Validating a phone number

The previous example showed how to incorporate the simple regular expression along with sed to replace characters in a data stream to process data. Often regular expressions are used to validate data to ensure that data is in the correct format for a script.

A common data validation application is checking phone numbers. Often data entry forms request phone numbers, and often customers fail to enter a properly formatted phone number. In the United States, there are several common ways to display a phone number:

```
(123)456-7890
(123) 456-7890
123-456-7890
123.456.7890
```

This leaves four possibilities for how customers can enter their phone number in a form. The regular expression must be robust enough to be able to handle either situation.

When building a regular expression, it's best to start on the left-hand side, and build your pattern to match the possible characters you'll run into. In this example, the first thing is that there may or may not be a left parenthesis in the phone number. This can be matched by using the pattern:

```
^\(?
```

The caret is used to indicate the beginning of the data. Since the left parenthesis is a special character, you must escape it to use it as a normal character. The question mark indicates that the left parenthesis may or may not appear in the data to match.

Next comes the three digit area code. In the United States area codes start with the number 2 (no area codes use the digits 0 or 1), and can go to 9. To match the area code, you'd use the pattern:

```
[2-9][0-9]{2}
```

This requires that the first character be a digit between 2 and 9, followed by any two digits. After the area code, the ending right parenthesis may or may not be there:

```
\)?
```

After the area code there can be a space, no space, a dash, or a dot. You can group those using a character group along with the pipe symbol:

```
( | |-|\.)
```

The very first pipe symbol appears immediately after the left parenthesis to match the no space condition. You must use the escape character for the dot; otherwise, it'll take on its special meaning of matching any character.

Next comes the three-digit phone exchange number. Nothing special required here:

```
[0-9]{3}
```

After the phone exchange number, you must match either a space, a dash, or a dot (this time you don't have to worry about matching no space, since there must be at least a space between the phone exchange number and the rest of the number):

```
( |-|\.)
```

Then to finish things off, you must match the four digit-local phone extension at the end of the string:

```
[0-9]{4}$
```

Putting the entire pattern together results in this:

```
^\(?[2-9][0-9]{2}\)?( | |-|\.)[0-9]{3}( |-|\.)[0-9]{4}$
```

You can use this regular expression pattern in the gawk program to filter out bad phone numbers. All you need to do now is create a simple script using the regular expression in a gawk program, then filter your phone list through the script. Remember, when you use regular expression intervals in the gawk program you must use the --re-interval command line option or you won't get the correct results.

Here's the script:

```
$ cat isphone
#!/bin/bash
# script to filter out bad phone numbers
gawk --re-interval '/^\(?[2-9][0-9]{2}\)?( | |-|\.)
[0-9]{3}( |-|\.)[0-9]{4}/{print $0}'
$
```

While you can't tell from this listing, the gawk command is on a single line in the shell script. You can then redirect phone numbers to the script for processing:

```
$ echo "317-555-1234" | ./isphone
317-555-1234
$ echo "000-555-1234" | ./isphone
$
```

Or you can redirect an entire file of phone numbers to filter out the invalid ones:

```
$ cat phonelist
000-000-0000
123-456-7890
212-555-1234
(317)555-1234
(202) 555-9876
33523
1234567890
234.123.4567
$ cat phonelist | ./isphone
212-555-1234
(317)555-1234
(202) 555-9876
234.123.4567
$
```

Only the valid phone numbers that match the regular expression pattern appear.

Parsing an e-mail address

In this day and age e-mail addresses have become a crucial form of communication. Trying to validate e-mail addresses has become quite a challenge for script builders, due to the myriad of ways to create an e-mail address. The basic form of an e-mail address is:

```
username@hostname
```

The *username* value can use any alphanumeric character, along with several special characters:

- Dot
- Dash
- Plus sign
- Underscore

These characters can appear in any combination in a valid e-mail userid. The *hostname* portion of the e-mail address consists of one or more domain names and a server name. The server and domain names must also follow strict naming rules, allowing only alphanumeric characters, along with the special characters:

- Dot
- Underscore

The server and domain names are each separated by a dot, with the server name specified first, any subdomain names specified next, and finally, the top-level domain name without a trailing dot.

At one time there were a fairly limited number of top-level domains, and regular expression pattern builders attempted to add them all in patterns for validation. Unfortunately, as the Internet grew so did the possible top-level domains. This technique is no longer a viable solution.

Let's start building the regular expression pattern from the left side. We know that there can be multiple valid characters in the username. This should be fairly easy:

```
^([a-zA-Z0-9_\-\.\+]+)@
```

This grouping specifies the allowable characters in the username, and the plus sign to indicate that there must be at least one character present. The next character is obviously going to be the @ symbol, no surprises there.

The hostname pattern uses the same technique to match the server name and the subdomain names:

```
([a-zA-Z0-9_\-\.]+)
```

This pattern matches the text:

```
server
server.subdomain
server.subdomain.subdomain
```

There are special rules for the top-level domain. Top-level domains are only alphabetic characters, and they must be no fewer than two characters (used in country codes) and no more than five characters in length. The regular expression pattern for the top-level domain is:

```
\.([a-zA-Z]{2,5})$
```

Putting the entire pattern together results in:

```
^([a-zA-Z0-9_\-\.\+]+)@([a-zA-Z0-9_\-\.]+)\.([a-zA-Z]{2,5})$
```

This pattern will filter out poorly formatted e-mail addresses from a data list. Now you can create your script to implement the regular expression:

```
$ echo "rich@here.now" | ./isemail
rich@here.now
$ echo "rich@here.now." | ./isemail
$
$ echo "rich@here.n" | ./isemail
$
$ echo "rich@here-now" | ./isemail
$
```

```
$ echo "rich.blum@here.now" | ./isemail
rich.blum@here.now
$ echo "rich_blum@here.now" | ./isemail
rich_blum@here.now
$ echo "rich/blum@here.now" | ./isemail
$
$ echo "rich#blum@here.now" | ./isemail
$
$ echo "rich*blum@here.now" | ./isemail
$
```

Summary

If you manipulate data files in shell scripts, you'll need to become familiar with regular expressions. Regular expressions are implemented in Linux utilities, programming languages, and applications using regular expression engines. There are a host of different regular expression engines available in the Linux world. The two most popular are the POSIX Basic Regular Expression (BRE) engine, and the POSIX Extended Regular Expression (ERE) engine. The sed editor conforms mainly to the BRE engine, while the gawk program utilizes most features found in the ERE engine.

A regular expression defines a pattern template that's used to filter text in a data stream. The pattern consists of a combination of standard text characters and special characters. The special characters are used by the regular expression engine to match a series of one or more characters, similarly to how wildcard characters work in other applications.

By combining characters and special characters, you can define a pattern to match most any type of data. You can then use the sed editor or gawk program to filter specific data from a larger data stream, or for validating data received from data entry applications.

The next chapter digs deeper into using the sed editor to perform advanced text manipulation. There are lots of advanced features available in the sed editor that make it useful for handling large data streams and filtering out just what you need.

Chapter 18

Advanced sed

Chapter 16 showed how to use the basics of the sed editor to manipulate text in data streams. The basic sed editor commands are capable of handling most of your everyday text-editing requirements. This chapter takes a look at the more advanced features that the sed editor has to offer. These are features that you might not use as often, but when you need them, it's nice to know that they're there and how to use them.

Multiline Commands

When using the basic sed editor commands you might have noticed a limitation. All of the sed editor commands perform functions on a single line of data. As the sed editor reads a data stream, it divides the data into lines based on the presence of newline characters. The sed editor processes each line of data one at a time, processing the defined script commands on a line of text, then moving on to the next line and repeating the process.

There are times when you need to perform actions on data that spans more than one line. This is especially true if you're trying to find or replace a phrase.

For example, if you're looking for the phrase *Linux System Administrators Group* in your data, it's quite possible that the phrase can be split into two lines between any of the words in the phrase. If you processed the text using a normal sed editor command, it would be impossible to detect how the phrase was split.

Fortunately, the designers behind the sed editor thought of that situation and devised a solution. The sed editor includes three special commands that you can use to process multiline text:

- N: Add the next line in the data stream to create a multiline group for processing.
- D: Delete a single line in a multiline group.
- P: Print a single line in a multiline group.

The following sections examine these multiline commands more closely and demonstrate how you can use them in your scripts.

The next commands

Before you can examine the multiline `next` command, you first need to take a look at how the single-line version of the `next` command works. Once you know what that command does, it's a lot easier to understand how the multiline version of the `next` command operates.

The single-line next command

The lower-case n command tells the sed editor to move to the next line of text in the data stream, without going back to the beginning of the commands. Remember, normally the sed editor processes all of the defined commands on a line before moving to the next line of text in the data stream. The single-line `next` command alters this flow.

This may sound somewhat complicated, and sometimes it is. Take a look at a simple example first to see just how this works:

```
$ cat data1
This is the header line.

This is a data line.

This is the last line.
$ sed '/header/{
> n
> d
> }' data1
This is the header line.
This is a data line.

This is the last line.
$
```

In this example, you have a data file that contains five lines, two of them empty. The goal is to remove the blank line after the header line but leave the blank line before the last line intact. If you write a sed script to just remove blank lines, you remove both blank lines:

```
$ sed '/^$/d' data1
This is the header line.
This is a data line.
This is the last line.
$
```

Since the line you want to remove is blank, you don't have any text you can search for to uniquely identify the line. The solution is to use the n command. The example script looks for the unique line before the blank line you want to remove, which is the header line. Once you identify that line, you use the n command to move the sed editor to the next line of text.

At that point, the sed editor continues processing the command list, which uses the d command to delete the line. When the sed editor reaches the end of the command script, it reads the next line of text from the data stream and starts processing commands from the top of the command script.

Combining lines of text

Now that you've seen the single-line next command, you can look at the multiline version. The single-line next command moves the next line of text from the data stream into the processing space (called the *pattern space*) of the sed editor. The multiline version of the next command (which uses a capital N) adds the next line of text to the text already in the pattern space.

This has the effect of combining two lines of text from the data stream into the same pattern space. The lines of text are still separated by a newline character, but the sed editor can now treat both lines of text as one line.

Here's a demonstration of how the N command operates:

```
$ cat data2
This is the header line.
This is the first data line.
This is the second data line.
This is the last line.
$ sed '/first/{
> N
> s/\n/ /
> }' data2
This is the header line.
This is the first data line. This is the second data line.
This is the last line.
$
```

The sed editor script searches for the line of text that contains the word first in it. When it finds the line, it uses the N command to combine the next line with that line. It then uses the substitution command (s) to replace the newline character with a space. The result is that the two lines in the text file appear as one line in the sed editor output.

This has a practical application if you're searching for a text phrase that may be split between two lines in the data file. Here's an example of what I mean:

```
$ cat data3
The first meeting of the Linux System
Administrator's group will be held on Tuesday.
All System Administrators should attend this meeting.
Thank you for your attendance.
$ sed 's/System Administrator/Desktop User/' data3
```

```
The first meeting of the Linux System
Administrator's group will be held on Tuesday.
All Desktop Users should attend this meeting.
Thank you for your attendance.
$
```

The substitution command is looking for the specific two-word phrase *System Administrator* in the text file. In the single line where the phrase appears, everything is fine; the substitution command can replace the text. But in the situation where the phrase is split between two lines, the substitution command doesn't recognize the matching pattern.

The N command helps solve this problem:

```
$ sed '
> N
> s/System.Administrator/Desktop User/
> ' data3
The first meeting of the Linux Desktop User's group will be held
on Tuesday.
All Desktop Users should attend this meeting.
Thank you for your attendance.
$
```

By using the N command to combine the next line with the line where the first word is found, you can detect when a line split occurs in the phrase.

Notice that the substitution command uses a wildcard pattern to match both the space and the newline situation. However, when it matched the newline character, it removed it from the string, causing the two lines to merge into one line. This may not be exactly what you want.

To solve this problem, you can use two substitution commands in the sed editor script, one to match the multiline occurrence and one to match the single-line occurrence:

```
$ sed '
> N
> s/System\nAdministrator/Desktop\nUser/
> s/System Administrator/Desktop User/
> ' data3
The first meeting of the Linux Desktop
User's group will be held on Tuesday.
All Desktop Users should attend this meeting.
Thank you for your attendance.
$
```

The first substitution command specifically looks for the newline character between the two search words and includes it in the replacement string. This allows you to add the newline character in the same place in the new text.

There's still one subtle problem with this script though. The script always reads the next line of text into the pattern space before executing the sed editor commands. When it reaches the last line of text, there isn't a next line of text to read, so the N command causes the sed editor to stop. If the matching text is on the last line in the data stream, the commands won't catch the matching data:

```
$ cat data4
The first meeting of the Linux System
Administrator's group will be held on Tuesday.
All System Administrators should attend this meeting.
$ sed '
> N
> s/System\nAdministrator/Desktop\nUser/
> s/System Administrator/Desktop User/
> ' data4
The first meeting of the Linux Desktop
User's group will be held on Tuesday.
All System Administrators should attend this meeting.
$
```

Since the *System Administrator* text appears in the last line in the data stream, the N command misses it, as there isn't another line to read into the pattern space to combine. You can easily resolve this problem by moving your single-line commands before the N command and having only the multiline commands appear after the N command, like this:

```
$ sed '
> s/System Administrator/Desktop User/
> N
> s/System\nAdministrator/Desktop\nUser/
> ' data4
The first meeting of the Linux Desktop
User's group will be held on Tuesday.
All Desktop Users should attend this meeting.
$
```

Now, the substitution command that looks for the phrase in a single line works just fine on the last line in the data stream, and the multiline substitution command covers the occurrence in the middle of the data stream.

The multiline delete command

Chapter 16 introduced the single-line delete command (d). The sed editor uses it to delete the current line in the pattern space. When working with the N command though, you must be careful when using the single-line delete command:

```
$ sed '
> N
```

```
> /System\nAdministrator/d
> ' data4
All System Administrators should attend this meeting.
$
```

The delete command looked for the words *System* and *Administrator* in separate lines and then deleted both of the lines in the pattern space. This may or may not have been what you intended.

The sed editor provides the multiline delete command (D) that only deletes the first line that is in the pattern space. It removes all characters up to and including the newline character:

```
$ sed '
> N
> /System\nAdministrator/D
> ' data3
Administrator's group will be held on Tuesday.
All System Administrators should attend this meeting.
$
```

The second line of text that's added to the pattern space by the N command remains intact. This comes in handy if you need to remove a line of text that appears before a line that you find a data string in.

Here's an example of removing a blank line that appears before the first line in a data stream:

```
$ cat data5

This is the header line.
This is a data line.

This is the last line.
$ sed '/^$/{
> N
> /header/D
> }' data5
This is the header line.
This is a data line.

This is the last line.
$
```

This sed editor script looks for blank lines and then uses the N command to add the next line of text into the pattern space. If the new pattern space contents contain the word header, the D command removes the first line in the pattern space. Without the combination of the N and D commands it would be impossible to remove the first blank line without removing all other blank lines.

The multiline print command

By now you're probably catching on to the difference between the single-line and multiline versions of the commands. The multiline print command (P) follows along using the same technique. It prints only the first line in a multiline pattern space. This includes all characters up to the newline character in the pattern space. It's used similarly to the single-line p command to display text when you use the -n option to suppress output from the script.

```
$ sed -n '
> N
> /System\nAdministrator/P
> ' data3
The first meeting of the Linux System
$
```

When the multiline match occurs, the P command prints only the first line in the pattern space.

The power of the multiline P command comes into play when you combine it with the N and D multiline commands.

The D command has a unique feature in that it forces the sed editor to return to the beginning of the script and repeat the commands on the same pattern space (it doesn't read a new line of text from the data stream). By including the N command in the command script, you can effectively single-step through the pattern space, matching multiple lines together.

Next, by using the P command, you can print the first line, and then using the D command, you can delete the first line and loop back to the beginning of the script. Once you are back at the script's beginning, the N command reads in the next line of text and starts the process all over again. This loop continues until you reach the end of the data stream.

The Hold Space

The *pattern space* is an active buffer area that holds the text examined by the sed editor while it processes commands. However, it isn't the only space available in the sed editor for storing text.

The sed editor utilizes another buffer area called the *hold space*. You can use the hold space to temporarily hold lines of text while working on other lines in the pattern space. There are five commands associated with operating with the hold space, shown in Table 18-1.

These commands let you copy text from the pattern space to the hold space. This frees up the pattern space to load another string for processing.

TABLE 18-1

The sed Editor Hold Space Commands

Command	Description
h	Copy pattern space to hold space
H	Append pattern space to hold space
g	Copy hold space to pattern space
G	Append hold space to pattern space
x	Exchange contents of pattern and hold spaces

Usually, after using the h or H commands to move a string to the hold space, eventually you want to use the g, G, or x commands to move the stored string back into the pattern space (otherwise, you wouldn't have cared about saving them in the first place).

With two buffer areas, trying to determine what line of text is in which buffer area can sometimes get confusing. Here's a short example that demonstrates using the h and g commands to move data back and forth between the sed editor buffer spaces:

```
$ cat data2
This is the header line.
This is the first data line.
This is the second data line.
This is the last line.
$ sed -n '/first/{
> h
> p
> n
> p
> g
> p
> }' data2
This is the first data line.
This is the second data line.
This is the first data line.
$
```

Take a look at this example step by step:

1. The sed script uses a regular expression in the address to filter the line containing the word first.

2. When the line containing the word first appears, the h command places the line in the hold space.

3. The p command prints the contents of the pattern space, which is still the first data line.

4. The n command retrieves the next line in the data stream and places it in the pattern space.

5. The p command prints the contents of the pattern space, which is now the second data line.

6. The g command places the contents of the hold space (the first data line) back in the pattern space, replacing the current text.

7. The p command prints the contents of the pattern space, which is now back to the first data line.

By shuffling the text lines around using the hold space, you are able to force the first data line to appear after the second data line in the output. If you just drop the first p command, you can output the two lines in reverse order:

```
$ sed -n '/first/{
> h
> n
> p
> g
> p
> }' data2
This is the second data line.
This is the first data line.
$
```

This is the start of something useful. You can use this technique to create a sed script that reverses an entire file of text lines! To do that though, you need to see the negating feature of the sed editor, which is what the next section is all about.

Negating a Command

Chapter 16 showed that the sed editor applies commands either to every text line in the data stream or to lines specifically indicated by either a single address or an address range. You can also configure a command to not apply to a specific address or address range in the data stream.

The exclamation mark command (!) is used to negate a command. What this means is that in situations where the command would normally have been activated, it isn't. Here's an example demonstrating this feature:

```
$ sed -n '/header/!p' data2
This is the first data line.
This is the second data line.
This is the last line.
$
```

The normal p command would have printed only the line in the data2 file that contained the word header. By adding the exclamation mark, all of the lines in the file printed except the one that contained the text referenced in the address.

There are several applications where using the exclamation mark comes in handy. Recall that earlier in the chapter, "The next commands" section showed a situation where a sed editor command wouldn't operate on the last line of text in the data stream because there wasn't a next line after it. You can use the exclamation point to fix that problem:

```
$ sed '{
$!N
s/System.Administrator/Desktop User/
}' data4
The first meeting of the Linux Desktop User's group will be held on
Tuesday.
All Desktop Users should attend this meeting.
$
```

This example shows the exclamation mark used with the N command, along with the dollar sign special address. The dollar sign represents the last line of text in the data stream, so when the sed editor reaches the last line, it doesn't execute the N command. For all other lines though, it does execute the command.

This is the technique you can use to reverse the order of text lines in a data stream. To reverse the order of the lines as they appear in the text stream (display the last line first and the first line last), you need to do some fancy footwork using the hold space.

The pattern you'll need to work with goes like this:

1. Place a line in the hold space.
2. Put the next line of text in the pattern space.
3. Append the hold space to the pattern space.
4. Place the pattern space into the hold space.
5. Repeat steps 2 through 4 until you've put all of the lines in reverse order in the hold space.
6. Retrieve the lines and print them.

Figure 18-1 diagrams what this looks like.

When using this technique, you do not want to print lines as they are processed. This means using the -n command line option for sed. The next thing to determine is how to append the hold space text to the pattern space text. This is done by using the G command. The only problem is that you don't want to append the hold space to the first line of text processed. This is easily solved by using the exclamation mark command:

```
1!G
```

FIGURE 18-1

Reversing the order of a text file using the hold space

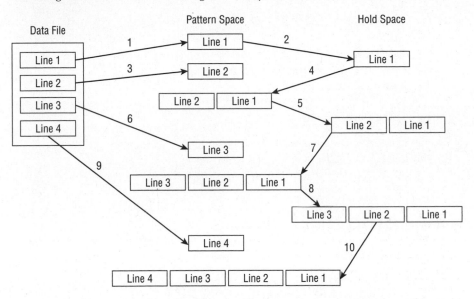

The next step is to place the new pattern space (the text line with the appended reverse lines) into the hold space. This is simple enough; just use the h command.

When you've got the entire data stream in the pattern space in reverse order, all you need to do is print the results. You know you've got the entire data stream in the pattern space when you've reached the last line in the data stream. To print the results, just use the command:

```
$p
```

Those are the pieces you need to create your line-reversing sed editor script. Now try it out in a test run:

```
$ cat data2
This is the header line.
This is the first data line.
This is the second data line.
This is the last line.
$ sed -n '{
1!G
h
$p
}' data2
```

483

```
This is the last line.
This is the second data line.
This is the first data line.
This is the header line.
$
```

The sed editor script performed as expected. The output from the script reverses the original lines in the text file. This demonstrates the power of using the hold space in your sed scripts. It provides an easy way to manipulate the order of lines in the script output.

> **NOTE** In case you're wondering, there's a Linux command that can perform the function of reversing a text file. The `tac` command displays a text file in reverse order. You probably noticed the clever name of the command, since it performs the reverse function of the `cat` command.

Changing the Flow

Normally, the sed editor processes commands starting at the top and proceeding toward the end of the script (the exception is the D command, which forces the sed editor to return to the top of the script without reading a new line of text). The sed editor provides a method for altering the flow of the command script, producing a result similar to that of a structured programming environment.

Branching

In the previous section, you saw how the exclamation mark command is used to negate the effect of a command on a line of text. The sed editor provides a way to negate an entire section of commands, based on an address, an address pattern, or an address range. This allows you to perform a group of commands only on a specific subset within the data stream.

The format of the branch command is:

```
[address]b [label]
```

The *address* parameter determines which line or lines of data trigger the branch command. The *label* parameter defines the location to branch to. If the *label* parameter is not present, the branch command proceeds to the end of the script.

```
$ sed '{
> 2,3b
> s/This is/Is this/
> s/line./test?/
> }' data2
Is this the header test?
This is the first data line.
```

```
This is the second data line.
Is this the last test?
$
```

The branch command skips the two substitution commands for the second and third lines in the data stream.

Instead of going to the end of the script you can define a label for the branch command to jump to. Labels start with a colon and can be up to seven characters in length:

```
:label2
```

To specify the label, just add it after the b command. Using labels allows you to skip commands that match the branch address but still process other commands in the script:

```
$ sed '{
> /first/b jump1
> s/ is/ might be/
> s/line/test/
> :jump1
> s/data/text/
> }' data2
This might be the header test.
This is the first text line.
This might be the second text test.
This might be the last test.
$
```

The branch command specifies that the program should jump to the script line labeled jump1 if the matching text first appears in the line. If the branch command pattern doesn't match, the sed editor continues processing commands in the script, including the command after the branch label. (Thus, all three substitution commands are processed on lines that don't match the branch pattern).

If a line matches the branch pattern, the sed editor branches to the branch label line. Thus, only the last substitution command is executed.

The example shows branching to a label further down in the sed script. You can also branch to a label that appears earlier in the script, thus creating a looping effect:

```
$ echo "This, is, a, test, to, remove, commas." | sed -n '{
> :start
> s/,//1p
> b start
> }'
This is, a, test, to, remove, commas.
This is a, test, to, remove, commas.
This is a test, to, remove, commas.
This is a test to, remove, commas.
```

485

```
This is a test to remove, commas.
This is a test to remove commas.
```

Each iteration of the script removes the first occurrence of a comma from the text string and prints the string. There's one catch to this script: it never ends. This situation creates an endless loop, searching for commas until you manually stop it by sending a signal with the Ctrl-C key combination.

To prevent this problem, you should specify an address pattern for the branch command to look for. If the pattern isn't present, the branching should stop:

```
$ echo "This, is, a, test, to, remove, commas." | sed -n '{
:start
s/,//1p
/,/b start
}'
This is, a, test, to, remove, commas.
This is a, test, to, remove, commas.
This is a test, to, remove, commas.
This is a test to, remove, commas.
This is a test to remove, commas.
This is a test to remove commas.
$
```

Now the branch command branches only if there's a comma in the line. After the last comma has been removed, the branch command won't execute, allowing the script to properly finish.

Testing

Similarly to the branch command, the test command (t) is also used to modify the flow of the sed editor script. Instead of jumping to a label based on an address, the test command jumps to a label based on the outcome of a substitution command.

If the substitution command successfully matches and substitutes a pattern, the test command branches to the specified label. If the substitution command doesn't match the specified pattern, the test command doesn't branch.

The test command uses the same format as the branch command:

```
[address]t [label]
```

Just like the branch command, if you don't specify a label sed branches to the end of the script if the test succeeds.

The test command provides a cheap way to perform a basic if-then statement on the text in the data stream. For example, if you don't need to make a substitution if another substitution was made, the test command can help:

```
$ sed '{
> s/first/starting/
> t
> s/line/test/
```

```
> }' data2
This is the header test.
This is the starting data line.
This is the second data test.
This is the last test.
$
```

The first substitution command looks for the pattern text first. If it matches the pattern in the line, it replaces the text, and the test command jumps over the subsequent substitution command. If the first substitution command doesn't match the pattern, the second substitution command is processed.

Using the test command, you can clean up the loop you tried using the branch command:

```
$ echo "This, is, a, test, to, remove, commas." | sed -n '{
:start
s/,//1p
t start
}'
This is, a, test, to, remove, commas.
This is a, test, to, remove, commas.
This is a test, to, remove, commas.
This is a test to, remove, commas.
This is a test to remove, commas.
This is a test to remove commas.
$
```

When there are no more substitutions to make, the test command doesn't branch and continues with the rest of the script.

Pattern Replacement

You've seen how to use patterns in the sed commands to replace text in the data stream. However, the problem is that sometimes when using wildcard characters it's not easy to know exactly what text will match the pattern.

For example, say that you want to place double quotation marks around a word you match in a line. That's simple enough if you're just looking for one word in the pattern to match:

```
$ echo "The cat sleeps in his hat." | sed 's/cat/"cat"/'
The "cat" sleeps in his hat.
$
```

But what if you use a wildcard character in the pattern to match more than one word:

```
$ echo "The cat sleeps in his hat." | sed 's/.at/".at"/g'
The ".at" sleeps in his ".at".
$
```

Well, that didn't work. The substitution string used the dot wildcard character to match any occurrence of a letter followed by at. Unfortunately, the replacement string doesn't match the wildcard character value of the matching word.

The ampersand

The sed editor has a solution for you. The ampersand symbol (&) is used to represent the matching pattern in the substitution command. Whatever text matches the pattern defined, you can use the ampersand symbol to recall it in the replacement pattern. This lets you manipulate whatever word matches the pattern defined:

```
$ echo "The cat sleeps in his hat." | sed 's/.at/"&"/g'
The "cat" sleeps in his "hat".
$
```

When the pattern matches cat, cat appears in the substituted word. When it matched hat, hat appears in the substituted word.

Replacing individual words

The ampersand symbol retrieves the entire string that matches the pattern you specify in the substitution command. There are times when you'll only want to retrieve a subset of the string. You can do that, too, but it's a little tricky.

The sed editor uses parentheses to define a substring component within the substitution pattern. You can then reference each substring component using a special character in the replacement pattern. The replacement character consists of a backslash and a number. The number indicates the position of the substring component. The sed editor assigns the first component the character \1, the second component the character \2, and so on.

> **CAUTION**   When you use parentheses in the substitution command, you must use the escape character to identify them as grouping characters and not normal parentheses. This is backwards from when you escape other special characters.

Take a look at an example of using this feature in a sed editor script:

```
$ echo "The System Administrator manual" | sed '
> s/\(System\) Administrator/\1 User/'
The System User manual
$
```

This substitution command uses one set of parentheses around the word System, identifying it as a substring component. It then uses the \1 in the replacement pattern to recall the first identified component. This wasn't too exciting, but it can really be useful when working with wildcard patterns.

If you need to replace a phrase with just a single word, that's a substring of the phrase, but that substring just happens to be using a wildcard character; using substring components is a lifesaver:

```
$ echo "That furry cat is pretty" | sed 's/furry \(.at\)/\1/'
That cat is pretty
$ echo "That furry hat is pretty" | sed 's/furry \(.at\)/\1/'
That hat is pretty
$
```

In this situation, you can't use the ampersand symbol, as it would replace the entire matching pattern. The substring component provides the answer, allowing you to select just which part of the pattern to use as the replacement pattern.

This feature can be especially helpful when you need to insert text between two or more substring components. Here's a script that uses substring components to insert a comma in long numbers:

```
$ echo "1234567" | sed '{
> :start
> s/\(.*[0-9]\)\([0-9]\{3\}\)/\1,\2/
> t start
> }'
1,234,567
$
```

The script divides the matching pattern into two components:

```
.*[0-9]
[0-9]{3}
```

This pattern looks for two substrings. The first substring is any number of characters, ending in a digit. The second substring is a series of three digits (see Chapter 17 for information about how to use braces in a regular expression). If this pattern is found in the text, the replacement text puts a comma between the two components, each identified by its component position. The script uses the test command to iterate through the number until all commas have been placed.

Using sed in Scripts

Now that you've seen the various parts of the sed editor, it's time to put them together and use them in your shell scripts. This section demonstrates some of the features that you should know about when using the sed editor in your bash shell scripts.

Using wrappers

You may have noticed that trying to implement a sed editor script can be cumbersome, especially if the script is long. Instead of having to retype the entire script each time you want to use it, you can place the sed editor command in a shell script *wrapper*. The wrapper acts as a go-between with the sed editor script and the command line.

Once inside the shell script, you can use normal shell variables and parameters with your sed editor scripts. Here's an example of using the command line parameter variable as the input to a sed script:

```
$ cat reverse
#!/bin/bash
# shell wrapper for sed editor script to reverse lines

sed -n '{
1!G
h
$p
}' "$1"
$
```

The shell script called `reverse` uses the sed editor script to reverse text lines in a data stream. It uses the $1 shell parameter to retrieve the first parameter from the command line, which should be the name of the file to reverse:

```
$ ./reverse data2
This is the last line.
This is the second data line.
This is the first data line.
This is the header line.
$
```

Now you can easily use the sed editor script on any file, without having to constantly retype the entire command line.

Redirecting sed output

By default the sed editor outputs the results of the script to STDOUT. You can employ all of the standard methods of redirecting the output of the sed editor in your shell scripts.

You can use backticks to redirect the output of your sed editor command to a variable for use later on in the script. Here's an example of using the sed script to add commas to the result of a numeric computation:

```
$ cat fact
#!/bin/bash
#add commas to numbers in factorial answer

factorial=1
counter=1
number=$1

while [ $counter -le $number ]
do
```

```
        factorial=$[ $factorial * $counter ]
        counter=$[ $counter + 1 ]
done

result=`echo $factorial | sed '{
:start
s/\(.*[0-9]\)\([0-9]\{3\}\)/\1,\2/
t start
}'`

echo "The result is $result"
$ ./fact 20
The result is 2,432,902,008,176,640,000
$
```

After you use the normal factorial calculation script, the result of that script is used as the input to the sed editor script, which adds commas. This value is then used in the echo statement to produce the result.

Creating sed Utilities

As you've seen in the short examples presented so far in this chapter, there are lots of cool data-formatting things you can do with the sed editor. This section shows a few handy well-known sed editor scripts for performing common data-handling functions.

Double spacing lines

To start things off, take a look at a simple sed script to insert a blank line between lines in a text file:

```
$ sed 'G' data2
This is the header line.

This is the first data line.

This is the second data line.

This is the last line.

$
```

That was pretty simple! The key to this trick is the default value of the hold space. Remember, the G command simply appends the contents of the hold space to the current pattern space contents. When you start the sed editor, the hold space contains an empty line. By appending that to an existing line, you create a blank line after the existing line.

You may have noticed that this script also adds a blank line to the last line in the data stream, producing a blank line at the end of the file. If you want to get rid of this, you can use the negate symbol and the last line symbol to ensure that the script doesn't add the blank line to the last line of the data stream:

```
$ sed '$!G' data2
This is the header line.

This is the first data line.

This is the second data line.

This is the last line.
$
```

Now that looks a little better. As long as the line isn't the last line, the G command appends the contents of the hold space. When the sed editor gets to the last line, it skips the G command.

Double spacing files that may have blanks

To take double spacing one step further, what if the text file already has a few blank lines, but you want to double space all of the lines? If you use the previous script, you'll get some areas that have too many blank lines, as each existing blank line gets doubled:

```
$ cat data6
This is line one.
This is line two.

This is line three.
This is line four.
$ sed '$!G' data6
This is line one.

This is line two.



This is line three.

This is line four.
$
```

Now you have three blank lines where the original blank line was located. The solution to this problem is to first delete any blank lines from the data stream and then use the G command to insert new blank lines after all of the lines. To delete existing blank lines, you just need to use the d command with a pattern that matches a blank line:

```
/^$/d
```

This pattern uses the start line tag (the caret) and the end line tag (the dollar sign). Adding this to the script produces the desired results:

```
$ sed '/^$/d;$!G' data6
This is line one.

This is line two.

This is line three.

This is line four.
$
```

Perfect!

Numbering lines in a file

Chapter 16 showed how to use the equal sign to display the line numbers of lines in the data stream:

```
$ sed '=' data2
1
This is the header line.
2
This is the first data line.
3
This is the second data line.
4
This is the last line.
$
```

This can be a little awkward to read, as the line number is on a line above the actual line in the data stream. A better solution would be to place the line number on the same line as the text.

Now that you've seen how to combine lines using the N command, it shouldn't be too hard to utilize that information in the sed editor script. The trick to this utility though is that you can't combine the two commands in the same script.

Once you have the output for the equal sign command, you can pipe the output to another sed editor script that uses the N command to combine the two lines. You also need to use the substitution command to replace the newline character with either a space or a tab character. Here's what the final solution looks like:

```
$ sed '=' data2 | sed 'N; s/\n/ /'
1 This is the header line.
2 This is the first data line.
3 This is the second data line.
4 This is the last line.
$
```

Now that looks much better. This is a great little utility to have around when working on programs where you need to see the line numbers used in error messages.

Printing last lines

So far you've seen how to use the p command to print all of the lines in a data stream or just lines that match a specific pattern. What if you just need to work with the last few lines of a long listing, such as a log file?

The dollar sign represents the last line of a data stream, so it's easy to display just the last line:

```
$ sed -n '$p' data2
This is the last line.
$
```

Now how can you use the dollar sign symbol to display a set number of lines at the end of the data stream? The answer is to create a *rolling window*.

A rolling window is a common way to examine blocks of text lines in the pattern space by combining them using the N command. The N command appends the next line of text to the text already in the pattern space. Once you have a block of 10 text lines in the pattern space, you can check if you're at the end of the data stream using the dollar sign. If you're not at the end, continue adding more lines to the pattern space, but removing the original lines (remember the D command, which deletes the first line in the pattern space).

By looping through the N and D commands, you add new lines to the block of lines in the pattern space, while removing old lines. The branch command is the perfect fit for the loop. To end the loop, just identify the last line and use the q command to quit.

Here's what the final sed editor script looks like:

```
$ sed '{
> :start
> $q
> N
> 11,$D
> b start
> }' /etc/passwd
mysql:x:415:416:MySQL server:/var/lib/mysql:/bin/bash
rich:x:501:501:Rich:/home/rich:/bin/bash
katie:x:502:506:Katie:/home/katie:/bin/bash
jessica:x:503:507:Jessica:/home/jessica:/bin/bash
testy:x:504:504:Test account:/home/testy:/bin/csh
barbara:x:416:417:Barbara:/home/barbara/:/bin/bash
ian:x:505:508:Ian:/home/ian:/bin/bash
emma:x:506:509:Emma:/home/emma:/bin/bash
bryce:x:507:510:Bryce:/home/bryce:/bin/bash
test:x:508:511::/home/test:/bin/bash
$
```

The script first checks if the line is the last line in the data stream. If it is, the quit command stops the loop. The N command appends the next line to the current line in the pattern space. The 11,$D command deletes the first line in the pattern space if the current line is after line 10. This creates the sliding window effect in the pattern space.

Deleting lines

Another useful utility for the sed editor is removing unwanted blank lines in a data stream. It's easy to remove all the blank lines from a data stream, but it takes a little ingenuity to selectively remove blank lines. This section shows a couple of quick sed editor scripts that you can use to help remove unwanted blank lines from your data.

Deleting consecutive blank lines

One nuisance is when extra blank lines crop up in data files. Often you have a data file that contains blank lines, but sometimes a data line is missing and produces too many blank lines (as you saw in the double spacing example earlier).

The easiest way to remove consecutive blank lines is to check the data stream using a range address. Chapter 16 showed how to use ranges in addresses, including how to incorporate patterns in the address range. The sed editor executes the command for all lines that match within the specified address range.

The key to removing consecutive blank lines is creating an address range that includes a non-blank line and a blank line. If the sed editor comes across this range, it shouldn't delete the line. However, for lines that don't match that range (two or more blank lines in a row), it should delete the lines.

Here's the script to do this:

```
/./,/^$/!d
```

The range is `/./` to `/^$/`. The start address in the range matches any line that contains at least one character. The end address in the range matches a blank line. Lines within this range aren't deleted.

Here's the script in action:

```
$ cat data6
This is the first line.


This is the second line.

This is the third line.



This is the fourth line.
$ sed '/./,/^$/!d' data6
This is the first line.
```

```
This is the second line.

This is the third line.

This is the fourth line.
$
```

No matter how many blank lines appear between lines of data in the file, the output only places one blank line between the lines.

Deleting leading blank lines

Another nuisance is data files containing multiple blank lines at the start of the file. Often when trying to import data from a text file into a database, the blank lines create null entries, throwing off any calculations using the data.

Removing blank lines from the top of a data stream is not too difficult of a task. Here's the script that accomplishes that function:

```
/./,$!d
```

The script uses an address range to determine what lines are deleted. The range starts with a line that contains a character and continues to the end of the data stream. Any line within this range is not deleted from the output. This means that any lines before the first line that contain a character are deleted.

Take a look at this simple script in action:

```
$ cat data7


This is the first line.

This is the second line.
$ sed '/./,$!d' data7
This is the first line.

This is the second line.
$
```

The test file contains two blank lines before the data lines. The script successfully removes both of the leading blank lines, while keeping the blank line within the data intact.

Deleting trailing blank lines

Unfortunately, deleting trailing blank lines is not as simple as deleting leading blank lines. Just like printing the end of a data stream, deleting blank lines at the end of a data stream requires a little ingenuity and looping.

Before I start the discussion, let me show you what the script looks like:

```
sed '{
:start
/^\n*$/{$d; N; b start }
}'
```

This may look a little odd to you at first. Notice that there are braces within the normal script braces. This allows you to group commands together within the overall command script. The group of commands applies to the specified address pattern. The address pattern matches any line that contains only a newline character. When one is found, if it's the last line, the delete command deletes it. If it's not the last line, the N command appends the next line to it, and the branch command loops to the beginning to start over.

Here's the script in action:

```
$ cat data8
This is the first line.
This is the second line.



$ sed '{
:start
/^\n*$/{$d ; N; b start }
}' data8
This is the first line.
This is the second line.
$
```

The script successfully removed the blank lines from the end of the text file.

Removing HTML tags

In this day and age it's not uncommon to download text from a Web site to save or use as data in an application. Sometimes, though, when you download text from the Web site, you also get the HTML tags used to format the data. This can be a problem when all you want to see is the data.

A standard HTML Web page contains several different types of HTML tags, identifying formatting features required to properly display the page information. Here's a sample of what an HTML file looks like:

```
$ cat data9
<html>
<head>
<title>This is the page title</title>
</head>
<body>
<p>
This is the <b>first</b> line in the Web page. This should provide
some <i>useful</i> information for us to use in our shell script.
</body>
</html>
$
```

HTML tags are identified by the less-than and greater-than symbols. Most HTML tags come in pairs. One tag starts the formatting process (for example, <b> for bolding), and another tag stops the formatting process (for example, </b> to turn off bolding).

Removing HTML tags creates a problem though if you're not careful. At first glance, you'd think that the way to remove HTML tags would be to just look for text that starts with the less-than symbol and ends with a greater-than symbol, with any data in between:

```
s/<.*>//g
```

Unfortunately, this command has some unintended consequences:

```
$ sed 's/<.*>//g' data9




This is the  line in the Web page. This should provide
some  information for us to use in our shell script.


$
```

Notice that the title text is missing, along with the text that was bolded and italicized. The sed editor literally interpreted the script to mean any text between the less-than and greater-than sign, including other less-than and greater-than signs! Every place where text was enclosed in HTML tags (such as <b>first</b>), the sed script removed the entire text.

The solution to this problem is to have the sed editor ignore any embedded greater-than signs between the original tags. To do that, you can create a character class that negates the greater-than sign. This changes the script to:

```
s/<[^>]*>//g
```

This script now works properly, displaying the data you need to see from the Web page HTML code:

```
$ sed 's/<[^>]*>//g' data9


This is the page title



This is the first line in the Web page. This should provide
some useful information for us to use in our shell script.


$
```

That's a little better. To clean things up some, you can add a delete command to get rid of those pesky blank lines:

```
$ sed 's/<[^>]*>//g;/^$/d' data9
This is the page title
This is the first line in the Web page. This should provide
some useful information for us to use in our shell script.
$
```

Now that's much more compact; there's only the data you need to see.

Summary

The sed editor provides some advanced features that allow you to work with text patterns across multiple lines. This chapter showed how to use the next command to retrieve the next line in a data stream and place it in the pattern space. Once in the pattern space you can perform complex substitution commands to replace phrases that span more than one line of text.

The multiline delete command allows you to remove the first line when the pattern space contains two or more lines. This is a convenient way to iterate through multiple lines in the data stream. Similarly, the multiline print command allows you to print just the first line when the pattern space contains two or more lines of text. The combination of the multiline commands allows you to iterate through the data stream and create a multiline substitution system.

Next, the chapter discussed the hold space. The hold space allows you to set aside a line of text while processing more lines of text. You can recall the contents of the hold space at any time and either replace the text in the pattern space or append the contents of the hold space to the text in the pattern space. Using the hold space allows you to sort through data streams, reversing the order of text lines as they appear in the data.

The chapter also discussed the sed editor flow control commands. The branch command provides a way for you to alter the normal flow of sed editor commands in the script, creating loops or skipping commands under certain conditions. The test command provides an if-then type of statement for your sed editor command scripts. The test command branches only if a prior substitution command succeeds in replacing text in a line.

The chapter finished by discussing how to use sed scripts in your shell scripts. A common technique for large sed scripts is to place the script in a shell wrapper. You can use command line parameter variables within the sed script to pass shell command line values. This creates an easy way to utilize your sed editor scripts directly from the command line, or even from other shell scripts.

The next chapter digs deeper into the gawk world. The gawk program supports many features of higher-level programming languages. You can create some pretty involved data manipulation and reporting programs just by using gawk. This chapter will describe the various programming features and demonstrate how to use them to generate your own fancy reports from simple data.

Chapter 19

Advanced gawk

C hapter 16 introduced the gawk program and demonstrated the basics of using it to produce formatted reports from raw data files. This chapter dives more deeply into customizing gawk to produce reports. The gawk program is a full-fledged programming language, providing features that allow you to write advanced programs to manipulate data. In this chapter, you'll see how to use the gawk programming language to write programs to handle just about any data formatting task you'll run into.

IN THIS CHAPTER

Reexamining gawk

Use variables in gawk

Structured commands

Format your printing

Functions

Using Variables

One important feature of any programming language is the ability to store and recall values using variables. The gawk programming language supports two different types of variables:

■ Built-in variables
■ User-defined variables

There are several built-in variables available for you to use in gawk. The built-in variables contain information used in handling the data fields and records in the data file. You can also create your own variables in your gawk programs. The following sections walk you through how to use variables in your gawk programs.

Built-in variables

The gawk program uses built-in variables to reference specific features within the program data. This section describes the built-in variables available for you to use in your gawk programs and demonstrates how to use them.

The field and record separator variables

Chapter 16 demonstrated one type of built-in variable available in gawk, the *data field variables*. The data field variables allow you to reference individual data fields within a data record using a dollar sign and the numerical position of the data field in the record. Thus, to reference the first data field in the record, you use the $1 variable. To reference the second data field, you use the $2 variable, and so on.

Data fields are delineated by a field separator character. By default the field separator character is a whitespace character, such as a space or a tab. Chapter 16 showed how to change the field separator character either on the command line by using the -F command line parameter or within the gawk program by using the special FS built-in variable.

The FS built-in variable belongs to a group of built-in variables that control how gawk handles fields and records in both input data and output data. Table 19-1 lists the built-in variables contained in this group.

The FS and OFS variables define how your gawk program handles data fields in the data stream. You've already seen how to use the FS variable to define what character separates data fields in a record. The OFS variable performs the same function but for the output by using the print command.

By default, gawk sets the OFS variable to a space, so when you use the command:

```
print $1,$2,$3
```

TABLE 19-1

The gawk Data Field and Record Variables

Variable	Description
FIELDWIDTHS	A space separated list of numbers defining the exact width (in spaces) of each data field.
FS	Input field separator character.
RS	Input record separator character.
OFS	Output field separator character.
ORS	Output record separator character.

you'll see the output as:

```
field1 field2 field3
```

You can see this in the following example:

```
$ cat data1
data11,data12,data13,data14,data15
data21,data22,data23,data24,data25
data31,data32,data33,data34,data35
$ gawk 'BEGIN{FS=","} {print $1,$2,$3}' data1
data11 data12 data13
data21 data22 data23
data31 data32 data33
$
```

The print command automatically places the value of the OFS variable between each data field in the output. By setting the OFS variable, you can use any string to separate data fields in the output:

```
$ gawk 'BEGIN{FS=","; OFS="-"} {print $1,$2,$3}' data1
data11-data12-data13
data21-data22-data23
data31-data32-data33
$ gawk 'BEGIN{FS=","; OFS="--"} {print $1,$2,$3}' data1
data11--data12--data13
data21--data22--data23
data31--data32--data33
$ gawk 'BEGIN{FS=","; OFS="<-->"} {print $1,$2,$3}' data1
data11<-->data12<-->data13
data21<-->data22<-->data23
data31<-->data32<-->data33
$
```

The FIELDWIDTHS variable allows you to read records without using a field separator character. In some applications, instead of using a field separator character, data is placed in specific columns within the record. In these instances, you must set the FIELDWIDTHS variable to the match the layout of the data in the records.

Once you set the FIELDWIDTHS variable, gawk ignores the FS and calculates data fields based on the provided field width sizes. Here's an example using field widths instead of field separator characters:

```
$ cat data1b
1005.3247596.37
115-2.349194.00
05810.1298100.1
$ gawk 'BEGIN{FIELDWIDTHS="3 5 2 5"}{print $1,$2,$3,$4}' data1b
100 5.324 75 96.37
```

```
115 -2.34 91 94.00
058 10.12 98 100.1
$
```

The FIELDWIDTHS variable defines four data fields, and gawk parses the data record accordingly. The string of numbers in each record is split based on the defined field width values.

> **CAUTION** It's important to remember that once you set the FIELDWIDTHS variable, those values must remain constant. This method can't accommodate variable-length data fields.

The RS and ORS variables define how your gawk program handles records in the data stream. By default, gawk sets the RS and ORS variables to the newline character. The default RS variable value indicates that each new line of text in the input data stream is a new record.

Sometimes you run into situations where data fields are spread across multiple lines in the data stream. A classic example of this is data that includes an address and phone number, each on a separate line:

```
Riley Mullen
123 Main Street
Chicago, IL 60601
(312)555-1234
```

If you try to read this data using the default FS and RS variable values, gawk will read each line as a separate record, and interpret each space in the record as a field separator. This isn't what you intended.

To solve this problem, you need to set the FS variable to the newline character. This indicates that each line in the data stream is a separate field and all of the data on a line belongs to the data field. However, now you have the problem of not knowing where a new record starts.

To solve this problem, set the RS variable to an empty string, then leave a blank line between data records in the data stream. The gawk program will interpret each blank line as a record separator.

Here's an example of using this technique:

```
$ cat data2
Riley Mullen
123 Main Street
Chicago, IL  60601
(312)555-1234

Frank Williams
456 Oak Street
Indianapolis, IN  46201
(317)555-9876

Haley Snell
4231 Elm Street
```

```
Detroit, MI 48201
(313)555-4938
$ gawk 'BEGIN{FS="\n"; RS=""} {print $1,$4}' data2
Riley Mullen (312)555-1234
Frank Williams (317)555-9876
Haley Snell (313)555-4938
$
```

Perfect, the gawk program interpreted each line in the file as a data field and the blank lines as record separators.

Data variables

Besides the field and record separator variables, gawk provides some other built-in variables to help you know what's going on with your data and extract information from the shell environment. Table 19-2 shows the other built-in variables in gawk.

TABLE 19-2

More gawk Built-in Variables

Variable	Description
ARGC	The number of command line parameters present.
ARGIND	The index in ARGV of the current file being processed.
ARGV	An array of command line parameters.
CONVFMT	The conversion format for numbers (see the printf statement). The default value is %.6g.
ENVIRON	An associative array of the current shell environment variables and their values.
ERRNO	The system error if an error occurs when reading or closing input files.
FILENAME	The file name of the data file used for input to the gawk program.
FNR	The current record number in the data file.
IGNORECASE	If set to a non-zero value, ignore the case of characters in strings used in the gawk command.
NF	The total number of data fields in the data file.
NR	The number of input records processed.
OFMT	The output format for displaying numbers. The default is %.6g.
RLENGTH	The length of the substring matched in the match function.
RSTART	The start index of the substring matched in the match function.

You should recognize a few of these variables from your shell script programming. The ARGC and ARGV variables allow you to retrieve the number of command line parameters and their values from the shell. This can be a little tricky though, as gawk doesn't count the program script as part of the command line parameters:

```
$ gawk 'BEGIN{print ARGC,ARGV[1]}' data1
2 data1
$
```

The ARGC variable indicates that there are two parameters on the command line. This includes the gawk command and the data1 parameter (remember, the program script doesn't count as a parameter). The ARGV array starts with an index of 0, which represents the command. The first array value is the first command line parameter after the gawk command.

> **NOTE**   Note that unlike shell variables, when you reference a gawk variable in the script, you don't add a dollar sign before the variable name.

The ENVIRON variable may seem a little odd to you. It uses an *associative array* to retrieve shell environment variables. An associative array uses text for the array index values instead of numeric values.

The text in the array index is the shell environment variable. The value of the array is the value of the shell environment variable. Here's an example of this:

```
$ gawk '
> BEGIN{
> print ENVIRON["HOME"]
> print ENVIRON["PATH"]
> }'
/home/rich
/usr/local/bin:/bin:/usr/bin:/usr/X11R6/bin
$
```

The ENVIRON["HOME"] variable retrieves the HOME environment variable value from the shell. Likewise, the ENVIRON["PATH"] variable retrieves the PATH environment variable value. You can use this technique to retrieve any environment variable value from the shell to use in your gawk programs.

The FNR, NF, and NR variables come in handy when you're trying to keep track of data fields and records in your gawk program. Sometimes you're in a situation where you don't know exactly how many data fields are in a record. The NF variable allows you to specify the last data field in the record without having to know its position:

```
$ gawk 'BEGIN{FS=":"; OFS=":"} {print $1,$NF}' /etc/passwd
rich:/bin/bash
testy:/bin/csh
mark:/bin/bash
dan:/bin/bash
```

```
mike:/bin/bash
test:/bin/bash
$
```

The NF variable contains the numerical value of the last data field in the data file. You can then use it as a data field variable by placing a dollar sign in front of it.

The FNR and NR variables are similar to each other, but slightly different. The FNR variable contains the number of records processed in the current data file. The NR variable contains the total number of records processed. Let's look at a couple of examples to see this difference:

```
$ gawk 'BEGIN{FS=","}{print $1,"FNR="FNR}' data1 data1
data11 FNR=1
data21 FNR=2
data31 FNR=3
data11 FNR=1
data21 FNR=2
data31 FNR=3
$
```

In this example, the gawk program command line defines two input files. (It specifies the same input file twice.) The script prints the first data field value and the current value of the FNR variable. Notice that the FNR value reset back to 1 when the gawk program processed the second data file.

Now, let's add the NR variable and see what that produces:

```
$ gawk '
> BEGIN {FS=","}
> {print $1,"FNR="FNR,"NR="NR}
> END{print "There were",NR,"records processed"}' data1 data1
data11 FNR=1 NR=1
data21 FNR=2 NR=2
data31 FNR=3 NR=3
data11 FNR=1 NR=4
data21 FNR=2 NR=5
data31 FNR=3 NR=6
There were 6 records processed
$
```

The FNR variable value reset when gawk processed the second data file, but the NR variable maintained its count into the second data file. The bottom line is that if you're only using one data file for input the FNR and NR values will be the same. If you're using multiple data files for input, the FNR value will reset for each data file, and the NR value will keep count throughout all the data files.

NOTE You'll notice when using gawk that often the gawk script can become larger than the rest of your shell script. In the examples in this chapter, for simplicity I just run the gawk scripts directly from the command line, using the multiline feature of the shell. When you use gawk in a shell script, you should place different gawk commands on separate lines. This'll make it much easier to read and follow, rather than trying to cram it all onto one line in the shell script.

User-defined variables

Just like any other self-respecting programming language, gawk allows you to define your own variables for use within the program code. A gawk user-defined variable name can be any number of letters, digits, and underscores, but it can't begin with a digit. It's also important to remember that gawk variable names are case sensitive.

Assigning variables in scripts

Assigning values to variables in gawk programs is similar to doing so in a shell script, using an *assignment statement*:

```
$ gawk '
> BEGIN{
> testing="This is a test"
> print testing
> }'
This is a test
$
```

The output of the print statement is the current value of the testing variable. Like shell script variables, gawk variables can hold either numeric or text values:

```
$ gawk '
> BEGIN{
> testing="This is a test"
> print testing
> testing=45
> print testing
> }'
This is a test
45
$
```

In this example, the value of the testing variable is changed from a text value to a numeric value.

Assignment statements can also include mathematical algorithms to handle numeric values:

```
$ gawk 'BEGIN{x=4; x= x * 2 + 3; print x}'
11
$
```

As you can see from this example, the gawk programming language includes the standard mathematical operators for processing numerical values. These can include the remainder symbol (%) and the exponentiation symbol (using either ∧ or **).

Assigning variables in the command line

You can also use the gawk command line to assign values to variables for the gawk program. This allows you to set values outside of the normal code, changing values on the fly. Here's an example of using a command line variable to display a specific data field in the file:

```
$ cat script1
BEGIN{FS=","}
{print $n}
$ gawk -f script1 n=2 data1
data12
data22
data32
$ gawk -f script1 n=3 data1
data13
data23
data33
$
```

This feature allows you to change the behavior of the script without having to change the actual script code. The first example displays the second data field in the file, while the second example displays the third data field, just by setting the value of the n variable in the command line.

There's one problem with using command line parameters to define variable values. When you set the variable, the value isn't available in the BEGIN section of the code:

```
$ cat script2
BEGIN{print "The starting value is",n; FS=","}
{print $n}
$ gawk -f script2 n=3 data1
The starting value is
data13
data23
data33
$
```

You can solve this using the -v command line parameter. This allows you to specify variables that are set before the BEGIN section of code. The -v command line parameter must be placed before the script code in the command line:

```
$ gawk -v n=3 -f script2 data1
The starting value is 3
data13
data23
data33
$
```

Now the n variable contains the value set in the command line during the BEGIN section of code.

Working with Arrays

Many programming languages provide arrays for storing multiple values in a single variable. The gawk programming language provides this using *associative arrays*.

Associative arrays are different from numerical arrays in that the index value can be any text string. You don't have to use sequential numbers to identify data elements contained in the array. Instead, an associative array consists of a hodge-podge of strings referencing values. Each index string must be unique and uniquely identifies the data element that's assigned to it.

The following sections walk you through using associative array variables in your gawk programs.

Defining array variables

You can define an array variable using a standard assignment statement. The format of the array variable assignment is:

```
var[index] = element
```

where *var* is the variable name, *index* is the associative array index value, and *element* is the data element value. Here are some examples of array variables in gawk:

```
capital["Illinois"] = "Springfield"
capital["Indiana"] = "Indianapolis"
capital["Ohio"] = "Columbus"
```

When you reference an array variable, you must include the index value to retrieve the appropriate data element value:

```
$ gawk 'BEGIN{
> capital["Illinois"] = "Springfield"
> print capital["Illinois"]
> }'
Springfield
$
```

When you reference the array variable, the data element value appears. This also works with numeric data element values:

```
$ gawk 'BEGIN{
> var[1] = 34
> var[2] = 3
> total = var[1] + var[2]
> print total
> }'
37
$
```

As you can see from this example, you can use array variables just as you would any other variable in the gawk program.

Iterating through array variables

The problem with associative array variables is that you might not have any way of knowing what the index values are. Unlike numeric arrays, which use sequential numbers for index values, an associative array index can be anything.

If you need to iterate through an associate array in gawk, you can use a special format of the `for` statement:

```
for (var in array)
{
    statements
}
```

The `for` statement loops through the statements, each time assigning the variable *var* the next index value from the *array* associative array. It's important to remember that the variable is the value of the index and not the data element value. You can easily extract the data element value by using the variable as the array index:

```
$ gawk 'BEGIN{
> var["a"] = 1
> var["g"] = 2
> var["m"] = 3
> var["u"] = 4
> for (test in var)
> {
>     print "Index:",test," - Value:",var[test]
> }
> }'
Index: u  - Value: 4
Index: m  - Value: 3
Index: a  - Value: 1
Index: g  - Value: 2
$
```

Notice that the index values aren't returned in any particular order, but they each reference the appropriate data element value. This is somewhat important to know, as you can't count on the returned values being in the same order, just that the index and data values match.

Deleting array variables

Removing an array index from an associative array requires a special command:

```
delete array[index]
```

The `delete` command removes the associative index value and the associated data element value from the array:

```
$ gawk 'BEGIN{
> var["a"] = 1
> var["g"] = 2
```

```
> for (test in var)
> {
>    print "Index:",test," - Value:",var[test]
> }
> delete var["g"]
> print "---"
> for (test in var)
>    print "Index:",test," - Value:",var[test]
> }'
Index: a  - Value: 1
Index: g  - Value: 2
---
Index: a  - Value: 1
$
```

Once you delete an index value from the associative array, you can't retrieve it.

Using Patterns

The gawk program supports several types of matching patterns to filter data records, similar to how the sed editor does. Chapter 16 already showed two special patterns in action. The BEGIN and END keywords are special patterns that execute statements before or after the data stream data has been read. Similarly, you can create other patterns to execute statements when matching data appears in the data stream.

This section demonstrates how to use matching patterns in your gawk scripts to limit what records a program script applies to.

Regular expressions

Chapter 17 showed how to use regular expressions as matching patterns. You can use either a Basic Regular Expression (BRE) or an Extended Regular Expression (ERE) to filter which lines in the data stream the program script applies to.

When using a regular expression, the regular expression must appear before the left brace of the program script that it controls:

```
$ gawk 'BEGIN{FS=","} /11/{print $1}' data1
data11
$
```

The regular expression /11/ matches records that contain the string 11 anywhere in the data fields. The gawk program matches the defined regular expression against all the data fields in the record, including the field separator character:

```
$ gawk 'BEGIN{FS=","} /,d/{print $1}' data1
data11
```

```
data21
data31
$
```

This example matches the comma used as the field separator in the regular expression. This is not always a good thing. It can lead to problems trying to match data specific to one data field that may also appear in another data field. If you need to match a regular expression to a specific data instance, you should use the matching operator.

The matching operator

The *matching operator* allows you to restrict a regular expression to a specific data field in the records. The matching operator is the tilde symbol (~). You specify the matching operator, along with the data field variable, and the regular expression to match:

```
$1 ~ /^data/
```

The $1 variable represents the first data field in the record. This expression filters records where the first data field starts with the text data. Here's an example of using it in a gawk program script:

```
$ gawk 'BEGIN{FS=","} $2 ~ /^data2/{print $0}' data1
data21,data22,data23,data24,data25
$
```

The matching operator compares the second data field with the regular expression /&data2/, which indicates the string starts with the text data2.

This is a powerful tool that is commonly used in gawk program scripts to search for specific data elements in a data file:

```
$ gawk -F: '$1 ~ /rich/{print $1,$NF}' /etc/passwd
rich /bin/bash
$
```

This example searches the first data field for the text rich. When it finds the pattern in a record, it prints the first and last data field values of the record.

You can also negate the regular expression match by using the ! symbol:

```
$1 !~ /expression/
```

If the regular expression isn't found in the record, the program script is applied to the record data:

```
$ gawk 'BEGIN{FS=","} $2 !~ /^data2/{print $1}' data1
data11
data31
$
```

In this example the gawk program script prints the first data field of records where the second data field doesn't start with the text data2.

Mathematical expressions

Besides regular expressions you can also use mathematical expressions in the matching pattern. This feature comes in handy when matching numerical values in data fields. For example, if you want to display all of the system users who belong to the root users group (group number 0), you could use this script:

```
$ gawk -F: '$4 == 0{print $1}' /etc/passwd
root
sync
shutdown
halt
operator
$
```

The script checks for records where the fourth data field contains the value 0. On my Linux system there are five user accounts that belong to the root user group.

You can use any of the normal mathematical comparison expressions:

- x == y: Value x is equal to y.
- x <= y: Value x is less than or equal to y.
- x < y: Value x is less than y.
- x >= y: Value x is greater than or equal to y.
- x > y: Value x is greater than y.

You can also use expressions with text data, but you must be careful. Unlike regular expressions, expressions are an exact match. The data must match exactly with the pattern:

```
$ gawk -F, '$1 == "data"{print $1}' data1
$
$ gawk -F, '$1 == "data11"{print $1}' data1
data11
$
```

The first test doesn't match any records as the first data field value isn't data in any of the records. The second test matches one record with the value data11.

Structured Commands

The gawk programming language supports the usual cast of structured programming commands. This section describes each of these commands and demonstrates how to use them within a gawk programming environment.

The if statement

The gawk programming language supports the standard if-then-else format of the if statement. You must define a condition for the if statement to evaluate, enclosed in parentheses. If the condition evaluates to a TRUE condition, the statement immediately following the if statement is executed. If the condition evaluates to a FALSE condition, the statement is skipped. This can use the format:

```
if (condition)
    statement1
```

or you can place it on one line, like this:

```
if (condition) statement1
```

Here's a simple example demonstrating this format:

```
$ cat data4
10
5
13
50
34
$ gawk '{if ($1 > 20) print $1}' data4
50
34
$
```

Not too complicated. If you need to execute multiple statements in the if statement, you must enclose them with braces:

```
$ gawk '{
> if ($1 > 20)
> {
>    x = $1 * 2
>    print x
> }
> }' data4
100
68
$
```

Be careful that you don't confuse the if statement braces with the braces used to start and stop the program script. The gawk program can detect missing braces and will produce an error message if you mess up:

```
$ gawk '{
> if ($1 > 20)
> {
>    x = $1 * 2
>    print x
> }' data4
gawk: cmd. line:7: (END OF FILE)
gawk: cmd. line:7: parse error
$
```

The gawk if statement also supports the else clause, allowing you to execute one or more statements if the if statement condition fails. Here's an example of using the else clause:

```
$ gawk '{
> if ($1 > 20)
> {
>    x = $1 * 2
>    print x
> } else
> {
>    x = $1 / 2
>    print x
> }}' data4
5
2.5
6.5
100
68
$
```

You can use the else clause on a single line, but you must use a semicolon after the if statement section:

```
if (condition) statement1; else statement2
```

Here's the same example using the single line format:

```
$ gawk '{if ($1 > 20) print $1 * 2; else print $1 / 2}' data4
5
2.5
6.5
100
68
$
```

This format is more compact but can be harder to follow.

The while statement

The while statement provides a basic looping feature for gawk programs. The format of the while statement is:

```
while (condition)
{
   statements
}
```

The `while` loop allows you to iterate over a set of data, checking a condition that stops the iteration. This is useful if you have multiple data values in each record that you must use in calculations:

```
$ cat data5
130 120 135
160 113 140
145 170 215
$ gawk '{
> total = 0
> i = 1
> while (i < 4)
> {
>    total += $i
>    i++
> }
> avg = total / 3
> print "Average:",avg
> }' data5
Average: 128.333
Average: 137.667
Average: 176.667
$
```

The `while` statement iterates through the data fields in the record, adding each value to the `total` variable, then incrementing the counter variable, `i`. When the counter value is equal to 4, the `while` condition becomes `FALSE`, and the loop terminates, dropping through to the next statement in the script. That statement calculates the average; then the average is printed. This process is repeated for each record in the data file.

The gawk programming language supports using the `break` and `continue` statements in while loops, allowing you to jump out of the middle of the loop:

```
$ gawk '{
> total = 0
> i = 1
> while (i < 4)
> {
>    total += $i
>    if (i == 2)
>        break
>    i++
> }
> avg = total / 2
> print "The average of the first two data elements is:",avg
> }' data5
```

```
The average of the first two data elements is: 125
The average of the first two data elements is: 136.5
The average of the first two data elements is: 157.5
$
```

The `break` statement is used to break out of the while loop if the value of the i variable is 2.

The do-while statement

The `do-while` statement is similar to the `while` statement but performs the statements before checking the condition statement. The format for the `do-while` statement is:

```
do
{
   statements
} while (condition)
```

This format guarantees that the statements are executed at least one time before the condition is evaluated. This comes in handy when you need to perform statements before evaluating the condition:

```
$ gawk '{
> total = 0
> i = 1
> do
> {
>    total += $i
>    i++
> } while (total < 150)
> print total }' data5
250
160
315
$
```

The script reads the data fields from each record and totals them until the cumulative value reaches 150. If the first data field is over 150 (as seen in the second record), the script is guaranteed to read at least the first data field before evaluating the condition.

The for statement

The `for` statement is a common method using in many programming languages for looping. The gawk programming language supports the C-style of `for` loops:

```
for( variable assignment; condition; iteration process)
```

This helps simplify the loop by combining several functions in one statement:

```
$ gawk '{
> total = 0
```

```
> for (i = 1; i < 4; i++)
> {
>    total += $i
> }
> avg = total / 3
> print "Average:",avg
> }' data5
Average: 128.333
Average: 137.667
Average: 176.667
$
```

By defining the iteration counter in the `for` loop, you don't have to worry about incrementing it yourself like you did when using the `while` statement.

Formatted Printing

You may have noticed that the `print` statement doesn't exactly give you much control over how gawk displays your data. About all you can do is control the output field separator character (`OFS`). If you're creating detailed reports, often you'll need to place data in a specific format and location.

The solution is to use the formatted printing command, called `printf`. If you're familiar with C programming, the `printf` command in gawk performs the same way, allowing you to specify detailed instructions on how to display data.

The format of the `printf` command is:

```
printf "format string", var1, var2...
```

The *format string* is the key to the formatted output. It specifies exactly how the formatted output should appear, using both text elements and *format specifiers*. A format specifier is a special code that indicates what type of variable is displayed and how to display it. The gawk program uses each format specifier as a placeholder for each variable listed in the command. The first format specifier matches the first variable listed, the second matches the second variable, and so on.

The format specifiers use the format:

```
%[modifier]control-letter
```

where *control-letter* is a one character code that indicates what type of data value will be displayed, and *modifier* defines an optional formatting feature.

Table 19-3 lists the control-letters that can be used in the format specifier.

TABLE 19-3

Format Specifier Control Letters

Control Letter	Description
c	Displays a number as an ASCII character.
d	Displays an integer value.
i	Displays an integer value (same as d).
e	Displays a number in scientific notation.
f	Displays a floating point value.
g	Displays either scientific notation or floating point, whichever is shorter.
o	Displays an octal value.
s	Displays a text string.
x	Displays a hexadecimal value.
X	Displays a hexadecimal value, but using capital letters for A through F.

Thus, if you need to display a string variable, you'd use the format specifier %s. If you need to display an integer variable, you'd use either %d or %i (%d is the C-style for decimals). If you want to display a large value using scientific notation, you'd use the %e format specifier:

```
$ gawk 'BEGIN{
> x = 10 * 100
> printf "The answer is: %e\n", x
> }'
The answer is: 1.000000e+03
$
```

In addition to the control-letters, there are three modifiers that you can use for even more control over your output:

- width: A numeric value that specifies the minimum width of the output field. If the output is shorter, printf pads the space with spaces, using right-justification for the text. If the output is longer than the specified width, it overrides the width value.

- prec: A numeric value that specifies the number of digits to the right of the decimal place in floating-point numbers, or the maximum number of characters displayed in a text string.

- – (minus sign): The minus sign indicates that left-justification should be used instead of right-justification when placing data in the formatted space.

When using the printf statement, you have complete control over how your output appears. For example, in the "Built-in variables" section, we used the print command to display data fields from our records:

```
$ gawk 'BEGIN{FS="\n"; RS=""} {print $1,$4}' data2
Riley Mullen (312)555-1234
Frank Williams (317)555-9876
Haley Snell (313)555-4938
$
```

You can use the printf command to help format the output so it looks better. First, let's just convert the print command to a printf command and see what that does:

```
$ gawk 'BEGIN{FS="\n"; RS=""} {printf "%s %s\n", $1, $4}' data 2
Riley Mullen  (312)555-1234
Frank Williams  (317)555-9876
Haley Snell  (313)555-4938
$
```

That produces the same output as the print command. The printf command uses the %s format specifier as a placeholder for the two string values.

Notice that you have to manually add the newline character at the end of the printf command to force a new line. Without it, the printf command will continue to use the same line on subsequent prints.

This is useful if you need to print multiple things on the same line, but using separate printf commands:

```
$ gawk 'BEGIN{FS=","} {printf "%s ", $1} END{printf "\n"}' data1
data11 data21 data31
$
```

Each of the printf outputs appears on the same line. To be able to terminate the line, the END section prints a single newline character.

Next, let's use a modifier to format the first string value:

```
$ gawk 'BEGIN{FS="\n"; RS=""} {printf "%16s  %s\n", $1, $4}' data2
    Riley Mullen  (312)555-1234
  Frank Williams  (317)555-9876
     Haley Snell  (313)555-4938
$
```

By adding the 16 modifier value, we force the output for the first string to use 16 spaces. By default, the printf command uses right-justification to place the data in the format space. To make it left-justified, just add a minus sign to the modifier:

```
$ gawk 'BEGIN{FS="\n"; RS=""} {printf "%-16s  %s\n", $1, $4}' data2
Riley Mullen      (312)555-1234
```

```
      Frank Williams    (317)555-9876
      Haley Snell       (313)555-4938
      $
```

Now that looks pretty professional!

The `printf` command also comes in handy when dealing with floating point values. By specifying a format for the variable, you can make the output look more uniform:

```
$ gawk '{
> total = 0
> for (i = 1; i < 4; i++)
> {
>    total += $i
> }
> avg = total / 3
> printf "Average: %5.1f\n",avg
> }' data5
Average: 128.3
Average: 137.7
Average: 176.7
$
```

By using the `%5.1f` format specifier, you can force the `printf` command to round the floating point values to a single decimal place.

Built-in Functions

The gawk programming language provides quite a few built-in functions that perform common mathematical, string, and even time functions. You can utilize these functions in your gawk programs to help cut down on the coding requirements in your scripts. This section walks you through the different built-in functions available in gawk.

Mathematical functions

If you've done programming in any type of language, you're probably familiar with using built-in functions in your code to perform common mathematical functions. The gawk programming language doesn't disappoint those looking for advanced mathematical features.

Table 19-4 shows the mathematical built-in functions available in gawk.

While it does not have an extensive list of mathematical functions, gawk does provide some of the basic elements you need for standard mathematical processing. The `int()` function produces the integer portion of a value, but it doesn't round the value. It behaves much like a floor function found in other programming languages. It produces the nearest integer to a value between the value and 0.

TABLE 19-4

The gawk Mathematical Functions

Function	Description
atan2(x, y)	The arctangent of x / y, with x and y specified in radians.
cos(x)	The cosine of x, with x specified in radians.
exp(x)	The exponential of x.
int(x)	The integer part of x, truncated toward 0.
log(x)	The natural logarithm of x.
rand()	A random floating point value larger than 0 and less than 1.
sin(x)	The sine of x, with x specified in radians.
sqrt(x)	The square root of x.
srand(x)	Specify a seed value for calculating random numbers.

This means that the int() function of the value 5.6 will return 5, while the int() function of the value −5.6 will return −5.

The rand() function is great for creating random numbers, but you'll need to use a trick to get meaningful values. The rand() function returns a random number, but only between the values 0 and 1 (not including 0 or 1). To get a larger number, you'll need to scale the returned value.

A common method for producing larger integer random numbers is to create an algorithm that uses the rand() function, along with the int() function:

```
x = int(10 * rand())
```

This returns a random integer value between (and including) 0 and 9. Just substitute the 10 in the equation with the upper limit value for your application, and you're ready to go.

Be careful when using some of the mathematical functions, as the gawk programming language does have a limited range of numeric values it can work with. If you go over that range, you'll get an error message:

```
$ gawk 'BEGIN{x=exp(100); print x}'
2.68812e+43
$ gawk 'BEGIN{x=exp(1000); print x}'
gawk: cmd. line:1: warning: exp argument 1000 is out of range
inf
$
```

The first example calculates the exponential of 100, which is a very large number but within the range of the system. The second example attempts to calculate the exponential of 1000, which goes over the numerical range limit of the system and produces an error message.

Besides the standard mathematical functions, gawk also provides a few functions for bitwise manipulating of data:

- and($v1$, $v2$): Performs a bitwise AND of values $v1$ and $v2$.
- compl(val): Performs the bitwise complement of val.
- lshift(val, count): Shifts the value val count number of bits left.
- or($v1$, $v2$): Performs a bitwise OR of values $v1$ and $v2$.
- rshift(val, count): Shifts the value val count number of bits right.
- xor($v1$, $v2$): Performs a bitwise XOR of values $v1$ and $v2$.
- The bit manipulation functions are useful when working with binary values in your data.

String functions

The gawk programming language also provides several functions you can use to manipulate string values, shown in Table 19-5.

Some of the string functions are fairly self-explanatory:

```
$ gawk 'BEGIN{x = "testing"; print toupper(x); print length(x) }'
TESTING
7
$
```

However, some of the string functions can get pretty complicated. The asort and asorti functions are new gawk functions that allow you to sort an array variable based on either the data element values (asort) or the index values (asorti). Here's an example of using asort:

```
$ gawk 'BEGIN{
> var["a"] = 1
> var["g"] = 2
> var["m"] = 3
> var["u"] = 4
> asort(var, test)
> for (i in test)
>     print "Index:",i," - value:",test[i]
> }'
Index: 4  - value: 4
Index: 1  - value: 1
Index: 2  - value: 2
Index: 3  - value: 3
$
```

TABLE 19-5

The gawk String Functions

Function	Description
asort(s [,d])	Sort an array s based on the data element values. The index values are replaced with sequential numbers indicating the new sort order. Alternatively, the new sorted array is stored in array d if specified.
asorti(s [,d])	Sort an array s based on the index values. The resulting array contains the index values as the data element values, with sequential number indexes indicating the sort order. Alternatively, the new sorted array is stored in array d if specified.
gensub(r, s, h [, t])	Search either the variable $0, or the target string t if supplied, for matches of the regular expression r. If h is a string beginning with either g or G, replaces the matching text with s. If h is a number, it represents which occurrence of r to replace.
gsub(r, s [,t])	Search either the variable $0, or the target string t if supplied, for matches of the regular expression r. If found, substitute the string s globally.
index(s, t)	Returns the index of the string t in string s, or 0 if not found.
length([s])	Returns the length of string s, or if not specified, the length of $0.
match(s, r [,a])	Returns the index of the string s where the regular expression r occurs. If array a is specified, it contains the portion of s that matches the regular expression.
split(s, a [,r])	Splits s into array a using either the FS character, or the regular expression r if supplied. Returns the number of fields.
sprintf(format, variables)	Returns a string similar to the output of printf using the format and variables supplied.
sub(r, s [,t])	Search either the variable $0, or the target string t, for matches of the regular expression r. If found, substitutes the string s for the first occurrence.
substr(s, i [,n])	Returns the nth character substring of s, starting at index i. If n is not supplied, the rest of s is used.
tolower(s)	Converts all characters in s to lower case.
toupper(s)	Converts all characters in s to upper case.

The new array, test, contains the newly sorted data elements of the original array, but the index values are now changed to numerical values, indicating the proper sort order.

The split() function is a great way to push data fields into an array for further processing:

```
$ gawk 'BEGIN{ FS=","}{
> split($0, var)
> print var[1], var[5]
> }' data1
data11 data15
data21 data25
data31 data35
$
```

The new array uses sequential numbers for the array index, starting with index value 1 containing the first data field.

Time functions

The gawk programming language contains a few functions to help you deal with time values, shown in Table 19-6.

The time functions are often used when working with log files that contain dates that you need to compare. By converting the text representation of a date to the epoch time (the number of seconds since January 1, 1970) you can easily compare dates.

Here's an example of using the time functions in a gawk program:

```
$ gawk 'BEGIN{
> date = systime()
> day = strftime("%A, %B %d, %Y", date)
> print day
> }'
Friday, December 28, 2007
$
```

TABLE 19-6

The gawk Time Functions

Function	Description
mktime(datespec)	Converts a date specified in the format YYYY MM DD HH MM SS [DST] into a timestamp value.
strftime(format [, timestamp])	Formats either the current time of day timestamp, or timestamp if provided, into a formatted day and date, using the date() shell function format.
systime()	Returns the timestamp for the current time of day.

This example uses the systime() function to retrieve the current epoch timestamp from the system, then uses the strftime() function to convert it into a human-readable format using the date shell command's date format characters.

User-Defined Functions

You're not limited to just using the built-in functions available in gawk. You can create your own functions for use in your gawk programs. This section shows how to define and use your own functions in your gawk programs.

Defining a function

To define you own function, you must use the function keyword:

```
function name([variables])
{
    statements
}
```

The function name must uniquely identify your function. You can pass one or more variables into the function from the calling gawk program:

```
function printthird()
{
    print $3
}
```

This function will print the third data field in the record.

The function can also return a value using the return statement:

```
return value
```

The value can be a variable, or an equation that evaluates to a value:

```
function myrand(limit)
{
    return int(limit * rand())
}
```

You can assign the value returned from the function to a variable in the gawk program:

```
x = myrand(100)
```

The variable will contain the value returned from the function.

Using your functions

When you define a function, it must appear by itself before you define any programming sections (including the BEGIN section). This may look a little odd at first, but it helps keep the function code separate from the rest of the gawk program:

```
$ gawk '
> function myprint()
> {
>     printf "%-16s - %s\n", $1, $4
> }
> BEGIN{FS="\n"; RS=""}
> {
>     myprint()
> }' data2
Riley Mullen      - (312)555-1234
Frank Williams    - (317)555-9876
Haley Snell       - (313)555-4938
$
```

The function defines the myprint() function, which formats the first and fourth data fields in the record for printing. The gawk program then uses the function to display the data from the data file.

Once you define a function, you can use it as often as necessary in the program section of the code. This saves lots of work when using long algorithms.

Creating a function library

Obviously, having to rewrite your gawk functions every time you need them is not all that pleasant of an experience. However, gawk provides a way for you to combine your functions into a single library file that you can use in all of your gawk programming.

First, you need to create a file that contains all of your gawk functions:

```
$ cat funclib
function myprint()
{
    printf "%-16s - %s\n", $1, $4
}

function myrand(limit)
{
    return int(limit * rand())
}

function printthird()
{
```

```
        print $3
    }
$
```

The `funclib` file contains three function definitions. To use them, you need to use the `-f` command line parameter. Unfortunately, you can't combine the `-f` command line parameter with an in-line gawk script, but you can use multiple -f parameters on the same command line.

Thus, to use your library, just create a file that contains your gawk program, and specify both the library file and your program file on the command line:

```
$ cat script4
BEGIN{ FS="\n"; RS=""}
{
     myprint()
}
[rich@test2 ch19]$ gawk -f funclib -f script4 data2
Riley Mullen        - (312)555-1234
Frank Williams      - (317)555-9876
Haley Snell         - (313)555-4938
$
```

Now all you need to do is add the `funclib` file to your gawk command line whenever you need to use a function defined in the library.

Summary

This chapter walked you through the more advanced features of the gawk programming language. Every programming language requires using variables, and gawk is no different. The gawk programming language includes some built-in variables that you can use to reference specific data field values and retrieve information about the number of data fields and records processed in the data file. You can also create your own variables for use in your scripts.

The gawk programming language also provides many of the standard structured commands you'd expect from a programming language. You can easily create fancy programs using `if-then` logic, `while`, and `do-while` loops, and `for` loops. Each of these commands allows you to alter the flow of your gawk program script to iterate through data field values to create detailed data reports.

The `printf` command is a great tool to have if you need to customize your report output. It allows you to specify the exact format for displaying data from the gawk program script. You can easily create formatted reports, placing data elements in exactly the correct position.

Finally, this chapter discussed the many built-in functions available in the gawk programming language, as well as showing how to create your own functions. The gawk program contains many useful functions for handling mathematical features, such as standard square roots and logarithms, as well as trigonometric functions. There are also several string-related functions that make extracting substrings from larger strings a breeze.

You aren't limited to the built-in functions in the gawk program. If you're working on an application that uses lots of specialized algorithms, you can create your own functions to process the algorithms, then use those functions in your own code. You can also set up a library file containing all of the functions you use in your gawk programs, saving you time and effort in all of your coding.

The next section of the book switches gears a little. It examines a few other shell environments you may run into in your Linux shell-scripting endeavors. While the bash shell is the most common shell used in Linux, it's not the only shell. It helps to know a little about some of the other shells available and how they differ from the bash shell.

Part IV

Alternative Linux Shells

Chapter 20

The ash Shell

N ow that you've seen the standard Linux bash shell, and what you can do with it, it's time to examine a few other shells available in the Linux world. The ash shell is a low-budget shell that offers basic features with a small footprint. This is perfect for low-memory applications, such as embedded Linux systems. This chapter describes the ash shell environment and shows you what you'll need to know to work with your scripts in an ash shell environment.

What Is the ash Shell?

The first trick to understanding the ash shell is figuring out what version of it you're using. The ash shell started out life as a simple copy of the original Bourne shell available on Unix systems (see Chapter 1). Kenneth Almquist created a small-scale version of the Bourne shell for Unix systems and called it the Almquist shell, which was then shortened to *ash*. This original version of the ash shell was extremely small, making it fast, but without many advanced features, such as command line editing or history features, making it difficult to use as an interactive shell.

The NetBSD Unix operating system adopted the ash shell and still uses it today as the default shell. The NetBSD developers customized the ash shell by adding several new features, making it closer to the Bourne shell. The new features include command line editing using both emacs and vi editor commands, as well as a history command to recall previously entered commands. This version of the ash shell is also used by the FreeBSD operating system as the default login shell.

533

The Debian Linux distribution created its own version of the ash shell (called Debian ash, or *dash*) for inclusion in its version of Linux. For the most part, dash copies the features of the NetBSD version of the ash shell, providing the advanced command line editing capabilities.

However, to help add to the shell confusion, the dash shell is actually not the default shell in many Debian-based Linux distributions. Due to the popularity of the bash shell in Linux, most Debian-based Linux distributions use the bash shell as the normal login shell, and only use the dash shell as a quick-start shell for the installation script to install the distribution files.

The exception is the popular Ubuntu distribution. This often confuses shell script programmers and causes a great number of problems with running shell scripts in a Linux environment. The Ubuntu Linux distribution uses the bash shell as the default interactive shell, but uses the dash shell as the default /bin/sh shell. This "feature" really confuses shell script programmers.

As you saw in Chapter 8, every shell script must start with a line that declares the shell used for the script. In our bash shell scripts, we've been using:

```
#!/bin/bash
```

This tells the shell to use the shell program located at /bin/bash to execute the script. In the Unix world, the default shell was always /bin/sh. Many shell script programmers familiar with the Unix environment copy this into their Linux shell scripts:

```
#!/bin/sh
```

On most Linux distributions, the /bin/sh file is a symbolic link (see Chapter 3) to the /bin/bash shell program. This allows you to easily port shell scripts designed for the Unix Bourne shell to the Linux environment without having to modify them.

Unfortunately, the Ubuntu Linux distribution links the /bin/sh file to the /bin/dash shell program. Since the dash shell only contains a subset of the commands available in the original Bourne shell, this can (and often does) cause some shell scripts to not work properly.

The remainder of this chapter walks you through the different versions of the ash shell you may run into in your Linux shell scripting travels, and shows you some tips on what to watch out for if you need to run your shell scripts in an ash or dash shell.

The Original ash Shell

Before looking at the newer, more advanced ash and dash shells, it's a good idea to understand what the original ash shell looked like. Even though you may not run into it in desktop or server Linux distributions, it still lives on today in some embedded Linux distributions, so it's good to know the limitations of the shell.

The Original ash command line parameters

The original ash shell uses command line parameters to control the behavior of the shell. Table 20-1 lists the command line parameters available in the original ash shell.

TABLE 20-1

The Original ash Shell Command Line Parameters

Parameter	Description
-c	Execute the specified shell command from the command line.
-e	Exit when a command terminates with a non-zero exit status.
-f	Disable filename generation.
-I	Ignore end-of-file characters.
-i	Force an interactive shell.
-j	Enable Berkeley job control (the default if using the -i parameter).
-n	Read commands but don't execute them.
-s	Read commands from STDIN.
-x	Display each command before executing it.
-z	Filename generation may generate zero files.

You can specify the command line parameters in any order, either individually, or together after a single dash.

The -e command line option allows you to force the ash shell to exit immediately if a command produces an error. This is a handy feature when trying to troubleshoot your shell scripts:

```
$ cat test1
#!/bin/ash -e
# exiting on an error
cp /home/badfile test
echo "Does this display?"
$ ./test1
cp: /home/badfile: No such file or directory
$
```

The cp command attempts to copy a file that doesn't exist, so it generates an error. When the ash shell detects the error, it immediately exits, causing the script to stop.

The -f command line option allows you to disable wildcard expansion in the shell. The shell treats the standard wildcard characters as normal characters:

```
$ ash -f
$ ls -al *.txt
ls: *.txt: No such file or directory
$
```

In this example, the shell is looking for a file called `*.txt`, instead of matching any file that ends with `.txt`.

The `-n` command line option is not used in interactive shells, but if you use it in your shell script, the ash shell will scan the script, but not actually run it. Here's a quick example:

```
$ cat test2
#!/bin/ash -n
# test run a script

echo "This is a test"
echo "This is a bad line.
$ ./test2
./test2: 5:Syntax error: Unterminated quoted string
$
```

The shell doesn't execute the good `echo` statement, since the bad `echo` statement contained an error. However, the shell does indicate that there's an error in the bad `echo` statement line, so at least you know where to look for the problem (the error message even tells you the line number). This is a great way to quickly troubleshoot coding problems in your ash shell scripts without having to actually run through the entire script line by line.

The original ash built-in commands

Since the original ash shell was designed to be lightweight, it contains just a subset of the Bourne shell built-in commands. The trick is knowing which commands you can use and which ones you can't. Table 20-2 shows the built-in commands available in the original ash shell.

As you can see from Table 20-2, the ash shell contains some of the bash commands that you're used to, but there are quite a few things missing. The original ash shell doesn't provide many bells and whistles in its command environment. It just provides a bare-bones environment for running programs. Of course, this feature is what makes it so popular in low-memory operations, such as embedded Linux devices.

Let's take a look at a few of the basic ash shell built-in commands that we haven't already explored in the bash shell.

The bltin command

You can use the `bltin` command when you want to run a built-in command in situations when there's another command available with the same name. When you're running shell scripts, if there's more than one script with the same name, you can just specify the full pathname to select the proper script. With a built-in command, you can't do that.

To solve this problem, the ash shell provides the `bltin` command (its name is changed to `builtin` in the bash shell). This forces the ash shell to look for a built-in command using the specified name instead of a shell script.

TABLE 20-2

The Original ash Shell Built-In Commands

Command	Description
bg	Continue the specified job in background mode.
bltin	Execute the specified built-in command.
cd	Change to the specified directory, to $HOME if none is specified.
eval	The supplied string is parsed as a shell command and executed.
exec	Replace the shell process with the specified program.
exit	Terminate the shell process.
export	Export the specified variable and value pair so that shell subprocesses can access it.
fg	Continue the specified job in foreground mode.
getopts	Retrieve the options and values specified on the shell command line.
hash	Display, remove, and use the contents of a command hash table.
jobid	Display the process IDs (PIDs) of the processes contained in the supplied job.
jobs	Display the background processes that are children of the current shell process.
lc	Re-execute the last command executed or define a specified function name to execute the last command executed.
pwd	Display the current working directory.
read	Read a line of data from STDIN and assign it to a variable.
readonly	Read a line of data from STDIN and assign it to a variable that can't be changed.
set	List values of shell variables, set (or clear) option flags, and set values of the shell's positional parameters.
setvar	Set a supplied value to a supplied variable name.
shift	Shift the positional parameters a specified number of times.
trap	Parse and execute a specified command when a specified signal is received.
umask	Set the default permissions used when creating files and directories.
unset	Unset the specified variable or options.
wait	Wait for the specified job to complete and return the exit status.

The hash command

The ash shell maintains a table of all commands you enter while in the shell process. The ash shell then uses this table (called the *hash* table) to quickly retrieve the location of recently used commands, instead of having to traverse all of the directories in the PATH environment variable looking for them.

You can display the current hash table just by using the hash command by itself:

```
$ hash
builtin hash
builtin pwd
/bin/ls
$
```

The hash table contains the commands starting with the most recently used command. As you can see from the example, it also remembers the built-in shell commands that you execute.

If you use the cd command to change your directory, the shell places an asterisk next to any commands in the hash table that use a pathname:

```
$ cd
$ hash
builtin hash
builtin pwd
builtin cd
/bin/ls*
$
```

The asterisk means that the pathname may no longer be valid due to the change of directory since the last time you executed the command.

You can use the -r parameter to remove individual items from the hash table:

```
$ hash -r /bin/ls
$ hash
builtin hash
builtin pwd
builtin cd
$
```

Sometimes you'll run into the problem of a command that's been moved, but the shell doesn't realize it and attempts to run the command from the location specified in the hash table. By removing the hash table entry for the command you force the shell to re-find the command.

The -v parameter tells the hash command to display the full location where it finds a command that you specify:

```
$ hash -v cd
builtin cd
$ hash -v ls
/bin/ls
$ hash -v fortune
```

```
/usr/games/fortune
$
```

This example also demonstrates that, if the command is a built-in shell command, the hash command will identify it as such.

The lc command

The lc command is a cute little utility that can save you some typing on the command line. It stands for *last command*, and its job is to execute the last command that you ran on the command line, including any command line arguments. Here's a few examples of using the lc command:

```
$ pwd
/home/rich/test
$ lc
/home/rich/test
$ ./test1
Your HOME directory exists
$ lc
Your HOME directory exists
$ ls -al
total 148
drwxr-xr-x    2 rich     rich          4096 Jan  7 08:15 .
drwxr-xr-x   17 rich     rich          4096 Jan  3 10:03 ..
-rwxr--r--    1 rich     rich            97 Jan  3 10:04 test1
-rwxr--r--    1 rich     rich            84 Jan  7 08:01 test2
$ lc
total 148
drwxr-xr-x    2 rich     rich          4096 Jan  7 08:15 .
drwxr-xr-x   17 rich     rich          4096 Jan  3 10:03 ..
-rwxr--r--    1 rich     rich            97 Jan  3 10:04 test1
-rwxr--r--    1 rich     rich            84 Jan  7 08:01 test2
$
```

The lc command works no matter what the last command was, whether it was a built-in shell command, an application program, or a shell script. As you can see from the example, the lc command also duplicates any command line arguments you supplied with the original command.

The ash shell files

Just like the bash shell, the ash shell uses default files to control its start environment. The default files allow you to define shell environment variables and settings when using the ash shell in an interactive mode.

There are three files that the ash shell uses:

■ The /etc/profile file
■ The $HOME/.profile file
■ A file defined in the ENV environment variable

If the ash shell detects that it's used as a login shell, it first executes the contents of the /etc/ profile file. This is the place to define system-wide environment variables that are set for all interactive users.

Next, the ash shell searches the contents of the user's HOME directory for a file named .profile. If it exists, the ash shell executes it. Finally, the ash shell checks if the ENV environment variable has been set (either before the ash shell is run or as part of the login script). If this variable is set, the ash shell attempts to execute the contents of the filename specified by the variable.

The dash Shell

The original ash shell was a great place to start for emulating the original Bourne shell features, but much needed to be added for a true interactive shell experience. The NetBSD Unix clone developers took the original ash shell and modified it for their own use. The Debian Linux distribution developers then took the NetBSD ash shell, and modified it to run in Debian Linux. This section describes the Debian version of the ash shell, called dash.

The dash command line parameters

The dash shell uses command line parameters to control its behavior. Table 20-3 lists the command line parameters and describes what each one does.

There are just a few additional command line parameters that Debian added to the original ash shell command line parameter list. The -E and -V command line parameters enable the special command line editing features of the dash shell.

The -E command line parameter allows you to use the emacs editor commands for editing command line text (see Chapter 7). You can use all of the emacs commands for manipulating text on a single line using the Ctrl and Meta key combinations.

The -V command line parameter allows you to use the vi editor commands for editing command line text (again, see Chapter 7). This feature allows you to switch between normal mode and vi editor mode on the command line by using the Esc key. When you're in vi editor mode, you can use all of the standard vi editor commands (such as x to delete a character, and i to insert text). Once you are finished editing the command line, you must hit the Esc key again to exit vi editor mode.

The dash environment variables

There are quite a few default environment variables that the dash shell uses to track information, and you can create your own environment variables as well. This section describes the environment variables and how dash handles them.

The dash Command Line Parameters

Parameter	Description
-a	Export all variables assigned to the shell.
-c	Read commands from a specified command string.
-e	If not interactive, exit immediately if any untested command fails.
-f	Display pathname wildcard characters.
-n	If not interactive, read commands but don't execute them.
-u	Write an error message to STDERR when attempting to expand a variable that is not set.
-v	Write input to STDERR as it is read.
-x	Write each command to STDERR as it's executed.
-I	Ignore EOF characters from the input when in interactive mode.
-i	Force the shell to operate in interactive mode.
-m	Turn on job control (enabled by default in interactive mode).
-s	Read commands from STDIN (the default behavior if no file arguments are present).
-E	Enable the emacs command line editor.
-V	Enable the vi command line editor.

Default environment variables

Table 20-4 shows the default dash environment variables and describes what they are used for.

TABLE 20-4

The dash Shell Environment Variables

Variable	Description
CDPATH	The search path used for the cd command.
HISTSIZE	The number of lines stored in the history file.
HOME	The user's default login directory.
IFS	The input field separator characters. The default value is a space, tab, and newline.

continued

TABLE 20-4	(continued)
Variable	**Description**
MAIL	The name of the user's mailbox file.
MAILCHECK	The frequency to check the mailbox file for new mail.
MAILPATH	A colon-separated list of multiple mailbox filenames. If set, this value overrides the MAIL environment variable.
OLDPWD	The value of the previous working directory.
PATH	The default search path for executable files.
PPID	The Process ID of the current shell's parent.
PS1	The primary shell command line interface prompt.
PS2	The secondary shell command line interface prompt.
PS4	A character printed before each line when an execution trace is enabled.
PWD	The value of the current working directory.
TERM	The default terminal setting for the shell.

You should notice that the dash environment variables are very similar to the environment variables used in bash (see Chapter 5). This is not by accident. Remember, both the dash and bash shells are extensions of the Bourne shell, so they both incorporate many of its features. However, because of its goal of simplicity, the dash shell contains significantly fewer environment variables than the bash shell. You need to take this into consideration when creating shell scripts in an ash shell environment.

The dash shell uses the set command to display environment variables:

```
$set
COLORTERM="
DESKTOP_SESSION='default'
DISPLAY=':0.0'
DM_CONTROL='/var/run/xdmctl'
GS_LIB='/home/atest/.fonts'
HOME='/home/atest'
IFS='
'
KDEROOTHOME='/root/.kde'
KDE_FULL_SESSION='true'
KDE_MULTIHEAD='false'
KONSOLE_DCOP='DCOPRef(konsole-5293,konsole)'
KONSOLE_DCOP_SESSION='DCOPRef(konsole-5293,session-1)'
LANG='en_US'
LANGUAGE='en'
```

```
LC_ALL='en_US'
LOGNAME='atest'
OPTIND='1'
PATH='/usr/local/sbin:/usr/local/bin:/usr/sbin:/usr/bin:/sbin:/bin'
PPID='5293'
PS1='$ '
PS2='> '
PS4='+ '
PWD='/home/atest'
SESSION_MANAGER='local/testbox:/tmp/.ICE-unix/5051'
SHELL='/bin/dash'
SHLVL='1'
TERM='xterm'
USER='atest'
XCURSOR_THEME='default'
_='ash'
$
```

Your default dash shell environment will most likely differ, as different Linux distributions assign different default environment variables at login.

Positional parameters

Besides the default environment variables, the dash shell also assigns special variables to any parameters defined in the command line. Here are the positional parameter variables available for use in the dash shell:

- $0: The name of the shell
- $n: The *n*th position parameter
- $*: A single value with the contents of all of the parameters, separated by the first character in the IFS environment variable, or a space if IFS isn't defined
- $@: Expands to multiple arguments consisting of all the command line parameters
- $#: The number of positional parameters
- $?: The exit status of the most recent command
- $-: The current option flags
- $$: The process ID (PID) of the current shell
- $!: The process ID (PID) of the most recent background command

All of the dash positional parameters mimic the same positional parameters available in the bash shell:

```
$ cat test3
#!/bin/dash
# testing positional parameters
```

```
number=$#
pid=$$
third=$3
echo "Passed $number parameters"
echo "The third parameter is $third"
echo "The PID is $pid"
$ ./test3 one two three
Passed 3 parameters
The third parameter is three
The PID is 10095
$
```

You can use each of the positional parameters in your shell scripts just as you would in the bash shell.

User-defined environment variables

The dash shell also allows you to set your own environment variables. As with bash, you can define a new environment variable on the command line by using the assign statement:

```
$ testing=10
$ echo $testing
10
$
```

By default, environment variables are only visible in the shell session in which they're defined. To allow an environment variable to be visible in a child shell or process, you must use the `export` command:

```
$ testing=10 ; export testing
$ dash
$ echo $testing
10
$
```

Without the `export` command, user-defined environment variables are only visible in the current shell or process.

CAUTION There's one huge difference between dash variables and bash variables. The dash shell doesn't support variable arrays. This small feature causes all sorts of problems for advanced shell script writers.

The dash built-in commands

Just as with the bash shell, the dash shell contains a set of built-in commands that it recognizes. You can use these commands directly from the command line interface or you can incorporate them in your shell scripts. Table 20-5 lists the dash shell built-in commands.

TABLE 20-5

The dash Shell Built-In Commands

Command	Description
alias	Create an alias string to represent a text string.
bg	Continue specified job in background mode.
cd	Switch to the specified directory.
echo	Display a text string and environment variables.
eval	Concatenate all arguments with a space.
exec	Replace the shell process with the specified command.
exit	Terminate the shell process.
export	Export the specified environment variable for use in all child shells.
fc	List, edit, or re-execute commands previously entered on the command line.
fg	Continue specified job in foreground mode.
getopts	Obtain options and arguments from a list of parameters.
hash	Maintain and retrieve a hash table of recent commands and their locations.
pwd	Display the value of the current working directory.
read	Read a line from STDIN and assign the value to a variable.
readonly	Read a line from STDIN to a variable that can't be changed.
printf	Display text and variables using a formatted string.
set	List or set option flags and environment variables.
shift	Shift the positional parameters a specified number of times.
test	Evaluate an expression and return 0 if true, or 1 if false.
times	Display the accumulated user and system times for the shell and all shell processes.
trap	Parse and execute an action when the shell receives a specified signal.
type	Interpret the specified name and display the resolution (alias, built-in, command, keyword).
ulimit	Query or set limits on processes.
umask	Set the value of the default file and directory permissions.
unalias	Remove the specified alias.
unset	Remove and unexport the specified variable or option flag.
wait	Wait for the specified job to complete and return the exit status.

You probably recognize all of these built-in commands from the bash shell. The dash shell supports many of the same built-in commands as the bash shell. You'll notice that there aren't any commands for the command history file, nor for the directory stack. The dash shell doesn't support these features.

The following two sections describe a couple of commands that are in the dash shell, but not in the ash shell.

The printf command

The echo command isn't the only way to display data from the command line, or your shell scripts. Chapter 10 demonstrated how to use the C programming language printf command in a gawk program.

The dash shell also incorporates the printf built-in command to allow you to customize your output. The printf command uses special formatting tags, which provide greater control over how and where data appears in the output.

The format of the printf command is:

```
printf "format string" var1 var2 ...
```

Notice that the dash version of the printf command doesn't use a comma between the format string and the variables. Just as in the gawk version, the format string is a string value that contains up to three elements:

- Standard text characters
- Format specifications
- Character escape sequences

The printf command displays each argument listed in the command line using a separate *format specification*. The format specification defines what type of data to display, and how to display it. The dash printf command uses the same format specifications as the gawk printf command discussed in Chapter 19.

Here's an example of using the printf command in a dash shell script:

```
$ cat test4
#!/bin/dash
# testing the printf command

factorial=1
value=1
while [ $value -le 10 ]
do
```

```
        count=1
        while [ $count -le $value ]
        do
            factorial=$(( $factorial * $count ))
            count=$(( $count + 1 ))
        done
        printf "The factorial of %d is %6.2e\n" $value $factorial
        factorial=1
        value=$(( $value + 1 ))
    done
```

The printf command allows us to format the output of the two variables, in this case displaying the factorial value using scientific notation:

```
$ ./test4
The factorial of 1 is 1.00e+00
The factorial of 2 is 2.00e+00
The factorial of 3 is 6.00e+00
The factorial of 4 is 2.40e+01
The factorial of 5 is 1.20e+02
The factorial of 6 is 7.20e+02
The factorial of 7 is 5.04e+03
The factorial of 8 is 4.03e+04
The factorial of 9 is 3.63e+05
The factorial of 10 is 3.63e+06
$
```

The %6.2e format specifies a six-position scientific notation value, with two places after the decimal point.

The ulimit command

The ulimit command is a great addition to the dash shell. It allows you to restrict system resources to prevent overuse in the shell. The limits you place apply to the shell from which the ulimit command is run.

There are two types of limits you can use in the dash shell:

- A hard limit, which can only be reset by the root user account.
- A soft limit, which can be reset by the owner user account for the shell.

When the shell violates a hard limit, an error occurs, blocking the operation. This is a great tool for preventing system users from overrunning the system.

The ulimit command uses several command line parameters to define the system resources to limit. These are shown in Table 20-6.

TABLE 20-6

The ulimit Command Line Parameters

Parameter	Description
-a	The currently active limits
-c	The largest core dump size (in KB)
-d	The largest data segment size of a process (in KB)
-f	The largest file block size (in 512-byte blocks)
-l	The largest amount of memory that can be locked (in KB)
-m	The largest amount of physical memory (in KB) that can be used
-n	The number of files the process can have open at one time
-p	The number of processes the user can have active at the same time
-s	The largest stack size of a process
-t	The CPU time limit
-H	Display or set a hard limit
-S	Display or set a soft limit

To display all of the currently set limits, use the -a parameter:

```
$ ulimit -a
time(seconds)         unlimited
file(blocks)          unlimited
data(kbytes)          unlimited
stack(kbytes)         8192
coredump(blocks)      0
memory(kbytes)        unlimited
locked memory(kbytes) unlimited
process               unlimited
nofiles               1024
vmemory(kbytes)       unlimited
locks                 unlimited
$
```

To set a limit, just add the number for the limit amount along with the appropriate parameter:

```
$ ulimit -f 2
$
```

This sets a soft limit on the number of blocks a new file can contain in the process. If you try to create a file larger than the limit, the shell will block the attempt and display a warning:

```
$ cat data1 >> data2
File size limit exceeded
$
```

If you want to set limits for the login shell for each user, you can use the ulimit command in the /etc/profile file, which the dash shell runs at each login. This is a great way to restrict system resources for users.

Scripting in dash

Unfortunately, the dash shell doesn't recognize all of the scripting features of the bash shell. Shell scripts written for the bash environment often fail when run on the ash or dash shells. This section describes the differences you'll need to be aware of to get your shell scripts to run properly in the ash or dash shell environments.

Creating ash and dash scripts

You probably guessed by now that creating shell scripts for the ash shell is pretty similar to creating shell scripts for the bash shell. You should always specify which shell you want to use in your script to ensure that the script runs with the proper shell.

You do this on the first line of the shell:

```
#!/bin/ash
```

or

```
#!/bin/dash
```

You can also specify a shell command line parameter on this line, as was demonstrated earlier in "The Original ash Shell" section with the -e command line parameter.

Things that won't work

Unfortunately, because the ash and dash shells are only a subset of the Bourne shell features, there are a few things in bash shell scripts that won't work in the ash or dash shells. These are often called *bashisms*. This section is a quick summary of bash shell features you may be used to using in your bash shell scripts that won't work if you're in an ash or dash shell environment.

Using arithmetic

Chapter 8 showed three ways to express a mathematical operation in the bash shell script:

- Using the expr command: expr operation
- Using square brackets: $[operation]
- Using double parentheses: $((operation))

The ash and dash shells support the expr command and the double parentheses method but don't support the square bracket method. This can be a problem if you've got lots of mathematical operations that use the square brackets:

```
$ cat test5
#!/bin/dash
# testing mathematical operations

value1=10
value2=15

value3=$[ $value1 * $value2 ]
echo "The answer is $value3"
$ ./test5
./test5: 7: value1: not found
The answer is
$
```

The proper format for performing mathematical operations in ash or dash shell scripts is to use the double parentheses method:

```
$ cat test5b
#!/bin/dash
# testing mathematical operations

value1=10
value2=15

value3=$(( $value1 * $value2 ))
echo "The answer is $value3"
$ ./test5b
The answer is 150
$
```

Now the shell can perform the calculation properly.

The test command

While the dash shell supports the test command, you must be careful how you use it. The bash shell version of the test command is slightly different than the dash shell version.

The bash shell `test` command allows you to use the double equal sign (==) to test if two strings are equal. This is an add-on to accommodate programmers familiar with using this format in other programming languages:

```
$ cat test6
#!/bin/bash
# testing the == comparison

test1=abcdef
test2=abcdef

if [ $test1 == $test2 ]
then
    echo "They're the same!"
else
    echo "They're different"
fi
$ ./test6
They're the same!
$
```

Simple enough. However, if you run this script in an ash or dash shell environment, you'll get an unwelcome outcome:

```
$ ./test6
[: ==: unexpected operator
They're different
$
```

The `test` command available in the ash and dash shells doesn't recognize the == symbol for text comparisons. Instead, it only recognizes the = symbol. If you change the text comparison symbol to just a single equal sign, things are just fine in all of the ash, bash, and dash shell environments:

```
$ cat test7
#!/bin/dash
# testing the = comparison

test1=abcdef
test2=abcdef

if [ $test1 = $test2 ]
then
    echo "They're the same!"
else
    echo "They're different"
fi
$ ./test7
They're the same!
$
```

This little bashism is responsible for many hours of frustration for shell programmers!

The echo statement options

The simple `echo` statement is also another source of frustration for dash shell programmers. It doesn't behave the same way in the dash and bash shells.

In the bash shell, if you want to display a special character in the output, you must use the `-e` command line parameter:

```
echo -e "This line contains\ta special character"
```

The `echo` statement contains the `\t` special character to represent a tab. Without the `-e` command line parameter, the bash version of the `echo` statement ignores the special character. Here's a test that demonstrates this in the bash shell:

```
$ cat test8
#!/bin/bash
# testing echo commands

echo "This is a normal test"
echo "This test uses a\tspecial character"
echo -e "This test uses a\tspecial character"
echo -n "Does this work: "
read test
echo "This is the end of the test"
$ ./test8
This is a normal test
This test uses a\tspecial character
This test uses a special character
Does this work: N
This is the end of the test
$
```

The `echo` statement that didn't use the `-e` command line parameter just displayed the `\t` character as normal text, so to get the tab character, you must use the `-e` command line parameter.

In the ash and dash shells, things are a little different. The `echo` statement in the ash and dash shells automatically recognizes and displays special characters. Because of this, there is no `-e` command line parameter. If you try to run the same script in an ash or dash environment, you get this output:

```
$ ./test8
This is a simple test
This line uses a       special character
-e This line uses a       special character
Does this work: N
This is the end of the test
$
```

As you can see from the output, the dash shell version of the echo command recognizes the special character in the line without the -e command line parameter just fine, but for the line that does contain the -e command line parameter, it gets confused and displays the -e as normal text.

CAUTION The -n command line parameter is also unreliable. While being supported in bash to suppress the newline character at the end of a line, it's not supported in all versions of the ash shell. The dash shell echo statement supports the -n parameter, but not all ash shell versions support it.

Unfortunately, there's no simple solution to this problem. If you must write scripts that work in both the bash and dash or ash environments, the best solution is to use the printf command to display text. This command works the same way in both shell environments, and it can display special characters just fine.

The function command

Chapter 14 showed how to define your own functions in your shell scripts. The bash shell supports two methods for defining functions. The first method is by using the function statement:

```
function name {
    commands
}
```

The name attribute defines a unique name assigned to the function. Each function you define in your script must be assigned a unique name.

The commands are one or more bash shell commands that make up your function. When you call the function, the bash shell executes each of the commands in the order they appear in the function, just as in a normal script.

The second format for defining a function in a bash shell script more closely follows how functions are defined in other programming languages:

```
name() {
commands
}
```

The empty parentheses after the function name indicate that you're defining a function. The same naming rules apply in this format as the original shell script function format.

The ash and dash shells don't support the first method of defining functions (they don't support the function statement). Instead, in the ash and dash shells you must define a function using the function name with parentheses. If you try to run a function designed for the bash shell in an ash or dash shell, you'll get an error message:

```
$ cat test9
#!/bin/dash
# testing functions

function func1() {
```

```
    echo "This is an example of a function"
}

count=1
while [ $count -le 5 ]
do
    func1
    count=$(( $count + 1 ))
done
echo "This is the end of the loop"
func1
echo "This is the end of the script"
$ ./test9
./test9: 4: Syntax error: "(" unexpected
$
$
```

Instead of assigning the function code to the function, the dash shell executed the code within the function definition, then complained about the format of the shell script.

If you're writing shell scripts that may be used in the ash or dash environment, always use the second method of defining your functions:

```
$ cat test10
#!/bin/dash
# testing functions

func1() {
    echo "This is an example of a function"
}

count=1
while [ $count -le 5 ]
do
    func1
    count=$(( $count + 1 ))
done
echo "This is the end of the loop"
func1
echo "This is the end of the script"
$ ./test10
This is an example of a function
This is an example of a function
This is an example of a function
This is an example of a function
This is an example of a function
This is the end of the loop
This is an example of a function
This is the end of the script
$
```

Now the dash shell recognized the function defined in the script just fine and was able to use it within the script.

Summary

This chapter discussed working in an ash shell environment. The ash shell is not a common shell you'll find in Linux distributions, but it does appear in the NetBSD and FreeBSD Unix distributions. A derivative of the ash shell is the dash shell, which is used in many Debian-based Linux distributions, although not as a login shell.

The ash and dash shells are smaller versions of the Bourne shell, so they don't support as many features as the bash shell. You need to take this into consideration if you're writing shell scripts that may be used in an ash or dash shell environment.

The next chapter discusses another Linux shell environment you may run into. The C shell is a popular shell in some Unix environments and has made its way over to the Linux world as the tcsh shell. We'll take a look at how the tcsh shell differs from the bash shell, and what you need to know to get your scripts to work in a tcsh shell environment.

Chapter 21

The tcsh Shell

Another popular alternative shell available in the Linux world is the C shell. The C shell, as you might guess, is somewhat of an attempt to incorporate features found in the C programming language into shell scripting. The most popular version of the C shell implemented in open source is the tcsh shell. This chapter discusses the tcsh shell, describing its features, and showing how to write shell scripts for it.

What Is the tcsh Shell?

The C shell was developed at the University of California, Berkeley by Bill Joy as a replacement for the original Unix shell created at AT&T Labs (before there was even a Bourne shell). Developers at Berkeley had designed and built a Unix system to compete with AT&T Unix, and the C shell was their choice for the default shell. This version of Unix is popularly called the Berkeley Software Distribution (or BSD Unix). The goal of the C shell was to provide a command line and scripting environment that C programmers would be comfortable with.

In the late 1970s Ken Greer created an extension to the C shell that added command line editing features found in the TENEX operating system. This is where the name tcsh came from. The tcsh shell has become a popular shell for many Unix systems patterned after BSD Unix (including early versions of the Mac OS X operating system; newer versions now use the bash shell as the default).

While the bash shell has become the default shell for most every Linux distribution, the tcsh shell is available as an option, and it can be easily

557

installed directly from source code if you desire. If you're migrating shell scripts from a BSD Unix environment to a Linux environment, it's helpful to use the tcsh shell.

Because the C shell was created before the Bourne shell, there are significant differences between the two. And because bash is based on the Bourne shell, there are significant differences between the tcsh and bash shells. Writing scripts that operate in both shell environments is close to impossible for all but the simplest of applications.

The following sections walk you through the components and features of the tcsh shell, and demonstrate how to write shell scripts for a tcsh environment.

The tcsh Shell Components

Just like the bash shell, the tcsh shell uses command line parameters, default files, environment variables, and built-in commands to define the shell operating environment. This section describes each of these features of the tcsh shell.

The tcsh command line parameters

The tcsh shell offers several command line parameters that allow you to customize how the shell operates. These command line parameters define just what features of the shell are available and how the shell behaves in the interactive environment. Table 21-1 lists the command line parameters available with the tcsh shell.

The tcsh shell uses a few of the same command line parameters as the bash shell, but also has a few of its own.

The -v and -V parameters are handy when you're trying to do some troubleshooting in the tcsh shell. They display commands as the shell executes them.

The -V parameter starts displaying commands as soon as the shell starts, including the login and startup shell files (see the "The tcsh files" section). The -v parameter doesn't display commands until after the startup and login files finish.

This isn't too useful for the command line, but it is pretty cool when dealing with shell scripts:

```
$ cat test1
#!/bin/tcsh -v
# test run a script

set testing=10
echo "This is a test"
echo "The value of testing is $testing"
$ ./test1
```

```
set testing=10
echo "This is a test"
This is a test
echo "The value of testing is $testing"
The value of testing is 10
$
```

TABLE 21-1

The tcsh Shell Command Line Parameters

Parameter	Description
-b	Breaks from option parameters, forcing any remaining parameters to be treated as non-option parameters.
-c	Commands are read from the specified argument.
-d	The shell loads the directory stack from the file $HOME/.cshdirs.
-e	The shell exits if a command terminates abnormally or with a non-zero exit status.
-f	The shell doesn't process the $HOME/.tcshrc file.
-i	Force an interactive shell session.
-l	Specify that the shell is used as a login shell.
-m	Forces the shell to execute the $HOME/.tcshrc file, even if it doesn't belong to the effective user.
-n	The shell parses commands but doesn't execute them.
-q	The shell accepts the SIGQUIT signal, and job control is disabled.
-s	Shell commands are taken from STDIN.
-t	The shell reads and executes a single line of input.
-v	Sets the verbose shell variable, so command input is echoed when using history substitution.
-V	Sets the verbose shell variable before executing the $HOME/.tcshrc file.
-x	Sets the echo shell variable, so commands are echoed immediately before execution.
-X	Sets the echo shell variable before executing the $HOME/.tcshrc file.
--help	Display a help message on STDOUT and exit.
--version	Display version information about the tcsh shell.

Using the -v parameter when defining the tcsh shell in the script causes the shell to display each statement before executing it.

The tcsh files

The tcsh shell automatically looks for several default files for setting environment variables and executing commands. If the any of the default files exist, the tcsh shell executes them at specific instances. There are three different types of default files the tcsh shell can handle:

- Login files
- Shell startup files
- Logout files

This section examines the myriad of possible files you can use for your tcsh shell.

The tcsh login files

If you use the tcsh shell as a login shell, it first looks for and executes the files:

- /etc/csh.login
- /etc/csh/login

You'll notice that all of these files use csh in the filename. Since the tcsh shell was designed as a replacement for the original C shell, it was designed to handle any of the default files that the C shell could. This made migrating from the C shell environment to the tcsh shell environment a snap.

These files are executed for all users who use the tcsh shell as their login shell. The files should contain system-wide environment variables that should be set for all users, and executable programs that all users should use (such as the umask command to set default file and directory permissions). Most likely if you're using a Linux distribution that supports the tcsh shell, one of these files already exists for setting system environment variables at login.

After executing either of these two files, the tcsh shell looks for a file in each user's $HOME directory:

    $HOME/.login

This file can contain user-specific environment variable settings, and executable commands that an individual user wants to run when logging into the system, before the command line interface prompt appears.

Any environment variable settings you make in the $HOME/.login shell will override any system-wide settings made in the /etc/csh.login file. You can test the order in which the tcsh shell executes these files by adding a simple echo statement to each one, then logging in:

```
$ telnet localhost
Trying 127.0.0.1...
Connected to localhost.localdomain.
Escape character is '^]'.
Welcome to testbox
login: test
Password:
Last login: Fri Jan 11 18:54:41 from localhost.localdomain
This is the /etc/csh.login file
This is the .login file
$
```

As you can see from the example, the tcsh shell executed the /etc/csh.login file first.

Shell startup files

If you don't use the tcsh shell as a login shell, but just an interactive shell, you must deal with a different set of files when the shell starts up.

The default system-wide startup file is:

* /etc/csh.cshrc

After executing this file (if it exists), the tcsh shell proceeds to the user's $HOME directory and looks for either of the following files:

- $HOME/.cshrc
- $HOME/.tcshrc

If both exist, it will only execute the .tcshrc file. You can test the order in which the tcsh shell executes these files by performing a simple test using the echo statement:

```
$ tcsh
This is the /etc/csh.cshrc file
This is the /home/test/.tcshrc file
$
```

When I started a new tcsh shell, it executed the /etc/csh.cshrc file first, then the .tcshrc file in the $HOME directory.

The shell startup files also execute if you use the tcsh shell for a shell script:

```
$ cat test2
#!/bin/tcsh
# test run a script
echo "This is a test"
$ ./test2
This is the /etc/csh/cshrc file
```

```
This is the /home/test/.tcshrc file
This is a test
$
```

Notice that before the output of the shell script appears, you see the `echo` statements from the tcsh shell startup files.

The startup files don't replace the login files, but add to them. If you have both set, when you log in with a new login shell you'll see that not only do the login shell files execute, but also the startup shell files:

```
$ telnet localhost
Trying 127.0.0.1...
Connected to localhost.localdomain.
Escape character is '^]'.
Welcome to testbox
login: test
Password:
Last login: Fri Jan 11 18:55:26 from localhost.localdomain
This is the /etc/csh.cshrc file
This is the /etc/csh.login file
This is the /home/test/.tcshrc file
This is the .login file
$
```

Notice the order in which the shell executes the default files:

1. The all-user startup file.
2. The all-user login file.
3. The private startup file.
4. The private login file.

This order is important to remember if you're setting environment variables, as if any of these files set the same environment variable values, the last value set wins.

The logout files

Besides the login and startup files, the tcsh shell also has the ability to execute commands in files when you log out from an interactive or login shell session. These files can be in the following locations:

-  /etc/csh.logout
- $HOME/.logout

As you probably figured out by now, every user on the system executes the commands in the /etc/csh.logout file at logout, while each individual user has a unique $HOME/.logout file. The tcsh shell will execute any commands in these files before logging out of the current shell.

This doesn't include just exiting from an interactive shell. Thus, if you just start another tcsh shell from an existing shell session, the tcsh shell won't execute the logout files when you exit the shell.

To test this feature, you can't just display text using the echo statement, as the shell will most likely go away too quickly for you to see. However, you can redirect the output to a file, then view the file after you've logged out.

Here's what my file looked like after I logged out from a tcsh shell session:

```
$ cat logout.txt
This is the /etc/csh.logout file
This is the /home/test/.logout file
$
```

The tcsh shell executed the commands in the /etc/csh.logout file first, then executed the commands in the $HOME/.logout file.

The tcsh environment variables

The tcsh shell environment variables can be somewhat confusing. The Bourne shell (and its derivatives bash, ash, and dash) uses a single class of environment variables to store system information. The tcsh shell contains two classes of environment variables:

- Shell variables
- System environment variables

The system environment variables consist of upper-case text strings that provide standard system information. The tcsh shell variables are lower case variables which have special meaning to the shell.

Shell variables

The special Table 21-2 shows the shell variables that tcsh uses to set behavior features in the shell.

That's quite a list of shell variables available for the tcsh shell! These variables demonstrate the power of the tcsh shell. It allows you to customize many different aspects of the shell just by setting shell variables.

563

TABLE 21-2

The tcsh Special Shell Variables

Variable	Description
addsuffix	If set (by default) filename completion adds a forward slash (/) to the end of directories, and a space to the end of normal filenames.
afsuser	If set, the autologout uses this value instead of the local username for Kerberos identification.
ampm	If set, all times are shown in 12-hour AM/PM format.
argv	The arguments supplied to the shell.
autocorrect	The shell invokes the spell-word editor automatically before each command.
autoexpand	If set, the shell invokes the expand-history editor automatically before each command.
autolist	If set, the shell lists possible commands after an ambiguous command.
autologout	Set to the number of minutes of inactivity before automatically logging out. An optional second parameter specifies the number of minutes of inactivity before locking the terminal.
backslash_quote	If set, the shell always quotes special characters (backslash, single, and double quotation marks) with a backslash character.
catalog	The filename of the message catalog.
cdpath	A list of directories that the cd command will search for subdirectories.
color	If set, enables color display for some commands.
colorcat	If set, color escape sequences for messages.
command	If set, the command passed to the shell using the -c command line parameter.
complete	Controls command completion. If set to enhance, completion ignores case and considers special characters. If set to igncase, completion just ignores case.
continue	If set to a list of commands, the shell will continue the list of commands instead of starting a new one.
continue_args	Same as continue, but the shell passes arguments.
correct	If set to cmd, commands are automatically spell-corrected. If set to complete, commands are automatically completed. If set to all, the entire command line is corrected.
csubstnonl	If set, newlines and carriage returns in commands are replaced with spaces.

continued

TABLE 21-2	*(continued)*
Variable	**Description**
cwd	The full pathname of the current directory.
dextract	If set, the pushd command extracts the nth entry from the directory stack instead of rotating it to the top.
dirsfile	The default location where the dirs command looks for a history file.
dirstack	An array of all the directories on the directory stack.
dspmbyte	Controls editing for multi-byte character sets.
dunique	If set, the pushd command removes any instances of the directory name from the stack.
echo	If set, the shell echoes each command before executing it.
echo_style	Defines the style of echo command (bsd, sysv, both, or none).
edit	If set, the command line editor is used.
ellipsis	If set, the %c, %, and %C prompt sequences in the prompt indicate skipped directories with ... (an ellipsis).
fignore	Lists filename suffixes to be ignored by completion.
filec	If the edit variable is not set, uses the traditional csh shell command completion.
gid	The user's read group ID.
group	The user's group name.
histchars	A string value determining the characters used in history substitution.
histdup	Controls handling of duplicates in the history file (all, prev, erase).
histfile	The default location of the history file.
histlit	If set, built-in and editor commands and savehist use the unexpanded form of lines in the history list.
history	The first entry indicates the number of history items to save. The optional second entry indicates the format in which history is printed.
home	The home directory of the user.
ignoreeof	If set to an empty string or 0, the Ctrl-D key combination doesn't exit the shell.
implicitcd	If set, typing a directory name on the command line acts as though you used the cd command with the directory name.
inputmode	Sets the editor to either insert or overwrite mode at the beginning of each line.

continued

TABLE 21-2	*(continued)*
Variable	**Description**
`killdup`	Controls duplicate entries in the kill ring. Can be set to `all`, `prev`, or `erase`.
`killring`	The number of killed strings to keep in memory (set to 30 by default).
`listflags`	List of flags to add to the `ls-F` command (can be x, a, or A).
`listjobs`	If set, all jobs are listed when a job is suspended. If set to `long`, the long format is used.
`listlinks`	If set, the `ls-F` command shows the type of file to which each symbolic link points.
`listmax`	The maximum number of items which the `list-choices` editor command will list.
`listmaxrows`	The maximum number of rows of items which the `list-choices` editor command will list.
`loginsh`	Set by the shell if it's a login shell.
`logout`	Set by the shell to `normal`, `automatic`, or `hangup`.
`mail`	The names of files or directories (separated by white space) to check for new mail.
`matchbeep`	Sets condition to generate a beep for completion match — `never`, `nomatch`, `ambiguous`, `notunique`.
`nobeep`	Beeping is disabled.
`noclobber`	If set, files are not automatically destroyed by redirection attempts.
`noding`	If set, disables the `DING!` display in the prompt time when the hour changes.
`noglob`	If set, filename substitution and directory stack substitution are disabled.
`nokanji`	If set and the shell supports Kanji, it is disabled so that the meta-key can be used.
`nonomatch`	If set, a filename substitution or directory stack substitution that doesn't match doesn't create an error.
`nostat`	A list of directories that should not be included in the `stat` command during a completion operation.
`notify`	If set, the shell announces job completions asynchronously.
`oid`	The users' real organization ID.
`owd`	The old working directory.
`path`	A list of directories to look for executable commands.

continued

TABLE 21-2   *(continued)*

Variable	Description
printexitvalue	If set in an interactive shell, the shell displays the non-zero exit status.
prompt	The string printed before each command line.
prompt2	The secondary command line prompt for command completions.
prompt3	The string used for automatic spelling corrections.
promptchars	A two-character string; if set the first character is used for the normal user prompt, and the second character is used for the root user prompt.
pushdtohome	If set, the pushd command pushes to the $HOME directory by default.
pushdsilent	If set, the pushd and popd commands don't print the directory stack.
recexact	If set, completion completes on an exact match even if a longer match is possible.
recognize_only_executables	If set, command listing displays only files in the path that are executable.
rmstar	If set, the user is prompted before the rm * command is executed.
rprompt	The string to display on the right side of the screen when the prompt is being displayed on the left side.
savedirs	If set, the shell performs a dirs -S command before exiting, saving the current dirs listing.
savehist	If set, the shell performs a history -S command before exiting, saving the current history listing.
sched	The format in which the sched command displays scheduled events.
shell	The filename of the shell program.
shlvl	The number of nested shells.
status	The exit status returned by the last command.
symlinks	Controls symbolic link resolution. Can be set to chase, ignore, or expand.
tcsh	The version number of the tcsh shell.
term	The terminal type.
time	If set to a number, the time command executes automatically after each command that takes longer than the specified CPU seconds.
tperiod	The time period, in minutes, between executions of the periodic special alias.
tty	The name of the current TTY device the shell is attached to.

continued

TABLE 21-2	(continued)
Variable	**Description**
uid	The user's real user ID.
user	The user's login name.
verbose	If set, the shell displays each command after history substitution.
version	Displays the tcsh shell version.
visiblebell	If set, a screen flash appears instead of an audible bell.
watch	Sets a list of user/terminal pairs to watch for logins and logouts (can use the any keyword). Reports if the user or terminal are used.
who	The format string used for watch messages.
wordchars	A list of nonalphanumeric characters to be considered as part of words by the editor commands.

To display the shell variables currently set in your shell, use the set command:

```
$ set
_        clear

addsuffix
argv    ()
autologout      60
cwd     /home/test
dirstack        /home/test
echo_style      both
edit
file    /etc/sysconfig/i18n
gid     511
group   test
history 1000
home    /home/test
loginsh
owd
path    (/usr/local/bin /bin /usr/bin /usr/X11R6/bin)
prompt  [%n@%m %c]$
prompt2 %R?
prompt3 CORRECT>%R (y|n|e|a)?
shell   /bin/tcsh
shlvl   1
sourced 1
status  0
tcsh    6.10.00
term    xterm
testing 10
```

```
tty     pts/0
uid     508
user    test
version tcsh 6.10.00 (Astron) 2000-11-19 (i386-intel-linux) options
8b,nls,dl,al,rh,color
$
```

Notice that the output of the tcsh set command is somewhat different from that produced when you list variables in the bash shell. The tcsh shell version shows the shell variable on the left side and the current value on the right side.

You should recognize many of these shell variables from their counterparts in the bash shell. Here are a couple of differences that you need to be aware of:

■ The tcsh shell uses the prompt shell variable (along with prompt2 and prompt3), instead of the PS1, PS2, and PS3 environment variables.

■ The path shell variable contains an indexed list of directories instead of a single string with values separated by colons.

To display or use the current value of a shell variable, you must precede it with a dollar sign:

```
$ echo $path
/usr/local/bin /bin /usr/bin /usr/X11R6/bin
$
```

The indexed string uses an array format to contain the individual values of the shell variable. You can use an array format to access the individual elements:

```
$ echo $path[1]
/usr/local/bin
$ echo $path[2]
/bin
$ echo $path[3]
/usr/bin
$
```

Notice that the array starts at index position 1.

It's important to remember that shell variables use all lower-case letters, while the environment variables use all upper-case letters. Confusing them can lead to problems.

Environment variables

The tcsh shell also maintains a set of environment variables, similarly to the Bourne shell. Table 21-3 lists the environment variables.

TABLE 21-3

The tcsh Shell Environment Variables

Variable	Description
AFSUSER	Equivalent to the afsuser shell variable.
COLUMNS	The number of columns available on the terminal.
DISPLAY	Pointer to the X Windows server for graphics windows.
EDITOR	Pathname to the default editor.
GROUP	Equivalent to the group shell variable.
HOME	Equivalent to the home shell variable.
HOST	The name of the system on which the shell process is running.
HOSTTYPE	The type of machine on which the shell process is running.
HPATH	A colon-separated list of directories in which the run-help editor command looks for command documentation.
LANG	Specifies the preferred character environment.
LC_CTYPE	If set, only ctype character handling is changed.
LINES	The number of lines in the terminal.
LS_COLORS	A colon-separated list of file type and color assignments used with the ls command.
MACHTYPE	The microprocessor class or machine model of the system.
OSTYPE	The operating system of the system.
PATH	A colon-separated list of directories used to locate executable files.
PWD	Equivalent to the cwd shell variable, but only updated after an actual directory change.
REMOTEHOST	If the current user has logged in remotely, the IP address of the remote host.
SHLVL	The number of nested shells (equivalent to the shlvl shell variable).
SYSTYPE	The current system type.
TERM	The terminal type (equivalent to the term shell variable).
TERMCAP	The terminal capability string.
USER	Equivalent to the user shell variable.
VENDOR	The vendor of the system processor.
VISUAL	The pathname of the full-screen editor.

Many of the tcsh environment variables are duplicates of the shell variable of the same name. This is to provide some compatibility with the Bourne shell environment (note the inclusion of the PATH environment variable, which uses the same format as the Bourne shell PATH environment variable).

However, the two aren't linked together. If you change one, the other won't change. Thus you can cause all sorts of problems by setting a shell variable (such as path) without setting the corresponding environment variable (PATH).

To display the current environment variables, you must use the setenv command:

```
$ setenv
USER=test
LOGNAME=test
HOME=/home/test
PATH=/usr/local/bin:/bin:/usr/bin:/usr/X11R6/bin:/usr/X11R6/bin
MAIL=/var/mail/test
SHELL=/bin/tcsh
TERM=xterm
HOSTTYPE=i386-linux
VENDOR=intel
OSTYPE=linux
MACHTYPE=i386
SHLVL=1
PWD=/home/test
GROUP=test
HOST=testbox
INPUTRC=/etc/inputrc
LESS=-MM
LESSKEY=/etc/.less
BSNUM=14
BACKSPACE=
HOSTNAME=testbox
LS_COLORS=no=00:fi=00:di=01;34:ln=01;36:pi=40;33:so=01;35:bd=40;33;01
:cd=40;33;01:or=01;05;37;41:mi=01;05;37;41:ex=01;32:*.cmd=01;32:*.exe
=01;32:*.com=01;32:*.btm=01;32:*.bat=01;32:*.tar=01;31:*.tgz=01;31:*.
tbz2=01;31:*.arc=01;31:*.arj=01;31:*.taz=01;31:*.lzh=01;31:*.lha=01;3
1:*.zip=01;31:*.z=01;31:*.Z=01;31:*.gz=01;31:*.bz2=01;31:*.bz=01;31:*
.tz=01;31:*.rpm=01;31:*.jpg=01;35:*.jpeg=01;35:*.gif=01;35:*.bmp=01;3
5:*.xbm=01;35:*.xpm=01;35:*.png=01;35:*.tif=01;35:*.tiff=01;35:
LC_CTYPE=en_US
LC_MONETARY=en_US
LANGUAGE=en_US:en
LC_TIME=en_US
LC_NUMERIC=en_US
LC_COLLATE=en_US
LC_MESSAGES=en_US
LANG=en
```

```
TMPDIR=/home/test/tmp
TMP=/home/test/tmp
$
```

Notice that the setenv command uses the same output format as the bash shell set command.

To display or use environment variable values you must also include the dollar sign:

```
$ echo $PATH
/usr/local/bin:/bin:/usr/bin:/usr/X11R6/bin
$
```

While the tcsh environment variables look and act a lot like their bash shell counterparts, there's a big catch to them. The next section describes what you need to do to set environment and shell variables in the tcsh shell.

Setting variables in tcsh

Setting variables in tcsh is one of the more complicated aspects of the shell. Depending on what data values you're trying to use, it can become a frustrating experience unless you're familiar with all of the rules.

Using the set command

For shell variables, you can use the set command to set a value for a shell variable. For a simple, one word data value, you use the format:

```
set variable=value
```

This is simple enough:

```
$ set testing=100
$ echo $testing
100
$ set test2=test
$ echo $test2
test
$
```

The tricky part comes into play when you need to work with indexed arrays values. If the index value already exists, it's easy to replace with a new value:

```
$ echo $path
/usr/local/bin /bin /usr/bin /usr/X11R6/bin
$ set path[4]=/home/test
$ echo $path
/usr/local/bin /bin /usr/bin /home/test
$
```

However, you can't use this technique to add a new element:

```
$ set path[5]=/home/test
set: Subscript out of range.
$
```

Instead, you must use parentheses to denote the new array: use $path to insert the existing array elements into the new array, then add the new array elements at the end:

```
$ set path=($path /home/test2)
$ echo $path
/usr/local/bin /bin /usr/bin /home/test /home/test2
$ echo $path[5]
/home/test2
$
```

Now the new array value contains the additional element.

Finally, the tcsh shell uses the at symbol (@) as an alias for the set command. You can use the at symbol in the same way you would the set command:

```
$ @ testing = 100
$ echo $testing
100
$
```

It's important to place a space after the at symbol, or else you'll get an error message.

Using the setenv command

You use the setenv command to set environment variable values in the tcsh shell. However, the format of the setenv command is slightly different from the set command:

```
setenv variable value
```

Notice that it doesn't use the equal sign to assign the value:

```
$ setenv TESTING 10
$ echo $TESTING
10
$ setenv TEST2 test
$ echo $TEST2
test
$
```

The oddity with the setenv command is when you want to append a value to a list of values (such as the PATH environment variable). If you attempt to do it as in the bash shell, you'll get an error message:

```
$ setenv PATH $PATH:/home/test
Bad : modifier in $ (/).
$
```

The tcsh shell interprets the colon as part of the shell variable. To add an element to the PATH environment variable, you need to use braces around the environment variable name:

```
$ setenv PATH ${PATH}:/home/test
$ echo $PATH
/usr/local/bin:/bin:/usr/bin:/usr/X11R6/bin:/home/test
$
```

Now the additional element is added to the PATH environment variable properly.

The tcsh built-in commands

The tcsh shell contains a host of built-in commands available both on the command line and in shell scripts. Table 21-4 describes the available commands.

TABLE 21-4

The tcsh Shell Built-in Commands

Command	Description
@	Display or set shell variables.
alias	Assign an alias name to a command.
alloc	Display the dynamic memory status.
bg	Place the current or specified job in background mode.
bindkey	Display or set editor commands to keyboard keys.
builtins	Displays the names of all built-in commands.
cd	Change to the home directory, or to the specified directory.
chdir	The same as the cd command.
complete	Display or manage command completion strings.
dirs	Display or save the current directory stack.
echo	Display a string to STDOUT.
echotc	Perform a terminal command on STDOUT.
eval	Treat the supplied string as input to the shell executes the commands.
exec	Execute the supplied command in place of the current shell.
exit	Terminate the current shell process.
fg	Continue the specified job in foreground mode.

continued

TABLE 21-4	*(continued)*
Command	**Description**
filetest	Apply a specified test to the specified file.
glob	Similar to echo, except doesn't recognize escape characters, and words are delimited with null characters.
hashstat	Display statistics on command line hash table hits.
history	Display and manage the command history file.
hup	Run specified command, and exit if a hangup signal is received.
jobs	Display active jobs.
kill	Send the specified signal to the specified process ID (PID).
limit	Limit the specified resource so as to not take more than the specified resource (CPU time, file space, memory size, and others).
log	Display the contents of the watch shell variable, and report on each user.
login	Terminates the shell and replaces it with the /bin/login process.
logout	Terminates the shell.
ls-F	Display files using the ls command and the -F parameter, identifying file types with special characters.
nice	Set the scheduling priority of the shell, or the specified command.
nohup	Run command and ignore hangup signals.
notify	Notify the user when status of the specified job(s) change(s).
onintr	Set the shell action when it receives an interrupt.
popd	Pop the directory stack and return to the new top directory.
printenv	Display the names and values of environment variables.
pushd	Exchange the top two elements of the directory stack.
rehash	Recompute the command hash table.
repeat	Execute the specified command a specified number of times.
sched	Display or manage the scheduled event list.
set	Display or manage shell variables.
setenv	Display or manage environment variables.
settc	Set the specified terminal capability feature to the specified value.
setty	Set the TTY modes that are not allowed to change.

continued

| TABLE 21-4 | (continued) |
Command	Description
shift	Shift the positional parameters one position.
source	Read and execute commands from the specified file.
stop	Stop the specified job or process executing in background mode.
suspend	Immediately stop the shell process using the SIGSTOP signal.
telltc	Display the values of all terminal capabilities.
time	Execute the specified command and display a time summary.
umask	Set the default permissions for new files and directories.
unalias	Remove all aliases that match the specified pattern.
uncomplete	Remove all completions that match the specified pattern.
unhash	Disable use of the hash table to find executable programs.
unlimit	Remove the resource restriction on a resource.
unset	Remove all shell variables whose names match the specified pattern.
unsetenv	Remove all environment variables whose names match the specified pattern.
wait	Wait for all background jobs to complete.
where	Display all known instances of the specified command, including aliases.
which	Display the command the shell will execute after matching the specified pattern.

The tcsh shell is no slouch in providing built-in commands! I'm sure that you recognize many of these commands from their bash counterparts. There are a few commands that the tcsh shell provides that aren't available in the bash shell.

The alloc command is an easy way to check up on the memory status on your Linux system:

```
$ alloc
tcsh current memory allocation:
free:        0    83    93     5    13     6     1     1     0     0     1     1
0     0     0     0     0     0     0     0     0     0     0     0     0     0
0     0     0
used:        0   173   611   347    35   834     7     7     5     1     1     1
0     0     0     0     0     0     0     0     0     0     0     0     0     0
0     0     0
         Total in use: 312176, total free: 33936
         Allocated memory from 0x80c31e0 to 0x8117c00.  Real top at
0x8117c00
$
```

The output from the `alloc` command is somewhat cryptic. The two sets of numbers show the list of memory blocks in increasing block sizes, starting at an 8-byte block, then a 16-byte block, and so on up to a 2 MB block of memory. Thus, in this example, there are eighty-three 16-byte blocks free, 93 32-byte blocks free, five 64-byte blocks free, and so on up to one 16 KB block free. The same process is used to display the used memory blocks. The result totals are shown at the end of the listing.

The `ls -F` command is another unique command to the tcsh shell. It produces the same output as if you use the `ls` command along with the `-F` parameter (which displays an indicator next to each entry showing executable files, linked files, and directories). Since it's a built-in command, it can produce the output much faster than the standard `ls` command.

The `bindkey` command is another interesting built-in command in the tcsh shell. It allows you to bind a key combination to any key sequence, or shell command. By default, the tcsh shell binds lots of key combinations to editor commands, allowing you to easily edit your command line entries using simple editor key combinations.

You can list all of the current key bindings just by entering the `bindkey` command by itself on the command line:

```
$ bindkey
Standard key bindings
"^@"          -> set-mark-command
"^A"          -> beginning-of-line
"^B"          -> backward-char
"^C"          -> tty-sigintr
"^D"          -> delete-char-or-list-or-eof
"^E"          -> end-of-line
```

This is just a partial list of the current key binding in my tcsh shell. The list is quite lengthy.

To define a new key binding, just list the desired key combination and the command or string you want to assign:

```
$ bindkey -c ^G ls-F
$
test1~*     test2*      tmp/
logout.txt  test2~*     test.txt
$
```

Now every time I hit the `Ctrl-G` key combination I get the `ls-F` listing!

Scripting in tcsh

Writing shell scripts in the tcsh shell isn't any more difficult than in the bash shell, just different. You'll need to get used to a slightly different method for performing many of the standard statements you're used to in bash.

Working with variables

You've already seen that when working with variables you need to use the `set` command. Other than that, you can use variables the same as with the bash shell. Remember to precede a variable with a dollar sign when you want to reference the variable value.

Array variables

The tcsh shell also supports one dimensional array variables using an index value:

```
$ set myarray = (one two three)
$ echo $myarray[1]
one
$ echo $myarray[2]
two
$ echo $myarray[3]
three
$
```

To create the new array, each element is placed within the parentheses, separated by spaces. The first element in the array must be referenced as item 1.

Handling mathematical operations

In the bash shell you could use the `expr` command, the double parentheses, or the square brackets to perform mathematical operations using variables. In the tcsh shell, you just need to use parentheses to perform any mathematical function. However, you can only perform mathematical operations using the at symbol alias of the `set` command:

```
$ set test1 = 10
$ set test2 = 15
$ @ test3 = ( $test1 * $test2 )
$ echo $test3
150
$
```

The only statement that must use the at symbol is the one that performs the mathematical operation. The statements that only assign values can use either the `set` command or the at symbol alias.

Structured commands

The tcsh shell supports the following structured commands:

- `if-then-else`
- `foreach`
- `while`
- `switch`

The following sections describe how to use each of these structured commands in your shell scripts.

The if statements

The tcsh if statement can use one of several formats. The first format looks like this:

```
if (expression) command
```

If the expression defined in the parentheses evaluates to a TRUE condition, the shell executes the command listed on the line:

```
$ cat test3
#!/bin/tcsh
# simple if statement test

set testing = 10

if ($testing == 10) echo "it worked"
echo "This is the end of the test"
$ ./test3
it worked
This is the end of the test
$
```

The if statement can also be used with the then clause to execute multiple statements if the expression is TRUE:

```
if (expression) then
    statements
endif
```

Similarly to the bash if statement, the tcsh if statement can incorporate the else clause to perform alternative statements if the expression is FALSE:

```
if (expression) then
    statements
else
    other statements
endif
```

And finally, you can link multiple if statements together by using another if statement on the else line:

```
if (expression1) then
    statement1
```

```
    else if (expression2) then
        statement2
    endif
```

The expression in the if statement uses standard C-style symbols for both mathematical and string comparisons, ==, !=, <, >, <=, >+, && (logical AND), and || (logical OR). In addition to the mathematical symbols, the tcsh if statement also supports two string symbols:

 =~ to match a string pattern.

■ !~ to not match a string pattern.

Here's an example of using the string expression:

```
$ cat test4
#!/bin/tcsh
# testing a string comparison

set testing=testing

if ( $testing =~ test* ) echo "it matched test*"
if ( $testing !~ test ) echo "it didn't match test"
$ ./test4
it matched test*
it didn't match test
$
```

There's also another expression symbol you'll probably find handy. The $? symbol tests if a variable has been set or not:

```
$ cat test5
#!/bin/tcsh
# using the $? symbol

set test1 = 10

if ($?test1) echo "The test1 variable has been set"
if ($?test2) echo "The test2 variable has been set"
$ ./test5
The test1 variable has been set
$
```

The tcsh shell also contains special tests for files and directories. These tests take the form:

```
-op file
```

where op is a one-character operation that defines the type of file operation to test.

Table 21-5 shows the file test operators available in tcsh.

TABLE 21-5

The tcsh File Test Operators

Operator	Description
r	Read access
w	Write access
x	Executable
X	Contained within the path or a built-in command
e	The file exists
o	The owner of the file
z	Has zero size
s	Has non-zero size
f	Plain file
d	Directory
l	Symbolic link

This provides an easy way to test the status of files in your shell scripts:

```
$ cat test6
#!/bin/tcsh
# testing for the $HOME directory and a file

if ( -d $HOME ) then
    echo "The HOME directory exists"
endif
if ( -f $HOME/test) then
    echo "The test file exists"
else
    echo "The test file doesn't exist"
endif
$ ./test6
The HOME directory exists
The test file doesn't exist
$ touch $HOME/test
$ ./test6
The HOME directory exists
The test file exists
$
```

Using the file test operators, you can easily determine the status of files before trying to use them in your scripts.

The foreach statement

The tcsh shell doesn't use the `for` statement, but it does contain a `foreach` statement for iterating through the values in an array variable or a list. The format of the `foreach` statement is:

```
foreach var1 (wordlist)
    statements
end
```

The parameter `wordlist` can be an array variable, or a list of values separated with spaces:

```
$ cat test7
#!/bin/tcsh
# testing the foreach statement

echo "The directories in your PATH are:"
foreach dir ($path)
    echo $dir
end
$ ./test7
The directories in your PATH are:
/usr/local/bin
/bin
/usr/bin
/usr/X11R6/bin
$
```

This is a great way to iterate through array variables, especially if you don't know how many elements are in the array.

The while statement

The `while` statement in tcsh allows you to loop until a specified expression evaluates to a `FALSE` condition. The format of the while command is:

```
while (expression)
    statements
end
```

The expression used in the `while` statement is the same format as for the `if` statement, using C-style mathematical comparison symbols, as well as the special `=~` and `!~` string comparison symbols:

```
$ cat test8
#!/bin/tcsh
# determining the factorial of a value

set value=$1
set factorial = 1
```

```
set counter = 1
while ( $counter <= $value )
   @ factorial = ( $factorial * $counter )
   @ counter += 1
end
echo "The factorial of $value is $factorial"
$ ./test8 5
The factorial of 5 is 120
$
```

The while statement continues looping through the statements until the expression evaluates to a FALSE condition.

The switch command

The switch command in the tcsh shell allows you to execute multiple statements based on the value of a string match. The format of the switch statement is:

```
switch (string)
case val1:
    statements
case val2:
    statements
default:
    statements
endsw
```

The shell compares the *string* value to the values listed in each case statement. If a case statement value matches *string*, the shell executes all of the statements contained in that case statement, plus all of the following case statements.

If you only want the shell to execute the statements in a single case section, you can use the breaksw command at the end of the case section. This causes the shell to jump to the end statement. If none of the case values match, the default section statements are executed.

Here's an example of using the switch statement in a shell script:

```
$ cat test9
#!/bin/tcsh
# reading input and using the switch statement

echo -n "Please enter a word: "
set input = $<
switch ($input)
case test:
   echo "This is a test"
   breaksw
case hello:
```

583

```
        echo "Hello world!"
        breaksw
    case exit:
        echo "Thank you for playing"
        breaksw
    default:
        echo "Sorry, I don't understand that command"
    endsw
$ ./test9
Please enter a word: test
This is a test
$ ./test9
Please enter a word: testing
Sorry, I don't understand that command
$ ./test9
Please enter a word: exit
Thank you for playing
$
```

Since the tcsh shell doesn't include a read statement like the bash shell, you must read an input value directly from STDIN. You do this using the $< symbol:

```
set input = $<
```

After retrieving the input, the switch statement compares the text to each case statement. If none match, it uses the default statement (if provided).

> **NOTE** In case you were wondering, the tcsh shell doesn't support functions in shell scripts. This can be a huge hindrance when converting bash shell scripts for the tcsh environment.

Summary

This chapter discussed the features found in the C shell. While the C shell is not overly popular in the Linux world, you may still run into it, so it's a good idea to know how it differs from the bash shell.

The most popular C shell implementation is the tcsh shell. While the tcsh shell is usually not the default shell in Linux, it's usually available as an installation file. This allows you to write and test scripts used in a Unix environment that uses the C shell.

The C shell uses two types of variables, shell variables and environment variables. Shell variables are lower case and contain system information and settings commonly used in the C shell. The environment variables are mostly used for compatibility with Bourne and bash shell scripts, and maintain simple values such as the path and shell name.

To set shell variables you must use the `set` statement. The C shell allows you use assign mathematical operations to variables, but you must use the `set` statement alias, the at symbol (@). Using this symbol you can write mathematical equations using standard math symbols and parentheses.

To set environment variables you must use the `setenv` statement.

The C shell provides most of the standard structured commands you're used to in the bash shell. Unfortunately they use a slightly different format, so you'll need to rewrite your bash shell scripts to get them to work properly in a C shell environment.

The next chapter examines yet another popular Unix shell that's made its way into the Linux world. The Korn shell is popular in the Sun Unix environment, and it is often used in Linux when it's necessary to port shell scripts from a Sun server to a Linux server.

Chapter 22

The Korn Shell

In exploring different Linux shells, no doubt sooner or later you'll run into the Korn shell. The Korn shell is popular in the Unix world, but not so much in the Linux world. The Korn shell offers an interesting mix of features from both the Bourne and C shell worlds. This chapter discusses the features of the Korn shell, and walks you through the most common version of the Korn shell, the ksh93 shell.

IN THIS CHAPTER

The Korn shell

Parts of the ksh93 shell

Scripting with the ksh93 shell

The Korn Shell History

The original Korn shell was developed by David Korn while working at AT&T Bell Labs in the 1980s. David developed the Korn shell (you can probably guess where its name comes from) to be a next-generation programming shell, incorporating the best features of the Bourne shell and the best features of the C shell. The Korn shell quickly became known as a programmer's shell. It supports advanced programming features missing from the Bourne and C shells, including associative arrays and floating-point arithmetic.

The original Korn shell was controlled by AT&T as a proprietary shell up until 2000. Since then it has been released as open source software.

There are two separate threads of the original Korn shell:

- ksh88
- ksh93

Most Korn shell implementations (including those found in Linux distributions) use the ksh93 shell. The exception is Sun Solaris. Sun uses a modified version of the ksh88 shell, which is somewhat different from the ksh93 shell. Because the Korn shell used in Linux distributions uses the ksh93 shell, that's the shell that's covered in this chapter.

> **NOTE**   The ksh93 shell is also referred to as the Enhanced Korn shell in some Linux distributions and Unix systems (such as IBM's AIX operating system).

There is one other version of the Korn shell you may run into in the Linux environment. During the time when the original Korn shell was proprietary software, a public domain version of the Korn shell (called the pdksh shell) was developed. The pdksh shell has most of the same features as the ksh88 shell, but it is missing the advanced mathematical features found in the ksh93 shell.

The Parts of the ksh93 Shell

Since the ksh93 shell is based upon the Bourne and C shells, you'll see lots of similarities between it and the bash and tcsh shells. This section describes the individual features of the ksh93 shell, including the command line parameters, environment variables, and built-in commands.

Command line parameters

As with other shells, the Linux ksh93 shell utilizes command line parameters to define how it behaves, both as an interactive shell, and a shell scripting shell. Table 22-1 shows the command line parameters you can use when starting a new ksh93 shell session.

TABLE 22-1

The ksh93 Command Line Parameters

Parameter	Description
-a	Automatically export shell variables.
-A	Assign values from the command line arguments to the specified array variable.
-b	Display job completion messages as soon as jobs change state.
-B	Enable brace pattern field generation.
-c	Read commands from the first argument.
-C	Prevent redirection from truncating existing files.
-D	Don't execute commands. Display double-quoted strings that are preceded by a dollar sign.
-e	If a command has a non-zero exit status, exit the shell.
-f	Disables filename generation.

TABLE 22-1	(continued)
Parameter	**Description**
-G	Cause the wildcard characters ** to match files and directories.
-h	Each command becomes a tracked alias.
-i	Interactive shell. All output goes to the terminal.
-m	Background jobs run as a separate process group.
-n	Read commands and check for errors, but don't execute them.
-o	Sets default shell options.
-p	Disables processing the $HOME/.profile file.
-P	Start the shell as a profile shell.
-r	Start the shell as a restricted shell.
-R	Generate a cross-reference database.
-s	Send all output to file descriptor 2.
-v	Display commands as they're read.
-x	Display commands and their arguments as they're executed.

The ksh93 command line parameters are pretty similar to the bash shell. Besides the command line parameters, you can customize the shell behavior using the -o command line parameter. There are quite a few shell options you can set with this parameter:

- allexport: Automatically export variables.
- errexit: Exit the shell if a command generates a non-zero exit status.
- bgnice: Run all background jobs at a lower priority.
- bracexpand: Enable brace pattern field generation.
- emacs: Use emacs editor mode for command line editing.
- ignoreeof: The shell doesn't exit on an EOF character.
- markdirs: All directory names resulting from filename generation use a trailing slash.
- monitor: Background jobs run as a separate process group.
- noclobber: Prevent redirection from overwriting files.
- noexec: Read commands and display errors, but don't execute them.
- noglob: Disable filename generation.
- nolog: Don't save functions in history log.
- notify: Display new status of jobs when they change status.
- nounset: Treat unset parameters as an error.

- `pipefail`: Pipelines won't complete until all components have completed.
- `privileged`: Disables processing of $HOME/.profile file.
- `verbose`: Display commands as the shell reads them.
- `trackall`: Each command becomes a tracked alias.
- `vi`: Use vi editor mode for command line editing.
- `viraw`: Process each character as it's typed in vi editor mode.
- `xtrace`: Display commands as the shell executes them.

You can set multiple command line options on the command line to set multiple features for the shell at once.

Default files

When you use the ksh93 shell as a login shell, it reads commands from two files:

- `/etc/profile`
- `$HOME/.profile`

You should store commands that are executed by all users in the `/etc/profile` file, while commands for individual users should be stored in the appropriate `$HOME/.profile` file.

Environment variables

The ksh93 shell uses environment variables to set features and provide information about the shell environment. Table 22-2 shows the default environment variables available in the ksh93 shell.

TABLE 22-2

The ksh93 Environment Variables

Variable	Description
CDPATH	The search path for the cd command
COLUMNS	The terminal width in characters for edit mode
EDITOR	The default editor used for command line editing
ENV	Defines a file used for specifying parameter expansion, command substitution, and arithmetic substitution (commonly $HOME/.kshrc)
FIGNORE	The set of filenames ignored when performing filename matching
FPATH	Search path for functions
HISTCMD	The number of the current command in the history file
HISTEDIT	The default editor for the history command

TABLE 22-2	*(continued)*
Variable	**Description**
HISTFILE	The file used to store command history
HOME	The user's default directory set at a login
IFS	Internal field separator, set to space, tab, and newline by default
LANG	The locale category used for functions not covered by an LC_ environment variable
LC_ALL	Overrides LANG and all LC_ environment value settings
LC_COLLATE	The language used for collation
LC_CTYPE	The language used for handling character sets
LC_NUMERIC	The language used for the decimal point character
LINES	The number of lines available on the terminal
LINENO	The current line in the script being processed
MAIL	The name of a mail file to check for new mail
MAILCHECK	How often (in seconds) to check the mail file specified by MAIL
MAILPATH	A colon-separated list of directories to check for the mail file specified by MAIL
OLDPWD	The previous working directory
PATH	A colon-separated list of directories to search for an executable command
PPID	The process ID of the parent process
PS1	The primary command line prompt string (default is $)
PS2	The secondary command line prompt string (default is >)
PS3	The select loop prompt (default is #?)
PS4	The prompt used in parameter evaluation, command substitution, and arithmetic substitution (default is +)
PWD	The current working directory
RANDOM	Generates a new random integer value each time it's accessed
SECONDS	The number of seconds since the shell was started
SHELL	The pathname of the current shell
TIMEFORMAT	A format string to specify how time is displayed
TMOUT	If non-zero, the default timeout for read commands
VISUAL	Allows you to enable the emacs, gmac, or vi editors

The ksh93 environment variables use the same format as the bash environment variables, in that system environment variables use all upper-case characters. You display the currently set environment variables using the set command:

```
$ set
_=/bin/ksh
COLORTERM=''
DBUS_SESSION_BUS_ADDRESS=unix:abstract=/tmp/dbus-
JlNamp8Rkt,guid=a1ed8c4706b2db3ebaa39969fed7c100
DESKTOP_SESSION=kde
DISPLAY=:0.0
DM_CONTROL=/var/run/xdmctl
ENV='$HOME/.kshrc'
FCEDIT=/bin/ed
GS_LIB=/home/rich/.fonts
GTK2_RC_FILES=/home/rich/.gtkrc-2.0
GTK_RC_FILES=/etc/gtk/gtkrc:/home/rich/.gtkrc:/home/rich/.kde/share/
config/gtkrc
HISTCMD=35
HOME=/home/rich
IFS=$' \t\n'
KDEDIR=/usr
KDE_FULL_SESSION=true
KDE_MULTIHEAD=false
KDEROOTHOME=/root/.kde
KONSOLE_DCOP='DCOPRef(konsole-4373,konsole)'
KONSOLE_DCOP_SESSION='DCOPRef(konsole-4373,session-1)'
LANG=en_US
LANGUAGE=en
LC_ALL=en_US
LINENO=1
LOGNAME=rich
MAILCHECK=600
OLDPWD=/home/rich
OPTIND=1
PATH=/bin:/sbin:/usr/bin:/usr/sbin:/usr/X11R6/bin:/usr/local/bin:/usr
/local/sbin
PPID=5619
PS1='$ '
PS2='> '
PS3='#? '
PS4='+ '
PWD=/home/rich/test
QTDIR=/usr/share/qt3
RANDOM=17445
SECONDS=1.291
SESSION_MANAGER=local/testbox:/tmp/.ICE-unix/4315
```

```
SHELL=/bin/ksh
SHLVL=3
SSH_AGENT_PID=4270
SSH_AUTH_SOCK=/tmp/ssh-HcqYkH4172/agent.4172
TERM=xterm
TMOUT=0
USER=rich
WINDOWID=35651589
XCURSOR_THEME=default
XDM_MANAGED=/var/run/xdmctl/xdmctl-
:0,maysd,mayfn,sched,rsvd,method=classic
$
```

You can also create your own environment variables in the ksh93 shell. It's common to use lower-case characters for user-defined variables, so as not to get them confused with the system environment variables.

To set an environment variable in the ksh93 shell, use the assignment operator:

```
$testing=10 ; export testing
$ ksh
$ echo $testing
10
$
```

The ksh93 shell uses the export command to export environment variables to child shells.

The next sections show some interesting features of the ksh93 environment variables.

Random numbers

The ksh93 shell uses the RANDOM variable as an easy way to generate random numbers in your scripts. The RANDOM variable produces a random integer between 0 and 32767 each time you reference it:

```
$ echo $RANDOM
13452
$ echo $RANDOM
12498
$ echo $RANDOM
31104
$
```

You can seed the random number generator by assigning an integer value to the RANDOM variable. Different seed values produce different sequences of random numbers. It's common practice to use the $$ variable as the seed value. This special variable represents the process ID (PID) of the shell and should be unique for each instance the shell runs.

Defining the variable type

A feature in the ksh93 shell that's not available in the bash shell is the `typeset` command. This command allows you to set attributes for variables and functions. One of the attributes you can set is the data type that the variable uses. Table 22-3 lists the parameters used with the `typeset` command.

The `typeset` command is a great way to convert numbers between different bases:

```
$ typeset -i2 a
$ typeset -i8 b
$ typeset -i16 c
$ a=100
$ b=100
$ c=100
$ echo $a $b $c
2#1100100 8#144 16#64
$
```

Each of the variables appears using a different base (the base appears before the pound sign when displaying the value).

TABLE 22-3

The typeset Command Parameters

Parameter	Description
-A	Make the variable an associative array.
-b	The variable can contain any number of data bytes.
-E*n*	Make the variable a double-precision floating-point number with *n* significant figures.
-F*n*	Make the variable a double-precision floating-point number with *n* decimal places.
-f	Assign a name for a function.
-i*n*	Make the variable an integer value with a base of *n*.
-l	Convert all upper-case characters to lower-case.
-L	Remove leading blanks and left-justify the text.
-n	Declare the variable to be a reference to another variable.
-r	Make the variable read-only.
-R	Add leading blanks to right-justify the text.
-u	Convert all lower-case characters to upper-case.
-x	Mark the variable for automatic exporting.
-Z	Right-justify and fill with leading zeros.

The `-l` and `-u` parameters work great in converting strings on the fly:

```
$ typeset -u testing
$ testing="This is a test"
$ echo $testing
THIS IS A TEST
$
```

It doesn't get any easier than that!

Use the `-n` parameter to allow one variable to reference the value in a separate variable. This can get confusing, so be careful when using it. Here's an example of how this works:

```
$ ntest1=100
$ typeset -n ntest1=ntest2
$ ntest2=1
$ echo $ntest1
1
$ ntest1=100
$ echo $ntest2
100
$
```

The `typeset` command forces the `ntest1` variable and the `ntest2` variable to reference the same memory location. Whatever value you assign to one, the other one also references. When I assigned a value of 1 to the `ntest2` variable, it replaced the existing value in `netst1`. When I displayed the value of the `ntest1` variable, it showed the same value as I assigned to `ntest2`. The same applied to `ntest2` when I assigned a value to the `ntest1` variable.

Using arrays

Just like the bash shell, the ksh93 shell supports the use of numerical array variables:

```
$ mytest=(one two three four five)
$ echo $mytest
one
$ echo ${mytest[2]}
three
$ echo ${mytest[*]}
one two three four five
$
```

The ksh93 shell also supports *associative arrays*. Associative arrays allow you to use strings as the index values instead of numbers. Before you can define the values in an associative array, you must declare the variable you'll use. You do that with the `typeset` command:

```
$ typeset -A test2
$
```

Once you declare the variable as an associative array, you can assign keys and values using the format:

```
variable=( [key1]=value1 [key2]=value2 ...)
```

Each key can be any length string, and each value can be a number or a text string:

```
$ test2=( [fruit]=banana [vegetable]=carrot [age]=18)
$
```

Once you define the elements in the associative array, you can access them based on the key:

```
$ echo ${test2[fruit]}
banana
$ echo ${test2[age]}
18
$
```

The problem with associative arrays is that unlike numeric arrays, where you can cycle through the index numbers, you have no way of knowing the key values that exist. To solve this problem, the ksh93 shell provides a special format for displaying just the key values of an associative array:

```
$ echo ${!test2[@]}
fruit age vegetable
$
```

Notice that the order the keys were printed in doesn't match the order in which they were defined. This is an important thing to remember. There's no guarantee that ksh93 will store the associative array values in the same order in which you define them.

While this may seem confusing, it's not really all that bad. When you display all of the element values, you'll see why:

```
$ echo ${test2[*]}
banana 18 carrot
$
```

When you display the element values, they appear in the same order as the keys. This allows you to easily match the keys with their values.

Associative arrays provide a method for you to match string keys with values in your shell scripts, which can be a very powerful tool.

Compound variables

The ksh93 shell supports yet another feature with variables called *compound variables*. A compound variable is similar to an associative array, but references the values in a slightly different manner.

To define a compound variable, you use the format:

```
variable=( subscript1=value1 subscript2=value2 ...)
```

The *subscript* is a text value, similar to the key in the associative array. The values can be any text or numerical values:

```
$ test3=( fruit=banana vegetable=carrot age=18)
$
```

Once you assign the subscripts and values, you can reference an individual subscript value with the format:

```
variable.subscript
```

Here's how this looks:

```
$ echo ${test3.fruit}
banana
$ echo ${test3.age}
18
$
```

Each individual subscript value can be extracted just by referencing the subscript name along with the variable.

Special variable subscripts

There are several special subscripts that are available in the ksh93 shell. These subscripts define current information about the shell, as well as current information about the currently running process in the shell. Table 22-4 lists the special ksh93 shell subscript variables.

Since the subscript variables use periods in their names, you must use braces around them when referencing them:

```
$ echo ${.sh.version}
Version M 1993-12-28 r-
$
```

The subscript variables used in discipline functions are discussed later in the "Discipline functions" section.

Built-in commands

The ksh93 built-in commands should look a lot like the bash commands, since they're both based on the Bourne shell. Table 22-5 shows the ksh93 built-in commands.

As you will see, the ksh93 shell contains a fair amount of built-in commands, making it a robust shell to use for scripting. You should recognize most of these commands from the bash shell.

The ksh93 shell uses the echo, print and printf commands for displaying data and text. The differences among these three commands can get confusing at times.

The echo command in ksh93 is somewhat unreliable. For the most part, it behaves similarly to the bash shell, but it's not guaranteed. Only the most basic use of the echo command is

TABLE 22-4

The ksh93 Subscript Variables

Variable	Description
.sh.command	The current command line about to run.
.sh.edchar	The value of the keyboard character entered for the last KEYBD trap.
.sh.edcol	The character position of the cursor at the last KEYBD trap.
.sh.edmode	Set to ESC when processing a key in vi editor mode, otherwise set to null.
.sh.edtext	The characters in the keyboard buffer when processing the last KEYBD trap.
.sh.file	The pathname of the file that contains the current command.
.sh.fun	The name of the function currently being executed.
.sh.match	An indexed array which stores the most recent match and subpattern matches.
.sh.name	The name of the variable at the time a discipline function is executed.
.sh.subscript	Set to the name subscript of the variable at the time a discipline function is executed.
.sh.subshell	The current depth of subshells and command substitution.
.sh.value	The value of the variable at the time a discipline function is executed.
.sh.version	The version of the shell.

recommended in the ksh93 shell. For more advanced formatted printing, you should use either the print or printf commands.

The print command uses the format:

```
print [ -Renprs ] [ -u unit] [ -f format ] [ arg ... ]
```

The command line parameters are:

- -R: Print all subsequent options and arguments other than -n.
- -e: Enable escape characters (such as \n and \t). This is the default behavior.
- -n: Don't add a newline character at the end of the line.
- -p: Write arguments onto the pipe of the spawned process instead of STDOUT.
- -r: Disable escape characters in the format string.
- -s: Write arguments into the history file instead of STDOUT.
- -u: Write the output to the specified file descriptor instead of STDOUT.
- -f: Use the specified C-style printf format string to display the arguments.

TABLE 22-5

The ksh93 Built-in Commands

Command	Description
alias	Defines an alias for a command.
bg	Starts the specified job in background mode.
builtin	Displays the built-in commands.
cd	Changes the current working directory.
command	Executes the specified command.
disown	Causes the shell to not send a HUP signal to the specified jobs when the shell terminates.
echo	Displays a text string and variables.
eval	The specified arguments are read into the shell and executed.
exec	The specified command is executed in place of the shell without creating a new process.
exit	Causes the shell to exit with the specified exit status.
export	Exports the specified environment variables to all child shells.
false	Exits with an exit status of 1.
fg	Starts the specified job in foreground mode.
getconf	Displays the current values of the shell configuration parameters
getopts	Retrieves the next option from a string of options each time it's called.
hist	Displays and edits the history file.
jobs	Displays information about the specified job, or all active jobs.
kill	Sends the specified signal (TERM if none specified) to the specified process ID.
let	Evaluates the specified arithmetic operation. Returns 0 if the value of the expression is non-zero, and 1 if otherwise.
newgrp	Equivalent to the /bin/newgrp utility.
print	Displays arguments on STDOUT.
printf	Displays arguments using a C-style formatting string.
pwd	Displays the current working directory.
read	Reads input from STDIN and stores it in a variable.

continued

TABLE 22-5	(continued)
Command	**Description**
readonly	Reads input from STDIN and stores it in a variable that can't be changed.
set	Sets shell features defined in the command line parameters.
shift	Renames positional parameters to shift the values down one parameter.
sleep	Suspends execution for the specified number of seconds.
trap	Intercepts the specified signal and performs the specified command.
true	Exits with an exit status of 0.
typeset	Sets attributes and values for shell variables and functions.
ulimit	Displays or sets a resource limit.
umask	Displays or sets the default permissions for new files and directories.
unalias	Removes a defined alias.
unset	Removes the value of the specified variable
wait	Waits until the specified job completes and reports its exit status.
whence	Displays how the specified command would be interpreted (built-in or utility location)

You can customize the output of the print command by using both the command line parameters and a printf C-style format string (see Chapter 19). By default the print command just prints out variables:

```
$ test=10
$ test2=15
$ print $test $test2
10 15
$
```

With the print command you can still use the same format as the echo command:

```
$ value1=10
$ value2=15
$ print "The first value is $value, while the second is $value2"
The first value is 10, while the second is 15
$
```

The print command also allows you to use the printf format string to display the variables in a formatted text string, much like the printf command:

```
$ test=testing
$ test2=10
```

```
$ print -f "This %s value is %d\n" $test $test2
This testing value is 10
$
```

The %s and %d control codes determine the format of the output for the associated variables in the print command list.

The printf command uses only the C-style printf format to display arguments by default. The format of the printf command is:

```
printf format [ arg ... ]
```

The *format* parameter is a text string that uses the standard symbols to denote specific data types and formats to use in the print (see Chapter 19). Each data symbol matches an argument supplied on the command line:

```
$ printf "This %s value is %d\n" $test $test2
This testing value is 10
$
```

The printf command provides a few extra formatting tricks than the print command:

- Reuses control codes until all of the listed variables are displayed.
- Can print time and date values using the same format as the date command.

If you supply more variables on the printf command line than control codes in the format string, the printf command automatically goes back to the first control code and repeats using the control codes with the additional variables. This is useful if you're trying to print a table of values. You only have to define the control codes for the first row, then list all of the variables on the same line:

```
$ test1=10
$ test2=15
$ test3=20
$ test4=25
$ printf "%d - %d\n" $test1 $test2 $test3 $test4
10 - 15
20 - 25
$
```

The printf command also allows you to easily reformat a date and time value into any format using the date command format:

```
$ value1='1/31/08'
$ print $value1
1/31/08
$ printf "%(%Y)T\n" $value1
2008
```

```
$ printf "%(%A, %B %d, %Y)T\n" $value1
Thursday, January 31, 2008
$ printf "%(%F)T\n" $value1
Thu Jan 31 12:42:11 EST 2008
$
```

It's pretty amazing what you can do with the %T format control code!

Scripting in the ksh93 Shell

For the most part, scripting in the ksh93 shell isn't much different than in the bash shell. Most of your bash shell scripts should work just fine in a ksh93 shell environment, and the ones that don't usually just need a little modification.

If you're writing scripts specifically for the ksh93 shell, there are a few additional things that you can use to make life a little easier for you. This section describes the major differences you'll find between the ksh93 shell and the bash shell.

Mathematical operations

A great feature of the ksh93 shell is the ease with which you can use mathematical operations. This section describes the features available in the ksh93 shell for manipulating numbers and performing mathematical operations.

Performing calculations

Mathematical calculations are performed using one of two methods:

- The let command
- Double parentheses

The let command allows you to assign the result of a mathematical operation directly to a variable:

```
$ let value1=4*5
$ echo $value1
20
$
```

Using this format, you can't have any spaces between the equal sign and the equation elements. Alternatively, you can enclose the equation in double quotation marks and use as many spaces as you want:

```
$ let value1=" 4 * 3 "
$ echo $value1
12
$
```

Probably the most useful feature of the ksh93 shell's mathematical abilities is that unlike the bash shell, it can handle floating point numbers:

```
$ let value1=" 10.5 * 0.5 "
$ echo $value1
5.25
$
```

This feature alone makes the ksh93 shell a favorite for many shell programmers.

Instead of the let command, you can also use the double parentheses method of defining mathematical operations:

```
$ value1=$(( 4 * 3 ))
$ echo value1
12
$
```

You can perform any mathematical operation you need within the double parentheses, using both numbers and variables:

```
$ value1=10.25
$ value2=$(( $value1 / 10 ))
$ echo $value2
1.025
$
```

If you try to perform something that's not valid, the ksh93 shell will let you know about it with an error message:

```
$ value1=0
$ value2=$(( 10.25 / $value1 ))
ksh93:  10.25 / 0 : divide by zero
$
```

Besides the error message, the ksh93 shell also returns a non-zero exit status to indicate that the operation failed.

Mathematical functions

The ksh93 shell includes several built-in mathematical functions you can use in your shell scripts. The mathematical library built into the ksh93 shell consists of the following functions:

- abs(x): Absolute value of x.
- acos(x): The arc cosine of x (in radians).
- asin(x): The arc sine of x (in radians).

- atan(x): The arc tangent of x (in radians).
- atan2(y, x): The arc tangent of y / x.
- cos(x): The cosine of x (in radians).
- cosh(x): The hyperbolic cosine of x (in radians).
- exp(x): The exponent of x.
- floor(x): The next lowest integer value by rounding down x.
- fmod(x, y): The floating-point remainder of x / y.
- hypot(x, y): The length of the hypotenuse of a right-angle triangle with sides x and y.
- int(x): The nearest integer between x and 0.
- log(x): The natural logarithm of x.
- pow(b, e): The result of b raised to the e power.
- sin(x): The sine of x (in radians).
- sinh(x): The hyperbolic sine of x (in radians).
- sqrt(x): The square root of x.
- tan(x): The tangent of x (in radians).
- tanh(x): The hyperbolic tangent of x (in radians).

That's a lot of functions for you to use! Using them is as easy as just including the function name and parameters in your shell script code:

```
$ cat test1
#!/bin/ksh93
# testing the ksh93 math functions

value1=9
value2=$(( sqt($value1) ))
value3=$(( int(10.52))
value4=$(( sin(45) ))
print "The square root of $value1 is $value2"
print "The integer part of 10.52 is $value3"
print "The sine of 45 is $value4"
$ ./test1
The square root of 9 is 3
The integer part of 10.52 is 10
The sine of 45 is 0.850903524534
$
```

As you can see from the examples, the ksh93 math functions can also work with floating-point numbers.

Structured commands

The ksh93 shell implements all of the structured commands you're familiar with in the bash shell:

- `if-then`
- `for` loops (including the C-style)
- `while` loops
- `until` loops
- `select` statements
- `case` statements

Each of these structured commands uses the same format as the Bourne shell (and thus the bash and ash shells), so I won't cover these in detail. However, the ksh93 shell provides a simpler method for specifying mathematical operations in the `if-then` statement and the `while`/`until` loops. The following sections take a closer look at these features.

The if-then-else statement

The `if-then` statement uses the same format as for the bash shell (see Chapter 9). The basic format of the `if-then` statement is:

```
if command then
    statements1
else
    statements2
fi
```

Just as with the bash shell, the ksh93 shell `if-then` statement executes the command provided, and if it returns a zero exit status, proceeds to execute the first set of statements. Otherwise, it executes the second set of statements.

The ksh93 shell also supports the `elif` statement, allowing you to chain `if-then-else` statements together:

```
if command1 then
    statements1
elif command2 then
    statements2
fi
```

The ksh93 `if-then` statement supports the `test` command (see Chapter 9), but it doesn't recognize the alternative `test` command format using the single brackets. Instead, the ksh93 shell supports using double parentheses for mathematical comparisons, and double brackets for non-mathematical comparisons. Here's an example of a math comparison:

```
$ cat test2
#!/bin/ksh93
# testing the test command
```

```
value1=10
value2=20
if (( $value1 < $value2 )) then
    print "The value $value1 is less than $value2"
else
    print "The value $value1 is greater than $value2"
fi
$ ./test2
The value 19 is less than 20
$
```

You'll also notice that similarly to the tcsh shell, the ksh93 shell supports using standard mathematical operators when comparing numerical values.

NOTE   The ksh93 shell also supports the bash-style numerical comparators (such as -gt, -lt, and -eq), but they're considered obsolete and may go away in future versions of the Korn shell.

The ksh93 shell uses the same file and directory tests as the bash shell, such as -d for directories, -f for files, -r for readable, and -x for executable. Here's an example using the directory comparison symbols:

```
$ cat test3
#!/bin/ksh93
# testing the non-math comparison

if [[ -d $HOME ]] && [[ -f $HOME/testing ]] then
    print "The file exists."
else
    print "Sorry, the file doesn't exist."
fi
$ ./test3
Sorry, the file doesn't exist.
$ touch $HOME/testing
$ ./test3
The file exists.
$
```

You can also see from this example that the ksh93 shell supports the use of logical AND (&&) symbols. It also supports using logical OR (| |) as well.

The while and until loops

The while and until loops require a condition to determine when the loop must stop. The ksh93 shell allows you to set the condition using the same mathematical comparators as the if-then statement:

```
$ cat test5
#!/bin/ksh93
```

```
# calculating factorials the ksh93 way

value=1
while (( $value <= 10 ))
do
    factorial=1
    counter=1
    while (( $counter <= $value ))
    do
        factorial=$(( $factorial * $counter ))
        counter=$(( $counter + 1 ))
    done
    print "The factorial of $value is $factorial"
    value=$(( $value + 1 ))
done
$ ./test5
The factorial of 1 is 1
The factorial of 2 is 2
The factorial of 3 is 6
The factorial of 4 is 24
The factorial of 5 is 120
The factorial of 6 is 720
The factorial of 7 is 5040
The factorial of 8 is 40320
The factorial of 9 is 362880
The factorial of 10 is 3628800
$
```

The `while` statements performed as expected in the shell script.

Command redirection

In the ksh93 shell you can't use the backtick to redirect the output of a command to a variable. Instead, you must use the format:

```
variable=$( command )
```

This format assigns the output of a command to the variable:

```
$ value1=$( date )
$ echo $value1
Mon Jan 14 19:23:14 EST 2008
$
```

This feature comes in handy in your shell scripts, when you need to extract data from the output of a command (more on that in Chapter 27).

Discipline functions

A ksh93 shell feature related to command redirection is a *discipline* function. A discipline function is a function that operates on a variable. There are three basic discipline functions:

- `get`: To get the value of the function variable.
- `set`: To set the value of the function variable.
- `unset`: To reset the value of a function variable.

You define a discipline function similarly to how you would define a normal function (the ksh93 shell uses the `function` command, similar to how the bash shell does it). The key for a discipline function is how it returns the resulting value.

If you're using the `get` discipline function for a variable, instead of using the `return` command, a discipline function uses the special `.sh.value` variable. This allows you to use the function just like a variable, as each time you reference the discipline function name, it returns the value stored in the `.sh.value` variable.

Here's an example of defining and using a discipline function:

```
$ function date.get {
> .sh.value=$( date +'%A, %B %d, %Y' )
> }
$
```

Now the `date` variable will return the formatted date any time you retrieve its value:

```
$ echo $date
Monday, January 14, 2008
$
```

You use the `set` discipline function to automatically alter the way a variable value is set in an assignment statement:

```
$ function sqrt.set {
> .sh.value=$(( sqrt(${.sh.value}) ))
}
$
```

Now whenever you assign a value to the `sqrt` variable, the discipline function automatically calculates the square root of the value and assigns the result to the variable:

```
$ sqrt=9
$ echo $sqrt
3
$ sqrt=16
$ echo $sqrt
4
$
```

This is a great way to create simple functions on the fly, both in your interactive shells and in your shell scripts.

NOTE   In case you're wondering, the ksh93 shell supports normal functions also. They use the same format as functions in the bash shell, either using the `function` command or using the double parentheses to define the function name.

Summary

This chapter introduced the Korn shell and discussed one of the most popular Korn shell implementations, the ksh93 shell. The ksh93 shell is an advanced version of the original Korn shell and provides lots of interesting features.

The ksh93 shell allows you to typeset variables, defining what type of data a variable can hold and how to process it. By typesetting variables, you can change the way the shell displays numeric values (such as the base used) and also modify the way text is stored (such as all upper or lower-case).

You can create both numeric and associative array variables in the ksh93 shell. Associative arrays allow you to assign a string key to a data value. To recall the value, just reference the string key in the array. The use of compound variables is similar in that you assign multiple values to a variable and reference the values using a subscript of the array.

The ksh93 shell also provides lots of built-in commands. One handy command is the `printf` command, which allows you to use C-style `printf` formatting features to format your output.

One of the highlights of the ksh93 shell is its support for math features. The ksh93 shell can perform mathematical operations using standard C-style math symbols, and even includes several advanced built-in math functions, such as square root, absolute value, and the standard trig functions. The selling feature of the ksh93 shell for many shell programmers is its full support of floating-point numbers. You can process floating-point values the same as integer values directly in your shell scripts!

Finally, the chapter discussed a unique feature of the ksh93 shell, discipline functions. Discipline functions allow you to modify how variables are set and the value they return when you reference them. By overriding the default behavior, you can assign any type of function to a variable. Whenever you reference the variable, the ksh93 shell automatically executes the function and assigns the appropriate values when it completes.

The next chapter finishes off our tour of alternate Linux shells by examining the Z shell (zsh). The Z shell is one of the newest shells, and shows it by including lots of advanced features.

Chapter 23

The zsh Shell

To wrap up our discussion on Linux shells, this chapter takes a look at the newest of them, the zsh shell. The zsh shell provides some amazing features, and sets the bar pretty high for any future shell development. This chapter discusses what makes the zsh shell so unique, and walks you through the various features available for use in your zsh shell scripts.

History of the zsh Shell

The Z shell (called zsh) is an open source Unix shell developed by Paul Falstad. It takes ideas from the Bourne, bash, ash, and tcsh shells and adds many unique features to create a full-blown advanced shell designed for programmers.

Some of the features that make the zsh shell unique are:

- Improved shell option handling
- Shell compatibility modes
- Loadable modules

Of all these features, loadable modules is the most advanced thought in shell design. As you've seen in the previous shell chapters, each shell contains a set of built-in commands that are available without the need of external utility programs. The benefit of built-in commands is execution speed. The shell doesn't have to load a utility program into memory before running it, the built-in commands are already in the shell memory, ready to go.

The zsh shell provides a core set of built-in commands, plus the ability to add additional *command modules*. Each command module provides a set of additional built-in commands for specific circumstances, such as network support and advanced math functions. You can add only the modules you think you need for your specific situation.

This feature provides a great way to either limit the size of the zsh shell for situations that require a small shell size and few commands, or expand the number of available built-in commands for situations that require faster execution speeds.

Parts of the zsh Shell

This section walks you through the basics of the zsh shell, showing the built-in commands that are available (or can be added by installing modules), as well as the command line parameters and environment variables used by the zsh shell.

Shell options

Most shells use command line parameters to define the behavior of the shell. The zsh shell uses a few command line parameters to define the operation of the shell, but mostly it uses *options* to customize the behavior of the shell. You can set shell options either on the command line, or within the shell itself using the set command.

Table 23-1 lists the command line parameters available for the zsh shell.

While this may seem like a small set of command line parameters, the -o parameter is somewhat misleading. It allows you to set shell options that define features within the shell. By far the zsh shell is the most customizable shell available. There are lots of features that you can alter for your shell environment. The different options fit into several general categories:

- **Changing directories:** Options that control how the cd and dirs commands handle directory changes
- **Completion:** Options that control command completion features
- **Expansion and globbing:** Options that control file expansion in commands
- **History:** Options that control command history recall
- **Initialization:** Options that control how the shell handles variables and startup files when started
- **Input/Output:** Options that control command handling
- **Job Control:** Options that dictate how the shell handles and starts jobs
- **Prompting:** Options that define how the shell works with command line prompts
- **Scripts and Functions:** Options that control how the shell processes shell scripts and defines shell functions

- **Shell Emulation:** Options that allow you to set the behavior of the zsh shell to mimic the behavior of other shell types
- **Shell State:** Options that define what type of shell to start
- **zle:** Options for controlling the zsh line editor (zle) feature
- **Option Aliases:** Special options that can be used as aliases for other option names

With this many different categories of shell options, you can imagine just how many actual options the zsh shell supports. The following sections show a sampling of the different zsh shell options available for you to use when customizing your zsh shell environment.

Shell state

There are six different zsh shell options that define the type of shell to start:

- interactive (-i): Provides a command line interface prompt for entering built-in commands and program names.
- login (-l): The default zsh shell type, processes the zsh shell startup files, and provides a command line interface prompt.
- privileged (-p): The default if the effective user ID (UID) of the user is not the same as the real UID (the user has become the root user). This option disables the user startup files.
- restricted (-r): Restricts the user to a specified directory structure in the shell.
- shin_stdin (-s): Commands are read from STDIN.
- single_command (-t): Executes a single command from STDIN and exits.

The shell states define whether or not the shell starts with a command line interface prompt, and what access the user has within the shell.

TABLE 23-1

The zsh Shell Command Line Parameters

Parameter	Description
-c	Execute only the specified command and exit.
-i	Start as an interactive shell, providing a command line interface prompt.
-s	Force the shell to read commands from STDIN.
-o	Specify command line options.

Shell emulation

The shell emulation options allow you to customize the zsh shell to perform similar to the csh or ksh shells. These options are:

- **bsd_echo:** Make the echo statement compatible with the C shell echo command.
- **csh_junkie_history:** Using the history command without a specifier references the previous command.
- **csh_junkie_loops:** Allow while and for loops to use end like the C shell instead of do and done.
- **csh_junkie_quotes:** Change the rules of using single and double quotation marks to match the C shell.
- **csh_nullcmd:** Don't use the values of the NULLCMD and READNULLCMD variables when executing redirections with no commands.
- **ksh_arrays:** Use Korn-style arrays, starting numeric arrays at 0, and require braces to reference array elements.
- **ksh_autoload:** Emulate the Korn shell autoload function feature.
- **ksh_option_print:** Emulate the Korn shell method of printing options.
- **ksh_typeset:** Alter the way that the typeset command arguments are processed.
- **posix_builtins:** Use the builtin command to execute built-in commands.
- **sh_file_expansion:** Perform filename expansion before any other expansion.
- **sh_nullcmd:** Don't use the NULLCMD and READNULLCMD variables when performing redirections.
- **sh_option_letters:** Interpret single letter shell command line options similar to the Korn shell.
- **sh_word_split:** Perform field splitting on unquoted parameter expansions.
- **traps_async:** While waiting for a program to exit, handle signals and run traps immediately.

By having multiple options you can pick and choose which csh or ksh shell feature you need to emulate in your zsh shell, instead of having to emulate the entire shell.

Initialization

There are a few options for handling the shell startup features:

- **all_export:** All parameters and variables are exported to child shell processes automatically.
- **global_export:** Parameters exported to the environment will not be made local to the function.

- **global_rcs:** If not set, the zsh shell doesn't run the global startup files, but it still runs local startup files.
- **rcs:** If not set, the zsh shell runs the /etc/zshenv startup file, but no others.

The initialization options allow you to specify which (if any) zsh shell startup files are run in your shell environment. You can also set these values within startup files themselves to limit which ones the shell executes.

Scripts and functions

The scripts and functions options allow you to customize the shell scripting environment in the zsh shell. This is a handy way to set the way functions perform within the shell.

- **c_bases:** Display hexadecimal numbers in C format (0xdddd) instead of shell format (16#dddd).
- **err_exit:** If a command exits with a non-zero exit status, perform the command in the ZERR trap and exit.
- **err_return:** If a command has a non-zero exit status, return immediately from the enclosing function.
- **eval_lineno:** If set, the line numbers of expressions evaluated using the eval built-in command are tracked separately from the rest of the shell environment.
- **exec:** Execute commands. If this option isn't set, read commands and report errors, but don't execute the commands.
- **function_argzero:** Set $0 to the name of the function or script.
- **local_options:** If set, when a shell function returns, all of the options that were set before the function are restored.
- **local_traps:** If set, when a signal trap is set within a function, the previous status of the trap is restored when the function exits.
- **multios:** Perform implicit tees or cats when multiple redirections are attempted.
- **octal_zeroes:** Interpret any integer string starting with a zero as an octal number.
- **typeset_silent:** If not set, using typeset with the name of a parameter displays the current value of the parameter.
- **verbose:** Displays shell input lines as they are read by the shell.
- **xtrace:** Displays commands and their arguments as the shell executes them.

The zsh shell allows you to customize lots of features that occur when you're exiting functions defined in the shell.

The zsh shell files

The zsh shell uses files at both login and logout to allow you to preset variables and features of the zsh shell. The zsh shell automatically looks for several default files for setting environment variables and executing commands. If the any of the default files exist, the zsh shell executes them at specific instances. There are four different types of default files the zsh shell can handle:

- Shell startup files
- Login files
- Interactive files
- Logout files

This section examines the myriad of possible files you can use for your zsh shell.

The shell startup files

When you start a new zsh shell as a login shell (either by logging into the system, or by running the zsh shell program), the zsh shell looks for commands in two files.

The default system-wide zsh shell startup file is:

```
/etc/zshenv
```

After executing this file (if it exists), the zsh shell proceeds to the user's $HOME directory and looks for the file:

```
$HOME/.zshenv
```

You can test the order in which the zsh shell executes these files by performing a simple test using the echo statement in each file:

```
% zsh
This is the /etc/zshenv file.
This is the .zshenv file in HOME.
%
```

When I started a new zsh shell, it executed the /etc/zshenv file first, then the .zshenv file in the $HOME directory.

The shell startup files also execute if you use the zsh shell for a shell script:

```
% cat test1
#!/bin/zsh
# test run a script
echo "This is a test"
% ./test1
This is the /etc/zshenv file.
This is the .zshenv file in HOME.
This is a test
%
```

Notice that before the output of the shell script appears, you see the echo statements from the zsh shell startup files.

> **NOTE** Some Linux distributions (such as Debian) create a zsh directory under the /etc directory to contain all of the zsh shell startup files, instead of placing them directly in the /etc folder.

The shell login files

If you use the zsh shell as a login shell, it first looks for and executes two files:

- /etc/zlogin
- /etc/zprofile

These files are executed for all users who use the zsh shell as their login shell. The files should contain system-wide environment variables that should be set for all users, and executable programs that all users should use (such as the umask command to set default file and directory permissions). Most likely if you're using a Linux distribution that supports the zsh shell, these files already exist for setting system environment variables at login.

After executing this file, the zsh shell looks for two files in each user's $HOME directory:

- $HOME/.zlogin
- $HOME/.zprofile

These files can contain user-specific environment variable settings, and executable commands that an individual user wants to run when logging in to the system, before the command line interface prompt appears.

Any environment variable settings you make in the $HOME/.zprofile shell will override any system-wide settings made in the /etc/zprofile file, and similarly for the .zlogin files. You can test the order in which the zsh shell executes these files by adding a simple echo statement to each one, then logging in:

```
% zsh -l
This is the /etc/zshenv file.
This is the .zshenv file in HOME.
This is the /etc/zprofie file.
This is the .zprofile file in HOME.
This is the /etc/zlogin file.
This is the .zlogin file in HOME.
%
```

As you can see from the example, the zsh shell executes the zshenv files first, then the zprofile files, and finally, the zlogin files.

The interactive shell files

If you start an interactive zsh shell session, there's another set of files that can hold startup variables and commands:

- `/etc/zshrc`
- `$HOME/.zshrc`

The zsh shell executes these files immediately after the startup files when starting an interactive shell:

```
% zsh
This is the /etc/zshenv file.
This is the .zshenv file in HOME.
This is the /etc/zshrc file.
This is the .zshrc file in HOME.
%
```

Since a login shell is also an interactive shell, the zsh shell executes the contents of the zshrc files as well:

```
% zsh -l
This is the /etc/zshenv file.
This is the .zshenv file in HOME.
This is the /etc/zprofie file.
This is the .zprofile file in HOME.
This is the /etc/zshrc file.
This is the .zshrc file in HOME.
This is the /etc/zlogin file.
This is the .zlogin file in HOME.
%
```

Notice the order in which the zsh shell executes the files. The `zshrc` file pair are executed after the `zprofile` files, but before the `zlogin` files.

The shell logout files

Besides the login and startup files, the zsh shell also has the ability to execute commands in files when you log out from an interactive or login shell session. These files can be in the following locations:

- `/etc/zlogout`
- `$HOME/.zlogout`

As you probably figured out by now, every user on the system executes the commands in the /etc/zlogout file at logout, while each individual user has a unique $HOME/.zlogout file. The zsh shell will execute any commands in these files before logging out of the current shell.

This doesn't include just exiting from an interactive shell. Thus, if you just start another zsh shell from an existing shell session, the zsh shell won't execute the logout files when you exit the shell. However, if you start a login shell, the logout files should execute upon exiting:

```
% zsh -l
This is the /etc/zshenv file.
This is the .zshenv file in HOME.
This is the /etc/zprofie file.
This is the .zprofile file in HOME.
This is the /etc/zshrc file.
This is the .zshrc file in HOME.
This is the /etc/zlogin file.
This is the .zlogin file in HOME.
% exit
This is the .zlogout file in HOME.
This is the /etc/zlogout file.
%
```

Notice that the shell executes the .zlogout file before the global zlogout file, which is in the opposite order from the other zsh file types.

Environment variables

Just like any other shell, the zsh provides standard environment variables for tracking system and shell information. The zsh uses a combination of lower-case variable names and upper-case variable names.

There are a few environment variables for which the zsh shell provides both a lower-case and upper-case version. The reason for this is in the way the zsh handles arrays, and compatibility with other shells.

The zsh shell uses a space-separated list of words to define an array. Many Bourne shell–derived shells use a colon to separate array elements in multi-value variables, such as the PATH variable in the bash shell.

To maintain compatibility, the zsh shell provides a lower-case path variable, which uses the zsh-style array, and an upper-case PATH variable, which uses the Bourne-style array. Table 23-2 lists the environment variables found in the zsh shell.

TABLE 23-2

The zsh Environment Variables

Variable	Description
!	The process ID of the last background command.
#	The number of parameters specified on the command line.
$	The process ID of the shell.
*	An array containing the command line positional parameters.
-	Options set on the command line.
argv	An array containing the command line positional parameters.
ARGV0	The value of argv[0] of external commands, which is usually the command name.
BAUD	The baud rate of the current connection.
cdpath	An array of directories used for the search path in the cd command.
CDPATH	The same as cdpath, but using a colon as the field separator.
COLUMNS	The number of columns in the terminal session.
CPUTYPE	The microprocessor class or model of the system.
DIRSTACKSIZE	The maximum size of the directory stack.
EGID	The effective group ID of the shell process.
ENV	If the shell is invoked as a Bourne or Korn shell, contains the location of the zprofile file.
ERRNO	The error status of the most recently failed system call.
EUID	The effective user ID of the shell process.
FCEDIT	The default editor used in the command history editor.
fignore	An array of file suffixes to ignore during file completion.
FIGNORE	The same as fignore, but using a colon as the field separator.
fpath	An array of directories specifying the search path for functions.
FPATH	The same as fpath, but using a colon as the field separator.
GID	The real group ID of the shell process.
histchars	Characters used by the history command.
HISTCMD	The current history line number.
HISTFILE	The file to save the history in when exiting an interactive shell.

Variable	Description
TABLE 23-2 *(continued)*	
HISTSIZE	The maximum number of events allowed in the history file.
HOME	The user's default working directory.
HOST	The current hostname.
IFS	The internal file separators, defaults to space, tab, newline, and the NUL character.
KEYTIMEOUT	The time the shell waits (in hundredths of a second) for another key to be pressed when reading multi-character sequences.
LANG	The locale category for any category not covered by a LC_ variable.
LC_ALL	The locale category that overrides all other defined locale categories.
LC_COLLATE	The locale category used to determine character collation.
LC_CTYPE	The locale category used to determine character handling functions.
LC_MESSAGES	The locale category used to display messages.
LC_NUMERIC	The locale category used to display decimal point and thousands separator characters.
LC_TIME	The locale category used to display dates and time.
LINES	The number of lines in the terminal session.
LINENO	The line number of the current command in the script or shell function.
LISTMAX	The number of matches to list in the line editor before asking for more.
LOGCHECK	The interval in seconds between checking for inactivity using the watch parameter.
LOGNAME	The login name corresponding to the current shell session.
MAIL	If set the shell checks for mail in the specified file.
MAILCHECK	The interval in seconds between mail checks.
mailpath	An array of filenames to check for mail.
MAILPATH	The same as mailpath, but using a colon as the field separator.
manpath	An array of directories not used by the zsh shell (relates to MANPATH used in the Bourne shell).
MANPATH	The same as manpath, but using a colon as the field separator.
module_path	An array of directories used by zmodload to load new zsh modules.
MODULE_PATH	The same as module_path, but using a colon as the field separator.

continued

TABLE 23-2	(continued)
Variable	**Description**
NULLCMD	The command name to assume if a redirection is specified with no command. The default is the cat command.
path	An array of directories to search for commands.
PATH	The same as path, but using a colon as the field separator.
POSTEDIT	A string to display whenever exiting the line editor.
PROMPT	The primary prompt string used by the shell.
PROMPT2	The secondary prompt string used when more input is required for a command.
PROMPT3	The selection prompt used in a select loop.
PROMTP4	The trace prompt used when tracing a command.
prompt	The same as PROMPT.
PS1	The same as PROMPT.
PS2	The same as PROMPT2.
PS3	The same as PROMPT3.
PS4	The same as PROMPT4.
psvar	An array whose first nine values are referenced by the associated prompt strings.
PSVAR	The same as psvar, but using a colon as the field separator.
RANDOM	A random number generator for integers between 0 and 32767.
READNULLCMD	The default command name if an input redirection is specified with no command. The default is the more command.
REPORTTIME	Array of commands to report timing statistics for.
reply	Reserved for passing string values between shell scripts and functions.
REPLY	The same as reply, but uses an array value rather than string values.
RPROMPT	A prompt displayed on the right side of the command line interface.
RPS1	The same as RPROMPT.
RPROMPT2	A prompt displayed on the right side of the command line interface when more input is required for a command.
RPS2	The same as RPROMPT2.
SAVEHIST	The maximum number of events to save in the history file.

TABLE 23-2	(continued)
Variable	**Description**
SECONDS	The number of seconds since the shell was created.
SHLVL	The level of subshells invoked.
SPROMPT	The prompt used for spelling corrections.
STTY	The value used to set up TTY sessions for the shell.
TERM	The type of terminal used for the shell session.
TIMEFMT	The format to use to process time requests.
TMOUT	The amount of time (in seconds) before issuing an alarm if no commands are entered.
TMPREFIX	The pathname prefix used for all temporary files. The default is /tmp/zsh.
USERNAME	The user login name corresponding to the real user ID of the shell process.
watch	An array of login and logout events to report.
WATCH	The same as watch, but using a colon as the field separator.
WATCHFMT	The format of the report generated if the watch variable is set.
WORDCHARS	A list of nonalphabetic characters considered part of a word by the line editor.
ZBEEP	A string of characters sent to the display instead of generating a beep for an alarm.
ZDOTDIR	The directory to search for zsh personal startup files. The default is the $HOME directory.

As you can see from Table 23-2 the zsh shell provides some unique features in the environment variables. One of my favorites is the right prompt (RPROMPT) variable.

The RPROMPT variable displays a prompt on the right side of the command line interface:

```
% RPROMPT='%d'
%                                                          /home/test
% cd test                                                  /home/test
%                                                     /home/test/test
```

The right prompt displays the defined prompt (set to the current working directory in this example) on the far right if the space isn't needed to display text. If the shell needs to display text, it doesn't display the right prompt.

The zsh shell supports the typeset command, which allows you to declare attributes for a variable before using it. Table 23-3 show the options available for the zsh typeset command.

TABLE 23-3

The typeset Command Parameters

Parameter	Description
-a	Create a numerical array variable.
-A	Create an associative array variable.
-E	Create a double-precision floating-point variable and display using scientific notation.
-f	Define a function name instead of a variable.
-F	Create a double-precision floating-point variable and display using fixed-point decimal notation.
-h	Create a hidden special variable.
-H	Don't display the value of the variable.
-i	Create an integer data type variable.
-l	Convert the variable value to lower case.
-L	Left-justify by removing leading blanks from a variable.
-r	Make the specified variables read-only.
-R	Right-justify by adding blanks on the left.
-t	Tag the specified variables.
-u	Convert the variable value to upper case.
-U	Keep only the first occurrence for each duplicated value in a numerical array.
-x	Mark the specified variable for automatic export.
-Z	Right-justify using leading zeroes.

As you can see from the typeset command parameters, the zsh shell supports arrays, both numeric and associative. If you're used to using numeric arrays in the bash and ksh shells, you'll have to be a little careful when using them in the zsh shell. The zsh shell starts arrays with an index value of 1 instead of 0:

```
% mytest=(one two three four)
% echo ${mytest[1]}
one
% echo ${mytest[2]}
two
%
```

Creating an associative array is also slightly different in the zsh shell. You must first declare it using the `typeset` command:

```
% typeset -A test
%
```

Once you've declared the variable as being an associative array, you can define keys and values. This is where things are a little different. In the zsh shell, you just alternate listing the keys and values:

```
variable=( key1 value1 key2 value2 ...)
```

Thus, to add data to the `test` array:

```
$ test=( fruit banana vegetable carrot age 18 )
$ echo ${test[fruit]}
banana
$ echo ${test[age]}
18
$
```

Because of this syntax, every key must be assigned a value in the zsh associative array.

Built-in commands

The zsh shell is unique in that it allows you to expand the built-in commands available in the shell. This provides for a wealth of speedy utilities at your fingertips for a host of different applications.

This section describes the core built-in commands, along with the various modules available at the time of this writing.

Core built-in commands

The core of the zsh shell contains the basic built-in commands you're used to seeing in other shells. Table 23-4 describes the built-in commands available for you.

The zsh shell is no slouch when it comes to providing built-in commands! You should recognize most of these commands from their bash counterparts. The most important features of the zsh shell built-in commands are modules.

Add-in modules

There's a long list of modules that provide additional built-in commands for the zsh shell, and the list continues to grow as resourceful programmers create new modules. Table 23-5 shows the currently available modules at the time of this writing.

TABLE 23-4

The zsh Core Built-In Commands

Command	Description
alias	Define an alternate name for a command and arguments.
autoload	Preload a shell function into memory for quicker access.
bg	Execute a job in background mode.
bindkey	Bind keyboard combinations to commands.
builtin	Execute the specified built-in command instead of an executable file of the same name.
bye	The same as exit.
cd	Change the current working directory.
chdir	Change the current working directory.
command	Execute the specified command as an external file instead of a function or built-in command.
declare	Set the data type of a variable (same as typeset).
dirs	Displays the contents of the directory stack.
disable	Temporarily disable the specified hash table elements.
disown	Remove the specified job from the job table.
echo	Display variables and text.
emulate	Set zsh to emulate another shell, such as the Bourne, Korn, or C shells.
enable	Enable the specified hash table elements.
eval	Execute the specified command and arguments in the current shell process.
exec	Execute the specified command and arguments replacing the current shell process.
exit	Exit the shell with the specified exit status. If none specified, use the exit status of the last command.
export	Allow the specified environment variable names and values to be used in child shell processes.
false	Returns an exit status of 1.
fc	Select a range of commands from the history list.

TABLE 23-4	*(continued)*
Command	**Description**
fg	Execute the specified job in foreground mode.
float	Set the specified variable for use as a floating point variable.
functions	Set the specified name as a function.
getln	Read the next value in the buffer stack and place it in the specified variable.
getopts	Retrieve the next valid option in the command line arguments and place it in the specified variable.
hash	Directly modify the contents of the command hash table.
history	List the commands contained in the history file.
integer	Set the specified variable for use as an integer value.
jobs	List information about the specified job, or all jobs assigned to the shell process.
kill	Send a signal (Default SIGTERM) to the specified process or job.
let	Evaluate a mathematical operation and assign the result to a variable.
limit	Set or display resource limits.
local	Set the data features for the specified variable.
log	Display all users currently logged in who are affected by the watch parameter.
logout	Same as exit, but only works when the shell is a login shell.
popd	Remove the next entry from the directory stack.
print	Display variables and text.
printf	Display variables and text using C-style format strings.
pushd	Change the current working directory, and put the previous directory in the directory stack.
pushln	Place the specified arguments into the editing buffer stack.
pwd	Display the full pathname of the current working directory.
read	Read a line and assign data fields to the specified variables using the IFS characters.
readonly	Assign a value to a variable that can't be changed.
rehash	Rebuild the command hash table.

continued

TABLE 23-4	(continued)
Command	**Description**
set	Set options or positional parameters for the shell.
setopt	Set the options for a shell.
shift	Read and delete the first positional parameter, then shift the remaining ones down one position.
source	Find the specified file and copy its contents into the current location.
suspend	Suspend the execution of the shell until it receives a SIGCONT signal.
test	Returns an exit status of 0 if the specified condition is TRUE.
times	Display the cumulative user and system times for the shell and processes that run in the shell.
trap	Block the specified signals from being processed by the shell, and execute the specified commands if the signals are received.
true	Return a zero exit status.
ttyctl	Lock and unlock the display.
type	Display how the specified command would be interpreted by the shell.
typeset	Set or display attributes of variables.
ulimit	Set or display resource limits of the shell or processes running in the shell.
umask	Set or display the default permissions for creating files and directories.
unalias	Remove the specified command alias.
unfunction	Remove the specified defined function.
unhash	Remove the specified command from the hash table.
unlimit	Remove the specified resource limit.
unset	Remove the specified variable attribute.
unsetopt	Remove the specified shell option.
wait	Wait for the specified job or process to complete.
whence	Display how the specified command would be interpreted by the shell.
where	Display the pathname of the specified command if found by the shell.
which	Display the pathname of the specified command using csh style output.
zcompile	Compile the specified function or script for faster autoloading.
zmodload	Performs operations on loadable zsh modules.

TABLE 23-5

The zsh Modules

Module	Description
zsh/cap	POSIX compatibility commands
zsh/clone	Commands to clone a running shell to another terminal
zsh/compctl	Commands to control command completion
zsh/complete	Command line completion commands
zsh/complist	Commands for command line completion listing extensions
zsh/computil	Utility commands for command line completion
zsh/datetime	Additional date and time commands and variables
zsh/deltochar	A line editor function replicating emacs functionality
zsh/files	Commands for basic file handling
zsh/mapfile	Access to external files via associative arrays
zsh/mathfunc	Additional scientific functions
zsh/parameter	Access to command hash tables via associative arrays
zsh/pcre	The extended regular expression library
zsh/sched	Scheduling commands for providing timed command execution
zsh/net/socket	Unix domain socket support
zsh/stat	Access to the stat system call to provide system statistics
zsh/system	Interface for various low-level system features
zsh/net/tcp	Access to TCP sockets
zsh/termcap	Interface to the termcap database
zsh/terminfo	Interface to the terminfo database
zsh/zftp	A specialized FTP client command
zsh/zle	The zshell line editor
zsh/zleparameter	Access to modify zle using variables
zsh/zprof	Allows profiling for shell functions
zsh/zpty	Start a command in a pseudo-terminal
zsh/zselect	Block and return when file descriptors are ready
zsh/zutil	Various shell utilities

The zsh shell modules cover a wide range of topics, from providing simple command line editing features to advanced networking functions. The idea behind the zsh shell is to provide a basic minimum shell environment and let you add on the pieces you need to accomplish your programming job.

Viewing, adding, and removing modules

The `zmodload` command is the interface to the zsh modules. You use this command to view, add, and remove modules from the zsh shell session.

Using the `zmodload` command without any command line parameters displays the currently installed modules in your zsh shell:

```
% zmodload
zsh/zutil
zsh/complete
zsh/main
zsh/terminfo
zsh/zle
zsh/parameter
%
```

Different zsh shell implementations include different modules by default. To add a new module, just specify the module name on the `zmodload` command line:

```
% zmodload zsh/zftp
%
```

Nothing indicates that the module loaded. You can perform another `zmodload` command, and the new module should appear in the list of installed modules.

Once you load a module, the commands associated with the module are available as built-in commands:

```
% zftp open myhost.com rich testing1
Welcome to the myhost FTP server.
% zftp cd test
% zftp dir
01-21-08 11:21PM     120823 test1
01-21-08 11:23PM     118432 test2
% zftp get test1 > test1.txt
% zftp close
%
```

The `zftp` command allows you to conduct a complete FTP session directly from your zsh shell command line! You can incorporate these commands into your zsh shell scripts to perform file transfers directly from your scripts.

To remove an installed module, use the `-u` parameter, along with the module name:

```
% zmodload -u zsh/zftp
% zftp
```

```
zsh: command not found: zftp
%
```

This allows you to easily manage your modules via the standard zsh shell startup files (see "The zsh shell files" section).

NOTE   It's a common practice to place `zmodload` commands in the `$HOME/.zshrc` file so that your favorite functions load automatically.

Scripting with zsh

The main purpose of the zsh shell was to provide an advanced programming environment for shell programmers. With that in mind, it's no surprise that the zsh shell offers many features that make shell scripting easier.

Mathematical operations

As you would expect, the zsh shell allows you to perform mathematical functions with ease. Similar to the ksh93 shell (see Chapter 22), the zsh shell has full support for floating-point numbers in all of its mathematical operations.

Performing calculations

The zsh shell supports the same two methods for performing mathematical operations as the ksh93 shell:

- The `let` command
- Double parentheses

When you use the `let` command you should enclose the operation in double quotation marks to allow for spaces:

```
% let value1=" 4 * 5.1 / 3.2 "
% echo $value1
6.3749999999999991
%
```

Notice that using floating point numbers introduces a precision problem. To solve this, it's always a good idea to use the `printf` command, and specify the decimal precision needed to correctly display the answer:

```
% printf "%6.3f\n" $value1
6.375
%
```

Now that's much better!

The second method is to use the double parentheses. This method incorporates two techniques for defining the mathematical operation:

```
% value1=$(( 4 * 5.1 ))
% (( value2 = 4 * 5.1 ))
% printf "%6.3f\n" $value1 $value2
20.400
20.400
%
```

Notice that you can place the double parentheses either around just the operation (preceded by a dollar sign) or around the entire assignment statement. Both methods produce the same results.

If you don't use the typeset command to declare the data type of a variable beforehand, the zsh shell attempts to automatically assign the data type. This can be dangerous when working with both integer and floating-point numbers. Take a look at this example:

```
% value=10
% value2=$(( $value1 / 3 ))
% echo $value2
3
%
```

Now that's probably not the answer you want to come out from the calculation. When you specify numbers without decimal places, the zsh shell interprets them as integer values, and performs integer calculations. To ensure that the result is a floating point number, you must specify the numbers with decimal places:

```
% value=10.
% value2=$(( $value1 / 3. ))
% echo $value2
3.3333333333333335
%
Now the result is in the floating point format.
```

Mathematical functions

With the zsh shell, built-in mathematical functions are either feast or famine. The default zsh shell doesn't include any special mathematical function. However, if you install the zsh/mathfunc module, you'll have more math functions than you'll most likely ever need:

```
% value1=$(( sqrt(9) ))
zsh: unknown function: sqrt
% zmodload zsh/mathfunc
% value1=$(( sqrt(9) ))
% echo $value1
3.
%
```

That was simple! Now you have an entire math library of functions at your fingertips.

> **NOTE** For a complete listing of all the math functions that the zsh/mathfunc module provides, look at the manual page for zshmodules.

Structured commands

The zsh shell provides the usual set of structured commands for your shell scripts:

- it-then-else statements
- for loops (including the C-style)
- while loops
- until loops
- select statements
- case statements

The zsh shell uses the same syntax for each of these structured commands that you're used to from the bash shell. The zsh shell also includes a different structured command called repeat. The repeat command uses the format:

```
repeat param
do
    commands
done
```

The param parameter must be a number or a mathematical operation that evaluates to a number. The repeat command then performs the specified commands that number of times:

```
% cat test1
#!/bin/zsh
# using the repeat command

value1=$(( 10 / 2 ))
repeat $value1
do
    echo "This is a test"
done
$ ./test1
This is a test
This is a test
This is a test
This is a test
This is a test
%
```

This command allows you to repeat sections of code for a set number of times based on a calculation.

Functions

The zsh shell supports creating your own functions using either the `function` command, or by defining the function name with parentheses:

```
% function functest1 {
> echo "This is the test1 function"
}
% functest2() {
> echo "This is the test2 function"
}
% functest1
This is the test1 function
% functest2
This is the test2 function
%
```

Just as with bash shell functions (see Chapter 14), you can define functions within your shell script and then either use global variables or pass parameters to your functions. Here's an example using a global variable:

```
% cat test3
#!/bin/zsh
# testing functions in zsh

dbl() {
    value=$(( $value * 2 ))
    return $value
}

value=10
dbl
echo The answer is $?
% ./test3
The answer is 20
%
```

You don't have to place your functions within your shell scripts. The zsh shell allows you to define your functions in separate files that it can access when trying to resolve a function name.

The zsh shell finds functions via the `fpath` environment variable. You can store your function files in any directory in this path. Here's the `fpath` value on my Linux workstation:

```
% echo $fpath
/usr/local/share/zsh/site-functions
/usr/share/zsh/4.2.5/functions/Completion
/usr/share/zsh/4.2.5/functions/Completion/AIX
/usr/share/zsh/4.2.5/functions/Completion/BSD
```

```
/usr/share/zsh/4.2.5/functions/Completion/Base
/usr/share/zsh/4.2.5/functions/Completion/Cygwin
/usr/share/zsh/4.2.5/functions/Completion/Darwin
/usr/share/zsh/4.2.5/functions/Completion/Debian
/usr/share/zsh/4.2.5/functions/Completion/Linux
/usr/share/zsh/4.2.5/functions/Completion/Mandrake
/usr/share/zsh/4.2.5/functions/Completion/Redhat
/usr/share/zsh/4.2.5/functions/Completion/Unix
/usr/share/zsh/4.2.5/functions/Completion/X
/usr/share/zsh/4.2.5/functions/Completion/Zsh
/usr/share/zsh/4.2.5/functions/MIME
/usr/share/zsh/4.2.5/functions/Misc
/usr/share/zsh/4.2.5/functions/Prompts
/usr/share/zsh/4.2.5/functions/TCP
/usr/share/zsh/4.2.5/functions/Zftp
/usr/share/zsh/4.2.5/functions/Zle
%
```

As you can see, there are lots of places the zsh shell goes hunting to resolve function names. On my system, I can place my functions in the /usr/local/share/zsh/site-functions directory, and the zsh shell will be able to resolve them.

However, before the zsh shell can resolve the function, you must use the autoload command. This command loads the function into memory for the shell to access.

Here's an example of a stand-alone function:

```
% cat dbl
#!/bin/zsh
# a function to double a value
dbl() {
    value=$(( $1 * 2 ))
    return $value
}
% cp dbl /usr/local/share/zsh/site-functions
%
```

Okay, now the function is created in a file and stored in a directory in the fpath. If I try to use it though, I'll get an error message until I load it into memory:

```
% dbl 5
zsh: command not found: dbl
% autoload dbl
% dbl 5
% echo $?
10
%
```

This also applies to shell scripts. If you have a function you need to use, you'll need to use the `autoload` command to make sure that it's available:

```
% cat test4
#!/bin/zsh
# testing an external function

autoload dbl

dbl $1
echo The answer is $?
% ./test4 5
The answer is 10
%
```

Another interesting feature of the zsh shell is the `zcompile` command. This command processes a function file and creates a "compiled" version for the shell. This isn't really the same type of compiling you're used to in other programming languages. It does, however, put the function into a binary format that the zsh shell can load more quickly.

When you run the `zcompile` command, it creates a `.zwc` version of the function file. When the `autoload` command looks for the command in the `fpath`, it'll see the `.zwc` version and load it instead of the text function file.

Summary

This chapter discussed the zsh shell. The zsh shell provides lots of advanced features for shell scripting, including many built-in commands available in loadable modules. The zsh shell provides several emulation modes, which allow it to closely emulate other common shells (such as the Bourne, csh, and ksh shells). This feature allows you to seamlessly run shell scripts written for other shell environments in the zsh shell.

The zsh shell uses the concept of loadable modules to expand the built-in commands available. There are several modules created for the zsh shell, which provide additional features such as command line editing, extended mathematical functions, and advanced network support. You can write complicated network scripts using the zsh shell's TCP module, without requiring any other type of network library.

This finishes our walk through the world of Linux shells. The next section of this book dives into some specific scripting applications you might run into in the Linux environment. The next chapter shows how to incorporate the two most popular database packages in the Linux world, MySQL and PostgreSQL, into your shell scripts.

Part V

Advanced Topics

Chapter 24

Using a Database

O ne of the problems with shell scripts is persistent data. You can store all the information you want in your shell script variables, but at the end of the script, they just go away. There are times when you'd like for your scripts to be able to store data that you can use later. In the old days, to store and retrieve data from a shell script required creating a file, reading data from the file, parsing the data, then saving the data back into the file. Trying to search for data in the file meant having to read every record in the file to look for your data. Nowadays with databases being all the rage, it's a snap to interface your shell scripts with professional-quality open source databases. The two most popular open source databases used in the Linux world are MySQL and PostgreSQL. This chapter shows how to get these databases running on your Linux system, then spends some time getting you used to working with them from the command line. It then goes on to show how to interact with each one using normal bash shell scripts.

IN THIS CHAPTER

Introducing MySQL

Introducing PostgreSQL

Creating database objects

Writing database shell scripts

The MySQL Database

By far the most popular database available in the Linux environment is the MySQL database. Its popularity has grown as a part of the Linux-Apache-MySQL-PHP (LAMP) server environment, which many Internet Web servers use for hosting online stores, blogs, and applications.

This section describes how to install a MySQL database in your Linux environment and how to create the necessary database objects to use in your shell scripts.

Installing MySQL

It's not uncommon for Linux distributions to use automated software installation programs. These programs not only allow you to easily download and install new software from network repositories, but also automatically check for updates for your installed software packages and install those too.

Figure 24-1 demonstrates the Add Software feature in the Fedora 8 Linux distribution.

You just have to select the option for MySQL, and Fedora downloads and installs the complete MySQL server and client software. It doesn't get any easier than that!

The openSuse 10.3 Linux distribution also uses an advanced software management system. Figure 24-2 shows the Software Management window, where you can select packages based on software category (the MySQL server is under Database Servers).

Again, selecting the option for the MySQL software downloads and installs the software packages required.

FIGURE 24-1

Installing MySQL on a Fedora 8 Linux system.

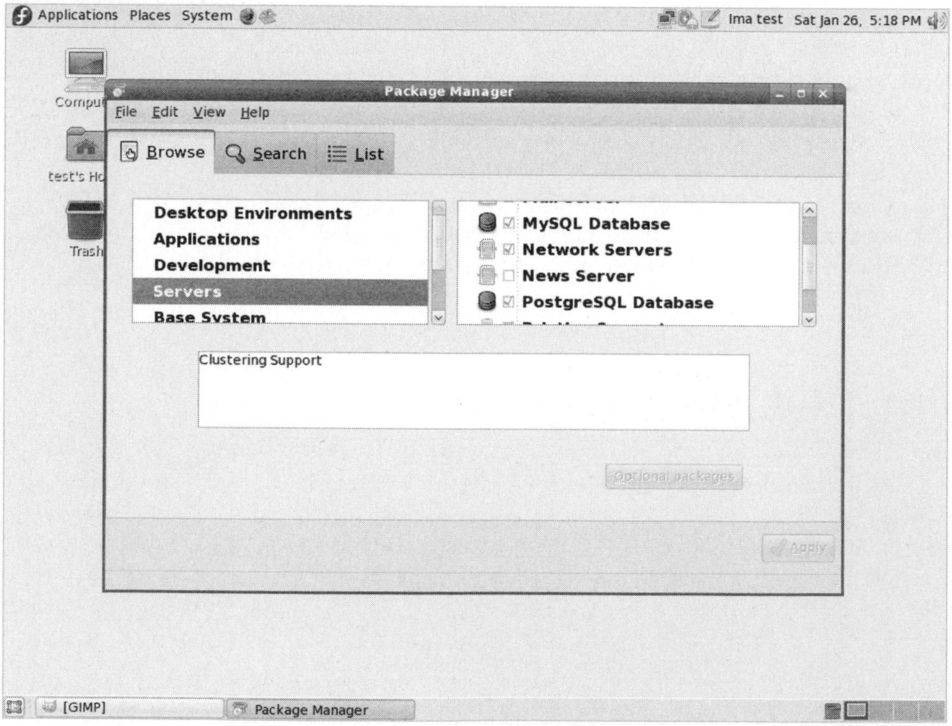

FIGURE 24-2

Installing MySQL on an openSuse 10.3 Linux system

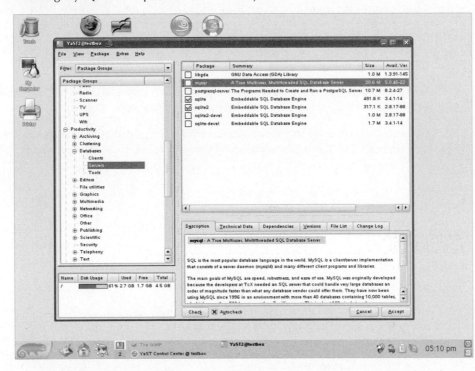

If you're using a Linux distribution that doesn't support automatic software loads, or you just want to have the latest-and-greatest version of the MySQL server, you can download an installation file directly from MySQL and install it yourself.

Here are the steps to download the installation file:

1. Open a browser window to the URL: www.mysql.com.

2. Click the *Downloads* link, located in the *Test Drive* section.

3. Under the *MySQL Community Server* section, select the link for the current release (5.0 at the time of this writing).

4. Select a link for your specific Linux platform. If a link for your specific platform exists, you can select it and install the software using your specific software installation program (such as .deb packages for Debian-based Linux systems, or .rpm packages for Red Hat–based Linux systems). If there isn't a link for your specific platform, select the *Linux (non RPM packages)* option to download the binary files without an installer package.

5. Select either the link to register, or download without registering.

6. Select a mirror location to start the download.

After the download completes, you should have a file on your system that looks something like this (the version number of the file you downloaded may vary):

```
mysql-5.0.45-linux-i686-tar.gz
```

If you remember from Chapter 4, the `.tar.gz` file extension indicates that the file is a gzipped tar file. It contains all of the files for the MySQL server archived into a single file using the `tar` command, then compressed using the `gzip` compression utility.

You'll need to extract it using the `tar` command into a directory to use the files in it contains. However, there are a few other steps you'll need to take first:

1. Create a unique user and group account responsible for the running MySQL server. Usually this account and group are called *mysql*. As the *root* Linux user account, perform these commands:

    ```
    # groupadd mysql
    # useradd -g mysql mysql
    ```

2. Select a directory where you want to place the MySQL software. The recommended location is `/usr/local`. Extract the files using the `tar` command, and create a link from the resulting obnoxiously long directory name to a directory simply called `mysql`:

    ```
    # cp mysql-5.0.45-linux-i686.tar.gz /usr/local
    # cd /usr/local
    # tar -zxvf mysql-5.0.45-linux-i686.tar.gz
    # ln -s mysql-5.0.45-linux-i686 mysql
    ```

3. Change the owner and group of the new `mysql` directory to the *mysql* user and group accounts you created:

    ```
    # cd mysql
    # chown -R mysql .
    # chgrp -R mysql .
    ```

So now you have your MySQL server and client files conveniently located in the `/usr/local/mysql` directory on your Linux system.

Completing the MySQL configuration

Between installing the MySQL software and using it to store your data, there are a few steps you need to perform. This section walks through what's necessary to get the MySQL server running on your Linux system.

Initializing the database files

The next step may or not be required on your system. If you've installed the MySQL server from your Linux distribution's software installation package, it created its own database files as part of the installation process, so you can skip this part.

88888888888888

If you've manually downloaded and installed the MySQL binary package, you'll need to create the default MySQL database files (these aren't included as part of the distribution package). As the Linux *root* user account, enter this command:

```
# /usr/local/mysql/scripts/mysql_install_db --user=mysql
```

After MySQL creates the default database, you can change the owner of everything but the database directory back to the root user using these commands:

```
# cd /usr/local/mysql
# chown -R root .
# chown -R mysql data
```

Now you're ready to start the MySQL server.

Starting the MySQL server

If you've installed MySQL using your Linux distribution's software installer, usually it's configured to start automatically the next time you boot your system. You can check by using our friend the ps command (see Chapter 4):

```
# ps ax | grep mysql
 2084 ?          S        0:00 /bin/sh /usr/bin/mysqld_safe --
datadir=/var/lib/mysql --socket=/var/lib/mysql/mysql.sock --log-
error=/var/log/mysqld.log --pid-file=/var/run/mysqld/mysqld.pid
 2141 ?          Sl       0:03 /usr/libexec/mysqld --basedir=/usr --
datadir=/var/lib/mysql --user=mysql --pid-
file=/var/run/mysqld/mysqld.pid --skip-external-locking --
socket=/var/lib/mysql/mysql.sock
 8825 pts/1     S+       0:00 grep mysql
#
```

The mysqld_safe script is used to start the MySQL server using the *mysql* user account.

If the MySQL server service isn't running, you'll need to start it. Many Linux distributions include some type of services utility that allows you to view the services that the system starts at boot time. In both Fedora 8 and openSuse 10.3 this feature is in the Administrative area.

Check to make sure that the MySQL server service on your Linux system is set to start automatically.

If you installed the software manually, you'll need to start the MySQL server yourself using the mysqld_safe script:

```
# /usr/local/mysql/bin/mysqld_safe --user=mysql &
```

This helper script starts the MySQL server in background mode, running as the new *mysql* user account. The MySQL installation also provides a script you can use to automatically start the MySQL server at boot time. Chapter 13 discusses how to place scripts so they automatically start when the Linux system boots. You can create a link in your distribution's startup script to reference the MySQL startup script, located at:

```
/usr/local/mysql/support-files/mysql.server
```

This script automatically starts the MySQL server using the mysql Linux user account.

Securing the MySQL user account

There's one final step for the MySQL server installation. The MySQL server maintains its own set of user accounts for controlling access to database objects. By default, the MySQL server has a master administrator account called *root*. Unfortunately, by default that account doesn't have a password. It's a very good idea to change the password for the root user account. You do this using the mysqladmin command at the Linux command line prompt:

```
$ mysqladmin -u root password newpasswd
```

where *newpasswd* is the text for the new password you're assigning to the root user account.

The MySQL client interface

The portal to the MySQL database is the mysql command line interface program. This section describes the mysql client program and shows how to use it to interact with your database.

Connecting to the server

The mysql client program allows you to connect to any MySQL database server anywhere on the network, using any user account and password. By default, if you enter the mysql program on a command line without any parameters it'll attempt to connect to a MySQL server running on the same Linux system, using the Linux login user name.

Most likely this isn't how you want to connect to the database. There are lots of command line parameters that allow you to control not only which MySQL server you connect to but also the behavior of the mysql interface. Table 24-1 shows the command line parameters you can use with the mysql program.

As you can see, there are quite a lot of command line options available for modifying how you log into the MySQL server.

By default, the mysql client program attempts to log in to the MySQL server using your Linux login name. If this name isn't configured in MySQL as a user account, you'll need to use the -u parameter to specify the name to log in as:

```
$ mysql -u root -p
Enter password:
Welcome to the MySQL monitor.  Commands end with ; or \g.
Your MySQL connection id is 7
Server version: 5.0.45 Source distribution

Type 'help;' or '\h' for help. Type '\c' to clear the buffer.

mysql>
```

TABLE 24-1

The mysql Command Line Parameters

Parameter	Description
-A	Disable automatic rehashing.
-b	Disable beep after error.
-B	Don't use a history file.
-C	Compress all information sent between the client and the server.
-D	Specify the database to use.
-e	Execute the specified statement and exit.
-E	Display query output vertically, one data field per line.
-f	Continue if an SQL error occurs.
-G	Enable named `mysql` commands.
-h	Specify the MySQL server hostname (the default is localhost).
-H	Display query output in HTML code.
-i	Ignore spaces after function names.
-N	Don't display column names in results.
-o	Ignore statements except those for the default database named on the command line.
-p	Specify the password for the user account.
-P	Specify the TCP port number to use for the network connection.
-q	Don't cache each query result.
-r	Display column values without escape conversion.
-s	Silent mode.
-S	Specify a socket for connection to the localhost.
-t	Display output in table form.
-T	Display debugging information, memory, and CPU statistics when the program exits.
-u	Specify the user account to log in as.
-U	Allow only `UPDATE` and `DELETE` statements that specify key values.
-v	Verbose mode.
-w	If the connection can't be established, wait and retry.
-X	Display query output in XHTML code.

The -p parameter tells MySQL to query for a password to use with the user account to log in. Once you're logged in to the server, you can start entering commands.

The mysql commands

The mysql program uses two different types of commands:

- Special mysql commands
- Standard SQL statements

The mysql program uses its own set of commands that let you easily control the environment and retrieve information about the MySQL server. Table 24-2 shows these commands.

You can use either the full command or the shortcut command directly from the mysql command prompt:

```
mysql> \s
--------------
mysql  Ver 14.12 Distrib 5.0.45, for redhat-linux-gnu (i386) using
readline 5.0

Connection id:          10
Current database:
Current user:           root@localhost
SSL:                    Not in use
Current pager:          stdout
Using outfile:          ''
Using delimiter:        ;
Server version:         5.0.45 Source distribution
Protocol version:       10
Connection:             Localhost via UNIX socket
Server characterset:    latin1
Db     characterset:    latin1
Client characterset:    latin1
Conn.  characterset:    latin1
UNIX socket:            /var/lib/mysql/mysql.sock
Uptime:                 4 hours 15 min 24 sec

Threads: 1  Questions: 53  Slow queries: 0  Opens: 23  Flush tables:
1  Open tables: 17  Queries per second avg: 0.003
--------------

mysql>
```

The mysql program implements all of the standard Structured Query Language (SQL) commands supported by the MySQL server. The "Creating MySQL database objects" section later on discusses this in more detail.

TABLE 24-2

The mysql Commands

Command	Shortcut	Description
?	\?	Help.
clear	\c	Clear command.
connect	\r	Connect to database and server.
delimiter	\d	Set SQL statement delimiter.
edit	\e	Edit the command with the command line editor.
ego	\G	Send the command to the MySQL server, and display results vertically.
exit	\q	Exit from the mysql program.
go	\g	Send command to MySQL server.
help	\h	Display help.
nopager	\n	Disable output pager and send output to STDOUT.
note	\t	Don't send output to output file.
pager	\P	Set pager command to specified program (use more as default).
print	\p	Print current command.
prompt	\R	Change the mysql command prompt.
quit	\q	Quit from the mysql program (same as exit).
rehash	\#	Rebuild the command completion hash table.
source	\.	Execute the SQL script in the specified file.
status	\s	Retrieve status information from the MySQL server.
system	\!	Execute a shell command on the system.
tee	\T	Append all output to the specified file.
use	\u	Use another database.
charset	\C	Change to another character set.
warnings	\W	Show warnings after every statement.
nowarning	\w	Don't show warnings after every statement.

One uncommon SQL command that the mysql program implements is the SHOW command. Using this command you can extract information about the MySQL server, such as the databases and tables created:

```
mysql> SHOW DATABASES;
+--------------------+
| Database           |
+--------------------+
| information_schema |
| mysql              |
+--------------------+
2 rows in set (0.04 sec)

mysql> USE mysql;
Database changed
mysql> SHOW TABLES;
+---------------------------+
| Tables_in_mysql           |
+---------------------------+
| columns_priv              |
| db                        |
| func                      |
| help_category             |
| help_keyword              |
| help_relation             |
| help_topic                |
| host                      |
| proc                      |
| procs_priv                |
| tables_priv               |
| time_zone                 |
| time_zone_leap_second     |
| time_zone_name            |
| time_zone_transition      |
| time_zone_transition_type |
| user                      |
+---------------------------+
17 rows in set (0.00 sec)

mysql>
```

In this example, I used the SHOW SQL command to display the databases currently configured on the MySQL server, then the USE SQL command to connect to a single database. Your mysql session can only be connected to one database at a time.

You'll notice that after each command I added a semicolon. The semicolon indicates the end of a command to the mysql program. If you don't use a semicolon, it prompts for more data:

```
mysql> SHOW
    -> DATABASES;
```

```
+---------------------+
| Database            |
+---------------------+
| information_schema  |
| mysql               |
+---------------------+
2 rows in set (0.00 sec)

mysql>
```

This feature can come in handy when you're working with long commands. You can enter part of the command on a line and press the Enter key, then continue on the next line. This can continue for as many lines as you like until you use the semicolon to indicate the end of the command.

NOTE Throughout this chapter you'll see me use upper-case letters for SQL commands. This has become a common way to write SQL commands, however, the `mysql` program allows you to specify SQL commands using either upper-case or lower-case.

Creating MySQL database objects

Before you can start writing your shell scripts to interact with a database, you'll need a few database objects to work with. At a minimum, you'll want to have:

- A unique database to store your application data
- A unique user account to access the database from your scripts
- One or more data tables to organize your data

You build all of these objects using the `mysql` program. The `mysql` program interfaces directly with the MySQL server, using SQL commands to create and modify each of the objects.

You can send any type of SQL commands to the MySQL server using the `mysql` program. This section walks through the different SQL statements you'll need to build the basic database objects for your shell scripts.

Creating a database

The MySQL server organizes data into *databases*. A database usually holds the data for a single application, separating it from other applications that use the database server. Creating a separate database for each shell script application helps eliminate confusion and data mix-ups.

The SQL statement required to create a new database is:

```
CREATE DATABASE name;
```

That's pretty simple. Of course, you must have the proper privileges to create new databases on the MySQL server. The easiest way to do that is to log in as the root user account:

```
$ mysql -u root -p
Enter password:
Welcome to the MySQL monitor.  Commands end with ; or \g.
```

```
Your MySQL connection id is 15
Server version: 5.0.45 Source distribution

Type 'help;' or '\h' for help. Type '\c' to clear the buffer.

mysql> CREATE DATABASE test;
Query OK, 1 row affected (0.00 sec)

mysql>
```

You can see if the new database was created by using the SHOW command:

```
mysql> SHOW DATABASES;
+--------------------+
| Database           |
+--------------------+
| information_schema |
| mysql              |
| test               |
+--------------------+
3 rows in set (0.01 sec)

mysql>
```

Yes, it was successfully created. You should now be able to connect to the new database:

```
mysql> USE test;
Database changed;
mysql> SHOW TABLES;
Empty set (0.00 sec)
mysql>
```

The SHOW TABLES command allows us to see if there are any tables created. The Empty set result indicates that there aren't any tables to work with yet. Before we start creating tables though, there's one other thing we need to do.

Creating a user account

So far you've seen how to connect to the MySQL server using the root administrator account. This account has total control over all of the MySQL server objects (much like how the *root* Linux account has complete control over the Linux system).

It's extremely dangerous to use the root MySQL account for normal applications. If there should be a breach of security and someone figures out the password for the root user account, all sorts of bad things could happen to your system (and data).

To prevent that, it's wise to create a separate user account in MySQL that only has privileges for the database used in the application. You do this with the GRANT SQL statement:

```
mysql> GRANT SELECT,INSERT,DELETE,UPDATE ON test.* TO test IDENTIFIED
by 'test';
```

```
Query OK, 0 rows affected (0.35 sec)

mysql>
```

That's quite a long command. Let's walk through the pieces and see what it's doing.

The first section defines the privileges the user account has on what database(s). This statement allows the user account to query the database data (the select privilege), insert new data records, delete existing data records, and update existing data records.

The test.* entry defines the database and tables the privileges apply to. This is specified in the format:

```
database.table
```

As you can see from this example, you're allowed to use wildcard characters when specifying the database and tables. This format applies the specified privileges to all of the tables contained in the database named test.

Finally, you specify the user account(s) the privileges apply to. The neat thing about the grant command is that if the user account doesn't exist, it creates it. The identified by portion allows you to set a default password for the new user account.

You can test the new user account directly from the mysql program:

```
$ mysql test -u test -p
Enter password:
Welcome to the MySQL monitor.  Commands end with ; or \g.
Your MySQL connection id is 3
Server version: 5.0.45 Source distribution

Type 'help;' or '\h' for help. Type '\c' to clear the buffer.

mysql>
```

The first parameter specifies the default database to use (test), and as you've already seen, the -u parameter defines the user account to log in as, along with the -p to query for the password. After entering the password assigned to the test user account, I'm connected to the server.

Now that you've got a database and a user account, you're ready to create some tables for the data. But first, let's take a look at the other database server you can use.

The PostgreSQL Database

The PostgreSQL database started out as an academic project, demonstrating how to incorporate advanced database techniques into a functional database server. Over the years, PostgreSQL has evolved into one of the most advanced open source database servers available for the Linux environment.

This section walks you through getting a PostgreSQL database server installed and running, then setting up a user account and database to work with in your shell scripts.

Installing PostgreSQL

Just like MySQL, you can install the PostgreSQL database server package either by using your system's automated software installation system, or manually by downloading it from the PostgreSQL Web site.

To use your Linux distribution's automated software installation, follow the same procedures outlined in the "Installing MySQL" section earlier. If you must manually download the PostgreSQL server software, unfortunately you'll have to do a little more work than with MySQL.

The only binary distribution for the PostgreSQL software uses the Red Hat RPM package management system. If your Linux system uses that package management system (or like the Debian distribution, has a utility to convert an RPM package into its own format), you can download the binary package and install it.

If not, you'll need to download the source code package for PostgreSQL, and manually compile it on your Linux system. This can be an interesting project.

NOTE Compiling a source code package requires that you have the C software development package loaded onto your Linux system. These days this is a fairly common thing for servers, but it may not be loaded if you're using a desktop Linux distribution. Please consult your individual Linux distribution documentation regarding compiling software, and what software packages are required for compiling C source code projects.

Here are the steps to obtain the PostgreSQL source code and install it on your system:

1. Open a browser window to the URL: www.postgresql.org.

2. Select the *Source* link for the latest PostgreSQL version at the top-right corner of the Web page.

3. Select the appropriate download file format (either using bzip2 or gzip) to download.

4. Select the download mirror site and method to begin the download.

After downloading the code, place it in a working directory on your Linux system (such as your $HOME directory), and extract the package files using the tar command:

```
tar -zxvf postgresql-8.2.6.tar.gz
```

The tar command creates the directory postgresql-8.2.6 (or whatever version you've downloaded) in your working directory and extracts the source code files. You're now ready to start building.

Here are the steps you'll need to follow to create the PostgreSQL server and client executable files:

1. Change to the new directory that contains the PostgreSQL source code.

```
$ cd postgresql-8.2.6
```

2. Run the configure script:

```
$ ./configure
```

This checks your system to ensure that you have the correct libraries needed to compile the source code. There are quite a few libraries that PostgreSQL needs. If it reports that you're missing something, you'll have to go out and install it on your Linux system.

3. Run the gmake utility to compile the source code:

```
$ gmake
```

4. Change to the root user, and run the install script using the gmake utility:

```
$ su
password:
# gmake install
```

This installs the PostgreSQL binary files in the /usr/local/pgsql directory.

5. Create a user named postgres, create a directory for the database files, and make that user the owner of that directory:

```
# adduser postgres
# mkdir /usr/local/postgres/data
# chown postgres /usr/local/postgres/data
```

Congratulations, you now have the PostgreSQL programs installed on your system! Before you can start PostgreSQL though, you'll need to initialize the PostgreSQL database files. There's a utility program for doing that, but you must be the postgres user to do that:

```
# su postgres
$ /usr/local/postgres/bin/initdb -D /usr/local/postgres/data
```

Now you're ready to start the PostgreSQL server. To start the PostgreSQL database and have it run in the background, you must again be the postgres user account:

```
# su postgres
# cd /usr/local/postgres/bin
# ./postgres -D /usr/local/postgres/data >logfile 2>&1 &
```

If you want the PostgreSQL server to automatically start at boot time, add these commands to the startup script for your Linux distribution.

Logging into the PostgreSQL server is slightly different from the MySQL server. If you remember, the MySQL server maintains its own internal database of users that can be granted access to database objects. While PostgreSQL also has this capability, most PostgreSQL implementations (including the default source code installation) utilize the existing Linux system user accounts to authenticate PostgreSQL users.

While this can sometimes be confusing, it does make for a nice, clean way to control user accounts in PostgreSQL. All you need to do is ensure each PostgreSQL user has a valid account on the Linux system, rather than having to worry about a whole separate set of user accounts.

Another major difference for PostgreSQL is that the administrator account in PostgreSQL is called *postgres*, not *root*. Thus the need for the postgres Linux system account, so the PostgreSQL administrative user account can exist.

Next we'll look at how to use the postgres account to access the PostgreSQL server.

The PostgreSQL command interface

The PostgreSQL command line client program is called psql. This program provides complete access to the database objects configured in the PostgreSQL server. This section describes the psql program and shows how to use it to interact with your PostgreSQL server.

Connecting to the server

The psql client program provides the command line interface to the PostgreSQL server. As you would expect, it uses command line parameters to control what features are enabled in the client interface. Each option uses either a long or short name format. Table 24-3 shows the command line parameters available.

TABLE 24-3

The psql Command Line Parameters

Short Name	Long Name	Description
-a	--echo-all	Display all SQL lines processed from a script file in the output.
-A	--no-align	Set the output format to unaligned mode. Data is not displayed as a formatted table.
-c	--command	Execute the specified SQL statement and exit.
-d	--dbname	Specify the database to connect with.
-e	--echo-queries	Echo all queries to the screen.
-E	--echo-hidden	Echo hidden psql meta-commands to the screen.
-f	--file	Execute SQL commands from the specified file and exit.
-F	--field-separator	Specify the character used to separate column data when in unaligned mode. The default is a comma.
-h	--host	Specify the IP address or hostname of the remote PostgreSQL server.

TABLE 24-3	(continued)	
Short Name	**Long Name**	**Description**
-l	--list	Display a list of available databases on the server and exit.
-o	--output	Redirect query output to the specified file.
-p	--post	Specify the PostgreSQL server TCP port to connect with.
-P	--pset	Set the table printing option specified to a specified value.
-q	--quiet	Quiet mode, doesn't display output messages.
-R	--record-separator	Use the specified character as the record separator. The default is the newline character.
-s	--single-step	Prompt to continue or cancel after every SQL query.
-S	--single-line	Specify that the Enter key defines the end of an SQL query instead of a semicolon.
-t	--tuples-only	Disables column headers and footers in table output.
-T	--table-attr	Use the HTML table tag specified when in HTML mode.
-U	--username	Use the specified user name to connect to the PostgreSQL server.
-v	--variable	Set the specified variable to a specified value.
-V	--version	Display the psql version number and exit.
-W	--password	Force a password prompt.
-x	--expanded	Enable expanded table output to display additional information for records.
-X	--nopsqlrc	Don't process the psql startup file.
-?	--help	Display the psql command line help and exit.

As mentioned in the previous section, the administrative account for PostgreSQL is called postgres. Since PostgreSQL uses Linux user accounts to validate users, you must be logged in as the postgres Linux account to access the PostgreSQL server as the postgres user.

Since the postgres user account is a special account, you shouldn't assign a password to it. That way no one can try to break into the system using that account. Instead, to log in using the postgres account, you must be the *root* user, then use the su command to change to the *postgres* user:

```
$ su
Password:
# su postgres
bash-3.2$ psql
Welcome to psql 8.2.6, the PostgreSQL interactive terminal.

Type:  \copyright for distribution terms
       \h for help with SQL commands
       \? for help with psql commands
       \g or terminate with semicolon to execute query
       \q to quit

postgres=#
```

The default psql prompt indicates the database you are connected to. The pound sign in the prompt indicates that you're logged in with the administrative user account. You're now ready to start entering some commands to interact with the PostgreSQL server.

The psql commands

Similarly to the mysql program, the psql program uses two different types of commands:

- Standard SQL statements
- PostgreSQL meta-commands

PostgreSQL meta-commands allow you to easily extract information about the database environment, plus set features for the psql session. A meta-command is indicted by using a backslash. There are lots of PostgreSQL meta-commands for lots of different settings and features, but there's no reason to start worrying about them all right away. The most commonly used ones are:

- \l to list the available databases
- \c to connect to a database
- \dt to list the tables in a database
- \du to list the PostgreSQL users
- \z to list table privileges
- \? to list all of the available meta-commands
- \h to list all of the available SQL commands
- \q to exit the database

If you ever need to find a meta-command, just enter the \? meta-command. You'll see a list, along with an explanation, of all the available meta-commands.

To test the meta-commands, use the \l meta-command to list the available databases:

```
postgres=# \l
        List of databases
   Name    |  Owner   | Encoding
-----------+----------+----------
 postgres  | postgres | UTF8
 template0 | postgres | UTF8
 template1 | postgres | UTF8
(3 rows)

postgres=#
```

These are the default databases provided by the PostgreSQL server. The postgres database maintains all of the system data for the server. The template0 and template1 databases provide default database templates for you to copy when creating a new database.

You're now ready to start working on your own data in PostgreSQL.

Creating PostgreSQL database objects

This section walks you through the process of creating your database and a user account to access it. You'll see that while some of the work in PostgreSQL is exactly the same as in MySQL, some of it is completely different.

Creating a database object

Creating a database is one of those actions that's the same as in MySQL. Remember to be logged in as the *postgres* administrative account to create the new database:

```
$ su
Password:
# su postgres
bash-3.2$ psql
Welcome to psql 8.2.6, the PostgreSQL interactive terminal.

postgres=# CREATE DATABASE test;
CREATE DATABASE
postgres=#
```

After you create the database, use the \l meta-command to see if it appears in the listing, then the \c meta-command to connect to it:

```
postgres=# \l
        List of databases
   Name    |  Owner   | Encoding
-----------+----------+----------
 postgres  | postgres | UTF8
 template0 | postgres | UTF8
```

```
  template1 | postgres | UTF8
  test      | postgres | UTF8
(4 rows)

postgres=# \c test
You are now connected to database "test".
test=#
```

When you connect to the test database, the psql prompt changes to indicate the new database name. This is a great reminder when you're ready to create your database objects, so you can easily tell where you are in the system.

> **NOTE** PostgreSQL adds another layer of control to the database called the *schema*. A database can contain multiple schemas, each schema containing multiple tables. This allows you to subdivide a database for specific applications or users.
>
> By default, every database contains one schema, called *public*. If you're only going to have one application use the database, you're fine with just using the public schema. If you'd like to really get fancy, you can create new schemas. For this example, I'll just use the public schema for my tables.

Creating user accounts

After creating the new database, the next step is to create a user account that has access to it for your shell scripts. As you've already seen, user accounts in PostgreSQL is one of those things that is significantly different from MySQL.

User accounts in PostgreSQL are called *Login Roles*. The PostgreSQL server matches Login Roles to the Linux system user accounts. Because of this, there are two common thoughts about creating Login Roles to run shell scripts that access the PostgreSQL database:

- Create a special Linux account with a matching PostgreSQL Login Role to run all your shell scripts.
- Create PostgeSQL accounts for each Linux user account that needs to run shell scripts to access the database.

For this example I'll choose the second method and create a PostgreSQL account that matches my Linux system account. This way, I can run shell scripts that access the PostgreSQL database directly from my Linux user account.

First, you must create the Login Role:

```
test=# CREATE ROLE rich login;
CREATE ROLE
test=#
```

That was simple enough. Without the login parameter, the role is not allowed to log in to the PostgreSQL server, but it can be assigned privileges. This type of role is called a *Group Role*.

Group Roles are great if you're working in a large environment with lots of users and tables. Instead of having to keep track of which user has which type of privileges for which tables, you just create Group Roles for specific types of access to tables, then assign the Login Roles to the proper Group Role.

For simple shell scripting, you most likely won't need to worry about creating Group Roles, and just assign privileges directly to the Login Roles. That's what I'll do in this example.

However, PostgreSQL handles privileges a bit differently than MySQL. It doesn't allow you to grant overall privileges to all objects in a database that filter down to the table level. Instead, you'll need to grant privileges for each individual table you create. While this is somewhat of a pain, it certainly helps enforce strict security policies. You'll have to hold off assigning privileges until you've created a table. That's the next step in our process.

Working with Tables

Now that you've got your MySQL or PostgreSQL server running, created a new database and a user account for accessing it, it's time to start working with data! Fortunately, both the mysql and psql programs use standard SQL to create and manage data tables. This section walks you through the SQL required to create tables, insert and remove data, and query existing data in both environments.

Creating a table

Both the MySQL and PostgreSQL servers are considered *relational* databases. In a relational database, data is organized by *data fields*, *records*, and *tables*. A data field is a single piece of information, such as an employee's last name, or a salary. A record is a collection of related data fields, such as the employee ID number, last name, first name, address, and salary. Each record indicates one set of the data fields.

The table contains all of the records that hold the related data. Thus, you'll have a table called Employees which holds the records for each employee.

To create a new table in the database, you need to use the CREATE TABLE SQL command:

```
$ mysql test -u root -p
Enter password:
mysql> CREATE TABLE employees (
    -> empid int not null,
    -> lastname varchar(30),
    -> firstname varchar(30),
    -> salary float,
    -> primary key (empid));
Query OK, 0 rows affected (0.14 sec)

mysql>
```

TABLE 24-4

MySQL and PostgreSQL Data Types

Data Type	Description
char	A fixed-length string value
varchar	A variable-length string value
int	An integer value
float	A floating-point value
Boolean	A Boolean true/false value
Date	A date value in YYYY-MM-DD format
Time	A time value in HH:mm:ss format
Timestamp	A date and time value together
Text	A long string value
BLOB	A large binary value, such as an image or video clip

First off, notice that to create the new table I needed to log in to MySQL using the *root* user account, since the *test* user doesn't have privileges to create a new table. The next item to notice is that I specified the test database on the mysql program command line. If I hadn't done that, I would need to use the USE SQL command to connect to the test database.

CAUTION   It's extremely important that you make sure you're in the right database before creating the new table. Also, make sure that you're logged in using the administrative user account (*root* for MySQL and *postgres* for PostgreSQL) to create the tables.

Each data field in the table is defined using a data type. The MySQL and PostgreSQL databases support lots of different data types. Table 24-4 shows some of the more popular data types you may need.

The empid data field also specifies a *data constraint*. A data constraint restricts what type of data you can enter to create a valid record. The not null data constraint indicates that every record must have an empid value specified.

Finally, the primary key defines a data field that uniquely identifies each individual record. This means that each data record must have a unique empid value in the table.

After creating the new table, you can use the appropriate command to ensure that it's created. In mysql, it's the show table command:

```
mysql> show tables;
+----------------+
| Tables_in_test |
+----------------+
```

```
| employees        |
+------------------+
1 row in set (0.00 sec)

mysql>
```

And in psql it's the \dt meta-command:

```
test=# \dt
            List of relations
  Schema |    Name    |  Type  |  Owner
 --------+------------+--------+----------
  public | employees  | table  | postgres
 (1 row)

test=#
```

If you remember from the "Creating PostgreSQL database objects" section earlier, in PostgreSQL we need to assign privileges at the table level. Now that you have a table, you'll need to give your Login Role access to it:

```
# su postgres
$ psql test
test=# GRANT SELECT,INSERT,DELETE,UPDATE ON public.employees TO rich;
GRANT
test=#
```

The format to specify the table must include the schema name, which by default is *public*. Also, remember to perform this command as the *postgres* Login Role.

With the table created you're now ready to start saving some data. The next section covers how to do that.

Inserting and deleting data

Not surprisingly, you use the INSERT SQL command to insert new data records into the table. Each INSERT command must specify the data field values for the MySQL or PostgreSQL server to accept the record.

The format of the INSERT SQL command is:

```
INSERT INTO table VALUES (...)
```

The values are a comma-separated list of the data values for each data field:

```
$ mysql test -u test -p
Enter password:

mysql>
Query OK, 1 row affected (0.35 sec)
```

or, in PostgreSQL:

```
[rich@testbox ~]$ psql test
Welcome to psql 8.2.6, the PostgreSQL interactive terminal.

test=> INSERT INTO employees VALUES (1, 'Blum', 'Rich', 25000.00);
INSERT 0 1
test=>
```

Since the new user account in both MySQL and PostgreSQL has privileges to insert data, you can log in using that account. The INSERT command pushes the data values you specify into the data fields in the table. If you attempt to add another record that duplicates the empid data field value, you'll get an error message:

```
mysql> INSERT INTO employees VALUES (1, 'Blum', 'Barbara', 45000.00);
ERROR 1062 (23000): Duplicate entry '1' for key 1
```

However, if you change the empid value to a unique value, everything should be OK:

```
mysql> INSERT INTO employees VALUES (2, 'Blum', 'Barbara', 45000.00);
Query OK, 1 row affected (0.00 sec)
```

You should now have two data records in your table.

If you need to remove data from your table, you use the DELETE SQL command. However, you need to be very careful with it.

The basic DELETE command format is:

```
DELETE FROM table;
```

where *table* specifies the table to delete records from. There's just one small problem with this command: it removes all of the records in the table.

To just specify a single record or a group of records to delete, you must use the WHERE clause. The WHERE clause allows you to create a filter that identifies which records to remove. You use the WHERE clause like this:

```
DELETE FROM employees WHERE empid = 2;
```

This restricts the deletion process to all of the records that have an empid value of 2. When you execute this command, the mysql program returns a message indicating how many records matched the filter:

```
mysql> DELETE FROM employees WHERE empid = 2;
Query OK, 1 row affected (0.29 sec)
```

As expected, only one record matched the filter and was removed.

Querying data

Once you've got all of your data in your database, it's time to start running reports to extract information.

The workhorse for all of your querying is the SQL SELECT command. The SELECT command is extremely versatile, but with versatility comes complexity.

The basic format of a SELECT statement is:

```
SELECT datafields FROM table
```

The datafields parameter is a comma-separated list of the data field names you want the query to return. If you want to receive all of the data field values, you can use an asterisk as a wildcard character.

You must also specify the specific table you want the query to search. To get meaningful results, you must match your query data fields with the proper table.

By default, the SELECT command returns all of the data records in the specified table:

```
mysql> SELECT * FROM employees;
+-------+----------+------------+--------+
| empid | lastname | firstname  | salary |
+-------+----------+------------+--------+
|     1 | Blum     | Rich       |  25000 |
|     2 | Blum     | Barbara    |  45000 |
|     3 | Blum     | Katie Jane |  34500 |
|     4 | Blum     | Jessica    |  52340 |
+-------+----------+------------+--------+
4 rows in set (0.00 sec)

mysql>
```

You can use one or more modifiers to define how the database server returns the data requested by the query. Here's a list of commonly used modifiers:

- WHERE: Displays a subset of records that meet a specific condition
- ORDER BY: Displays records in a specified order
- LIMIT: Displays only a subset of records

The WHERE clause is the most common SELECT command modifier. It allows you to specify conditions to filter data from the result set. Here's an example of using the WHERE clause:

```
mysql> SELECT * FROM employees WHERE salary > 40000;
+-------+----------+-----------+--------+
| empid | lastname | firstname | salary |
+-------+----------+-----------+--------+
|     2 | Blum     | Barbara   |  45000 |
|     4 | Blum     | Jessica   |  52340 |
+-------+----------+-----------+--------+
2 rows in set (0.01 sec)

mysql>
```

Now you can see the power of adding database access to your shell scripts! You can easily control your data management needs just with a few SQL commands and the mysql or psql programs. The next section describes how you can incorporate these features into your shell scripts.

Using the Database in Your Scripts

Now that you've got a working database going, it's finally time to turn our attention back to the shell scripting world. This section describes what you need to do to interact with your databases using shell scripts.

Connecting to the databases

Obviously, to connect to the databases you'll need to somehow utilize the mysql or psql programs in your shell script. This isn't too complicated of a process, but there are a few things you'll need to watch out for.

Finding the programs

The first hurdle you'll need to complete is to figure out just where the mysql and psql command line client programs are on the Linux system. The one downside to Linux software installs is that often different Linux distributions place software packages in different locations.

Fortunately, there's the which command. The which command tells you where the shell would find a command if it attempted to run it from the command line:

```
$ which mysql
/usr/bin/mysql
$ which psql
/usr/bin/psql
$
```

The easiest way to handle this information is to assign it to an environment variable, then use that in your shell script when you want to reference the appropriate program:

```
MYSQL=`which mysql`
PSQL=`which psql`
```

Now the $MYSQL variable points to the executable for the mysql program, and the $PSQL variable points to the executable for the psql program.

Logging into the server

After finding the location of the client programs, you can use them in your scripts to access the database servers. For the PostgreSQL server, this is easy:

```
[rich@testbox]$ cat ptest1
#!/bin/bash
# test connecting to the PostgreSQL server

PSQL=`which psql`

$PSQL test
[rich@testbox]$ ./ptest1
Welcome to psql 8.2.6, the PostgreSQL interactive terminal.

Type:  \copyright for distribution terms
       \h for help with SQL commands
       \? for help with psql commands
       \g or terminate with semicolon to execute query
       \q to quit

test=>
```

Since I'm running the script from my Linux user account, all I need to specify on the psql command line is the name of the database to connect with. The ptest1 script connected to the test database and left you at the psql prompt inside that database.

If you've created a special user account in MySQL for your shell scripts, you'll need to specify that on the mysql command line:

```
$ cat mtest1
#!/bin/bash
# test connecting to the MySQL server

MYSQL=`which mysql`

$MYSQL test -u test -p
$ ./mtest1
Enter password:
Welcome to the MySQL monitor.  Commands end with ; or \g.
Your MySQL connection id is 15
Server version: 5.0.45 Source distribution

Type 'help;' or '\h' for help. Type '\c' to clear the buffer.

mysql>
```

665

That worked, but not all that well for a non-interactive script. The -p command line parameter caused mysql to pause and ask for the password. You can solve that problem by including the password on the command line:

```
$MYSQL test -u test -ptest
```

This however, is not a good idea. Anyone who has access to your script will know the user account and password for your database.

To solve this problem, you can use a special configuration file used by the mysql program. The mysql program uses the $HOME/.my.cnf file to read special startup commands and settings. One of those settings is the default password for mysql sessions started by the user account.

To set the default password in this file, just create the following:

```
$ cat .my.cnf
[client]
password = test
$ chmod 400 .my.cnf
$
```

The chmod command is used to restrict the .my.cnf file so that only you can view it. You can test this now from the command line:

```
$ mysql test -u test
Welcome to the MySQL monitor.  Commands end with ; or \g.
Your MySQL connection id is 15
Server version: 5.0.45 Source distribution

Type 'help;' or '\h' for help. Type '\c' to clear the buffer.

mysql>
```

Perfect! Now you don't have to include the password on the command line in your shell scripts.

Sending commands to the server

After establishing the connection to the server, you'll want to send commands to interact with your database. There are two methods to do this:

- Send a single command and exit
- Send multiple commands

To send a single command, you must include the command as part of the mysql or psql command line.

For the mysql command, you do this using the -e parameter:

```
$ cat mtest2
#!/bin/bash
# send a command to the MySQL server
```

```
MYSQL=`which mysql`

$MYSQL test -u test -e 'select * from employees'
$ ./mtest2
+-------+----------+------------+---------+
| empid | lastname | firstname  | salary  |
+-------+----------+------------+---------+
|     1 | Blum     | Rich       | 25000   |
|     2 | Blum     | Barbara    | 45000   |
|     3 | Blum     | Katie Jane | 34500   |
|     4 | Blum     | Jessica    | 52340   |
+-------+----------+------------+---------+
$
```

For the psql command, you do this using the -c parameter:

```
$ cat ptest2
#!/bin/bash
# send a command to the PostgreSQL server

PSQL=`which psql`

$PSQL test -c 'select * from employees'
$ ./ptest2
 empid | lastname | firstname  | salary
-------+----------+------------+--------
     1 | Blum     | Rich       | 25000
     2 | Blum     | Barbara    | 45000
     3 | Blum     | Katie Jane | 34500
     4 | Blum     | Jessica    | 52340
(4 rows)
$
```

The database servers return the results from the SQL commands to the shell scripts, which display them in STDOUT.

If you need to send more than one SQL command, you can use file redirection (see Chapter 12). To redirect lines in the shell script, you must define an *end of file* string. The end of file string indicates the beginning and end of the redirected data.

Here's an example of defining an end of file string, with data in it:

```
$ cat mtest3
#!/bin/bash
# sending multiple commands to MySQL

MYSQL="$(which mysql)"
$MYSQL test -u test <<EOF
```

```
  show tables;
  select * from employees where salary > 40000;
  EOF
  $ ./mtest3
  Tables_in_test
  employees
  empid      lastname      firstname      salary
  2          Blum          Barbara        45000
  4          Blum          Jessica        52340
  $
```

The shell redirects everything with the EOF delimiters to the mysql command, which executes the lines as if you typed them yourself at the prompt. Using this method, you can send as many commands to the MySQL server as you need. You'll notice though that there's no separation between the output from each command. In the next section, "Formatting data," you'll see how to fix this problem.

NOTE You should also notice that the mysql program changed the default output style when you used the redirected input method. Instead of creating the ASCII symbol boxes around the data, the mysql program detected that the input was redirected, so it returned just the raw data. This will come in handy when you need to extract the individual data elements.

The same technique also works for the psql program:

```
  $ cat ptest3
  #!/bin/bash
  # sending multiple commands to PostgreSQL

  PSQL="$(which psql)"

  $PSQL test <<EOF
  \dt
  select * from employees where salary > 40000;
  EOF
  $ ./ptest3
              List of relations
   Schema |    Name    | Type  |  Owner
  --------+------------+-------+----------
   public | employees  | table | postgres
  (1 row)

   empid | lastname | firstname | salary
  -------+----------+-----------+--------
       2 | Blum     | Barbara   |  45000
       4 | Blum     | Jessica   |  52340
  (2 rows)
  $
```

The `psql` program displays the output from each command directly to STDOUT in the order in which you specify them.

Of course, you're not limited to just retrieving data from the tables. You can use any type of SQL command in your script, such as an INSERT statement:

```
$ cat mtest4
#!/bin/bash
# send data to the table in the MySQL database

MYSQL=`which mysql`

if [ $# -ne 4 ]
then
    echo "Usage: mtest4 empid lastname firstname salary"
else
    statement="INSERT INTO employees VALUES ($1, '$2', '$3', $4)"
    $MYSQL test -u test << EOF
    $statement
EOF
    if [ $? -eq 0 ]
    then
        echo Data successfully added
    else
        echo Problem adding data
    fi
fi
$ ./mtest4
Usage: mtest4 empid lastname firstname salary
$ ./mtest4 5 Blum Jasper 100000
Data added successfully
$
$ ./mtest4 5 Blum Jasper 100000
ERROR 1062 (23000) at line 1: Duplicate entry '5' for key 1
Problem adding data
$
```

This example demonstrates a few things about using this technique. When you specify the end of file string, it must be the only thing on the line, and the line must start with the string. If I had indented the EOF text to match the rest of the if-then indentation, it wouldn't work.

Also, notice how I used the special $? variable to test the exit status of the mysql program. This helps you determine whether the command failed or not.

Just sending output from the commands to STDOUT is not the easiest way to manage and manipulate the data. The next section shows you some tricks you can use to help your scripts capture data retrieved from the database.

Formatting data

The standard output from the mysql and psql commands doesn't lend itself too much for data retrieval. If you need to actually do something with the data you retrieve, you'll need to do some fancy data manipulation. This section describes some of the tricks you can use to help extract data from your database reports.

Assigning output to a variable

The first step in trying to capture database data is to redirect the output from the mysql and psql commands in an environment variable. This allows you to use the output information in other commands. Here's an example:

```
$ cat mtest5
#!/bin/bash
# redirecting SQL output to a variable

MYSQL=`which mysql`

dbs=`$MYSQL test -u test -Bse 'show databases'`
for db in $dbs
do
    echo $db
done
$ ./mtest5
information_schema
test
$
```

This example uses two additional parameters on the mysql program command line. The -B parameter specifies for the mysql program to work in batch mode, and in combination with the -s (silent) parameter, the column headings and formatting symbols are suppressed.

By redirecting the output of the mysql command to a variable, this example is able to step through the individual values of each returned record.

Using formatting tags

In the previous example, you saw how adding the -B and -s parameters to the mysql program command line allows you to suppress the output heading information, so all you get is data. There are a few other parameters that you can use to help make life easier for you.

Generating data for Web pages is a popular thing these days. Both the mysql and psql programs provide an option to display the output using HTML format. In both, this is enabled using the -H command line parameter:

```
$ psql test -H -c 'select * from employees where empid = 1'
<table border="1">
  <tr>
    <th align="center">empid</th>
```

```
      <th align="center">lastname</th>
      <th align="center">firstname</th>
      <th align="center">salary</th>
    </tr>
    <tr valign="top">
      <td align="right">1</td>
      <td align="left">Blum</td>
      <td align="left">Rich</td>
      <td align="right">25000</td>
    </tr>
</table>
<p>(1 row)<br />
</p>
$
```

The `mysql` program also supports an additional popular format, called the Extensible Markup Language (XML). This language uses HTML-like tags to identify data names and values.

For the `mysql` program, you do this using the `-X` command line parameter:

```
$ mysql test -u test -X -e 'select * from employees where empid = 1'
<?xml version="1.0"?>

<resultset statement="select * from employees
">
  <row>
  <field name="empid">1</field>
  <field name="lastname">Blum</field>
  <field name="firstname">Rich</field>
  <field name="salary">25000</field>
  </row>
</resultset>
$
```

Using XML, you can easily identify individual rows of data, along with the individual data values in each record.

Summary

This chapter discussed the ability to save, modify, and retrieve data from your shell scripts in databases. You can easily access both the MySQL and PostgreSQL database servers directly from your shell scripts.

After installing the MySQL and PostgreSQL servers, you can use their respective client programs to access the servers from the command line, or from shell scripts. The `mysql` client program provides the command line interface to the MySQL server. You can send SQL commands as well as customized MySQL commands to the server from your shell scripts, then retrieve the results.

The `psql` client program operates the same way for the PostgreSQL server. There are plenty of command line parameters you can use to help format your data in just the right way.

Both client programs allow you to send either a single command to the server, or use input redirection to send a batch of commands. The programs normally send the output data from the server to STDOUT, but you can redirect the output to a variable, and use that information in your shell script.

The next chapter examines the World Wide Web. Getting your shell scripts to interface with Web sites on the Internet is a tricky task, but once you master it the world is yours to retrieve data from.

Using the Web

Often when you think of shell script programming the last thing you think of is the Internet. The command line world often seems foreign to the fancy, graphical world of the Internet. There are, however, several different utilities you can easily use in your shell scripts to gain access to data content on the Web, as well as on other network devices. This chapter walks you through three popular methods for getting your shell scripts to interact with the network world.

The Lynx Program

Almost as old as the Internet itself, the Lynx program was created in 1992 by students at the University of Kansas as a text-based browser. Since it's text-based, the Lynx program allows you to browse Web sites directly from a terminal session, replacing the fancy graphics on Web pages with HTML text tags. This allows you to surf the Internet from just about any type of Linux terminal. A sample Lynx screen is shown in Figure 25-1.

Lynx uses the standard keyboard keys to navigate around the Web page. Links appear as highlighted text within the Web page. Using the right arrow key allows you to follow a link to the next Web page.

You may be wondering how you can use a graphical text program in your shell scripts. The Lynx program also provides a feature that allows you to dump the text contents of a Web page to STDOUT. This feature is great for mining for data contained within a Web page. This section describes how to use the Lynx program within your shell scripts to extract data from Internet Web sites.

673

FIGURE 25-1

Viewing a Web page using Lynx

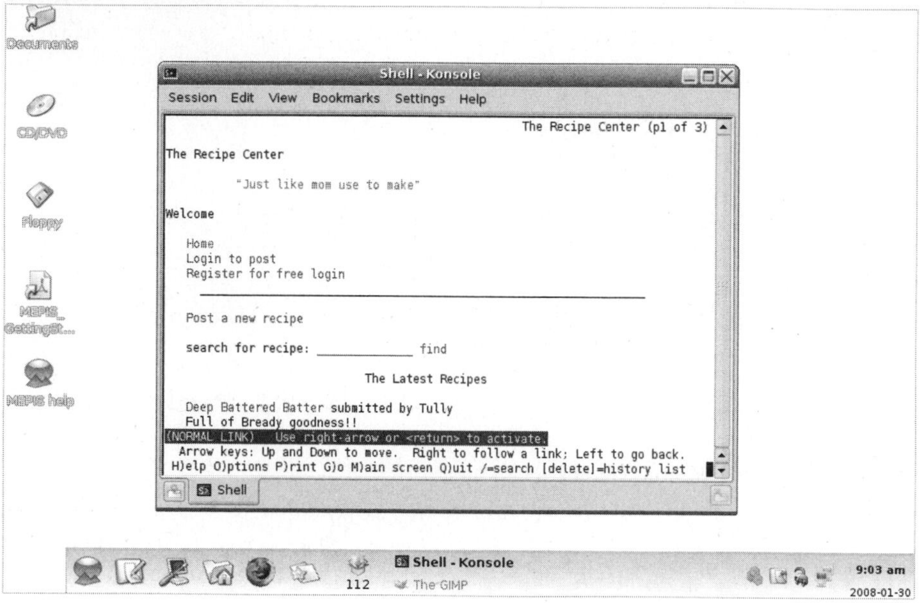

Installing Lynx

Even though the Lynx program is somewhat old, it's still in active development. At the time of this writing, the latest version of Lynx is version 2.8.6, released in October of 2006, with a new release in development. Due to its popularity among shell script programmers, many Linux distributions install the Lynx program in their default installations.

If you're using an installation that doesn't provide the Lynx program, check your distribution's installation packages. Most likely you'll find it there for easy installation.

If your distribution doesn't include the Lynx package, or if you just want the latest version, you can download the source code and compile it yourself (assuming that you've got the C development libraries installed on your Linux system).

NOTE   The Lynx program uses the curses text-graphics library in Linux. Most distributions have this installed by default. If your distribution doesn't, consult your particular distribution's instructions on installing the curses library before trying to compile Lynx.

Follow these steps to download, compile, and install Lynx on your Linux system:

1. The Web page for the Lynx project is located at `lynx.isc.org`. From there you can find links to the latest release and development versions. Download the latest version in the compression format of your choice (such as `.tar.gz` or `.zip`).

2. Extract the download file into a working directory on your Linux system (such as your $HOME folder):

```
tar -zxvf lynx2.8.6.tar.gz
```

3. Change to the resulting working directory (called lynx2.8.6 in this example):

```
cd lynx2.8.6
```

4. Execute the configure script in the directory:

```
./configure
```

5. Execute the make utility to compile the source code and create the executable file:

```
make
```

6. As the *root* user, copy the lynx executable file to a common directory in your PATH, such as the /usr/local/bin directory.

The next section describes how to use the lynx command from the command line.

The lynx command line

The lynx command is extremely versatile in what information it can retrieve from the remote Web site. When you view a Web page in your browser, you're only seeing part of the information that's transferred to your browser. Web pages consist of three types of data elements:

■ HTTP headers

■ Cookies

■ HTML content

HTTP headers provide information about the type of data sent in the connection, the server sending the data, and the type of security used in the connection. If you're sending special types of data, such as video or audio clips, the server identifies that in the HTTP headers. The Lynx program allows you to view all of the HTTP headers sent within a Web page session.

If you've done any type of Web browsing, no doubt you're familiar with Web page *cookies*. Web sites use cookies to store data about your Web site visit for future use. Each individual site can store information, but only access the information that it sets. The lynx command provides options for you to view cookies sent by Web servers, as well as reject or accept specific cookies sent from servers.

The Lynx program allows you to view the actual HTML content of the Web page in three different formats:

■ In a text-graphics display on the terminal session using the curses graphical library.

■ As a text file, dumping the raw data from the Web page.

■ As a text file, dumping the raw HTML source code from the Web page.

For shell scripts, viewing the raw data or HTML source code is a gold mine. Once you capture the data retrieved from a Web site, you can easily extract individual pieces of information.

As you can see, the Lynx program is extremely versatile in what it can do. However, with versatility comes complexity, especially when it comes to command line parameters. The Lynx program is one of the more complex programs you'll run into in the Linux world.

The basic format of the `lynx` command is:

```
lynx options URL
```

where *URL* is the HTTP or HTTPS destination you want to connect to, and *options* are one or more options that modify the behavior of Lynx as it interacts with the remote Web site. There are options for just about any type of Web interaction required by Lynx. Table 25-1 shows all of the available command line parameters you can use with the `lynx` command.

As you can see, you can control just about any type of HTTP or HTML setting directly from the command line. For example, if you want to post data to a Web form using the HTTP POST method, you just include your data in the `-post-data` parameter. If you want to store the cookies received by the Web site in a special location, you use the `-cookie_save_file` parameter.

Many of the command line parameters define behaviors that control Lynx when you're using it in full-screen mode, allowing you to customize the behavior of Lynx as you're traversing Web pages.

There are often groups of command line parameters that you find useful in your normal browsing environment. Instead of having to enter these parameters on the command line every time you use Lynx, Lynx provides a general configuration file that defines the base behavior when you use Lynx. This configuration file is discussed in the next section.

The Lynx configuration file

The `lynx` command reads a configuration file for many of its parameter settings. By default, this file is located at `/usr/local/lib/lynx.cfg`, although you'll find that many Linux distributions change this to the `/etc` directory (`/etc/lynx.cfg`).

The `lynx.cfg` configuration file groups related parameters together into sections to make finding parameters easier. The format of an entry in the configuration file is:

```
PARAMETER:value
```

where *PARAMETER* is the full name of the parameter (often, but not always in upper-case letters), and *value* is the value associated with the parameter.

Perusing this file, you'll find many parameters that are similar to the command line parameters, such as the `ACCEPT_ALL_COOKIES` parameter, which is equivalent to setting the `-accept_all_cookies` command line parameter.

There are also a few configuration parameters that are similar in function, but different in name. The `FORCE_SSL_COOKIES_SECURE` configuration file parameter setting can be overridden by the `-force_secure` command line parameter.

TABLE 25-1

The Lynx Command Parameters

Parameter	Description
-	Receive options and arguments from STDIN.
-accept_all_cookies	Accept cookies without prompting if Set-Cookie handling is on. Set to off by default.
-anonymous	Apply restrictions for anonymous account.
-assume_charset=*name*	Default charset for documents that don't specify one.
-assume_local_charset=*name*	Default charset for local files.
-assume_unrec_charset=*name*	Default charset to use instead of unrecognized charsets.
-auth=id:pw	Authentication information for protected documents.
-base	Prepend a request URL comment and BASE tag to text/HTML outputs for -source dumps
-bibhost=*URL*	Local bibp server URL (default http://bibhost/).
-book	Use the bookmark page as the startfile. Set to off by default.
-buried_news	Toggle scanning of news articles for buried references. Set to on by default.
-cache=*n*	Number of documents cached in memory.
-case	Enable case-sensitive user searching. Set to off by default.
-center	Toggle center alignment in HTML <table> tags. Set to off by default.
-cfg=*filename*	Specify a configuration file other than the default lynx.cfg file.
-child	Exit on left-arrow in startfile, and disable save to disk.
-cmd_log=*filename*	Log keystroke commands to the specified file.
-cmd_script=*filename*	Read keystroke commands from the specified file.
-connect_timeout=n	Set the connection timeout (in seconds). The default is 18000 seconds.
-cookie_file=*filename*	Specify the file to use to read cookies.
-cookie_save_file=*filename*	Specify the file to use to store cookies.

continued

TABLE 25-1 *(continued)*

Parameter	Description
-cookies	Toggle handling of Set-Cookie headers. Set to on by default.
-core	Toggle forced core dumps on fatal errors. Set to off by default.
-crawl	With -traversal, output each page to a file with -dump, format output as with -traversal, but to STDOUT.
-curses_pads	Use curses pad feature to support left/right shifting. Set to on by default.
-debug_partial	Display incremental display stages with MessageSecs delay. Set to off by default.
-delay=n	Set delay at statusline message (in seconds). Set to 0.000 by default.
-display=display	Set the display variable for X Window programs.
-display_charset=name	The charset for the terminal output.
-dont_wrap_pre	Don't wrap text in \<pre\> sections when -dump and -crawl set. Mark wrapped lines in interactive session. Set to on by default.
-dump	Dump the first URL to STDOUT and exit.
-editor=editor	Enable edit mode with the specified editor.
-emacskeys	Enable emacs-like key movement. Set to off by default.
-enable_scrollback	Toggle compatibility with scrollback keys. Set to off by default.
-error_file=filename	Write the HTTP status code to the specified file.
-exec	Enable local program execution.
-force_empty_hrefless_a	Force \<a\> elements without an href attribute to be empty. Set to off by default.
-force_html	Force the first document to be interpreted as HTML. Set to off by default.
-force_secure	Require the secure flag for SSL cookies. Set to off by default.
-forms_options	Use forms-based options menu. Set to on by default.

TABLE 25-1 *(continued)*

Parameter	Description
-from	Enable transmission of From headers. Set to on by default.
-ftp	Disable ftp access. Set to off by default.
-get_data	Read data for get forms from STDIN, terminated by ---.
-head	Send a HEAD request. Set to off by default.
-help	Print usage message.
-hiddenlinks=*option*	Specify how to handle hidden links. *Option* can be merge, listonly, or ignore.
-historical	Use '>' instead of '-->' as terminator for comments. Set to off by default.
-homepage=URL	Set homepage separate from start page.
-image_links	Enable inclusion of links for all images. Set to off by default.
-index=URL	Set the default index filename.
-ismap	Include ISMAP links when client-side MAPs are present. Set to off by default.
-link=n	Set the starting count for lnk#.dat files produced by -crawl. Set to 0 by default.
-localhost	Disable URLs that point to remote hosts. Set to off by default.
-locexec	Enable local program execution from local files only. Set to off by default.
-mime_header	Include mime headers and force source dump.
-minimal	Use minimal instead of valid comment parsing. Set to off by default.
-nested_tables	Use nested-tables logic. Set to off by default.
-newschunksize=n	Set the number of articles in chunked news listings.
-newsmaxchunk=n	Set the maximum number of news articles in listings before chunking.
-nobold	Disable bold video-attribute.
-nobrowse	Disable directory browsing.

continued

TABLE 25-1 *(continued)*

Parameter	Description
-nocc	Disable Cc: prompts for self-copies of mailings. Set to off by default.
-nocolor	Disable color support.
-noexec	Disable local program execution. Set to on by default.
-nofilereferer	Disable transmission of Referer headers for file URLs. Set to on by default.
-nolist	Disable the link list feature in dumps. Set to off by default.
-nolog	Disable mailing of error messages to document owners. Set to on by default.
-nonrestarting_sigwinch	Make window size change handler non-restarting. Set to off by default.
-nopause	Disable forced pauses for statusline messages.
-noprint	Disable some print functions, like -restrictions=print. Set to off by default.
-noredir	Don't follow Location: redirection. Set to off by default.
-noreferer	Disable transmission of Referer headers. Set to off by default.
-noreverse	Disable reverse video-attribute.
-nostatus	Disable the miscellaneous information messages. Set to off by default.
-nounderline	Disable underline video-attribute
-number_fields	Force numbering of links as well as form input fields. Set to off by default.
-number_links	Force numbering of links. Set to off by default.
-partial	Display partial pages while downloading. Set to on by default.
-partial_thres=*n*	Set the number of lines to render before repainting display with partial-display logic. Set to -1 by default, which disables this feature.
-pauth=id:pw	Set the authentication information for a protected proxy server.
-popup	Handle single-choice SELECT options via popup windows instead of lists of radio buttons. Set to off by default.

TABLE 25-1	*(continued)*
Parameter	**Description**
-post_data	Read data for post forms from stdin, terminated by ---.
-preparsed	Show parsed text/html with -source and in source view to visualize how Lynx behaves with invalid HTML. Set to off by default.
-prettysrc	Use syntax highlighting and hyperlink handling in source view. Set to off by default.
-print	Enable print functions, the opposite of -noprint. Set to on by default.
-pseudo_inlines	Use pseudo-ALTs for inlines with no ALT string. Set to on by default.
-raw	Use default setting of 8-bit character translations or CJK mode for the startup character set. Set to off by default.
-realm	Restrict access to URLs in the starting realm. Set to off by default.
-reload	Flush the cache on a proxy server (only the first document affected). Set to off by default.
-restrictions=*options*	Set restriction options. Use -restrictions with no parameters to see list.
-resubmit_posts	Force resubmissions (no-cache) of forms with method POST when the documents they returned are sought with the PREV_DOC command or from the History List. Set to off by default.
-rlogin	Disable rlogin feature. Set to off by default.
-selective	Require .www_browsable files to browse directories.
-short_url	Enable examination of beginning and end of long URL in status line. Set to off by default.
-show_cursor	When set to off, hide the cursor in the lower right corner, otherwise show cursor. Set to on by default.
-show_rate	Display the transfer rate. Set to on by default.
-soft_dquotes	Use emulation of old Netscape and Mosaic bug, which treated '>' as a co-terminator for double quotation marks and tags. Set to off by default.
-source	Dump the source of the first URL to STDOUT and exit.
-stack_dump	Disable SIGINT cleanup handler. Set to off by default.

continued

TABLE 25-1 *(continued)*

Parameter	Description
-startfile_ok	Allow non-HTTP startfile and homepage with -validate. Set to off by default.
-stdin	Read startfile from STDIN. Set to off by default.
-tagsoup	Use TagSoup rather than SortaSGML parser. Set to off by default.
-telnet	Disable Telnet sessions. Set to off by default.
-term=term	Specify the terminal type to emulate.
-tlog	Use a Lynx Trace Log for the current session. Set to on by default.
-tna	Use "Textfields Need Activation" mode. Set to off by default.
-trace	Use Lynx trace mode. Set to off by default.
-trace_mask	Customize Lynx trace mode. Set to 0 by default.
-traversal	Traverse all HTTP links derived from startfile.
-trim_input_fields	Trim input text/textarea fields in forms. Set to off by default.
-underline_links	Use an underline/bold attribute for links. Set to off by default.
-underscore	Use an underline format in dumps. Set to off by default.
-use_mouse	Enable mouse support. Set to off by default.
-useragent=Name	Set alternate Lynx User-Agent header.
-validate	Accept only http URLs (meant for validation) implies more restrictions than -anonymous, but goto is allowed for http and https. Set to off by default.
-verbose	Use [LINK], [IMAGE], and [INLINE] comments with filenames of these images. Set to on by default.
-version	Display Lynx version information
-vikeys	Enable vi-like key movement. Set to off by default.
-width=n	Set the screen width for formatting of dumps. The default is 80 columns.
-with_backspaces	Emit backspaces in output if using -dump or -crawl parameters. Set to off by default.

However, you'll also find quite a few configuration parameters that don't match with command line parameters. These values can only be set from the configuration file.

The most common configuration parameters that you can't set on the command line are for the *proxy servers*. Some networks (especially corporate networks) use a proxy server as a middleman between the client's browser and the destination Web site server. Instead of sending HTTP requests directly to the remote Web server, client browsers must send their requests to the proxy server. The proxy server in turn sends the requests to the remote Web server, retrieves the results, and forwards them back to the client browser.

While this may seem somewhat of a waste of time, it's a vital function in protecting clients from dangers on the Internet. A proxy sever can filter inappropriate content, malicious coding, or even detect sites used for Internet data phishing schemes (rogue servers pretending to be someone else in order to capture customer data). Proxy servers can also help reduce Internet bandwidth usage, as they cache commonly viewed Web pages and return them to clients instead of having to download the original page again.

The configuration parameters used to define proxy servers are:

```
http_proxy:http://some.server.dom:port/
https_proxy:http://some.server.dom:port/
ftp_proxy:http://some.server.dom:port/
gopher_proxy:http://some.server.dom:port/
news_proxy:http://some.server.dom:port/
newspost_proxy:http://some.server.dom:port/
newsreply_proxy:http://some.server.dom:port/
snews_proxy:http://some.server.dom:port/
snewspost_proxy:http://some.server.dom:port/
snewsreply_proxy:http://some.server.dom:port/
nntp_proxy:http://some.server.dom:port/
wais_proxy:http://some.server.dom:port/
finger_proxy:http://some.server.dom:port/
cso_proxy:http://some.server.dom:port/
no_proxy:host.domain.dom
```

You can define a different proxy server for any network protocol supported by Lynx. The NO_PROXY parameter is a comma-separated list of Web sites that you prefer to have direct access to, without using the proxy server. These are often internal Web sites that don't require filtering.

The Lynx environment variables

As you can see from the wealth of command line options and configuration file parameters, the Lynx program is extremely customizable. However, the customization doesn't stop there. You can override many configuration file parameters using environment variables. If you're working in an environment where you don't have access to the lynx.cfg configuration file, you can override some default parameters by setting your local environment variables. Table 25-2 lists the more common Lynx environment variables that you might need to use when using Lynx in a restricted environment.

TABLE 25-2	

The Lynx Environment Variables

Variable	Description
LYNX_CFG	Specify the location of an alternate configuration file.
LYNX_LSS	Specify the location of the default Lynx character set style sheet.
LYNX_SAVE_SPACE	Specify the location for saving files to disk.
NNTPSERVER	Specify the server to use for retrieving and posting USENET news.
PROTOCOL_PROXY	Override the proxy server for the specified protocol.
SSL_CERT_DIR	Specify the directory containing trusted certificates for accessing trusted sites.
SSL_CERT_FILE	Specify the file containing your trusted certificates.
WWW_HOME	Define the default URL for Lynx to use at startup.

You set these environment variables just as you would any other environment variable before using the Lynx program:

```
$ http_proxy=http://myproxy.com:8080
$ lynx
```

To specify a proxy server, you must provide the protocol, the server name, and the port used to communicate with the proxy server. If you need this variable setting, it's usually a good idea to include it in a common startup file for your shell (such as the .bashrc file for the bash shell), so you don't have to enter it every time.

Capturing data from Lynx

When you use Lynx in a shell script, most likely you're trying to obtain a specific piece (or pieces) of information from a Web page. The technique to accomplish this is called *screen scraping*. In screen scraping, you're trying to programmatically find data in a specific location on a graphical screen so you can capture it and use it in your shell script.

The easiest way to perform screen scraping with lynx is to use the -dump option. This option doesn't bother trying to display the Web page on the terminal screen. Instead, it displays the Web page text data directly to STDOUT:

```
$ lynx -dump http://localhost/RecipeCenter/

The Recipe Center

        "Just like mom use to make"
```

```
Welcome

   [1]Home
   [2]Login to post
   [3]Register for free login
   _____

   [4]Post a new recipe
```

Each link is identified by a tag number, and Lynx displays a listing of all the tag references after the Web page data.

Once you have all of the text data from the Web page, you probably know what tools we're going to get out of the toolbox to start work on extracting data. That's right, our old friends the sed and gawk programs (see Chapter 16).

First, let's find some interesting data to collect. The Yahoo! weather Web page is a great source for finding the current weather conditions anywhere in the world. Each location uses a separate URL to display weather information for that city (you can find the specific URL for your city by going to the site in a normal browser, and entering in your city's information). The Lynx command for finding the weather in Chicago, Illinois, is:

```
lynx -dump http://weather.yahoo.com/forecast/USILO225.html
```

This command dumps lots and lots of data from the Web page. The first step is to find the precise information you want. To do that, redirect the output from the lynx command to a file, then search the file for your data. After doing that with the above command, I found this text in the output file:

```
     Current conditions as of 1:54 pm EDT

Light Drizzle

     Feels Like:
          50°

     Barometer:
          29.34 in and falling

     Humidity:
          93%

     Visibility:
          4 mi

     Dewpoint:
          48°

     Wind:
          S 16 mph
```

That's just about all the information about the current weather that you'll need. There's just one small problem with this output. You'll notice that the numbers are on a line below the heading. Trying to just extract individual numbers will be difficult. Chapter 18 discussed how to deal with a problem just like this.

The key to solving this is to write a sed script that can search for the data heading first. When you find it, you can then go to the correct line to extract the data. We're fortunate in this example in that all of the data we need are on lines by themselves. We should be able to solve this with just the sed script. If there had also been other text on the same line, we'd need to get out the gawk tool to filter out just the data we needed.

First, you need to create a sed script that will look for the *Current conditions* text, then skip two lines to get the text that describes the current weather condition, and print it. Here's what that looks like:

```
$ cat sedcond
/Current conditions/{
n
n
p
}
$
```

The address specifies to look for the line with the desired text. If sed finds it, the two n commands skip the next two lines, then the p command prints the contents of the following line, which is the text describing the current weather conditions of the city.

Next, you'll need a sed script that can search for the *Feels Like:* text, then go to the next line to print the temperature:

```
$ cat sedtemp
/Feels Like:/{
n
p
}
$
```

Perfect. Now, you can use these two sed scripts in a shell script that first captures the lynx output of the Web page to a temporary file, then applies the two sed scripts to the Web page data to extract only the data you're looking for. Here's an example of how to do that:

```
$ cat weather
#!/bin/bash
# extract the current weather for Chicago, IL

URL="http://weather.yahoo.com/forecast/USIL0225.html"
LYNX=`which lynx`
TMPFILE=`mktemp tmpXXXXXX`
$LYNX -dump $URL > $TMPFILE
```

```
conditions=`cat $TMPFILE | sed -n -f sedcond`
temp=`cat $TMPFILE | sed -n -f sedtemp`
rm -f $TMPFILE
echo "Current conditions: $conditions"
echo The current temp outside is: $temp
$ ./weather
Current conditions: Light Rain
The current temp outside is: 49°
$
```

The weather script connects to the Yahoo! weather Web page for the desired city, saves the Web page to a temporary file, extracts the appropriate text, removes the temporary file, then displays the weather information. The beauty of this is that once you've extracted the data from a Web site you can do whatever you want with it, such as create a table of temperatures. You can then create a cron job (see Chapter 13) that runs every day to track daily temperatures.

CAUTION The Internet is a dynamic place. Don't be surprised if you spend hours working out the precise location of data on a Web page, only to find that it's moved a couple of weeks later, breaking your scripts. In fact, it's quite possible that my example won't work by the time you read this book. The important thing is to know the process for extracting data from Web pages. You can then apply that principle to any situation.

The cURL Program

The popularity of Lynx has spawned another similar product, called cURL. The cURL program allows you to automatically transfer files from the command line using a specified URL. It currently supports the FTP, FTPS, HTTP, HTTPS, SCP, SFTP, TFTP, Telnet, DICT, LDAP, LDAPS, and FILE protocols as specified in URLs.

While cURL isn't used as a Web page browser per se, it allows you to easily send or retrieve data unattended directly from the command line, or your shell scripts, just by using a simple command. This provides a great tool to have in your shell scripting toolbox.

This section walks you through the process of installing and using cURL in your shell scripts.

CAUTION There's also a programming language called curl, owned and marketed by the Sumisho Computer System Corporation. Don't confuse cURL with the curl programming language.

Installing cURL

With it's growing popularity, cURL is installed by default in many Linux distributions. If it's not available for your Linux distribution, or if you just want to use the latest version, you can download the source code and compile it on your Linux system. Again, the standard disclaimers apply; you must have the C development libraries installed on your Linux system for this to work.

Here are the steps for downloading and installing cURL:

1. Go to the main cURL Web site at `curl.haxx.se`, and click the Download link on the left side of the page.

2. Click the link for the latest version of cURL in the archive format of your choice (such as `.tar.gz`).

3. Change to the resulting working directory (called `curl-7.18.0` in this example):

   ```
   cd curl-7.18.0
   ```

4. Execute the configure script in the directory:

   ```
   ./configure
   ```

5. Execute the make utility to compile the source code and create the executable file:

   ```
   make
   ```

6. As the *root* user, copy the `curl` executable file to a common directory in your PATH, such as the `/usr/local/bin` directory.

The next section describes how to use the `curl` program from the command line.

The cURL command line

Just like the Lynx program command line, the curl command line can get messy. There are lots of options available for controlling exactly how you want cURL to interface with the remote server. Table 25-3 shows the command line parameters available for cURL.

The list of command line parameters is similar to the Lynx program. Most of the parameters define how to interact with the remote server.

Now let's take a look at what we can do with the `curl` command.

Exploring with curl

By default, cURL returns the complete HTML code for the Web page to STDOUT:

```
$ curl http://localhost/RecipeCenter/
<!DOCTYPE html PUBLIC "-//W3C//DTD XHTML 1.0 Transitional//EN"
"http://www.w3.org/TR/xhtml1/DTD/xhtml1-transitional.dtd">
<html xmlns="http://www.w3.org/1999/xhtml">
<head>
<link rel="stylesheet" type="text/css" href="mystyle.css" />
<link rel="stylesheet" media="print" type="text/css" href="print.css"
/>
<title>The Recipe Center</title>
</head>

<body>
<table width="100%" border="0">
```

```
<tr>
  <td id="header" height="90" colspan="3">
      <h1><br>
  The Recipe Center</h1>
<h4>            
<em> "Just like mom use to make"</em></h4></td>
  </tr>
  <tr>
    <td id="nav" width="15%" valign="top">
        <table width="100%" cellpadding="3">
  <tr>
    <td><h3>Welcome</h3></td>
  </tr>
  <tr>
[ listing truncated ]
```

TABLE 25-3

The cURL Command Line Parameters

Long Parameter	Short Parameter	Description
--append	-a	Append to target file when uploading.
--user-agent *name*	-A	User-Agent to send to server.
--anyauth		Use the ANY authentication method.
--cookie *name=string*	-b	Cookie string or file to read cookies from.
--basic		Use HTTP Basic Authentication.
--use-ascii	-B	Transfer data using ASCII.
--cookie-jar *file*	-c	Write cookies to the specified file after operation.
--continue-at offset	-C	Resume file transfer at *offset*.
--data data	-d	Send *data* using the HTTP POST method.
--data-ascii *data*		Send ASCII data using the HTTP POST method.
--data-binary *data*		Send binary data using the HTTP POST method.
--negotiate		Use HTTP Negotiate Authentication.
--digest		Use HTTP Digest Authentication.
--disable-eprt		Disable using EPRT or LPRT.
--disable-epsv		Disable using EPSV.

continued

TABLE 25-3   *(continued)*

Long Parameter	Short Parameter	Description
`--dump-header` *file*	`-D`	Write the HTTP session headers to the specified file.
`--egd-file` *file*		Specify a EGD socket path for random data.
`--tcp-nodelay`		Use the TCP`NODELAY option.
`--referer`	`-e`	Referer URL.
`--cert cert:passwd`	`-E`	Specify a client certificate file and password.
`--cert-type` *type*		Specify a certificate file type (DER/PEM/ENG).
`--key key`		Specify the private key file.
`--key-type` *type*		Specify the private key file type (DER/PEM/ENG).
`--pass` *pass*		Specify the passphrase for the private key.
`--engine` *eng*		Specify the crypto engine to use.
`--cacert` *file*		Specify a CA certificate to verify the remote peer.
`--capath` *dir*		Specify a CA directory to verify the remote peer.
`--ciphers` *list*		Specify a list of SSL ciphers to use in an SSL connection.
`--compressed`		Request compressed response.
`--connect-timeout` *sec*		Specify the maximum time allowed for connection (in seconds).
`--create-dirs`		Create necessary local directory hierarchy.
`--crlf`		Convert LF to CRLF in upload.
`--fail`	`-f`	Fail silently on HTTP errors.
`--ftp-create-dirs`		Create the remote dirs if not present.
`--ftp-pasv`		Use PASV/EPSV instead of PORT in FTP transfers.
`--ftp-skip-pasv-ip`		Skip the IP address for PASV.
`--ftp-ssl`		Enable SSL/TLS for the FTP transfer.
`--form name=`*content*	`-F`	Specify HTTP multipart POST data.
`--form-string name=`*string*		Specify HTTP multipart POST data.
`--globoff`	`-g`	Disable URL sequences and ranges using {} and [].
`--get`	`-G`	Send the `-d` data with a HTTP GET.

TABLE 25-3   *(continued)*

Long Parameter	Short Parameter	Description
--help	-h	Display the help text file.
--header *header*	-H	Specify a custom HTTP header to pass to the server.
--ignore-content-length		Ignore the HTTP Content-Length header.
--include	-i	Include protocol headers in the output.
--head	-I	Show document info only.
--junk-session-cookies	-j	Ignore session cookies read from file.
--interface *int*		Specify network interface to use.
--krb4 level		Enable krb4 with specified security level.
--insecure	-k	Allow connections to SSL sites without certs.
--config	-K	Specify which config file to read.
--list-only	-l	List only names of an FTP directory.
--limit-rate *rate*		Limit transfer speed to *rate* bits per second.
--location	-L	Follow HTTP Location: headers.
--location-trusted		Follow Location: and send authentication even to other hostnames.
--max-time *sec*	-m	Maximum time allowed for the file transfer (in seconds)
--max-redirs *num*		Maximum number of redirects allowed.
--max-filesize *bytes*		Maximum file size to download (in bytes)
--manual	-M	Display the full manual.
--netrc	-n	Must read .netrc for user name and password.
--netrc-optional		Use either .netrc or UR. Overrides -n.
--ntlm		Use HTTP NTLM authentication.
--no-buffer	-N	Disable buffering of the output stream.
--output *file*	-o	Write output to *file* instead of STDOUT.
--remote-name	-O	Write output to a file named as the remote file.
--proxytunnel	-p	Operate through a HTTP proxy tunnel.
--proxy-anyauth		Use the Any proxy authentication method.

continued

TABLE 25-3 *(continued)*

Long Parameter	Short Parameter	Description
`--proxy-basic`		Use `Basic` authentication on the proxy.
`--proxy-digest`		Use `Digest` authentication on the proxy.
`--proxy-ntlm`		Use `NTLM` authentication on the proxy.
`--ftp-port address`	`-P`	Use TCP port *address* instead of PASV for FTP.
	`-q`	If used as the first parameter, disables reading `.curlrc` file.
`--quote cmd`	`-Q`	Sends command *cmd* to server before file transfer.
`--range range`	`-r`	Retrieve a byte range from a HTTP/1.1 or FTP server.
`--random-file file`		Specify a file for reading random data for SSL.
`--remote-time`	`-R`	Set the remote file's time on the local output.
`--retry num`		Retry request *num* times if transient problems occur.
`--retry-delay sec`		When retrying, wait *sec* seconds between each attempt.
`--retry-max-time sec`		Retry only within *sec* period (in seconds).
`--silent`	`-s`	Silent mode. Doesn't output anything.
`--show-error`	`-S`	Show error. With `-s`, show errors when they occur.
`--socks host:port`		Use `SOCKS5` proxy on specified host and port.
`--stderr file`		Specify a file to redirect `STDERR`. Using `-` redirects to `STDOUT`.
`--telnet-option OPT=val`	`-t`	Set Telnet option.
`--trace file`		Write a debug trace to the specified file.
`--trace-ascii file`		Like `--trace` but without the hex output.
`--trace-time`		Add timestamps to trace/verbose output.
`--upload-file file`	`-T`	Specify file to transfer to remote site.
`--url URL`		Specify the URL to connect with.
`--user user:password`	`-u`	Specify a user ID and password for the remote server.
`--proxy-user user:password`	`-U`	Specify the user ID and password required for proxy server.
`--verbose`	`-v`	Display more output information if available.

	Short	
Long Parameter	**Parameter**	**Description**
`--version`	`-V`	Display version number and exit.
`--write-out` *format*	`-w`	Specify text to display after completion.
`--proxy` *host:port*	`-x`	Specify the HTTP proxy server hostname and port.
`--request` *cmd*	`-X`	Specify a request command to use.
`--speed-time`	`-y`	Time (in seconds) needed to trigger a `--speed-limit` abort. Default is 30.
`--speed-limit`	`-Y`	Stop transfer if below `speed-limit` for `--speed-time` setting.
`--time-cond` *time*	`-z`	Set a time condition for the transfer.
`--http1.0`	`-0`	Use HTTP 1.0.
`--tlsv1`	`-1`	Use TLSv1.
`--sslv2`	`-2`	Use SSLv2.
`--sslv3`	`-3`	Use SSLv3.
`--3p-quote`		Similar to `-Q` for the source URL for third-party transfer.
`--3p-url`		Source URL to activate third-party transfer.
`--3p-user`		User and password for source third-party transfer.
`--ipv4`	`-4`	Resolve name to IPv4 address.
`--ipv6`	`-6`	Resolve name to IPv6 address.
`--progress-bar`	`-#`	Display transfer progress as a progress bar.

Just as with the Lynx program, you can use the standard shell scripting techniques to extract individual data elements from the dumped Web page.

What I like using cURL for is batch downloading files. These days it seems like I'm constantly downloading the latest Linux distribution ISO file. Since the ISO files are so large, I need to start the download and walk away while it's downloading. Once I know the URL for an ISO file, I can create a simple shell script using cURL to automate the process:

```
$ cat downld
#!/bin/bash
# download latest cURL file automatically
```

```
curl -s -o /home/rich/curl-7.18.0.tar.gz
http://curl.haxx.se/downloads/curl-7.18.0.tar.gz
$
```

Note that the `curl` command is all one line in the script. This simple script just goes out and directly downloads the file from the cURL Web site. I can now use the at or cron commands (see Chapter 13) to schedule the download to take place in the evening when I'm not using my PC or network.

Networking with zsh

Chapter 23 describes all of the features available in the zsh shell. The zsh shell is a newer shell available for the Linux and Unix environments. One of the features of the zsh shell is plug-in modules. Instead of trying to combine lots of features into the core zsh shell, it uses specialty modules, so you can pick and choose what commands you need to load. One of those is the TCP module.

The TCP module in the zsh shell provides some pretty amazing network capabilities directly from the command line. You can create a full TCP network session with another network device directly from your command line (or shell script). This section discusses the features of the zsh TCP module, and shows a simple client/server application you can build using a zsh shell script.

The TCP module

The zsh shell uses modules to add additional features to the core zsh shell. Each module contains built-in commands that specialize in a specific area. The TCP module provides built-in commands for a plethora of networking features.

To install the TCP module in a zsh shell, do the following:

```
% zmodload zsh/net/tcp
%
```

And that's all there is to bring in the module! If you use the TCP module in your shell script, remember to include this line in your script. The module only applies to the current shell.

Once you load the TCP module, you have access to the `ztcp` command. The format for the `ztcp` command is:

```
ztcp [-acflLtv] [ -d fd] [args]
```

The command line options available are:

- `-a`: Accept a new connection.
- `-c`: Close an existing connection.
- `-d`: Use the specified file descriptor for the connection.
- `-f`: Force a connection to close.

- ■ -l: Open a new socket for listening.
- ■ -L: List currently connected sockets.
- ■ -t: Exit if no connection is pending.
- ■ -v: Display verbose information about the connection.

The ztcp program uses a file descriptor to interact with an open TCP connection. By default, the zsh referenced the file descriptor using the environment variable $RESULT. All you need to do is send data to the file descriptor specified in the $RESULT variable, and the TCP module will forward it to the remote host. Likewise, if the remote host sends you any data, all you need to do is read it from the file descriptor specified in the $RESULT variable. Network programming doesn't get any easier than that!

The client/server paradigm

Before diving into creating a client/server program using the zsh shell, it's a good idea to have an understanding of how exactly client and server programs operate. Obviously, they each have different responsibilities in the connection and transfer of data.

A *server* program listens to the network for requests coming from *clients*. A client initiates a request to the server for a connection. Once the server accepts the connection request, a two-way communication channel is available for each device to send and receive data. This process is shown in Figure 25-2.

As you can see from Figure 25-2, the server must perform two functions before it can communicate with the client. First, it must set up a specific TCP port to listen for incoming requests. When a connection request comes in, it must accept the connection.

The client's responsibility is much simpler. All it must do is attempt to connect to a server on the specific TCP port on which the server is listening. If the server accepts the connection, the two-way communication is available and data can be sent.

Once a connection is established between the server and the client, there must be some sort of communication process (or rule) used between the two devices. If both devices attempt to listen for a message at the same time, they'll deadlock and nothing will happen. Likewise, if they both attempt to send a message at the same time, nothing will be accomplished.

It's your job as the network programmer to decide the protocol rules that your client and server programs must follow.

Client/server programming with zsh

To demonstrate creating a client/server program using ztcp, let's set up a simple network application. The server program we'll create will listen for connection requests on TCP port 5150. When a connection request comes in, the server will accept it, then send a welcome message to the client.

FIGURE 25-2

The client/server communication diagram

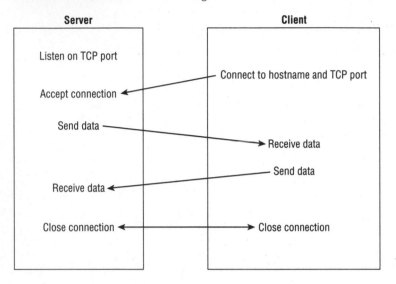

The server program will then wait to receive a message from the client. If it receives a message, the server will display the message, then send the same message back to the client. After sending the message, the server will loop back to listen for another message. This loop will continue until the server receives a message that consists of the text *exit*. When that happens the server will terminate the session.

The client program we'll create will send a connection request to the server on TCP port 5150. When a connection is established, the client will need to receive the servers' welcome message.

After receiving the message, the client displays it, then will query the user for data to send to the server. After getting the message from the user, the client program will send it to the server, and wait to receive the message back. If the message comes back, the client displays the message and loops back to request another message from the user. This loop will continue until the user enters the text *exit*. When this occurs, the client sends the exit text to the server, then terminates the session.

The next sections show the server and client programs.

The server program

Here's the code for the server program:

```
% cat server
#!/bin/zsh
# zsh TCP server script
zmodload zsh/net/tcp
```

```
ztcp -l 5150
fd=$REPLY

echo "Waiting for a client..."
ztcp -a $fd
clientfd=$REPLY
echo "client connected"

echo "Welcome to my server" >& $clientfd

while [ 1 ]
do
   read line <& $clientfd
   if [[ $line = "exit" ]]
   then
      break
   else
      echo Received: $line
      echo $line >& $clientfd
   fi
done
echo "Client disconnected session"
ztcp -c $fd
ztcp -c $clientfd
%
```

The server program follows the client/server paradigm shown in Figure 25-2. It first uses the -l parameter to listen on the specified port (5150). The $RESULT variable contains the file descriptor that the Linux system returns to identify the connection. The server uses the -a parameter to accept a new connection request. This command waits until a new connection request comes in (called *blocking*). The script won't progress unless a connection request is accepted.

Each client connection uses a separate file descriptor from the listening port file descriptor. This allows you to maintain multiple client connections if you so desire (we don't in this simple exercise).

After accepting the connection, the server redirects a welcome message to the client's file descriptor:

```
echo "Welcome to my server" >& $clientfd
```

The zsh shell TCP module handles all of the mechanics of ensuring the data is sent to the remote client.

Next, the server program enters an endless loop. It uses the read command to wait for data to come back from the client:

```
read line <& $clientfd
```

This command also blocks execution of the script until it receives data from the client. This could be a bad thing if the client has lost connection to the network. To prevent this problem, you can use the -t option in the read line to specify a timeout value (in seconds). If the server doesn't receive data from the client in the timeout period, it continues on.

If the server receives data from the client, it displays the data on STDOUT, then sends it back to the client. If the data is equal to the text string *exit*, the server exits the loop, and uses the -c parameter in ztcp to close both the client's file descriptor, and the listening port's file descriptor. If you prefer to have your server listen for another connection, after you close the client's file descriptor you can loop back to waiting to accept a new connection.

The client program

Here's the code for the client shell script program:

```
% cat client
#!/bin/zsh
# zsh TCP client program
zmodload zsh/net/tcp

ztcp localhost 5150
hostfd=$REPLY

read line <& $hostfd
echo $line

while [ 1 ]
do
   echo -n "Enter text: "
   read phrase
   echo Sending $phrase to remote host...
   echo $phrase >& $hostfd
   if [[ $phrase = "exit" ]]
   then
      break
   fi
   read line <& $hostfd
   echo "   Received: $line"
done
ztcp -c $hostfd
%
```

The client program must specify the IP address (or hostname) of the system the server program is running on, and the proper TCP port number the server is listening to. When the server accepts the connection, the ztcp program sets the file descriptor for the connection and saves the value in the $REPLY variable. The client program reads the server's welcome message, then displays it:

```
read line <& $hostfd
echo $line
```

Next the client program enters a `while` loop, querying the user for text to send to the server, reading the text entered, and sending the text to the server. After sending the text, it checks to see if the text entered was *exit*. If so, it breaks out of the loop and closes the file descriptor, which closes the TCP connection. If the text wasn't *exit*, it waits for the response from the server, then displays it.

Running the programs

You can either run these programs on two separate Linux systems on your network, or from two different terminal sessions on the same system. You must start the server program first so that it's available to listen for incoming connections when the client starts:

```
% ./server
Waiting for a client...
```

Then you can start the client:

```
% ./client
Welcome to my server
Enter text: test
Sending test to remote host...
   Received: test
```

When the client connects, you'll see this on the server:

```
client connected
Received: test
```

This will continue until the user enters the text exit on the client:

```
Enter text: exit
Sending exit to remote host...
%
```

Then you should see the server automatically exit:

```
Client disconnected session
%
```

You now have the beginnings of a full-fledged network program! With zsh shell and the TCP module it's easy sending data between shell scripts operating on separate systems on a network.

Summary

This chapter walked you through the world of interfacing shell scripts to the Internet. One of the most popular tools for doing that is the Lynx program. Lynx is a command line program that can display Web site information in a terminal session using text-mode graphics. Besides that feature, Lynx also provides a way to retrieve just the raw data from a Web site, and display it to STDOUT. You can use Lynx to extract data from a Web site, then parse the data using standard Linux text-handling tools such as sed and gawk to find specific information.

The cURL program is another handy tool to have when interfacing with the Internet. The cURL program also allows you to dump data from a Web site, and it also provides a way to easily script file downloads from many different types of servers.

Finally, the chapter showed you how to use the TCP module of the zsh shell to write your own network programs. The zsh shell provides an easy way to communicate between shell scripts that are located on separate systems on the network, just as easily as reading and writing data to a file.

In the next chapter, we'll examine how to utilize e-mail in your shell scripts. Often when you use shell scripts to automate processes, it's nice to get a message indicating if the process failed or succeeded. By knowing how to work with the installed e-mail software on your system, you can easily send automated messages to anyone in the world.

Chapter 26

Using E-Mail

With the popularity of e-mail, these days just about everyone has an e-mail address. Because of that, people often expect to receive data via e-mail instead of seeing files or printouts. That's no different in the shell script world. If you generate any type of report from your shell script, most likely at some point you'll be asked to e-mail the results to someone. This chapter shows you just how to set up your Linux system to support e-mailing directly from your shell scripts. It also shows you how to make sure that your Linux system can send outbound mail messages, and how to make sure you have a mail client that can do that from the command line. But first, the chapter presents a brief overview of the way Linux handles e-mails in general.

IN THIS CHAPTER

E-mail and Linux

Setting up an e-mail server

Sending simple messages

Using attachments with Mutt

The Basics of Linux E-Mail

Sometimes the hardest part of using e-mail in your shell scripts is understanding just how the e-mail system works in Linux. Knowing what software packages perform what tasks is crucial in getting e-mails from your shell script to your inbox. This section walks you through the basics of how Linux systems use e-mail, and what you need to have in place before you can use it.

E-Mail in Linux

The Linux system derives its e-mail system from the Unix environment. One of the main goals of the Unix operating system was to modularize software. Instead of having one monolithic program that handles all of the required pieces of a function, Unix developers created smaller programs each of which handles a smaller piece of the total functionality of the system.

FIGURE 26-1

Linux modular e-mail environment

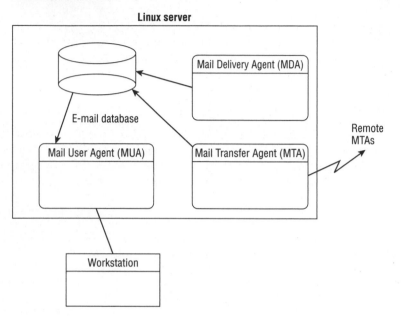

This philosophy was used when implementing the e-mail systems used in Unix, and was carried over to the Linux environment. In Linux, e-mail functions are divided into separate pieces, each assigned to separate programs. Figure 26-1 shows how most open source e-mail software modularizes e-mail functions in the Linux environment.

As you can see in Figure 26-1, in the Linux environment the e-mail process is normally divided into three functions:

- The Mail Transfer Agent (MTA)
- The Mail Delivery Agent (MDA)
- The Mail User Agent (MUA)

The lines between these three functions are often fuzzy. Some e-mail packages combine functionality for the MDA and MTA functions, whereas others combine the MDA and MUA functions. The following sections describe these basic e-mail components and how they are implemented in Linux systems in more detail.

The Mail Transfer Agent

The MTA software is the core of the Linux e-mail system. It's responsible for handling both incoming and outgoing mail messages on the system. For each outgoing mail message the MTA must determine the destination of the recipient addresses. If the destination host is the local system, the MTA can either deliver it to the local mailbox directly or pass the message off to the local MDA for delivery.

However, if the destination host is a remote mail server, the MTA must establish a communication link with the MTA software on the remote host to transfer the message. There are two common methods that MTA software packages use to deliver mail to remote hosts:

- Direct delivery
- Proxy delivery

If your Linux system is directly connected to the Internet, it can often deliver messages destined for recipients on remote hosts directly to the remote host. The MTA software uses the Domain Name System (DNS) to resolve the proper network IP address to deliver the mail message, then establishes the TCP connection using the Simple Mail Transfer Protocol (SMTP).

There are plenty of times when a host is not directly connected to the Internet, or it doesn't want to communicate directly with other remote hosts. In those situations, it usually uses a *smart host*. The smart host is a proxy server that accepts mail messages from your Linux system, then attempts to directly deliver them to the intended recipient.

NOTE Smart hosts are becoming more difficult to work with on the Internet due to relay spam. A rogue server sends relay spam by bouncing thousands of unsolicited commercial e-mail (UCE) messages off of a smart host to hide its identity. Most smart hosts now require some type of authentication before forwarding messages to other hosts.

For incoming messages, the MTA must be able to accept connection requests from remote mail servers and receive messages destined for local users. Again, the most common protocol used for this process is SMTP.

The Linux environment has many different types of open source MTA programs. Each program offers different features that distinguish it from the others. By far the two most popular you'll run into are:

- sendmail
- Postfix

We'll examine both of these e-mail MTA packages in detail in the "Setting Up Your Server" section.

The Mail Delivery Agent

The MDA program's responsibility is to deliver a message destined for a local user. It receives messages from the MTA program and must determine exactly how and where those messages should be delivered. Figure 26-2 demonstrates how the MDA program interacts with the MTA program to deliver mail.

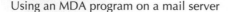

FIGURE 26-2

Using an MDA program on a mail server

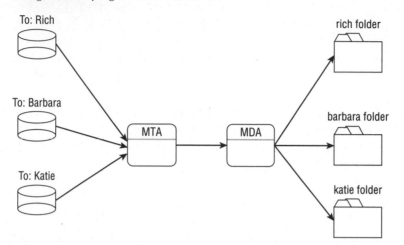

While sometimes the MDA function is performed within the MTA program itself, often Linux e-mail implementations rely on a separate stand-alone MDA program to deliver messages to local users. Because these MDA programs concentrate only on delivering mail to local users, they can add additional bells and whistles that aren't available on MTA programs that include MDA functionality. This enables the mail administrator to offer additional mail features to mail users, such as mail filtering for spam, out-of-office redirections, and automatic mail sorting.

When the MDA program receives a message, it must ensure that the message is delivered to the proper location, either to the local user's mailbox or to an alternate location defined by the local user.

There are currently three different types of user mailboxes commonly used on Linux systems:

- `/var/spool/mail` or `/var/mail` files
- `$HOME/mail` files
- Maildir-style mailbox directories

Each mailbox type has its own features that make it attractive to use. Most Linux distributions use either the `/var/spool/mail` or `/var/mail` directories to contain individual mailbox files, one file for each user account on the system. This is a central location for all mailbox files so that MUA programs know where to find everyone's mailbox file.

A few Linux distributions allow you to move the individual mailbox files to each user's `$HOME` directory. This provides greater security, in that each mailbox file is located in an area already set with the proper access privileges.

Maildir-style mailboxes are a relatively new feature supported by some more advanced MTA, MDA, and MUA applications. Instead of each message being part of a mailbox file, the mailbox is a directory, and each message is a separate file in that directory. This helps cut down on mailbox corruption, as a single message won't corrupt the entire mailbox.

While Maildir-style mailbox directories offer increased performance, security, and fault tolerance, there are many popular MDA and MUA programs that aren't able to use them. Just about all MDA and MUA programs can use the /var/spool/mail mailbox files.

NOTE The original Unix location for mailboxes is /var/spool/mail. Most Linux distributions use this file-naming convention; however, there are a few Linux distributions that use /var/mail instead.

If your system does use a special MDA program to process incoming mail messages, most likely it's the popular Procmail program. Procmail allows each individual user to create a customized configuration file to define mail filters, out-of-office destinations, and separate mailboxes.

The Mail User Agent

So far we've followed the e-mail traffic from the remote host to the local host to an individual user's mailbox. The next step in the process is to allow individual users to view their e-mail messages.

The Linux e-mail model uses a local mailbox file or directory for each user to hold messages for that user. The job of the MUA program is to provide a method for users to interface with their mailboxes to read their messages.

It's important to remember that MUAs don't receive messages; they only display messages that are already in the mailbox. Many MUA programs also offer the ability to create separate mail folders so the user can move mail from the default mailbox (often called the *inbox*) to separate folders for organization.

Most MUA programs also provide the ability to send messages. This part gets a little fuzzy, because as you've already seen, sending e-mail messages is the job of the MTA program.

To perform this function, most MUA programs utilize the smart host feature in SMTP. Either the MUA program automatically delivers messages to the local MTA program for delivery, or you must define a remote smart host in the MUA configuration for it to send messages to for delivery.

Throughout the years, many different open source MUA programs have been available for the Linux platform. The following sections describe some of the more popular MUA programs you'll run across in Linux.

Mailx

The Mailx program is the most popular command line MUA program in use for the Linux environment. The name Mailx comes from its being an improvement over the original mail program developed for Unix. In all installations the Mailx program installs with the executable file mail, indicating that it's a replacement for the mail program, rather than a separate program.

The Mailx program allows users to access their mailboxes to read stored messages, as well as to send messages to other mail users, all from the command line. Here's a sample Mailx session.

```
$ mail
Mail version 8.1.2 01/15/2001.  Type ? for help.
"/var/mail/rich": 2 messages 2 new
>N  1 atest@testbox      Fri Feb  1 17:42    16/664   This is a test
 N  2 atest@testbox      Fri Feb  1 17:43    16/676   This is another
test
& 1
Message 1:
From atest@testbox  Fri Feb  1 17:42:56 2008
Date: Fri, 1 Feb 2008 17:42:56 -0500
From: atest@testbox
To: rich@localhost.localdomain
Subject: This is a test

This is a test message.

& d
& q
Held 1 message in /var/mail/rich
$mail Barbara
Subject: This is a test message
This is a test message that I'm sending to Barbara.
.
Cc:
$
```

The first line shows the Mailx program being executed with no command line options. By default this allows the user to check the messages in his mailbox. After entering the `mail` command, a summary of all of the messages in the user's mailbox is displayed. The Mailx program can only read messages in the `/var/mail` format or `$HOME/mail` format. It's not able to process mail using the Maildir mail folder format.

Each user has a separate file that contains all of his messages. The filename is usually the system login name of the user and is located in the system mailbox directory. Thus, all messages for user name *rich* are stored in the file `/var/mail/rich` on the Linux system. As new messages are received for the user, they are appended to the end of the file.

The second use of the `mail` command demonstrates sending a mail message to another user from the command line. The name of the recipient is included on the command line with the program name. The Mailx program queries for the message subject, then allows you to type in the text of the message. To terminate the message, enter a line with a single period. To finish, the Mailx program queries if there should be any additional recipients to receive a copy of the message, then it terminates and attempts to pass the message to the MTA program for delivery.

Mutt

As advancements were made to the Unix environment, MUA programs became fancier. One of the first attempts at graphics on Unix systems was the ncurses graphics library. Using ncurses a program could manipulate the location of a cursor on the terminal screen and place characters almost anywhere on the terminal.

One MUA program that takes advantage of the ncurses library is the Mutt program. When you start Mutt it paints a user-friendly menu on the terminal display, listing the messages similar to the output of the Mailx program. You can select a message and view it in the display, as shown in Figure 26-3.

The Mutt program uses key combinations to perform standard functions, such as read a message and start a new message. Possibly the most useful feature for shell script programmers is the ability to send messages directly from the command line, without going into text-graphics mode. We'll be covering the Mutt program in much more detail later on in "The Mutt Program" section.

Graphical e-mail clients

Almost all Linux systems support the graphical X Window environment. There are many e-mail MUA programs that utilize the X Window system to display message information. The two most popular graphical MUA programs available are:

- KMail for the KDE windows environment
- Evolution for the GNOME windows environment

FIGURE 26-3

The Mutt program

FIGURE 26-4

The KMail MUA program main screen

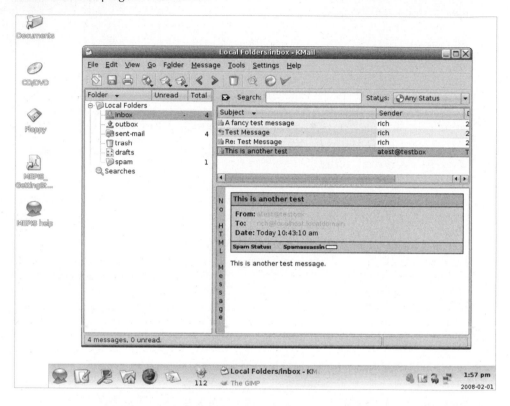

Each of these packages allows you to interact with your local Linux mailbox, as well as connect to remote mail servers to read mail messages. Figure 26-4 shows a sample KMail session screen.

To connect with remote servers, both KMail and Evolution support the Post Office Protocol (POP), and the more advanced Internet Message Access Protocol (IMAP). While the KMail and Evolution MUA programs are great for desktop Linux, they aren't so useful in shell scripting.

Setting Up Your Server

Before you can start sending your automated e-mail messages off to the universe, you'll need to ensure that your Linux system has an MTA package running and that it's configured correctly. This is no small task in itself, but fortunately, some Linux distributions provide some basic tools to help you out.

This section walks you through the basics of the two most popular e-mail MTA programs used in Linux: sendmail and Postfix. While there have been complete books written on properly configuring each of these packages, we'll just look at the basics to see how to get e-mails off the Linux system and into your inbox.

sendmail

The sendmail MTA package is one of the most popular open source MTA packages used by Internet mail servers. In the past it had been plagued with stories about backdoors and security flaws; however, it has been rewritten not only to remove the security flaws but also to incorporate many newer MTA features such as spam control. The newer versions of the sendmail program have proven to be secure as well as versatile.

Parts of the sendmail program

The main executable program is called `sendmail`. It normally runs in background mode, listening for SMTP connections from remote mail servers, and forwarding outbound messages from local users.

Besides the main `sendmail` program, there's a configuration file and several tables that it uses to contain information used while processing incoming and outgoing mail messages. Table 26-1 lists all the parts used in a normal sendmail installation.

Unless you're running the main mail server for a corporation or Internet service provider, all you'll need to worry about is the `sendmail.cf` configuration file. In fact, many Linux distributions that use sendmail create and configure a core `sendmail.cf` configuration file for you automatically that should work just fine in most simple applications.

The sendmail.cf file

The sendmail program needs to be told how to handle messages as the server receives them. As an MTA, sendmail processes incoming mail and redirects it to another mail package, either on a remote system or on the local system. The configuration file is used to direct sendmail how to manipulate the destination mail addresses to determine where and how to forward the messages. The default location for the configuration file is `/etc/mail/sendmail.cf`.

The `sendmail.cf` file consists of rule sets that parse the incoming mail message and determine what actions to take. Each rule set is used to identify certain mail formats and instruct sendmail how to handle that message.

As the sendmail program receives a message, it parses the message header and passes the message through the various rule sets to determine an action to take on the message. The sendmail configuration file includes rules that allow sendmail to handle mail in many different formats. Mail received from an SMTP host has different header fields than mail received from a local user. The sendmail program must know how to handle any mail situation.

TABLE 26-1

The sendmail Configuration Files

File	Description
sendmail.cf	Text file that controls the behavior of the sendmail program.
sendmail.cw	Text file which contains a list of domain names that the sendmail program will receive messages for.
sendmail.ct	Text file which contains a list of trusted users that can control the sendmail operations.
aliases	Binary file which contains a list of valid local mail addresses that can redirect mail to another user, a file, or a program.
newaliases	Executable program that creates a new aliases database file from a text file.
mailq	Executable program that checks the mail queue and prints any messages.
mqueue	A directory used to store messages waiting to be delivered.
mailertable	Text file used to specify route paths for specific domains.
domaintable	Text file used to map old domain names to new ones.
virtusertable	Text file used to map users and domains to alternate addresses.
relay-domains	Text file used to list specific hosts that are allowed to relay messages through the sendmail program.
access	Text file that lists specific domains from which received messages are either allowed or refused.

Rules also have helper functions defined in the configuration file. There are three different types of helper functions that you can define:

- Classes define common phrases that are used to help the rule sets identify certain types of messages.
- Macros are values that are set to simplify the typing of long strings in the configuration file.
- Options are defined to set parameters for the sendmail program's operation.

The configuration file is made up of a series of classes, macros, options, and rule sets. Each function is defined as a single text line in the configuration file.

Each line in the configuration file begins with a single character that defines the action for that line. Lines that begin with a space or a tab are continuation lines from a previous action line. Lines that begin with a pound sign (#) indicate comments and are not processed by sendmail.

TABLE 26-2	

sendmail Configuration File Lines

Configuration Line	Description
C	Defines classes of text
D	Defines a macro
F	Defines files containing classes of text
H	Defines header fields and actions
K	Defines databases that contain text to search
M	Defines mailers
O	Defines sendmail options
P	Defines sendmail precedence values
R	Defines rule sets to parse addresses
S	Defines rule set groups

The action at the beginning of the text line defines what the line is used for. Table 26-2 shows the standard sendmail actions and what they represent.

As I mentioned, most likely you won't have to start from scratch with your sendmail.cf configuration file, the Linux distribution should create a standard template file for you. Figure 26-5 shows part of the sendmail.cf configuration file from a Debian-based Linux system.

Most likely, the only piece you'll have to worry about is if you must use a smart host to forward mail for you. The DS configuration line controls this feature:

```
DSmyisp.com
```

Just add the hostname of the smart host immediately after the DS tag.

Postfix

The Postfix software package is quickly becoming one of the more popular e-mail packages available for Unix and Linux systems. Postfix was developed by Wietse Venema to provide an alternative MTA for standard Unix-type servers. The Postfix software is capable of turning any Unix or Linux system into a fully functional e-mail server.

It is the responsibility of the MTA package to manage messages that come into or leave the mail server. Postfix accomplishes this message tracking by using several different modular programs, and a system of mail queue directories. Each program processes messages through the various message queues until they are delivered to their final destinations. If at any time the mail server crashes during a message transfer, Postfix can determine what queue the message was last successfully placed in and attempt to continue the message processing.

Parts of the Postfix system

The Postfix system consists of several mail queue directories and executable programs, all interacting with each other to provide mail service. Figure 26-6 shows a block diagram of the core Postfix parts.

Each piece of the Postfix block diagram provides a different function for the whole e-mail process. The following sections describe the different pieces of the Postfix block diagram in more detail.

The Postfix package utilizes a `master` program that runs as a background process at all times. The master program allows Postfix to spawn programs that scan the mail queues for new messages and send them to the proper destinations. The core programs can be configured to remain running for set times after they are utilized. This allows the master program to reutilize a running helper program if necessary, saving processing time. After a set time limit, the helper program quietly stops itself.

FIGURE 26-5

The sendmail.cf configuration file in Debian Linux

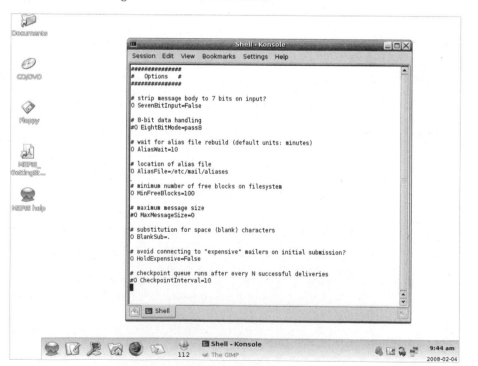

FIGURE 26-6

Block diagram of Postfix

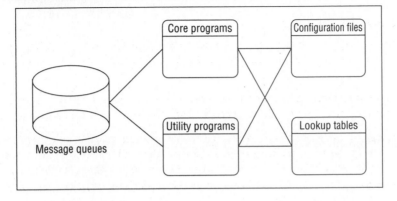

The master program is used to control the overall operation of Postfix. It is responsible for starting other Postfix processes as needed. The qmgr and pickup programs are configured to remain as background processes longer than other core programs. The pickup program determines when messages are available to be routed by the Postfix system. The qmgr program is responsible for the central message routing system for Postfix.

Table 26-3 shows other core programs that Postfix uses to transfer mail messages.

TABLE 26-3

The Postfix Core Programs

Program	Description
bounce	Posts a log in the bounce message queue for bounced messages and returns the bounced message to the sender
cleanup	Processes incoming mail headers and places messages in the incoming queue
error	Processes message delivery requests from qmgr, forcing messages to bounce
flush	Processes messages waiting to be retrieved by a remote mail server
local	Delivers messages destined for local users
pickup	Waits for messages in the maildrop queue and sends them to the cleanup program to begin processing
pipe	Forwards messages from the queue manager program to external programs

continued

TABLE 26-3	(continued)
Program	**Description**
postdrop	Moves an incoming message to the maildrop queue when that queue is not writable by normal users
qmgr	Processes messages in the incoming queue, determining where and how they should be delivered and spawns programs to deliver them
sendmail	Provides a sendmail compatible interface for programs to send messages to the maildrop queue
showq	Reports Postfix mail queue status
smtp	Forwards messages to external mail hosts using the SMTP protocol
smtpd	Receives messages from external mail hosts using the SMTP protocol
trivial-rewrite	Receives messages from the cleanup program to ensure header addresses are in a standard format for the qmgr program, and used by the qmgr program to resolve remote host addresses

Unlike some other MTA packages, Postfix uses several different message queues for managing e-mail messages as they are processed. Each message queue contains messages in a different message state in the Postfix system. Table 26-4 lists the message queues that are used by Postfix.

If the Postfix system should be shut down at any time, messages remain in the last queue in which they were placed. When Postfix is restarted, it will automatically begin processing messages from the queues.

TABLE 26-4	

Postfix Message Queues

Queue	Description
maildrop	New messages waiting to be processed, received from local users.
incoming	New messages waiting to be processed, received from remote hosts, as well as processed messages from local users.
active	Messages that are ready to be delivered by Postfix.
deferred	Messages that have failed on an initial delivery attempt and are waiting for another attempt.
flush	Messages that are destined for remote hosts that will connect to the mail server to retrieve them.
mail	Delivered messages stored for local users to read.

TABLE 26-5

Postfix Configuration Files

File	Description
install.cf	Contains information from the install parameters used when Postfix was installed.
main.cf	Contains parameters used by the Postfix programs when processing messages.
master.cf	Contains parameters used by the Postfix master program when running core programs.

Postfix configuration files

The next block in the diagram is the Postfix configuration files. The configuration files contain information that the Postfix programs use when processing messages. Unlike some other MTA programs, it's possible to change configuration information while the Postfix server is running and issue a command to have Postfix load the new information without completely downing the mail server.

There are three Postfix configuration files, which are located in a common Postfix directory. Often the default location for this directory is /etc/postfix. Usually, all users have access to view the configuration files, whereas only the *root* user has the ability to change values within the files. Of course, this can be modified for your own security situation. Table 26-5 lists the Postfix configuration files.

The install.cf configuration file allows you to retrieve installation parameters that were used when the Postfix software was first installed on the system. This provides an easy way to determine which features are or aren't available in the software setup.

The master.cf configuration file controls the behavior of the core Postfix programs. Each program is listed in a separate line along with the parameters to control its operation. Here's a sample master.cf file with default settings.

```
# =================================================================
#service type  private unpriv  chroot  wakeup  maxproc command + args
#             (yes)   (yes)   (yes)   (never) (50)
# =================================================================
smtp      inet  n    -    n    -    -   smtpd
pickup    fifo  n    -    n    60   1   pickup
cleanup   unix  -    -    n    -    0   cleanup
qmgr      fifo  n    -    n    300  1   qmgr
rewrite   unix  -    -    n    -    -   trivial-rewrite
bounce    unix  -    -    n    -    0   bounce
defer     unix  -    -    n    -    0   bounce
trac      unix  -    -    n    -    0   bounce
verify    unix  -    -    n    -    1   verify
```

```
flush      unix   n   -   n   1000  0   flush
proxymap   unix   -   -   n    -    -   proxymap
smtp       unix   -   -   n    -    -   smtp
relay      unix   -   -   n    -    -   smtp -o fallback_relay=
showq      unix   n   -   n    -    -   showq
error      unix   -   -   n    -    -   error
local      unix   -   n   n    -    -   local
virtual    unix   -   n   n    -    -   virtual
lmtp       unix   -   -   n    -    -   lmtp
anvil      unix   -   -   n    -    1   anvil
scache     unix   -   -   n    -    1   scache
```

The `master.cf` configuration file also includes lines for directing Postfix on how to interface with external MDA software, such as Procmail.

The Postfix operational parameters are set in the `main.cf` configuration file. All of the Postfix operational parameters have default values that are implied within the Postfix system. If a parameter value is not present in the `main.cf` file, its value is preset by Postfix. If a parameter value is present in the `main.cf` file, its contents override the default value.

Each Postfix parameter is listed on a separate line in the configuration file along with its value, in the form:

```
parameter = value
```

Both `parameter` and `value` are plain text strings that can be easily read and changed if necessary. The Postfix `master` program reads the parameter values in the `main.cf` file when Postfix is first started, and again whenever a postfix `reload` command is issued.

Two examples of Postfix parameters are the `myhostname` and `mydomain` parameters. If they are not specified in the `main.cf` configuration file, the `myhostname` parameter assumes the results of a `gethostname()` command on the Linux system, whereas `mydomain` assumes the domain part of the default `myhostname` parameter. Often a single mail server will handle mail for an entire domain. This is an easy setting in the Postfix configuration file:

```
myhostname = mailserver.smallorg.org
mydomain = smallorg.org
```

When Postfix starts, it will recognize the local mail server as `mailserver.smallorg.org` and the local domain as `smallorg.org` and will ignore any system set values.

If you need to specify a smart host, do that with the `relayhost` parameter:

```
relayhost = myisp.com
```

You can also specify an IP address here, but it must be enclosed in square brackets.

TABLE 26-6

The Mailx Command Line Parameters

Parameter	Description
-a	Specify additional SMTP header lines.
-b	Add a BCC: recipient to the message.
-c	Add a CC: recipient to the message.
-e	Don't send the message if it's empty.
-i	Ignore TTY interrupt signals.
-I	Force Mailx to run in interactive mode.
-n	Don't read the /etc/mail.rc startup file.
-s	Specify a Subject line.
-v	Display details of the delivery on the terminal

Sending a Message with Mailx

The main tool you have available for sending e-mail messages from your shell scripts is the Mailx program. Not only can you use it interactively to read and send messages, but you can also use the command line parameters to specify how to send a message.

The format for the Mailx program's command line for sending messages is:

```
mail [-eIinv] [-a header] [-b addr] [-c addr] [-s subj] to-addr
```

The mail command uses the command line parameters shown in Table 26-6.

As you can see from Table 26-6, you can pretty much create an entire e-mail message just from the command line parameters. The only thing you need to add is the message body.

To do that, you need to redirect text to the mail command. Here's a simple example of how to create and send an e-mail message directly from the command line:

```
$ echo "This is a test message" | mail -s "Test message" rich
$ mail
Mail version 8.1.2 01/15/2001.  Type ? for help.
"/var/mail/rich": 1 message 1 new
>N  1 rich@testbox        Fri Feb  1 19:12   16/664    Test message
&
Message 1:
From rich@testbox  Fri Feb  1 14:12:03 2008
```

```
Date: Fri, 1 Feb 2008 19:12:02 -0500
From: rich <rich@testbox>
To: rich@localhost.localdomain
Subject: Test message

This is a test message

&
```

The Mailx program sent the text from the echo command as the message body. This provides an easy way for you to send messages from your shell scripts. Here's a quick example:

```
$ cat factmail
#!/bin/bash
# mailing the answer to a factorial

MAIL=`which mail`

factorial=1
counter=1

read -p "Enter the number: " value
while [ $counter -le $value ]
do
    factorial=$[$factorial * $counter]
    counter=$[$counter + 1]
done

echo The factorial of $value is $factorial | mail -s "Factorial
answer" $USER
echo "The result has been mailed to you."
```

The first thing this script does is not assume that the Mailx program is located in the standard location. It uses the which command to determine just where the mail program is.

After calculating the result of the factorial function, the shell script uses the mail command to send the message to the user-defined $USER environment variable, which should be the person executing the script.

```
$ ./factmail
Enter the number: 5
The result has been mailed to you.
$
```

All you need to do is check your mail to see if the answer arrived:

```
$ mail
Mail version 8.1.2 01/15/2001.  Type ? for help.
"/var/mail/rich": 1 message 1 new
```

```
>N  1 rich@testbox        Fri Feb  1 19:24   16/671   Factorial answer
&
Message 1:
From rich@testbox  Fri Feb  1 14:24:33 2008
Date: Fri, 1 Feb 2008 19:24:33 -0500
From: rich <rich@testbox>
To: rich@localhost.localdomain
Subject: Factorial answer

The factorial of 5 is 120

&
```

It's not always convenient to send just one line of text in the message body. Often you'll need to send an entire output as the e-mail message. In those situations, you can always redirect text to a temporary file, then use the `cat` command and redirect the output to the mail program.

Here's an example of sending a larger amount of data in an e-mail message:

```
$ cat diskmail
#!/bin/bash
# sending the current disk statistics in an e-mail message

date=`date +%m/%d/%Y`
MAIL=`which mail`
TEMP=`mktemp tmp.XXXXXX`

df -k > $TEMP
cat $TEMP | $MAIL -s "Disk stats for $date" $1
rm -f $TEMP
$ ./diskmail rich
$ mail
Mail version 8.1.1 6/6/93.  Type ? for help.
"/var/spool/mail/rich": 1 message 1 new
>N  1 rich@test2.dfas.mil   Mon Feb  3 14:15  15/594   "Disk stats
for 02/03/"
&
Message 1:
From rich  Mon Feb  3 14:15:57 2008
Delivered-To: rich@test2.dfas.mil
To: rich@test2.dfas.mil
Subject: Disk stats for 02/03/2008
Date: Mon,  3 Feb 2008 14:15:57 -0500 (EST)
From: rich@test2.dfas.mil (Rich)

Filesystem           1k-blocks     Used Available Use% Mounted on
/dev/hda1              3526172  1464476   1882576  44% /
/dev/hda6             16002168  6570168   8619116  43% /home

&
```

The diskmail program gets the current date using the `date` command (along with some special formatting), finds the location of the Mailx program, then creates a temporary file. After all that, it uses the `df` command to display the current disk space statistics (see Chapter 4), redirecting the output to the temporary file.

It then redirects the temporary file to the `mail` command, using the first command line parameter for the destination address, and the current date in the Subject header.

The Mutt Program

The Mutt program is another popular e-mail client package for the Linux command line, developed in 1995 by Michael Elkins. It has one feature that's not available in the Mailx program which makes it a good tool to have handy for your shell scripts.

The Mutt program has the ability to send files as attachments in your e-mail messages. Instead of having to incorporate a long text file in the body of your e-mail message as we did with Mailx, you can use the Mutt program and include the text file as a separate attachment to the main message body. This feature is great for e-mailing long files, such as log files.

This section walks through installing Mutt on your Linux system, and using it to attach files to e-mail messages in your shell scripts.

Installing Mutt

The Mutt program is not a popular package in this day of fancy graphical e-mail clients such as KMail or Evolution, so it's a good bet that your Linux distribution doesn't have it installed by default. However, most Linux distributions include it in the normal distribution files for installation using the standard software installation methods.

If your Linux distribution doesn't include the Mutt package, or you just want to install the latest version, here are the steps to do that:

1. Go to the Mutt package Web site at `www.mutt.org`. From here, select the Downloading link to go to the download page.

2. On the download page, there are compiled binary executable packages for specific Linux distributions, as well as a source code distribution package. If your Linux distribution has a compiled binary executable package, download that and follow the appropriate steps for installing software on your Linux distribution. Otherwise, download the current source code distribution (there are two packages, a stable release and a development release).

3. After downloading the source code package, extract it into a working directory using the `tar` command:

    ```
    tar -zxvf mutt-1.4.2.3.tar.gz
    ```

4. Change to the newly created directory:

    ```
    cd mutt-1.4.2.3
    ```

5. Run the configure script to build the necessary files for compiling Mutt on your system:

```
./configure
```

6. As the *root* user, run the `make` utility with the `install` option to create and install Mutt:

```
make install
```

This will install the Mutt program on your Linux system for you to use from the command line.

The Mutt command line

The `mutt` command provides parameters for you to use to control how Mutt operates. Table 26-7 shows the command line parameters available to you.

With the myriad of command line parameters you can customize your e-mail message directly from the command line, which is exactly what you'll want to do in your shell scripts.

Much as with the Mailx program, there's one thing that you can't specify on the command line with the Mutt program, and that's the message body text. If you don't redirect text to the Mutt program, it'll start in text-graphics mode with an editor window for you to type the message body in.

This is not a good thing for the shell script, so you'll always want to redirect some type of text for the message body, even if you're using the attachment option to specify a file to attach. The next section demonstrates how to do this.

Using Mutt

Now you're ready to start using the Mutt program in your shell scripts. To create the basic `mutt` command in your shell script, you'll want to include command line options that specify the subject of the message, the attachment file, and all the recipients of the message:

```
mutt -s Subject -a file recipients
```

The *recipients* list is a space-separated list of the e-mail addresses to send the message to. If you want to attach more than one file, you'll need to use multiple `-a` options, as each option can only declare one filename. The *file* parameter must be an absolute pathname, or a relative pathname relative to the current working directory from which you're running the `mutt` command.

There's one other catch with the `mutt` command. If you don't redirect text for the message body, Mutt will automatically go to full-screen mode for you to enter the text in an editor window. Most likely this is not what you want to do, so be sure to redirect some text for the message body, even if it's an empty file:

```
# echo "Here's the log file" | mutt -s "Log file" -a
/var/log/messages rich
```

TABLE 26-7

The Mutt Command Line Parameters

Parameter	Description
-A *alias*	Pass an expanded version of the specified alias to STDOUT.
-a *file*	Attach the specified file to your message using the MIME protocol.
-b *address*	Specify a blind-carbon-copy (BCC) recipient.
-c *address*	Specify a carbon-copy (CC) recipient.
-D	Print the value of all configuration options to STDOUT.
-e *command*	Specify a configuration command to be run after processing of initialization files.
-f *mailbox*	Specify a mailbox file to load.
-F *muttrc*	Specify an initialization file to read instead of $HOME/.muttrc
-h	Display help text.
-H *draft*	Specify a draft file that contains header and body to use to send a message.
-i *include*	Specify a file to include in the body of a message.
-m *type*	Specify a default mailbox type.
-n	Ignore the system configuration file.
-p	Resume a postponed message.
-Q *query*	Query a configuration variable value. The query is executed after all configuration files have been parsed and any commands given on the command line have been executed.
-R	Open a mailbox in read-only mode.
-s *subject*	Specify the subject of the message.
-v	Display the Mutt version number and compile-time definitions.
-x	Emulate the Mailx compose mode.
-y	Start with a listing of all mailboxes specified by the mailboxes command.
-z	When used with -f, don't start if there are no messages in the mailbox.
-Z	Open the first mailbox specified by the mailboxes command that contains new mail.

FIGURE 26-7

Using KMail to view a message with an attachment

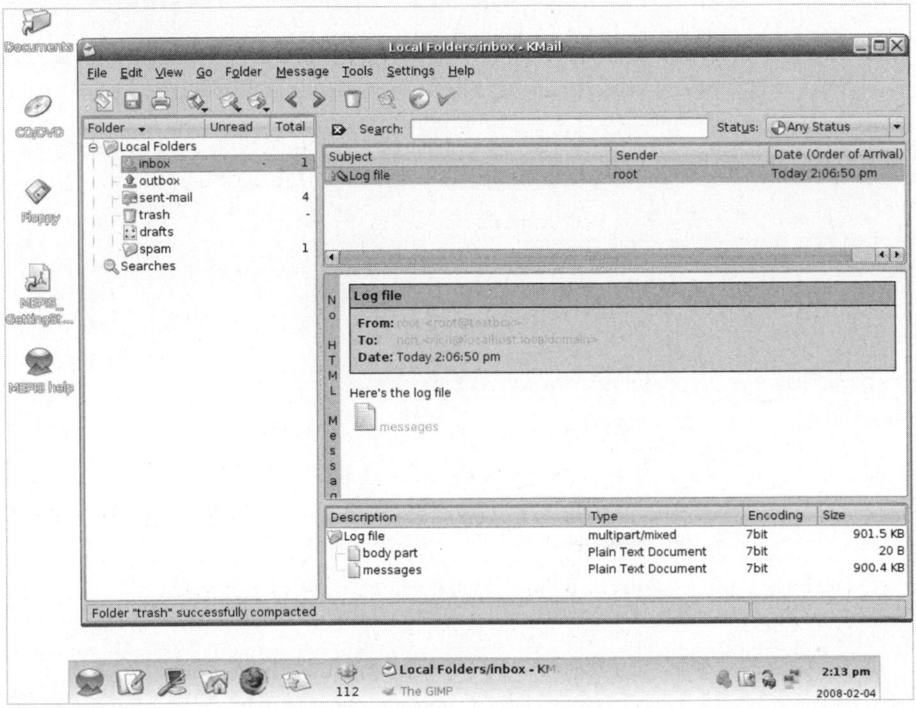

This command sends the system log file as an attachment to the e-mail address `rich` on the local system. Note that you must also have the proper permissions to access the file you want to attach. Figure 26-7 shows the received e-mail message in the KMail mail client.

Notice that the message includes the body text from the `echo` statement, along with a separate icon for the attached file. You can save the attached file directly from the KMail client.

CAUTION If you look at the name of the attached file, you'll notice that Mutt uses the basename of the attached file as the filename in the attachment. Be careful when using temporary files, as Mutt will use the temporary filename as the attachment filename. You'll be better off saving temporary files using more descriptive names rather than using temporary filenames.

Summary

This chapter discusses how to incorporate e-mail in your shell scripts. The ability to regularly e-mail reports to customers is a great feature to offer in your shell scripts.

Before using the command line to send e-mail messages, you'll need to know how e-mail works in the Linux environment, and what applications you'll need to have installed and configured. The Linux e-mail environment consists of three elements, a Mail Transport Agent (MTA) program, a Mail Delivery Agent (MDA) program (which often is part of the MTA program), and a Mail User Agent (MUA) program.

The MTA program is responsible for sending and receiving mail messages for the Linux system. It must know how to pass incoming mail messages to the proper user mailboxes, as well as know how to send outbound mail messages destined for users on remote mail servers. Often the MTA program will use a proxy server (also called a smart host) to do the detailed mail delivery. It forwards any message destined for a user on a remote mail server to the smart host for delivery. It can rely on the smart host to make the delivery on its own.

The MDA program is responsible for ensuring that mail destined for local users ends up in the proper local mailbox. Sometimes this function is performed directly by the MTA program. However, if you require advanced mail delivery features, such as out-of-office notifications or spam filtering, you can configure the MTA program to pass messages to the MDA program, which often has these capabilities built in.

The MUA program allows individual system users to access messages in their mailboxes and pass outbound messages to other users to the MTA for delivery. These programs can range from simple command line programs, such as Mailx and Mutt, to fancy graphical programs such as KMail and Evolution.

The easiest way to send e-mails from your shell script is to use the Mailx program. This program allows you to specify the subject header and one or more recipients on the command line. You create the message body by redirecting text to the Mailx program. You can do this using either the echo command for single line text, or the cat command to redirect the contents of a file to the mail message.

The Mutt program is a more advanced command line MUA program that provides the ability to attach files to the mail message, rather than including text inside the message body. This allows you to attach large text files that your customers can easily save to disk for examination in other programs, such as spreadsheets or word processing packages.

The last chapter in this section covers an important part of shell scripts, the administration functions. If you're a Linux system administrator, most likely you'll run into a situation where you'll want to regularly monitor the status of a system feature. By creating a shell script and placing it in a cron job, you can easily monitor what's going on in your Linux system.

Shell Scripts for Administrators

There's no place where shell script programming is more useful than for the Linux system administrator. The typical Linux system administrator has a myriad of jobs that need to be done daily, from monitoring disk space and users to backing up important files. Shell scripts can make the life of the system administrator much easier! You can accomplish all of the basic system administration functions automatically using simple shell scripts. This chapter demonstrates some of the capabilities you have using shell scripts.

IN THIS CHAPTER

Managing statistics

Performing backups

Working with users

Monitoring System Statistics

One of the core responsibilities of the Linux system administrator is to ensure that the system is running properly. To accomplish this task, there are lots of different system statistics that you must monitor. Creating automated shell scripts to monitor specific situations can be a lifesaver.

This section shows how to create simple shell scripts that monitor and report problems as soon as possible, without you even having to be logged in to the Linux system.

Monitoring disk free space

One of the biggest problems with multi-user Linux systems is the amount of available disk space. In some situations, such as in a file sharing server, disk space can fill up almost immediately just because of one careless user.

This shell script will monitor the available disk space on a specific volume, and send out an e-mail message if the available disk space goes below a set threshold.

The required functions

To automatically monitor the available disk space, you'll first need to use a command that can display that value. The best command to monitor disk space is the df command (see Chapter 4). The basic output of the df command looks like this:

```
$ df
Filesystem            1K-blocks       Used Available Use% Mounted on
/dev/hda1              3197228     2453980    580836  81% /
varrun                 127544         100    127444   1% /var/run
varlock                127544           4    127540   1% /var/lock
udev                   127544          44    127500   1% /dev
devshm                 127544           0    127544   0% /dev/shm
/dev/hda3              801636      139588    621328  19% /home
$
```

The df command shows the current disk space statistics for all of the real and virtual disks on the system. For the purposes of this exercise, we'll monitor the size of the root filesystem. We'll first need to parse the results of the df command to extract only the line for the root filesystem.

There are a couple of different ways to do this. Probably the easiest is to use the sed command to search for the line that ends with a forward slash:

```
/dev/hda1              3197228     2453980    580836  81% /
```

The sed script to build this uses the dollar sign (to indicate the end of the line), and the forward slash (which you'll need to escape since it's a sed special character). That will look like this:

```
$ df | sed -n '/\/$/p'
/dev/hda1              3197228     2453980    580836  81% /
$
```

Now that you've got the statistics for the root filesystem volume, the next step is to isolate the percentage used value in the line. To do that, you'll need to use the gawk command:

```
$ df | sed -n '/\/$/p' | gawk '{print $5}'
81%
$
```

This is close, but there's still one small problem. The gawk command let you filter out the fifth data field, but the value also includes the percent symbol. You'll need to remove that so you can use the value in a mathematical equation. That's easily accomplished by using the sed command again:

```
$ df | sed -n '/\/$/p' | gawk '{print $5}' | sed 's/%//'
81
$
```

Now you're in business! The next step is to use this information to create the script.

Creating the script

Now that you know how to extract the used disk space value, you can use that formula to store the value to a variable. You can then check the variable against a predetermined number to indicate when the used space has exceeded your set limit.

Here's an example of code using this technique:

```
$ cat diskmon
#!/bin/bash
# monitor available disk space

SPACE=`df | sed -n '/\/$/p' | gawk '{print $5}' | sed 's/%//'`

if [ $SPACE -ge 90 ]
then
    echo "Disk space on root at $SPACE% used" | mail -s "Disk warning"
rich
fi
$
```

And there you have it. A simple shell script that'll check the available disk space on the root filesystem and send an e-mail message if the used space is at 90% or more.

Running the script

Before having the diskmon script run automatically, you'll want to test it out a few times manually to ensure that it does what you think it should do. To test it, change the value that it checks against to a value lower than the current disk usage percentage:

```
if [ $SPACE -ge 40 ]
When you run the script, it should send you a mail message:
$ ./diskmon
$ mail
Mail version 8.1.2 01/15/2001.  Type ? for help.
"/var/mail/rich": 1 message 1 new
>N  1 rich@testbox        Tue Feb  5 06:22   16/672    Disk warning
&
Message 1:
From rich@testbox  Tue Feb  5 06:22:26 2008
Date: Tue, 5 Feb 2008 06:22:26 -0500
From: rich <rich@testbox>
To: rich@localhost.localdomain
Subject: Disk warning

Disk space on root at 81% used

&q
$
```

It worked! Now you can set the shell script to execute at a set number of times to monitor the disk activity. You do this using the cron table (see Chapter 13).

How often you need to run this script depends on how active your file server is. For a low-volume file server, you may only have to run the script once a day:

```
30 0 * * * /home/rich/diskmon
```

This cron table entry runs the shell script every day at 12:30 AM. For a high-volume file server environment, you may have to monitor this a few times a day:

```
30 0,8,12,16 * * * /home/rich/diskmon
```

This cron table entry runs the shell script four times a day, at 12:30 AM, 8:30 AM, 12:30 PM, and 4:30 PM.

Catching disk hogs

If you're responsible for a Linux server with lots of users, one problem that you'll often bump up against is who's using all of the disk space. This age-old administration question is sometimes harder to figure out than others.

Unfortunately, for the importance of tracking user disk space usage, there's no one Linux command that can provide that information for you. Instead, you need to write a shell script piecing other commands together to extract the information you're looking for. This section walks you through this process.

The required functions

The first tool you'll need to use is the du command (see Chapter 4). This command displays the disk usage for individual files and directories. The -s option lets you summarize totals at the directory level. This will come in handy when calculating the total disk space used by an individual user. Just use this command for the /home directory contents to summarize for each user's $HOME directory:

```
# du -s /home/*
40       /home/barbara
9868     /home/jessica
40       /home/katie
40       /home/lost+found
107340   /home/rich
5124     /home/test
#
```

Okay, that's a start. You can now see the total listing (in KB) for the $HOME directory totals. Depending on how your /home directory is mounted, you may or may not also see a special directory called lost+found, which isn't a user account.

NOTE   To get statistics for all of the user $HOME directories, you must be logged in as the root user account when running this script.

To get rid of that, we use the grep command with the -v option, which prints all of the lines except ones that contain the specified text:

```
# du -s /home/* | grep -v lost
40        /home/barbara
9868      /home/jessica
40        /home/katie
107340    /home/rich
5124      /home/test
#
```

Next, let's get rid of the full pathname so all we see are the user names. This sounds like a job for the sed command:

```
# du -s /home/* | grep -v lost | sed 's/\/home\///'
40        barbara
9868      jessica
40        katie
107340    rich
5124      test
#
```

Much better. Now, let's sort this output so that it appears in descending order:

```
# du -s /home/* | grep -v lost | sed 's/\/home\///' | sort -g -r
107340    rich
9868      jessica
5124      test
40        katie
40        barbara
#
```

The sort command sorts numerical values when you use the -g option, and will sort in descending order when you include the -r option.

There's just one more piece of information that you're interested in, and that's the total amount of space used for all of the users. Here's how to get that value:

```
# du -s /home
122420 /home
#
```

This is all the information you'll need to create the disk hogs report. Now you're ready to push this into a shell script.

Creating the script

Now that you know how to extract the raw data for the report, it's time to figure out a script that can read the report, parse the raw data values, and display it in a format that's presentable to a user.

The easiest way to manipulate data for reports is with the gawk command. The report will have three sections:

- A header with text identifying the columns
- The body of the report, showing the user, their total disk space used, and a percentage of the total they're consuming
- A footer which shows the total disk space usage for all users

The gawk command can perform all of these functions as a single command, using the BEGIN and END tags (see Chapter 16).

Here's the diskhogs script that puts all of the elements together:

```
# cat diskhogs
#!/bin/bash
# calculate disk usage and report per user

TEMP=`mktemp -t tmp.XXXXXX`
du -s /home/* | grep -v lost | sed 's/\/home\///' | sort -g -r >
$TEMP
TOTAL=`du -s /home | gawk '{print $1}'`
cat $TEMP | gawk -v n="$TOTAL" '
BEGIN {
        print "Total Disk Usage by User";
        print "User\tSpace\tPercent"
}

{
      printf "%s\t%d\t%6.2f%\n", $2, $1, ($1/n)*100
}

END {
        print "---------------------------";
        printf "Total\t%d\n", n
}'
rm -f $TEMP
#
```

The script sends the result from the formula used to generate the raw data to a temporary file, then stores the result of the total disk space formula in the variable $TOTAL.

Next, the script retrieves the raw data in the temporary file, and sends it to the gawk command. The gawk command retrieves the $TOTAL value and assigns it to a local variable called n.

The code in the gawk command first creates the report header in the BEGIN section:

```
BEGIN {
        print "Total Disk Usage by user";
```

```
            print User\tSpace\tPercent"
    }
```

It then uses the `printf` command to format and rearrange the text from the raw data:

```
    {
        printf "%s\t%d\t%6.2f%\n", $2, $1, ($1/n)*100
    }
```

This is the section that processes each line of output from the `du` command. The `printf` command allows us to format the output to make a nice table. If you happen to have long usernames on your system, you may need to fudge the formatting some to get it to turn out.

The other trick here is that the diskhogs script passes the `$TOTAL` variable value to the gawk script via the gawk command line parameter:

```
    -v n=$TOTAL
```

Now the gawk variable *n* is equal to the total user disk space, and you can the use that value anywhere in the gawk script.

Finally, the script ends the output display by showing the total amount of user disk spaced used:

```
    END {
        print "--------------------------";
        printf "Total\t%d\n", n
    }'
```

This uses the n variable, which contains the value from the `$TOTAL` shell variable.

Running the script

Putting it all together, when you run the script you should get a nice report:

```
    # ./diskhogs
    Total Disk Usage by user
    User    Space   Percent
    rich    107340  87.68%
    jessica 9868     8.06%
    test    5124     4.19%
    katie   40       0.03%
    barbara 40       0.03%
    --------------------------
    Total   122420
    #
```

Now you've got a report that you can send off to your boss and feel proud of!

NOTE If you really do have disk hogs on your system, it may take a long time for the `du` command to calculate all the space they're using. This causes quite a delay before you see any output from the `diskhogs` script. Be patient!

Watching CPU and memory usage

The core statistics of any Linux system are the CPU and memory usage. If these values start getting out of control, things can go wrong very quickly on the system. This section demonstrates how to write scripts to help you monitor and track the CPU and memory usage on your Linux system, using a couple of basic shell scripts.

The required functions

As with the other scripts shown so far in this chapter, the first step is to determine exactly what data you want to produce with your scripts. There are a few different commands that you can use to extract CPU and memory information for the system.

The most basic system statistics command is the `uptime` command:

```
$ uptime
 09:57:15 up  3:22,  3 users,  load average: 0.00, 0.08, 0.28
$
```

The `uptime` command gives us a few different basic pieces of information that we can use:

- The current time
- The number of days, hours, and minutes the system has been operational
- The number of users currently logged into the system
- The one, five, and fifteen minute load averages

Another great command for extracting system information is the `vmstat` command. Here's an example of the output from the `vmstat` command:

```
$ vmstat
procs- ----memory--------- ---swap-- --io-- --system-- -----cpu------
 r  b  swpd  free  buff cache si  so  bi  bo   in   cs us sy id  wa st
 0  0 178660 13524 4316 72076  8  10  80  22  127  124  3  1 92   4  0
$
```

The first time you run the `vmstat` command, it displays the average values since the last reboot. To get the current statistics, you must run the `vmstat` command with command line parameters:

```
$ vmstat 1 2
procs- ----memory--------- ---swap-- --io-- --system-- -----cpu------
 r  b  swpd  free  buff cache si  so  bi  bo   in   cs us sy id  wa st
 0  0 178660 13524 4316 72076  8  10  80  22  127  124  3  1 92   4  0
 0  0 178660 12845 4245 71890  8  10  80  22  127  124  3  1 86  10  0
$
```

The second line contains the current statistics for the Linux system. As you can see, the output from the `vmstat` command is somewhat cryptic. Table 27-1 explains what each of the symbols mean.

TABLE 27-1	

The vmstat Output Symbols

Symbol	Description
r	The number of processes waiting for CPU time
b	The number of processes in uninterruptible sleep
swpd	The amount of virtual memory used (in MB)
free	The amount of physical memory not used (in MB)
buff	The amount of memory used as buffer space (in MB)
cache	The amount of memory used as cache space (in MB)
si	The amount of memory swapped in from disk (in MB)
so	The amount of memory swapped out to disk (in MB)
bi	Number of blocks received from a block device
bo	Number of blocks sent to a block device
in	The number of CPU interrupts per second
cs	The number of CPU context switches per second
us	Percent of CPU time spent running non-kernel code
sy	Percent of CPU time spent running kernel code
id	Percent of CPU time spent idle
wa	Percent of CPU time spent waiting for I/O
st	Percent of CPU time stolen from a virtual machine

This is a lot of information. You probably don't need to record all of the values from the vmstat command; just a few will do. The free memory, and percent of CPU time spent idle, should give you a good snapshot of the system status (and by now you can probably guess exactly how we'll extract those values from the output).

You may have also noticed that the output from the vmstat command includes table heading information, which we obviously don't want in our data. To solve that problem, you can use the sed command to display only lines that have a numerical value in them:

```
$ vmstat 1 2 | sed -n '/[0-9]/p'
1  0  172028  8564  5276  62244   9 13   98  28   160  157  5  2 89  5  0
0  0  178660 12845  4245  71890   8 10   80  22   127  124  3  1 86 10  0
$
```

733

That's better, but now we need to get only the second line of data. Another call to the sed editor can solve that problem:

```
$ vmstat | sed -n '/[0-9]/p' | sed -n '2p'
 0  0 178660 12845 4245 71890  8  10  80  22  127  124  3  1 86 10  0
$
```

Now you can easily extract the data value you want using the gawk program.

Finally, you'll want to tag each data record with a date and timestamp to indicate when the snapshots were taken. The date command is handy, but the default output from the date command might be a little cumbersome. You can simplify the date command output by specifying another format:

```
$ date +"%m/%d/%Y %k:%M:%S"
02/05/2008 19:19:26
$
```

That should look much better in our output. Speaking of the output, you should also consider how you want to record the data values.

For data that you sample on a regular basis, often it's best to output the data directly to a log file. You can create the log file in your $HOME directory, appending data each time you run the shell script. When you want to see the results, you can just view the log file.

You should also spend some time considering the format of the log file. You'll want to ensure that the data in the log file can be read easily (after all that's the whole purpose of this script).

There are many different methods you can use to format the data in the log file. A popular format is comma-separated values (CSV). This format places each record of data on a separate line, and separates the data fields in the record with commas. This is a popular format for people who love spreadsheets, as it's easily imported into a spreadsheet.

However, staring at a CSV file of data is not the most exciting thing in the world. If you want to provide a more aesthetically appealing report, you can create an HTML document.

HTML has been the standard method for formatting Web pages for years. It uses simple tags to delineate data types within the Web page. However, HTML is not just for Web pages. You'll often find HTML used in e-mail messages as well. Depending on the MUA client (see Chapter 26), you may or may not be able to view an embedded HTML e-mail document. A better solution is to create the HTML report, and attach it to the e-mail message.

The script will save data in a CSV-formatted file, so you can always access the raw data to import into a spreadsheet. When the system administrator runs the report script, that will reformat the data into an HTML report. How cool is that?

Creating the capture script

Since you need to sample system data at a regular interval, you'll need two separate scripts. One script will capture the data and save it to the log file. This script should be run on a regular basis from the cron table. The frequency depends on how busy your Linux system is. For most systems, running the script once an hour should be fine.

The second script should output the report data and e-mail it to the appropriate individual(s). Most likely you won't want to e-mail a new report every time you get a new data sampling. You'll probably want to run the second script as a cron job at a lower frequency, such as once a day, first thing in the day.

The first script, used to capture the data, is called `capstats`. Here's what it looks like:

```
$ cat capstats
#!/bin/bash
# script to capture system statistics

OUTFILE=/home/rich/capstats.csv
DATE=`date +%m/%d/%Y`
TIME=`date +%k:%M:%S`

TIMEOUT=`uptime`
VMOUT=`vmstat 1 2`

USERS=`echo $TIMEOUT | gawk '{print $4}'`
LOAD=`echo $TIMEOUT | gawk '{print $9}' | sed 's/,//'`
FREE=`echo $VMOUT |sed -n '/[0-9]/p' |sed -n '2p' |gawk '{print $4}'`
IDLE=`echo $VMOUT |sed -n '/[0-9]/p' |sed -n '2p'|gawk '{print $15}'`

echo "$DATE,$TIME,$USERS,$LOAD,$FREE,$IDLE" >> $OUTFILE
$
```

This script mines the statistics from the `uptime` and `vmstat` commands and saves them in variables. The script then writes the values to the file defined by the `$OUTFILE` variable. For this example, I just saved the file in my `$HOME` directory. You should modify this location to what suits your environment best.

After creating the capstats script, you should probably test it from the command line before having it run regularly from your cron table:

```
$ ./capstats
$ cat capstats.csv
02/06/2008,10:39:57,4,0.26,57076,87
$
```

The script created the new file, and placed the statistic values in the proper places. Just to make sure that subsequent runs of the script don't overwrite the file, test it again:

```
$ ./capstats
$ cat capstats.csv
02/06/2008,10:39:57,4,0.26,57076,87
02/06/2008,10:41:52,4,0.14,46292,88
$
```

As hoped, the second time the script ran it appended the new statistics data to the end of the file. Now you're ready to place this in the cron table. To run it once every hour, create this cron table entry:

```
0 * * * * /home/rich/capstats
```

You'll need to use the full pathname of where you place your capstats shell script file for the cron table. Now you're capturing statistics once every hour without having to do anything else!

Generating the report script

Now that you have a file full of raw data, you can start working on the script to generate a fancy report for your boss. The best tool for this is the gawk command.

The gawk command allows you to extract raw data from a file and present it in any manner necessary. First, test this from the command line, using the new capstats.csv file created by the capstats script:

```
$ cat capstats.csv | gawk -F, '{printf "%s %s - %s\n", $1, $2, $4}'
02/06/2008 10:39:57 - 0.26
02/06/2008 10:41:52 - 0.14
02/06/2008 10:50:01 - 0.06
02/06/2008 11:00:01 - 0.18
02/06/2008 11:10:01 - 0.03
02/06/2008 11:20:01 - 0.07
02/06/2008 11:30:01 - 0.03
$
```

You need to use the -F option for the gawk command to define the comma as the field separator character in your data. After that, you can retrieve each individual data field and display it as you need.

For the report, we'll be using HTML format. This allows us to create a nicely formatted report with a minimum amount of work. The browser that displays the report will do all the hard work of formatting and displaying the report. All you need to do is insert the appropriate HTML tags to format the data.

The easiest way to display spreadsheet data in HTML is using the <table> tag. The table tag allows you to create a table with rows and cells (called divisions in HTML-speak). You define the start of a row using the <tr> tag, and the end of the row with the </tr> tag. Similarly, you define cells using the <td> and </td> tag pair.

The HTML for a full table looks like this:

```
<html>
<body>
<h2>Report title</h2>
<table border="1">
```

```
<tr>
   <td>Date</td><td>Time</td><td>Users</td>
   <td>Load</td><td>Free Memory</td><td>%CPU Idle</td>
</tr>
<tr>
   <td>02/05/2008</td><td>11:00:00</td><td>4</td>
   <td>0.26</td><td>57076</td><td>87</td>
</tr>
</table>
</body>
</html>
```

Each data record is part of a `<tr>/</tr>` tag pair. Each data field is within its own `<td>/</td>` tag pair.

When you display the HTML report in a browser, the browser creates the table automatically for you, as shown in Figure 27-1.

FIGURE 27-1

Displaying data in an HTML table

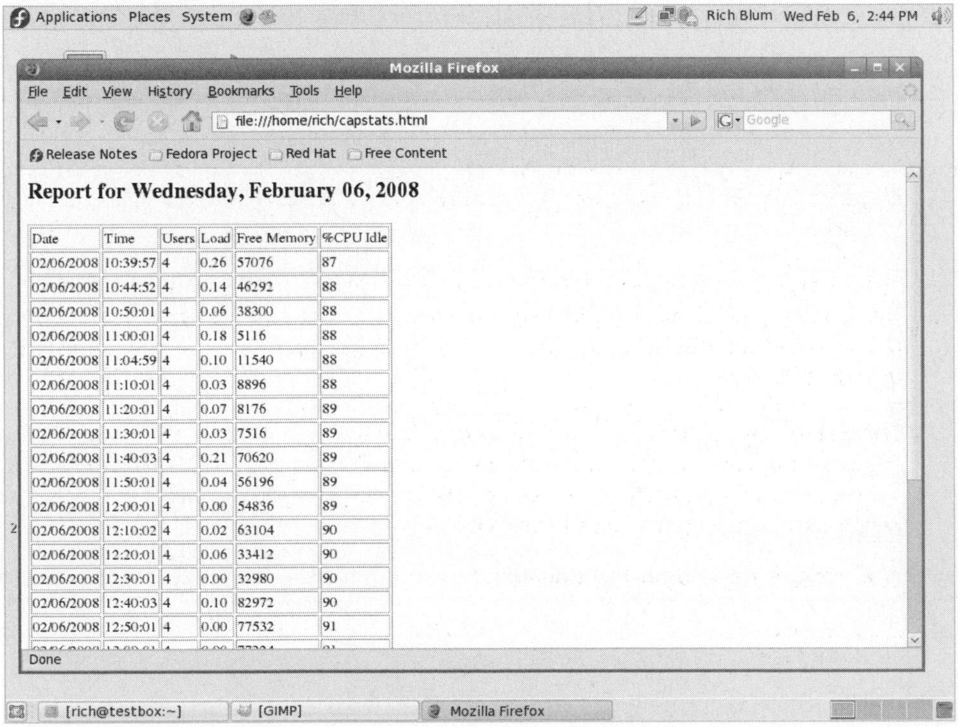

For the script, all you need to do is generate the HTML heading code by using `echo` commands, generate the data HTML code by using the `gawk` command, then close out the table, again by using `echo` commands.

Once you have your HTML report generated, you'll want to redirect it to a file for mailing. The `mutt` command (see Chapter 26) is a great tool for easily sending e-mail attachments.

Here's the `reportstats` script, which will generate the HTML report and mail it off:

```
$ cat reportstats
#!/bin/bash
# parse capstats data into daily report

FILE=/home/rich/capstats.csv
TEMP=/home/rich/capstats.html
MAIL=`which mutt`
DATE=`date +"%A, %B %d, %Y"`

echo "<html><body><h2>Report for $DATE</h2>" > $TEMP
echo "<table border=\"1\">" >> $TEMP
echo "<tr><td>Date</td><td>Time</td><td>Users</td>" >> $TEMP
echo "<td>Load</td><td>Free Memory</td><td>%CPU Idle</td></tr>" >>
$TEMP
cat $FILE | gawk -F, '{
    printf "<tr><td>%s</td><td>%s</td><td>%s</td>", $1, $2, $3;
    printf "<td>%s</td><td>%s</td><td>%s</td>\n</tr>\n", $4, $5, $6;
    }' >> $TEMP
echo "</table></body></html>" >> $TEMP
$MAIL -a $TEMP -s "Stat report for $DATE" rich < /dev/null
rm -f $TEMP
$
```

Since the `mutt` command uses the file name of the attached file as the attachment file name, it's best not to create the report file using the `mktemp` command. Instead, I gave the file a more descriptive name. The script deletes the file at the end, so it's not too important where you create the file.

CAUTION Most e-mail clients can automatically detect the type of file attachment by the file extension. For this reason, you should end your report file name with `.html`.

Running the script

After creating the reportstats script, give it a test run from the command line and see what happens:

```
$ ./reportstats
$
```

FIGURE 27-2

Viewing the report attachment in Evolution

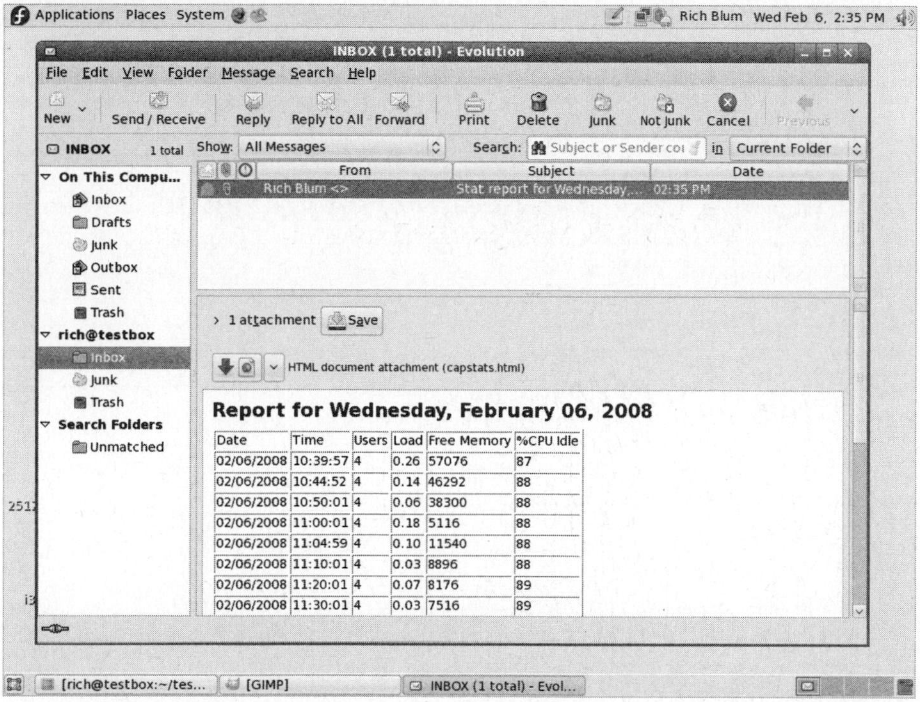

Well, that wasn't too exciting. The real test now is to view your mail message, preferably in a graphical e-mail client such as KMail or Evolution. Figure 27-2 demonstrates viewing the message from the Evolution e-mail client.

The Evolution e-mail client provide the option of either viewing the attachment separate from the client window, or within the client window. Figure 27-2 demonstrates viewing the attached report within the client window. Notice how the data is all nicely formatted using the HTML tables, just as it was when viewing from the browser!

Performing Backups

Whether you're responsible for a Linux system in a business environment or just using it in a home environment, a loss of data can be catastrophic. To help prevent bad things from happening to your data, it's always a good idea to perform regular backups.

However, what's a good idea and what's practical are often two separate things. Trying to arrange a backup schedule to store important files can be a challenge. This is another place where shell scripts often come to the rescue.

This section demonstrates two different methods for using shell scripts to back up data on your Linux system.

Archiving data files

Often the cause for lost data isn't a catastrophic system failure. Many times, data is lost in that "oh no" moment. You know, that millisecond of time just after you click the Delete button. For this reason, it's always a good idea to have a separate archived copy of data you're working on laying around on the system.

If you're using your Linux system to work on an important project, you can create a shell script that automatically takes snapshots of your working directories, then stores them in a safe place on the system. While not a protection against a catastrophic hardware failure, this is a great safeguard against file corruption or accidental deletions.

This section shows how to create an automated shell script that can take snapshots of your working directory and keep an archive of past versions of your data.

The required functions

The workhorse for archiving data in the Linux world is the `tar` command (see Chapter 4). The `tar` command is used to archive an entire directory into a single file. Here's an example of creating an archive file of a working directory using the `tar` command:

```
$ tar -cf archive.tar /home/rich/test
tar: Removing leading `/' from member names
$
```

The `tar` command responds with a warning message that it's removing the leading forward slash from the pathname to convert it from an absolute pathname to a relative pathname. This allows you to extract the tar archive file anywhere you want in your filesytem. You'll probably want to get rid of that message in your script. You do that by redirecting STDERR to the `/dev/null` file (see Chapter 12):

```
$ tar -cf archive.tar /home/rich/test 2> /dev/null
$
```

Now it's ready to be used in a script.

CAUTION   If you're using a Linux distribution that includes a graphical desktop, be careful about archiving your $HOME directory. While this may be tempting, the $HOME directory contains lots of configuration and temporary files related to the graphical desktop, and it will create a much larger archive file than you probably intended. Pick a subdirectory in which to store your working files, and use that as the archive directory.

After creating the archive file you can send it to your favorite compression utility to reduce its size:

```
$ ls -l archive.tar
-rw-rw-r-- 1 rich rich 30720 2008-02-06 12:26 archive.tar
$ gzip archive.tar
$ ls -l archive*
-rw-rw-r-- 1 rich rich 2928 2008-02-06 12:26 archive.tar.gz
$
```

You now have the first component to your archive system.

The next step is to create a rolling archive system. If you save your working directory on a regular basis, you may not necessarily want the newest archive copy to immediately overwrite the previous archive copy.

To prevent this, you'll need to create a method to automatically provide a unique filename for each archive copy. The easiest way to do that is to incorporate the date and time in your filenames.

As you've seen from the "Monitoring System Statistics" section, you can format the date command to produce information in just about any format you desire. This comes in handy when creating unique filenames.

For example, if you want to create a filename using the two-digit year, the month, and the date, you'd do something like this:

```
$ DATE=`date +%y%m%d`
$ FILE=tmp$DATE
$ echo $FILE
tmp080206
$
```

While it may look odd to squish the $DATE variable at the end of a text string, it's perfectly legal in the bash shell. The shell appends the variable's value to the string, creating a unique filename.

NOTE Using a date to uniquely identify a file can get tricky when looking for the most recent file version. Make that sure you remember the format you use to tag the date (such as month-day-year or year-month-day). Often when sorting file names it is good to specify the year first, then the month, and finally, the day.

You should now have enough information to start building the script. The next section walks you through creating the archive script.

Creating a daily archive script

The archdaily script automatically creates an archived version of your working directory in a separate location, using the day to uniquely identify the file. Here's the code for that script:

```
$ cat archdaily
#!/bin/bash
```

```
# archive a working directory

DATE=`date +%y%m%d`
FILE=archive$DATE
SOURCE=/home/rich/test
DESTINATION=/home/rich/archive/$FILE

tar -cf $DESTINATION $SOURCE 2> /dev/null
gzip $DESTINATION
$
```

The archdaily script generates a unique filename based on the year, month, and day that it runs. It also uses environment variables to define the source directory to archive, so that can be easily changed. You can even use a command line parameter to make the archdaily program even more versatile.

The $DESTINATION variable appends the full pathname for the archived file. This too can be easily changed to an alternative directory if needed.

Testing the archdaily script is pretty straightforward:

```
$ ./archdaily
$ ls -al /home/rich/archive
total 24
drwxrwxr-x  2 rich rich 4096 2008-02-06 12:50 .
drwx------ 37 rich rich 4096 2008-02-06 12:50 ..
-rw-rw-r--  1 rich rich 3046 2008-02-06 12:50 archive080206.gz
$
```

The data is now safely archived away.

Creating an hourly archive script

If you're in a high-volume production environment where files are changing rapidly, a daily archive might not be good enough. If you want to increase the archiving frequency to hourly, you'll need to take another item into consideration.

If you're backing up files hourly, and trying to use the date command to timestamp each file name, things can get pretty ugly pretty quickly. I don't thing you'd want to have to sift through a directory of files with filenames looking like this:

```
archive080206110233.gz
```

Instead of placing all of the archive files in the same folder, you'd be better off creating a directory hierarchy for your archived files. Figure 27-3 demonstrates this principle.

The archive directory contains directories for each month of the year, using the month number as the directory name. Each month's directory in turn contains folders for each day of the month (using the day's numerical value as the directory name). This allows you to just timestamp the individual archive files, then place them in the appropriate directory for the day and month.

FIGURE 27-3

Creating an archive directory hierarchy

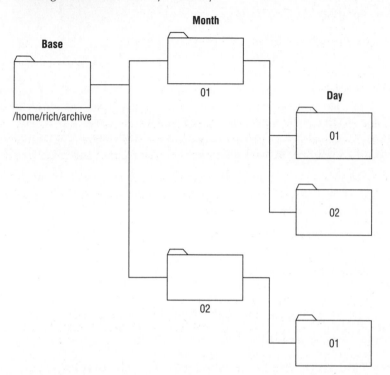

Now you have a new challenge to solve. Your script must create the individual month and day directories automatically, and know that if they already exist, they don't need to be created. As it turns out, this isn't as hard as it sounds!

If you peruse the command line options for the mkdir command (see Chapter 3), you'll find the -p command line option. This option allows you to create directories and subdirectories in a single command, plus the added benefit in that it doesn't produce an error message if the directory already exists. Perfect!

We're now ready to create the archhourly script. Here's what it looks like:

```
$ cat archhourly
#!/bin/bash
# archive a working directory hourly

DAY=`date +%d`
MONTH=`date +%m`
TIME=`date +%k%M`
```

```
SOURCE=/home/rich/test
BASEDEST=/home/rich/archive

mkdir -p $BASEDEST/$MONTH/$DAY

DESTINATION=$BASEDEST/$MONTH/$DAY/archive$TIME
tar -cf $DESTINATION $SOURCE 2> /dev/null
gzip $DESTINATION
$
```

The script retrieves the day and month values from the date command, along with the timestamp used to uniquely identify the archive file. It then uses that information to create the archive directory for the day (or just silently exit if it already exists). Finally, the script uses the tar and gzip commands to create the archive and compress it.

Just as with the archdaily script, it's a good idea to test the archhourly script before putting it in the cron table:

```
$ ./archhourly
$ ls -al /home/rich/archive/02/06
total 32
drwxrwxr-x 2 rich rich 4096 2008-02-06 13:20 .
drwxrwxr-x 3 rich rich 4096 2008-02-06 13:19 ..
-rw-rw-r-- 1 rich rich 3145 2008-02-06 13:19 archive1319.gz
$ ./archhourly
$ ls -al /home/rich/archive/02/06
total 32
drwxrwxr-x 2 rich rich 4096 2008-02-06 13:20 .
drwxrwxr-x 3 rich rich 4096 2008-02-06 13:19 ..
-rw-rw-r-- 1 rich rich 3145 2008-02-06 13:19 archive1319.gz
-rw-rw-r-- 1 rich rich 3142 2008-02-06 13:20 archive1320.gz
$
```

The script worked fine the first time, creating the appropriate month and day directories, then creating the archive file. Just to test things out, I ran it a second time to see if it would have a problem with the existing directories. The script again ran just fine and created the second archive file. It's now ready for the cron table!

Storing backups off-site

While creating archives of important files is a good idea, it's certainly no replacement for a full backup that's stored in a separate location. In large commercial Linux environments, system administrators often have the luxury of tape drives to copy important files off of the server for safe storage.

For smaller environments this is not always an option. Just because you can't afford a fancy backup system doesn't mean that you have to have your important data at risk. You can put together a shell script that automatically creates an archive file, then sends it outside of the Linux system. This section describes just how to do that.

The required functions

You've already seen the core of the archiving system, the `tar` and `gzip` commands. The trick is getting the compressed archive file off of the Linux system. If you have the e-mail system configured (see Chapter 26) that can be your portal to the outside world!

While system administrators don't often think of e-mail as a way to archive data, it's a perfectly acceptable method in a snap for getting your archived data to another safe location. I wouldn't recommend trying to archive your entire Linux system and send it out as an e-mail attachment, but archiving a working directory and using it as an attachment should not be a problem.

Let's take a look at this script and see how it works.

Creating the script

The mailarch script creates a normal archive file as you did with the archdaily and archhourly scripts. Once it creates the archive file, it uses the Mutt e-mail client to send the file to a remote e-mail address.

Here's the `mailarch` script:

```
$ cat mailarch
#!/bin/bash
# archive a working directory and e-mail it out

MAIL=`which mutt`
DATE=`date +%y%m%d`
FILE=archive$DATE
SOURCE=/home/rich/test
DESTINATION=/home/rich/archive/$FILE
ZIPFILE=$DESTINATION.zip

tar -cf $DESTINATION $SOURCE 2> /dev/null
zip $ZIPFILE $DESTINATION
$MAIL -a $ZIPFILE -s "Archive for $DATE" rich@myhost.com < /dev/null
$
```

One thing you may notice about the mailarch script is that I use the zip compression utility instead of the `gzip` command. This allows you to create a .zip file that is more easily handled on non-Linux systems, such as Microsoft Windows workstations.

Running the script

The mailarch script runs the same was as the archdaily script, by placing it in the cron table to run at a specific time of the day (usually late at night). When the script runs, it creates the archive file, compresses it using the `zip` command, then sends it off in an e-mail message. Figure 27-4 demonstrates what the e-mail message you receive should look like.

Congratulations, you now have a method for backing up your important files from your Linux system.

FIGURE 27-4

E-mail message with archive file

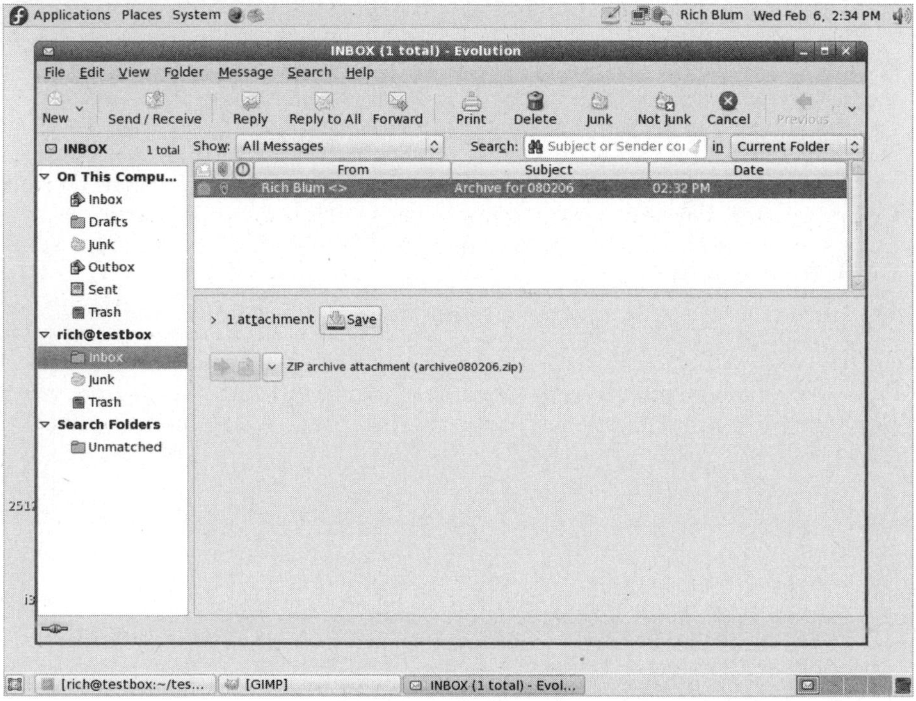

Summary

This chapter put some of the shell-scripting information presented in the book to good use in the Linux system administration world. When you're responsible for managing a Linux system, whether it's a large multi-user system or your own system, there are lots of things you need to watch. Instead of pouring over log files, and manually running commands, you can create shell scripts to do the work for you.

The chapter demonstrated how to use the df command to determine available disk space, then use the sed and gawk commands to retrieve specific information from the data. Passing the output from a command to sed and gawk to parse data is a common function in shell scripts, so it's a good idea to know how to do it.

Next the chapter showed how to use the du command to determine the disk space used by individual users. The output from the du command was again passed to the sed and gawk commands to help filter out just the data that we were interested in.

The next section walked you through the world of creating system logs and reports. The capstats shell script captured vital system statistics on a regular basis, extracted the data from the commands, and stored it in a comma-separated value file. This data could then be imported into a spreadsheet, but instead you saw how to create another script to create a formatted report from the data. The reportstats shell script used HTML formatting to place the raw system data into an HTML table, then used the Mutt e-mail client to send the file to a remote user.

The chapter closed out by discussing using shell scripts for archiving and backing up data files on the Linux system. The `tar` and `gzip` commands are popular commands for archiving data. The chapter showed how to use them in shell scripts to create archive files, and manage the archive files in an archive directory. Finally, you saw how to e-mail an archive file to a remote user as a crude form of backup for important data files.

Thanks for joining me on this journey through the Linux command line and shell scripting. I hope that you've enjoyed the journey and have learned how to get around on the command line, and how to create shell scripts to save you time. But don't stop your command line education there. There's always something new being developed in the open source world, whether it's a new command line utility, or a full-blown shell. Stay in touch with the Linux community, and follow along with the new advances and features.

Appendix A

Quick Guide to bash Commands

As you've seen throughout this book, the bash shell contains lots of features and thus has lots of commands available. This appendix provides a concise guide to allow you to quickly look up a feature or command that you can use from the bash command line or from a bash shell script.

Built-In Commands

The bash shell includes many popular commands built into the shell. This provides for faster processing times when using these commands. Table A-1 shows the built-in commands available directly from the bash shell.

The built-in commands provide higher performance than external commands, but the more built-in commands that are added to a shell, the more memory it consumes with commands that you may never use. The bash shell also contains external commands that provide extended functionality for the shell. These are discussed in the next section.

Bash Commands

Besides the built-in commands, the bash shell utilizes external commands to allow you to maneuver around the filesystem and manipulate files and directories. Table A-2 shows the common external commands you'll want to use when working in the bash shell.

You can accomplish just about any task you need to on the command line using these commands.

bash Built-in Commands

Command	Description
alias	Define an alias for the specified command.
bg	Resume a job in background mode.
bind	Bind a keyboard sequence to a readline function or macro.
break	Exit from a for, while, select, or until loop.
builtin	Execute the specified shell built-in command.
cd	Change the current directory to the specified directory.
caller	Return the context of any active subroutine call.
command	Execute the specified command without the normal shell lookup.
compgen	Generate possible completion matches for the specified word.
complete	Display how the specified words would be completed.
continue	Resume the next iteration of a for, while, select, or until loop.
declare	Declare a variable or variable type.
dirs	Display a list of currently remembered directories.
disown	Remove the specified jobs from the jobs table for the process.
echo	Display the specified string to STDOUT.
enable	Enable or disable the specified built-in shell command.
eval	Concatenate the specified arguments into a single command, then execute the command.
exec	Replace the shell process with the specified command.
exit	Force the shell to exit with the specified exit status.
export	Set the specified variables to be available for child shell processes.
fc	Select a list of commands from the history list.
fg	Resume a job in foreground mode.
getopts	Parse the specified positional parameters.
hash	Find and remember the full pathname of the specified command.
help	Display a help file.

TABLE A-1	*(continued)*
Command	**Description**
history	Display the command history.
jobs	List the active jobs.
kill	Send a system signal to the specified process ID (PID).
let	Evaluate each argument in a mathematical expression.
local	Create a limited-scope variable in a function.
logout	Exit a login shell.
popd	Remove entries from the directory stack.
printf	Display text using formatted strings.
pushd	Add a directory to the directory stack.
pwd	Display the pathname of the current working directory.
read	Read one line of data from STDIN and assign it to a variable.
readonly	Read one line of data from STDIN and assign it to a variable that can't be changed.
return	Force a function to exit with a value that can be retrieved by the calling script.
set	Set and display environment variable values and shell attributes.
shift	Rotate positional parameters down one position.
shopt	Toggle the values of variables controlling optional shell behavior.
suspend	Suspend the execution of the shell until a SIGCONT signal is received.
test	Return an exit status of 0 or 1 based on the specified condition.
times	Display the accumulated user and system.
trap	Execute the specified command if the specified system signal is received.
type	Display how the specified word would be interpreted and used as a command.
ulimit	Set a limit on the specified resource for system users.
umask	Set default permissions for newly created files and directories.
unalias	Remove the specified alias.
unset	Remove the specified environment variable or shell attribute.
wait	Wait for the specified process to complete, and return the exit status.

The bash Shell External Commands

Command	Description
bzip2	Compression using the Burrows-Wheeler block sorting text compression algorithm and Huffman coding.
cat	List the contents of the specified file.
chage	Change the password expiration date for the specified system user account.
chfn	Change the specified user account's comment information.
chgrp	Change the default group of the specified file or directory.
chmod	Change system security permissions for the specified file or directory.
chown	Change the default owner of the specified file or directory.
chpasswd	Reads a file of login name and password pairs and updates the passwords.
chsh	Change the specified user account's default shell.
compress	Original Unix file compression utility.
cp	Copy the specified files to an alternate location.
df	Display current disk space statistics for all mounted devices.
du	Display disk usage statistics for the specified filepath.
file	View the file type of the specified file.
finger	Display information about user accounts on the Linux system or a remote system.
grep	Search a file for the specified text string.
groupadd	Create a new system group.
groupmod	Modify an existing system group.
gzip	The GNU Project's compression using Lempel-Ziv compression.
head	Display the first portion of the specified file's contents.
killall	Send a system signal to a running process based on process name.
less	Advanced viewing of file contents.
link	Create a link to a file using an alias name.
ls	List directory contents.

TABLE A-2	*(continued)*
Command	**Description**
mkdir	Create the specified directory under the current directory.
more	List the contents of the specified file, pausing after each screen of data.
mount	Display or mount disk devices into the virtual file system.
passwd	Change the password for a system user account.
ps	Display information about the running processes on the system.
pwd	Display the current directory.
mv	Rename a file.
rm	Delete the specified file.
rmdir	Delete the specified directory.
sort	Organize data in a data file based on the specified order.
stat	View the file statistics of the specified file.
tail	Display the last portion of the specified file's contents.
tar	Archive data and directories into a single file.
touch	Create a new empty file, or update the timestamp on an existing file.
umount	Remove a mounted disk device from the virtual file system.
useradd	Create a new system user account.
userdel	Remove an existing system user account.
usermod	Modify an existing system user account.
zip	Unix version of the Windows PKZIP program.

Environment Variables

The bash shell also utilizes many environment variables. While environment variables aren't commands, they often affect how shell commands operate, so it's important to know the shell environment variables. Table A-3 shows the default environment variables available in the bash shell.

You display the environment variables using the set built-in command. The default shell environment variables set at boot time can and often do vary between different Linux distributions.

TABLE A-3

bash Shell Environment Variables

Variable	Description
$*	Contains all of the command line parameters as a single text value.
$@	Contains all of the command line parameters as separate text values.
$#	The number of command line parameters.
$?	The exit status of the most recently used foreground process.
$-	The current command line option flags.
$$	The process ID (PID) of the current shell.
$!	The PID of the most recently executed background process.
$0	The name of the command from the command line.
$_	The absolute pathname of the shell.
BASH	The full filename used to invoke the shell.
BASH_ARGC	The number of parameters in the current subroutine.
BASH_ARGV	An array containing all of the command line parameters specified.
BASH_COMMAND	The name of the command currently being executed.
BASH_ENV	When set, each bash script attempts to execute a startup file defined by this variable before running.
BASH_EXECUTION_STRING	The command used in the -c command line option.
BASH_LINENO	An array containing the line numbers of each command in the script.
BASH_REMATCH	An array containing text elements that match a specified regular expression.
BASH_SOURCE	An array containing source filenames for the declared functions in the shell.
BASH_SUBSHELL	The number of subshells spawned by the current shell.
BASH_VERSION	The version number of the current instance of the bash shell.
BASH_VERSINFO	A variable array that contains the individual major and minor version numbers of the current instance of the bash shell.
COLUMNS	Contains the terminal width of the terminal used for the current instance of the bash shell.

TABLE A-3   *(continued)*

Variable	Description
COMP_CWORD	An index into the variable COMP_WORDS, which contains the current cursor position.
COMP_LINE	The current command line.
COMP_POINT	The index of the current cursor position relative to the beginning of the current command.
COM_WORDBREAKS	A set of characters used as word separators when performing word completion.
COMP_WORDS	A variable array that contains the individual words on the current command line.
COMPREPLY	A variable array that contains the possible completion codes generated by a shell function.
DIRSTACK	A variable array that contains the current contents of the directory stack.
EUID	The numeric effective user ID of the current user.
FCEDIT	The default editor used by the fc command.
FIGNORE	A colon-separated list of suffixes to ignore when performing filename completion.
FUNCNAME	The name of the currently executing shell function.
GLOBIGNORE	A colon-separated list of patterns defining the set of filenames to be ignored by filename expansion.
GROUPS	A variable array containing the list of groups of which the current user is a member.
histchars	Up to three characters that control history expansion.
HISTCMD	The history number of the current command.
HISTCONTROL	Controls what commands are entered in the shell history list.
HISTFILE	The name of the file to save the shell history list (.bash_history by default).
HISTFILESIZE	The maximum number of lines to save in the history file.
HISTIGNORE	A colon-separated list of patterns used to decide which commands are ignored for the history file.
HISTSIZE	The maximum number of commands stored in the history file.

continued

TABLE A-3	*(continued)*
Variable	**Description**
HOSTFILE	Contains the name of the file that should be read when the shell needs to complete a hostname.
HOSTNAME	The name of the current host.
HOSTTYPE	A string describing the machine the bash shell is running on.
IGNOREEOF	The number of consecutive EOF characters the shell must receive before exiting. If this value doesn't exist, the default is one.
INPUTRC	The name of the Readline initialization file (the default is .inputrc).
LANG	The local category for the shell.
LC_ALL	Overrides the LANG variable, defining a local category.
LC_COLLATE	Sets the collation order used when sorting string values.
LC_CTYPE	Determines the interpretation of characters used in filename expansion and pattern matching.
LC_MESSAGES	Determines the local setting used when interpreting double-quoted strings preceded by a dollar sign.
LC_NUMERIC	Determines the local setting used when formatting numbers.
LINENO	The line number in a script currently executing.
LINES	Defines the number of lines available on the terminal.
MACHTYPE	A string defining the system type in *cpu-company-system* format.
MAILCHECK	How often (in seconds) the shell should check for new mail (default is 60).
OLDPWD	The previous working directory used in the shell.
OPTERR	If set to 1, the bash shell displays errors generated by the getopts command.
OSTYPE	A string defining the operating system the shell is running on.
PIPESTATUS	A variable array containing a list of exit status values from the processes in the foreground process.
POSIXLY_CORRECT	If set, bash starts in POSIX mode.
PPID	The process ID (PID) of the bash shell's parent process.
PROMPT_COMMAND	If set, the command to execute before displaying the primary prompt.

TABLE A-3	*(continued)*
Variable	**Description**
PS1	The primary command line prompt string.
PS2	The secondary command line prompt string.
PS3	The prompt to use for the select command.
PS4	The prompt displayed before the command line is echoed if the bash -x parameter is used.
PWD	The current working directory.
RANDOM	Returns a random number between 0 and 32767. Assigning a value to this variable seeds the random number generator.
REPLY	The default variable for the read command.
SECONDS	The number of seconds since the shell was started. Assigning a value resets the timer to the value.
SHELLOPTS	A colon-separated list of enabled bash shell options.
SHLVL	Indicates the shell level, incremented by one each time a new bash shell is started.
TIMEFORMAT	A format specifying how the shell displays time values.
TMOUT	The value of how long (in seconds) the select and read commands should wait for input. The default of zero indicates to wait indefinitely.
UID	The numeric real user ID of the current user.

Appendix B

Quick Guide to sed and gawk

I f you do any type of data handling in your shell scripts, most likely you'll need to use either the sed or gawk programs (and sometimes both). This appendix provides a quick reference for sed and gawk commands that come in handy when working with data in your shell scripts.

The sed Editor

The sed editor can manipulate data in a data stream based on commands you either enter into the command line or store in a command text file. It reads one line of data at a time from the input and matches that data with the supplied editor commands, changes data in the stream as specified in the commands, then outputs the new data to STDOUT.

Starting the sed editor

The format for using the sed command is:

```
sed options script file
```

The *options* parameters allow you to customize the behavior of the sed command, and include the options shown in Table B-1.

The *script* parameter specifies a single command to apply against the stream data. If more than one command is required, you must use either the -e option to specify them in the command line or the -f option to specify them in a separate file.

759

TABLE B-1

The sed Command Options

Option	Description
-e *script*	Add commands specified in *script* to the commands run while processing the input.
-f *file*	Add the commands specified in the file *file* to the commands run while processing the input.
-n	Don't produce output for each command, but wait for the print command.

sed commands

The sed editor script contains commands that sed processes for each line of data in the input stream. This section describes some of the more common sed commands you'll want to use.

Substitution

The s command substitutes text in the input stream. The format of the s command is:

s/*pattern*/*replacement*/*flags*

where *pattern* is the text to replace, and *replacement* is the new text that sed will insert in its place.

The *flags* parameter controls how the substitution takes place. There are four types of substitution flags available:

- A number, indicating the pattern occurrence that should be replaced.
- g: Indicates that all occurrences of the text should be replaced.
- p: Indicates that the contents of the original line should be printed.
- w *file*: Indicates that the results of the substitution should be written to a file.

In the first type of substitution, you can specify which occurrence of the matching pattern that the sed editor should replace, such as a 2 to indicate to replace only the second occurrence of the pattern.

Addressing

By default, the commands you use in the sed editor apply to all lines of the text data. If you only want to apply a command to a specific line, or a group of lines, you must use *line addressing*.

There are two forms of line addressing in the sed editor:

- A numeric range of lines
- A text pattern that filters out a line

Both forms use the same format for specifying the address:

[*address*]*command*

When using numeric line addressing, you reference lines by their line position in the text stream. The sed editor assigns the first line in the text stream as line number one and continues sequentially for each new line.

```
$ sed '2,3s/dog/cat/' data1
```

The other method of restricting which lines a command applies to is a bit more complicated. The sed editor allows you to specify a text pattern that it uses to filter lines for the command. The format for this is:

```
/pattern/command
```

You must encapsulate the *pattern* you specify in forward slashes. The sed editor only applies the command to lines that contain the text pattern that you specify.

```
$ sed '/rich/s/bash/csh/' /etc/passwd
```

This filter finds the line that contains the text *rich*, and replaces the text *bash* with *csh*.

You can also group more than one command together for a specific address:

```
address {
    command1
    command2
    command3
}
```

The sed editor applies each of the commands you specify only to lines that match the address specified. The sed editor will process each command listed on the address line(s):

```
$ sed '2{
> s/fox/elephant/
> s/dog/cat/
> }' data1
```

The sed editor applies each of the substitutions to the second line in the data file.

Deleting lines

The delete command, d, pretty much does what it says. It'll delete any text lines that match the addressing scheme supplied. Be careful with the delete command, for if you forget to include an addressing scheme, all of the lines will be deleted from the stream:

```
$ sed 'd' data1
```

The delete command is obviously most useful when used in conjunction with a specified address. This allows you to delete specific lines of text from the data stream, either by line number:

```
$ sed '3d' data6
```

or a specific range of lines:

```
$ sed '2,3d' data6
```

761

The pattern-matching feature of the sed editor also applies to the delete command:

```
$ sed '/number 1/d' data6
```

Only lines matching the specified text are deleted from the stream.

Inserting and appending text

As you would expect, like any other editor, the sed editor allows you to insert and append text lines to the data stream. The difference between the two actions can be confusing:

- The insert command (i) adds a new line before the specified line.
- The append command (a) adds a new line after the specified line.

A confusing thing about these two commands is their formats. You can't use these commands on a single command line. You must specify the line to insert or append on a separate line by itself. The format for doing this is:

```
sed '[address]command\
new line'
```

The text in *new line* appears in the sed editor output in the place you specify. Remember, when you use the insert command, the text appears before the data stream text:

```
$ echo "testing" | sed 'i\
> This is a test'
This is a test
testing
$
```

And when you use the append command, the text appears after the data stream text:

```
$ echo "testing" | sed 'a\
> This is a test'
testing
This is a test
$
```

This allows you to insert text at the end of the normal text.

Changing lines

The change command allows you to change the contents of an entire line of text in the data stream. It works the same as the insert and append commands, in that you must specify the new line separately from the rest of the sed command:

```
$ sed '3c\
> This is a changed line of text.' data6
```

The backslash character is used to indicate the new line of data in the script.

Transform command

The transform command (y) is the only sed editor command that operates on a single character. The transform command uses the format:

```
[address]y/inchars/outchars/
```

The transform command performs a one-to-one mapping of the *inchars* and the *outchars* values. The first character in *inchars* is converted to the first character in *outchars*. The second character in *inchars* is converted to the second character in *outchars*. This mapping continues throughout the length of the specified characters. If the *inchars* and *outchars* are not the same length, the sed editor will produce an error message.

Printing lines

Similar to the p flag in the substitution command, the p command prints a line in the sed editor output. The most common use for the print command is for printing lines that contain matching text from a text pattern:

```
$ sed -n '/number 3/p' data6
This is line number 3.
$
```

The print command allows you to filter only specific lines of data from the input stream.

Writing to a file

The w command is used to write lines to a file. The format for the w command is:

```
[address]w filename
```

The *filename* can be specified as either a relative or absolute pathname, but in either case the person running the sed editor must have write permissions for the file. The *address* can be any type of addressing method used in sed, such as a single line number, a text pattern, or a range of line numbers or text patterns.

Here's an example that prints only the first two lines of a data stream to a text file:

```
$ sed '1,2w test' data6
```

The output file test contains only the first two lines from the input stream.

Reading from a file

You've already seen how to insert and append text into a data stream from the sed command line. The read command (r) allows you to insert data contained in a separate file.

The format of the read command is:

```
[address]r filename
```

The `filename` parameter specifies either an absolute or relative pathname for the file that contains the data. You can't use a range of addresses for the read command. You can only specify a single line number or text pattern address. The sed editor inserts the text from the file after the address.

```
$ sed '3r data' data2
```

The sed editor inserts the complete text from the `data` file into the `data2` file, starting at line 3 of the `data2` file.

The gawk program

The gawk program is the GNU version of the original awk program in Unix. The awk program takes stream editing one step further than the sed editor by providing a programming language instead of just editor commands. This section describes the basics of the gawk program as a quick reference to its abilities.

The gawk command format

The basic format of the gawk program is:

```
gawk options program file
```

Table B-2 shows the options available with the gawk program.

TABLE B-2

The gawk Options

Option	Description
-F fs	Specify a file separator for delineating data fields in a line.
-f file	Specify a filename to read the program from.
-v var=value	Define a variable and default value used in the gawk program.
-mf N	Specify the maximum number of fields to process in the data file.
-mr N	Specify the maximum record size in the data file.
-W keyword	Specify the compatibility mode or warning level for gawk. Use help to list all the available keywords.

The command line options provide an easy way to customize features in the gawk program.

Using gawk

You can use gawk either directly from the command line or from within your shell scripts. This section demonstrates how to use the gawk program, and how to enter scripts for gawk to process.

Reading the program script from the command line

A gawk program script is defined by an opening and closing brace. You must place script commands between the two braces. Since the gawk command line assumes that the script is a single text string, you must also enclose your script in single quotation marks. Here's an example of a simple gawk program script specified on the command line:

```
$ gawk '{print $1}'
```

This script will display the first data field in every line of the input stream.

Using multiple commands in the program script

A programming language wouldn't be very useful if you could only execute one command. The gawk programming language allows you to combine commands into a normal program. To use multiple commands in the program script specified on the command line, just place a semicolon between each command:

```
$ echo "My name is Rich" | gawk '{$4="Dave"; print $0}'
My name is Dave
$
```

The script performs two commands: first it replaces the fourth data field with a different value, then it displays the entire data line in the stream.

Reading the program from a file

Just as with the sed editor, the gawk editor allows you to store your programs in a file and refer to them in the command line:

```
$ cat script2
{ print $5 "'s userid is " $1 }
$ gawk -F: -f script2 /etc/passwd
```

The gawk program processes all of the commands specified in the file on the input stream data.

Running scripts before processing data

The gawk program also allows you to specify when the program script is run. By default, gawk reads a line of text from the input, then executes the program script on the data in the line of text. Sometimes you may need to run a script before processing data, such as to create a header section for a report. To do that you use the BEGIN keyword. This forces gawk to execute the program script specified after the BEGIN keyword before reading the data:

```
$ gawk 'BEGIN {print "This is a test report"}'
This is a test report
$
```

You can place any type of gawk command in the BEGIN section, such as assigning default values to variables.

Running scripts after processing data

Similar to the BEGIN keyword, the END keyword allows you to specify a program script that gawk executes after reading the data:

```
$ gawk 'BEGIN {print "Hello World!"} {print $0} END {print
    "byebye"}'
Hello World!
This is a test
This is a test
This is another test.
This is another test.
byebye
$
```

The gawk program executes the code in the BEGIN section first, then processes any data in the input stream, then executes the code in the END section.

The gawk variables

The gawk program is more than just an editor; it's a complete programming environment. As such, there are lots of commands and features associated with gawk. This section shows the main features you'll need to know for programming with gawk.

Built-in variables

The gawk program uses built-in variables to reference specific features within the program data. This section describes the gawk built-in variables available for you to use in your gawk programs, and demonstrates how to use them.

The gawk program defines data as records and data fields. A record is a line of data (delineated by the newline characters by default), and a data field is a separate data element within the line (delineated by a white space character, such as a space or tab, by default).

The gawk program uses data field variables to reference data elements within each record. Table B-3 describes these variables.

TABLE B-3

The gawk Data Field and Record Variables

Variable	Description
$0	The entire data record.
$1	The first data field in the record.
$2	The second data field in the record.
$n	The nth data field in the record.
FIELDWIDTHS	A space separated list of numbers defining the exact width (in spaces) of each data field.
FS	Input field separator character.
RS	Input record separator character.
OFS	Output field separator character.
ORS	Output record separator character.

Besides the field and record separator variables, gawk provides some other built-in variables to help you know what's going on with your data and extract information from the shell environment. Table B-4 shows the other built-in variables in gawk.

You can use the built-in variables anywhere in the gawk program script, including the BEGIN and END sections.

Assigning variables in scripts

Assigning values to variables in gawk programs is similar to how you do it in a shell script, using an *assignment statement*:

```
$ gawk '
> BEGIN{
> testing="This is a test"
> print testing
> }'
This is a test
$
```

Once you assign a value to a variable, you can use that variable anywhere in your gawk script.

TABLE B-4

More gawk Built-In Variables

Variable	Description
ARGC	The number of command line parameters present.
ARGIND	The index in ARGV of the current file being processed.
ARGV	An array of command line parameters.
CONVFMT	The conversion format for numbers (see the printf statement). The default value is %.6g.
ENVIRON	An associative array of the current shell environment variables and their values.
ERRNO	The system error if an error occurs reading or closing input files.
FILENAME	The file name of the data file used for input to the gawk program.
FNR	The current record number in the data file.
IGNORECASE	If set to a non-zero value, gawk all string functions (including regular expressions); ignore the case of characters.
NF	The total number of data fields in the data file.
NR	The number of input records processed.
OFMT	The output format for displaying numbers. The default is %.6g.
RLENGTH	The length of the substring matched in the match function.
RSTART	The start index of the substring matched in the match function.

Assigning variables in the command line

You can also use the gawk command line to assign values to variables for the gawk program. This allows you to set values outside of the normal code, changing values on the fly. Here's an example of using a command line variable to display a specific data field in the file:

```
$ cat script1
BEGIN{FS=","}
{print $n}
$ gawk -f script1 n=2 data1
$ gawk -f script1 n=3 data1
```

This feature is a great way to process data from your shell scripts in the gawk script.

The gawk program features

There are a few features of the gawk program that make it handy for manipulating data, allowing you to create gawk scripts that can parse just about any type of text file, such as log files.

Regular expressions

You can use either a Basic Regular Expression (BRE) or an Extended Regular Expression (ERE) to filter which lines in the data stream the program script applies to.

When using a regular expression, the regular expression must appear before the left brace of the program script that it controls:

```
$ gawk 'BEGIN{FS=","} /test/{print $1}' data1
This is a test
$
```

The matching operator

The *matching operator* allows you to restrict a regular expression to a specific data field in the records. The matching operator is the tilde symbol (~). You specify the matching operator, along with the data field variable, and the regular expression to match:

```
$1 ~ /^data/
```

This expression filters records where the first data field starts with the text data.

Mathematical expressions

Besides regular expressions you can also use mathematical expressions in the matching pattern. This feature comes in handy when matching numerical values in data fields. For example, if you want to display all of the system users who belong to the root users group (group number 0), you could use this script:

```
$ gawk -F: '$4 == 0{print $1}' /etc/passwd
```

This script displays the first data field value for all lines that contain the value 0 in the fourth data field.

Structured commands

The gawk program supports the following structured commands:

The if-then-else statement:

```
if (condition) statement1; else statement2
```

The while statement:

```
while (condition)
{
    statements
}
```

The `do-while` statement:

```
do
{
    statements
} while (condition)
```

The `for` statement:

```
for( variable assignment; condition; iteration process)
```

This provides a wealth of programming opportunities for the gawk script programmer. You can write gawk programs that rival the functions of just about any higher-level language program.

Appendix C

Comparing Shells

With the wealth of shells available in the Linux environment, sometimes it's hard to decide which shell best suits your needs. Other times you're limited to using a specific shell and need to determine which features that you use in shell scripts in your default shell are available in the new shell and which ones aren't supported. This appendix provides a quick comparison between the features of the different shells that are commonly used in the Linux environment.

Variables

Each shell supports environment and user-defined variables, but they differ on just how they support variables. This section describes the things you need to watch out for when working with variables in your shell scripts.

Environment variables

The bash, dash, ksh93, and zsh shells all use all uppercase letters for environment variables. The zsh shell provides both upper- and lower-case environment variables for the common variables, so if you refer to upper-case environment variables in your script, they'll work just fine in the zsh shell.

Unfortunately, the tcsh shell uses lower-case variables for special shell variables. However, it does provide a limited number of upper-case environment variables that match some of the basic Bourne shell environment variables to provide limited compatibility. If your shell script relies heavily on bash shell environment variables, you'll want to check to make sure that those variables are available in the tcsh shell.

One thing to watch out for is that the tcsh shell sets environment variables differently from the other shells. It uses the `setenv` command for setting environment variables:

```
setenv variable value
```

This is different from the `set` command (described in the "User-defined variables" section next), which the other shells use for environment variables.

User-defined variables

All shells allow users to define their own variables both on the command line and in shell scripts. All of the shells except the tcsh shell allow you to set variables directly from the command prompt without a special command:

```
$ testing=100
```

In the tcsh shell you must use the `set` command:

```
$ set testing=100
```

You can also use the `set` command in other shells as well, but it's not required. The tcsh shell also uses the at symbol for setting variables:

```
$ @ testing=100
```

In all shells, to make a variable accessible by child shells and processes, you must use the `export` command:

```
$ export testing
```

The `typeset` command is available in all shells to declare attributes for the variable before using it. In the ksh93 and zsh shells you must use the `typeset` command to define associative array variables:

```
$ typeset -A testing
```

The ksh93 and zsh shells also allow you to define floating-point variables using the `typeset` command.

Array variables

All of the shells support one-dimensional numeric arrays:

```
$ mytest=(one two three four five)
$ echo $mytest
one
$ echo ${mytest[2]}
three
$ echo ${mytest[*]}
one two three four five
$
```

In the bash, ksh93, and tcsh shells, numeric arrays start at 0 for the first element. The zsh shell starts arrays with an index value of 1 instead of 0.

The ksh93 and zsh shells also support associative arrays, which allow you to use a text value as the array index. In the ksh93 shell, you define an associative array like this:

```
$ typeset -A test2
$ test2=( [fruit]=banana [vegetable]=carrot [age]=18 )
```

whereas in the zsh shell you do it like this:

```
% typeset -A test
% test=( fruit banana vegetable carrot age 18 )
```

Notice the subtle difference in the way that the data elements are defined.

Structured Commands

All of the shells support the basic structured commands for manipulating the flow of the shell script. Some of them use a slightly different syntax though. This section discusses the differences between the shells.

The if-then, while, and until statements

The bash, dash, ksh93, and zsh shells use the same format for if-then, while, and until statements. The format for the if-then statement is:

```
if command
then
    commands
else
    commands
fi
```

The same format applies to the while and until statements. Each statement executes a command, then checks the exit status of the command. The if-then statement executes the first set of commands if the exit status is zero, and the second set of commands if the exit status is non-zero.

The while and until statements loop through the specified commands until the exit status of the evaluation command is zero.

The tcsh shell uses a slightly different format for each of these statements:

```
if (expression) then
    commands
else
    commands
endif
```

The while and until statements use a similar format, using the *expression* instead of a command as the evaluation. In both formats, the result of the *expression* determines which section the shell executes. If the *expression* exits with an exit status of 0, the shell executes the commands in the then section. If the *expression* exits with a non-zero exit status, the shell executes the commands in the else section.

The bash, dash, ksh93, and zsh shells use the test command (or its alias, [ ]) to evaluate values and files:

```
if [ -d $HOME ]
then
    echo "Your HOME directory exists"
else
    echo "There's a problem with your HOME directory"
fi
```

The tcsh shell uses this expression, which incorporates testing expressions similar to those used by the test command:

```
if ( -d $HOME ) then
    echo "The HOME directory exists"
endif
```

This subtle difference can cause all sorts of problems for shell scripts.

The for statement

The for statement is another problem area. The bash, dash, ksh93, and zsh shells all use the same format for the basic for statement:

```
for var in list
do
    commands
done
```

The bash and zsh shells also support the C-style for statements:

```
for (( variable assignment ; condition ; iteration process ))
```

However, the tcsh shell doesn't support the for statement. Instead, it uses the foreach statement:

```
foreach var1 (wordlist)
    statements
end
```

This is a huge compatibility problem when migrating shell scripts within the tcsh environment.

Mathematical Operations

All of the shells allow you to perform some level of mathematical operations within them. This is the area where the ksh93 and zsh shells shine.

The bash and dash shells use the `expr` command to evaluate a mathematical expression:

```
$ expr 1 + 5
6
```

They both also provide the `$[]` and `$(())` shortcuts for defining mathematical operations:

```
$ var1=$[1 + 5]
$ echo $var1
6
```

The tcsh shell uses the at symbol for defining mathematical operations:

```
$ set test1 = 10
$ set test2 = 15
$ @ test3 = ( $test1 * $test2 )
$ echo $test3
150
$
```

The bash, dash, and tcsh shells can only perform integer mathematical operations.

Both the ksh93 and zsh shells use two methods for defining mathematical operations. The `let` command:

```
% let value1=" 4 * 5.1 / 3.2 "
% echo $value1
6.3749999999999991
```

and the `$(())` shortcut:

```
% value1=$(( 4 * 5.1 ))
% (( value2 = 4 * 5.1 ))
% printf "%6.3f\n" $value1 $value2
20.400
20.400
%
```

Also, both the ksh93 and zsh shells fully support floating-point arithmetic in all mathematical operations.

The ksh93 shell includes many common mathematical functions built into the shell:

```
$ value1=$(( sqt(9) ))
$ echo $value1
3
```

The zsh shell doesn't include mathematical functions built-in, but provides them as a separate loadable module:

```
% zmodload zsh/mathfunc
% value1=$(( sqrt(9) ))
% echo $value1
3.
```

Obviously, if you're interested in writing shell scripts with advanced mathematical functions, you'll want to choose the ksh93 or zsh shells over the others.

Index

A

L

Q

R

W